AMERICAN GOVERNMENT

Readings and Cases

SEVENTEENTH EDITION

Peter Woll
Brandeis University

New York San Francisco Boston
London Toronto Sydney Tokyo Singapore Madrid
Mexico City Munich Paris Cape Town Hong Kong Montreal

This book is dedicated to Ellen and to Jill and Mac.

Editor-In-Chief: Eric Stano
Senior Marketing Manager: Elizabeth Fogarty
Production Manager: Eric Jorgensen
Project Coordination, Text Design, and Electronic Page Makeup: Pre-Press Company, Inc.
Senior Cover Design Manager/Cover Designer: Nancy Danahy
Cover Image: © Robert Harding World Imagery/Getty Images, Inc.
Senior Manufacturing Buyer: Dennis J. Para
Supplements Editor: Brian Belardi
Printer and Binder: R. R. Donnelley & Sons Company
Cover Printer: R. R. Donnelley & Sons Company

For permission to use copyrighted material, grateful acknowledgment is made to the copyright holders on pp. 445–46 which are hereby made part of this copyright page.

Library of Congress Cataloging-in-Publication Data

American government : readings and cases / [edited by] Peter Woll. -- 17th ed.
p. cm.
Includes bibliographical references.
ISBN 0-321-47314-0
1. United States--Politics and government. I. Woll, Peter, 1933-
JK21.A445 2008
320.473--dc22

2006039073

Please visit us at www.ablongman.com

ISBN 0-321-47314-0

ISBN 13: 978-0-321-47314-1

4 5 6 7 8 9 10—DOC 10 09 08

Contents

Chapter 8 Congress 321

Preface

Welcome to the new edition of *American Government: Readings and Cases*. The text is a major source book for students of American government, providing them with classic and current readings and Supreme Court cases.

The seventeenth edition includes important new readings that interpret constitutional and political issues that continue from the past and have come to the fore in the post–9/11 political world. Students will learn that, while the world often changes in frightening ways, the Constitution remains our steadfast beacon of freedom and democracy. This is not the first time our nation has confronted and surmounted a crisis, always becoming stronger in the process. By learning about our constitutional and political heritage, our classic and enduring theories of constitutional government, students will better understand how a great nation not only survives but also progresses through troubling times.

The text continues to provide key classic and contemporary readings and cases that introduce students to the theoretical underpinnings and current practices of American government. It complements regular textbooks by illustrating and amplifying important issues and concepts, and at the same time, due to the organization and design of the book, it is suitable for use as a core textbook. Included are extensive notes that prepare for, connect, and comment on the readings and point out their significance within the broader context of American government.

The new edition:

- Contains the classic articles on the politics of the Constitutional Convention and the way the Founding Fathers explained the constitutional system of balanced powers and deliberative government
- Retains such precedent-setting cases in the constitutional history of federalism as *McCulloch v. Maryland* (1819) and *Gibbons v. Ogden* (1824) and depicts how the Founders viewed federalism
- Illustrates the politics and the constitutional debate that continues today over the boundaries of national and state powers by including the contrasting views of Supreme Court Justices in the California medical marijuana case, *Gonzales v. Raich* (2005)
- Extends readings to help students understand the constitutional privacy issue by adding a short excerpt from the historic 1890 article by Samuel Warren and Louis Brandeis on privacy that appeared in the *Harvard Law Review*. The addition of Justice William O. Douglas's opinion for the Supreme Court in *Griswold v. Connecticut* (1965) explains the constitutional basis of privacy
- Now focuses, with regard to the constitutional issue of affirmative action, on Justice Powell's centrist opinion in *Regents of the University of California v Bakke* (1978), to give students the principal precedent used in later cases

- Adds depth to the section on the party model of government by adding a reading on the constitutional and political requirements for a responsible two-party system that many political scientists propose as necessary for a healthy democracy
- Analyzes how presidents define their leadership styles in a new reading by leading presidential scholar Stephen Skowronek, using President George Bush as his case study
- Updates Sidney Milkis' reading on the presidency and political parties to review the Bush presidency
- Uses *Ex Parte Milligan* (1866) as the precedent students should know to understand the constitutionality of military tribunals
- Adds a commentary by former presidential counsel John Dean on how the presidency can become a "constitutional dictator" in times of national crisis. His analysis references and gives the theories of presidential power from Hamilton to Rossiter a contemporary relevance
- Contains the classic readings on the bureaucracy and Congress that remain the best sources for understanding the constitutional context and politics of these institutions
- Introduces students to the common law background of our judicial system with a selection from William Blackstone's *Commentaries on the Laws of England, 1765*.

The core readings and cases of this text have always given students a real sense and understanding of their great heritage. Without detailing each and every selection, the highlights of what students learn from this text are:

- John Locke's theory of government by consent
- Madison's constitutional model of balance and deliberative government in the national interest
- Hamilton's model of strong presidential government, energy in the executive being the definition of good government
- The Supreme Court's role in constitutional interpretation and how it shapes our government and politics
- The Bill of Rights and how the Supreme Court has interpreted its meaning
- The constitutional and political basis of our federal system, highlighted by contemporary developments
- The importance of *Federalist 10* and Madison's view of factions and special interests
- The party model of government and the role of parties in the political process
- How special interests shape our governmental process and policies
- The characteristics of the presidency and contrasting theories of presidential power
- Edmund Burke's *Speech to the Electors of Bristol* on the proper role of elected representatives
- The theories of David Mayhew, Richard Fenno, Morris Fiorina, Lawrence Dodd, and Nelson Polsby, which explain Congress

- How Supreme Court Justices think as they write their opinions, citing examples from William H. Rehnquist, Sandra Day O'Connor, and Antonin Scalia in the privacy area.

An **Instructor's Manual** (ISBN: 0321468139) accompanies the text. Students and professors can also access wide-ranging web resources that complement the text using links at http://people.brandeis.edu/~woll/wollwebsites.html. My websites also link to my introductory American Government course syllabus and extensive lecture notes using this reader.

PowerPoint Slides to accompany this text are available on the Instructor Resource Center at http://www.ablongman.com/irc. Please contact your local Longman representative for access to the Instructor Resource Center.

MyPoliSciLab for American Government. If this reader has been ordered alongside one of Longman's American government textbooks, qualified college adopters may also be able to avail themselves of a wealth of resources contained in this online product. MyPoliSciLab is a state-of-the-art, interactive solution for your course. Available as a Web site or as part of several course management systems (CourseCompass, Blackboard, and WebCT), MyPoliSciLab offers students a huge array of simulations, videos, interactive exercises, and assessment tools—all integrated with one of Longman's online e-books. For each chapter of the online text, students will navigate through a pre-test, post-test, chapter review, and a full chapter exam, so they can assess, review, and improve their understanding of the concepts within the chapters. In addition to the online chapter content and assessment, students will have access to simulations, debate and roundtable videos, a weekly poll and news review, an hourly feed from the *New York Times*, Research Navigator, writing resources (including how to avoid plagarism), visual literacy exercises, interactive timelines, comparative exercises, and more!

To find out if the Longman text you are using is accompanied by MyPoliSciLab, visit us www.mypoliscilab.com.

Acknowledgments

My Longman editor Eric Stano has skillfully and professionally guided the new edition, as he did with its predecessors. Eric mans his post at all hours and is himself an example of instant messaging as he immediately answers my e-mails to him, even at 8 A.M.! That is the kind of support every author appreciates.

I would also like to thank the other talented professionals at Longman and Pre-Press Company who helped this text move smoothly through the production process.

Political scientists nationwide have helpfully reviewed the text and made suggestions for the new edition: Cary Covington, University of Iowa; Jennifer Jensen, University of Albany, State University of New York; Daniel Klinghard, College of Charleston; Keith Knutson, Viterbo University; Kevin Parsneau, University of Minnesota; Donald Robert Raber II, Furman University; Diane Schmidt, California State University, Chico; Maurice Sheppard, Alma College; and Alexander Tan, University of Canterbury.

Peter Woll

PART ONE

THE SETTING OF THE AMERICAN SYSTEM

CHAPTER 1

CONSTITUTIONAL GOVERNMENT

The Founding Fathers were consummate politicians, but also brilliant political philosophers in their own right. They did not hesitate to draw upon the rich Western tradition of political philosophy as they searched for an ideal model of government. Above all, they wanted a government that was responsive to the people but also of balanced and limited powers.

CONSTITUTIONAL DEMOCRACY: THE RULE OF LAW

Western political heritage has emphasized the importance of democracy and the rule of law. Aristotle's *Politics* stressed the viability of democracy, provided there are sufficient checks upon unlimited popular rule.

The American constitutional tradition reflects the beliefs of many political philosophers. One of the most dominating figures is John Locke. It is not suggested that Locke was read by most of the colonists, but only that his ideas invariably found their way into many writings of eighteenth-century America, most importantly the Declaration of Independence. In a letter to Henry Lee in 1825, Thomas Jefferson wrote:

"When forced . . . to resort to arms for redress, an appeal to the tribunal of the world was deemed proper for our justification. This was the object of the Declaration of Independence. Not to find out new principles, or new arguments, never before thought of, not merely to say things which had never been said before; but to place before mankind the common sense of the subject, in terms so plain and firm as to command their assent, and to justify ourselves in the independent stand we are compelled to take. Neither aiming at originality of principle or sentiment, nor yet copied from any particular and previous writing, it was intended to be an expression of the American mind, and to give to that expression the proper tone and spirit called for by the occasion. All its authority rests then on the harmonizing sentiments of the day, whether expressed in conversation, in letters, printed essays, or in the elementary books of public right [such] as Aristotle, Cicero, Locke, Sidney, etc. . . . "

In May 1790, Jefferson wrote: "Locke's little book on government is perfect as far as it goes." Although Jefferson's admiration of Locke was perhaps greater than that of many other colonists, his views did reflect a mood of eighteenth-century America. Locke's *Second Treatise, Of Civil Government* attempted to trace the reasons why people enter into political societies in the first place. The eighteenth century, no less than the twentieth, was an era characterized by attempts to be "scientific" in political formulations. Locke's *Second Treatise,* first published in 1690, reflected the scientific emphasis that was to prevail so widely beginning in the eighteenth century. To Locke, natural law was objectively valid, and therefore once this law was ascertained, governments based upon it would have a superior claim to legitimacy. Locke is notable for his discussions of natural law, from which he derived the "best" form of government. In reading Locke, one should observe how much importance he placed upon property rights and the right of the people to dissolve a government that no longer meets their legitimate expectations.

1

SECOND TREATISE, OF CIVIL GOVERNMENT

John Locke

Of the State of Nature

To understand political power aright, and derive it from its original, we must consider what estate all men are naturally in, and that is, a state of perfect freedom to order their actions, and dispose of their possessions and persons as they think fit, within the bounds of the laws of Nature, without asking leave or depending upon the will of any other man.

A state also of equality, wherein all the power and jurisdiction is reciprocal, no one having more than another, there being nothing more evident than that creatures of the same species and rank, promiscuously born to all the same advantages of Nature, and the use of the same faculties, should also be equal one amongst another, without subordination or subjection, unless the lord and master of them all should, by any manifest declaration of his will, set one above another, and confer on him, by an evident and clear appointment, an undoubted right to dominion and sovereignty. . . .

But though this be a state of liberty, yet it is not a state of license; though man in that state have an uncontrollable liberty to dispose of his person or possessions, yet he had not liberty to destroy himself, or so much as any creature in his possession, but where some nobler use than its bare preservation calls for it. The state of Nature has a law of Nature to govern it, which obliges every one, and reason, which is that law, teaches all mankind who will but consult it, that being all equal and independent, no one ought to harm another in his life, health, liberty or possessions. . . . And, being furnished with like faculties, sharing all in one community of Nature, there cannot be supposed any such subordination among us that may authorize us to destroy one another, as if we were made for one another's uses, as the inferior ranks of creatures are for ours. Every one as he is bound to preserve himself, and not to quit his station wilfully, so by the like reason, when his own preservation comes not in competition, ought he as much as he can to preserve the rest of mankind, and not unless it be to do justice on an offender, take away or impair the life, or what tends to the preservation of life, the liberty, health, limb, or goods of another.

And that all men may be restrained from invading others' rights, and from doing hurt to one another, and the law of Nature be observed, which willeth the peace and preservation of all mankind, the execution of the law of Nature is in that state put into every man's hands, whereby every one has a right to punish the transgressors of that law to such a degree as may hinder its violation. For the law of Nature would, as all other laws that concern men in this world, be in vain if there were nobody that in the state of Nature had a power to execute that law, and thereby preserve the innocent and restrain offenders; and if any one in the state of Nature may punish another for any evil he has done, every one may do so. For in that state of perfect equality, where naturally there is no superiority or jurisdiction of one over another, what any may do in prosecution of that law, every one must needs have a right to do.

And thus, in the state of Nature, one man comes by a power over another, but yet no absolute or arbitrary power to use a criminal, when he has got him in his hands, according to the passionate heats or boundless extravagancy of his own will, but only to retribute him so far as calm reason and conscience dictate, what is proportionate to his transgression, which is so much as may serve for reparation and restraint. . . .

Every offence that can be committed in the state of Nature may, in the state of Nature, be also punished equally, and as far forth, as it may, in a commonwealth. For—though it would be beside my present purpose to enter here into the particulars of the law of Nature, or its measures of punishment, yet it is certain there is such a law, and that too as intelligible and plain to a rational creature and a studier of that law as the positive laws of commonwealths, nay, possibly plainer; as much as reason is easier to be understood than the fancies and intricate contrivances of men, following contrary and hidden interests put into words. . . .

Of the Ends of Political Society and Government

If man in the state of Nature be so free as has been said, if he be absolute lord of his own person and possessions, equal to the greatest and subject to nobody, why will he part with his freedom, this empire, and subject himself to the dominion and control of any other power? To which it is obvious to answer, that though in the state of Nature he hath such a right, yet the enjoyment of it is very uncertain and constantly exposed to the invasion of others; for all being kings as much as he, every man his equal, and the greater part no strict observers of equity and justice, the enjoyment of the property he has in this state is very unsafe, very insecure. This makes him willing to quit this condition which, however free, is full of fears and continual dangers; and it is not without reason that he seeks out and is willing to join in society with others who are already united, or have a mind to unite for the mutual preservation of their lives, liberties, and estates, which I call by the general name—property.

The great and chief end, therefore, of men uniting into commonwealths, and putting themselves under government, is the preservation of their property; to which in the state of Nature there are many things wanting.

Firstly, there wants an established, settled, known law, received and allowed by common consent to be the standard of right and wrong, and the common measure to decide all controversies between them. For though the law of Nature be plain and intelligible to all rational creatures, yet men, being biased by their interest, as well as ignorant for want of study of it, are not apt to allow of it as a law binding to them in the application of it to their particular cases.

Secondly, in the state of Nature there wants a known and indifferent judge, with authority to determine all differences according to the established law. For every one in that state being both judge and executioner of the law of Nature, men being partial to themselves, passion and revenge is very apt to carry them too far, and with too much heat in their own cases, as well as negligence and unconcernedness, make them too remiss in other men's.

Thirdly, in the state of Nature there often wants power to back and support the sentence when right, and to give it due execution. They who by any injustice offended will seldom fail where they are able by force to make good their injustice. Such resistance many times makes the punishment dangerous, and frequently destructive to those who attempt it.

Thus mankind, notwithstanding all the privileges of the state of Nature, being but in an ill condition while they remain in it are quickly driven into society. Hence it comes to pass, that we seldom find any number of men live any time together in this state. The inconveniences that they are therein exposed to by the irregular and uncertain exercise of the power every man has of punishing the transgressions of others, make them take sanctuary under the established laws of government, and therein seek the preservation of their property. It is this makes them so willingly give up every one his single power of punishing to be exercised by such alone as shall be appointed to it amongst them, and by such rules as the community, or those authorised by them to that purpose, shall agree on. And in this we have the original right and rise of both the legislative and executive power as well as of the governments and societies themselves.

For in the state of Nature to omit the liberty he has of innocent delights, a man has two powers. The first is to do whatsoever he thinks fit for the preservation of himself and others within the permission of the law of Nature; by which law, common to them all, he and all the rest of mankind are one community, make up one society distinct from all other creatures, and were it not for the corruption and viciousness of degenerate men, there would be no need for any other, no necessity that men should separate from this great and natural community, and associate into lesser combinations. The other power a man has in the state of Nature is the power to punish the crimes committed against that law. Both these he gives up when he joins in a private, if I may so call it, or particular political society, and incorporates into any commonwealth separate from the rest of mankind.

The first power—viz., of doing whatsoever he thought fit for the preservation of himself and the rest of mankind, he gives up to be regulated by laws made by the society, so far forth as the preservation of himself and the rest of that society shall require; which laws of the society in many things confine the liberty he had by the law of Nature.

Secondly, the power of punishing he wholly gives up, and engages his natural force, which he might before employ in the execution of the law of Nature, by his own single authority, as he thought fit, to assist the executive power of the society as the law thereof shall require. For being now in a new state, wherein he is to enjoy many conveniences from the labor, assistance, and society of others in the same community, as well as protection from its whole strength, he is to part also with as much of his natural liberty, in providing for himself, as the good, prosperity, and safety of the society shall require, which is not only necessary but just, since the other members of the society do the like.

But though men when they enter into society give up the equality, liberty, and executive power they had in the state of Nature into the hands of the society, to be so far disposed of by the legislative as the good of the society shall require, yet it being only with an intention in every one the better to preserve himself, his liberty and property (for no rational creature can be supposed to change his condition with an intention to be worse), the power of the society or legislative constituted by them can never be supposed to extend farther than the common against those three defects above mentioned that made the state of Nature so unsafe and uneasy. And so, whoever has the legislative or supreme power of any commonwealth, is bound to govern by established standing laws, promulgated and known to the people, and not by extemporary decrees, by indifferent and upright judges, who are to decide controversies by those laws; and to employ the force of the community at home only in the execution of such laws, or abroad to prevent or redress foreign injuries and secure the community from inroads and invasion. And all this to be directed to no other end but the peace, safety, and public good of the people. . . .

Of the Extent of the Legislative Power

The great end of men's entering into society being the enjoyment of their properties in peace and safety, and the great instrument and means of that being the laws established in that society, the first and fundamental positive law of all commonwealths is the establishing of the legislative power, as the first and fundamental natural law, which is to govern even the legislative itself, is the preservation of the society and (as far as will consist with the public good) of every person in it. This legislative is not only the supreme power of the commonwealth, but sacred and unalterable in the hands where the community have once placed it. Nor can any edict of anybody else, in what form soever conceived, or by what power soever backed, have the force and obligation of a law which has not its sanction from that legislative which the public has chosen and appointed it; for without this the law could not have that which is absolutely necessary to its being a law, the consent of the society, over whom nobody can have a power to make laws but by their own consent and by authority received from them. . . .

These are the bounds which the trust that is put in them by the society and the law of God and Nature have set to the legislative power of every commonwealth, in all forms of government. First: They are to govern by promulgated established laws, not to be varied in particular cases, but to have one rule for rich and poor, for the favorite at Court and the countryman at plough. Secondly: These laws also ought to be designed for no other end ultimately but the good of the people. Thirdly: They must not raise taxes on the property of the people without the consent of the people given by themselves or their deputies. And this properly concerns only such governments where the legislative is always in being, or at least where the people have not reserved any part of the legislative to deputies, to be from time to time chosen by themselves. Fourthly: Legislative neither must nor can transfer the power of making laws to anybody else, or place it anywhere but where the people have. . . .

Of the Dissolution of Government

The constitution of the legislative [authority] is the first and fundamental act of society, whereby provision is made for the continuation of their union under the direction of persons and bonds of laws, made by persons authorised thereunto, by the consent and appointment of the people, without which no one man, or number of men, amongst them can have authority of making laws that shall be binding to the rest. When any one, or more, shall take upon them to make laws whom the people have not appointed so to do, they make laws without authority, which the people are not therefore bound to obey; by which means they come again to be out of subjection, and may constitute to themselves a new legislative, as they think best, being in full liberty to resist the force of those who, without authority, would impose anything upon them. . . .

Whosoever uses force without right—as every one does in society who does it without law—puts himself into a state of war with those against whom he so uses it, and in that state all former ties are cancelled, all other rights cease, and every one has a right to defend himself, and to resist the aggressor. . . .

Here it is like the common question will be made: Who shall be judge whether the prince or legislative act contrary to their trust? This, perhaps, ill-affected and factious men may spread amongst the people, when the prince only makes use of his due prerogative. To this I reply, The people shall be judge; for who shall be judge whether his trustee or deputy acts well and according to the trust reposed in him, but he who deputes him and must, by having deputed him, have still a power to discard him when he fails in his trust? If this be reasonable in particular cases of private men, why should it be otherwise in that of the greatest moment, where the welfare of millions is concerned and also where the evil, if not prevented, is greater, and the redress very difficult, dear, and dangerous? . . .

To conclude. The power that every individual gave the society when he entered into it can never revert to the individuals again, as long as the society lasts, but will always remain in the community; because without this there can be no community—no commonwealth, which is contrary to the original agreement; so also when the society hath placed the legislative in any assembly of men, to continue in them and their successors, with direction and authority for providing such successors, the legislative can never revert to the people whilst that government lasts; because, having provided a legislative with power to continue for ever, they have given up their political power to the legislative, and cannot resume it. But if they have set limits to the duration of their legislative, and made this supreme power in any person or assembly only temporary; or else when, by the miscarriages of those in authority, it is forfeited; upon the forfeiture of their rulers, or at the determination of the time set, it reverts to the society, and the people have a right to act as supreme, and continue the legislative in themselves or place it in a new form, or new hands, as they think good.

The influence of John Locke goes far beyond his impact on the thinking of the Founding Fathers of the United States, such as Thomas Jefferson. Some scholars (among them Louis Hartz, *The Liberal Tradition in America*) have interpreted the American political tradition in terms of the pervasive attachment to the ideas and values set forth in the writings of Locke. There is little question that American political life has been uniquely characterized by widespread adherence to the fundamental principles about the relations among people, society, and government expressed in Locke's writings.

It is not just that we have a representative government, with institutions similar in structure and function to those of the constitutional democracy described in Locke's *Second Treatise*, but that through the years we have maintained, probably more than any other society, a widespread agreement about the fundamental human values cherished by Locke. His emphasis on the sanctity of private property has been paramount in the American political tradition from the very beginning. Moreover, Locke's views on the nature of man are shared by most Americans. All our governmental institutions, processes, and traditions rest upon principles such as the primacy of the individual, man's inborn ability to exercise reason in order to discern truth and higher principles of order and justice, and a political and social equality among people in which no person shall count for more than another in determining the actions of government and its application. We may not have always practiced these ideals, but we have been *theoretically* committed to them.

FRAMING THE CONSTITUTION: ELITIST OR DEMOCRATIC PROCESS?

A remarkable fact about the United States government is that it has operated for two hundred years on the basis of a written Constitution. Does this suggest unusual sagacity on the part of the Founding Fathers, or exceptional luck? What was involved in framing the Constitution?

In the following selection John P. Roche suggests that the framing of the Constitution was essentially a democratic process involving the reconciliation of a variety of state, political, and economic interests. Roche writes that "the Philadelphia Convention was not a College of Cardinals or a council of Platonic guardians working in a manipulative, predemocratic framework; it was a *nationalist* reform caucus that had to operate with great delicacy and skill in a political cosmos full of enemies to achieve one definitive goal—popular approbation." Roche recognizes that the framers, collectively, were an elite, but he is careful to point out that they were a political elite dedicated for the most part to establishing an effective and at the same time controlled national government that would be able to overcome the weaknesses of the Articles of Confederation. The framers were not, says Roche, a cohesive elite dedicated to a particular set of political or economic assumptions beyond the simple need to create a national government that would be capable of reconciling disparate state interests. The Constitution was "a vivid demonstration of effective democratic political action, and of the forging of a national elite which literally persuaded its countrymen to hoist themselves by their own bootstraps."

2

THE FOUNDING FATHERS: A REFORM CAUCUS IN ACTION

John P. Roche

Over the last century and a half, the work of the Constitutional Convention and the motives of the Founding Fathers have been analyzed under a number of different ideological auspices. To one generation of historians, the hand of God was moving in the assembly; under a later dispensation, a dialectic (at various levels of philosophical sophistication) replaced the Deity. "relationships of production" moved into the niche previously reserved for Love of Country. Thus in counterpart to the *zeitgeist*, the framers have undergone miraculous metamorphoses: at one time acclaimed as liberals and bold social engineers, today they appear in the guise of sound Burkean conservatives, men who in our time would subscribe to *Fortune*, look to Walter Lippmann for political theory, and chuckle patronizingly at the antics of Barry Goldwater. The implicit assumption is that if James Madison were among us, he would be President of the Ford Foundation, while Alexander Hamilton would chair the Committee for Economic Development.

The "Fathers" have thus been admitted to our best circles; the revolutionary ferocity which confiscated all Tory property in reach and populated New Brunswick with outlaws has been converted by the "Miltown School" of American historians into a benign dedication to "consensus" and "prescriptive rights." The Daughters of the American Revolution have, through the ministrations of Professors Boorstin, Hartz, and Rossiter, at last found ancestors worthy of their descendants. It is not my purpose here to argue that the "Fathers" were, in fact, radical revolutionaries; that proposition has been brilliantly demonstrated by Robert R. Palmer in his *Age of the Democratic Revolution*. My concern is with the future position that not only were they revolutionaries, but also they were democrats. Indeed, in my view, there is one fundamental truth about the Founding Fathers that *every* generation of zeitgeisters has done its best to obscure: they were first and foremost superb democratic politicians. I suspect that in a contemporary setting, James Madison would be Speaker of the House of Representatives and Hamilton would be the *eminence grise* dominating (*pace* Theodore Sorensen or Sherman Adams) the Executive Office of the President. They were, with their colleagues, *political men*—not metaphysicians, disembodied conservatives or Agents of History—and as recent research into the nature of American politics in the 1780s confirms, they were committed (perhaps willy-nilly) to working within the democratic framework, within a universe of public approval. Charles Beard *and* the filiopietists to the contrary notwithstanding, the Philadelphia Convention was not a College of Cardinals or a council of Platonic guardians working within a manipulative, predemocratic framework; it was a *nationalist* reform caucus which had to operate with great delicacy and skill in a political cosmos full of enemies to achieve the one definitive goal—popular approbation.

Perhaps the time has come, to borrow Walton Hamilton's fine phrase, to raise the framers from immortality to mortality, to give them credit for their magnificent demonstration of the art of democratic politics. The point must be reemphasized: they *made* history and did it within the limits of consensus. There was nothing inevitable about the future in 1787; the *zeitgeist*, that fine Hegelian technique of begging causal questions, could only be discerned in retrospect. What they did was to hammer out a pragmatic compromise which would both bolster the "national interest" and be acceptable to the people. What inspiration they got came from their collective experience as professional politicians in a democratic society. As John Dickinson put it to his fellow delegates on August 13, "Experience must be our guide. Reason may mislead us."

In this context, let us examine the problems they confronted and the solutions they evolved. The Convention has been described picturesquely as a counter-revolutionary junta and the Constitution as a coup d'état, but this has been accomplished by withdrawing the whole history of the movement for constitutional reform from its true context. No doubt the goals of the constitutional elite were "subversive" to the existing political order, but it is overlooked that their subversion could only have succeeded if the people of the United States endorsed it by regularized procedures. Indubitably they were "plotting" to establish a much stronger central government than existed under the Articles, but only in the sense in which one could argue equally well that John F. Kennedy was, from 1956 to 1960, "plotting" to become President. In short, on the fundamental *procedural* level, the Constitutionalists had to work according to the prevailing rules of the game. Whether they liked it or not is a topic for spiritualists—and is irrelevant: one may be quite certain that had Washington agreed to play the de Gaulle (as the Cincinnati once urged), Hamilton would willingly have held his horse, but such fertile speculation in no way alters the actual context in which events took place.

I

When the Constitutionalists went forth to subvert the Confederation, they utilized the mechanisms of political legitimacy. And the roadblocks which confronted them were formidable. At the same time, they were endowed with certain potent political assets. The history of the United States from 1786 to 1790 was largely one of a masterful employment of political expertise by the Constitutionalists as against bumbling, erratic behavior by the opponents of reform. Effectively, the Constitutionalists had to induce the states, by democratic techniques of coercion, to emasculate themselves. To be specific, if New York had refused to join the new Union, the project was doomed; yet before New York was safely in, the reluctant state legislature had *sua sponte* to take the following steps: (1) agree to send delegates to the Philadelphia Convention; (2) provide maintenance for these delegates (these were distinct stages: New Hampshire was early in naming delegates, but did not provide for their maintenance until July); (3) set up the special ad hoc convention to decide on ratification; and (4) concede to the decision of the ad hoc convention that New York should participate. New York admittedly was a tricky state, with a strong interest in a status quo which permitted her to exploit New Jersey and Connecticut, but the same legal hurdles existed in every state. And at the risk of becoming boring, it must be reiterated that the *only* weapon in the Constitutionalist arsenal was an effective mobilization of public opinion.

The group which undertook this struggle was an interesting amalgam of a few dedicated nationalists with the self-interested spokesmen of various parochial bailiwicks. The Georgians, for example, wanted a strong central authority to provide military protection for their huge, underpopulated state against the Creek Confederacy; Jerseymen and Connecticuters wanted to escape from economic bondage to New York; the Virginians hoped to establish a system which would give that great state its rightful place in the councils of the republic. The dominant figures in the politics of these states therefore cooperated in the call for the Convention. In other states, the thrust towards national reform was taken up by opposition groups who added the "national interest" to their weapons system; in Pennsylvania, for instance, the group fighting to revise the Constitution of 1776 came out four square behind the Constitutionalists, and in New York, Hamilton and the Schuyler *ambiance* took the same tack against George Clinton. There was, of course, a large element of personality in the affair: there is reason to suspect that Patrick Henry's opposition to the Convention and the Constitution was founded on his conviction that Jefferson was behind both, and a close study of local politics elsewhere would surely reveal that others supported the Constitution for the simple (and politically quite sufficient) reason that the "wrong" people were against it.

To say this is not to suggest that the Constitution rested on a foundation of impure or base motives. It is rather to argue that in politics there are no immaculate conceptions, and that in the drive for a stronger general government, motives of all sorts played a part. Few men in the history of mankind have espoused a view of the "common good" or "public interest" that militated against their private status; even Plato with all his reverence for disembodied reason managed to put philosophers on top of the pile. Thus it is not surprising that a number of diversified private interests joined to push the nationalist public interest; what would have been surprising was the absence of such a pragmatic united front. And the fact remains that, however motivated, these men did demonstrate a willingness to compromise their parochial interest in behalf of an ideal which took shape before their eyes and under their ministrations.

As Stanley Elkins and Eric McKitrick have suggested in a perceptive essay [76 *Political Science Quarterly* 181 (1961)], what distinguished the leaders of the Constitutionalist caucus from their enemies was a "Continental" approach to political, economic and military issues. To the extent that they shared an institutional base of operations, it was the Continental Congress (thirty-nine of the delegates to the Federal Convention had served in Congress), and this was hardly a locale which inspired respect for the state governments. Robert de Jouvenal observed French politics half a century ago and noted that a revolutionary Deputy had more in common with a non-revolutionary Deputy than he had with a revolutionary non-Deputy; similarly one can surmise that membership in the Congress under the Articles of Confederation worked to establish a Continental frame of reference, that a Congressman from Pennsylvania and one from South Carolina would share a universe of discourse which provided them with a conceptual common denominator vis-à-vis their respective state legislatures. This was particularly true with respect to external affairs: the average state legislator was probably about as concerned with foreign policy then as he is today, but Congressmen were constantly forced to take the broad view of American prestige, were compelled to listen to the reports of Secretary John Jay and to the dispatches and pleas from their frustrated envoys in Britain, France, and Spain. From considerations such as these, a "Continental" ideology developed which seems to have demanded a revision of our domestic institutions primarily on the ground that only by invigorating our general government could we assume our rightful place in the international arena. Indeed, an argument with great force—particularly since Washington was its incarnation—urged that our very survival in the Hobbesian jungle of world politics depended upon a reordering and strengthening of our national sovereignty.

The great achievement of the Constitutionalists was their ultimate success in convincing the elected representatives of a majority of the white male population that change was imperative. A small group of political leaders with a Continental vision and essentially a consciousness of the United States' *international* impotence, provided the matrix of the movement. To their standard other leaders rallied with their own parallel ambitions. Their great assets were (1) the presence in their caucus of the one authentic American "father figure," George Washington, whose prestige was enormous; (2) the energy and talent of their leadership (in which one must include the towering intellectuals of the time, John Adams and Thomas Jefferson, despite their absence abroad), and their communications "network," which was far superior to anything on the opposition side; (3) the preemptive skill which made "their" issue The Issue and kept the locally oriented opposition permanently on the defensive; and (4) the subjective consideration that these men were spokesmen of a new and compelling credo: *American* nationalism, that ill-defined but nonetheless potent sense of collective purpose that emerged from the American Revolution.

Despite great institutional handicaps, the Constitutionalists managed in the mid-1780s to mount an offensive which gained momentum as years went by. Their greatest problem was lethargy, and paradoxically, the number of barriers in their path may have proved an advantage in the long run. Beginning with the initial battle to get the Constitutional Convention called, the delegates appointed, they could never relax, never let up the pressure. In practical terms, this meant that the local "organizations" created by the Constitutionalists were perpetually in movement building up their cadres for the next fight. (The word *organization* has to be used with great caution: a political organization in the United States—as in contemporary England—generally consisted of a magnate and his following, or a coalition of magnates. This did not necessarily mean that it was "undemocratic" or "aristocratic," in the Aristotelian sense of the word: while a few magnates such as the Livingstons could draft their followings, most exercised their leadership without coercion on the basis of popular endorsement. The absence of organized opposition did not imply the impossibility of competition any more than low public participation in elections necessarily indicated an undemocratic suffrage.)

The Constitutionalists got the jump on the "opposition" (a collective noun: oppositions would be more correct) at the outset with demand for a Convention. Their opponents were caught in an old political trap: they were not being asked to approve any specific program of reform, but only to endorse a meeting to discuss and recommend needed reforms. If they took a hard line at the first stage, they were put in the position of glorifying the status quo and of denying the need for *any* changes. Moreover, the Constitutionalists could go to the people with a persuasive argument for "fair play"—"How can you condemn reform before you know precisely what is involved?" Since the state legislatures obviously would have the final say on any proposals that might emerge from the Convention, the Constitutionalists were merely reasonable men asking for a chance. Besides, since they did not make any concrete proposals at that stage, they were in a position to capitalize on every sort of generalized discontent with the Confederation.

Perhaps because of their poor intelligence system, perhaps because of overconfidence generated by the failure of all previous efforts to alter the Articles, the opposition awoke too late to the dangers that confronted them in 1787. Not only did the Constitutionalists manage to get every state but Rhode Island (where politics was enlivened by a party system reminiscent of the "Blues" and the "Greens" in the Byzantine Empire) to appoint delegates to Philadelphia, but when the results were in, it appeared that they dominated the delegations. Given the apathy of the opposition, this was a natural phenomenon: in an ideologically nonpolarized political atmosphere those who get appointed to a special committee are likely to be the men who supported the movement for its creation. Even George Clinton, who seems to have been the first opposition leader to awake to the possibility of trouble, could not prevent the New York legislature from appointing Alexander Hamilton—though he did have the foresight to send two of his henchmen to dominate the delegation. Incidentally, much has been made of the fact that the delegates to Philadelphia were not elected by the people; some have adduced this fact as evidence of the "undemocratic" character of the gathering. But put in the context of the time, this argument is wholly specious: the central government under the Articles was considered a creature of the component states and in all the states but Rhode Island, Connecticut, and New Hampshire, members of the national Congress were chosen by the state legislatures. This was not a consequence of elitism or fear of the mob; it was a logical extension of states' rights doctrine to guarantee that the national institution did not end-run the state legislatures and make direct contact with the people.

II

With delegations safely named, the focus shifted to Philadelphia. While waiting for a quorum to assemble, James Madison got busy and drafted the so-called Randolph or Virginia Plan with the aid of the Virginia delegation. This was a political masterstroke. Its consequence was that once business got underway, the framework of the discussion was established on Madison's terms. There was no interminable argument over agenda; instead the delegates took the Virginia Resolutions—"just for purposes of discussion"—as their point of departure. And along with Madison's proposals, many of which were buried in the course of the summer, went his major premise: a new start on a Constitution rather than piecemeal amendment. This was not necessarily revolutionary—but Madison's proposal that this "lump sum" amendment go into effect after approval by nine states (the Articles required unanimous state approval for any amendment) was thoroughly subversive.

Standard treatments of the Convention divide the delegates into "nationalists" and "states' righters" with various improvised shadings ("moderate nationalists," etc.), but these are *a posteriori* categories which obfuscate more than they clarify. What is striking to one who analyzes the Convention as a case study in democratic politics is the lack of clear-cut ideological divisions in the Convention. Indeed, I submit that the evidence—Madison's *Notes*, the correspondence of the delegates, and debates on ratification—indicates that this was a remarkably homogeneous body on the ideological level. Yates and Lansing, Clinton's two chaperones for Hamilton, left in disgust on July 10. (Is there anything more tedious than sitting through endless disputes on matters one deems fundamentally misconceived? It takes an iron will to spend a hot summer as an ideological *agent provocateur.*) Luther Martin, Maryland's bibulous narcissist, left on September 4 in a huff when he discovered that others did not share his self-esteem; others went home for personal reasons. But the hard core of delegates accepted a grinding regimen throughout the attrition of a Philadelphia summer precisely because they shared the Constitutionalist goal.

Basic differences of opinion emerged, of course, but these were not ideological; they were *structural*. If the so-called "states' rights" group had not accepted the fundamental purposes of the Convention, they could simply have pulled out and by doing so have aborted the whole enterprise. Instead of bolting, they returned day after day to argue and to compromise. An interesting symbol of this basic homogeneity was the initial agreement on secrecy: these professional politicians did not want to become prisoners of publicity; they wanted to retain that freedom of maneuver which is only possible when men are not forced to take public stands in the preliminary stages of negotiation. There was no legal means of binding the tongues of the delegates: at any stage in the game a delegate with basic principled objections to the emerging project could have taken the stump (as Luther Martin did after his exit) and denounced the Convention to the skies. Yet Madison did not even inform Thomas Jefferson in Paris of the course of the deliberations and available correspondence indicates that the delegates generally observed the injunction. Secrecy is certainly uncharacteristic of any assembly marked by strong ideological polarization. This was noted at the time: the *New York Daily Advertiser*, August 14, 1787, commented that the "profound secrecy hitherto observed by the Convention [we consider] a happy omen, as it demonstrates that the spirit of party on any great and essential point cannot have arisen to any height."

Commentators on the Constitution who have read *The Federalist* in lieu of reading the actual debates have credited the Fathers with the invention of a sublime concept called "Federalism." Unfortunately, *The Federalist* is probative evidence for only one proposition: that Hamilton and Madison were inspired propagandists with a genius for retrospective symmetry. Federalism, as the theory is generally defined, was an improvisation which was later promoted into a political theory. Experts on "federalism" should take to heart the advice of David Hume, who warned in his *Of the Rise and Progress of the Arts and Sciences* that "there is no subject in which we must proceed with more caution than in [history], lest we assign causes which never existed and reduced what is merely contingent to stable and universal principles." In any event, the final balance in the Constitution between the states and the nation must have come as a great disappointment to Madison, while Hamilton's unitary views are too well known to need elucidation.

It is indeed astonishing how those who have glibly designated James Madison the "father" of Federalism have overlooked the solid body of fact which indicates that he shared Hamilton's quest for a unitary central government. To be specific, they have avoided examining the clear import of the Madison-Virginia Plan, and have disregarded Madison's dogged inch-by-inch retreat from the bastions of centralization. The Virginia Plan envisioned a unitary national government effectively freed from and dominant over the states. The lower house of the national legislature was to be elected directly by the people of the states with membership proportional to population. The upper house was to be selected by the lower and two chambers would elect the executive and choose the judges. The national government would be thus cut completely loose from the states.

The structure of the general government was freed from state control in a truly radical fashion, but the scope of the authority of the national sovereign as Madison initially formulated it was breathtaking—it was a formulation worthy of the Sage of Malmesbury himself. The national legislature was to be empowered to disallow the acts of state legislatures, and the central government was vested, in addition to the powers of the nation under the Articles of Confederation, with plenary authority wherever "the separate States are incompetent or in which the harmony of the United States may be interrupted by the exercise of individual legislation." Finally, just to lock the door against state intrusion, the national Congress was to be given the power to use military force on recalcitrant states. This was Madison's "model" of an ideal national government, though it later received little publicity in *The Federalist*.

The interesting thing was the reaction of the Convention to this militant program for a strong autonomous central government. Some delegates were startled, some obviously leery of so comprehensive a project of reform, but nobody set off any fireworks and nobody walked out. Moreover, in the two weeks that followed, the Virginia Plan received substantial endorsement *en principe;* the initial temper of the gathering can be deduced from the approval "without debate or dissent," on May 31, of the Sixth Resolution which granted Congress the authority to disallow state legislation "contravening *in its opinion* the Articles of Union." Indeed, an amendment was included to bar states from contravening national treaties.

The Virginia Plan may therefore be considered, in ideological terms, as the delegates' Utopia, but as the discussions continued and became more specific, many of those present began to have second thoughts. After all, they were not residents of Utopia or guardians in Plato's Republic who could simply impose a philosophical ideal on subordinate strata of the population. They were practical politicians in a democratic society, and no matter what their private dreams might be, they had to take home an acceptable package and defend it—and their own political futures—against predictable attack. On June 14 the breaking point between dream and reality took place. Apparently realizing that under the Virginia Plan, Massachusetts, Virginia, and Pennsylvania could virtually dominate the national government—and probably appreciating that to sell this program to "the folks back home" would be impossible—the delegates from the small states dug in their heels and demanded time for a consideration of alternatives. One gets a graphic sense of the inner politics from John Dickinson's reproach to Madison: "You see the consequences of pushing things too far. Some of the members from the small States wish for two branches in the General Legislature and are friends to a good National Government; but we would sooner submit to a foreign power than . . . be deprived of an equality of suffrage in both branches of the Legislature, and thereby be thrown under the domination of the large States."

The bare outline of the *Journal* entry for Tuesday, June 14, is suggestive to anyone with extensive experience in deliberative bodies. "It was moved by Mr. Patterson [*sic*, Paterson's name was one of those consistently misspelled by Madison and everybody else] seconded by Mr. Randolph that the further consideration of the report from the Committee of the whole House [endorsing the Virginia Plan] be postponed till tomorrow and before the question for postponement was taken. It was moved by Mr. Randolph and seconded by Mr. Patterson that the House adjourn." The House adjourned by obvious prearrangement of the two principals: since the preceding

Saturday when Brearley and Paterson of New Jersey had announced their fundamental discontent with the representational features of the Virginia Plan, the informal pressure had certainly been building up to slow down the steamroller. Doubtless there were extended arguments at the Indian Queen between Madison and Paterson, the latter insisting that events were moving rapidly towards a probably disastrous conclusion, towards a political suicide pact. Now the process of accommodation was put into action smoothly—and wisely, given the character and strength of the doubters. Madison had the votes, but this was one of those situations where the enforcement of mechanical majoritarianism could easily have destroyed the objectives of the majority: the Constitutionalists were in quest of a qualitative as well as a quantitative consensus. This was hardly from deference to local Quaker custom; it was a political imperative if they were to attain ratification.

III

According to the standard script, at this point the "states' rights" group intervened in force behind the New Jersey Plan, which has been characteristically portrayed as a reversion to the status quo under the Articles of Confederation with but minor modifications. A careful examination of the evidence indicates that only in a marginal sense is this an accurate description. It is true that the New Jersey Plan put the states back into the institutional picture, but one could argue that to do so was a recognition of political reality rather than an affirmation of states' rights. A serious case can be made that the advocates of the New Jersey Plan, far from being ideological addicts of states' rights, intended to substitute for the Virginia Plan a system which would both retain strong national power and have a chance of adoption in the states. The leading spokesman for the project asserted quite clearly that his views were based more on counsels of expediency than on principle; said Paterson on June 16: "I came here not to speak my own sentiments, but the sentiments of those who sent me. Our object is not such a Government as may be best in itself, but such a one as our Constituents have authorized us to prepare, and as they will approve." This is Madison's version; in Yates's transcription, there is a crucial sentence following the remarks above: "I believe that a little practical virtue is to be preferred to the finest theoretical principles, which cannot be carried into effect." In his preliminary speech on June 9, Paterson had stated "to the public mind we must accommodate ourselves," and in his notes for this and his later effort as well, the emphasis is the same. The *structure* of government under the Articles should be retained:

> 2. Because it accords with the Sentiments of the People.
>
> [Proof:] 1. Coms. [Commissions from state legislatures defining the jurisdiction of the delegates]
>
> 2. News-papers—Political Barometer. Jersey never would have sent Delegates under the first [Virginia] Plan—
>
> Not here to sport Opinions of my own. Wt. [What] can be done. A little practical Virtue preferable to Theory.

This was a defence of political acumen, not of states' rights. In fact, Paterson's notes of his speech can easily be construed as an argument for attaining the substantive objectives of the Virginia Plan by a sound political route, i.e., pouring the new wine in the old bottles. With a shrewd eye, Paterson queried:

> Will the Operation, and Force of the [central] Govt. depend upon the mode of Representn.—No—it will depend upon the Quantum of Power lodged in the leg. ex. and judy. Departments—Give [the existing] Congress the same Powers that you intend to give the two Branches, [under the Virginia Plan] and I apprehend they will act with as much Propriety and more Energy. . . .

In other words, the advocates of the New Jersey Plan concentrated their fire on what they held to be the *political liabilities* of the Virginia Plan—which were matters of institutional structure—rather than on the proposed scope of national authority. Indeed, the Supremacy Clause of the Constitution first saw the light of day in Paterson's Sixth Resolution; the New Jersey Plan contemplated the use of military force to secure compliance with national law; and finally Paterson made clear his view that under either the Virginia or the New Jersey systems, the general government would ". . . act on individuals and not on states." From the states' rights viewpoint, this was heresy: the fundament of that doctrine was the proposition that any central government had as its constituents the states, not the people, and could only reach the people through the agency of the state government.

Paterson then reopened the agenda of the Convention, but he did so within a distinctly nationalist framework. Paterson's position was one of favoring a strong central government in principle, but opposing one which in fact *put the big states in the saddle*. (The Virginia Plan, for all its abstract merits, did very well by Virginia.) As evidence for this speculation, there is a curious and intriguing proposal among Paterson's preliminary drafts of the New Jersey Plan:

> Whereas it is necessary in Order to form the People of the U.S. of America in to a Nation, that the States should be consolidated, by which means all the Citizens thereof will become equally intitled to and will equally participate in the same Privileges and Rights . . . it is therefore resolved, that all the Lands contained within the Limits of each state individually, and of the U.S. generally be considered as constituting one Body or Mass, and be divided into thirteen or more integral parts.
>
> Resolved, That such Divisions or integral Parts shall be styled Districts.

This makes it sound as though Paterson was prepared to accept a strong unified central government along the lines of the Virginia Plan if the existing states were eliminated. He may have gotten the idea from his New Jersey colleague Judge David Brearley, who on June 9 had commented that the only remedy to the dilemma over representation was "that a map of the U.S. be spread out, that all the existing boundaries be erased, and that a new partition of the whole be made into 13 equal parts." According to Yates, Brearley added at this point, "then a government on the present [Virginia Plan] system will be just."

This proposition was never pushed—it was patently unrealistic—but one can appreciate its purpose: it would have separated the men from the boys in the large-state delegations. How attached would the Virginians have been to their reform principles if Virginia were to disappear as a component geographical unit (the largest) for representational purposes? Up to this point, the Virginians had been in the happy position of supporting high ideals with that inner confidence born of knowledge that the "public interest" they endorsed would nourish their private interest. Worse, they had shown little willingness to compromise. Now the delegates from the small states announced that they were unprepared to be offered up as sacrificial victims to a "national interest" which reflected Virginia's parochial ambition. Caustic Charles Pinckney was not far off when he remarked sardonically that "the whole [conflict] comes to this": "Give N. Jersey an equal vote, and she will dismiss her scruples, and concur in the Natl. system." What he rather unfairly did not add was that the Jersey delegates were not free agents who could adhere to their private convictions; they had to take back, sponsor and risk their reputations on the reforms approved by the Convention—and in New Jersey, not in Virginia.

Paterson spoke on Saturday, and one can surmise that over the weekend there was a good deal of consultation, argument, and caucusing among the delegates. One member at least prepared a full-length address: on Monday Alexander Hamilton, previously mute, rose and delivered a six-hour oration. It was a remarkably apolitical speech; the gist of his position was that *both* the Virginia and New Jersey Plans were inadequately centralist, and he detailed a reform program which was reminiscent of the Protectorate under the Cromwellian *Instrument of Government* of 1653. It has been suggested that Hamilton did this in the best political tradition to emphasize the moderate character of the Virginia Plan, to give the cautious delegates something *really* to worry about; but this interpretation seems somehow too clever. Particularly since the sentiments Hamilton expressed happened to be completely consistent with those he privately—and sometimes publicly—expressed throughout his life. He wanted, to take a striking phrase from a letter to George Washington, a "strong well mounted government"; in essence, the Hamilton Plan contemplated an elected life monarch, virtually free of public control, on the Hobbesian ground that only in this fashion could strength and stability be achieved. The other alternatives, he argued, would put policy-making at the mercy of the passions of the mob; only if the sovereign was beyond the reach of selfish influence would it be possible to have government in the interests of the whole community.

From all accounts, this was a masterful and compelling speech, but (aside from furnishing John Lansing and Luther Martin with ammunition for later use against the Constitution) it made little impact. Hamilton was simply transmitting on a different wavelength from the rest of the delegates; the latter adjourned after his great effort, admired his rhetoric, and then returned to business. It was rather as if they had taken a day off to attend the opera. Hamilton, never a particularly patient man or much of a negotiator, stayed for another ten days and then left, in considerable disgust, for New York. Although he came back to Philadelphia sporadically and attended the last two weeks of the Convention, Hamilton played no part in the laborious task of hammering out the Constitution. His day came later when he led the New York Constitutionalists into the savage imbroglio over ratification—an arena in which his unmatched talent for dirty political infighting may well have won the day. For instance, in the New York Ratifying Convention, Lansing threw back into Hamilton's teeth the sentiments the latter had expressed in his June 18 oration in the Convention. However, having since retreated to the fine defensive positions immortalized in *The Federalist*, the Colonel flatly denied that he had ever been an enemy of the states, or had believed that conflict between states and nation was inexorable! As Madison's authoritative *Notes* did not appear until 1840, and there had been no press coverage, there was no way to verify his assertions, so in the words of the reporter, "a warm personal altercation between [Lansing and Hamilton] engrossed the remainder of the day [June 28, 1788]."

IV

On Tuesday morning, June 19, the vacation was over. James Madison led off with a long, carefully reasoned speech analyzing the New Jersey Plan which, while intellectually vigorous in its criticisms, was quite conciliatory in mood. "The great difficulty," he observed, "lies in the affair of Representation; and if this could be adjusted, all others would be surmountable." (As events were to demonstrate, this diagnosis was correct.) When he finished, a vote was taken on whether to continue with the Virginia Plan as the nucleus for a new constitution: seven states voted "Yes"; New York, New Jersey, and Delaware voted "No"; and Maryland, whose position often depended on which delegates happened to be on the floor, divided. Paterson, it seems, lost decisively; yet in a fundamental sense he and his allies had achieved their purpose: from that day onward, it could never be forgotten that the state governments loomed ominously in the background and that no verbal incantations could exorcise their power. Moreover, nobody bolted the Convention: Paterson and his colleagues took their defeat in stride and set to work to modify the Virginia Plan, particularly with respect to its provisions on representation in the national legislature. Indeed, they won an immediate rhetorical bonus; when Oliver Ellsworth of Connecticut rose to move that the word "national" be expunged from the Third Virginia Resolution ("Resolved that a *national* Government ought to be established consisting of a *supreme* Legislative, Executive and Judiciary"), Randolph agreed and the motion passed unanimously. The process of compromise had begun.

For the next two weeks, the delegates circled around the problem of legislative representation. The Connecticut delegation appears to have evolved a possible compromise quite early in the debates, but the Virginians and particularly Madison (unaware that he would later be acclaimed as the prophet of "federalism") fought obdurately against providing for equal representation of states in the second chamber. There was a good deal of acrimony and at one point Benjamin Franklin—of all people—proposed the institution of a daily prayer; practical politicians in the gathering, however, were meditating more on the merits of a good committee than on the utility of Divine intervention. On July 2, the ice began to break when through a number of fortuitous events—and one that seems deliberate—the majority against equality of representation was converted into a dead tie. The Convention had reached the stage where it was "ripe" for a solution (presumably all the therapeutic speeches had been made), and the South Carolinians proposed a committee. Madison and James Wilson wanted none of it, but with only Pennsylvania dissenting, the body voted to establish a working party on the problem of representation.

The members of this committee, one from each state, were elected by the delegates—and a very interesting committee it was. Despite the fact that the Virginia

Plan had held majority support up to that date, neither Madison nor Randolph was selected (Mason was the Virginian) and Baldwin of Georgia, whose shift in position had resulted in the tie, was chosen. From the composition, it was clear that this was not to be a "fighting" committee: the emphasis in membership was on what might be described as "second-level political entrepreneurs." On the basis of the discussions up to that time, only Luther Martin of Maryland could be described as a "bitter-ender." Admittedly, some divination enters into this sort of analysis, but one does get a sense of the mood of the delegates from these choices—including the interesting selection of Benjamin Franklin, despite his age and intellectual wobbliness, over the brilliant and incisive Wilson or the sharp, polemical Gouverneur Morris, to represent Pennsylvania. His passion for conciliation was more valuable at this juncture than Wilson's logical genius, or Morris's acerbic wit.

There is a common rumor that the framers divided their time between philosophical discussions of government and reading the classics in political theory. Perhaps this is as good a time as any to note that their concerns were highly practical, that they spent little time canvassing abstractions. A number of them had some acquaintance with the history of political theory (probably gained from reading John Adams's monumental compilation *A Defense of the Constitutions of Government*, the first volume of which appeared in 1786), and it was a poor rhetorician indeed who could not cite Locke, Montesquieu, or Harrington *in support* of a desired goal. Yet up to this point in the deliberations, no one had expounded a defense of states' rights or the "separation of powers" on anything resembling a theoretical basis. It should be reiterated that the Madison model had no room either for the states or for the "separation of powers": effectively *all* governmental power was vested in the national legislature. The merits of Montesquieu did not turn up until *The Federalist;* and although a perverse argument could be made that Madison's ideal was truly in the tradition of John Locke's *Second Treatise of Government*, the Locke whom the American rebels treated as an honorary president was a pluralistic defender of vested rights, not of parliamentary supremacy.

It would be tedious to continue a blow-by-blow analysis of the work of the delegates; the critical fight was over representation of the states and once the Connecticut Compromise was adopted on July 17, the Convention was over the hump. Madison, James Wilson, and Gouverneur Morris of New York (who was there representing Pennsylvania!) fought the compromise all the way in a last-ditch effort to get a unitary state with parliamentary supremacy. But their allies deserted them and they demonstrated after their defeat the essential opportunist character of their objections—using "opportunist" here in a nonpejorative sense, to indicate a willingness to swallow their objections and get on with the business. Moreover, once the compromise had carried (by five states to four, with one state divided), its advocates threw themselves vigorously into the job of strengthening the general government's substantive powers—as might have been predicted, indeed, from Paterson's early statements. It nourishes an increased respect for Madison's devotion to the art of politics, to realize that this dogged fighter could sit down six months later and prepare essays for *The Federalist* in contradiction to his basic convictions about the true course the Convention should have taken.

V

Two tricky issues will serve to illustrate the later process of accommodation. The first was the institutional position of the Executive. Madison argued for an executive chosen by the national legislature and on May 29 this had been adopted with a provision that after his seven-year term was concluded, the chief magistrate should not be eligible for reelection. In late July this was reopened and for a week the matter was argued from several different points of view. A good deal of desultory speech-making ensued, but the gist of the problem was the opposition from two sources to election by the legislature. One group felt that the states should have a hand in the process; another small but influential circle urged direct election by the people. There were a number of proposals: election by the people, election by state governors, by electors chosen by state legislatures, by the national legislature (James Wilson, perhaps ironically, proposed at one point that an Electoral College be chosen by lot from the national legislature!), and there was some resemblance to three-dimensional chess in the dispute because of the presence of two other variables, length of tenure and reeligibility. Finally, after opening, reopening, and re-reopening the debate, the thorny problem was consigned to a committee for absolution.

The Brearley Committee on Postponed Matters was a superb aggregation of talent and its compromise on the Executive was a masterpiece of political improvisation. (The Electoral College, its creation, however, had little in its favor as an *institution*—as the delegates well appreciated.) The point of departure for all discussion about the presidency in the Convention was that in immediate terms, the problem was nonexistent; in other words, everybody present knew that under any system devised, George Washington would be President. Thus they were dealing in the future tense and to a body of working politicians the merits of the Brearley proposal were obvious: everybody got a piece of cake. (Or to put it more academically, each viewpoint could leave the Convention and argue to its constituents that it had *really* won the day.) First, the state legislatures had the right to determine the mode of selection of the electors; second, the small states received a bonus in the Electoral College in the form of a guaranteed minimum of three votes while the big states got acceptance of the principle of proportional power; third, if the state legislatures agreed (as six did in the first presidential election), the people could be involved directly in the choice of electors; and finally, if no candidate received a majority in the College, the right of decision passed to the national legislature with each state exercising equal strength. (In the Brearley recommendation, the election went to the Senate, but a motion from the floor substituted the House; this was accepted on the ground that the Senate already had enough authority over the executive in its treaty and appointment powers.)

This compromise was almost too good to be true, and the framers snapped it up with little debate or controversy. No one seemed to think well of the College as an *institution*; indeed, what evidence there is suggests that there was an assumption that once Washington had finished his tenure as President, the electors would cease to produce majorities and the Chief Executive would usually be chosen in the House. George Mason observed casually that the selection would be made in the House nineteen times in twenty and no one seriously disputed this point. The vital aspect of the Electoral College was that it got the Convention over the hurdle and protected everybody's interests. The future was left to cope with the problem of what to do with this Rube Goldberg mechanism.

In short, the framers did not in their wisdom endow the United States with a college of Cardinals—the Electoral College was neither an exercise in applied Platonism nor an experiment in indirect government based on elitist distrust of the masses. It was merely a jerry-rigged improvisation which has subsequently been endowed with a high theoretical content. When an elector from Oklahoma in 1960 refused to cast his vote for Nixon (naming Byrd and Goldwater instead) on the ground that the Founding Fathers intended him to exercise his great independent wisdom, he was indulging in historical fantasy. If one were to indulge in counter-fantasy, he would be tempted to suggest that the Fathers would be startled to find the College still in operation—and perhaps even dismayed at their descendants' lack of judgment or inventiveness.

The second issue on which some substantial practical bargaining took place was slavery. The morality of slavery was, by design, not at issue; but in its other concrete aspects, slavery colored the arguments over taxation, commerce, and representation. The "Three-Fifths Compromise," that three-fifths of the slaves would be counted both for representation and for purposes of direct taxation (which was drawn from the past—it was a formula of Madison's utilized by Congress in 1783 to establish the basis of state contributions to the Confederation treasury), had allayed some Northern fears about Southern overrepresentation (no one then foresaw the trivial role that direct taxation would play in later federal financial policy), but doubts still remained. The Southerners, on the other hand, were afraid that Congressional control over commerce would lead to the exclusion of slaves or to their excessive taxation as imports. Moreover, the Southerners were disturbed over "navigation acts," i.e., tariffs, or special legislation providing, for example, that exports be carried only in American ships; as a section depending upon exports, they wanted protection from the potential voracity of their commercial brethren of the Eastern states. To achieve this end, Mason and others urged that the Constitution include a proviso that navigation and commercial laws should require a two-thirds vote in Congress.

These problems came to a head in late August and, as usual, were handed to a committee in the hope that, in Gouverneur Morris's words, "these things may form a bargain among the Northern and Southern States." The Committee reported its measures of reconciliation on August 25, and on August 29 the package was wrapped up and delivered. What occurred can best be described in George Mason's dour version (he anticipated Calhoun in his conviction that permitting navigation acts to pass by majority vote would put the South in economic bondage to the North—it was mainly on this ground that he refused to sign the Constitution):

> The Constitution as agreed to till a fortnight before the Convention rose was such a one as he would have set his hand and heart to. . . . [Until that time] The 3 New England States were constantly with us in all questions . . . so that it was these three States with the 5 Southern ones against Pennsylvania, Jersey and Delaware. With respect to the importation of slaves, [decision-making] was left to Congress. This disturbed the two Southern-most States who knew the Congress would immediately

> suppress the importation of slaves. Those two States therefore struck up a bargain with the three New England States. If they would join to admit slaves for some years, the two Southern-most States would join in changing the clause which required the 2/3 of the Legislature in any vote [on navigation acts]. It was done.

On the floor of the Convention there was a virtual love-feast on this happy occasion. Charles Pinckney of South Carolina attempted to overturn the committee's decision, when the compromise was reported to the Convention, by insisting that the South needed protection from the imperialism of the Northern states. But his Southern colleagues were not prepared to rock the boat and General C. C. Pinckney arose to spread oil on the suddenly ruffled waters; he admitted that:

> It was in the true interest of the S[outhern] States to have no regulation of commerce; but considering the loss brought on the commerce of the Eastern States by the Revolution, their liberal conduct towards the views of South Carolina [on the regulation of the slave trade] and the interests the weak Southn. States had in being united with the strong Eastern states, he thought it proper that no fetters should be imposed on the power of making commercial regulations; *and that his constituents, though prejudiced against the Eastern States, would be reconciled to this liberality*. He had himself prejudices against the Eastern States before he came here, but would acknowledge that he had found them as liberal and candid as any men whatever. (Italics added.)

Pierce Butler took the same tack, essentially arguing that he was not too happy about the possible consequences, but that a deal was a deal. Many Southern leaders were later—in the wake of the "Tariff of Abominations"—to rue this day of reconciliation; Calhoun's *Disquisition on Government* was little more than an extension of the argument in the Convention against permitting a Congressional majority to enact navigation acts.

VI

Drawing on their vast collective political experience, utilizing every weapon in the politician's arsenal, looking constantly over their shoulders at their constituents, the delegates put together a Constitution. It was a makeshift affair; some sticky issues (for example, the qualification of voters) they ducked entirely; others they mastered with that ancient instrument of political sagacity, studied ambiguity (for example, citizenship); and some they just overlooked. In this last category, I suspect, fell the matter of the power of the federal courts to determine the constitutionality of acts of Congress. When the judicial article was formulated (Article III of the Constitution), deliberations were still in the stage where the legislature was endowed with broad power under the Randolph formulation, authority which by its own terms was scarcely amenable to judicial review. In essence, courts could hardly determine when "the separate States are incompetent or . . . the harmony of the United States may be interrupted"; the national legislature, as critics pointed out, was free to define its own jurisdiction. Later the definition of legislative authority was changed into the form we know, a series of stipulated powers, *but the delegates never seriously reexamined the jurisdiction of the judiciary under this new limited formulation*. All arguments on the intention of the framers in this matter are thus deductive and *a posteriori*, though some obviously make more sense than others.

The framers were busy and distinguished men, anxious to get back to their families, their positions, and their constituents, not members of the French Academy devoting a lifetime to a dictionary. They were trying to do an important job, and do it in such a fashion that their handiwork would be acceptable to very diverse constituencies. No one was rhapsodic about the final document, but it was a beginning, a move in the right direction, and one they had reason to believe the people would endorse. In addition, since they had modified the impossible amendment provisions of the Articles (the requirement of unanimity which could always be frustrated by "Rogues Island") to one demanding approval by only three-quarters of the states, they seemed confident that gaps in the fabric which experience would reveal could be rewoven without undue difficulty.

So with a neat phrase introduced by Benjamin Franklin (but devised by Gouverneur Morris) which made their decision sound unanimous, and an inspired benediction by the Old Doctor urging doubters to doubt their own infallibility, the Constitution was accepted and signed. Curiously, Edmund Randolph, who had played so vital a role throughout, refused to sign, as did his fellow Virginian George Mason and Elbridge Gerry of Massachusetts. Randolph's behavior was eccentric, to say the least—his excuses for refusing his signature have a factitious ring even at this late date; the best explanation seems to be that he was afraid that the Constitution would prove to be a liability in Virginia politics, where Patrick Henry was burning up the countryside with impassioned denunciations. Presumably, Randolph wanted to check the temper of the populace before he risked his reputation, and perhaps his job, in a fight with both Henry and Richard Henry Lee. Events lend some justification to this speculation: after much temporizing and use of the conditional subjunctive tense, Randolph endorsed ratification in Virginia and ended up getting the best of both worlds.

Madison, despite his reservations about the Constitution, was the campaign manager in ratification. His first task was to get the Congress in New York to light its own funeral pyre by approving the "amendments" to the Articles and sending them on to the state legislatures. Above all, momentum had to be maintained. The anti-Constitutionalists, now thoroughly alarmed and no novices in politics, realized that their best tactic was attrition rather than direct opposition. Thus they settled on a position expressing qualified approval but calling for a second Convention to remedy various defects (the one with the most demagogic appeal was the lack of a Bill of Rights). Madison knew that to accede to this demand would be equivalent to losing the battle, nor would he agree to conditional approval (despite wavering even by Hamilton). This was an all-or-nothing proposition: national salvation or national impotence with no intermediate positions possible. Unable to get Congressional approval, he settled for second best: a unanimous resolution of Congress transmitting the Constitution to the states for whatever action they saw fit to take. The opponents then moved from New York and the Congress, where they had attempted to attach amendments and conditions, to the states for the final battle.

At first the campaign for ratification went beautifully: within eight months after the delegates set their names to the document, eight states had ratified. Only in Massachusetts had the result been close (187–168). Theoretically, a ratification by one more state convention would set the new government in motion, but in fact until Virginia and New York acceded to the new Union, the latter was a fiction. New Hampshire was the next to ratify; Rhode Island was involved in its characteristic political convulsions (the legislature there sent the Constitution out to the towns for decision by popular vote and it got lost among a series of local issues); North Carolina's convention did not meet until July and then postponed a final decision. This is hardly the place for an extensive analysis of the conventions of New York and Virginia. Suffice it to say that the Constitutionalists clearly outmaneuvered their opponents, forced them into impossible political positions, and won both states narrowly. The Virginia Convention could serve as a classic study in effective floor management: Patrick Henry had to be contained, and a reading of the debates discloses a standard two-stage technique. Henry would give a four- or five-hour speech denouncing some section of the Constitution on every conceivable ground (the federal district, he averred at one point, would become a haven for convicts escaping from state authority!); when Henry subsided, "Mr. Lee of Westmoreland" would rise and literally poleax him with sardonic invective (when Henry complained about the militia power, "Lighthorse Harry" really punched below the belt: observing that while the former Governor had been sitting in Richmond during the Revolution, *he* had been out in the trenches with the troops and thus felt better qualified to discuss military affairs). Then the gentlemanly Constitutionalists (Madison, Pendleton, and Marshall) would pick up the matters at issue and examine them in the light of reason.

Indeed, modern Americans who tend to think of James Madison as a rather desiccated character should spend some time with this transcript. Probably Madison put on his most spectacular demonstration of nimble rhetoric in what might be called "The Battle of the Absent Authorities." Patrick Henry in the course of one of his harangues alleged that Jefferson was known to be opposed to Virginia's approving the Constitution. This was clever: Henry hated Jefferson, but was prepared to use any weapon that came to hand. Madison's riposte was superb: First, he said that with all due respect to the great reputation of Jefferson, he was not in the country and therefore could not formulate an adequate judgment; second, no one should utilize the reputation of an outsider—the Virginia Convention was there to think for itself; third, if there were to be recourse to outsiders, the opinions of George Washington should certainly be taken into consideration; and finally, he knew from privileged personal communications from Jefferson that in fact the latter *strongly favored* the Constitution. To devise an assault route into this rhetorical fortress was literally impossible.

VII

The fight was over; all that remained now was to establish the new frame of government in the spirit of its framers. And who were better qualified for this task than the framers themselves? Thus victory for the Constitution meant simultaneous victory for the Constitutionalists; the anti-Constitutionalists either capitulated or vanished into limbo—soon Patrick Henry would be offered a seat on the Supreme Court and Luther Martin would be known as the Federalist "bull-dog." And irony of ironies, Alexander Hamilton and James Madison would shortly accumulate a reputation as the formulators of what is often alleged to be our political theory, the concept of "federalism." Also, on the other side of the ledger, the arguments would soon appear over what the framers "really meant"; while these disputes have assumed the proportions of a big scholarly business in the last century, they began almost before the ink on the Constitution was dry. One of the best early ones featured Hamilton versus Madison on the scope of presidential power, and other framers characteristically assumed positions in this and other disputes on the basis of their political convictions.

Probably our greatest difficulty is that we know so much more about what the framers *should have meant* than they themselves did. We are intimately acquainted with the problems that their Constitution should have been designed to master; in short, we have read the mystery story backwards. If we are to get the right "feel" for their time and their circumstances, we must in Maitland's phrase, "think ourselves back into a twilight." Obviously, no one can pretend completely to escape from the solipsistic web of his own environment, but if the effort is made, it is possible to appreciate the past roughly on its own terms. The first step in this process is to abandon the academic premise that because we can ask a question, there must be an answer.

Thus we can ask what the framers meant when they gave Congress the power to regulate interstate and foreign commerce, and we emerge, reluctantly perhaps, with the reply that they may not have known what they meant, that there may not have been any semantic consensus. The Convention was not a seminar in analytic philosophy or linguistic analysis. Commerce was *commerce*—and if different interpretations of the word arose, later generations could worry about the problem of definition. The delegates were in a hurry to get a new government established; when definitional arguments arose, they characteristically took refuge in ambiguity. If different men voted for the same proposition for varying reasons, that was politics (and still is); if later generations were unsettled by this lack of precision, that would be their problem.

There was a good deal of definitional pluralism with respect to the problems the delegates did discuss, but when we move to the question of extrapolated intentions, we enter the realm of spiritualism. When men in our time, for instance, launch into elaborate talmudic exegesis to demonstrate that federal aid to parochial schools is (or is not) in accord with the intentions of the men who established the Republic and endorsed the Bill of Rights, they are engaging in historical Extra-Sensory Perception. (If one were to join this E.S.P. contingent for a minute, he might suggest that the hard-boiled politicians who wrote the Constitution and Bill of Rights would chuckle scornfully at such an invocation of authority: obviously a politician would chart his course on the intentions of the living, not of the dead, and count the number of Catholics in his constituency.)

The Constitution, then, was not an apotheosis of "constitutionalism," a triumph of architectonic genius; it was a patch-work sewn together under the pressure of both time and events by a group of extremely talented democratic politicians. They refused to attempt the establishment of a strong, centralized sovereignty on the principle of legislative supremacy for the excellent reason that the people would not accept it. They risked their political fortunes by opposing the established doctrines of state sovereignty because they were convinced that the existing system was leading to national impotence and probably foreign domination. For two years, they worked to get a convention established. For over three months, in what must have seemed to the faithful participants an endless process of give-and-take, they reasoned, cajoled, threatened, and bargained amongst themselves. The result was a Constitution which the people, in fact, by democratic processes, did accept, and a new and far better national government was established.

Beginning with the inspired propaganda of Hamilton, Madison, and Jay, the ideological build-up got under way. *The Federalist* had little impact on the ratification of the Constitution, except perhaps in New York, but this volume had enormous influence on the image of the Constitution in the minds of future generations, particularly on historians and political scientists who have an innate fondness for theoretical symmetry. Yet, while the shades of Locke and Montesquieu *may* have been hovering in the background, and the delegates *may* have been unconscious instruments of a transcendent *telos*, the careful observer of the day-to-day work of the Convention finds no overarching principles. The "separation of powers" to him seems to be a by-product of suspicion, and "federalism" he views as a *pis aller*, as the farthest point the delegates felt they could go in the destruction of state power without themselves inviting repudiation.

To conclude, the Constitution was neither a victory for abstract theory nor a great practical success. Well over half a million men had to die on the battlefields of the Civil War before certain constitutional principles could be defined—a baleful consideration which is somehow overlooked in our customary tributes to the farsighted genius of the framers and to the supposed American talent for "constitutionalism." The Constitution was, however, a vivid demonstration of effective democratic political action, and of the forging of a national elite which literally persuaded its countrymen to hoist themselves by their own boot straps. American pro-consuls would be wise not to translate the Constitution into Japanese, or Swahili, or treat it as a work of semi-Divine origin; but when students of comparative politics examine the process of nation-building in countries newly freed from colonial rule, they may find the American experience instructive as a classic example of the potentialities of a democratic elite.

John Roche's article on the framing of the Constitution was written as an attack upon a variety of views that suggested the Constitution was not so much a practical political document as an expression of elitist views based upon political philosophy and economic interests. One such elitist view was that of Charles A. Beard, who published his famous *An Economic Interpretation of the Constitution* in 1913. He suggested that the Constitution was nothing more than the work of an economic elite that was seeking to preserve its property. This elite, according to Beard, consisted of landholders, creditors, merchants, public bondholders, and wealthy lawyers. Beard demonstrated that many of the delegates to the convention fell into one of these categories.

According to Beard's thesis, as the delegates met, the primary concern of most of them was to limit the power of popular majorities and thus protect their own property interests. To Beard, the antimajoritarian attributes that he felt existed in the Constitution were a reflection of the small creditor class attempting to protect itself against incursions by the majority. Specific provisions as well were put into the Constitution with a view toward protecting property, such as the clause prohibiting states from impairing contracts, coining money, or emitting bills of credit. Control over money was placed in the hands of the national government, and in Article VI of the Constitution it was provided that the new government was to guarantee all debts that had been incurred by the national government under the Articles of Confederation.

Ironically, Beard, like Roche, was attempting to dispel the prevailing notions of his time that the Constitution had been formulated by philosopher kings whose wisdom could not be challenged. But while Roche postulates a loosely knit practical political elite, Beard suggests the existence of a cohesive and even conspiratorial economic elite. The limitation on majority rule was an essential component of this economic conspiracy.

The Constitution does contain many provisions that limit majority rule. Beard claimed that the Constitution, from initial adoption to final ratification, was never supported by the majority of the people. The holding of a constitutional convention in the first place was never submitted to a popular vote, nor was the Constitution that was finally agreed upon ratified by a popular referendum. The selection of delegates to state ratifying conventions was not executed through universal suffrage, but on the basis of the suffrage qualifications that applied in the states and that were within the discretion of state legislatures. The limited suffrage in the states severely restricted popular participation in ratification of the Constitution.

Beard's thesis was startling at the time it was published in 1913. As it came under close examination, it was revealed that the evidence simply did not support Beard's hypothesis. Key leaders of the convention, including Madison, were not substantial property owners. Several important opponents to ratification of the Constitution were the very members of the economic elite that Beard said conspired to thrust the Constitution upon an unknowing public.

Before Beard presented his narrow thesis in 1913, he had published *The Supreme Court and the Constitution* in 1912. The major theme of the book was that the Supreme Court was intended to have the authority to review acts of Congress under the terms of the original Constitution. At the same time, the book presents Beard's elitist view of the framing of the Constitution in a somewhat broader context than it was presented in *An Economic Interpretation of the Constitution*, published a year later. But the earlier work clearly contains the economic theme, as in the passage where Beard states that the framers of the Constitution were "anxious above everything else to safeguard the rights of private property against any levelling tendencies on the part of the propertyless masses." The following selection contains Beard's overview of the framing and adoption of the Constitution and highlights his economic theme and his belief in the antimajoritarian attributes of the Constitution.

3

FRAMING THE CONSTITUTION

Charles A. Beard

As Blackstone* shows by happy illustration the reason and spirit of a law are to be understood only by an inquiry into the circumstances of its enactment. The underlying purposes of the Constitution [of the United States], therefore, are to be revealed only by a study of the conditions and events which led to its formation and adoption.

At the outset it must be remembered that there were two great parties at the time of the adoption of the Constitution—one laying emphasis on strength and efficiency in government and the other on its popular aspects. Quite naturally the men who led in stirring up the revolt against Great Britain and in keeping the fighting temper of the Revolutionists at the proper heat were the boldest and most radical thinkers—men like Samuel Adams, Thomas Paine, Patrick Henry, and Thomas Jefferson. They were not, generally speaking, men of large property interests or of much practical business experience. In a time of disorder, they could consistently lay more stress upon personal liberty than upon social control; and they pushed to the extreme limits those doctrines of individual rights which had been evolved in England during the struggles of the small landed proprietors and commercial classes against royal prerogative, and which corresponded to the economic conditions prevailing in America at the close of the eighteenth century. They associated strong government with monarchy, and came to believe that the best political system was one which governed least. A majority of the radicals viewed all government, especially if highly centralized, as a species of evil, tolerable only because necessary and always to be kept down to an irreducible minimum by a jealous vigilance.

Jefferson put the doctrine in concrete form when he declared that he preferred newspapers without government to government without newspapers. The Declaration of Independence, the first state Constitutions, and the Articles of Confederation bore the impress of this philosophy. In their anxiety to defend the individual against all federal interference and to preserve to the states a large sphere of local autonomy, these Revolutionists had set up a system too weak to accomplish

*Compiler's note: Blackstone, Sir William (1723–1780). Distinguished commentator on the laws of England, judge, and teacher.

the accepted objects of government; namely, national defense, the protection of property, and the advancement of commerce. They were not unaware of the character of their handiwork, but they believed with Jefferson that "man was a rational animal endowed by nature with rights and with an innate sense of justice and that he could be restrained from wrong and protected in right by moderate powers confided to persons of his own choice." Occasional riots and disorders, they held, were preferable to too much government.

The new American political system based on these doctrines had scarcely gone into effect before it began to incur opposition from many sources. The close of the Revolutionary struggle removed the prime cause for radical agitation and brought a new group of thinkers into prominence. When independence had been gained, the practical work to be done was the maintenance of social order, the payment of the public debt, the provision of a sound financial system, and the establishment of conditions favorable to the development of the economic resources of the new country. The men who were principally concerned in this work of peaceful enterprise were not the philosophers, but men of business and property and the holders of public securities. For the most part they had had no quarrel with the system of class rule and the strong centralization of government which existed in England. It was on the question of policy, not of governmental structure, that they had broken with the British authorities. By no means all of them, in fact, had even resisted the policy of the mother country, for within the ranks of the conservatives were large numbers of Loyalists who had remained in America, and, as was to have been expected, cherished a bitter feeling against the Revolutionists, especially the radical section which had been boldest in denouncing the English system root and branch. In other words, after the heat and excitement of the War of Independence were over and the new government, state and national, was tested by the ordinary experiences of traders, financiers, and manufacturers, it was found inadequate, and these groups accordingly grew more and more determined to reconstruct the political system in such a fashion as to make it subserve their permanent interests.

Under the state constitutions and the Articles of Confederation established during the Revolution, every powerful economic class in the nation suffered either immediate losses or from impediments placed in the way of the development of their enterprises. The holders of the securities of the Confederate government did not receive the interest on their loans. Those who owned Western lands or looked with longing eyes upon the rich opportunities for speculation there chaffed at the weakness of the government and its delays in establishing order on the frontiers. Traders and commercial men found their plans for commerce on a national scale impeded by local interference with interstate commerce. The currency of the states and the nation was hopelessly muddled. Creditors everywhere were angry about the depreciated paper money which the agrarians had made and were attempting to force upon those from whom they had borrowed specie. In short, it was a war between business and populism. Under the Articles of Confederation populism had a free hand, for majorities in the state legislatures were omnipotent. Anyone who reads the economic history of the time will see why the solid conservative interests of the country were weary of talk about the "rights of the people" and bent upon establishing firm guarantees for the rights of property.

The Congress of the Confederation was not long in discovering the true character of the futile authority which the Articles had conferred upon it. The necessity for new sources of revenue became apparent even while the struggle for independence was yet undecided, and, in 1781, Congress carried a resolution to the effect that it should be authorized to lay a duty of five percent on certain goods. This moderate proposition was defeated because Rhode Island rejected it on the grounds that "she regarded it the most precious jewel of sovereignty that no state shall be called upon to open its purse but by the authority of the state and by her own officers." Two years later Congress prepared another amendment to the Articles providing for certain import duties, the receipts from which, collected by state officers, were to be applied to the payment of the public debt; but three years after the introduction of the measure, four states, including New York, still held out against its ratification, and the project was allowed to drop. At last, in 1786, Congress in a resolution declared that the requisitions for the last eight years had been so irregular in their operation, so uncertain in their collection, and so evidently unproductive, that a reliance on them in the future would be no less dishonorable to the understandings of those who entertained it than it would be dangerous to the welfare and peace of the Union. Congress, thereupon, solemnly added that it had become its duty "to declare most explicitly that the crisis had arrived when the people of the United States, by whose will and for whose benefit the federal government was instituted, must decide whether they will support their rank as a nation by maintaining the public faith at home and abroad, or whether for the want of a timely exertion in establishing a general review and thereby giving strength to the Confederacy, they will hazard not only the existence of the Union but those great and invaluable privileges for which they have so arduously and so honorably contended."

In fact, the Articles of Confederation had hardly gone into effect before the leading citizens also began to feel that the powers of Congress were wholly inadequate. In 1780, even before their adoption, Alexander Hamilton proposed a general convention to frame a new constitution, and from that time forward he labored with remarkable zeal and wisdom to extend and popularize the idea of a strong national government. Two years later, the Assembly of the State of New York recommended a convention to revise the Articles and increase the power of Congress. In 1783, Washington, in a circular letter to the governors, urged that it was indispensable to the happiness of the individual states that there should be lodged somewhere a supreme power to regulate and govern the general concerns of the confederation. Shortly afterward (1785), Governor Bowdoin, of Massachusetts, suggested to his state legislature the advisability of calling a national assembly to settle upon and define the powers of Congress; and the legislature resolved that the government under the Articles of Confederation was inadequate and should be reformed, but the resolution was never laid before Congress.

In January, 1786, Virginia invited all the other states to send delegates to a convention at Annapolis to consider the question of duties on imports and commerce in general. When this convention assembled in 1786, delegates from only five states were present, and they were disheartened at the limitations on their powers and the lack of interest the other states had shown in the project. With characteristic foresight, however, Alexander Hamilton seized the occasion to secure the adoption of a recommendation advising the states to choose representatives for another convention to meet in Philadelphia the following year "to consider the Articles of Confederation and to propose such changes therein as might render them adequate to the exigencies of the union." This recommendation was cautiously worded, for Hamilton did not want to raise any unnecessary alarm. He doubtless believed that a complete revolution in the old system was desirable, but he knew that, in the existing state of popular temper, it was not expedient to announce his complete program. Accordingly no general reconstruction of the political system was suggested; the Articles of Confederation were merely to be "revised"; and the amendments were to be approved by the state legislatures as provided by that instrument.

The proposal of the Annapolis convention was transmitted to the state legislatures and laid before Congress. Congress thereupon resolved in February, 1787, that a convention should be held for the sole and express purpose of revising the Articles of Confederation and reporting to itself and the legislatures of the several states such alterations and provisions as would when agreed to by Congress and confirmed by the states render the federal constitution adequate to the exigencies of government and the preservation of the union.

In pursuance of this call, delegates to the new convention were chosen by the legislatures of the states or by the governors in conformity to authority conferred by the legislative assemblies.[1] The delegates were given instructions of a general nature by their respective states, none of which, apparently, contemplated any very far-reaching changes. In fact, almost all of them expressly limited their representatives to a mere revision of the Articles of Confederation. For example, Connecticut authorized her delegates to represent and confer for the purpose mentioned in the resolution of Congress and to discuss such measures "agreeable to the general principles of Republican government" as they should think proper to render the Union adequate. Delaware, however, went so far as to provide that none of the proposed alterations should extend to the fifth part of the Articles of Confederation guaranteeing that each state should be entitled to one vote.

It was a truly remarkable assembly of men that gathered in Philadelphia on May 14, 1787, to undertake the work of reconstructing the American system of government. It is not merely patriotic pride that compels one to assert that never in the history of assemblies has there been a convention of men richer in political experience and in practical knowledge, or endowed with a profounder insight into the springs of human action and the intimate essence of government. It is indeed an astounding fact that at one time so many men skilled in statecraft could be found on the very frontiers of civilization among a population numbering about four million whites. It is no less a cause for admiration that their instrument of government should have survived the trials and crises of a century that saw the wreck of more than a score of paper constitutions.

All the members had had a practical training in politics. Washington, as commander-in-chief of the Revolutionary forces, had learned well the lessons and problems of war, and mastered successfully the no less difficult problems of

---

[1]Rhode Island alone was unrepresented. In all, sixty-two delegates were appointed by the states; fifty-five of these attended sometime during the sessions; but only thirty-nine signed the finished document.

administration. The two Morrises had distinguished themselves in grappling with financial questions as trying and perplexing as any which statesmen had ever been compelled to face. Seven of the delegates had gained political wisdom as governors of their native states; and no less than twenty-eight had served in Congress either during the Revolution or under the Articles of Confederation. These were men trained in the law, versed in finance, skilled in administration, and learned in the political philosophy of their own and all earlier times. Moreover, they were men destined to continue public service under the government which they had met to construct—Presidents, Vice-Presidents, heads of departments, Justices of the Supreme Court were in that imposing body. . . .

As Woodrow Wilson had concisely put it, the framers of the Constitution represented "a strong and intelligent class possessed of unity and informed by a conscious solidarity of interests."[2] . . .

The makers of the federal Constitution represented the solid, conservative, commercial and financial interests of the country—not the interests which denounced and proscribed judges in Rhode Island, New Jersey, and North Carolina, and stoned their houses in New York. The conservative interests, made desperate by the imbecilities of the Confederation and harried by state legislatures, roused themselves from the lethargy, drew together in a mighty effort to establish a government that would be strong enough to pay the national debt, regulate interstate and foreign commerce, provide for national defense, prevent fluctuations in the currency created by paper emissions, and control the propensities of legislative majorities to attack private rights. . . . The radicals, however, like Patrick Henry, Jefferson, and Samuel Adams, were conspicuous by their absence from the convention.* . . .

[The makers of the Constitution were convened] to frame a government which would meet the practical issues that had arisen under the Articles of Confederation. The objections they entertained to direct popular government, and they were undoubtedly many, were based upon their experience with popular assemblies during the immediately preceding years. With many of the plain lessons of history before them, they naturally feared that the rights and privileges of the minority would be insecure if the principle of majority rule was definitely adopted and provisions made for its exercise. Furthermore, it will be remembered that up to that time the right of all men, as men, to share in the government had never been recognized in practice. Everywhere in Europe the government was in the hands of a ruling monarch or at best a ruling class; everywhere the mass of the people had been regarded principally as an arms-bearing and tax-paying multitude, uneducated, and with little hope or capacity for advancement. Two years were to elapse after the meeting of the grave assembly at Philadelphia before the transformation of the Estates General into the National Convention in France opened the floodgates of revolutionary ideas on human rights before whose rising tide old landmarks of government are still being submerged. It is small wonder, therefore, that, under the

---

[2]Woodrow Wilson, *Division and Reunion* (New York: Longmans, Green, & Co., 1893), p. 12.

**Compiler's note.* The contents of this paragraph have been taken from positions on pp. 75–76 and 88 of the original text of *The Supreme Court and the Constitution* and placed here to emphasize the economic theme.

circumstances, many of the members of that august body held popular government in slight esteem and took the people into consideration only as far as it was imperative "to inspire them with the necessary confidence," as Mr. Gerry frankly put it.[3]

Indeed, every page of the laconic record of the proceedings of the convention preserved to posterity by Mr. Madison shows conclusively that the members of that assembly were not seeking to realize any fine notions about democracy and equality, but were striving with all the resources of political wisdom at their command to set up a system of government that would be stable and efficient, safeguarded on one hand against the possibilities of despotism and on the other against the onslaught of majorities. In the mind of Mr. Gerry, the evils they had experienced flowed "from the excess of democracy," and he confessed that while he was still republican, he "had been taught by experience the danger of the levelling spirit."[4] Mr. Randolph in offering to the consideration of the convention his plan of government, observed "that the general object was to provide a cure for the evils under which the United States labored; that, in tracing these evils to their origin, every man had found it in the turbulence and follies of democracy; that some check therefore was to be sought for against this tendency of our governments; and that a good Senate seemed most likely to answer the purpose."[5] Mr. Hamilton, in advocating a life term for Senators, urged that "all communities divide themselves into the few and the many. The first are rich and well born and the other the mass of the people who seldom judge or determine right."

Gouverneur Morris wanted to check the "precipitancy, changeableness, and excess" of the representatives of the people by the ability and virtue of men "of great and established property—aristocracy; men who from pride will support consistency and permanency. . . . Such an aristocratic body will keep down the turbulence of democracy." While these extreme doctrines were somewhat counter-balanced by the democratic principles of Mr. Wilson who urged that "the government ought to possess, not only first, the force, but second the mind or sense of the people at large," Madison doubtless summed up in a brief sentence the general opinion of the convention when he said that to secure private rights against majority factions, and at the same time to preserve the spirit and form of popular government, was the great object to which their inquiries had been directed.[6]

They were anxious above everything else to safeguard the rights of private property against any leveling tendencies on the part of the propertyless masses. Gouverneur Morris, in speaking on the problem of apportioning representatives, correctly stated the sound historical fact when he declared: "Life and liberty were generally said to be of more value than property. An accurate view of the matter would, nevertheless, prove that property was the main object of society. . . . If property, then, was the main object of government, certainly it ought to be one measure of the influence due to those who were to be affected by the government."[7] Mr. King also agreed that "property was the

---

[3]Jonathan Elliot, *The Debates in the Several State Conventions on the Adoption of the Federal Constitution* (Washington, D.C.: The Editor, 1827–1830), vol. v, p. 160.

[4]Ibid., vol. v, p. 136.

[5]Ibid., vol. v, p. 138.

[6]*The Federalist*, No. 10.

[7]Elliot's *Debates*, op. cit., vol. v, p. 279.

primary object of society,"[8] and Mr. Madison warned the convention that in framing a system which they wished to last for ages they must not lose sight of the changes which the ages would produce in the forms and distribution of property. In advocating a long term in order to give independence and firmness to the Senate, he described these impending changes: "An increase of population will of necessity increase the proportion of those who will labor under all the hardships of life and secretly sigh for a more equal distribution of its blessings. These may in time outnumber those who are placed above the feelings of indigence. According to the equal laws of suffrage, the power will slide into the hands of the former. No agrarian attempts have yet been made in this country, but symptoms of a levelling spirit, as we have understood have sufficiently appeared, in a certain quarter, to give notice of the future danger."[9] And again, in support of the argument for a property qualification on voters, Madison urged: "In future times, a great majority of the people will not only be without landed, but any other sort of property. These will either combine, under the influence of their common situation,—in which case the rights of property and the public liberty will not be secure in their hands,—or what is more probable, they will become the tools of opulence and ambition; in which case there will be equal danger on another side."[10] Various projects for setting up class rule by the establishment of property qualifications for voters and officers were advanced in the convention, but they were defeated. . . .

> The absence of such property qualifications is certainly not due to any belief in Jefferson's free-and-equal doctrine. It is due rather to the fact that the members of the convention could not agree on the nature and amount of the qualifications. Naturally a landed qualification was suggested, but for obvious reasons it was rejected. Although it was satisfactory to the landed gentry of the South, it did not suit the financial, commercial, and manufacturing gentry of the North. If it was high, the latter would be excluded; if it was low it would let in the populistic farmers who had already made so much trouble in the state legislatures with paper-money schemes and other devices for "relieving agriculture." One of the chief reasons for calling the convention and framing the Constitution was to promote commerce and industry and to protect personal property against the "depredations" of Jefferson's noble freeholders. On the other hand a personal-property qualification, high enough to please merchant princes like Robert Morris and Nathaniel Gorham, would shut out the Southern planters. Again, an alternative of land or personal property, high enough to afford safeguards to large interests, would doubtless bring about the rejection of the whole Constitution by the troublemaking farmers who had to pass upon the question of ratification.* . . .

Nevertheless, by the system of checks and balances placed in the government, the convention safeguarded the interests of property against attacks by majorities.

---

[8]Ibid., p. 280.

[9]Ibid., p. 243.

[10]Ibid., p. 387.

**Compiler's note:* This single paragraph from "Whom Does Congress Represent?" *Harper's Magazine*, Jan. 1930, pp. 144–152, has been inserted here because of its value in amplifying the passages from *The Supreme Court and the Constitution*. Reprinting from this article by Beard has been done with the permission of *Harper's Magazine*.

The House of Representatives, Mr. Hamilton pointed out, "was so formed as to render it particularly the guardian of the poorer orders of citizens,"[11] while the Senate was to preserve the rights of property and the interests of the minority against the demands of the majority.[12] In the tenth number of *The Federalist*, Mr. Madison argued in a philosophic vein in support of the proposition that it was necessary to base the political system on the actual conditions of "natural inequality." Uniformity of interests throughout the state, he contended, was impossible on account of the diversity in the faculties of men, from which the rights of property originated; the protection of these faculties was the first object of government; from the protection of different and unequal faculties of acquiring property the possession of different degrees and kinds of property immediately resulted; from the influence of these on the sentiments and views of the respective proprietors ensued a division of society into different interests and parties; the unequal distribution of wealth inevitably led to a clash of interests in which the majority was liable to carry out its policies at the expense of the minority; hence, he added, in concluding this splendid piece of logic, "the majority, having such coexistent passion or interest, must be rendered by their number and local situation unable to concert and carry into effect schemes of oppression"; and in his opinion it was the great merit of the newly framed Constitution that it secured the rights of the minority against "the superior force of an interested and overbearing majority."

This very system of checks and balances, which is undeniably the essential element of the Constitution, is built upon the doctrine that the popular branch of the government cannot be allowed full sway, and least of all in the enactment of laws touching the rights of property. The exclusion of the direct popular vote in the election of the President; the creation, again by indirect election, of a Senate which the framers hoped would represent the wealth and conservative interests of the country;* and the establishment of an independent judiciary appointed by the President with the concurrence of the Senate—all these devices bear witness to the fact that the underlying purpose of the Constitution was not the establishment of popular government by means of parliamentary majorities.

Page after page of *The Federalist* is directed to that portion of the electorate which was disgusted with the "mutability of the public councils." Writing on the presidential veto Hamilton says: "The propensity of the legislative department to intrude upon the rights, and absorb the powers, of other departments has already been suggested and repeated. . . . It may perhaps be said that the power of preventing bad laws included the power of preventing good ones; and may be used to the one purpose as well as the other. But this objection will have little weight with those who can properly estimate the mischiefs of that inconstancy and mutability in the laws which form the greater blemish in the character and genius of our governments. They will consider every institution calculated to restrain the excess of law-making and to keep things in the same state in which they happen to be at any given period,

---

[11]Elliot's *Debates*, *op. cit.*, vol. v, p. 244.

[12]Ibid., vol. v, p. 203.

**Compiler's note:* Popular election of senators was achieved in 1913 through the Seventeenth Amendment to the Constitution.

as more likely to do good than harm; because it is favorable to greater stability in the system of legislation. The injury which may be possibly done by defeating a few good laws will be amply compensated by the advantage of preventing a number of bad ones."

When the framers of the Constitution had completed the remarkable instrument which was to establish a national government capable of discharging effectively certain great functions and checking the propensities of popular legislatures to attack the rights of private property, a formidable task remained before them—the task of securing the adoption of the new frame of government by states torn with popular dissensions. They knew very well that the state legislatures which had been so negligent in paying their quotas [of money] under the Articles [of Confederation] and which had been so jealous of their rights, would probably stick at ratifying such a national instrument of government. Accordingly they cast aside that clause in the Articles requiring amendments to be ratified by the legislatures of all the states; and advised that the new Constitution should be ratified by conventions in the several states composed of delegates chosen by the voters.* They furthermore declared—and this is a fundamental matter—that when the conventions of nine states had ratified the Constitution the new government should go into effect so far as those states were concerned. The chief reason for resorting to ratifications by conventions is laid down by Hamilton in the twenty-second number of *The Federalist:* "It has not a little contributed to the infirmities of the existing federal system that it never had a ratification by the people. Resting on no better foundation than the consent of the several legislatures, it has been exposed to frequent and intricate questions concerning the validity of its powers; and has in some instances given birth to the enormous doctrine of a right of legislative repeal. Owing its ratification to the law of a state, it has been contended that the same authority might repeal the law by which it was ratified. However gross a heresy it may be to maintain that a party to a compact has a right to revoke that compact, the doctrine itself has respectable advocates. The possibility of a question of this nature proves the necessity of laying the foundations of our national government deeper than in the mere sanction of delegated authority. The fabric of American empire ought to rest on the solid basis of the consent of the people. The streams of national power ought to flow immediately from that pure original foundation of all legitimate authority."

Of course, the convention did not resort to the revolutionary policy of transmitting the Constitution directly to the conventions of the several states. It merely laid the finished instrument before the Confederate Congress with the suggestion that it should be submitted to "a convention of delegates chosen in each state by the people thereof, under the recommendation of its legislature, for their assent and ratification; and each convention assenting thereto and ratifying the same should give notice thereof to the United States in Congress assembled." The convention

*Compiler's note: The original text (p. 75) comments, "It was largely because the framers of the Constitution knew the temper and class bias of the state legislatures that they arranged that the new Constitution should be ratified by conventions."

went on to suggest that when nine states had ratified the Constitution, the Confederate Congress should extinguish itself by making provision for the elections necessary to put the new government into effect. . . .

After the new Constitution was published and transmitted to the states, there began a long and bitter fight over ratification. A veritable flood of pamphlet literature descended upon the country, and a collection of these pamphlets by Hamilton, Madison, and Jay, brought together under the title of *The Federalist*—though clearly a piece of campaign literature—has remained a permanent part of the contemporary sources on the Constitution and has been regarded by many lawyers as a commentary second in value only to the decisions of the Supreme Court. Within a year the champions of the new government found themselves victorious, for on June 21, 1788, the ninth state, New Hampshire, ratified the Constitution, and accordingly the new government might go into effect as between the agreeing states. Within a few weeks, the nationalist party in Virginia and New York succeeded in winning these two states, and in spite of the fact that North Carolina and Rhode Island had not yet ratified the Constitution, Congress determined to put the instrument into effect in accordance with the recommendations of the convention. Elections for the new government were held; the date March 4, 1789, was fixed for the formal establishment of the new system; Congress secured a quorum on April 6; and on April 30 Washington was inaugurated at the Federal Hall in Wall Street, New York.

Charles A. Beard suggests that there is a dichotomy between the values of the Constitution and those of the Declaration of Independence, between Jefferson and his followers on the one hand, and Madison and Hamilton on the other. He suggests that Jefferson and the Revolutionists supported political equality and individual freedom and opposed a strong central government. The spirit of the Revolution, argues Beard, spawned the Articles of Confederation, which purposely created a weak and ineffective government. The Revolutionists, in general, were not men of property and thus did not believe that a strong central government was necessary to protect their interests. By contrast, the framers of the Constitution reflected the spirit of Alexander Hamilton, who ironically was not a man of substantial property himself, but who advocated an energetic and dominant national government. Hamilton, like many of the framers, was a strong proponent of governmental protection of property interests.

LIMITATION OF GOVERNMENTAL POWER AND OF MAJORITY RULE

The most accurate and helpful way to characterize our political system is to call it a constitutional democracy. The term implies a system in which the government is regulated by laws that control and limit the exercise of political power. In a constitutional democracy people participate in government on a limited basis. A distinction should be made between an unlimited democratic government and a constitutional democracy. In the former, the people govern through the operation of a principle such as majority rule without legal restraint; in the latter, majority rule is curtailed and checked through various legal devices. A constitutional system is one in which the formal authority of government is restrained. The checks upon government in a constitutional society customarily include a division or fragmentation of authority that prevents government from controlling all sectors of human life.

Hamilton noted in *Federalist 1*, "It seems to have been reserved to the people of this country, to decide by their conduct and example, the important question, whether societies of men are really capable or not, of establishing good government from reflection and choice, or whether they are forever destined to depend, for their political constitutions, on accident and force." The framers of our Constitution attempted to structure the government in such a way that it would meet the needs and aspirations of the people and at the same time check the arbitrary exercise of political power. The doctrine of the separation of powers was designed to prevent any one group from gaining control of the national governmental apparatus. The selections reprinted here from *The Federalist*, which was written between October 1787 and August 1788, outline the theory and mechanism of the separation of powers.

4

FEDERALIST 47, 48, 51

James Madison

Federalist 47

I proceed to examine the particular structure of this government, and the distribution of this mass of power among its constituent parts.

One of the principal objections inculcated by the more respectable adversaries to the constitution, is its supposed violation of the political maxim, that the legislative, executive, and judiciary departments, ought to be separate and distinct. In the structure of the federal government, no regard, it is said, seems to have been paid to this essential precaution in favor of liberty. The several departments of power are distributed and blended in such a manner, as at once to destroy all symmetry and beauty of form; and to expose some of the essential parts of the edifice to the danger of being crushed by the disproportionate weight of other parts.

No political truth is certainly of great intrinsic value, or is stamped with the authority of more enlightened patrons of liberty, than that on which the objection is founded. The accumulation of all powers, legislative, executive, and judiciary, in the same hands, whether of one, a few, or many, and whether hereditary, self-appointed, or elective, may justly be pronounced the very definition of tyranny. Were the federal constitution, therefore, really chargeable with this accumulation of power, or with a mixture of powers, having a dangerous tendency to such an accumulation, no further arguments would be necessary to inspire a universal reprobation of the system. I persuade myself, however, that it will be made apparent to every one, that the charge cannot be supported, and that the maxim on which it relies has been totally misconceived and misapplied.

The oracle who is always consulted and cited on this subject, is the celebrated Montesquieu. If he be not the author of this invaluable precept in the science of politics, he has the merit of at least displaying and recommending it most effectually to the attention of mankind. . . .

From . . . facts, by which Montesquieu was guided, it may clearly be inferred, that in saying, "there can be no liberty, where the legislative and executive powers are united in the same person, or body of magistrates"; or "if the power of judging, be not separated from the legislative and executive powers," he did not mean that these departments ought to have no *partial agency* in, or no *control* over, the acts of each other. His meaning . . . can amount to no more than this, that where the *whole* power of one department is exercised by the same hands which possess the *whole* power of another department, the fundamental principles of a free constitution are subverted. . . .

If we look into the constitutions of the several states, we find, that notwithstanding the emphatical, and, in some instances, the unqualified terms in which this axiom has been laid down, there is not a single instance in which the several departments of power have been kept absolutely separate and distinct. . . .

The constitution of Massachusetts has observed a sufficient, though less pointed caution, in expressing this fundamental article of liberty. It declares, "that the legislative department shall never exercise the executive and judicial powers, or either of them: the executive shall never exercise the legislative and judicial powers, or either of them: the judicial shall never exercise the legislative and executive powers, or either of them." This declaration corresponds precisely with the doctrine of Montesquieu. . . . It goes no farther than to prohibit any one of the entire departments from exercising the powers of another department. In the very constitution to which it is prefixed, a partial mixture of powers has been admitted. . . .

Federalist 48

. . . I shall undertake in the next place to show, that unless these departments be so far connected and blended, as to give to each a constitutional control over the others, the degree of separation which the maxim requires, as essential to a free government, can never in practice be duly maintained.

It is agreed on all sides, that the powers properly belonging to one of the departments ought not to be directly and completely administered by either of the other departments. It is equally evident, that neither of them ought to possess, directly or indirectly, an overruling influence over the others in the administration of their respective powers. It will not be denied, that power is of an encroaching nature, and that it ought to be effectually restrained from passing the limits assigned to it. After discriminating, therefore, in theory, the several classes of power, as they may in their nature be legislative, executive, or judiciary; the next, and most difficult task, is to provide some practical security for each, against the invasion of the others. What this security ought to be, is the great problem to be solved.

Will it be sufficient to mark, with precision, the boundaries of these departments, in the constitution of the government, and to trust to these parchment barriers against the encroaching spirit of power? This is the security which appears to have been principally relied on by the compilers of most American constitutions. But experience assures us, that the efficacy of the provision has been greatly overrated; and that some more adequate defense is indispensably necessary for the more feeble, against the more powerful members of the government. The legislative department is everywhere extending the sphere of its activity, and drawing all power into its impetuous vortex. . . .

In a government where numerous and extensive prerogatives are placed in the hands of an hereditary monarch, the executive department is very justly regarded as the source of danger, and watched with all the jealousy which a zeal for liberty ought to inspire. In a democracy, where a multitude of people exercise in person the legislative functions, and are continually exposed, by their incapacity for regular deliberation and concerted measures, to the ambitious intrigues of their executive magistrates, tyranny may well be apprehended on some favorable emergency, to start up in the same quarter. But in a representative republic, where the executive magistracy is carefully limited, both in the extent and the duration of its power; and where the legislative is exercised by an assembly, which is inspired by a supposed influence over the people, with an intrepid confidence in its own strength; which is sufficiently numerous to feel all the passions which actuate a multitude; yet not so numerous as to be incapable of pursuing the objects of its passions, by means which reason prescribes; it is against the enterprising ambition of this department, that the people ought to indulge all their jealousy and exhaust all their precautions.

The legislative department derives a superiority in our governments from other circumstances. Its constitutional powers being at once more extensive, and less susceptible of precise limits, it can, with the greater facility, mask, under complicated and indirect measures, the encroachment which it makes on the coordinate departments. It is not infrequently a question of real nicety in legislative bodies, whether the operation of a particular measure will, or will not, extend beyond the legislative sphere. On the other side, the executive power being restrained within a narrower compass, and being more simple in its nature; and the judiciary being described by landmarks, still less uncertain, projects of usurpation by either of these departments would immediately betray and defeat themselves. Nor is this all: as the legislative department alone has access to the pockets of the people, and has in some constitutions full discretion, and in all a prevailing influence over the pecuniary rewards of those who fill the other departments; a dependence is thus created in the latter, which gives still greater facility to encroachment of the former. . . .

Federalist 51

To what expedient then shall we finally resort, for maintaining in practice the necessary partition of power among the several departments, as laid down in the constitution? The only answer that can be given is, that as all these exterior provisions are found to be inadequate, the defect must be supplied, by so contriving the interior structure of the government, as that its several constituent parts may, by their mutual relations, be the means of keeping each other in their proper places. . . .

In order to lay a due foundation for that separate and distinct exercise of the different powers of government, which, to a certain extent, is admitted on all hands to be essential to the preservation of liberty, it is evident that each department should have a will of its own; and consequently should be so constituted, that the members of each should have as little agency as possible in the appointment of the members of the others. . . .

It is equally evident, that the members of each department should be as little dependent as possible on those of the others, for the emoluments annexed to their offices. Were the executive magistrate, or the judges, not independent of the legislature in this particular, their independence in every other, would be merely nominal.

But the great security against a gradual concentration of the several powers in the same department, consists in giving to those who administer each department, the necessary constitutional means, and personal motives, to resist encroachments of the others. The provision for defense must in this, as in all other cases, be made commensurate to the danger of attack. Ambition must be made to counteract ambition. The interest of the man must be connected with the constitutional rights of the place. It may be a reflection on human nature, that such devices should be necessary to control the abuses of government. But what is government itself, but the greatest of all reflections on human nature? If men were angels, no government would be necessary. If angels were to govern men, neither external nor internal controls on government would be necessary. In framing a government, which is to be administered by men over men, the great difficulty lies in this: you must first enable the government to control the governed; and in the next place, oblige it to control itself. A dependence on the people is, no doubt, the primary control on the government; but experience has taught mankind the necessity of auxiliary precautions.

This policy of supplying by opposite and rival interests, the defect of better motives, might be traced through the whole system of human affairs, private as well as public. We see it particularly displayed in all the subordinate distributions of power, where the constant aim is, to divide and arrange the several offices in such a manner, as that each may be a check on the other; that the private interest of every individual, may be a sentinel over the public rights. These inventions of prudence cannot be less requisite to the distribution of the supreme powers of the state.

But it is not possible to give each department an equal power of self-defense. In republican government, the legislative authority necessarily predominates. The remedy for this inconvenience is, to divide the legislature into different branches; and to render them by different modes of election, and different principles of action, as little connected with each other, as the nature of their common functions, and their common dependence on the society will admit. It may even be necessary to guard against dangerous encroachments, by still further precautions. As the weight of the legislative authority requires that it should be thus divided, the weakness of the executive may require, on the other hand, that it should be fortified. An absolute negative on the legislature, appears, at first view, to be the natural defense with which the executive magistrate should be armed. But perhaps it would be neither altogether safe, nor alone sufficient. On ordinary occasions, it might not be exerted with the requisite firmness; and on extraordinary occasions, it might be perfidiously abused. May not this defect of an absolute negative be supplied by some qualified connection between this weaker department, and the weaker branch of the stronger department, by which the latter may be led to support the constitutional rights of the former, without being too much detached from the rights of its own department?

INTERPRETING THE CONSTITUTION

The preceding selections have offered contrasting views on the framing, nature, and purpose of the Constitution. As background, John Locke's political philosophy expressed in his *Second Treatise, Of Civil Government* (1690) supported the political beliefs of many eighteenth-century Americans in government as a social contract between rulers and ruled to protect the natural rights of citizens to life, liberty, and, very importantly, property.

To John Roche the Constitution was a practical political document reflecting compromises among state delegations with contrasting political and economic interests and among advocates of strong national power and proponents of states' rights. Charles Beard saw the Constitution as a reflection of the interests of property owners and creditors who feared that the rule of the debtor majority would inflate currency, cancel debts, and deprive creditors of their rightful property. James Madison's selections from *The Federalist* suggest a mistrust of government, a wary view of both political leaders and the people, and an emphasis upon the need for governmental checks and balances to prevent the arbitrary exercise of political power. Madison also distrusted what he termed "faction," by which he meant political parties or special-interest groups, which he considered to be intrinsically opposed to the national interest (see *Federalist 10,* Chapter 4).

The separation of powers among the executive, legislative, and judicial branches is an outstanding characteristic of our constitutional system. A uniquely American separation of powers incorporated an *independent* executive, pitting the president against Congress and requiring their cooperation to make the government work. The separation of powers was a constitutional filter through which political demands had to flow before they could be translated into public policies.

James Madison clearly saw the separation-of-powers system, incorporating checks and balances among the branches of government, as a process that would help to prevent arbitrary and excessive governmental actions. The three branches of the government, but particularly the president and Congress, would have independent political bases, motivations, and powers that would both enable and encourage them to compete with each other.

While Madison saw the separation of powers as an important limit upon arbitrary government, Alexander Hamilton represented a different point of view. He viewed the independent presidency, a central component of the separation of powers, as an office that could make the national government energetic and effective. "Energy in the executive is the definition of good government," wrote Hamilton in *Federalist 70*, and the constitutional separation of powers would provide that energy rather than simply making the president of a co-equal branch subject to congressional whims or Supreme Court constraints.

History has, at different times, borne out the views of both Madison and Hamilton regarding the effect of the separation of powers. During times of relative political tranquility the president and Congress have often been stalemated in a deadlock of democracy. But Hamilton's imperial presidency has taken charge in times of crisis, such as during the Civil War, Franklin D. Roosevelt's New Deal in the 1930s, and the Second World War in the 1940s.

The Constitution is a frugal, bare-bones document that has, almost miraculously and with very few amendments, remained in place for over 200 years. It was not, however, a perfect governmental plan, for the nation had to fight a bloody Civil War to establish the principle of *e pluribus unum* once and for all.

While reverence for the Constitution is an important strand in our political history, it has not prevented sharp political controversy over how the Constitution should be interpreted. The framers themselves did not see eye to eye on many constitutional provisions, interpreting them in different ways. To buttress their positions political opponents have often cited the Constitution, claiming that it supports their side. For example, during George Washington's presidency Thomas Jefferson argued that the Constitution should be strictly interpreted to limit Congress to its explicit Article I powers, which did not allow establishment of a national bank. Secretary of the Treasury Alexander Hamilton took the "loose" constructionist approach in support of the bank. Hamilton argued that while Article I of the Constitution did not explicitly give Congress the authority to create a national bank, Congress could imply such authority under its enumerated power to regulate commerce among the states. Both men were using the same Constitution to support their contrasting political positions.

The historic debate over whether or not the Constitution should be read "strictly" or "loosely" has metamorphosed into another and related debate over the importance of "original intent" in constitutional interpretation. Strict constructionists argue that the Supreme Court has often erred in not following the original intent of the framers. The authors of the following selection, however, claim that the framers of the Constitution knew they had forged a flexible document that future generations would be able to adapt to their values and needs.

5

HOW NOT TO READ THE CONSTITUTION

Laurence H. Tribe and Michael C. Dorf

From its very creation, the Constitution was perceived as a document that sought to strike a delicate balance between, on the one hand, governmental power to accomplish the great ends of civil society and, on the other, individual liberty. As James Madison put it in *The Federalist Papers*, "[i]f men were angels, no government would be necessary. If angels were to govern men, neither external nor internal controls on government would be necessary. In framing a government which is to be administered by men over men, the great difficulty lies in this: you must first enable the government to control the governed; and in the next place oblige it to control itself. A dependence on the people is, no doubt, the primary control on the government; but experience has taught mankind the necessity of auxiliary precautions." Although Madison initially opposed the inclusion of a Bill of Rights in the Constitution, as his correspondence with Thomas Jefferson shows, he became convinced that judicially enforceable rights are among the necessary "auxiliary precautions" against tyranny.

In the Constitution of the United States, men like Madison bequeathed to subsequent generations a framework for balancing liberty against power. However, it is only a framework; it is not a blueprint. Its Eighth Amendment prohibits the infliction of "cruel and unusual punishment," but gives no examples of permissible or impermissible punishments. Article IV requires that "[t]he United States shall guarantee to every State in this Union a Republican Form of Government," but attempts no definition of republican government. The Fourteenth Amendment proscribes state abridgments of the "privileges or immunities of citizens of the United States," but contains no catalogue of privileges or immunities.

How then ought we to go about the task of finding concrete commandments in the Constitution's majestically vague admonitions? If there is genuine controversy over how the Constitution should be read, certainly it cannot be because the disputants have access to different bodies of information. After all, they all have exactly the same text in front of them, and that text has exactly one history, however complex, however multifaceted. But of course different people believe different things about how that history bears on the enterprise of constitutional interpretation. . . .

Perhaps the disputants agree on what *counts* as "the Constitution," but simply approach the same body of textual and historical materials with different visions, different premises, and different convictions. But *that* assumption raises an obvious question: How are those visions, premises, and convictions relevant to how this brief text ought to be read? Is reading the text just a *pre*text for expressing the reader's vision in the august, almost holy terms of constitutional law? Is the Constitution simply a mirror in which one sees what one wants to see? . . .

Reading the Constitution or Writing One?

The belief that we must look beyond the specific views of the Framers to apply the Constitution to contemporary problems is not necessarily a "liberal" position. Indeed, not even the most "conservative" justices today believe in a jurisprudence of original intent that looks only to the Framers' unenacted views about particular institutions or practices. Consider the following statement made by a Supreme Court justice in 1976:

> The framers of the Constitution wisely spoke in general language and left to succeeding generations the task of applying that language to the unceasingly changing environment in which they would live. . . . Where the framers . . . used general language, they [gave] latitude to those who would later interpret the instrument to make that language applicable to cases that the framers might not have foreseen.

The author was not Justice William Brennan or Justice Thurgood Marshall, but then-Justice William Rehnquist. Or consider the statement by Justice White, joined by Justice Rehnquist in a 1986 opinion for the Court: "As [our] prior cases clearly show, . . . this Court does not subscribe to the simplistic view that constitutional interpretation can possibly be limited to the 'plain meaning' of the Constitution's text or to the subjective intention of the Framers. The Constitution," wrote Justice White, "is not a deed setting forth the precise metes and bounds of its subject matter; rather, it is a document announcing fundamental principles in value-laden terms that leave ample scope for the exercise of normative judgment by those charged with interpreting and applying it."

So the "conservatives" on the Court, no less than the "liberals," talk as though *reading* the Constitution requires much more than passively discovering a fixed meaning planted there generations ago. Those who wrote the document, and those who voted to ratify it, were undoubtedly projecting their wishes into an indefinite future. If writing is wish-*projection*, is reading merely an exercise in wish-*fulfillment*—not fulfillment of the wishes of the *authors*, who couldn't have begun to foresee the way things would unfold, but fulfillment of the wishes of *readers*, who perhaps use the language of the Constitution simply as a mirror to dress up their own political or moral preferences in the hallowed language of our most fundamental document? Justice Joseph Story feared that that might happen when he wrote in 1845: "How easily men satisfy themselves that the Constitution is exactly what they wish it to be."

To the extent that this is so, it is indefensible. The authority of the Constitution, its claim to obedience and the force that we permit it to exercise in our law and over our lives, would lose all legitimacy if it really were only a mirror for the readers' ideals and ideas. Just as the original intent of the Framers—even if it could be captured in the laboratory, bottled, and carefully inspected under a microscope—will not yield a satisfactory determinate interpretation of the Constitution, so too at the other end of the spectrum we must also reject as completely unsatisfactory the idea of an empty, or an infinitely malleable, Constitution. We must find principles of interpretation that can anchor the Constitution in some more secure, determinate, and external reality. But that is no small task.

One basic problem is that the text itself leaves so much room for the imagination. Simply consider the preamble, which speaks of furthering such concepts as "Justice" and the "Blessings of Liberty." It is not hard, in terms of concepts that fluid and that plastic, to make a linguistically plausible argument in support of more than a few surely incorrect conclusions. Perhaps a rule could be imposed that it is improper to refer to the preamble in constitutional argument on the theory that it is only an introduction, a preface, and not part of the Constitution *as enacted*. But even if one were to invent such a rule, which has no apparent grounding in the Constitution itself, it is hardly news that the remainder of the document is filled with lively language about "liberty," "due process of law," "unreasonable searches and seizures," and so forth—words that, although not *infinitely* malleable, are capable of supporting meanings at opposite ends of virtually any legal, political, or ideological spectrum.

It is therefore not surprising that readers on both the right and left of the American political center have invoked the Constitution as authority for strikingly divergent conclusions about the legitimacy of existing institutions and practices, and that neither wing has found it difficult to cite chapter and verse in support of its "reading" of our fundamental law. As is true of other areas of law, the materials of constitutional law require construction, leave room for argument over meaning, and tempt the reader to import his or her vision of the just society into the meaning of the materials being considered. . . .

When all of the Constitution's supposed unities are exposed to scrutiny, criticisms of its inconsistency with various readers' sweeping visions of what it ought to be become considerably less impressive. Not all need be reducible to a single theme. Inconsistency—even inconsistency with democracy—is hardly earth-shattering. Listen to Walt Whitman: "Do I contradict myself? Very well then, I contradict myself." "I am large, I contain multitudes," the Constitution replies.

CHAPTER 2

FEDERALISM

Federalism is a constitutional division of authority between a national government and state or constituent governments. The Constitution created a federal form of government in order to establish a powerful national government that would replace the weak government of the Articles of Confederation. In the eighteenth century federalism meant national power over the states but not unlimited national authority. Article I of the Constitution enumerates congressional powers but does not *define* them. An endless debate in all political venues has occurred throughout our history over the definition of the boundaries of national authority.

In the twenty-first century students of American government do not, to say the least, view federalism as a hot political topic. They do not return to their dorm rooms at night worrying that they may lose their freedom because the national government is undermining the foundations of federalism. But throughout our history politics has been all about federalism, in the states, on Capitol Hill, in the White House and in litigation before the Supreme Court, and, sadly, on the bloody battlefields of the Civil War. The politics of federalism was also deeply intertwined with slavery.

The political issue of the late eighteenth century was federalism and the question of whether or not state sovereignty should surrender to the proposed powerful national government of the Constitution. The paramount political issue throughout the nineteenth century was federalism and the boundaries of national and state powers. Federalism continued to be a major issue in the twentieth century well into FDR's New Deal, which in the end marked what appeared to be final state capitulation to a dominant national government.

While federalism became a dormant political issue for a while after the New Deal apparently settled the question of national power, it would not disappear. After all, the Tenth Amendment explicitly provided for the federal form of government that the original Constitution seemed to imply.

The Supreme Court's historic desegregation decision in *Brown v. Board of Education* in 1954 deeply affected federalism by nationalizing a constitutional standard of equal protection under the law that overturned state segregation laws throughout the South and in the

District of Columbia. In the 1960s the Supreme Court completed the nationalization of most of the Bill of Rights that significantly diminished state power.

The nationalization of the Bill of Rights and the Supreme Court's latter New Deal acceptance of virtually unlimited congressional authority to regulate commerce and define the boundaries of taxation appeared to end, once and for all, the political debate over federalism. John Roche's constitutional nationalists (see Chapter 1) were finally victorious, or so it seemed.

In the 1990s politics by other means in the form of litigation before the Supreme Court successfully resurrected the issue of states rights of the distant past. A razor thin Court majority declared unconstitutional congressional laws regulating guns in school zones and allowing women to bring federal lawsuits against defendants who had committed acts of violence against them. The Court found the laws exceeded congressional authority under the commerce clause of Article I and thereby invaded state sovereignty. In other cases the Court upheld state sovereign immunity, overturning legislation that permitted suits against the states for damages if the plaintiffs could prove violations of federal law.

Chief Justice Rehnquist summarized the position of the Court's majority on the issue of federalism in *United States v. Lopez* (1995), which overturned legislation that prohibited carrying guns in and around schools:

> We start with first principles. The Constitution creates a Federal Government of enumerated powers. See U.S. Const., Art. I, 8. As James Madison wrote, "[t]he powers delegated by the proposed single Constitution to the federal government are few and defined. Those which are to remain in the State governments are numerous and indefinite." . . . This constitutionally mandated division of authority "was adopted by the Framers to ensure protection of our fundamental liberties." *Gregory v. Ashcroft*, 501 U.S. 452, 458 (1991) . . . "Just as the separation and independence of the coordinate branches of the Federal Government serves to prevent the accumulation of excessive power in any one branch, a healthy balance of power between the States and the Federal Government will reduce the risk of tyranny and abuse from either front."

CONSTITUTIONAL BACKGROUND: NATIONAL VERSUS STATE POWER

No subject attracted greater attention or was more carefully analyzed at the time of the framing of the Constitution than federalism. *The Federalist* devoted a great deal of space to proving the advantages of a federal form of government relative to a confederacy, since the Constitution was going to take some of the power traditionally within the jurisdiction of state governments and give it to a newly constituted national government.

The victory of the nationalists at the Constitutional Convention of 1787, which resulted in sovereign states giving up a significant portion of their authority to a new national government, is remarkable by any standard of measurement. Today, when the creation of the Union is largely taken for granted, it is difficult to appreciate the environment of the Revolutionary period, a time when the states wanted at all costs to protect their newly won freedom from an oppressive British government. The Constitution of 1787 was accepted as a matter of necessity as much as desire.

It was against the background of the Articles of Confederation that Hamilton wrote in *The Federalist* about the advantages of the new "federal" system that would be created by the Constitution. The Articles of Confederation had been submitted to the states in 1777 and were finally ratified by all of the states in 1781, Maryland being the only holdout after 1779. The "League of Friendship" that had been created among the states by the Articles had proved inadequate to meeting even the minimum needs of union. The government of the Articles of Confederation had many weaknesses, for it was essentially a league of sovereign states, joined together more in accordance with principles of international agreement than in accordance with the rules of nation-states. Most of the provisions of the Articles of Confederation concerned the foreign relations of the new government and matters of national defense and security. For this purpose a minimum number of powers were granted to the national government, which, however, had no executive or judicial authority and was therefore incapable of independent enforcement. National actions were dependent upon the states for enforcement, and under Article 2 "each state retains its sovereignty, freedom and independence, and every power, jurisdiction and right, which is not by this confederation expressly delegated to the United States, in Congress assembled." The paucity of authority delegated to the central government under the Articles left the sovereignty of the states intact. And the national government was totally dependent upon the states as agents of enforcement of what little authority it could exercise. The government of the Articles of Confederation then, without an executive or judicial branch, and without such crucial authority as the power to tax and regulate commerce, required a drastic overhaul if it was to become a national government in fact as well as in name.

In the following selections from *The Federalist,* Alexander Hamilton argues the advantages of the new federal Constitution, and at the same time attempts to alleviate his opponents' fears that the new government would intrude upon and possibly eventually destroy the sovereignty of the states. The national government, he wrote, must be able to act directly upon the citizens of the states to regulate the common concerns of the nation. He found the system of the Articles of Confederation too weak, allowing state evasion of national power. Augmenting the authority of the national government would not destroy state sovereignty, because of the inherent strength of the individual states (which at the time, Hamilton wrote, were singly and collectively far more powerful than any proposed national government). Moreover, there would be no incentives for ambitious politicians to look to the states to realize their goals, for the scope of national power was sufficient to occupy temptations for political aggrandizement.

6

FEDERALIST 16, 17

Alexander Hamilton

Federalist 16

The . . . death of the confederacy . . . is what we now seem to be on the point of experiencing, if the federal system be not speedily renovated in a more substantial form. It is not probable, considering the genius of this country, that the complying states would often be inclined to support the authority of the union, by engaging in a war against the non-complying states. They would always be more ready to pursue the milder course of putting themselves upon an equal footing with the delinquent members, by an imitation of their example. And the guilt of all would thus become the security of all. Our past experience has exhibited the operation of this spirit in its full light. There would, in fact, be an insuperable difficulty in ascertaining when force would with propriety be employed. In the article of pecuniary contribution, which would be the most usual source of delinquency, it would often be impossible to decide whether it had proceeded from disinclination, or inability. The pretense of the latter would always be at hand. And the case must be very flagrant in which its fallacy could be detected with sufficient certainty to justify the harsh expedient of compulsion. It is easy to see that this problem alone, as often as it should occur, would open a wide field to the majority that happened to prevail in the national council, for the exercise of factious views, of partiality, and of oppression.

It seems to require no pains to prove that the states ought not to prefer a national constitution, which could only be kept in motion by the instrumentality of a large army, continually on foot to execute the ordinary requisitions or decrees of the government. And yet this is the plain alternative involved by those who wish to deny it the power of extending its operations to individuals. Such a scheme, if practicable at all, would instantly degenerate into a military despotism; but it will be found in every light impracticable. The resources of the union would not be equal to the maintenance of any army considerable enough to confine the larger states within the limits of their duty; nor would the means ever be furnished of forming such an army in the first instance. Whoever considers the populousness and strength of several of these states singly at the present juncture, and looks forward to what they will become, even at the distance of half a century, will at once dismiss as idle and visionary any scheme which aims at regulating their movements by laws, to operate upon them in their collective capacities, and to be executed by a coercion applicable to them in the same capacities. A project of this kind is little less romantic than the monster-taming spirit attributed to the fabulous heroes and demigods of antiquity. . . .

The result of these observations to an intelligent mind must clearly be this, that if it be possible at any rate to construct a federal government capable of regulating the common concerns, and preserving the general tranquility, it must be founded, as to the objects committed to its case, upon the reverse of the principle contended for by the opponents of the proposed constitution [i.e., a confederacy]. It must carry its agency to the persons of the citizens. It must stand in need of no intermediate legislations; but must itself be empowered to employ the arm of the ordinary magistrate to execute its own resolutions. The majesty of the national authority must be manifested through the medium of the courts of justice. The government of the union, like that of each state, must be able to address itself immediately to the hopes and fears of individuals; and to attract to its support, those passions which have the strongest influence upon the human heart. It must, in short, possess all the means, and have a right to resort to all the methods, of executing the powers with which it is entrusted, that are possessed and exercised by the governments of the particular states.

To this reasoning it may perhaps be objected, that if any state should be disaffected to the authority of the union, it could at any time obstruct the execution of its laws, and bring the matter to the same issue of force, with the necessity of which the opposite scheme is reproached.

The plausibility of this objection will vanish the moment we advert to the essential difference between a mere noncompliance and a direct and active resistance. If the interposition of the state legislatures be necessary to give effect to a measure of the union [as in a confederacy], they have only not to act, or to act evasively, and the measure is defeated. This neglect of duty may be disguised under affected but unsubstantial provisions so as not to appear, and of course not to excite any alarm in the people for the safety of the constitution. The state leaders may even make a merit of their surreptitious invasions of it, on the ground of some temporary convenience, exemption, or advantage.

But if the execution of the laws of the national government should not require the intervention of the state legislatures; if they were to pass into immediate operation upon the citizens themselves, the particular governments could not interrupt their progress without an open and violent exertion of an unconstitutional power. No omission, nor evasions, would answer the end. They would be obliged to act, and in such a manner, as would leave no doubt that they had encroached on the national rights. An experiment of this nature would always be hazardous in the face of a constitution in any degree competent to its own defense, and of the people enlightened enough to distinguish between a legal exercise and an illegal usurpation of authority. The success of it would require not merely a factious majority in the legislature, but the concurrence of the courts of justice, and of the body of the people. . . .

Federalist 17

An objection, of a nature different from that which has been stated and answered in my last address, may, perhaps, be urged against the principle of legislation for the individual citizens of America. It may be said, that it would tend to render the government of the union too powerful, and to enable it to absorb those residuary authorities, which it might be judged proper to leave with the states for local purposes. Allowing the utmost latitude to the love of power, which any reasonable man can require, I confess I am at a loss to discover what temptation the persons entrusted with the administration of the general government could ever feel to divest the states of the authorities of that description. The regulation of the mere domestic police of a state, appears to me to hold out slender allurements to ambition. Commerce, finance, negotiation, and war, seem to comprehend all the objects which have charms for minds governed by that passion; and all the powers necessary to those objects, ought, in the first instance, to be lodged in the national depository. The administration of private justice between the citizens of the same state; the supervision of agriculture, and of other concerns of a similar nature; all those things, in short, which are proper to be provided for by local legislation, can never be desirable cares of a general jurisdiction. It is therefore improbable, that there should exist a disposition in the federal councils, to usurp the powers with which they are connected; because the attempt to exercise them would be as troublesome as it would be nugatory; and the possession of them, for that reason, would contribute nothing to the dignity, to the importance, or to the splendor, of the national government.

But let it be admitted, for argument's sake, that mere wantonness, and lust of domination, would be sufficient to beget that disposition; still, it may be safely affirmed, that the sense of the constituent body of the national representatives, or in other words, of the people of the several states, would control the indulgence of so extravagant an appetite. It will always be far more easy for the state governments to encroach upon the national authorities, than for the national government to encroach upon the state authorities. The proof of this proposition turns upon the greater degree of influence which the state governments, if they administer their affairs with uprightness and prudence, will generally possess over the people; a circumstance which at the same time teaches us, that there is an inherent and intrinsic weakness in all federal constitutions; and that too much pain cannot be taken in their organization, to give them all the force which is compatible with the principles of liberty.

The superiority of influence in favor of the particular governments, would result partly from the diffusive construction of the national government; but chiefly from the nature of the objects to which the attention of the state administrations would be directed.

It is a known fact in human nature, that its affections are commonly weak in proportion to the distance of diffusiveness of the object. Upon the same principle that a man is more attached to his family than to his neighborhood, to his neighborhood than to the community at large, the people of each state would be apt to feel a strong bias towards their local governments, than towards the government of the union, unless the force of that principle should be destroyed by a much better administration of the latter.

This strong propensity of the human heart, would find powerful auxiliaries in the objects of state regulation.

The variety of more minute interests, which will necessarily fall under the superintendence of the local administrations, and which will form so many rivulets of influence, running through every part of the society, cannot be particularized, without involving a detail too tedious and uninteresting to compensate for the instruction it might afford.

There is one transcendent advantage belonging to the province of the state governments, which alone suffices to place the matter in a clear and satisfactory light—I mean the ordinary administration of criminal and civil justice. This, of all others, is the most powerful, most universal and most attractive source of popular obedience and attachment. It is this, which, being the immediate and visible guardian of life and property; having its benefits and its terrors in constant activity before the public eye; regulating all those personal interests, and familiar concerns, to which the sensibility of individuals is more immediately awake; contributes, more than any other circumstance, to impress upon the minds of the people affection, esteem, and reverence towards the government. This great cement of society, which will diffuse itself almost wholly through the channels of the particular governments, independent of all other causes of influence, would insure them so decided an empire over their respective citizens, as to render them at all times a complete counterpoise, and not infrequently dangerous rivals to the power of the union.

The Federalist Papers were a brilliant and comprehensive analysis of the politics and theory of the Constitution. James Madison and Alexander Hamilton had no peers when it came to persuasive explanations of every nook and cranny of the Constitution. As was customary at the time, Madison and Hamilton signed *The Federalist Papers* with the *nom de plume* Publius. Between October 1787 and May 1788 they produced eighty-five papers (John Jay authored a few of *The Federalist Papers* but dropped out of the endeavor early due to illness), almost all of which appeared in New York newspapers.

Opponents of the new Constitution, the Anti-Federalists, also wrote a series of essays that various newspapers around the country published. They expressed their concerns in the ratifying conventions and other venues as well. In contrast with the Federalists and the nationalists, the Anti-Federalists had no unified direction, theme, or plan of action. Publius authored *The Federalist*, but a wide range of Anti-Federalists from "Brutus" to "Country Boy," "Cato," "Republicus," "An Old Whig," "A Plebeian," and "A Federal Farmer" wrote the Anti-Federalist "papers." The Anti-Federalist criticisms were disjointed and often employed shrill adjectives that could also be used to describe the Anti-Federalist forces that failed in the end to defeat the ratification of the Constitution. History gave Madison, Hamilton, and *The Federalist* an A+, a grade History also awarded to the nationalist political strategy. After all, the spoils of History always go to the victors. The Anti-Federalists received a failing grade for their political theory and politics.

Both Federalists and Anti-Federalists recognized the importance of constitutional text. They knew that once ratified, the Constitution would dictate the balance of political power between the national government and the states. Eighteenth-century Americans believed that government should be one of law, not men. They were the first nation in history to adopt a written Constitution and to accept it as the supreme law of the land. The debates between Federalists and Anti-Federalists started with the text of the Constitution and proceeded to how that text could be interpreted to expand or limit national and state powers.

One particularly important part of the text of Article I is the necessary and proper or implied powers clause. It states that Congress shall have the power "to make all laws which shall be necessary and proper for carrying into execution the foregoing [enumerated] powers, and all other powers vested by this Constitution in the government of the United States, or in any department or office thereof." The Anti-Federalists viewed this clause as a grant of absolute power to the national government over the states.

7

THE ANTI-FEDERALIST PAPERS NO. 17

Federalist Power Will Ultimately Subvert State Authority

This [new] government is to possess absolute and uncontrollable powers, legislative, executive and judicial, with respect to every object to which it extends, for by the last clause of section eighth, article first, it is declared, that the Congress shall have power "to make all laws which shall be necessary and proper for carrying into execution the foregoing powers, and all other powers vested by this Constitution in the government of the United States, or in any department or office thereof." And by the sixth article, it is declared, "that this Constitution, and the laws of the United States, which shall be made in pursuance thereof, and the treaties made, or which shall be made, under the authority of the United States, shall be the supreme law of the land; and the judges in every State shall be bound thereby, any thing in the Constitution or law of any State to the contrary notwithstanding." It appears from these articles, that there is no need of any intervention of the State governments, between the Congress and the people, to execute any one power vested in the general government, and that the Constitution and laws of every State are nullified and declared void, so far as they are or shall be inconsistent with this Constitution, or the laws made in pursuance of it, or with treaties made under the authority of the United States. The government, then, so far as it extends, is a complete one, and not a confederation. It is as much one complete government as that of New York or Massachusetts, has as absolute and perfect powers to make and execute all laws, to appoint officers, institute courts, declare offenses, and annex penalties, with respect to every object to which it extends, as any other in the world. So far, therefore, as its powers reach, all ideas of confederation are given up and lost. It is true this government is limited to certain objects, or to speak more properly, some small degree of power is still left to the States; but a little attention to the powers vested in the general government, will convince every candid man, that if it is capable of being executed, all that is reserved for the individual States must very soon be annihilated, except so far as they are barely necessary to the organization of the general government. The powers of the general legislature extend to every case that is of the least importance—there is nothing valuable to human nature, nothing dear to freemen, but what is within its power. It has the authority to make laws which will affect the lives, the liberty, and property of every man in the United States; nor can the Constitution or laws of any State, in any way prevent or impede the full and complete execution of every power given. The legislative power is competent to lay taxes, duties, imposts, and excises;—there is no limitation to this power, unless it be said that the clause which directs the use to which those taxes and duties shall be applied, may be said to be a limitation. But this is no restriction of the power at all, for by this clause they are to be applied to pay the debts and provide for the common defense and general welfare of the United States; but the legislature have authority to contract debts at their discretion; they are the sole judges of what is necessary to provide for the common defense, and they only are to determine what is for the general welfare. This power, therefore, is neither more nor less than a power to lay and collect taxes, imposts, and excises, at their pleasure; not only the power to lay taxes unlimited as to the amount they may require, but it is perfect and absolute to raise them in any mode they please. No State legislature, or any power in the State governments, have any more to do in carrying this into effect than the authority of one State has to do with that of another. In the business, therefore, of laying and collecting taxes, the idea of confederation is totally lost, and that of one entire republic is embraced. It is proper here to remark, that the authority to lay and collect taxes is the most important of any power that can be granted; it connects with it almost all other powers, or at least will in process of time draw all others after it; it is the great mean of protection, security, and defense, in a good government, and the great engine of oppression and tyranny in a bad one. This cannot fail of being the case, if we consider the contracted limits which are set by this Constitution, to the State governments, on this article of raising money. No State can emit paper money, lay any duties or imposts, on imports, or exports, but by consent of the Congress; and then the net produce shall be for the benefit of the United States. The only means, therefore, left for any State to support its government and discharge its debts, is by direct taxation; and the United States have also power to lay and collect taxes, in any way they please. Everyone who has thought on the subject, must be convinced that but small sums of money can he collected in any country, by direct tax; when the federal government begins to exercise the right of taxation in all its parts, the legislatures of the several states will find it impossible to raise monies to support their governments. Without money they cannot be supported, and they must dwindle away, and, as before observed, their powers be absorbed in that of the general government.

It might be here shown, that the power in the federal legislature, to raise and support armies at pleasure, as well in peace as in war, and their control over the militia, tend not only to a consolidation of the government, but the destruction of liberty. I shall not, however, dwell upon these, as a few observations upon the judicial power of this government, in addition to the preceding, will fully evince the truth of the position.

The judicial power of the United States is to be vested in a supreme court, and in such inferior courts as Congress may, from time to time, ordain and establish. The powers of these courts are very extensive; their jurisdiction comprehends all civil causes, except such as arise between citizens of the same State; and it extends to all cases in law and equity arising under the Constitution. One inferior court must be established, I presume, in each State, at least, with the necessary executive officers appendant thereto. It is easy to see, that in the common course of things, these courts will eclipse the dignity, and take away from the respectability, of the State courts. These courts will be, in themselves, totally independent of the States, deriving their authority from the United States, and receiving from them fixed salaries; and in the course of human events it is to be expected that they will swallow up all the powers of the courts in the respective States.

How far the clause in the eighth section of the first article may operate to do away with all idea of confederated States, and to effect an entire consolidation of the whole into one general government, it is impossible to say. The powers given by this article are very general and comprehensive, and it may receive a construction to justify the passing of almost any law. A power to make all laws, which shall be necessary and proper, for carrying into execution all powers vested by the Constitution in the government of the United States, or any department or officer thereof, is a power very comprehensive and definite, and may, for aught I know, be exercised in such manner as entirely to abolish the State legislatures. Suppose the legislature of a State should pass a law to raise money to support their government and pay the State debt; may the Congress repeal this law, because it may prevent the collection of a tax which they may think proper and necessary to lay, to provide for the general welfare of the United States? For all laws made, in pursuance of this Constitution, are the supreme law of the land, and the judges in every State shall be bound thereby, anything in the Constitution or laws of the different States to the contrary notwithstanding. By such a law, the government of a particular State might be overturned at one stroke, and thereby be deprived of every means of its support.

It is not meant, by stating this case, to insinuate that the Constitution would warrant a law of this kind! Or unnecessarily to alarm the fears of the people, by suggesting that the Federal legislature would be more likely to pass the limits assigned them by the Constitution, than that of an individual State, further than they are less responsible to the people. But what is meant is, that the legislature of the United States are vested with the great and uncontrollable powers of laying and collecting taxes, duties, imposts, and excises; of regulating trade, raising and supporting armies, organizing, arming, and disciplining the militia, instituting courts, and other general powers; and are by this clause invested with the power of making all laws, proper and necessary, for carrying all these into execution; and they may so exercise this power as entirely to annihilate all the State governments, and reduce this country to one single government. And if they may do it, it is pretty certain they will; for it will be found that the power retained by individual States, small as it is, will be a clog upon the wheels of the government of the United States; the latter, therefore, will be naturally inclined to remove it out of the way. Besides, it is a truth confirmed by the unerring experience of ages, that every man, and every body of men, invested with power, are ever disposed to increase it, and to acquire a superiority over everything that stands in their way. This disposition, which is implanted in human nature, will operate in the Federal legislature to lessen and ultimately to subvert the State authority, and having such advantages, will most certainly succeed, if the Federal government succeeds at all. It must be very evident, then, that what this Constitution wants of being a complete consolidation of the several parts of the union into one complete government, possessed of perfect legislative, judicial, and executive powers, to all intents and purposes, it will necessarily acquire in its exercise in operation.

BRUTUS

The following Federalist papers address the Anti-Federalist concerns over the implications of Article I powers and the necessary and proper clause. The Federalists considered "implied powers" an essential part of Article I congressional powers to create an effective national government. The Anti-Federalists, as the preceding reading illustrates, argued that Article I enumerated powers in combination with the necessary and proper clause and the supremacy clause would destroy state sovereignty. How Congress and the Supreme Court interpreted Article I powers and the supremacy clause defined the boundaries of national and state powers throughout U.S. history.

8

FEDERALIST 44

James Madison

. . . The sixth and last class [class of powers, lodged in the general government] consists of the several powers and provisions by which efficacy is given to all the rest.

1. Of these the first is, the "power to make all laws which shall be necessary and proper for carrying into execution the foregoing powers, and all other powers vested by this Constitution in the government of the United States, or in any department or officer thereof."

Few parts of the Constitution have been assailed with more intemperance than this; yet on a fair investigation of it, no part can appear more completely invulnerable. Without the substance of this power, the whole Constitution would be a dead letter. Those who object to the article, therefore, as a part of the Constitution, can only mean that the form of the provision is improper. But have they considered whether a better form could have been substituted?

There are four other possible methods which the Constitution might have taken on this subject. They might have copied the second article of the existing Confederation, which would have prohibited the exercise of any power not expressly delegated; they might have attempted a positive enumeration of the powers comprehended under the general terms "necessary and proper"; they might have attempted a negative enumeration of them, by specifying the powers excepted from the general definition; they might have been altogether silent on the subject, leaving these necessary and proper powers to construction and inference.

Had the convention taken the first method of adopting the second article of Confederation, it is evident that the new Congress would be continually exposed, as their predecessors have been, to the alternative of construing the term "expressly" with so much rigor, as to disarm the government of all real authority whatever, or with so much latitude as to destroy altogether the force of the restriction. It would be easy to show, if it were necessary, that no important power, delegated by the articles of Confederation, has been or can be executed by Congress, without recurring more or less to the doctrine of construction or implication. As the powers delegated under the new system are more extensive, the government which is to administer it would find itself still more distressed with the alternative of betraying the public interests by doing nothing, or of violating the Constitution by exercising powers indispensably necessary and proper, but, at the same time, not expressly granted.

Had the convention attempted a positive enumeration of the powers necessary and proper for carrying their other powers into effect, the attempt would have involved a complete digest of laws on every subject to which the Constitution relates; accommodated too, not only to the existing state of things, but to all the possible changes which futurity may produce; for in every new application of a general power, the particular powers, which are the means of attaining the object of the general power, must always necessarily vary with that object, and be often properly varied whilst the object remains the same.

Had they attempted to enumerate the particular powers or means not necessary or proper for carrying the general powers into execution, the task would have been no less chimerical, and would have been liable to this further objection, that every defect in the enumeration would have been equivalent to a positive grant of authority. If, to avoid this consequence, they had attempted a partial enumeration of the exceptions, and described the residue by the general terms, not necessary or proper, it must have happened that the enumeration would comprehend a few of the excepted powers only; that these would be such as would be least likely to be assumed or tolerated, because the enumeration would of course select such as would be least necessary or proper; and that the unnecessary and improper powers included in the residuum, would be less forcibly excepted, than if no partial enumeration had been made.

Had the Constitution been silent on this head, there can be no doubt that all the particular powers requisite as means of executing the general powers would have resulted to the government, by unavoidable implication. No axiom is more clearly established in law, or in reason, than that wherever the end is required, the means are authorized; wherever a general power to do a thing is given, every particular power necessary for doing it is included. Had this last method, therefore, been pursued by the convention, every objection now urged against their plan would remain in all its plausibility; and the real inconveniency would be incurred of not removing a pretext which may be seized on critical occasions for drawing into question the essential powers of the Union.

If it be asked what is to be the consequence, in case the Congress shall misconstrue this part of the Constitution, and exercise powers not warranted by its true meaning, I answer, the same as if they should misconstrue or enlarge any other power vested in them; as if the general power had been reduced to particulars, and any one of these were to be violated; the same, in short, as if the State legislatures should violate the irrespective constitutional authorities. *In the first instance, the success of the usurpation will depend on the executive and judiciary departments, which are to expound and give effect to the legislative acts; and in the last resort a remedy must be obtained from the people who can, by the election of more faithful representatives, annul the acts of the usurpers.* The ultimate redress may be more confided in against unconstitutional acts of the federal government than of the State legislatures, for this plain reason, that as every such act of the former will be an invasion of the rights of the latter, these will be ever ready to mark the innovation, to sound the alarm to the people, and to exert their local influence in effecting a change of federal representatives. There being no such intermediate body between the State legislatures and the people interested in watching the conduct of the former, violations of the State constitutions are more likely to remain unnoticed and unredressed. [Italics added.]

9

FEDERALIST 45

James Madison

The Alleged Danger From the Powers of the Union to the State Governments Considered

To the People of the State of New York:

HAVING shown that no one of the powers transferred to the federal government is unnecessary or improper, the next question to be considered is, whether the whole mass of them will be dangerous to the portion of authority left in the several States.

The adversaries to the plan of the convention, instead of considering in the first place what degree of power was absolutely necessary for the purposes of the federal government, have exhausted themselves in a secondary inquiry into the possible consequences of the proposed degree of power to the governments of the particular States. But if the Union, as has been shown, be essential to the security of the people of America against foreign danger; if it be essential to their security against contentions and wars among the different States; if it be essential to guard them against those violent and oppressive factions which embitter the blessings of liberty, and against those military establishments which must gradually poison its very fountain; if, in a word, the Union be essential to the happiness of the people of America, is it not preposterous, to urge as an objection to a government, without which the objects of the Union cannot be attained, that such a government may derogate from the importance of the governments of the individual States? Was, then, the American Revolution effected, was the American Confederacy formed, was the precious blood of thousands spilt, and the hard-earned substance of millions lavished, not that the people of America should enjoy peace, liberty, and safety, but that the government of the individual States, that particular municipal establishments, might enjoy a certain extent of power, and be arrayed with certain dignities and attributes of sovereignty? We have heard of the impious doctrine in the Old World, that the people were made for kings, not kings for the people. Is the same doctrine to be revived in the New, in another shape that the solid happiness of the people is to be sacrificed to the views of political institutions of a different form? It is too early for politicians to presume on our forgetting that the public good, the real welfare of the great body of the people, is the supreme object to be pursued; and that no form of government whatever has any other value than as it may be fitted for the attainment of this object. Were the plan of the convention adverse to the public happiness, my voice would be, Reject the plan. Were the Union itself inconsistent with the public happiness, it would be, Abolish the Union. In like manner, as far as the sovereignty of the States cannot be reconciled to the happiness of the people, the voice of every good citizen must be, Let the former be sacrificed to the latter. How far the sacrifice is necessary, has been shown. How far the unsacrificed residue will be endangered, is the question before us. . . .

The State government will have the advantage of the Federal government, whether we compare them in respect to the immediate dependence of the one on the other; to the weight of personal influence which each side will possess; to the powers respectively vested in them; to the predilection and probable support of the people; to the disposition and faculty of resisting and frustrating the measures of each other.

The State governments may be regarded as constituent and essential parts of the federal government; whilst the latter is nowise essential to the operation or organization of the former. Without the intervention of the State legislatures, the President of the United States cannot be elected at all. They must in all cases have a great share in his appointment, and will, perhaps, in most cases, of themselves determine it. The Senate will be elected absolutely and exclusively by the State legislatures. Even the House of Representatives, though drawn immediately from the people, will be chosen very much under the influence of that class of men, whose influence over the people obtains for themselves an election into the State legislatures. Thus, each of the principal branches of the federal government will owe its existence more or less to the favor of the State governments, and must consequently feel a dependence, which is much more likely to beget a disposition too obsequious than too overbearing towards them. On the other side, the component parts of the State governments will in no instance be indebted for their appointment to the direct agency of the federal government, and very little, if at all, to the local influence of its members.

The number of individuals employed under the Constitution of the United States will be much smaller than the number employed under the particular States. There will consequently be less of personal influence on the side of the former than of the latter. The members of the legislative, executive, and judiciary departments of thirteen and more States, the justices of peace, officers of militia, ministerial officers of justice, with all the county, corporation, and town officers, for three millions and more of people, intermixed, and having particular acquaintance with every class and circle of people, must exceed, beyond all proportion, both in number and influence, those of every description who will be employed in the administration of the federal system. . . .

The powers delegated by the proposed Constitution to the federal government are few and defined. Those which are to remain in the State governments are numerous and indefinite. The former will be exercised principally on external objects, as war, peace, negotiation, and foreign commerce; with which last the power of taxation will, for the most part, be connected. The powers reserved to the several States will extend to all the objects which, in the ordinary course of affairs, concern the lives, liberties, and properties of the people, and the internal order, improvement, and prosperity of the State.

The operations of the federal government will be most extensive and important in times of war and danger; those of the State governments, in times of peace and security. . . .

If the new Constitution be examined with accuracy and candor, it will be found that the change which it proposes consists much less in the addition of NEW POWERS to the Union, than in the invigoration of its ORIGINAL POWERS. The regulation of commerce, it is true, is a new power; but that seems to be an addition which few oppose, and from which no apprehensions are entertained. The powers relating to war and peace, armies and fleets, treaties and finance, with the other more considerable powers, are all vested in the existing Congress by the articles of Confederation. The proposed change does not enlarge these powers; it only substitutes a more effectual mode of administering them. The change relating to taxation may be regarded as the most important; and yet the present Congress have as complete authority to REQUIRE of the States indefinite supplies of money for the common defense and general welfare, as the future Congress will have to require them of individual citizens; and the latter will be no more bound than the States themselves have been, to pay the quotas respectively taxed on them. Had the States complied punctually with the articles of Confederation, or could their compliance have been enforced by as peaceable means as may be used with success towards single persons, our past experience is very far from countenancing an opinion, that the State governments would have lost their constitutional powers, and have gradually undergone an entire consolidation. To maintain that such an event would have ensued, would be to say at once, that the existence of the State governments is incompatible with any system whatever that accomplishes the essential purposes of the Union.

PUBLIUS

In *Federalist 39,* James Madison stated that the new Constitution was both federal and national. He attempted to answer arguments that the Constitution destroyed the confederacy of sovereign states and replaced it with a national government. In answering this argument Madison used the term federal as it was used by the objectors to the Constitution he was attempting to answer. They essentially used federal and confederacy interchangeably, each term referring to a system requiring agreement among the states before certain actions could be taken. Because agreement was required among the states for ratification, for example, Madison referred to the establishment of the Constitution as a federal and not a national act. Madison suggested that the character of the House of Representatives, which derives its powers from the people, was national rather than federal. Conversely, the Senate, representing the states equally, was federal, not national. With regard to the powers of the national government, Madison claimed that in operation they are national because they allow the national government to act directly upon the people, but in extent they are federal because they are limited, the states having agreed to delegate only a certain number of powers to the national government. A truly national government would not be limited in the scope of its powers.

10

FEDERALIST 39

James Madison

The last paper having concluded the observations which were meant to introduce a candid survey of the plan of government reported by the convention, we now proceed to the execution of that part of our undertaking.

The first question that offers itself is whether the general form and aspect of the government be strictly republican. It is evident that no other form would be reconcilable with the genius of the people of America; with the fundamental principles of the Revolution; or with that honorable determination which animates every votary of freedom to rest all our political experiments on the capacity of mankind for self-government. If the plan of the convention, therefore, be found to depart from the republican character, its advocates must abandon it as no longer defensible.

What, then, are the distinctive characters of the republican form? Were an answer to this question to be sought, not by recurring to principles but in the application of the term by political writers to the constitutions of different States, no satisfactory one would ever be found. Holland, in which no particle of the supreme authority is derived from the people, has passed almost universally under the denomination of a republic. The same title has been bestowed on Venice, where absolute power over the great body of the people is exercised in the most absolute manner by a small body of hereditary nobles. Poland, which is a mixture of aristocracy and of monarchy in their worst forms, has been dignified with the same appellation. The government of England, which has one republican branch only, combined with an hereditary aristocracy and monarchy, has with equal impropriety been frequently placed on the list of republics. These examples, which are nearly as dissimilar to each other as to a genuine republic, show the extreme inaccuracy with which the term has been used in political disquisitions.

If we resort for a criterion to the different principles on which different forms of government are established, we may define a republic to be, or at least may bestow the name on, a government which derives all its powers directly or indirectly from the great body of the people, and is administered by persons holding their offices during pleasure for a limited period, or during good behavior. It is essential to such a government that it be derived from the great body of the society, not from an inconsiderable proportion or a favored class of it; otherwise a handful of tyrannical nobles, exercising their oppressions by a delegation of their powers, might aspire to the rank of republicans and claim for their government the honorable title of republic. It is sufficient for such a government that the persons administering it be appointed, either directly or indirectly, by the people; and that they hold their appointments by either of the tenures just specified; otherwise every government in the United States, as well as every other popular government that has been or can be well organized or well executed, would be degraded from the republican character. According to the constitution of every State in the Union, some or other of the officers of government are appointed indirectly only by the people. According to most of them, the chief magistrate himself is so appointed. And according to one, this mode of appointment is extended to one of the coordinate branches of the legislature. According to all the constitutions, also, the tenure of the highest offices is extended to a definite period, and in many instances, both within the legislative and executive departments, to a period of years. According to the provisions of most of the constitutions, again, as well as according to the most respectable and received opinions on the subject, the members of the judiciary department are to retain their offices by the firm tenure of good behavior.

On comparing the Constitution planned by the convention with the standard here fixed, we perceived at once that it is, in the most rigid sense, conformable to it. The House of Representatives, like that of one branch at least of all the State legislatures, is elected immediately by the great body of the people. The Senate, like the present Congress and the Senate of Maryland, derives its appointment indirectly from the people. The President is indirectly derived from the choice of the people, according to the example in most of the States. Even the judges, with all other officers of the Union, will, as in the several States, be the choice, though a remote choice, of the people themselves. The duration of the appointments is equally conformable to the republican standard and to the model of State constitutions. The House of Representatives is periodically elective, as in all the States; and for the period of two years, as in the State of South Carolina. The Senate is elective for the period of six years, which is but one year more than the period of the Senate of Maryland, and but two more than that of the Senators of New York and Virginia. The President is to continue in office for the period of four years; as in New York and Delaware the chief magistrate is elected for three years, and in South Carolina for two years. In the other States the election is annual. In several of the States, however, no explicit provision is made for the impeachment of the chief magistrate. And in Delaware and Virginia he is not impeachable till out of office. The President of the United States is impeachable at any time during his continuance in office. The tenure by which the judges are to hold their places is, as it unquestionably ought to be, that of good behavior. The tenure of the ministerial offices generally will be a subject of legal regulation, conformable to the reason of the case and the example of the State constitutions.

Could any further proof be required of the republican complexion of this system, the most decisive one might be found in its absolute prohibition of titles of nobility, both under the federal and the State governments; and in its express guaranty of the republican form to each of the latter.

"But it was not sufficient," say the adversaries of the proposed Constitution, "for the convention to adhere to the republican form. They ought with equal care to have preserved the federal form, which regards the Union as a Confederacy of sovereign states; instead of which they have framed a national government, which regards the Union as a consolidation of the States." And it is asked by what authority this bold and radical innovation was undertaken. The handle which has been made of this objection requires that it should be examined with some precision.

Without inquiring into the accuracy of the distinction on which the objection is founded, it will be necessary to a just estimate of its force, first, to ascertain the real character of the government in question; secondly, to inquire how far the convention were authorized to propose such a government; and thirdly, how far the duty they owed to their country could supply any defect of regular authority.

First.—In order to ascertain the real character of the government, it may be considered in relation to the foundation on which it is to be established; to the sources from which its ordinary powers are to be drawn; to the operation of those powers; to the extent of them; and to the authority by which future changes in the government are to be introduced.

On examining the first relation, it appears, on one hand, that the Constitution is to be founded on the assent and ratification of the people of America, given by deputies elected for the special purpose; but, on the other, that this assent and ratification is to be given by the people, not as individuals composing one entire nation, but as composing the distinct and independent States to which they respectively belong. It is to be the assent and ratification of the several States, derived from the supreme authority in each State—the authority of the people themselves. The act, therefore, establishing the Constitution will not be a national but a federal act.

That it will be a federal and not a national act, as these terms are understood by the objectors—the act of the people, as forming so many independent States, not as forming one aggregate nation—is obvious from this single consideration: that it is to result neither from the decision of a majority of the people of the Union, nor from that of a majority of the States. It must result from the unanimous assent of the several States that are parties to it, differing not otherwise from their ordinary assent than in its being expressed, not by the legislative authority, but by that of the people themselves. Were the people regarded in this transaction as forming one nation, the will of the majority of the whole people of the United States would bind the minority, in the same manner as the majority in each State must bind the minority; and the will of the majority must be determined either by a comparison of the individual votes, or by considering the will of the majority of the States as evidence of the will of a majority of the people of the United States. Neither of these rules has been adopted. Each State, in ratifying the Constitution, is considered as a sovereign body independent of all others, and only to be bound by its own voluntary act. In this relation, then, the new Constitution will, if established, be a federal and not a national constitution.

The next relation is to the sources from which the ordinary powers of government are to be derived. The House of Representatives will derive its powers from the people of America; and the people will be represented in the same proportion and on the same principle as they are in the legislature of a particular State. So far the government is national, not federal. The Senate, on the other hand, will derive its powers from the States as political and coequal societies, and these will be represented on the principle of equality in the Senate, as they now are in the existing Congress. So far the government is federal, not national. The executive power will be derived from a very compound source. The immediate election of the President is to be made by the States in their political characters. The votes allotted to them are in a compound ratio, which considers them partly as distinct and coequal societies, partly as unequal members of the same society. The eventual election, again, is to be made by that branch of the legislature which consists of the national representatives; but in this particular act they are to be thrown into the form of individual delegations from so many distinct and coequal bodies politic. From this aspect of the government it appears to be of a mixed character, presenting at least as many federal as national features.

The difference between a federal and national government, as it relates to the operation of the government, is by the adversaries of the plan of the convention supposed to consist in this, that in the former the powers operate on the political bodies composing the confederacy in their political capacities; in the latter, on the individual citizens composing the nation in their individual capacities. On trying the Constitution by this criterion, it falls under the national not the federal character; though perhaps not so completely as has been understood. In several cases, and particularly in the trial of controversies to which States may be parties, they must be viewed and proceeded against in their collective and political capacities only. But the operation of the government on the people in their individual capacities, in its ordinary and most essential proceedings, will, in the sense of its opponents, on the whole, designate it, in this relation, a national government.

But if the government be national with regard to the operation of its powers, it changes its aspect again when we contemplate it in relation to the extent of its powers. The idea of a national government involves in it not only an authority over the individual citizens, but an indefinite supremacy over all persons and things, so far as they are objects of lawful government. Among a people consolidated into one nation, this supremacy is completely vested in the national legislature. Among communities united for particular purposes, it is vested partly in the general and partly in the municipal legislatures. In the former case, all local authorities are subordinate to the supreme; and may be controlled, directed, and abolished by it at pleasure. In the latter, the local or municipal authorities form distinct and independent portions of the supremacy, no more subject, within their respective spheres, to the general authority than the general authority is subject to them, within its own sphere. In this relation, then, the proposed government cannot be deemed a national one; since its jurisdiction extends to certain enumerated objects only, and leaves to the several States a residuary and inviolable sovereignty over all other objects. It is true that in controversies relating to the boundary between the two jurisdictions, the tribunal which is ultimately to decide is to be established under the general government. But this does not change the principle of the case. The decision is to be impartially made, according to the rules of the Constitution; and all the usual and most effectual precautions are taken to secure this impartiality. Some such tribunal is clearly essential to prevent an appeal to the sword and a dissolution of the compact; and that it ought to be established under the general rather than under the local governments, or, to speak more properly, that it could be safely established under the first alone, is a position not likely to be combated.

If we try the Constitution by its last relation to the authority by which amendments are to be made, we find it neither wholly national nor wholly federal. Were it wholly national, the supreme and ultimate authority would reside in the majority of the people of the Union; and this authority would be competent at all times, like that of a majority of every national society to alter or abolish its established government. Were it wholly federal, on the other hand, the concurrence of each State in the Union would be essential to every alteration that would be binding on all. The mode provided by the plan of the convention is not founded on either of these principles. In requiring more than a majority, and particularly in computing the proportion by States, not by citizens, it departs from the national and advances towards the federal character; in rendering the concurrence of less than the whole number of States sufficient, it loses again the federal and partakes of the national character.

The proposed Constitution, therefore, even when tested by the rules laid down by its antagonists, is, in strictness, neither a national nor a federal Constitution, but a composition of both. In its foundation it is federal, not national; in the sources from which the ordinary powers of the government are drawn, it is partly federal and partly national; in the operation of these powers, it is national, not federal; in the extent of them, again, it is federal, not national; and, finally in the authoritative mode of introducing amendments, it is neither wholly federal nor wholly national.

PUBLIUS

In *The Federalist,* Alexander Hamilton and James Madison were careful to point out the advantages of the federal form of government that would be established by the Constitution, both over the government that had existed under the Articles of Confederation and in general terms. Because many state political leaders were highly suspicious of the national government that would be created by the new Constitution, much of the efforts of Hamilton and Madison were directed toward allaying these fears. Above all, they both stated, the energy of the national government would never be sufficient to coerce the states into giving up any portion of their sovereignty. Moreover, Hamilton stated in *Federalist 17* that there would be no incentive for national politicians to take away the reserved powers of the states. The sphere of national power, although limited, was considered entirely adequate to absorb even the most ambitious politicians. And James Madison, in *Federalist 39,* was careful to point out that the jurisdiction of the national government extended only to certain enumerated objects, implying that the residual sovereignty of the states was in fact greater than the sovereignty of the national government.

Federalism Viewed as a Political Experiment

The great nineteenth-century Scotsman, scholar, politician, and world traveler James Bryce made the great American political experiment in all its dimensions the focus of his book, *The American Commonwealth.* Published in 1888, and later revised twice, *The American Commonwealth* was widely acclaimed and read in both England and America and influenced nineteenth-century views of American political institutions.

Bryce's nineteenth-century analysis of American federalism in the following selection is as sharply relevant in the twenty-first century as it was at the end of the nineteenth century.

11

THE MERITS OF THE FEDERAL SYSTEM

James Bryce

. . . There are two distinct lines of argument by which their Federal system was recommended to the framers of the Constitution, and upon which it is still held forth for imitation to other countries. These lines have been so generally confounded that it is well to present them in a precise form.

The first set of arguments point to Federalism proper, and are the following:—

1. That Federalism furnishes the means of uniting commonwealths into one nation under one national government without extinguishing their separate administrations, legislatures, and local patriotisms. As the Americans of 1787 would probably have preferred complete State independence to the fusion of their States into a unified government, Federalism was the only resource. So when the new Germanic Empire, which is really a Federation, was established in 1871, Bavaria and Würtemberg could not have been brought under a national government save by a Federal scheme. Similar suggestions, as every one knows, have been made for re-settling the relations of Ireland to Great Britain, and of the self-governing British colonies to the United Kingdom. There are causes and conditions which dispose independent or semi-independent communities, or peoples living under loosely compacted governments, to form a closer union in a Federal form. There are other causes and conditions which dispose the subjects of one government, or sections of these subjects, to desire to make their governmental union less close by substituting a Federal for a unitary system. In both sets of cases, the centripetal or centrifugal forces spring from the local position, the history, the sentiments, the economic needs of those among whom the problem arises; and that which is good for one people or political body is not necessarily good for another. Federalism is an equally legitimate resource whether it is adopted for the sake of tightening or for the sake of loosening a pre-existing bond.

2. That Federalism supplies the best means of developing a new and vast country. It permits an expansion whose extent, and whose rate and manner of progress, cannot be foreseen to proceed with more variety of methods, more adaptation of laws and administration to the circumstances of each part of the territory, and altogether in a more truly natural and spontaneous way, than can be expected

under a centralized government, which is disposed to apply its settled system through all its dominions. Thus the special needs of a new region are met by the inhabitants in the way they find best: its laws can be adapted to the economic conditions which from time to time present themselves, its special evils can be cured by special remedies, perhaps more drastic than an old country demands, perhaps more lax than an old country would tolerate; while at the same time the spirit of self-reliance among those who build up these new communities is stimulated and respected.

3. That Federalism prevents the rise of a despotic central government, absorbing other powers, and menacing the private liberties of the citizen. This may now seem to have been an idle fear, so far as America was concerned. It was, however, a very real fear among the ancestors of the present Americans, and nearly led to the rejection even of so undespotic an instrument as the Federal Constitution of 1789. Congress (or the President, as the case may be) is still sometimes described as a tyrant, by the party which does not control it, simply because it is a central government: and the States are represented as bulwarks against its encroachments.

The second set of arguments relate to and recommend not so much Federalism as local self-government. I state them briefly because they are familiar.

4. Self-government stimulates the interest of people in the affairs of their neighbourhood, sustains local political life, educates the citizen in his daily round of civic duty, teaches him that perpetual vigilance and the sacrifice of his own time and labour are the price that must be paid for individual liberty and collective prosperity.

5. Self-government secures the good administration of local affairs by giving the inhabitants of each locality due means of overseeing the conduct of their business. . . .

Three further benefits to be expected from a Federal system may be mentioned, benefits which seem to have been unnoticed or little regarded by those who established it in America.

6. Federalism enables a people to try experiments in legislation and administration which could not be safely tried in a large centralized country. A comparatively small commonwealth like an American State easily makes and unmakes its laws; mistakes are not serious, for they are soon corrected; other States profit by the experience of a law or a method which has worked well or ill in the State that has tried it.

7. Federalism, if it diminishes the collective force of a nation, diminishes also the risks to which its size and the diversities of its parts expose it. A nation so divided is like a ship built with water-tight compartments. When a leak is sprung in one compartment, the cargo stowed there may be damaged, but the other compartments remain dry and keep the ship afloat. So if social discord or an economic crisis has produced disorders or foolish legislation in one member of the Federal body, the mischief may stop at the State frontier instead of spreading through and tainting the nation at large.

8. Federalism, by creating many local legislatures with wide powers, relieves the national legislature of a part of that large mass of functions which might otherwise prove too heavy for it. Thus business is more promptly despatched, and the great central council of the nation has time to deliberate on those questions which most nearly touch the whole country.

All of these arguments recommending Federalism have proved valid in American experience. . . .

. . . The problem which all federalized nations have to solve is how to secure an efficient central government and preserve national unity, while allowing free scope for the diversities, and free play to the authorities, of the members of the federation. It is, to adopt that favourite astronomical metaphor which no American panegyrist of the Constitution omits, to keep the centrifugal and centripetal forces in equilibrium, so that neither the planet States shall fly off into space, nor the sun of the Central government draw them into its consuming fires. The characteristic merit of the American Constitution lies in the method by which it has solved this problem. It has given the National government a direct authority over all citizens, irrespective of the State governments, and has therefore been able safely to leave wide powers in the hands of those governments. And by placing the Constitution above both the National and the State governments, it has referred the arbitrament of disputes between them to an independent body, charged with the interpretation of the Constitution, a body which is to be deemed not so much a third authority in the government as the living voice of the Constitution, the unfolder of the mind of the people whose will stands expressed in that supreme instrument.

The application of these two principles, unknown to, or at any rate little used by, any previous federation, has contributed more than anything else to the stability of the American system, and to the reverence which its citizens feel for it, a reverence which is the best security for its permanence. Yet even these devices would not have succeeded but for the presence of a mass of moral and material influences stronger than any political devices, which have maintained the equilibrium of centrifugal and centripetal forces. On the one hand there has been the love of local independence and self-government; on the other, the sense of community in blood, in language, in habits and ideas, a common pride in the national history and the national flag. . . .

IMPLIED POWERS AND THE SUPREMACY OF NATIONAL LAW

Tracing the historical development of nation-state relationships, one finds that there has been constant strife over the determination of the boundaries of national power in relation to the reserved powers of the states. The Civil War did not settle once and for all the difficult question of national versus state power. The Supreme Court has played an important role in the development of the federal system, and some of its most historic opinions have upheld national power at the expense of the states. In the early period of the Court, Chief Justice John Marshall in *McCulloch v. Maryland*, 4 Wheaton 316 (1819), stated two doctrines that have had a profound effect upon the federal system: (1) the doctrine of implied powers, and (2) the doctrine of the supremacy of national law. The former enables Congress to expand its power into numerous areas affecting states directly. By utilizing the commerce clause, for example, Congress may now regulate what is essentially intrastate commerce, for the Court has held that this is implied in the original clause giving Congress the power to regulate commerce among the several states. The immediate issues in *McCulloch v. Maryland* were, first, whether or not Congress had the power to incorporate, or charter, a national bank; and second, if Congress did have such a power, although nowhere stated in the Constitution, did the existence of such a bank prevent state action that would interfere in its operation?

12

McCULLOCH V. MARYLAND

4 Wheaton 316 (1819)

Mr. Chief Justice Marshall delivered the opinion of the Court, saying in part:

In the case now to be determined, the defendant, a sovereign state, denies the obligation of a law enacted by the legislature of the Union; and the plaintiff, on his part, contests the validity of an act which has been passed by the legislature of that state. The Constitution of our country, in its most interesting and vital parts, is to be considered; the conflicting powers of the government of the Union and of its members, as marked in that Constitution, are to be discussed; and an opinion given, which may essentially influence the great operations of the government. . . .

If any one proposition could command the universal assent of mankind, we might expect it would be this: that the government of the Union, though limited in its powers, is supreme within its sphere of action. This would seem to result necessarily from its nature. It is the government of all; its powers are delegated by all; it represents all, and acts for all. Though any one state may be willing to control its operations, no state is willing to allow others to control them. The nation, on those subjects on which it can act, must necessarily bind its component parts. But this question is not left to mere reason: the people have, in express terms, decided it, by saying, "this Constitution, and the laws of the United States, which shall be made in pursuance thereof," "shall be the supreme law of the land," and by requiring that the members of the state legislatures, and the officers of the executive and judicial departments of the states, shall take the oath of fidelity to it. . . .

A constitution, to contain an accurate detail of all the subdivisions of which its great powers will admit, and of all the means by which they may be carried into execution, would partake of the prolixity of a legal code, and could scarcely be embraced by the human mind. It would probably never be understood by the public. Its nature, therefore, requires that only its great outlines should be marked, its important objects designated, and the minor ingredients which compose those objects be deduced from the nature of the objects themselves. That this idea was entertained by the framers of the American Constitution, is not only to be inferred from the nature of the instrument, but from the language. . . .

Although, among the enumerated powers of government, we do not find the word "bank," or "incorporation," we find the great powers to lay and collect taxes; to borrow money; to regulate commerce; to declare and conduct a war; and to raise and support armies and navies. The sword and the purse, all the external relations, and no inconsiderable portion of the industry of the nation, are entrusted to its government. It can never be pretended that these vast powers draw after them others of inferior importance, merely because they are inferior. Such an idea can never be advanced. But it may, with great reason, be contended, that a government, entrusted with such ample powers, on the due execution of which the happiness and prosperity of the nation so vitally depends, must also be entrusted with ample means for their execution. The power being given, it is the interest of the nation to facilitate its execution. It can never be their interest, and cannot be presumed to have been their intention, to clog and embarrass its execution by withholding the most appropriate means. Throughout this vast republic, from the St. Croix to the Gulf of Mexico, from the Atlantic to the Pacific, revenue is to be collected and expended, armies are to be marched and supported. The exigencies of the nation may require, that the treasure raised in the North should be transported to the South, that raised in the East conveyed to the West, or that this order should be reversed. Is that construction of the Constitution to be preferred which would render these operations difficult, hazardous, and expensive? Can we adopt that construction (unless the words imperiously require it) which would impute to the framers of that instrument, when granting these powers for the public good, the intention of impeding their exercise by withholding a choice of means? If, indeed, such be the mandate of the Constitution, we have only to obey; but that instrument does not profess to enumerate the means by which the powers it confers may be executed; nor does it prohibit the creation of a corporation, if the existence of such a being be essential to the beneficial exercise of those powers. It is, then, the subject of fair inquiry, how far such means may be employed. . . .

We admit, as all must admit, that the powers of the government are limited, and that its limits are not to be transcended. But we think the sound construction of the Constitution must allow to the national legislature that discretion, with respect to the means by which the powers it confers are to be carried into execution, which will enable that body to perform the high duties assigned to it, in the manner most beneficial to the people. Let the end be legitimate, let it be within the scope of the

Constitution, and all means which are appropriate, which are plainly adapted to that end, which are not prohibited, but consist with the letter and spirit of the Constitution, are constitutional. . . .

It being the opinion of the court that the act incorporating the bank is constitutional; and that the power of establishing a branch in the state of Maryland might be properly exercised by the bank itself, we proceed to inquire:

Whether the state of Maryland may, without violating the Constitution, tax that branch? . . .

That the power of taxation is one of vital importance; that it is retained by the states; that it is not abridged by the grant of a similar power to the government of the Union; that it is to be concurrently exercised by the two governments: are truths which have never been denied. But, such is the paramount character of the Constitution, that its capacity to withdraw any subject from the action of even this power, is admitted. The states are expressly forbidden to lay any duties on imports or exports, except what may be absolutely necessary for executing their inspection laws. If the obligation of this prohibition must be conceded—if it may restrain a state from the exercise of its taxing power of imports and exports; the same paramount character would seem to restrain, as it certainly may restrain, a state from such other exercise of this power, as is in its nature incompatible with, and repugnant to, the constitutional laws of the Union. A law, absolutely repugnant to another, as entirely repeals that other as if express terms of repeal were used.

On this ground the counsel for the bank place its claim to be exempted from the power of a state to tax its operations. There is no express provision for the case, but the claim has been sustained on a principle which so entirely pervades the Constitution, is so intermixed with the materials which compose it, so interwoven with its web, so blended with its texture, as to be incapable of being separated from it, without rending it into shreds.

This great principle is, that the Constitution and the laws made in pursuance thereof are supreme; that they control the Constitution and laws of the respective states, and cannot be controlled by them. From this, which may be almost termed an axiom, other propositions are deduced as corollaries, on the truth or error of which, and on their application to this case, the cause has been supposed to depend. These are, 1. That a power to create implies a power to preserve. 2. That a power to destroy, if wielded by a different hand, is hostile to, and incompatible with, these powers to create and preserve. 3. That where this repugnancy exists, that authority which is supreme must control, not yield to that over which it is supreme. . . .

If we apply the principle for which the state of Maryland contends, to the Constitution generally, we shall find it capable of changing totally the character of that instrument. We shall find it capable of arresting all the measures of the government, and of prostrating it at the foot of the states. The American people have declared their Constitution, and the laws made in pursuance thereof, to be supreme; but this principle would transfer the supremacy, in fact, to the states. . . .

The court has bestowed on this subject its most deliberate consideration. The result is a conviction that the states have no power, by taxation or otherwise, to retard, impede, burden, or in any manner control, the operations of the constitutional laws enacted by Congress to carry into execution the powers vested in the general government. That is, we think, the unavoidable consequence of that supremacy which the Constitution has declared. . . .

Interpretation of the Commerce Clause Decides the Balance of National and State Powers Under the Constitution

Chief Justice John Marshall's expansive interpretation of the Article I powers of Congress in *McCulloch v. Maryland* (1819) continued in the first major case interpreting the commerce clause, *Gibbons v. Ogden* (1824). Constitutional doctrine defining the power of the national government to regulate commerce among the states was to become a major political issue that would decide the balance of powers between the national government and the states.

At issue is the interpretation of Congress' Article I power to "regulate commerce with foreign nations, and among the several States."

The seminal case supporting the supremacy of the national government in commercial regulation was *Gibbons v. Ogden,* 9 Wheaton 1 (1824). The New York legislature, in 1798, granted Robert R. Livingston the exclusive privilege to navigate by steam the rivers and other waters of the state, provided he could build a boat that would travel at four miles an hour against the current of the Hudson River. A two-year time limitation was imposed, and the conditions were not met; however, New York renewed its grant for two years in 1803 and again in 1807. In 1807 Robert Fulton, who now held the exclusive license with Livingston, completed and put into operation a steamboat that met the legislative conditions. The New York legislature now provided that a five-year extension of their monopoly would be given to Livingston and Fulton for each new steamboat they placed into operation on New York waters. The monopoly could not exceed thirty years, but during that period anyone wishing to navigate New York waters by steam had first to obtain a license from Livingston and Fulton, who were given the power to confiscate unlicensed boats. New Jersey and Connecticut passed retaliatory laws, the former authorizing confiscation of any New York ship for each ship confiscated by Livingston and Fulton, the latter prohibiting boats licensed in New York from entering Connecticut waters. Ohio also passed retaliatory legislation. Open commercial warfare seemed a possibility among the states of the union.

In 1793 Congress passed an act providing for the licensing of vessels engaged in the coasting trade, and Gibbons obtained under this statute a license to operate boats between New York and New Jersey. Ogden was engaged in a similar operation under an exclusive license issued by Livingston and Fulton, and thus sought to enjoin Gibbons from further operation. The New York court upheld the exclusive grants given to Livingston and Fulton, and Gibbons appealed to the Supreme Court. Chief Justice Marshall made it quite clear that (1) states cannot interfere with a power granted to Congress by passing conflicting state legislation, and (2) the commerce power includes anything affecting "commerce among the states" and thus may include intrastate as well as interstate commerce. In this way the foundation was laid for broad national control over commercial activity.

13

GIBBONS V. OGDEN

9 Wheaton 1 (1824)

Chief Justice John Marshall delivered the opinion of the Court:

The appellant [Gibbons] contends that this decree [of the New York State Court upholding Ogden's monopoly under state law] is erroneous because the laws which purport to give the exclusive privilege it sustains are repugnant to the Constitution and laws of the United States. They are said to be repugnant: first, to that clause in the Constitution which authorizes Congress to regulate commerce; second, to that which authorizes Congress to promote the progress of science and useful arts.

As preliminary to the very able discussions of the Constitution which we have heard from the bar, and as having some influence on its construction, reference has been made to the political situation of these states, anterior to its formation. It has been said that they were sovereign, were completely independent, and were connected with each other only by a league. This is true. But, when these allied sovereigns converted their league into a government, when they converted their congress of ambassadors, deputed to deliberate on their common concerns, and to recommend measures of general utility, into a legislature, empowered to enact laws on the most interesting subjects, the whole character in which the states appear underwent a change, the extent of which must be determined by a fair consideration of the instrument [Constitution] by which that change was effected.

This [Constitution] contains an enumeration of powers expressly granted by the people to their government. It has been said that these powers ought to be construed strictly. But why ought they to be so construed? Is there one sentence in the Constitution which gives countenance to this rule? In the last of the enumerated powers [of Article I] , that which grants, expressly, the means for carrying all others into execution, Congress is authorized *to make all laws which shall be necessary and proper* for the purpose. . . .

What do gentlemen mean by a strict construction? If they contend only against that enlarged construction which would extend words beyond their natural and obvious import, we might question the application of the term, but should not controvert the principle. If they contend for that narrow construction which, in support of some theory not to be found in the Constitution, would deny to the government those powers which the words of the grant, as usually understood, import, and which are consistent with the general views and objects of the instrument; for that narrow construction, which would cripple the government, and render it unequal to the objects for which it is declared to be instituted, and to which the powers given, as fairly understood, render it competent; then we cannot perceive the propriety of this strict construction, nor adopt it as the rule by which the Constitution is to be expounded. As men whose intentions require no concealment generally employ the words which most directly and aptly express the ideas they intend to convey, the enlightened patriots who framed our Constitution, and the people who adopted it, must be understood to have employed words in their natural sense, and to have intended what they have said.

If, from the imperfection of human language, there should be serious doubts respecting the extent of any given power, it is a well-settled rule that the objects for which it was given, especially when those objects are expressed in the instrument itself, should have great influence in the construction. We know of no reason for excluding this rule from the present case. The grant does not convey power which might be beneficial to the grantor, if retained by himself, or which can inure solely to the benefit of the grantee, but is an investment of power for the general advantage in the hands of agents selected for that purpose; which power can never be exercised by the people themselves, but must be placed in the hands of agents, or lie dormant. We know of no rule for construing the extent of such powers other than is given by the language of the instrument which confers them, taken in connection with the purposes for which they were conferred.

The words are: *Congress shall have power to regulate commerce with foreign nations, and among the several states, and with the Indian tribes*. The subject to be regulated is commerce; and our Constitution being, as was aptly said at the bar, one of enumeration and not of definition, to as certain the extent of the power it becomes necessary to settle the meaning of the word.

Commerce, undoubtedly, is traffic, but it is something more—it is intercourse. It describes the commercial intercourse between nations, and parts of nations, in all its branches, and is regulated by prescribing rules for carrying on that intercourse. The mind can scarcely conceive a system for regulating commerce between nations which shall exclude all laws concerning navigation, which shall be silent on the admission of the vessels of the one nation into the ports of the other, and be confined to prescribing rules for the conduct of individuals in the actual employment of buying and selling or of barter. If commerce does not include navigation, the government of the Union has no direct power over that subject, and can make no law prescribing what shall constitute American vessels, or requiring that they shall be navigated by American seamen.

Yet this power has been exercised from the commencement of the government, has been exercised with the consent of all, and, has been understood by all to be a commercial regulation. All America understands, and has uniformly understood, the word *commerce* to comprehend navigation.

The word used in the Constitution, then, comprehends, and has been always understood to comprehend, navigation within its meaning; and a power to regulate navigation is as expressly granted as if that term had been added to the word *commerce*. To what commerce does this power extend? The Constitution informs us to commerce *with foreign nations, and among the several states, and with the Indian tribes*. It has, we believe, been universally admitted that these words comprehend every species of commercial intercourse between the United States and foreign nations. No sort of trade can be carried on between this country and any other to which this power does not extend. It has been truly said that commerce, as the word is used in the Constitution, is a unit, every part of which is indicated by the term. If this be the admitted meaning of the word in its application to foreign nations, it must carry the same meaning throughout the sentence and remain a unit, unless there be some plain intelligible cause which alters it.

The subject to which the power is next applied is to commerce *among the several states*. The word *among* means intermingled with. A thing which is among others is intermingled with them. Commerce among the states cannot stop at the external boundary line of each state, but may be introduced into the interior. It is not intended to say that these words comprehend that commerce which is completely internal, which is carried on between man and man in a state, or between different parts of the same state, and which does not extend to or affect other states. Such a power would be inconvenient and is certainly unnecessary. Comprehensive as the word *among* is, it may very properly be restricted to that commerce which concerns more states than one. The phrase is not one which would probably have been selected to indicate the completely interior traffic of a state, because it is not an apt phrase for that purpose; and the enumeration of the particular classes of commerce to which the power was to be extended would not have been made had the intention been to extend the power to every description. The enumeration presupposes something not enumerated; and that something, if we regard the language or the subject of the sentence, must be the exclusively internal commerce of a state.

The genius and character of the whole government seem to be that its action is to be applied to all the external concerns of the nation and to those internal concerns which affect the states generally; but not to those which are completely within a particular state, which do not affect other states, and with which it is not necessary to interfere for the purpose of executing some of the general powers of the government. The completely internal commerce of a state, then, may be considered as reserved for the state itself.

But, in regulating commerce with foreign nations, the power of Congress does not stop at the jurisdictional lines of the several states. It would be a very useless power if it could not pass those lines. The commerce of the United States with foreign nations is that of the whole United States. Every district has a right to participate in it. The deep streams which penetrate our country in every direction pass through the interior of almost every state in the Union, and furnish the means of exercising this right. If Congress has the power to regulate it, that power must be exercised whenever the subject exists. If it exists within the states, if a foreign voyage may commence or terminate at a port within a state, then the power of Congress may be exercised within a state.

This principle is, if possible, still more clear, when applied to commerce *among the several states*. They either join each other, in which case they are separated by a mathematical line, or they are remote from each other, in which case other states lie between them. What is commerce *among* them, and how is it to be conducted? Can a trading expedition between two adjoining states commence and terminate outside of each? And if the trading intercourse be between two states remote from each other, must it not commence in one, terminate in the other, and probably pass through a third? Commerce among the states must, of necessity, be commerce with the states. In the regulation of trade with the Indian tribes, the action of the law, especially, when the Constitution was made, was chiefly within a state.

The power of Congress, then, whatever it may be, must be exercised within the territorial jurisdiction of the several states. The sense of the nation on this subject is unequivocally manifested by the provisions made in the laws for transporting goods by land between Baltimore and Providence, between New York and Philadelphia, and between Philadelphia and Baltimore.

We are now arrived at the inquiry—What is this power? It is the power to regulate, that is, to prescribe the rule by which commerce is to be governed. This power, like all others vested in Congress, is complete in itself, may be exercised to its utmost extent, and acknowledges no limitations other than are prescribed in the Constitution. These are expressed in plain terms and do not affect the questions which arise in this case, or which have been discussed at the bar. If, as has always been understood, the sovereignty of Congress, though limited to specified objects, is plenary as to those objects, the power over commerce with foreign nations and among the several states is vested in Congress as absolutely as it would be in a single government, having in its constitution the same restrictions on the exercise of the power as are found in the Constitution of the United States.

The wisdom and the discretion of Congress, their identity with the people, and the influence which their constituents possess at elections are, in this as in many other instances, as that, for example, of declaring war, the sole restraints on which they have relied to secure them from its abuse. They are the restraints on which the people must often rely solely in all representative governments. The power of Congress, then, comprehends navigation within the limits of every state in the Union so far as that navigation may be, in any manner, connected with *commerce with foreign nations, or among the several States, or with the Indian tribes*. It may, of consequence, pass the jurisdiction line of New York, and act upon the very waters to which the prohibition now under consideration applies.

But it has been urged with great earnestness that, although the power of Congress to regulate commerce with foreign nations and among the several states be coextensive with the subject itself, and have no other limits than are prescribed in the Constitution, yet the states may severally exercise the same power within their respective jurisdictions. In support of this argument, it is said that they possessed it as an inseparable attribute of sovereignty before the formation of the Constitution, and still retain it, except so far as they have surrendered it by that instrument; that this principle results from the nature of the government, and is secured by the Tenth Amendment; that an affirmative grant of power is not exclusive, unless in its own nature it be such that the continued exercise of it by the former possessor is inconsistent with the grant, and that this is not of that description.

The appellant, conceding these postulates except the last, contends that full power to regulate a particular subject implies the whole power and leaves no residuum; that a grant of the whole is incompatible with the existence of a right in another to any part of it. Both parties have appealed to the Constitution, to legislative acts, and judicial decisions; and have drawn arguments from all these sources to support and illustrate the propositions they respectively maintain.

In discussing the question, whether this power is still in the states, in the case under consideration, we may dismiss from it the inquiry, whether it is surrendered by the mere grant to Congress, or is retained until Congress shall exercise the power. We may dismiss that inquiry because it has been exercised, and the regulations which Congress deemed it proper to make are now in full operation. The sole question is—Can a state regulate commerce with foreign nations and among the states while Congress is regulating it?

The counsel for the respondent answer this question in the affirmative, and rely very much on the restrictions in the 10th Section as supporting their opinion. They say, very truly, that limitations of a power furnish a strong argument in favor of the existence of that power, and that the section which prohibits the states from laying duties on imports or exports proves that this power might have been exercised had it not been expressly forbidden; and, consequently, that any other commercial regulation, not expressly forbidden, to which the original power of the state was competent, may still be made. That this restriction shows the opinion of the Convention, that a state might impose duties on exports and imports, if not expressly forbidden, will be conceded; but that it follows, as a consequence from this concession, that a state may regulate commerce with foreign nations and among the states cannot be admitted. . . .

It has been contended by the counsel for the appellant that, as the word *to regulate* implies in its nature full power over the thing to be regulated, it excludes, necessarily, the action of all others that would perform the same operation on the same thing. That regulation is designed for the entire result, applying to those parts which remain as they were, as well as to those which are altered. It produces a uniform whole, which is as much disturbed and deranged by changing what the regulating power designs to leave untouched as that on which it has operated. There is great force in this argument, and the court is not satisfied that it has been refuted.

Since, however, in exercising the power of regulating their own purely internal affairs, whether of trading or police, the states may sometimes enact laws, the validity of which depends on their interfering with, and being contrary to, an act of Congress passed in pursuance of the Constitution, the court will enter upon the inquiry, whether the laws of New York, as expounded by the highest tribunal of that state, have, in their application to this case, come into collision with an act of Congress, and deprived a citizen of a right to which that act entitles him. Should this collision exist, it will be immaterial whether those laws were passed in virtue of a concurrent power *to regulate commerce with foreign nations and among the several states*, or in virtue of a power to regulate their domestic trade and police.

In one case and the other the acts of New York must yield to the law of Congress; and the decision sustaining the privilege they confer against a right given by a law of the Union must be erroneous. This opinion has been frequently expressed in this court, and is founded as well on the nature of the government as on the words of the Constitution. In argument, however, it has been contended that, if a law passed by a state in the exercise of its acknowledged sovereignty comes into conflict with a law passed by Congress in pursuance of the Constitution, they affect the subject and each other like equal opposing powers.

But the framers of our Constitution foresaw this state of things and provided for it by declaring the supremacy not only of itself but of the laws made in pursuance of it. The nullity of any act inconsistent with the Constitution is produced by the declaration that the Constitution is supreme law. The appropriate application of that part of the clause which confers the same supremacy on laws and treaties is to such acts of the state legislatures as do not transcend their powers, but though enacted in the execution of acknowledged state powers, interfere with, or are contrary to, the laws of Congress, made in pursuance of the Constitution or some treaty made under the authority of the United States. In every such case, the act of Congress or the treaty is supreme; and the law of the state, though enacted in the exercise of powers not controverted, must yield to it.

Decree

This court is of opinion that so much of the several laws of the state of New York as prohibits vessels, licensed according to the laws of the United States, from navigating the waters of the state of New York, by means of fire or steam, is repugnant to the said Constitution and void. This court is, therefore, of opinion that the decree of the court of New York for the trial of impeachments and the correction of errors, affirming the decree of the chancellor of that state is erroneous and ought to be reversed, and the same is hereby reversed and annulled. And this court doth further direct, order, and decree that the bill of the said Aaron Ogden be dismissed, and the same is hereby dismissed accordingly.

NATIONAL POWER OVER THE STATES: A RECURRING CONSTITUTIONAL DEBATE

Put simply, the Constitution created federalism by delegating powers to the national government and then, in the Tenth Amendment, providing that "The powers not delegated to the United States by the Constitution, nor prohibited by it to the states, are reserved to the states respectively, or to the people."* The law-making powers of the

---

**Compilers note:* Interestingly, the states did not ratify the Tenth Amendment until 1798. Textually, then, the original Constitution did not reserve any powers to the states. But the states were sovereign at the time of the ratification of the Constitution, and clearly they would not have entered into any compact that would have taken away all of their sovereign powers.

national government are those enumerated powers of Congress found in Article I. The most important of these are the commerce and war powers and the power to tax and provide for the general welfare.

Constitutional and political debate during the nineteenth and much of the twentieth centuries focused upon the issue of national versus state power. Over 650,000 young men lost their lives in the Civil War because of the failure of the political system to resolve national-state conflict.

Constitutional Changes in the Balance of Federalism: The Civil War Amendments

The "Civil War amendments," the Thirteenth, Fourteenth, and Fifteenth Amendments, added an important new constitutional dimension to federalism. The amendments abolished slavery (thirteenth); granted citizenship to all persons born in the United States (fourteenth); prohibited states from denying persons life, liberty, or property without due process of law or equal protection of the laws (fourteenth), barred states from denying the privileges and immunities of citizens of the United States (fourteenth); and prohibited both the federal government and the states from denying the right to vote on account of race, nationality, or previous condition of servitude (fifteenth).

Especially important to federalism were the Enforcement Clauses of the Civil War amendments, which gave Congress the authority to enforce each of the amendments by "appropriate legislation." The new enforcement powers vastly expanded Congress' potential authority over the states. The Civil War had settled the question of Union once and for all time in favor of national power. The Civil War amendments were the constitutional recognition of national victory over state sovereignty in the determination of civil rights.

However, as seemingly clear as the nationalist Civil War amendments were, they did not automatically settle the political question of the scope of national power over the states. As with the original Constitution, the amendments provided an outline, not a blueprint, of congressional powers and protected rights. Absent a clear national majority reflected in disciplined political parties, the courts once again became the supreme interpreters of the amendments and hence of the boundaries of national and state powers within their context. Litigation became politics by other means to settle disputes over national versus state power. Litigation over the constitutional authority of Congress over the states now encompassed not only the meaning of the commerce clause and other Article I powers, but also what constituted "appropriate legislation" under the enforcement clauses of the Civil War amendments.

Litigation continues to be the avenue for the resolution of political conflict over the scope of national and state powers, particularly on the part of advocates of states' rights who were dissatisfied with what they viewed as increasing national encroachments upon state powers and rights. Of course, Congress represents, and some would argue overrepresents in the Senate, the states, and therefore is unlikely to pass legislation that unduly interferes with states' rights. But in the highly pluralistic American political system there will always be interests that are dissatisfied with national policies, and if they have the resources they will use litigation to challenge the constitutionality of congressional laws.

Gibbons v. Ogden Revisited: Federalism and the Commerce Clause

Throughout its history the Supreme Court has interpreted the commerce clause both to expand and to contract the authority of the national government. After Chief Justice John Marshall's era ended in 1836, the Court gradually adopted a more restrictive view of the national commerce power, protecting state sovereignty over many areas of commercial regulation that Marshall clearly would have allowed Congress to regulate. The Supreme Court did not fully return to the broad commerce clause interpretation of the *Gibbons* case until 1937, when it reluctantly capitulated to Franklin D. Roosevelt's New Deal and the centralized government it represented. The restoration of the Marshall Court's definition of the commerce power removed constitutional restraints upon Congress.

Since 1937 the Supreme Court has essentially upheld congressional interpretations of its own authority under the Commerce Clause. While the commerce power is generally used to support economic regulation, Congress turned to the Commerce Clause for the legal authority to enact the Civil Rights Act of 1964. The public accommodations section of the bill, Title II, banned discrimination in public establishments, including inns, hotels, motels, restaurants, motion-picture houses, and theaters. The law declared that the "operations of an establishment affects commerce . . . if . . . it serves or offers to serve interstate travelers or a substantial portion of the food which it serves or gasoline or other products which it sells, has moved in commerce . . . [or if] it customarily presents films, performances, athletic teams, exhibitions, or other sources of entertainment which move in commerce." In *Heart of Atlanta Motel, Inc. v. United States*, 379 U.S. 241 (1964), the Supreme Court upheld the law under the Commerce Clause. The motel-plaintiff contended that it was in no way involved in interstate commerce, arguing that while some of its guests might be occasionally engaged in commerce, "persons and people are not part of trade or commerce . . . people conduct commerce and engage in trade, but people are not part of commerce and trade." But the Court accepted the government's argument that racial discrimination in public accommodations impedes interstate travel by those discriminated against, causing disruption of interstate commerce which Congress has the authority to prevent.

The Supreme Court did briefly resurrect the Commerce Clause as a limit on congressional power over the states in *National League of Cities v. Usery*, 426 U.S. 833 (1976). A sharply divided Court held that Congress could not regulate governmental activities that were an integral part of state sovereignty. The decision overturned provisions of the Fair Labor Standards Act that governed state employees. The Court's majority opinion argued that states had traditionally controlled their employees, a responsibility within state sovereignty because the states through their own democratic processes should have the autonomy to decide for themselves how they would manage their public sector.

It was not long, however, before the Court reversed the *National League of Cities* decision, holding in *Garcia v. San Antonio Metropolitan Transit Authority*, 469 U.S. 528 (1985), that Congress could apply minimum-wage requirements to the states and their localities. Again the vote was closely divided, 5–4, and this time the majority opinion struck a distinct note of judicial self-restraint, concluding: "We doubt that courts ultimately can identify principled constitutional limitations on the scope of Congress' Commerce Clause powers over the states merely by relying on a priori definitions of state sovereignty." The Court found nothing in the Fair Labor Standards Act that violated state sovereignty, implying that it was up to Congress and not the courts to determine the extent of its power under the Commerce Clause. Sharp dissents were registered in the case, indicating that if in the future the issue was raised a more conservative Supreme Court majority might uphold some Commerce Clause restraints against national regulation of state governments. The *Garcia* decision was directly in line with Court precedents since 1937 that have supported virtually unlimited congressional authority under the Commerce Clause.

The *Garcia* decision appeared yet once again to have settled the constitutional question of the scope of congressional authority under the Commerce Clause. But the conservative Supreme Court of the 1990s refused to grant Congress the benefit of the doubt in applying a "rational-basis" test in reviewing legislation under the Commerce Clause. The New Deal political victory embedded in the *Wickard v. Filburn* (1942) case doctrine where the Supreme Court deferred to congressional interpretation of its commerce power ended in *United States v. Lopez* (1995). In *Lopez* the Supreme Court, by a vote of 5–4, with the conservatives in the majority, overturned the Gun-Free School Zones Act of 1990 on the ground that Congress did not have the authority to enact it under its commerce power. The law made it a federal crime "for any individual knowingly to possess a firearm at a place that the individual knows, or has reasonable cause to believe, is a school zone." Chief Justice Rehnquist's opinion for the Court flatly stated: "The Act neither regulates a commercial activity nor contains a requirement that the possession be connected in any way to interstate commerce. We hold that the Act exceeds the authority of Congress '[t]o regulate Commerce . . . among the several States. . . .'" Justice Rehnquist and his brethren in the majority were particularly concerned that Congress did not make findings that tied the possession of guns in school zones to interstate commerce. Congress merely assumed that it had the power to enact the law. The government argued before the Court that since gun possession might affect commerce among the states the law was constitutional. But Rehnquist concluded, "To uphold the Government's contentions here, we would have to pile inference upon inference in a manner that would bid fair to convert congressional authority under the Commerce Clause to a general police power of the sort retained by the States."

The Supreme Court Redefines "Necessary and Proper" Congressional Power for the Twenty-First Century

The Supreme Court once again confronted the question of the scope of Congress' commerce power, as well as congressional enforcement power under section 5 of the Fourteenth Amendment, when it reviewed the constitutionality of the Violence Against Women Act of 1994 in *United States v. Morrison* (2000). A vast majority of the states supported the law, reflecting strong political support throughout the nation. Would a majority of only five Supreme Court Justices follow the *Lopez* precedent and overturn the law on the ground that Congress did not have the constitutional authority to enact it?

The law stated that "[a]ll persons within the United States shall have the right to be free from crimes of violence motivated by gender." The enforcement section declared: "A person . . . who commits a crime of violence motivated by gender . . . shall be liable to the party injured, in an action for the recovery of compensatory and punitive damages, injunctive and declaratory relief, and such other relief as a court may deem appropriate. . . ." The law defined a "crim[e] of violence motivated by gender" as "a crime of violence committed because of gender or on the basis of gender, and due, at least in part, to an animus based on the victim's gender."

Unlike the gun control legislation the Court voided in *Lopez* in *United States v. Morrison* Congress made extensive findings to connect violence against women with interstate commerce.

These congressional findings are called legislative facts. They are empirical in nature and Congress uses them to make policy. Empirical findings support but do not dictate policy.

In the following case note how the dissent stresses the importance of the extensive congressional findings that connected violence against women with interstate commerce. These findings, the dissenters held, supported congressional authority under the Commerce Clause to enact the legislation.

14

UNITED STATES V. MORRISON

529 U.S. 59 (2000)

Chief Justice Rehnquist delivered the opinion of the Court.

In these cases we consider the constitutionality of 42 U.S.C. §13981 [of the Violence Against Women Act of 1994], which provides a federal civil remedy for the victims of gender-motivated violence. The United States Court of Appeals for the Fourth Circuit, sitting en banc, struck down §13981 because it concluded that Congress lacked constitutional authority to enact the section's civil remedy. Believing that these cases are controlled by our decisions in *United States v. Lopez*, we affirm.

I

Petitioner Christy Brzonkala enrolled at Virginia Polytechnic Institute (Virginia Tech) in the fall of 1994. In September of that year, Brzonkala met respondents Antonio Morrison and James Crawford, who were both students at Virginia Tech and members of its varsity football team. Brzonkala alleges that, within 30 minutes of meeting Morrison and Crawford, they assaulted and repeatedly raped her. After the attack, Morrison allegedly told Brzonkala, "You better not have any . . . diseases." In the months following the rape, Morrison also allegedly announced in the dormitory's dining room that he "like[d] to get girls drunk and. . . . " The omitted portions, quoted verbatim in the briefs on file with this Court, consist of boasting, debased remarks about what Morrison would do to women, vulgar remarks that cannot fail to shock and offend.

Brzonkala alleges that this attack caused her to become severely emotionally disturbed and depressed. She sought assistance from a university psychiatrist, who prescribed antidepressant medication. Shortly after the rape Brzonkala stopped attending classes and withdrew from the university.

In early 1995, Brzonkala filed a complaint against respondents under Virginia Tech's Sexual Assault Policy. During the school-conducted hearing on her complaint, Morrison admitted having sexual contact with her despite the fact that she had twice told him "no." After the hearing, Virginia Tech's Judicial Committee found insufficient evidence to punish Crawford, but found Morrison guilty of sexual assault and sentenced him to immediate suspension for two semesters.

Virginia Tech's dean of students upheld the judicial committee's sentence. However, in July 1995, Virginia Tech informed Brzonkala that Morrison intended to initiate a court challenge to his conviction under the Sexual Assault Policy. University officials told her that a second hearing would be necessary to remedy the school's error in prosecuting her complaint under that policy, which had not been widely circulated to students. The university therefore conducted a second hearing under its Abusive Conduct Policy, which was in force prior to the dissemination of the Sexual Assault Policy. Following this second hearing the Judicial Committee again found Morrison guilty and sentenced him to an identical 2-semester suspension. This time, however, the description of Morrison's offense was, without explanation, changed from "sexual assault" to "using abusive language."

Morrison appealed his second conviction through the university's administrative system. On August 21, 1995, Virginia Tech's senior vice president and provost set aside Morrison's punishment. She concluded that it was " 'excessive when compared with other cases where there has been a finding of violation of the Abusive Conduct Policy.' " Virginia Tech did not inform Brzonkala of this decision. After learning from a newspaper that Morrison would be returning to Virginia Tech for the fall 1995 semester, she dropped out of the university.

In December 1995, Brzonkala sued Morrison, Crawford, and Virginia Tech in the United States District Court for the Western District of Virginia. Her complaint alleged that Morrison's and Crawford's attack violated §13981 and that Virginia Tech's handling of her complaint violated Title IX of the Education Amendments of 1972, 86 Stat. 373–375, 20 U.S.C. §§1681–1688. Morrison and Crawford moved to dismiss this complaint on the grounds that it failed to state a claim and that §13981's civil remedy is unconstitutional. The United States, petitioner in No. 99–5, intervened to defend §13981's constitutionality.

The District Court dismissed Brzonkala's Title IX claims against Virginia Tech for failure to state a claim upon which relief can be granted. See *Brzonkala v. Virginia Polytechnic and State Univ.*, 935 F. Supp. 772 (WD Va. 1996). It then held that

Brzonkala's complaint stated a claim against Morrison and Crawford under §13981, but dismissed the complaint because it concluded that Congress lacked authority to enact the section under either the Commerce Clause or §5 of the Fourteenth Amendment. *Brzonkala v. Virginia Polytechnic and State Univ.*, 935 F. Supp. 779 (WD Va. 1996).

A divided panel of the Court of Appeals reversed the District Court, reinstating Brzonkala's §13981 claim and her Title IX hostile environment claim. *Brzonkala v. Virginia Polytechnic and State Univ.*, 132 F. 3d 949 (CA4 1997). The full Court of Appeals vacated the panel's opinion and reheard the case en banc. The en banc court then issued an opinion affirming the District Court's conclusion that Brzonkala stated a claim under §13981 because her complaint alleged a crime of violence and the allegations of Morrison's crude and derogatory statements regarding his treatment of women sufficiently indicated that his crime was motivated by gender animus. Nevertheless, the court by a divided vote affirmed the District Court's conclusion that Congress lacked constitutional authority to enact §13981's civil remedy. *Brzonkala v. Virginia Polytechnic and State Univ.*, 169 F. 3d 820 (CA4 1999). Because the Court of Appeals invalidated a federal statute on constitutional grounds, we granted certiorari. 527 U.S. 1068 (1999).

Section 13981 was part of the Violence Against Women Act of 1994. It states that "[a]ll persons within the United States shall have the right to be free from crimes of violence motivated by gender." . . .

Every law enacted by Congress must be based on one or more of its powers enumerated in the Constitution. "The powers of the legislature are defined and limited; and that those limits may not be mistaken or forgotten, the constitution is written." *Marbury v. Madison*, 1 Cranch 137, 176 (1803) (Marshall, C. J.). Congress explicitly identified the sources of federal authority on which it relied in enacting §13981. It said that a "federal civil rights cause of action" is established "[p]ursuant to the affirmative power of Congress . . . under section 5 of the Fourteenth Amendment to the Constitution, as well as under [the Commerce Clause,] section 8 of Article I of the Constitution." We address Congress' authority to enact this remedy under each of these constitutional provisions in turn.

II

Due respect for the decisions of a coordinate branch of Government demands that we invalidate a congressional enactment only upon a plain showing that Congress has exceeded its constitutional bounds. . . . With this presumption of constitutionality in mind, we turn to the question whether §13981 falls within Congress' power under Article I, §8, [the Commerce Clause] of the Constitution. Brzonkala and the United States rely upon the third clause of the Article, which gives Congress power "[t]o regulate Commerce with foreign Nations, and among the several States, and with the Indian Tribes."

As we discussed at length in *Lopez*, our interpretation of the Commerce Clause has changed as our Nation has developed. . . . We need not repeat that detailed review of the Commerce Clause's history here; it suffices to say that, in the years since *NLRB v. Jones & Laughlin Steel Corp.*, 301 U.S. 1 (1937), Congress has had considerably greater latitude in regulating conduct and transactions under the Commerce Clause than our previous case law permitted. . . .

[Using the] principles underlying our Commerce Clause jurisprudence as reference points, the proper resolution of the present cases is clear. Gender motivated crimes of violence are not, in any sense of the phrase, economic activity. While we need not adopt a categorical rule against aggregating the effects of any noneconomic activity in order to decide these cases, thus far in our Nation's history our cases have upheld Commerce Clause regulation of intrastate activity only where that activity is economic in nature. . . .

In contrast with the lack of congressional findings that we faced in *Lopez*, §13981 is supported by numerous findings regarding the serious impact that gender-motivated violence has on victims and their families. . . . But the existence of congressional findings is not sufficient, by itself, to sustain the constitutionality of Commerce Clause legislation. As we stated in *Lopez*, " '[S]imply because Congress may conclude that a particular activity substantially affects interstate commerce does not necessarily make it so.' " . . .

Congress found that gender-motivated violence affects interstate commerce by deterring potential victims from traveling interstate, from engaging in employment in interstate business, and from transacting with business, and in places involved in interstate commerce; . . . by diminishing national productivity, increasing medical and other costs, and decreasing the supply of and the demand for interstate products.

Given these findings and petitioners' arguments, the concern that we expressed in *Lopez* that Congress might use the Commerce Clause to completely obliterate the Constitution's distinction between national and local authority seems well founded. The reasoning that petitioners advance seeks to follow the but-for causal chain from the initial occurrence of violent crime (the suppression of which has always been the prime object of the States' police power) to every attenuated effect upon interstate commerce. If accepted, petitioners' reasoning would allow Congress to regulate any crime as long as the nationwide, aggregated impact of that crime has substantial effects on employment, production, transit, or consumption. Indeed, if Congress may regulate gender-motivated violence, it would be able to regulate murder or any other type of violence since gender-motivated violence, as a subset of all violent crime, is certain to have lesser economic impacts than the larger class of which it is a part.

Petitioners' reasoning, moreover, will not limit Congress to regulating violence but may, as we suggested in *Lopez*, be applied equally as well to family law and other areas of traditional state regulation since the aggregate effect of marriage, divorce, and childrearing on the national economy is undoubtedly significant. . . .

We accordingly reject the argument that Congress may regulate noneconomic, violent criminal conduct based solely on that conduct's aggregate effect on interstate commerce. The Constitution requires a distinction between what is truly national and what is truly local. . . .

Because we conclude that the Commerce Clause does not provide Congress with authority to enact §13981, we address petitioners' alternative argument that the section's civil remedy should be upheld as an exercise of Congress' remedial power under §5 of the Fourteenth Amendment. As noted above,

Congress expressly invoked the Fourteenth Amendment as a source of authority to enact §13981. . . .

. . . [T]he language and purpose of the Fourteenth Amendment place certain limitations on the manner in which Congress may attack discriminatory conduct. These limitations are necessary to prevent the Fourteenth Amendment from obliterating the Framers' carefully crafted balance of power between the States and the National Government. . . . Foremost among these limitations is the time-honored principle that the Fourteenth Amendment, by its very terms, prohibits only state action. "[T]he principle has become firmly embedded in our constitutional law that the action inhibited by the first section of the Fourteenth Amendment is only such action as may fairly be said to be that of the States. That Amendment erects no shield against merely private conduct, however discriminatory or wrongful." *Shelley v. Kraemer*, 334 U.S. 1, 13, and n. 12 (1948). . . .

. . . Section 13981 is not aimed at proscribing discrimination by officials which the Fourteenth Amendment might not itself proscribe; it is directed not at any State or state actor, but at individuals who have committed criminal acts motivated by gender bias. . . .

. . . [We conclude that Congress' power under §5 does not extend to the enactment of §13981.]

IV

Petitioner Brzonkala's complaint alleges that she was the victim of a brutal assault. But Congress' effort in §13981 to provide a federal civil remedy can be sustained neither under the Commerce Clause nor under §5 of the Fourteenth Amendment. If the allegations here are true, no civilized system of justice could fail to provide her a remedy for the conduct of respondent Morrison. But under our federal system that remedy must be provided by the Commonwealth of Virginia, and not by the United States. The judgment of the Court of Appeals is Affirmed.

Justice Souter, with whom Justice Stevens, Justice Ginsburg, and Justice Breyer join, dissenting.

The Court says both that it leaves Commerce Clause precedent undisturbed and that the Civil Rights Remedy of the Violence Against Women Act of 1994, 42 U.S.C. §13981, exceeds Congress's power under that Clause. I find the claims irreconcilable and respectfully dissent.

Our cases, which remain at least nominally undisturbed, stand for the following propositions. Congress has the power to legislate with regard to activity that, in the aggregate, has a substantial effect on interstate commerce. See *Wickard v. Filburn*, 317 U.S. 111, 124–128 (1942). The fact of such a substantial effect is not an issue for the courts in the first instance, but for the Congress, whose institutional capacity for gathering evidence and taking testimony far exceeds ours. By passing legislation, Congress indicates its conclusion, whether explicitly or not, that facts support its exercise of the commerce power. The business of the courts is to review the congressional assessment, not for soundness but simply for the rationality of concluding that a jurisdictional basis exists in fact. Any explicit findings that Congress chooses to make, though not dispositive of the question of rationality, may advance judicial review by identifying factual authority on which Congress relied. Applying those propositions in these cases can lead to only one conclusion.

One obvious difference from *United States v. Lopez*, 514 U.S. 549 (1995), is the mountain of data assembled by Congress, here showing the effects of violence against women on interstate commerce. Passage of the Act in 1994 was preceded by four years of hearings, which included testimony from physicians and law professors; from survivors of rape and domestic violence; and from representatives of state law enforcement and private business.

The record includes reports on gender bias from task forces in 21 States, and we have the benefit of specific factual findings in the eight separate Reports issued by Congress and its committees over the long course leading to enactment. . . .

II

The Act would have passed muster at any time between *Wickard* in 1942 and *Lopez* in 1995, a period in which the law enjoyed a stable understanding that congressional power under the Commerce Clause, complemented by the authority of the Necessary and Proper Clause, Art. I. §8 cl. 18, extended to all activity that, when aggregated, has a substantial effect on interstate commerce. . . .

Amendments that alter the balance of power between the National and State Governments, like the Fourteenth, or that change the way the States are represented within the Federal Government, like the Seventeenth, are not rips in the fabric of the Framers' Constitution, inviting judicial repairs. The Seventeenth Amendment may indeed have lessened the enthusiasm of the Senate to represent the States as discrete sovereignties, but the Amendment did not convert the judiciary into an alternate shield against the commerce power. . . .

III

As our predecessors learned then, the practice of such ad hoc review [as the majority has practiced in this case] cannot preserve the distinction between the judicial and the legislative, and this Court, in any event, lacks the institutional capacity to maintain such a regime for very long. This one will end when the majority realizes that the conception of the commerce power for which it entertains hopes would inevitably fail the test expressed in Justice Holmes' statement that "[t]he first call of a theory of law is that it should fit the facts." O. Holmes, *The Common Law 167* (Howe ed. 1963). The facts that cannot be ignored today are the facts of integrated national commerce and a political relationship between States and Nation much affected by their respective treasuries and constitutional modifications adopted by the people. The federalism of some earlier time is no more adequate to account for those facts today than the theory of laissez-faire was able to govern the national economy 70 years ago.

WHAT STATE ACTIONS ARE BEYOND FEDERAL REGULATION? CALIFORNIA'S MEDICAL MARIJUANA LAW

California voters, through the state's initiative process, passed a proposition in 1996 that legalized the use of marijuana for a limited class of medical conditions. The state legislature followed with a law that authorized the medical use of marijuana.

The California law conflicted with the federal Controlled Substances Act, which was Title II of the Comprehensive Drug Abuse Prevention and Control Act of 1970. The law categorically prohibited the cultivation, sale, and possession of marijuana. Congress cited the Commerce Clause in conjunction with the Necessary and Proper Clause as its authority to pass the law, claiming that the cultivation, distribution, and possession of marijuana were activities that rationally could be considered to have a "substantial effect" on commerce in controlled substances among the states. Since Congress could prohibit the latter, it could prohibit the former.

The following case involved a challenge to enforcement of the federal law on the ground that it exceeded congressional authority under the Commerce Clause by regulating a purely local activity.

15

GONZALES V. RAICH

U.S. Supreme Court (2005)

Justice Stevens delivered the opinion of the Court.

California is one of at least nine States that authorize the use of marijuana for medicinal purposes. The question presented in this case is whether the power vested in Congress by Article I, §8, of the Constitution "[t]o make all Laws which shall be necessary and proper for carrying into Execution" its authority to "regulate Commerce with foreign Nations, and among the several States" includes the power to prohibit the local cultivation and use of marijuana in compliance with California law.

I

California has been a pioneer in the regulation of marijuana. In 1913, California was one of the first States to prohibit the sale and possession of marijuana, and at the end of the century, California became the first State to authorize limited use of the drug for medicinal purposes. In 1996, California voters passed Proposition 215, now codified as the Compassionate Use Act of 1996.The proposition was designed to ensure that "seriously ill" residents of the State have access to marijuana for medical purposes, and to encourage Federal and State Governments to take steps towards ensuring the safe and affordable distribution of the drug to patients in need. The Act creates an exemption from criminal prosecution for physicians, as well as for patients and primary caregivers who possess or cultivate marijuana for medicinal purposes with the recommendation or approval of a physician. A "primary caregiver" is a person who has consistently assumed responsibility for the housing, health, or safety of the patient.

Respondents Angel Raich and Diane Monson are California residents who suffer from a variety of serious medical conditions and have sought to avail themselves of medical marijuana pursuant to the terms of the Compassionate Use Act. They are being treated by licensed, board-certified family practitioners, who have concluded, after prescribing a host of conventional medicines to treat respondents' conditions and to alleviate their associated symptoms, that marijuana is the only drug available that provides effective treatment. Both women have been using marijuana as a medication for several years pursuant to their doctors' recommendation, and both rely heavily on cannabis to function on a daily basis. Indeed, Raich's physician believes that forgoing cannabis treatments would certainly cause Raich excruciating pain and could very well prove fatal.

Respondent Monson cultivates her own marijuana, and ingests the drug in a variety of ways including smoking and using a vaporizer. Respondent Raich, by contrast, is unable to cultivate her own, and thus relies on two caregivers, litigating as "John Does," to provide her with locally grown marijuana at no charge. These caregivers also process the cannabis into hashish or keif, and Raich herself processes some of the marijuana into oils, balms, and foods for consumption.

On August 15, 2002, county deputy sheriffs and agents from the federal Drug Enforcement Administration (DEA) came to Monson's home. After a thorough investigation, the county officials concluded that her use of marijuana was entirely lawful as a matter of California law. Nevertheless, after a 3-hour standoff, the federal agents seized and destroyed all six of her cannabis plants.

Respondents thereafter brought this action against the Attorney General of the United States and the head of the DEA seeking injunctive and declaratory relief prohibiting the enforcement of the federal Controlled Substances Act (CSA). . . .

III

Respondents in this case do not dispute that passage of the CSA, as part of the Comprehensive Drug Abuse Prevention and Control Act, was well within Congress' commerce power. . . . Nor do they contend that any provision or section of the CSA amounts to an unconstitutional exercise of congressional authority. Rather, respondents' challenge is actually quite limited; they argue that the CSA's categorical prohibition of the manufacture and possession of marijuana as applied to the intrastate manufacture and possession of marijuana for medical purposes pursuant to California law exceeds Congress' authority under the Commerce Clause.

In assessing the validity of congressional regulation, none of our Commerce Clause cases can be viewed in isolation. As charted in considerable detail in *United States v. Lopez*, our understanding of the reach of the Commerce Clause, as well as Congress' assertion of authority thereunder, has evolved over time. The Commerce Clause emerged as the Framers' response to the central problem giving rise to the Constitution itself: the absence of any federal commerce power under the Articles of Confederation. For the first century of our history, the primary use of the Clause was to preclude the kind of discriminatory state legislation that had once been permissible. Then, in response to rapid industrial development and an increasingly interdependent national economy, Congress "ushered in a new era of federal regulation under the commerce power," beginning with the enactment of the Interstate Commerce Act in 1887, and the Sherman Antitrust Act in 1890. . . .

Our case law firmly establishes Congress' power to regulate purely local activities that are part of an economic "class of activities" that have a substantial effect on interstate commerce. See, *Wickard v. Filburn*, 317 U.S. 111(1942). As we stated in *Wickard*, "even if appellee's activity be local and though it may not be regarded as commerce, it may still, whatever its nature, be reached by Congress if it exerts a substantial economic effect on interstate commerce." We have never required Congress to legislate with scientific exactitude. When Congress decides that the "total incidence" of a practice poses a threat to a national market, it may regulate the entire class. . . .

In assessing the scope of Congress' authority under the Commerce Clause, we stress that the task before us is a modest one. We need not determine whether respondents' activities, taken in the aggregate, substantially affect interstate commerce in fact, but only whether a "rational basis" exists for so concluding . . . Given the enforcement difficulties that attend distinguishing between marijuana cultivated locally and marijuana grown elsewhere, and concerns about diversion into illicit channels, we have no difficulty concluding that Congress had a rational basis for believing that failure to regulate the intrastate manufacture and possession of marijuana would leave a gaping hole in the CSA. Thus, as in *Wickard*, when it enacted comprehensive legislation to regulate the interstate market in a fungible commodity, Congress was acting well within its authority to "make all Laws which shall be necessary and proper" to "regulate Commerce . . . among the several States." U.S. Const., Art. I,§8. That the regulation ensnares some purely intrastate activity is of no moment. As we have done many times before, we refuse to excise individual components of that larger scheme. . . .

Justice O'Connor, with whom The Chief Justice and Justice Thomas join as to all but Part III, dissenting.

We enforce the "outer limits" of Congress' Commerce Clause authority not for their own sake, but to protect historic spheres of state sovereignty from excessive federal encroachment and thereby to maintain the distribution of power fundamental to our federalist system of government. . . . One of federalism's chief virtues, of course, is that it promotes innovation by allowing for the possibility that "a single courageous State may, if its citizens choose, serve as a laboratory; and try novel social and economic experiments without risk to the rest of the country."

This case exemplifies the role of States as laboratories. The States' core police powers have always included authority to define criminal law and to protect the health, safety, and welfare of their citizens. . . . Exercising those powers, California (by ballot initiative and then by legislative codification) has come to its own conclusion about the difficult and sensitive question of whether marijuana should be available to relieve severe pain and suffering. Today the Court sanctions an application of the federal Controlled Substances Act that extinguishes that experiment, without any proof that the personal cultivation, possession, and use of marijuana for medicinal purposes, if economic activity in the first place, has a substantial effect on interstate commerce and is therefore an appropriate subject of federal regulation. In so doing, the Court announces a rule that gives Congress a perverse incentive to legislate broadly pursuant to the Commerce Clause—nestling questionable assertions of its authority into comprehensive regulatory schemes—rather than with precision. That rule and the result it produces in this case are irreconcilable with our decisions in *Lopez, supra,* and *United States v. Morrison*, 529 U.S. 598 (2000). Accordingly I dissent. . . .

STATE POLITICS AND CONSTITUTIONAL GOVERNMENT

In the following selection a celebrated national columnist and political observer finds that the growing use of initiative petitions in state politics threatens the Madisonian system of balanced government.

16

A REPUBLIC SUBVERTED

David Broder

At the start of a new century and millennium a new form of government is spreading in the United States. It is alien to the spirit of the Constitution and its careful system of checks and balances. Though derived from a reform favored by Populists and Progressives as a cure for special interest influence, this method of lawmaking has become the favored tool of millionaires and interest groups that use their wealth to achieve their own policy goals—missing a lucrative business for a new set of political entrepreneurs.

Exploiting the public's disdain for politics and distrust of politicians, it is now the most uncontrolled and unexamined arena of power politics. It has given the United States something that seems unthinkable, not a government of laws but laws without government. The initiative process, an import now just over one hundred years old, threatens to challenge or even subvert the American system of government in the next few decades.

To be sure, change is the order of the day in the United States and elsewhere in the advanced countries of the world. The computer and the Internet are revolutionizing the economy. The speed of communications and the reduction in barriers to trade are making national boundaries less and less meaningful. The end of the Cold War has brought an outbreak of ethnic warfare and has heightened awareness of the dangers of terrorism by extremist groups on every continent.

Amid these changes, American life looks like an island of strength and stability. One reason in addition to the vitality of our business and entrepreneurial culture, the incredible productivity of our farms, the quality of our great research universities, and the energy and vigor of our people is the time tested solidity and flexibility of our system of government. The United States Constitution, in this third century of our national life, continues to provide a durable foundation for our governing institutions. The presidency, Congress, the Supreme Court, the federal system, the rule of law, have been tested by many challenges. Twice in the twentieth century we fought world wars. Twice we faced efforts to impeach and remove our chief executive. We overcame the Great Depression and led the reconstruction of Europe. Repeatedly we wrestled with the terrible legacy of the almost indelible moral stain left by slavery. And we have managed to absorb and integrate waves of immigration from lands far distant from our European roots, giving this nation a richer variety of ethnic and racial groups than ever before.

But even as the system of government invented by the founders—a system based on the separation of powers and a complex matrix of procedures designed to require the creation of consensus before the enactment of laws—has proved its worth in crisis after crisis, public impatience with "the system" has grown. Some argue that the science of public opinion and the speed of electronic communications make the political arrangements of the eighteenth century Constitution as outdated as the one horse shay. With journalism focused on the foibles in the private lives of political leaders, disdain for those in government has mounted with each new scandal. Political campaigns have become demolition derbies, in which even the winners emerge with ruined reputations. The trust between governors and governed, on which representative democracy depends, has been badly depleted. Polls consistently show an alarmingly small percentage of Americans believe the government in Washington will do what is right all or even most of the time. With the end of the Cold War, that distrust of Washington has brought about a significant shift in political power. Fewer of the decisions that determine the quality and character of our lives and communities are being made in Washington, D.C.

Responsibilities are being transferred to state capitols and city halls. Except for Social Security and Medicare, federal spending is smaller than that of state and local governments. Only 13 percent of public employees are on the federal payroll. And states have become the innovators in vital areas of domestic policy, from welfare to education to growth policies.

In half our states—including the giant of them all, California—and in hundreds of municipalities, from New York City to Nome, policies are being made not by government but by initiative. In a single year, 1998, voters across America used the initiative process to pass laws or to amend state constitutions, achieving a wide variety of goals. They ended affirmative action, raised the minimum wage, banned billboards, decriminalized a wide range of hard drugs and permitted thousands of patients to obtain prescriptions for marijuana, restricted campaign spending and contributions, expanded casino gambling, banned many forms of hunting, prohibited some abortions, and allowed adopted children to obtain the names of their biological parents.

At the local level, things were even busier. No less than 226 conservation measures—for parks and greenways, open space, zoning, land use and "smart growth" regulations—were on local ballots, and 163 of them were approved. That was a 50 percent increase over 1996 and committed more than a billion dollars in local revenues. Voters in New York tried to force a referendum on building a new Yankee Stadium, and Cincinnati voted on the location of its own new ballpark. The ballpark issue was also put to a vote in Round Rock, Texas, while Kenosha, Wisconsin, voters decided on a proposed gambling initiative. Nude dancing and thong bathing suits were the issues in Seminole County, Florida. And in August of 1999, voters in Beverly Hills decided on an initiative promoted by animal rights advocates that would have required fur shops on Rodeo Drive, and other swank venues, to place on each garment a tag saying it was "made with fur from animals that may have been killed by electrocution, gassing, neck breaking, poisoning, clubbing, stomping, or drowning and may have been trapped in steel jaw leghold traps." Backers, including Sid Caesar, Jack Lemmon, and Buddy Hackett, raised $75,000 and distributed 5,000 videotapes of hidden camera scenes in which merchants assured customers the animals had died humanely. But the fur makers, bolstered by the city council and the Beverly Hills Chamber of Commerce, spent even more—$81,000. It was the only issue in an election that cost the city $60,000, and it failed, 3,363 to 1,908, with barely more than a quarter of the registered voters participating.

Not one of these decisions was made through the time-consuming process of passing and signing bills into laws—the method prescribed by the Constitution, which guaranteed the nation and each of the states "the republican form of government." Rather, they were made by the voters themselves or whatever fraction of them constituted the majority on Election Day. This is the new form of government—an increasingly popular one.

Government by initiative is not only a radical departure from the Constitution's system of checks and balances, it is also a big business, in which lawyers and campaign consultants, signature gathering firms and other players sell their services to affluent interest groups or millionaire do gooders with private policy and political agendas. These players, often not even residents of the states whose laws and constitutions they are rewriting, have learned that the initiative is a far more efficient way of achieving their ends than the cumbersome process of supporting candidates for public office and then lobbying them to pass or sign the measures they seek.

The process had its roots in the beginning of the last century, when Populist and Progressive reformers promoted the initiative use along with its cousin, the referendum; popular primaries; direct election of senators; and recall of errant officeholders as a remedy for the corruption rampant in the legislatures, the state capitols, and the city halls of their day. The initiative let voters, by petition, place legislation or constitutional amendments of their own devising on the ballot. The referendum made enactments of the legislature subject to up-or-down votes by the public. . . .

The great defense of [our original] scheme of government can be found in *The Federalist* papers, written to persuade the states and their people to ratify the new Constitution. In *Federalist 10*, James Madison, one of the principal architects of the Constitution, gave the classic argument for its careful effort to balance democratic impulses with safeguards against heedless majorities.

He wrote:

> Complaints are everywhere heard from our most considerate and virtuous citizens, equally the friends of public and private faith and of public and personal liberty, that our governments are too unstable, that the public good is disregarded in the conflicts of rival parties, and that measures are too often decided, not according to the rules of justice and the rights of the minor party, but by the superior force of an interested and overbearing majority. However anxiously we may wish that these complaints had no foundation, the evidence of known facts will not permit us to deny that they are in some degree true.

Their reading of history had convinced them that the Greek city states had failed because they had tried to govern themselves by vote of the people. Madison further wrote:

> It may be concluded that a pure democracy, by which I mean a society consisting of a small number of citizens, who assemble and administer the government in person, can admit of no cure for the mischiefs of faction. A common passion or interest will, in almost every case, be felt by a majority of the whole; a communication and concert results from the form of government itself; and there is nothing to check the inducements to sacrifice the weaker party or an obnoxious individual. Hence it is that such democracies have ever been spectacles of turbulence and contention; have ever been found incompatible with personal security or the rights of property; and have in general been as short in their lives as they have been violent in their deaths.

They also argued that while direct democracy might be appropriate for a small, compact civil society, it would be impractical, let alone inconvenient, in a nation the size of the United States. Yet, as children of the Enlightenment and believers in natural law, they were convinced that individual rights preceded the formation of the state and were superior to the edicts and laws of any ruler. Thus, they wanted the government they were creating to derive its powers from "the consent of the governed."

Translating that phrase into reality became the great work of the Constitutional Convention. No one there argued for direct democracy. Instead, their solution was representative government based on election of officials who would exercise power within the limits set forth by the constitutions of the nation and the states and under the discipline of frequent elections, which would require them to defend their actions to their constituents and allow the people to replace them if they abused their power or exercised it in ways that did not meet public approval. As Madison said at the 1788 Virginia ratifying convention, "I go on the great republican principle that the people will have the virtue and intelligence to select men of virtue and wisdom."

In *The Federalist,* he wrote:

> A republic, by which I mean a government in which the scheme of representation takes place, opens a different prospect and promises the cure for which we are seeking. Let us examine the points in which it varies from pure democracy, and we shall comprehend both the nature of the cure and the efficacy which it must derive from the Union.
>
> The two great points of difference between a democracy and a republic are: first, the delegation of the government, in the latter, to a small number of citizens elected by the rest; secondly, the greater number of citizens and greater sphere of country over which the latter may be extended. The effect of the first difference is, on the one hand, to refine and enlarge the public views by passing them through the medium of a chosen body of citizens, whose wisdom may best discern the true interest of their country and whose patriotism and love of justice will be least likely to sacrifice it to temporary or partial considerations. Under such a regulation, it may well happen that the public voice, pronounced by the representatives of the people, will be more consonant to the public good than if pronounced by the people themselves, convened for the purpose.

Madison conceded that there was a risk that "men of factious tempers, of local prejudices, or of sinister designs, may, by intrigue, by corruption or by other means" come to office and abuse their powers. But that risk, he said, is reduced by the size and diversity of the American Republic. "Extend the sphere and you take in a greater variety of parties and interests; you make it less probable that a majority of the whole will have a common motive to invade the rights of other citizens; or if such a common motive exists, it will be more difficult for all who feel it to discover their own strength and to act in unison with each other. . . . Hence, it clearly appears that the same advantage which a republic has over a democracy in controlling the effect of faction is enjoyed by a large over a small republic . . . [and] is enjoyed by the Union over the states composing it."

Thus, the rationale for making the United States a republic, rather than a democracy, rested on a healthy apprehension of the dangers of direct democracy and the manifold risks of relying on simple majority rule. Direct democracy, Fisher Ames of Massachusetts wrote, "would be very burdensome, subject to factions and violence; decisions would often be made by surprise, in the precipitancy of passion. . . . It would be a government not by laws but by men." The threats, as the founders envisaged them, ranged from raids on the treasury and shifting of tax burdens from one constituency to another, to the infringement of civil liberties, the submersion of minority viewpoints and interests, and even the destabilization of the entire political order.

All of those effects except the last can be seen in a number of California initiative campaigns. Proposition 13, for example, relieved many businesses and almost all apartment owners of property taxes and shifted the cost of government on to those with more transient addresses. Other initiatives commandeered high percentages of the state budget for education, requiring stringent economies in health and welfare programs that might otherwise have competed for available funds. In 1994, Proposition 187 denied education and health benefits to the families of illegal immigrants, a relatively weak minority group. And in 1996, Proposition 209 ended affirmative action, or racial and gender preferences for minorities and women, restricting education opportunities for those groups and closing down job and contract opportunities for them.

What the founders never could have foreseen, however, was the growth of a lucrative initiative industry, in which a variety of firms make handsome profits from drafting the language, collecting the signatures, managing the campaigns, and creating the media that result in the passage or defeat of these ballot measures.

A review of records for the 1998 election cycle—not one of the busiest of recent years—discloses that more than a quarter billion dollars was raised and spent on this unevenly regulated and fitfully reported arena of politics. Even more than candidate elections, initiative campaigns have become a money game, where average citizens are subjected to advertising blitzes of distortion and half truths and are left to figure out for themselves which interest groups pose the greatest threats to their self-interest.

It is a far cry from the dream of direct democracy cherished by the early nineteenth century reformers who imported this peculiar institution and installed it in this country, hoping it would cleanse our politics. They might be the first to throw up their hands in horror at what their noble experiment has produced.

Is it compatible with our form of government . . . or an alien growth? One answer comes from the distinguished historian Charles A. Beard, who was a great advocate of popular democracy in all its forms. In a book on the initiative, which he published with Birl E. Shultz in 1912, *Documents on the StateWide Initiative, Referendum, and Recall,* Beard wrote that "it is idle to speculate whether [the framers of the Constitution] would have regarded a system of initiative and referendum, such as now existing in Oregon, as repugnant to the republican form. They were not called upon to consider any such proposition."

But Beard immediately went on to quote the warnings Madison and other Founding Fathers voiced in Philadelphia about what Elbridge Gerry called "the excess of democracy." Beard wrote:

> In the face of such evidence, which may easily be multiplied by citations from the records of the convention, the *Federalist,* and other writings of this period, no one has any warrant for assuming that the founders of our federal system would have shown the slightest countenance to a system of initiative and referendum applied either to state or national affairs. If some state had possessed such a system at that time, it is questionable whether they would have been willing to have compromised with it, as they did with the slave states, in order to secure its adherence to the Union. Democracy, in the sense of simple direct majority rule, was undoubtedly more odious to most of the delegates to the convention than was slavery.
>
> When the judges of the Supreme Court are called upon to interpret the "republican" clause of the Constitution as applied to a system of initiative and referendum, it is evident they cannot discover what was the intention of the

> Fathers, for the latter can scarcely be said to have had any intention about a matter which had not yet come within their ken in anything approaching the form which it has now assumed. If the court, however, wishes to apply the spirit of the federal Constitution as conceived by its framers, it can readily find justification in declaring a scheme of statewide initiative and referendum contrary to the principles of that great instrument.

Beard hastened to write that such a verdict "hardly seems possible," because in a number of cases the Supreme Court said that it was up to Congress, in exercising its authority to admit states to the Union, and not to the Court, to determine whether the state constitution was satisfactory. As early as 1912, in a pair of cases challenging the constitutionality of the initiative process, *Pacific States Telephone and Telegraph v. Oregon* and *Kiernan v. City of Portland*, the justices held this was a political question, not subject to judicial review. Over the decades courts have overturned numerous individual initiatives as violating rights guaranteed by state constitutions or the Constitution. But the process itself remains constitutionally protected. And Congress has admitted to the Union states such as Oklahoma and Alaska which had the initiative process in their original constitutions.

Some legal scholars have argued that the Supreme Court rulings do not relieve state supreme courts of the right or responsibility to weigh whether the initiative process is compatible with a republican form of government, but so far no court has taken up their challenge.

The growing reliance on initiatives in the half of the country where they are available is part of the increasing alienation of Americans from the system of representative government that has served this nation for over two hundred years. As the new century begins, the reputation of elected officials at all levels has rarely been worse. Our citizens always have had a healthy skepticism about the people in public office; the whole Constitution rests on the assumption that the exercise of power is a dangerous intoxicant; hence, those in authority must be checked by clear delineation of their authority and balanced against one another, lest anyone commandeer too much power.

But what we have in the country today goes well beyond healthy skepticism to a pervasive distrust of those we ourselves have elected to exercise temporarily the authority we have given them. As a young woman attending a session of the North Carolina Institute of Political Leadership—a wonderful skills training program for community leaders who are preparing to enter elective politics—told me in 1999, "The reaction I get from people I've known for years is, 'You're such a nice person. Why would you want to go into politics?'"

The general disdain for politics and politicians is especially fierce when it comes to legislatures (including Congress) and their members. While many voters are prepared to exempt their own representative from the blanket indictment, the pervasive attitude is that our lawmakers are selfish, self-centered partisans, controlled by special interests and constantly on the lookout for ways to line their own pockets and pay off their pals and political sponsors.

One expression of that disdain has been the term-limits movement, which swept across the country during the last two decades, usually implemented by the mechanism of the initiative campaign. In that combination of initiatives and term limits, we have seen the clearest expression of the revolt against representative government. It is a command to "Clear out of there, you bums. You're none of you worth saving. We want to clean house of the lot of you. And we'll take over the job of writing the laws ourselves."

Many Americans and presumably many of those who read this will heartily endorse those sentiments and shout "Good riddance!" to the ousted legislators. In every state I visited in my reporting, the initiative process was viewed as sacrosanct. In most of them, the legislature (even though term-limited) was in disrepute.

[My] argument . . . is that representative government is not something to be discarded quite so casually. We need to examine what really happens in direct legislation by initiative. And we must ask ourselves about the implications of a weakening of our republican form of government. Is California the model we want for the nation? Or is there enduring wisdom in the founders' design?

C H A P T E R 3

CIVIL LIBERTIES AND CIVIL RIGHTS

The Bill of Rights has become the best-known part of the Constitution, although few can recite its provisions. Before beginning this chapter, go to the Constitution (Appendix I) and read the Bill of Rights, the first ten constitutional amendments. The first eight amendments list the operative provisions of the Bill of Rights.

Since the Bill of Rights *limits* Congress, arguably the Supreme Court not only is but also *should be* the court of last resort in interpreting what the Bill of Rights means. The Bill of Rights acts as a shield *against* political majorities. The judiciary should be diligent and actively uphold civil liberties and rights against legislative action that would diminish them. Judicial activism in protecting individual rights and liberties conforms to the idea of natural law and natural rights that are inalienable.

CONSTITUTIONAL BACKGROUND

The delegates to the Constitutional Convention of 1787 were not concerned with adding a Bill of Rights to the Constitution, although they did create a committee to consider it. But virtually no references were made to a Bill of Rights during the entire convention proceedings. A handful of delegates did briefly address the pros and cons of a Bill of Rights in post-Convention proceedings before state ratifying conventions and legislatures.

The Constitutional Convention was not about protecting civil liberties and rights but about creating a powerful and balanced national government. Representative government and the separation of powers and checks and balances system protected the people against a despotic national government. The states had their own Bills of Rights that guaranteed extensive civil rights and liberties at the state level. The existence of natural laws and rights, and the common law, along with the extensive political checks on the national government, made a Bill of Rights unnecessary to the Federalists.

Nevertheless, Thomas Jefferson expressed a view widely held outside of the Constitutional Convention, that a major defect of the new Constitution was the lack of a separate Bill of Rights. As the ratification debates began, the Federalists promised to add a Bill of Rights as an informal condition of ratification.

The following anti-federalist paper by "Brutus" vigorously argues that a major failing of the new Constitution is the lack of a Bill of Rights.

17

ANTI-FEDERALIST PAPER NO. 84

On the Lack of a Bill of Rights

When a building is to be erected which is intended to stand for ages, the foundation should be firmly laid. The Constitution proposed to your acceptance is designed, not for yourselves alone, but for generations yet unborn. The principles, therefore, upon which the social compact is founded, ought to have been clearly and precisely stated, and the most express and full declaration of rights to have been made. But on this subject there is almost an entire silence. . . .

. . . Those who have governed, have been found in all ages ever active to enlarge their powers and abridge the public liberty. This has induced the people in all countries, where any sense of freedom remained, to fix barriers against the encroachments of their rulers. The country from which we have derived our origin, is an eminent example of this. Their magna charta and bill of rights have long been the boast, as well as the security of that nation. I need say no more, I presume, to an American, than that this principle is a fundamental one, in all the Constitutions of our own States; there is not one of them but what is either founded on a declaration or bill of rights, or has certain express reservation of rights interwoven in the body of them. From this it appears, that at a time when the pulse of liberty beat high, and when an appeal was made to the people to form Constitutions for the government of themselves, it was their universal sense, that such declarations should make a part of their frames of government. It is, therefore, the more astonishing, that this grand security to the rights of the people is not to be found in this Constitution. . . .

For the security of life, in criminal prosecutions, the bills of rights of most of the States have declared, that no man shall be held to answer for a crime until he is made fully acquainted with the charge brought against him; he shall not be compelled to accuse, or furnish evidence against himself—the witnesses against him shall be brought face to face, and he shall be fully heard by himself or counsel. That it is essential to the security of life and liberty, that trial of facts be in the vicinity where they happen. Are not provisions of this kind as necessary in the general government, as in that of a particular State? The powers vested in the new Congress extend in many cases to life; they are authorized to provide for the punishment of a variety of capital crimes, and no restraint is laid upon them in its exercise, save only, that "the trial of all crimes, except in cases of impeachment, shall be by jury; and such trial shall be in the State where the said crimes shall have been committed." No man is secure of a trial in the county where he is charged to have committed a crime; he may be brought from Niagara to New York, or carried from Kentucky to Richmond for trial for an offense supposed to be committed. What security is there, that a man shall be furnished with a full and plain description of the charges against him? That he shall be allowed to produce all proof he can in his favor? That he shall see the witnesses against him face to face, or that he shall be fully heard in his own defense by himself or counsel?

For the security of liberty it has been declared, "that excessive bail should not be required, nor excessive fines imposed, nor cruel or unusual punishments inflicted. That all warrants, without oath or affirmation, to search suspected places, or seize any person, his papers or property, are grievous and oppressive."

These provisions are as necessary under the general government as under that of the individual States; for the power of the former is as complete to the purpose of requiring bail, imposing fines, inflicting punishments, granting search warrants, and seizing persons, papers, or property, in certain cases, as the other.

For the purpose of securing the property of the citizens, it is declared by all the States, "that in all controversies at law, respecting property, the ancient mode of trial by jury is one of the best securities of the rights of the people, and ought to remain sacred and inviolable."

Does not the same necessity exist of reserving this right under their national compact, as in that of the States? Yet nothing is said respecting it. In the bills of rights of the States it is declared, that a well regulated militia is the proper and natural defense of a free government; that as standing armies in time of peace are dangerous, they are not to be kept up, and that the military should be kept under strict subordination to, and controlled by, the civil power.

The same security is as necessary in this Constitution, and much more so; for the general government will have the sole power to raise and to pay armies, and are under no control in the exercise of it; yet nothing of this is to be found in this new system.

I might proceed to instance a number of other rights, which were as necessary to be reserved, such as, that elections should be free, that the liberty of the press should be held sacred. . . .

I cannot help suspecting that persons who attempt to persuade people that such [rights] were less necessary under this Constitution than under those of the States, are willfully endeavoring to deceive, and to lead you into an absolute state of vassalage.

BRUTUS

After the ratification of the Constitution, James Madison proposed amendments to create a Bill of Rights. He was carrying out the Federalist promises made at the ratifying conventions.

The following reading is Madison's speech before the House of Representatives in the 1st Congress supporting a Bill of Rights and recommending its contents.

18

SPEECH BEFORE THE HOUSE OF REPRESENTATIVES IN 1789 PROPOSING AMENDMENTS TO ADD A BILL OF RIGHTS TO THE CONSTITUTION

James Madison

It appears to me that this house is bound by every motive of prudence, not to let the first session pass over without proposing to the state legislatures some things to be incorporated into the constitution, as will render it as acceptable to the whole people of the United States, as it has been found acceptable to a majority of them. I wish, among other reasons why something should be done, that those who have been friendly to the adoption of this constitution, may have the opportunity of proving to those who were opposed to it, that they were as sincerely devoted to liberty and a republican government, as those who charged them with wishing the adoption of this constitution in order to lay the foundation of an aristocracy or depotism. . . .

It cannot be a secret to the gentlemen in this house, that, notwithstanding the ratification of this system of government by eleven of the thirteen United States, in some cases unanimously, in others by large majorities; yet still there is a great number of our constituents who are dissatisfied with it; among whom are many respectable for their talents, their patriotism, and respectable for the jealousy they have for their liberty, which, though mistaken in its object, is laudable in its motive. There is a great body of the people falling under this description, who as present feel much inclined to join their support to the cause of federalism, if they were satisfied in this one point: We ought not to disregard their inclination, but, on principles of amity and moderation, conform to their wishes, and expressly declare the great rights of mankind secured under this constitution. . . .

There have been objections of various kinds made against the constitution: Some were levelled against its structure, because the president was without a council; because the senate, which is a legislative body, had judicial powers in trials on impeachments; and because the powers of that body were compounded in other respects, in a manner that did not correspond with a particular theory; because it grants more power than is supposed to be necessary for every good purpose; and controls the ordinary powers of the state governments. I know some respectable characters who opposed this government on these grounds; but I believe that the great mass of the people who opposed it, disliked it because it did not contain effectual provison against encroachments on particular rights, and those safeguards which they have been long accustomed to have interposed between them and the magistrate who exercised the sovereign power: nor ought we to consider them safe, while a great number of our fellow citizens think these securities necessary.

It has been a fortunate thing that the objection to the government has been made on the ground I stated; because it will be practicable on that ground to obviate the objection, so far as to satisfy the public mind that their liberties will be perpetual, and this without endangering any part of the constitution, which is considered as essential to the existence of the government by those who promoted its adoption.

The amendments which have occurred to me, proper to be recommended by congress to the state legislatures are these:

First.

That there be prefixed to the constitution a declaration—That all power is originally vested in, and consequently derived from the people.

That government is instituted, and ought to be exercised for the benefit of the people; which consists in the enjoyment of life and liberty, with the right of acquiring and using property, and generally of pursuing and obtaining happiness and safety.

That the people have an indubitable, unalienable, and indefeasible right to reform or change their government, whenever it be found adverse or inadequate to the purposes of its institution.

[Madison's second and third proposed amendments that are not part of his Bill of Rights are omitted.]

Fourthly.

That in article 2st, section 9, between clauses 3 and 4, be inserted these clauses, to wit, The civil rights of none shall be abridged on account of religious belief or worship, nor shall any national religion be established, nor shall the full and equal rights of conscience by in any manner, or on any pretext infringed.

The people shall not be deprived or abridged of their right to speak, to write, or to publish their sentiments; and the freedom of the press, as one of the great bulwarks of liberty, shall be inviolable.

The people shall not be restrained from peaceably assembling and consulting for their common good, nor from applying to the legislature by petitions, or remonstrances for redress of their grievances.

The right of the people to keep and bear arms shall not be infringed; a well armed, and well regulated militia being the best security of a free country: but no person religiously scrupulous of bearing arms, shall be compelled to render military service in person.

No soldier shall in time of peace be quartered in any house without the consent of the owner; nor at any time, but in a manner warranted by law.

No person shall be subject, except in cases of impeachment, to more than one punishment, or one trial for the same office; nor shall be compelled to be a witness against himself; nor be deprived of life, liberty, or property without due process of law; nor be obliged to relinquish his property, where it may be necessary for public use, without a just compensation.

Excessive bail shall not be required, nor excessive fines imposed, nor cruel and unusual punishments inflicted.

The rights of the people to be secured in their persons, their houses, their papers, and their other property from all unreasonable searches and seizures, shall not be violated by warrants issued without probable cause, supported by oath or affirmation, or not particularly describing the places to be searched, or the persons or things to be seized.

In all criminal prosecutions, the accused shall enjoy the right to a speedy and public trial, to be informed of the cause and nature of the accusation, to be confronted with his accusers, and the witnesses against him; to have a compulsory process for obtaining witnesses in his favor; and to have the assistance of counsel for his defense.

The exceptions here or elsewhere in the constitution, made in favor of particular rights, shall not be so construed as to diminish the just importance of other rights retained by the people; or as to enlarge the powers delegated by the constitution; but either as actual limitations of such powers, or as inserted merely for greater caution.

Fifthly.

That in article 2st, section 10, between clauses 1 and 2, be inserted this clause, to wit:

No state shall violate the equal rights of conscience, or the freedom of the press, or the trial by jury in criminal cases.

Sixthly.

That article 3d, section 2, be annexed to the end of clause 2d, these words to wit: but no appeal to such court shall be allowed where the value in controversy shall not amount to dollars: nor shall any fact triable by jury, according to the course of common law, be otherwise re-examinable than may consist with the principles of common law.

Seventhly.

That in article 3d, section 2, the third clause be struck out, and in its place be inserted the classes following, to wit:

The trial of all crimes (except in cases of impeachments, and cases arising in the land or naval forces, or the militia when on actual service in time of war or public danger) shall be by an impartial jury of freeholders of the vicinage, with the requisite of unanimity for conviction, of the right of challenge, and other accustomed requisites; and in all crimes punishable with loss of life or member, presentment or indictment by a grand jury, shall be an essential preliminary, provided that in cases of crimes committed within any county which may be in possession of an enemy, or in which a general insurrection may prevail, the trial may by law be authorised in some other county of the same state, as near as may be to the seat of the offence.

In cases of crimes committed not within any county, the trial may by law be in such county as the laws shall have prescribed. In suits at common law, between man and man, the trial by jury, as one of the best securities to the rights of the people, ought to remain inviolate.

Eighthly.

That immediately after article 6th, be inserted, as article 7th, the clauses following, to wit:

The powers delegated by this constitution, are appropriated to the departments to which they are respectively distributed: so that the legislative department shall never exercise the powers vested in the executive or judicial; nor the executive exercise the powers vested in the legislative or judicial; nor the judicial exercise the powers vested in the legislative or executive departments.

The powers not delegated by this constitution, nor prohibited by it to the states, are reserved to the States respectively.

Ninthly.

That article 7th, be numbered as article 8th.

The first of these amendments, relates to what may be called a bill of rights; I will own that I never considered this provision so essential to the federal constitution, as to make it improper to ratify it, until such an amendment was added; at the same time, I always conceived, that in a certain form and to a certain extent, such a provision was neither improper nor altogether useless. I am aware, that a great number of the most respectable friends to the government and champions for republican liberty, have thought such a provision, not only unnecessary, but even improper, nay, I believe some have gone so far as to think it even dangerous. Some policy has been made use of perhaps by gentlemen on both sides of the question: I acknowledge the ingenuity of those arguments which were drawn against the constitution, by a comparison with the policy of Great-Britain, in establishing a declaration of rights; but there is too great a difference in the case to warrant the comparison: therefore the arguments drawn from that source, were in a great measure inapplicable. In the declaration of rights which that country has established, the truth is, they have gone no farther, than to raise a barrier against the power of the crown; the power of the legislature is left altogether indefinite. Altho' I know whenever the great rights, the trial by jury, freedom of the press, or liberty of conscience, came in question in that body, the invasion of them is resisted by able advocates, yet their Magna Charta does not contain any one provision for the security of those rights, respecting which, the people of America are most alarmed. The freedom of the press and rights of conscience, those choicest privileges of the people, are unguarded in the British constitution.

But although the case may be widely different, and it may not be thought necessary to provide limits for the legislative power in that country, yet a different opinion prevails in the United States. The people of many states, have thought it necessary to raise barriers against power in all forms and departments of government . . .

It has been objected . . . against a bill of rights, that, by enumerating particular exceptions to the grant of power, it would disparage those rights which were not placed in that enumeration, and it might follow by implication, that those rights which were not singled out, were intended to be assigned into the hands of the general government, and were consequently insecure. This is one of the most plausible arguments I have ever heard urged against the admission of a bill of rights into this system; but, I conceive, that may be guarded against. I have attempted it, as gentlemen may see by turning to the last clause of the 4th resolution.

. . . If [a Bill of Rights is] incorporated into the constitution, independent tribunals of justice will consider themselves in a peculiar manner the guardians of those rights; they will be an impenetrable bulwark against every assumption of power in the legislative or executive; they will be naturally led to resist every encroachment upon rights expressly stipulated for in the constitution by the declaration of rights. . . . I conclude from this view of the subject, that it will be proper in itself, and highly politic, for the tranquility of the public mind, and the stability of the government, that we should offer something, in the form I have proposed, to be incorporated in the system of government, as a declaration of the rights of the people.

THE NATIONALIZATION OF THE BILL OF RIGHTS

It is clear from the debate over the inclusion of the Bill of Rights in the Constitution of 1787 that its provisions were certainly never intended to be prohibitions upon state action. The Bill of Rights was added to the Constitution to satisfy state governments that the same rights that they generally accorded to their own citizens under state constitutions would apply with respect to the national government and act as a check upon abridgments by the national government of civil liberties and civil rights. Proponents of a separate bill of rights wanted specific provisions to limit the powers of the national government, which, in its own sphere, could act directly upon citizens of the states.

Article X, which is not so much a part of the Bill of Rights as an expression of the balance of authority that exists between the national government and the states in the Constitution, provides that "the powers not delegated to the United States by the Constitution, nor prohibited by it to the States, are reserved to the states respectively, or to the people." Under the federal system each member of the community is both (1) a citizen of the United States and (2) a citizen of the particular state in which he or she resides. The rights and obligations of each citizenship class are determined by the legal divisions of authority set up in the Constitution. Apart from specific limits upon state power to abridge civil liberties and civil rights, as for example the prohibitions of Section 10 against state passage of any bills of attainder or ex post facto laws, there is nothing in the main body of the Constitution or the Bill of Rights that controls state action. Originally, it was up to the states to determine the protections they would give to their own citizens against state actions. The applicability of the Bill of Rights to national action only was affirmed in *Barron v. Baltimore*, 7 Peters 243 (1833). Barron claimed that the city of Baltimore's actions in paving its streets had diverted streams in such a way as to cause dirt to be deposited at the base of his wharf, changing deep water to shallow, which rendered it useless. He argued that under the Fifth Amendment "taking" clause the city should compensate him for taking his property. The state supreme court held that the Fifth Amendment did not apply to state action. On appeal to the United States Supreme Court Chief Justice John Marshall's opinion in Barron v. Balitmore stated that both the text and intent of the Framers clearly was to limit the applicability of the Bill of Rights to the national government.

THE FOURTEENTH AMENDMENT

The adoption of the Fourteenth Amendment in 1868 potentially limited the discretion that the states had possessed to determine the civil liberties and rights of citizens within their sphere of authority. The Fourteenth Amendment provided that:

> 1. All persons born or naturalized in the United States, and subject to the jurisdiction thereof, are citizens of the United States and of the state wherein they reside. No state shall make or enforce any law which shall abridge the privileges or immunities of citizens of the United States; nor shall any state deprive any person of life, liberty, or property, without due process of law; nor deny to any person within its jurisdiction the equal protection of the laws. . . .
>
> 5. *The Congress shall have power to enforce, by appropriate legislation, the provisions of this article.* (Italics added)

Although the Fourteenth Amendment appeared to be a tough restriction upon state action, both Congress and the Supreme Court needed to define the amendment's "privileges and immunities," "due process," and "equal protection" clauses. Although the congressional sponsors of the amendment stipulated that *Congress* would enforce it, inevitably the Supreme Court had the final say in defining the law.

The history of the Fourteenth Amendment suggested that it was designed to protect the legal and political rights of blacks against state encroachment, and was not to have a broader application. In the *Slaughterhouse Cases*, 16 Wallace 36 (1873), the Supreme Court held that the privileges and immunities clause of the Fourteenth Amendment did nothing to alter the authority of the states to determine the rights and obligations of citizens subject to state action. Under this doctrine the Bill of Rights could not be made applicable to the states.

It was not until *Gitlow v. New York*, 268 U.S. 652 (1925), that the Court finally announced that the substantive areas of freedom of speech and of press of the First Amendment are part of the "liberty" protected by the Fourteenth Amendment Due Process Clause, however, in Gitlow's case the Court found that the procedures that had been used in New York to restrict his freedom of speech did not violate due process. In *Near v. Minnesota*, 283 U.S. 697 (1931), the Court for the first time overturned a state statute as a violation of the Fourteenth Amendment Due Process Clause because it permitted prior censorship of the press. *Gitlow* and *Near* were limited because they incorporated only the freedom of speech and press provisions of the First Amendment under the due process clause of the Fourteenth Amendment. The cases marked the beginning of a slow and tedious process of "incorporation" of most of the provisions of the Bill of Rights as part of the Due Process Clause of the Fourteenth Amendment. The process of incorporation did not begin in earnest until the Warren Court, and then not until the 1960s. By the late 1970s all of the Bill of Rights was incorporated as protections against state action, with the exceptions of the rights to grand jury indictment, trial by jury in civil cases, the right to bear arms, protection against excessive bail and fines, and protection against involuntary quartering of troops in private homes.

The following case presents an example of incorporation of the right to counsel under the Due Process Clause of the Fourteenth Amendment. In cases prior to *Gideon v. Wainwright,* decided in 1963, the Court had upheld an ad hoc right to counsel in individual cases. That is, it had held that the facts of a particular case warranted granting the right to counsel as part of due process under the Fourteenth Amendment for that particular case only. By such ad hoc determinations, the Court was able to exercise self-restraint in relation to federal-state relations, by not requiring a general right to counsel in all state criminal cases. *Powell v. Alabama,* 287 U.S. 45 (1932), was an example of such an ad hoc inclusion of the right to counsel in a specific case, where, in a one-day trial, seven black men had been convicted of raping two white girls and sentenced to death. The Court held that under the circumstances of the case the denial of counsel by the Alabama courts to the defendants violated the Due Process Clause of the Fourteenth Amendment. In Powell, however, the Court did not incorporate the right to counsel in all criminal cases under this Due Process Clause. It only provided that "in a capital case, where the defendant is unable to employ counsel, and is incapable adequately of making his own defense because of ignorance, feeblemindedness, illiteracy, or the like, it is the duty of the court, whether requested or not, to assign counsel for him as a necessary requisite of due process of law. . . . " The *Powell* case was widely interpreted as nationalizing (incorporating) the right to counsel in all capital cases. The Court reaffirmed its refusal to incorporate the right to counsel in all criminal cases in *Betts v. Brady,* 316 U.S. 455 (1942). There the Court held that the Sixth Amendment applies only to trials in federal courts and that the right to counsel is not a fundamental right, essential to a fair trial, and therefore is not required in all cases under the Due Process Clause of the Fourteenth Amendment. The Court emphasized that whether or not the right to counsel would be required depended upon the circumstances of the case in which it was requested.

In *Gideon v. Wainwright* the Court finally nationalized the right to counsel in all criminal cases under the Due Process Clause of the Fourteenth Amendment. The case represented, in 1963, an important step in the progression toward nationalization of most of the Bill of Rights. While Justice Roberts, writing for the majority of the Court in the *Betts* case in 1942, found that the right to counsel was not fundamental to a fair trial, Justice Black, who had dissented in the *Betts* case, writing for the majority in *Gideon v. Wainwright* in 1962, held that the right to counsel was fundamental and essential to a fair trial and therefore was protected by the Due Process Clause of the Fourteenth Amendment. In *Gideon,* Justice Black noted:

> We accept the *Brady* assumption, based as it was on our prior cases, that a provision of the Bill of Rights which is "fundamental and essential to a fair trial" is made obligatory upon the states by the Fourteenth Amendment. We think the Court in *Betts* was wrong, however, in concluding that the Sixth Amendment's guarantee of counsel is not one of the fundamental rights.

The history of Supreme Court interpretation of the Fourteenth Amendment Due Process Clause reveals the Court acting both politically and ideologically. In the period from 1868 to 1925 the Court was careful to exercise judicial self-restraint in interpreting the Fourteenth Amendment, in part because of the conservative views of most of the justices that the Court should not impose national standards of civil liberties and civil rights upon the states. The Court did not believe in self-restraint in all areas, as is demonstrated by its use of the Due Process Clause of the Fourteenth Amendment to impose its own views on the proper relationship between the states and business. The Court read the Fourteenth Amendment Due Process Clause in such a way as to protect the property interests of business against state regulation. Many such laws were found to be taking the liberty or property of business without due process. Beginning with *Gitlow v. New York* in 1925, the Court for the first time added substance to the Due Process Clause of the Fourteenth Amendment in the area of civil liberties by including First Amendment freedoms of speech and press as part of the "liberty" of the Due Process Clause.

While the Supreme Court is sensitive to the political environment in which it functions, the ways in which it has interpreted the Due Process Clause of the Fourteenth Amendment suggest that ideological convictions are more important than pressure from political majorities. During the era of economic substantive due process under the Fourteenth Amendment, which ended in 1937, the Court was really taking an elitist position that did not agree with the political majorities in many states that were behind the regulatory laws that the Court struck down. Nor can it be said that when the Court began to add substance in civil liberties and civil rights to the Due Process Clause and extend procedural protection that it was supported by political majorities. In fact, the Warren Court's extension of the Fourteenth Amendment Due Process Clause, particularly in the area of criminal rights, caused a political outcry among the states and their citizens who felt that law enforcement efforts would be unduly impeded. When the Court, in *Griswold v. Connecticut* in 1965, went beyond the explicit provisions of the Bill of Rights to find a right of privacy to strike down Connecticut's birth control statute that prevented the use of contraceptives in the state, even Justice Black, a strong supporter of incorporating the Bill of Rights under the Due Process Clause, took objection. He found in the *Griswold* decision a return to substantive due process in a form that was unacceptable, because it was adding substance to the clause that was not explicitly provided for in the intent of the Fourteenth Amendment, which he had held in *Adamson v. California* in 1946 to be total inclusion of the Bill of Rights. The Griswold decision was not unpopular politically, but when the Court in *Roe v. Wade* in 1973 used the right of privacy to strike down a Texas abortion statute, and in effect declare all state laws that absolutely prohibited abortion to be unconstitutional, a nationwide antiabortion movement was organized to overturn the decision by mobilizing political support behind a constitutional amendment. The Supreme Court has certainly not, in the area of interpretation of the Fourteenth Amendment, acted solely out of political motives.

The following case presents an example of the way in which the Supreme Court gradually incorporated the Bill of Rights under the Fourteenth Amendment. Behind the decision to nationalize the right to counsel in *Gideon v. Wainwright* a fascinating series of events had occurred.* By the time the *Gideon* case was called up, the Court was

---

**Compiler's note:* The story of the case is brilliantly told by Anthony Lewis in *Gideon's Trumpet* (New York: Random House, 1964).

purposely looking for an appropriate case from which it could incorporate the right to counsel under the Due Process Clause of the Fourteenth Amendment. The Court felt that Gideon's case presented the kind of circumstances that would be publicly accepted as requiring the right to counsel to ensure fairness. In granting certiorari to Gideon's in forma pauperis petition ("in the manner of the pauper," a permission to sue without incurring liability for costs) the Court had in effect already made up its mind about the decision. By the appointment of attorney Abe Fortas, later to become a member of the Court (although eventually forced to resign because of conflict-of-interest charges), one of the most distinguished lawyers in the country, the Court guaranteed an eloquent and persuasive brief for the petitioner, Earl Gideon. The Court felt that the right to counsel was a right whose time had come by 1963.

19

GIDEON V. WAINWRIGHT*

372 U.S. 335 (1963)

. . . Mr. Justice Black delivered the opinion of the Court, saying in part:

Petitioner was charged in a Florida state court with having broken and entered a poolroom with intent to commit a misdemeanor. This offense is a felony under Florida law. Appearing in court without funds and without a lawyer, petitioner asked the court to appoint counsel for him, whereupon the following colloquy took place:

> The Court: Mr. Gideon, I am sorry, but I cannot appoint Counsel to represent you in this case. Under the laws of the State of Florida, the only time the Court can appoint Counsel to represent a Defendant is when that person is charged with a capital offense. I am sorry, but I will have to deny your request to appoint Counsel to defend you in this case. The Defendant: The United States Supreme Court says I am entitled to be represented by Counsel.

Put to trial before a jury, Gideon conducted his defense about as well as could be expected from a layman. He made an opening statement to the jury, cross-examined

*Compiler's note: In this selection some footnotes are omitted: all are renumbered.

the State's witnesses, presented witnesses in his own defense, declined to testify himself, and made a short argument "emphasizing his innocence to the charge contained in the Information filed in this case." The jury returned a verdict of guilty, and petitioner was sentenced to serve five years in the state prison. Later, petitioner filed in the Florida Supreme Court this habeas corpus petition attacking his conviction and sentence on the ground that the trial court's refusal to appoint counsel for him denied him rights "guaranteed by the Constitution and the Bill of Rights by the United States Government."[1] Treating the petition for habeas corpus as properly before it, the State Supreme Court, "upon consideration thereof" but without an opinion, denied all relief. Since 1942, when *Betts v. Brady*, 316 U.S. 455 . . . was decided by a divided Court, the problem of a defendant's federal constitutional right to counsel in a state court has been a continuing source of controversy and litigation in both state and federal courts. To give this problem another review here, we granted certiorari. 370 U.S. 908. . . . Since Gideon was proceeding in forma pauperis, we appointed counsel to represent him and requested both sides to discuss in their briefs and oral arguments the following: "Should this Court's holding in *Betts v. Brady* . . . be reconsidered?"

I

The facts upon which Betts claimed that he had been unconstitutionally denied the right to have counsel appointed to assist him are strikingly like the facts upon which Gideon here bases his federal constitutional claim. Betts was indicted for robbery in a Maryland state court. On arraignment, he told the trial judge of his lack of funds to hire a lawyer and asked the court to appoint one for him. Betts was advised that it was not the practice in that county to appoint counsel for indigent defendants except in murder and rape cases. He then pleaded not guilty, had witnesses summoned, cross-examined the State's witnesses, examined his own, and chose not to testify himself. He was found guilty by the judge, sitting without a jury, and sentenced to eight years in prison. Like Gideon, Betts sought release by habeas corpus, alleging that he had been denied the right to assistance of counsel in violation of the Fourteenth Amendment. Betts was denied any relief, and on review this Court affirmed. It was held that a refusal to appoint counsel for an indigent defendant charged with a felony did not necessarily violate the Due Process Clause of the Fourteenth Amendment, which for reasons given the Court deemed to be the only applicable federal constitutional provision. The Court said:

> Asserted denial [of due process] is to be tested by an appraisal of the totality of facts in a given case. That which may, in one setting, constitute a denial of fundamental fairness, shocking to the universal sense of justice, may, in other circumstances, and in the light of other considerations, fall short of such denial. 316 U.S., at 462. . . .

---

[1]Later in the petition for habeas corpus, signed and apparently prepared by the petitioner himself, he stated, "I, Clarence Earl Gideon, claim that I was denied the rights of the 4th, 5th and 14th amendments of the Bill of Rights."

Treating due process as "a concept less rigid and more fluid than those envisaged in other specific and particular provisions of the Bill of Rights," the Court held that refusal to appoint counsel under the particular facts and circumstances in the Betts case was not so "offensive to the common and fundamental ideas of fairness" as to amount to a denial of due process. Since the facts and circumstances of the two cases are so nearly indistinguishable, we think the *Betts v. Brady* holding if left standing would require us to reject Gideon's claim that the Constitution guarantees him the assistance of counsel. Upon full reconsideration we conclude that *Betts v. Brady* should be overruled.

II

The Sixth Amendment provides, "In all criminal prosecutions, the accused shall enjoy the right . . . to have the Assistance of Counsel for his defence." We have construed this to mean that in federal courts counsel must be provided for defendants unable to employ counsel unless the right is competently and intelligently waived. Betts argued that this right is extended to indigent defendants in state courts by the Fourteenth Amendment. In response the Court stated that, while the Sixth Amendment laid down "no rule for the conduct of the states, the question recurs whether the constraint laid by the amendment upon the national courts expresses a rule so fundamental and essential to a fair trial, and so, to due process of law, that it is made obligatory upon the states by the Fourteenth Amendment." 316 U.S., at 465. . . . In order to decide whether the Sixth Amendment's guarantee of counsel is of this fundamental nature, the Court in Betts set out and considered "[r]elevant data on the subject . . . afforded by constitutional and statutory provisions subsisting in the colonies and the states prior to the inclusion of the Bill of Rights in the national Constitution, and in the constitutional, legislative, and judicial history of the states to the present date." 316 U.S., at 465. . . . On the basis of this historical data the Court concluded that "appointment of counsel is not a fundamental right, essential to a fair trial." 316 U.S., at 471. . . . It was for this reason the Betts Court refused to accept the contention that the Sixth Amendment's guarantee of counsel for indigent federal defendants was extended to or, in the words of that Court, "made obligatory upon the states by the Fourteenth Amendment." Plainly, had the Court concluded that appointment of counsel for an indigent criminal defendant was "a fundamental right, essential to a fair trial," it would have held that the Fourteenth Amendment requires appointment of counsel in a state court, just as the Sixth Amendment requires in a federal court.

We think the Court in Betts had ample precedent for acknowledging that those guarantees of the Bill of Rights which are fundamental safeguards of liberty immune from federal abridgment are equally protected against state invasion by the Due Process Clause of the Fourteenth Amendment. This same principle was recognized, explained, and applied in *Powell v. Alabama,* 287 U.S. 45 (1932), a case upholding the right of counsel, where the Court held that despite sweeping language to the contrary in *Hurtado v. California*, 110 U.S. 516 (1884), the Fourteenth Amendment "embraced" those "fundamental principles of liberty and justice which lie at the base of all our civil and political institutions," even though they had been "specifically dealt with in another part of the Federal Constitution." 287 U.S., at 67. . . . In many cases other than Powell and Betts, this Court has looked to the fundamental nature of original Bill of Rights guarantees to decide whether the Fourteenth Amendment makes them obligatory on the States. Explicitly recognized to be of this "fundamental nature" and therefore made immune from state invasion by the Fourteenth, or some part of it, are the First Amendment's freedoms of speech, press, religion, assembly, association, and petition for redress of grievances. For the same reason, though not always in precisely the same terminology, the Court has made obligatory on the States the Fifth Amendment's command that private property shall not be taken for public use without just compensation, the Fourth Amendment's prohibition of unreasonable searches and seizures, and the Eighth's ban on cruel and unusual punishment. On the other hand, this Court in *Palko v. Connecticut*, 301 U.S. 319 . . . (1937), refused to hold that the Fourteenth Amendment made the double jeopardy provision of the Fifth Amendment obligatory on the States. In so refusing, however, the Court, speaking through Mr. Justice Cardozo, was careful to emphasize that "immunities that are valid as against the federal government by force of the specific pledges of particular amendments have been found to be implicit in the concept of ordered liberty, and thus, through the Fourteenth Amendment, become valid as against the states" and that guarantees "in their origin . . . effective against the federal government alone" had by prior cases "been taken over from the earlier articles of the Federal Bill of Rights and brought within the Fourteenth Amendment by a process of absorption." 302 U.S., at 324–325, 326. . . .

We accept *Betts v. Brady*'s assumption, based as it was on our prior cases, that a provision of the Bill of Rights which is "fundamental and essential to a fair trial" is made obligatory upon the States by the Fourteenth Amendment. We think the Court in Betts was wrong, however, in concluding that the Sixth Amendment's guarantee of counsel is not one of these fundamental rights. Ten years before *Betts v. Brady*, this Court, after full consideration of all the historical data examined in Betts, had unequivocally declared that "the right to the aid of counsel is of this fundamental character." *Powell v. Alabama*, 287 U.S. 45 . . . (1932). While the Court at the close of its Powell opinion did by its language, as this Court frequently does, limit its holding to the particular facts and circumstances of that case, its conclusions about the fundamental nature of the right to counsel are unmistakable. Several years later, in 1936, the Court reemphasized what it had said about the fundamental nature of the right to counsel in this language:

> We concluded that certain fundamental rights, safeguarded by the first eight amendments against federal action, were also safeguarded against state action by the due process of law clause of the Fourteenth Amendment, and among them the fundamental right of the accused to the aid of counsel in a criminal prosecution. *Grosjean v. American Press Co.*, 297 U.S. 233 . . . (1936).

And again in 1938 this Court said:

> [The assistance of counsel] is one of the safeguards of the Sixth Amendment deemed necessary to insure fundamental human rights of life and liberty. . . . The Sixth Amendment stands as a constant admonition that if the constitutional safeguards it provides be lost, justice will not 'still be done.' *Johnson v. Zerbst*, 304 U.S. 458 . . . (1938). To the same effect, see *Avery v. Alabama*, 308 U.S. 444 . . . (1940), and *Smith v. O'Grady*, 312 U.S. 329 . . . (1941).

In light of these and many other prior decisions of this Court, it is not surprising that the Betts Court, when faced with the contention that "one charged with crime, who is unable to obtain counsel, must be furnished counsel by the state," conceded that "[e]xpressions in the opinions of this court lend color to the argument . . . " 316 U.S., at 462–463. . . . The fact is that in deciding as it did—that "appointment of counsel is not a fundamental right, essential to a fair trial"—the Court in *Betts v. Brady* made an abrupt break with its own well-considered precedents. In returning to these old precedents, sounder we believe than the new, we but restore constitutional principles established to achieve a fair system of justice. Not only these precedents but also reason and reflection require us to recognize that in our adversary system of criminal justice, any person hailed into court, who is too poor to hire a lawyer, cannot be assured a fair trial unless counsel is provided for him. This seems to us to be an obvious truth. Governments, both state and federal, quite properly spend vast sums of money to establish machinery to try defendants accused of crime. Lawyers to prosecute are everywhere deemed essential to protect the public's interest in an orderly society. Similarly, there are few defendants charged with crime, few indeed, who fail to hire the best lawyers they can get to prepare and present their defenses. That government hires lawyers to prosecute and defendants who have the money hire lawyers to defend are the strongest indications of the widespread belief that lawyers in criminal courts are necessities, not luxuries. The right of one charged with crime to counsel may not be deemed fundamental and essential to fair trials in some countries, but it is in ours. From the very beginning, our state and national constitutions and laws have laid great emphasis on procedural and substantive safeguards designed to assure fair trials before impartial tribunals in which every defendant stands equal before the law. This noble ideal cannot be realized if the poor man charged with crime has to face his accusers without a lawyer to assist him. A defendant's need for a lawyer is nowhere better stated than in the moving words of Mr. Justice Sutherland in *Powell v. Alabama:*

> The right to be heard would be, in many cases, of little avail if it did not comprehend the right to be heard by counsel. Even the intelligent and educated layman has small and sometimes no skill in the science of law. If charged with crime, he is incapable, generally, of determining for himself whether the indictment is good or bad. He is unfamiliar with the rules of evidence. Left without the aid of counsel he may be put on trial without a proper charge, and convicted upon incompetent evidence, or evidence irrelevant to the issue or other wise inadmissible. He lacks both the skill and knowledge adequately to prepare his defense, even though he have a perfect one. He requires the guiding hand of

> counsel at every step in the proceedings against him. Without it, though he be not guilty, he faces the danger of conviction because he does not know how to establish his innocence. 287 U.S., at 68–69. . . .

The Court in *Betts v. Brady* departed from the second wisdom upon which the Court's holding in *Powell v. Alabama* rested. Florida, supported by two other States, has asked that *Betts v. Brady* be left intact. Twenty-two States, as friends of the Court, argue that Betts was "an anachronism when handed down" and that it should now be overruled. We agree.

The judgment is reversed and the cause is remanded to the Supreme Court of Florida for further action not inconsistent with this opinion. Chief Justice Warren, and Justices Brennan, Stewart, White, and Goldberg join in the opinion of the Court.

Mr. Justice Douglas joins the opinion, giving a brief historical resume of the relation between the Bill of Rights and the Fourteenth Amendment. Mr. Justice Clark concurs in the result. Mr. Justice Harlan concurs in the result.

FREEDOM OF SPEECH AND PRESS

Justice Oliver Wendell Holmes, in *Schenck v. United States,* 249 U.S. 47 (1919), stated his famous "clear and present danger" test, which subsequently was applied at both the national and state levels, for deciding whether or not Congress could abridge freedom of speech under the First Amendment:

> The most stringent protection of free speech would not protect a man in falsely shouting fire in a theatre and causing a panic. It does not protect a man from an injunction against uttering words that may have all the effects of force. . . . The question in every case is whether the words used are used in such circumstances and are of such a nature as to create a clear and present danger that they will bring about the substantive evils that Congress has a right to prevent. It is a question of proximity and degree. When a nation is at war many things that might be said in time of peace are such a hindrance to its efforts that their utterance will not be endured so long as men fight and that no Court could regard them as protected by any constitutional right.

The freedoms of the First Amendment are uniquely American. They are rooted in the Colonial and Revolutionary experiences. The colonists used the press, pamphlets, and newspapers to criticize British rule. But the British statutory and common law, while not dictating what opinions could be held, punished the *expression* of ideas that would undermine government or damage the reputations of both government officials and private individuals.

The great English jurist Sir William Blackstone in his *Commentaries* (1765–1769), summarized the law of the press in the eighteenth century: "The liberty of the press is indeed essential to the nature of a free state; but this consists in laying no previous restraints on publications, and not in freedom from censure for criminal matter when published. Every freeman has an undoubted right to lay what sentiments he pleases before the public; to forbid this is to destroy the freedom of the press: but if he publishes what is improper, mischievous, or illegal, he must take the consequences of his own temerity."*

Colonial America suppressed speech and press as vigorously as Britain. Leonard W. Levy writes of this period: "Where vigorously expressed nonconformist opinions were suffered to exist by the community, they were likely to run afoul of the law. In colonial America, as in England, the common law of criminal libel was strung out like a chicken wire of constraint against the captious and the chancy, making open discussion of public issues hazardous, if not impossible, except when public opinion opposed administration policy."†

Nineteenth- and the first half of twentieth-century America continued sedition and libel laws as well as common law that punished unpopular and in Blackstone's words "improper, mischievous, or illegal" expression. In many states in nineteenth-century America legislatures, prosecutors, and courts punished speech that had a "bad tendency," one that might undermine the community morals, safety, and general well-being.

Governments and political majorities are on the side of suppression of speech and press. The courts stand between government and individual expression and interpret the constitutional boundaries of political and other forms of expression.

First Amendment cases are extensive and encompass a broad landscape. First Amendment litigation characterized the twentieth, not the nineteenth century. There was never a constitutional challenge in the Supreme Court to the first sedition law, the Alien and Sedition Acts of 1798, although Jefferson backed the Virginia and Kentucky Resolutions that declared the law unconstitutional. World War I began a period of a half-century of congressional and state sedition legislation, criminal anarchy, and other statutes that resulted in prosecutions that defendants appealed to the Supreme Court in many cases. State and local prosecutions under breach-of-the-peace laws added to the jurisprudence of the First Amendment.

The Evolution of the Clear and Present Danger Test

Until the late 1950s the Supreme Court applied Oliver Wendell Holmes' clear and present danger test from *Schenck v. United States* (1919) to *uphold* both federal and state sedition statutes and convictions under them. Ironically, Holmes' most famous dissent in *Abrams v. United States* (1919), decided just eight months after Schenck, revised his clear and present danger test to expand constitutional protection of political speech. His revised formula required the Supreme Court itself to decide if the facts of the case warranted a finding of clear and *imminent* danger to a clear governmental interest, such as national security. His dissent did not become law until *Brandenburg v. Ohio* (1969). It remains a classic expression of the importance of free expression of ideas.

**Compiler's note:* Blackstone, *Commentaries*, Vol. 4, pp. 151–152.

†Compiler's note: Leonard W. Levy, *Legacy of Suppression* (Cambridge, Mass.: Belknap Press of Harvard University Press, 1960), p. 19.

20

THE NEED TO MAINTAIN A FREE MARKETPLACE OF IDEAS

Oliver Wendell Holmes

Abrams v. United States 250 U.S. 616 (1919)

Justice Oliver Wendell Holmes, dissenting:

This indictment is founded wholly upon the publication of two leaflets which I shall describe in a moment. The first count charges a conspiracy pending the war with Germany to publish abusive language about the form of government of the United States, laying the preparation and publishing of the first leaflet as overt acts. The second count charges a conspiracy pending the war to publish language intended to bring the form of government into contempt, laying the preparation and publishing of the two leaflets as overt acts. The third count alleges a conspiracy to encourage resistance to the United States in the same war and to attempt to effectuate the purpose by publishing the same leaflets. The fourth count lays a conspiracy to incite curtailment of production of things necessary to the prosecution of the war and to attempt to accomplish it by publishing the second leaflet to which I have referred.

The first of these leaflets says that the President's cowardly silence about the intervention in Russia reveals the hypocrisy of the plutocratic gang in Washington. It intimates that "German militarism combined with allied capitalism to crush the Russian revolution"—goes on that the tyrants of the world fight each other until they see a common enemy—working class enlightenment, when they combine to crush it; and that now militarism and capitalism combined, though not openly, to crush the Russian revolution. It says that there is only one enemy of the workers of the world and that is capitalism; that it is a crime for workers of America, etc., to fight the workers' republic of Russia, and ends "Awake! Awake, you workers of the world! Revolutionists." A note adds "It is absurd to call us pro-German. We hate and despise German militarism more than do you hypocritical tyrants. We have more reason for denouncing German militarism than has the coward of the White House."

The other leaflet, headed "Workers—Wake Up," with abusive language says that America together with the Allies will march for Russia to help the Czecko-Slovaks in their struggle against the Bolsheviki, and that this time the hypocrites shall not fool the Russian emigrants and friends of Russia in America. It tells the Russian emigrants that they now must spit in the face of the false military propaganda by which their sympathy and help to the prosecution of the war have been called forth and says that with the money they have lent or are going to lend "they will make bullets not only for the Germans but also for the Workers Soviets of Russia," and further, "Workers in the ammunition factories, you are producing bullets, bayonets, cannon to murder not only the Germans, but also your dearest, best, who are in Russia fighting for freedom." It then appeals to the same Russian emigrants at some length not to consent to the "inquisitionary expedition in Russia," and says that the destruction of the Russian revolution is "the politics of the march on Russia." The leaflet winds up by saying "Workers, our reply to this barbaric intervention has to be a general strike!" and after a few words on the spirit of revolution, exhortations not to be afraid, and some usual tall talk ends "Woe unto those who will be in the way of progress. Let solidarity live! The Rebels."

No argument seems to be necessary to show that these pronunciamentos in no way attack the form of government of the United States, or that they do not support either of the first two counts. What little I have to say about the third count may be postponed until I have considered the fourth. With regard to that it seems too plain to be denied that the suggestion to workers in the ammunition factories that they are producing bullets to murder their dearest, and the further advocacy of a general strike, both in the second leaflet, do urge curtailment of production of things necessary to the prosecution of the war within the meaning of the Act of May 16, 1918, c. 75, 40 Stat. 553, amending section 3 of the earlier Act of 1917 (Comp. St. 10212c). But to make the conduct criminal that statute requires that it should be "with intent by such curtailment to cripple or hinder the United States in the prosecution of the war." It seems to me that no such intent is proved.

I am aware of course that the word "intent" as vaguely used in ordinary legal discussion means no more than knowledge at the time of the act that the consequences said to be intended will ensue. Even less than that will satisfy the general principle of civil and criminal liability. A man may have to pay damages, may be sent to prison, at common law might be hanged, if at the time of his act he knew facts from which common experience showed that the consequences would follow, whether he individually could foresee them or not. But, when words are used exactly, a deed is not done with intent to produce a consequence unless that consequence is the aim of the deed. It may be obvious, and obvious to the actor, that the consequence will follow, and he may be liable for it even if he regrets it, but he does not do the act with intent to produce it unless the aim to produce it is the proximate motive of the specific act, although there may be some deeper motive behind.

It seems to me that this statute must be taken to use its words in a strict and accurate sense. They would be absurd in any other. A patriot might think that we were wasting money on aeroplanes, or making more cannon of a certain kind than we needed, and might advocate curtailment with success, yet even if it turned out that the curtailment hindered and was thought by other minds to have been obviously likely to hinder the United States in the prosecution of the war, no one would hold such conduct a crime. I admit that my illustration does not answer all that might be said but it is enough to show what I think and to let me pass to a more important aspect of the case. I refer to the First Amendment to the Constitution that Congress shall make no law abridging the freedom of speech.

I never have seen any reason to doubt that the questions of law that alone were before this Court in the Cases of *Schenck* (249 U.S. 47, 29 Sup. Ct. 247), *Frohwerk* (249 U.S. 204, 39 Sup. Ct. 249), and *Debs* (249 U.S. 211, 39 Sup. Ct. 252), were rightly decided. I do not doubt for a moment that by the same reasoning that would justify punishing persuasion to murder, the United States constitutionally may punish speech that produces or is intended to produce a clear and imminent danger that it will bring about forthwith certain substantive evils that the United States constitutionally may seek to prevent. The power undoubtedly is greater in time of war than in time of peace because war opens dangers that do not exist at other times.

But as against dangers peculiar to war, as against others, the principle of the right to free speech is always the same. It is only the present danger of *immediate* evil or an intent to bring it about that warrants Congress in setting a limit to the expression of opinion where private rights are not concerned. Congress certainly cannot forbid all effort to change the mind of the country. Now nobody can suppose that the surreptitious publishing of a silly leaflet by an unknown man, without more, would present any immediate danger that its opinions would hinder the success of the government arms or have any appreciable tendency to do so. Publishing those opinions for the very purpose of obstructing, however, might indicate a greater danger and at any rate would have the quality of an attempt. So I assume that the second leaflet if published for the purposes alleged in the fourth count might be punishable. But it seems pretty clear to me that nothing less than that would bring these papers within the scope of this law. An actual intent in the sense that I have explained is necessary to constitute an attempt, where a further act of the same individual is required to complete the substantive crime, for reasons given in *Swift & Co. v. United States*, 196 U.S. 375, 396, 25 S. Sup. Ct. 276. It is necessary where the success of the attempt depends upon others because if that intent is not present the actor's aim may be accomplished without bringing about the evils sought to be checked. An intent to prevent interference with the revolution in Russia might have been satisfied without any hindrance to carrying on the war in which we were engaged.

I do not see how anyone can find the intent required by the statute in any of the defendant's words. The second leaflet is the only one that affords even a foundation for the charge, and there, without invoking the hatred of German militarism expressed in the former one, it is evident from the beginning to the end that the only object of the paper is to help Russia and stop American intervention there against the popular government—not to impede the United States in the war that it was carrying on. To say that two phrases taken literally might import a suggestion of conduct that would have interference with the war as an indirect and probably undesired effect seems to me by no means enough to show an attempt to produce that effect.

I return for a moment to the third count. That charges an intent to provoke resistance to the United States in its war with Germany. Taking the clause in the statute that deals with that in connection with the other elaborate provisions of the Act, I think that resistance to the United States means some forcible act of opposition to some proceeding of the United States in pursuance of the war. I think the intent must be the specific intent that I have described and for the reasons that I have given I think that no such intent was proved or existed in fact. I also think that there is no hint at resistance to the United States as I construe the phrase.

In this case sentences of twenty years imprisonment have been imposed for the publishing of two leaflets that I believe the defendants had as much right to publish as the Government has to publish the Constitution of the United States now vainly invoked by them. Even if I am technically wrong and enough can be squeezed from these poor and puny anonymities to turn the color of legal litmus paper; I will add, even if what I think the necessary intent were shown; the most nominal punishment seems to me all that possible could be inflicted, unless the defendants are to be made to suffer not for what the indictment alleges but for the creed that they avow—a creed that I believe to be the creed of ignorance and immaturity when honestly held, as I see no reason to doubt that it was held here but which, although made the subject of examination at the trial, no one has a right even to consider in dealing with the charges before the Court.

Persecution for the expression of opinions seems to me perfectly logical. If you have no doubt of your premises or your power and want a certain result with all your heart you naturally express your wishes in law and sweep away all opposition. To allow opposition by speech seems to indicate that you think the speech impotent, as when a man says that he has squared the circle, or that you do not care whole heartedly for the result, or that you doubt either your power or your premises. But when men have realized that time has upset many fighting faiths, they may come to believe even more than they believe the very foundations of their own conduct that the ultimate good desired is better reached by free trade in ideas—that the best test of truth is the power of the thought to get itself accepted in the competition of the market, and that truth is the only ground upon which their wishes safely can be carried out. That at any rate is the theory of our Constitution. It is an experiment, as all life is an experiment. Every year if not every day we have to wager our salvation upon some prophecy based upon imperfect knowledge. While that experiment is part of our system I think that we should be eternally vigilant against attempts to check the expression of opinions that we loathe and believe to be fraught with death, unless they so imminently threaten immediate interference with the lawful and pressing purposes of the law that an immediate check is required to save the country. I wholly disagree with the argument of the Government that the First Amendment left the common law as to seditious libel in force. History seems to me against the notion. I had conceived that the United States through many years had shown its repentance for the Sedition Act of 1798 (Act July 14, 1798, c. 73, 1 Stat. 596), by repaying fines that it imposed. Only the emergency that makes it immediately dangerous to leave the correction of evil counsels to time without making any exception to the sweeping command, "Congress shall make no law abridging the freedom of speech." Of course I am speaking only of expressions of opinion and exhortations, which were all that were uttered here, but I regret that I cannot put into more impressive words my belief that in their conviction upon this indictment the defendants were deprived of their rights under the Constitution of the United States.

EXPANDING THE BOUNDARIES OF PERMISSIBLE CRITICISM OF GOVERNMENT AND PUBLIC OFFICIALS

In *New York Times v. Sullivan* (1964) the Court overturned the historic common law of criminal and civil libel that was embedded in state statutory law. The opinion of Justice William J. Brennan for the Court had enormous implications for freedom of the press. The common law of libel that statutory law repeated was the principal shield preventing unrestrained press and speech criticism of government and public officials in particular. The *Sullivan* case was indeed a watershed event in constitutional law and First Amendment jurisprudence.

21

NEW YORK TIMES CO. V. SULLIVAN

376 U.S. 254 (1964)

Mr. Justice Brennan delivered the opinion of the Court.

We are required in this case to determine for the first time the extent to which the constitutional protections for speech and press limit a State's power to award damages in a libel action brought by a public official against critics of his official conduct.

Respondent L. B. Sullivan is one of the three elected Commissioners of the City of Montgomery, Alabama. He testified that he was "Commissioner of Public Affairs and the duties are supervision of the Police Department, Fire Department, Department of Cemetery and Department of Scales." He brought this civil libel action against the four individual petitioners, who are Negroes and Alabama clergymen, and against petitioner the New York Times Company, a New York corporation which publishes the *New York Times*, a daily newspaper. A jury in the Circuit Court of Montgomery County awarded him damages of $500,000, the full amount claimed, against all the petitioners, and the Supreme Court of Alabama affirmed.

Respondent's complaint alleged that he had been libeled by statements in a full-page advertisement that was carried in the *New York Times* on March 29, 1960. Entitled "Heed Their Rising Voices," the advertisement began by stating that "As the whole world knows by now, thousands of Southern Negro students are engaged in widespread non-violent demonstrations in positive affirmation of the right to live in human dignity as guaranteed by the U.S. Constitution and the Bill of Rights." It went on to charge that "in their efforts to uphold these guarantees, they are being met by an unprecedented wave of terror by those who would deny and negate that document which the whole world looks upon as setting the pattern for modern freedom. . . . " Succeeding paragraphs purported to illustrate the "wave of terror" by describing certain alleged events. The text concluded with an appeal for funds for three purposes: support of the student movement, "the struggle for the right-to vote," and the legal defense of Dr. Martin Luther King, Jr., leader of the movement, against a perjury indictment then pending in Montgomery.

The text appeared over the names of 64 persons, many widely known for their activities in public affairs, religion, trade unions, and the performing arts. Below these names, and under a line reading "We in the south who are struggling daily for dignity and freedom warmly endorse this appeal," appeared the names of the four individual petitioners and of 16 other persons, all but two of whom were identified as clergymen in various Southern cities. The advertisement was signed at the bottom of the page by the "Committee to Defend Martin Luther King and the Struggle for Freedom in the South," and the officers of the Committee were listed.

Of the 10 paragraphs of text in the advertisement, the third and a portion of the sixth were the basis of respondent's claim of libel. They read as follows:

> Third paragraph:
>
> "In Montgomery, Alabama, after students sang 'My Country, 'Tis of Thee' on the State Capitol steps, their leaders were expelled from school, and truckloads of police armed with shotguns and tear-gas ringed the Alabama State College Campus. When the entire student body protested to state authorities by refusing to re-register, their dining hall was padlocked in an attempt to starve them into submission."
>
> Sixth paragraph:
>
> "Again and again the Southern violators have answered Dr. King's peaceful protests with intimidation and violence. They have bombed his home almost killing his wife and child. They have assaulted his person. They have arrested him seven

> times—for 'speeding,' 'loitering' and similar 'offenses.' And now they have charged him with 'perjury'—a felony under which they could imprison him for ten years. . . . "

Although neither of these statements mentions respondent by name, he contended that the word "police" in the third paragraph referred to him as the Montgomery Commissioner who supervised the Police Department, so that he was being accused of "ringing" the campus with police. He further claimed that the paragraph would be read as imputing to the police, and hence to him, the padlocking of the dining hall in order to starve the students into submission. As to the sixth paragraph, he contended that since arrests are ordinarily made by the police, the statement "They have arrested [Dr. King] seven times" would be read as referring to him; he further contended that the "They" who did the arresting would be equated with the "They" who committed the other described acts and with the "Southern violators." Thus, he argued, the paragraph would be read as accusing the Montgomery police, and hence him, of answering Dr. King's protests with "intimidation and violence," bombing his home, assaulting his person, and charging him with perjury. Respondent and six other Montgomery residents testified that they read some or all of the statements as referring to him in his capacity as Commissioner.

It is uncontroverted that some of the statements contained in the paragraphs were not accurate descriptions of events which occurred in Montgomery. . . .

The trial judge submitted the case to the jury under instructions that the statements in the advertisement were "libelous per se" and were not privileged, so that petitioners might be held liable if the jury found that they had published the advertisement and that the statements were made "of and concerning" respondent. The jury was instructed that, because the statements were libelous per se, "the law . . . implies legal injury from the bare fact of publication itself," "falsity and malice are presumed," "general damages need not be alleged or proved but are presumed," and "punitive damages may be awarded by the jury even though the amount of actual damages is neither found nor shown." An award of punitive damages—as distinguished from "general" damages, which are compensatory in nature—apparently requires proof of actual malice under Alabama law, and the judge charged that "mere negligence or carelessness is not evidence of actual malice or malice in fact, and does not justify an award of exemplary or punitive damages." He refused to charge, however, that the jury must be "convinced" of malice, in the sense of "actual intent" to harm or "gross negligence and recklessness," to make such an award, and he also refused to require that a verdict for respondent differentiate between compensatory and punitive damages. The judge rejected petitioners' contention that his rulings abridged the freedoms of speech and of the press that are guaranteed by the First and Fourteenth Amendments.

In affirming the judgment, the Supreme Court of Alabama sustained the trial judge's rulings and instructions in all respects . . .

. . . We reverse the judgment. We hold that the rule of law applied by the Alabama courts is constitutionally deficient for failure to provide the safeguards for freedom of speech and of the press that are required by the First and Fourteenth

Amendments in a libel action brought by a public official against critics of his official conduct. . . .

The general proposition that freedom of expression upon public questions is secured by the First Amendment has long been settled by our decisions. The constitutional safeguard, we have said, "was fashioned to assure unfettered interchange of ideas for the bringing about of political and social changes desired by the people." . . . "The maintenance of the opportunity for free political discussion to the end that government may be responsive to the will of the people and that changes may be obtained by lawful means, an opportunity essential to the security of the Republic, is a fundamental principle of our constitutional system." . . .

"[I]t is a prized American privilege to speak one's mind, although not always with perfect good taste, on all public institutions," . . . and this opportunity is to be afforded for "vigorous advocacy" no less than "abstract discussion." . . . The First Amendment, said Judge Learned Hand, "presupposes that right conclusions are more likely to be gathered out of a multitude of tongues, than through any kind of authoritative selection. To many this is, and always will be, folly; but we have staked upon it our all."

. . . Mr. Justice Brandeis, in his concurring opinion in *Whitney v. California*, 274 U.S. 357, 375–376, gave the principle its classic formulation:

> "Those who won our independence believed . . . that public discussion is a political duty; and that this should be a fundamental principle of the American government. They recognized the risks to which all human institutions are subject. But they knew that order cannot be secured merely through fear of punishment for its infraction; that it is hazardous to discourage thought, hope and imagination; that fear breeds repression; that repression breeds hate; that hate menaces stable government; that the path of safety lies in the opportunity to discuss freely supposed grievances and proposed remedies; and that the fitting remedy for evil counsels is good ones. Believing in the power of reason as applied through public discussion, they eschewed silence coerced by law—the argument of force in its worst form. Recognizing the occasional tyrannies of governing majorities, they amended the Constitution so that free speech and assembly should be guaranteed."

Thus we consider this case against the background of a profound national commitment to the principle that debate on public issues should be uninhibited, robust, and wide-open, and that it may well include vehement, caustic, and sometimes unpleasantly sharp attacks on government and public officials. . . . The present advertisement, as an expression of grievance and protest on one of the major public issues of our time, would seem clearly to qualify for the constitutional protection. The question is whether it forfeits that protection by the falsity of some of its factual statements and by its alleged defamation of respondent.

Authoritative interpretations of the First Amendment guarantees have consistently refused to recognize an exception for any test of truth—whether administered by judges, juries, or administrative officials—and especially one that puts the burden of proving truth on the speaker. . . . The constitutional protection does not turn upon "the truth, popularity, or social utility of the ideas and beliefs which are offered." . . . As Madison said, "Some degree of abuse is inseparable from the proper use of every thing; and in no instance is this more true than in that of the press." . . .

That erroneous statement is inevitable in free debate, and . . . it must be protected if the freedoms of expression are to have the "breathing space" that they "need . . . to survive." . . .

Injury to official reputation affords no more warrant for repressing speech that would otherwise be free than does factual error. . . .

A rule compelling the critic of official conduct to guarantee the truth of all his factual assertions—and to do so on pain of libel judgments virtually unlimited in amount—leads to a comparable "self-censorship." Allowance of the defense of truth, with the burden of proving it on the defendant, does not mean that only false speech will be deterred. . . .

The constitutional guarantees require, we think, a federal rule that prohibits a public official from recovering damages for a defamatory falsehood relating to his official conduct unless he proves that the statement was made with "actual malice"—that is, with knowledge that it was false or with reckless disregard of whether it was false or not. . . .

Such a privilege for criticism of official conduct is appropriately analogous to the protection accorded a public official when he is sued for libel by a private citizen. In *Barr v. Matteo*, 360 U.S. 564, 575, this Court held the utterance of a federal official to be absolutely privileged if made "within the outer perimeter" of his duties. . . .

We conclude that such a privilege [for criticism of public officials] is required by the First and Fourteenth Amendments.

III

We hold today that the Constitution delimits a State's power to award damages for libel in actions brought by public officials against critics of their official conduct. Since this is such an action, the rule requiring proof of actual malice is applicable. . . .

Applying these standards, we consider that the proof presented to show actual malice lacks the convincing clarity which the constitutional standard demands, and hence that it would not constitutionally sustain the judgment for respondent under the proper rule of law. The case of the individual petitioners requires little discussion. Even assuming that they could constitutionally be found to have authorized the use of their names on the advertisement, there was no evidence whatever that they were aware of any erroneous statements or were in any way reckless in that regard. The judgment against them is thus without constitutional support.

As to the *Times*, we similarly conclude that the facts do not support a finding of actual malice. The statement by the *Times*' Secretary that, apart from the padlocking allegation, he thought the advertisement was "substantially correct," affords no constitutional warrant for the Alabama Supreme Court's conclusion that it was a "cavalier ignoring of the falsity of the advertisement [from which] the jury could not have but been impressed with the bad faith of the *Times*, and its maliciousness inferable therefrom." The statement does not indicate malice at the time of the publication; even if the advertisement was not "substantially correct"—although respondent's own proofs tend to show that it was—that opinion was at least a reasonable one, and there was no evidence to impeach the witness' good faith in holding it. The *Times*' failure to retract upon respondent's demand, although it later retracted upon the demand of Governor Patterson, is likewise not adequate evidence of malice for constitutional purposes. Whether or not a failure to retract may ever constitute such evidence, there are two reasons why it does not here. First, the letter written by the *Times* reflected a reasonable doubt on its part as to whether the advertisement could reasonably be taken to refer to respondent at all. Second, it was not a final refusal, since it asked for an explanation on this point—a request that respondent chose to ignore. Nor does the retraction upon the demand of the Governor supply the necessary proof. It may be doubted that a failure to retract which is not itself evidence of malice can retroactively become such by virtue of a retraction subsequently made to another party. But in any event that did not happen here, since the explanation given by the *Times*' Secretary for the distinction drawn between respondent and the Governor was a reasonable one, the good faith of which was not impeached.

Finally, there is evidence that the *Times* published the advertisement without checking its accuracy against the news stories in the *Times*' own files. The mere presence of the stories in the files does not, of course, establish that the *Times* "knew" the advertisement was false, since the state of mind required for actual malice would have to be brought home to the persons in the *Times*' organization having responsibility for the publication of the advertisement. With respect to the failure of those persons to make the check, the record shows that they relied upon their knowledge of the good reputation of many of those whose names were listed as sponsors of the advertisement, and upon the letter from A. Philip Randolph, known to them as a responsible individual, certifying that the use of the names was authorized. There was testimony that the persons handling the advertisement saw nothing in it that would render it unacceptable under the *Times*' policy of rejecting advertisements containing "attacks of a personal character"; their failure to reject it on this ground was not unreasonable. We think the evidence against the *Times* supports at most a finding of negligence in failing to discover the misstatements, and is constitutionally insufficient to show the recklessness that is required for a finding of actual malice. . . .

We also think the evidence was constitutionally defective in another respect: it was incapable of supporting the jury's finding that the allegedly libelous statements were made "of and concerning" respondent. . . .

. . . [T]he Supreme Court of Alabama . . . , in holding that the trial court "did not err in overruling the demurrer [of the *Times*] in the aspect that the libelous matter was not of and concerning the [plaintiff,]" based its ruling on the proposition that:

> "We think it common knowledge that the average person knows that municipal agents, such as police and firemen, and others, are under the control and direction of the city governing body, and more particularly under the direction and control of a single commissioner. In measuring the performance or deficiencies of such groups, praise or criticism is usually attached to the official in complete control of the body." . . .

This proposition has disquieting implications for criticism of governmental conduct. For good reason, "no court of last resort in this country has ever held, or even suggested, that prosecutions for libel on government have any place in the American system of jurisprudence." . . . The present proposition would sidestep this obstacle by transmuting criticism of government, however impersonal it may seem on its face, into personal criticism, and hence potential libel, of the officials of whom the government is composed. . . . Raising as it does the possibility that a good-faith critic of government will be penalized for his criticism, the proposition relied on by the Alabama courts strikes at the very center of the constitutionally protected area of free expression. We hold that such a proposition may not constitutionally be utilized to establish that an otherwise impersonal attack on governmental operations was a libel of an official responsible for those operations. Since it was relied on exclusively here, and there was no other evidence to connect the statements with respondent, the evidence was constitutionally insufficient to support a finding that the statements referred to respondent.

The judgment of the Supreme Court of Alabama is reversed and the case is remanded to that court for further proceedings not inconsistent with this opinion.

Reversed and remanded.

EQUAL PROTECTION OF THE LAWS: SCHOOL DESEGREGATION

The Supreme Court announced the "separate but equal" doctrine in *Plessy v. Ferguson*, 163 U.S. 537 (1896). The plaintiff challenged a Louisiana segregation statute on the ground that it was state action in violation of the Fourteenth Amendment's Equal Protection Clause which provided: No state shall deny "to any person within its jurisdiction the equal protection of the laws." The *Plessy* case stated that separate but equal accommodations, required by state law to be established on railroads in Louisiana, did not violate the Equal Protection of the Laws Clause of the Fourteenth Amendment.

22

PLESSY V. FERGUSON

163 U.S. 537 (1896)

Mr. Justice Brown delivered the opinion of the court.

This case turns upon the constitutionality of an act of the general assembly of the state of Louisiana, passed in 1890, providing for separate railway carriages for the white and colored races.

The constitutionality of this act is attacked upon the ground that it conflicts both with the Thirteenth Amendment of the constitution, abolishing slavery, and the Fourteenth Amendment [Equal Protection Clause which prohibits state action depriving any person within its jurisdiction the equal protection of the laws].

That it does not conflict with the Thirteenth Amendment, which abolished slavery and involuntary servitude, except a punishment for crime, is too clear for argument. Slavery implies involuntary servitude,—a state of bondage; the ownership of mankind as a chattel, or, at least, the control of the labor and services of one man for the benefit of another, and the absence of a legal right to the disposal of his own person, property, and services. . . .

[The claim of deprivation of equal protection of the laws under the Fourteenth Amendment is unfounded.] The object of the amendment was undoubtedly to enforce the absolute equality of the two races before the law, but, in the nature of things, it could not have been intended to abolish distinctions based upon color, or to enforce social, as distinguished from political, equality, or a commingling of the two races upon terms unsatisfactory to either. Laws permitting, and even requiring, their separation, in places where they are liable to be brought into contact, do not necessarily imply the inferiority of either race to the other, and have been generally, if not universally, recognized as within the competency of the state legislatures in the exercise of their police power. The most common instance of this is connected with the establishment of separate schools for white and colored children, which have been held to be a valid exercise of the legislative power even by courts of states where the political rights of the colored race have been longest and most earnestly enforced. . . .

Laws forbidding the intermarriage of the two races may be said in a technical sense to interfere with the freedom of contract, and yet have been universally recognized as within the police power of the state. . . .

The distinction between laws interfering with the political equality of the negro and those requiring the separation of the two races in schools, theaters, and railway carriages has been frequently drawn by this court. . . .

In the Civil Rights Cases [1883], it was held that an act of congress entitling all persons within the jurisdiction of the United States to the full and equal enjoyment of the accommodations, advantages, facilities, and privileges of inns, public conveyances, on land or water, theaters, and other places of public amusement, and made applicable to citizens of every race and color, regardless of any previous condition of servitude, was unconstitutional and void, upon the ground that the Fourteenth Amendment was prohibitory upon the states only, and the legislation authorized to be adopted by congress for enforcing it was not direct legislation on matters respecting which the states were prohibited from making or enforcing certain laws, or doing certain acts, but was corrective legislation. . . .

So far, then, as a conflict with the Fourteenth Amendment is concerned, the case reduces itself to the question whether the statute of Louisiana is a reasonable regulation, and with respect to this there must necessarily be a large discretion on the part of the legislature. In determining the question of reasonableness, it is at liberty to act with reference to the established usages, customs, and traditions of the people, and with a view to the promotion of their comfort, and the preservation of the public peace and good order. Gauged by this standard, we cannot say that a law which authorizes or even requires the separation of the two races in public conveyances is unreasonable, or more obnoxious to the Fourteenth Amendment than the acts of congress requiring separate schools for colored children in the District of Columbia, the constitutionality of which does not seem to have been questioned, or the corresponding acts of state legislatures. . . .

Mr. Justice Harlan dissenting.

. . . [I]n view of the constitution, in the eye of the law, there is in this country no superior, dominant, ruling class of citizens. There is no caste here. Our constitution is color-blind, and neither knows nor tolerates classes among citizens. In respect of civil rights, all citizens are equal before the law. The humblest is the peer of the most powerful. The law regards man as man, and takes no account of his surroundings or of his color when his civil rights as guaranteed by the supreme law of the land are involved. It is therefore to be regretted that this high tribunal, the final expositor of the fundamental law of the land, has reached the conclusion that it is competent for a state to regulate the enjoyment by citizens of their civil rights solely upon the basis of race.

In my opinion, the judgment this day rendered will, in time, prove to be quite as pernicious as the decision made by this tribunal in the *Dred Scott Case*. . . .

The sure guaranty of the peace and security of each race is the clear, distinct, unconditional recognition by our governments, national and state, of every right that inheres in civil freedom, and of the equality before the law of all citizens of the United States, without regard to race. State enactments regulating the enjoyment of civil rights upon the basis of race, and cunningly devised to defeat legitimate results of the war, under the pretense of recognizing equality of rights, can have no other result than to render permanent peace impossible, and to keep alive a conflict of races, the continuance of which must do harm to all concerned. . . .

The Supreme Court overruled *Plessy v. Ferguson* in *Brown v. Board of Education*, 347 U.S. 483 (1954). The case is an outstanding example of how litigation becomes politics by other means. The NAACP's lawyers, led by Thurgood Marshall, who would himself later be appointed to the Supreme Court, knew they had no chance to persuade what at the time was a Southern controlled Congress to overturn school segregation laws. But the NAACP strategists observed a string of Supreme Court decisions overturning segregated state law schools as a violation of the Fourteenth Amendment's Equal Protection Clause.* The Court found that state law school segregation was inherently unequal. Segregated law schools put African American law graduates at a professional disadvantage, because it cut them off from a large portion of future lawyers at a critical time when they should be making social contacts.

The NAACP strategists thought they might have a chance to overturn segregated public education in the seventeen Southern and border states if they could bring one successful case that would set a precedent for challenging all segregation laws. As a general precedent *Plessy v. Ferguson* was a major barrier to success. The Court's decisions regarding law schools did not overrule the "separate but equal" *Plessy* precedent. In fact the opinions accepted the rule by holding that separate law schools for African Americans were intrinsically *unequal.* The segregation of the schools was not a problem per se, but became one only because of the intrinsic inequality of the schools. There was no way a state could make a segregated law school equal for the minority segregated class because of the *social* consequences of segregation.

Somehow Thurgood Marshall and his team would have to persuade the court, first, to accept the case because an injured party had made a legitimate constitutional claim under the Fourteenth Amendment Equal Protection Clause. Far more difficult would be the need to persuade a majority of the Supreme Court that segregated public education at the elementary and high school levels is intrinsically unequal, not because of unequal physical facilities but due to the inevitable social or psychological injury to minority segregated students. The NAACP lawyers would have to put aside what they learned at their respective law schools and marshal *empirical* evidence of social and psychological harm to segregated children.

**Compiler's note:* See, for example, *McLaurin v. Oklahoma State Regents* (1950), and *Sweatt v. Painter* (1950).

23

BROWN V. BOARD OF EDUCATION OF TOPEKA

347 U.S. 483 (1954)

Mr. Chief Justice Warren delivered the opinion of the Court, saying in part:

These cases come to us from the states of Kansas, South Carolina, Virginia, and Delaware. They are premised on different facts and different local conditions, but a common legal question justifies their consideration together in this consolidated opinion.

In each of the cases, minors of the Negro race, through their legal representatives, seek the aid of the courts in obtaining admission to the public schools of their community on a nonsegregated basis. In each instance, they had been denied admission to schools attended by white children under laws requiring or permitting segregation according to race. This segregation was alleged to deprive the plaintiffs of the equal protection of the laws under the Fourteenth Amendment. In each of the cases other than the Delaware case, a three-judge federal district court denied relief to the plaintiffs on the so-called "separate but equal" doctrine announced by this Court in *Plessy v. Ferguson*. . . .

The plaintiffs contend that segregated public schools are not "equal" and cannot be made "equal," and that hence they are deprived of the equal protection of the laws. Because of the obvious importance of the question presented, the Court took jurisdiction. . . .

In the first cases in this Court construing the Fourteenth Amendment, decided shortly after its adoption, the Court interpreted it as proscribing all state-imposed discriminations against the Negro race. The doctrine of "separate but equal" did not make its appearance in this Court until 1896 in the case of *Plessy v. Ferguson*, supra, involving not education but transportation. American courts have since labored with the doctrine for over half a century. In this Court, there have been six cases involving the "separate but equal" doctrine in the field of public education. . . . In more recent cases, all on the graduate school level, inequality was found in that specific benefits enjoyed by white students were denied to Negro students of the same educational qualifications. . . . In none of these cases was it necessary to reexamine the doctrine to grant relief to the Negro plaintiff. And in *Sweatt v. Painter* [339 U.S. 629 (1950)], the Court expressly reserved decision on the question whether *Plessy v. Ferguson* should be held inapplicable to public education.

In the instant cases, that question is directly presented. Here, unlike *Sweatt v. Painter,* there are findings below that the Negro and white schools involved have been equalized, or are being equalized, with respect to buildings, curricula, qualifications and salaries of teachers, and other "tangible" factors. Our decision, therefore, cannot turn on merely a comparison of these tangible factors in the Negro and white schools involved in each of the cases. We must look instead to the effect of segregation itself on public education.

In approaching this problem, we cannot turn the clock back to 1868 when the Amendment was adopted, or even to 1896 when *Plessy v. Ferguson* was written. We must consider public education in the light of its full development and its present place in American life throughout the Nation. Only in this way can it be determined if segregation in public schools deprives these plaintiffs of the equal protection of the laws.

Today, education is perhaps the most important function of state and local governments. Compulsory school attendance laws and the great expenditures for education both demonstrate our recognition of the importance of education to our democratic society. It is required in the performance of our most basic public responsibilities, even service in the armed forces. It is the very foundation of good citizenship. Today it is a principal instrument in awakening the child to cultural values, in preparing him for later professional training, and in helping him to adjust normally to his environment. In these days, it is doubtful that any child may reasonably be expected to succeed in life if he is denied the opportunity of an education. Such an opportunity, where the state has undertaken to provide it, is a right which must be made available to all on equal terms.

We come then to the question presented: Does segregation of children in public schools solely on the basis of race, even though the physical facilities and other "tangible" factors may be equal, deprive the children of the minority group of equal educational opportunities? We believe that it does.

In *Sweatt v. Painter,* supra, in finding that a segregated law school for Negroes could not provide them equal educational opportunities, this Court relied in large part on "those qualities which are incapable of objective measurement but which make for greatness in a law school." In *MacLaurin v. Oklahoma State Regents*, supras [339 U.S. 637 (1950)], the Court, in requiring that a Negro admitted to a white graduate school be treated like all other students, again resorted to intangible considerations: "his ability to study, to engage in discussions and exchange views with other students, and, in general, to learn his profession." Such considerations apply with added force to children in grade and high schools. To separate them from others of similar age and qualifications solely because of their race generates a feeling of inferiority as to their status in the community that may affect their hearts and minds in a way unlikely ever to be undone. The effect of this separation of their educational opportunities was well stated by a finding in the Kansas case by a court which nevertheless felt compelled to rule against the Negro plaintiffs:

> Segregation of white and colored children in public schools has a detrimental effect upon the colored children. The impact is greater when it has the sanction of the law; for the policy of separating the races is usually interpreted as denoting the inferiority of the Negro group. A sense of inferiority affects the motivation of a child to learn. Segregation with the sanction of law, therefore, has a tendency to retard the educational and mental development of Negro children and to deprive them of some of the benefits they would receive in a racially integrated school system.

Whatever may have been the extent of psychological knowledge at the time of *Plessy v. Ferguson*, this finding is amply supported by modern authority. Any language in *Plessy v. Ferguson* contrary to this finding is rejected.

We conclude that in the field of public education the doctrine of "separate but equal" has no place. Separate educational facilities are inherently unequal. Therefore, we hold that the plaintiffs and others similarly situated for whom the actions have been brought are by reason of the segregation complained of, deprived of the equal protection of the laws guaranteed by the Fourteenth Amendment. This disposition makes unnecessary any discussion whether such segregation also violates the Due Process Clause of the Fourteenth Amendment.

Because these are class actions, because of the wide applicability of this decision, and because of the great variety of local conditions, the formulation of decrees in these cases presents problems of considerable complexity. On reargument, the consideration of appropriate relief was necessarily subordinate to the primary question—the constitutionality of segregation in public education. We have now announced that such segregation is a denial of the equal protection of the laws. In order that we may have the full assistance of the parties in formulating decrees, the cases will be restored to the docket, and the parties are requested to present further argument on Questions 4 and 5 previously propounded by the Court for the re-argument this Term [which deal with the implementation of desegregation]. The Attorney General of the United States is again invited to participate. The Attorneys General of the states requiring or permitting segregation in public education will also be permitted to appear as amici curiae upon request to do so by September 15, 1954, and submission of briefs by October 1, 1954.

On the same day the decision was announced in the *Brown* case (1954), the Court held that segregation in the District of Columbia was unconstitutional on the basis of the Due Process Clause of the Fifth Amendment. [See *Bolling v. Sharpe*, 347 U.S. 497 (1954).] This situation reversed the normal one in that a protection explicitly afforded citizens of states was not expressly applicable against the national government, and could be made so only through interpreting it into the concept of due process of law.

After hearing the views of all interested parties in the *Brown* case, the Court, on May 31, 1955, announced its decision concerning the implementation of desegregation in public schools.

24

BROWN V. BOARD OF EDUCATION OF TOPEKA

349 U.S. 294 (1955)

Mr. Chief Justice Warren delivered the opinion of the Court, saying in part:

These cases were decided on May 17, 1954. The opinions of that date, declaring the fundamental principle that racial discrimination in public education is unconstitutional, are incorporated herein by reference. All provisions of federal, state, or local law requiring or permitting such discrimination must yield to this principle. There remains for consideration the manner in which relief is to be accorded.

Because these cases arose under different local conditions and their disposition will involve a variety of local problems, we requested further argument on the question of relief. . . . The parties, the United States, and the states of Florida, North Carolina, Arkansas, Oklahoma, Maryland, and Texas filed briefs and participated in the oral argument.

These presentations were informative and helpful to the Court in its consideration of the complexities arising from the transition to a system of public education freed of racial discrimination. The presentations also demonstrated that substantial steps to eliminate racial discrimination in public schools have already been taken, not only in some of the communities in which these cases arose, but in some of the states appearing as amici curiae, and in other states as well. Substantial progress has been made in the District of Columbia and in the communities in Kansas and Delaware involved in this litigation. The defendants in the cases coming to us from South Carolina and Virginia are awaiting the decision of this Court concerning relief.

Full implementation of these constitutional principles may require solution of varied local school problems. School authorities have the primary responsibility for elucidating, assessing, and solving these problems; courts will have to consider whether the action of school authorities constitutes good faith implementation of the governing constitutional principles. Because of their proximity to local conditions and the possible need for further hearings, the courts which originally heard these cases can best perform this judicial appraisal. Accordingly, we believe it appropriate to remand the cases to those courts.

In fashioning and effectuating the decrees, the courts will be guided by equitable principles. Traditionally, equity has been characterized by a practical flexibility in shaping its remedies and by a facility for adjusting and reconciling public and private needs. These cases call for the exercise of these traditional attributes of equity power. At stake is the personal interest of the plaintiffs in admission to public schools as soon as practicable on a nondiscriminatory basis. To effectuate this interest may call for elimination of a variety of obstacles in making the transition to school systems operated in accordance with the constitutional principles set forth in our May 17, 1954, decision. Courts of equity may properly take into account the public interest in the elimination of such obstacles in a systematic and effective manner. But it should go without saying that the vitality of these constitutional principles cannot be allowed to yield simply because of disagreement with them.

While giving weight to these public and private considerations, the courts will require that the defendants make a prompt and reasonable start toward full compliance with our May 17, 1954, ruling. Once such a start has been made, the courts may find that additional time is necessary to carry out the ruling in an effective manner. The burden rests upon the defendants to establish such time as is necessary in the public interest and is consistent with good faith compliance at the earliest practicable date. To that end, the courts may consider problems related to administration, arising from the physical condition of the school plant, the school transportation system, personnel, revision of school districts and attendance areas into compact units to achieve a system of determining admission to the public schools on a nonracial basis, and revision of local laws and regulations which may be necessary in solving the foregoing problems. They will also consider the adequacy of any plans the defendants may propose to meet these problems and to effectuate a transition to a racially nondiscriminatory school system. During this period of transition, the courts will retain jurisdiction of these cases.

The judgments below, except that in the *Delaware* case, are accordingly reversed and the cases are remanded to the District Courts to take such proceedings and enter such orders and decrees consistent with this opinion as are necessary and proper to admit to public schools on a racially nondiscriminatory basis with all deliberate speed the parties to these cases. The judgment in the *Delaware case*—ordering the immediate admission of the plaintiffs to schools previously attended only by white children—is affirmed on the basis of the principles stated in our May 17, 1954, opinion, but the case is remanded to the Supreme Court of Delaware for such further proceedings as that Court may deem necessary in the light of this opinion.

After the second decision of the Supreme Court in *Brown v. Board of Education* in 1955, it soon became clear that many Southern states would proceed with deliberate speed not to implement the desegregation of public schools but to obstruct the intent of the Supreme Court. The Southern Manifesto, signed by 101 members of Congress from eleven Southern states in 1956, clearly indicated the line that would be taken by many Southern members of

Congress to justify defiance of the Supreme Court. The gist of the manifesto was simply that the Supreme Court did not have the constitutional authority to interfere in an area such as education, which falls within the reserved powers of the states.

After the two *Brown* decisions in 1954 and 1955, the implementation of desegregation in the South was very slow. Ten years later, less than 10 percent of the black pupils in the lower educational levels in the Southern states that had had legally segregated education before *Brown* were enrolled in integrated schools. It was not until 1970 that substantial progress was made in the South. Between 1968 and 1970 the percentage of black students in all-black schools in eleven Southern states decreased from 68.0 percent to 18.4 percent. One device that was used to circumvent the Supreme Court's decisions was the establishment of de facto dual school systems, similar to those that exist in most Northern cities, whereby students are assigned to schools on the basis of the neighborhoods in which they live. Such systems are not de jure segregation because they are not based upon a law requiring segregation per se, but simply upon school board regulations assigning pupils on the basis of where they live. De facto school systems can be as segregated as were the de jure systems previously existing in the South, but the question is, to what extent can courts interfere to break up de facto segregation patterns, since they are not based upon legal stipulations?

In *Swann v. Charlotte-Mecklenburg County Board of Education*, 402 U.S. 1 (1971), the Supreme Court held that in Southern states with a history of legal segregated education the district courts have broad power to assure "unitary" school systems by requiring (1) reassignment of teachers, so that each school faculty will reflect a racial balance similar to that which exists in the community as a whole; (2) reassignment of pupils to reflect a racial ratio similar to that which exists within the total community; (3) the use of noncontiguous school zones and the grouping of schools for the purpose of attendance to bring about racial balance; and (4) the use of busing of elementary and secondary school students within the school system to achieve racial balance.

This case and companion cases were referred to at the time as school "busing" cases; they caused tremendous controversy within the South because communities felt they were not being treated on an equal basis with their Northern counterparts, where de facto segregation is for the most part not subject to judicial intervention. The Nixon administration, which favored neighborhood schools, was firmly opposed to the transportation of students beyond normal geographic school zones to achieve racial balance. Democratic Senator Ribicoff of Connecticut attempted to attach an amendment that would have required nationwide integration of pupils from inner-city schools with children from the suburbs to an administration-sponsored bill providing $1.5 billion to aid school districts in the South in the desegregation of facilities. The amendment was defeated on April 21, 1971, by a vote of 51 to 35, with most Republicans voting against it and 13 of 34 Northern Democrats opposed. Busing remains a highly controversial political issue.

Swann v. Charlotte-Mecklenburg County Board (1971) held that the courts could order busing of schoolchildren within the limits of the city school district if necessary to achieve desegregated educational facilities. In the case of *Charlotte-Mecklenburg*, the limits of the city school district included the surrounding county. However, only 18 of the country's 100 largest city school districts contained both the inner city and the surrounding county. In cities such as San Francisco, Denver, Pasadena, and Boston, court-ordered busing plans pertained only to the central city school district. In 1974 the Supreme Court reviewed a busing plan for Detroit ordered by a federal district court and sustained by the court of appeals that would have required the busing of students among fifty-four separate school districts in the Detroit metropolitan area to achieve racially balanced schools. The decision of the lower federal court in the Detroit case set a new precedent that required busing among legally separate school districts. Proponents of the Detroit busing plan argued that the central city of Detroit was 70 percent black and that the only way integration could be achieved would be to link the school district of Detroit with the surrounding white suburban school districts. In *Milliken v. Bradley*, 418 U.S. 717 (1974), the Supreme Court held that the court-ordered Detroit busing plan could not be sustained under the Equal Protection Clause of the Fourteenth Amendment, which was the constitutional provision relied upon in the lower court's decision to require busing. The Supreme Court found that there was no evidence of disparate treatment of white and black students among the fifty-three outlying school districts that surrounded Detroit. The only evidence of discrimination was within the city limits of Detroit itself. Therefore, since the outlying districts did not violate the Equal Protection Clause they could not be ordered to integrate their systems with that of Detroit. Since discrimination was limited to Detroit, the court order to remedy the situation had to be limited to Detroit also. The effect of the decision was to leave standing court orders for busing within school districts, but prevented the forced merger of inner-city schools with legally separate suburban school districts.

THE JUDICIAL SOURCES OF POLITICAL CONTROVERSIES OVER CIVIL LIBERTIES AND RIGHTS

Chief Justice John Marshall laid the groundwork in the early nineteenth century for Supreme Court involvement in politics when he declared that "it is emphatically the province and duty of the Judicial Department to say what the law is." Ironically, in the same case he invented the doctrine of "political questions," proclaiming that the courts should not become involved in those matters the Constitution delegated to Congress and the President. Marshall muted that note of judicial self-restraint, however, by his implicit recognition that the courts, and not legislatures, ultimately would decide what matters fell within their jurisdiction.

Chief Justice Marshall's proclamation of judicial power in *Marbury v. Madison* also incorporated the doctrine of judicial review. The authority to declare what the law is included the power to review acts of Congress and judge their constitutionality. The *Marbury* case, however, did not involve a major confrontation with Congress. The Court merely held that Congress could not grant it the mandamus power in original jurisdiction, which had been done in the Judiciary Act of 1789. Essentially the Court was interpreting the scope of its own powers, not those of Congress.

Inevitably, however, the power of judicial review pushed the Supreme Court, and lower federal courts as well, into political controversies as they ruled not only on congressional laws but far more importantly on the actions of state legislatures and courts. As of early 1985 the Supreme Court had held only 135 provisions of federal laws to be unconstitutional in whole or in part out of a total of approximately 91,000 public and private bills that had been passed. By contrast, the Court had overturned on constitutional grounds 970 state laws and provisions of state constitutions, with 800 of these rulings coming after 1870. By far the greatest political controversies have been over Supreme Court rulings affecting the states, as the nation for most of its history struggled over the question of how far national power should intrude upon state sovereignty.

Controversies surrounding Supreme Court decisions on civil liberties and civil rights have almost entirely involved Supreme Court rulings on the permissible scope of state power. In the early nineteenth century Chief Justice John Marshall's decisions in the historic cases of *McCulloch v. Maryland* (1819) and *Gibbons v. Ogden* (1823) raised the ire of states' rights advocates who widely proclaimed that the Court's actions would bring about the dissolution of the Union. The Supreme Court had unequivocally upheld national supremacy and wide congressional powers over the states.

Almost a century and a half after the *McCulloch* decision, the Supreme Court was again embroiled in a political controversy, not concerning the extent of congressional power over the states, an issue that had finally been settled in favor of the national government during the New Deal, but over how far national civil liberties and rights standards should be applied to the states. Under the chief justiceship of former California governor Earl Warren, an activist and interventionist Supreme Court in the 1960s completed the process of applying most of the provisions of the Bill of Rights to the states under the Due Process Clause of the Fourteenth Amendment. Before the Warren era the Court had been very reluctant to extend parts of the Bill of Rights to the states, weighing heavily against such action considerations of federalism that supported state sovereignty. It nationalized only what in the view of a majority of the justices were fundamental freedoms and rights without which the democratic process and individual liberty could not survive.

THE ESTABLISHMENT CLAUSE AND THE ISSUE OF SCHOOL PRAYER

As early as 1940 the Supreme Court nationalized the Free Exercise Clause of the First Amendment, but it was not until 1947 that a majority of justices agreed that the Establishment Clause of the First Amendment was also a fundamental liberty protected by the Due Process Clause of the Fourteenth Amendment.*

The First Amendment provision embodying the Establishment and Free Exercise Clauses states: "Congress shall make no law respecting an establishment of religion, or prohibiting the free exercise thereof." While little controversy surrounded the Supreme Court's nationalization of these provisions, its 1962 decision in *Engel v. Vitale*, given in the following selection, holding that religious freedom required a ban on prayers in public schools, caused a political backlash that continued into the 1980s, one that seemed to grow in intensity as the years passed. As the Moral Majority and the Christian Right became politically active in the 1980s, one of their major goals was the restoration of prayers in public schools. They supported state

---

**Compiler's note:* Henry J. Abraham, *The Judiciary: The Supreme Court in the Governmental Process*, 6th ed. (Boston: Allyn & Bacon, 1983), p. 164.

efforts to pass legislation that would get around the school prayer decision by requiring moments of silence rather than prayers to open school days. However, the Supreme Court held in 1985 that an Alabama moment-of-silence statute authorizing public school teachers to hold a one minute period of silence for "meditation or voluntary prayer" each school day violated the Establishment Clause of the First Amendment.*

Of particular concern to the Court were statements by the sponsors of the legislation that they intended the law to restore prayer to public schools. Even conservative justices, such as Sandra Day O'Connor, who supported completely voluntary moments of silence in public schools during which prayers might be given, agreed that the Alabama statute had no secular effect and was an impermissible official encouragement of prayers. The following case originated the school prayer controversy.

25

ENGEL V. VITALE

370 U.S. 421 (1962)

Mr. Justice Black delivered the opinion of the Court, saying in part:

The respondent Board of Education of Union Free School District No. 9, New Hyde Park, New York, acting in its official capacity under state law, directed the School District's principal to cause the following prayer to be said aloud by each class in the presence of a teacher at the beginning of each school day.

> Almighty God, we acknowledge our dependence upon Thee, and we beg Thy blessings upon us, our parents, our teachers and our country.

This daily procedure was adopted on the recommendation of the State Board of Regents, a governmental agency created by the state Constitution to which the New York Legislature has granted broad supervisory, executive, and legislative powers over the state's public school system. These state officials composed the prayer which they recommended and published as a part of their "Statement on Moral and Spiritual Training in the Schools," saying: "We believe that this

*Compiler's note: *Wallace v. Jaffree*, 86 L Ed. 2d 29 (1985).

Statement will be subscribed to by all men and women of good will, and we call upon all of them to aid in giving life to our program."

Shortly after the practice of reciting the Regents' prayer was adopted by the School District, the parents of ten pupils brought this action in a New York State Court insisting that use of this official prayer in the public schools was contrary to the beliefs, religions, or religious practices of both themselves and their children. Among other things, these parents challenged the constitutionality of both the state law authorizing the School District to direct the use of prayer in public schools and the School District's regulation ordering the recitation of this particular prayer on the ground that these actions of official governmental agencies violate that part of the First Amendment of the federal Constitution which commands that "Congress shall make no law respecting an establishment of religion"—a command which was "made applicable to the state of New York by the Fourteenth Amendment of the said Constitution." The New York Court of Appeals, over the dissents of Judges Dye and Fuld, sustained an order of the lower state courts which had upheld the power of New York to use the Regents' prayer as a part of the daily procedures of its public schools so long as the schools did not compel any pupil to join in the prayer over his or her parents' objection. We granted certiorari to review this important decision involving rights protected by the First and Fourteenth Amendments.

We think that by using its public school system to encourage recitation of the Regents' prayer, the state of New York has adopted a practice wholly inconsistent with the Establishment Clause. There can, of course, be no doubt that New York's program of daily classroom invocation of God's blessings as prescribed in the Regents' prayer is a religious activity. It is a solemn avowal of divine faith and supplication for the blessings of the Almighty. The nature of such a prayer has always been religious, none of the respondents has denied this and the trial court expressly so found. . . .

The petitioners contend among other things that the state laws requiring or permitting use of the Regents' prayer must be struck down as a violation of the Establishment Clause because the prayer was composed by governmental officials as a part of a governmental program to further religious beliefs. For this reason, petitioners argue, the state's use of the Regents' prayer in its public school system breaches the constitutional wall of separation between church and state. We agree with that contention since we think that the constitutional prohibition against laws respecting an establishment of religion must at least mean that in this country it is no part of the business of government to compose official prayers for any group of the American people to recite as a part of a religious program carried on by government.

It is a matter of history that this very practice of establishing governmentally composed prayers for religious services was one of the reasons which caused many of our early colonists to leave England and seek religious freedom in America. The *Book of Common Prayer*, which was created under governmental direction and which was approved by Acts of Parliament in 1548 and 1549, set out in minute detail the accepted form and content of prayer and other religious ceremonies to be used in the established, tax-supported Church of England. The controversies over the Book and what should be its content repeatedly threatened to disrupt the peace of that country as the accepted forms of prayer in the established church changed with the views of the particular ruler that happened to be in control at the time. Powerful groups representing some of the varying religious views of the people struggled among themselves to impress their particular views upon the government and obtain amendments of the Book more suitable to their respective notions of how religious services should be conducted in order that the official religious establishment would advance their particular religious beliefs. Other groups, lacking the necessary political power to influence the government on the matter, decided to leave England and its established church and seek freedom in America from England's governmentally ordained and supported religion.

It is an unfortunate fact of history that when some of the very groups which had most strenuously opposed the established Church of England found themselves sufficiently in control of colonial governments in this country to write their own prayers into law, they passed laws making their own religion the official religion of their respective colonies. Indeed, as late as the time of the Revolutionary War, there were established churches in at least eight of the thirteen former colonies and established religions in at least four of the other five. But the successful Revolution against English political domination was shortly followed by intense opposition to the practice of establishing religion by law. . . .

By the time of the adoption of the Constitution, our history shows that there was a widespread awareness among many Americans of the dangers of a union of church and state. . . . The First Amendment was added to the Constitution to stand as a guarantee that neither the power nor the prestige of the federal government would be used to control, support or influence the kinds of prayer the American people can say—that the people's religions must not be subjected to the pressures of government for change each time a new political administration is elected to office. Under that amendment's prohibition against governmental establishment of religion, as reinforced by the provisions of the Fourteenth Amendment, government in this country, be it state or federal, is without power to prescribe by law any particular form of prayer which is to be used as an official prayer in carrying on any program of governmentally sponsored religious activity.

There can be no doubt that New York's state prayer program officially establishes the religious beliefs embodied in the Regents' prayer. The respondents' argument to the contrary, which is largely based upon the contention that the Regents' prayer is "nondenominational" and the fact that the program, as modified and approved by state courts, does not require all pupils to recite the prayer but permits those who wish to do so to remain silent or be excused from the room, ignores the essential nature of the program's constitutional defects. Neither the fact that the prayer may be denominationally neutral, nor the fact that its observance on the part of the students is voluntary can serve to free it from the limitations of the Establishment Clause, as it might from the Free Exercise Clause, of the First Amendment, both of which are operative against the states by virtue of the Fourteenth Amendment. Although these two clauses may in certain instances overlap, they forbid two quite different kinds of governmental encroachment upon religious freedom. The Establishment Clause, unlike the Free Exercise Clause, does not depend upon any showing of direct governmental compulsion and is violated by the enactment of laws which establish an official religion whether those laws operate directly to coerce nonobserving individuals or not. This is not to say, of course, that laws officially prescribing a particular form of religious worship do not involve coercion of such individuals. When the power, prestige and financial support of government is placed behind a particular religious belief, the indirect coercive pressure upon religious minorities to conform to the prevailing officially approved religion is plain. But the purposes underlying the Establishment Clause go much further than that. Its first and most immediate purpose rested on the belief that a union of government and religion tends to destroy government and to degrade religion. The history of governmentally established religion, both in England and in this country, showed that whenever government had allied itself with one particular form of religion, the inevitable result has been that it had incurred the hatred, disrespect and even contempt of those who held contrary beliefs. That same history showed that many people had lost their respect for any religion that had relied upon the support of government to spread its faith. The Establishment Clause thus stands as an expression of principle on the part of the Founders of our Constitution that religion is too personal, too sacred, too holy, to permit its "unhallowed perversion" by a civil magistrate. Another purpose of the Establishment Clause rested upon an awareness of the historical fact that governmentally established religions and religious persecutions go hand in hand. The founders knew that only a few years after the *Book of Common Prayer* became the only accepted form of religious services in the established Church of England, an Act of Uniformity was passed to compel all Englishmen to attend those services and to make it a criminal offense to conduct or attend religious gatherings of any other kind—a law which was consistently flouted by dissenting religious groups in England and which contributed to widespread persecutions of people like John Bunyan who persisted in holding "unlawful [religious] meetings . . . to the great disturbance and distraction of the good subjects of this kingdom. . . . " And they knew that similar persecutions had received the sanction of law in several of the colonies in this country soon after the establishment of official religions in those colonies. It was in large part to get completely away from this sort of systematic religious persecution that the Founders brought into being our Nation, our Constitution, and our Bill of Rights with its prohibition against any governmental establishment of religion. The New York laws officially prescribing the Regents' prayer are inconsistent with both the purposes of the Establishment Clause and with the Establishment Clause itself.

It has been argued that to apply the Constitution in such a way as to prohibit state laws respecting an establishment of religious services in public schools is to indicate a hostility toward religion or toward prayer. Nothing, of course, could be more wrong. The history of man is inseparable from the history of religion. And perhaps it is not too much to say that since the beginning of that history many people have devoutly believed that "More things are wrought by prayer than this world dreams of." It was doubtless largely due to men who believed this that there grew up a sentiment that caused men to leave the crosscurrents of officially established state religions and religious persecution in Europe and come to this country filled with the hope that they could find a place in which they could pray when they pleased to the God of their faith in the language they chose. And there were men of this same faith in the power of prayer who led the fight for adoption of our Constitution and also for our Bill of Rights with the very guarantees of religious freedom that forbid the sort of governmental activity which New York has attempted here. These men knew that the First Amendment, which tried to put an end to governmental control of religion and of prayer, was not written to destroy either. They knew rather that it was written to quiet well-justified fears which nearly all of them felt arising out of an awareness that governments of the past had shackled men's tongues to make them speak only the religious thoughts that government wanted them to speak and to pray only to the God that government wanted them to pray to. It is neither sacrilegious nor antireligious to say that each separate government in this country should stay out of the business of writing or sanctioning official prayers and leave that purely religious function to the people themselves and to those the people choose to look to for religious guidance.

It is true that New York's establishment of its Regents' prayer as an officially approved religious doctrine of that state does not amount to a total establishment of one particular religious sect to the exclusion of all others—that, indeed, the governmental endorsement of that prayer seems relatively insignificant when compared to the governmental encroachments upon religion which were common-place 200 years ago. To those who may subscribe to the view that because the Regents' official prayer is so brief and general there can be no danger to religious freedom in its governmental establishment, however, it may be appropriate to say in the words of James Madison, the author of the First Amendment:

> [I]t is proper to take alarm at the first experiment on our liberties. . . . Who does not see that the same authority which can establish Christianity, in exclusion of all other Religions, may establish with the same ease any particular sect of Christians, in exclusion of all other Sects? That the same authority which can force a citizen to contribute three pence only of his property for the support of any one establishment, may force him to conform to any other establishment in all cases whatsoever?

The judgment of the Court of Appeals of New York is reversed and the cause remanded for further proceedings not inconsistent with this opinion.

Mr. Justice Frankfurter took no part in the decision of this case.

Mr. Justice White took no part in the consideration or decision of this case.

Mr. Justice Douglas concurred in a separate opinion.

Mr. Justice Stewart, dissenting:

A local school board in New York has provided that those pupils who wish to do so may join in a brief prayer at the beginning of each school day, acknowledging their dependence upon God and asking His blessing upon them and upon their parents, their teachers, and their country. The court today decides that in permitting this brief nondenominational prayer the school board has violated the Constitution of the United States. I think this decision is wrong.

The Court does not hold, nor could it, that New York has interfered with the free exercise of anybody's religion. For the state courts have made clear that those who object to reciting the prayer must be entirely free of any compulsion to do so, including any "embarrassments and pressure." Cf. *West Virginia State Board of Education v. Barnette*,

319 U.S. 624. But the Court says that in permitting school children to say this simple prayer, the New York authorities have established "an official religion."

With all respect, I think the Court has misapplied a great constitutional principle. I cannot see how an "official religion" is established by letting those who want to say a prayer say it. On the contrary, I think that to deny the wish of these school children to join in reciting this prayer is to deny them the opportunity of sharing in the spiritual heritage of our nation.

The Court's historical review of the quarrels over the *Book of Common Prayer* in England throws no light for me on the issue before us in this case. England had then and has now an established church. Equally unenlightening, I think, is the history of the early establishment and later rejection of an official church in our own states. For we deal here not with the establishment of a state church, which would, of course, be constitutionally impermissible, but with whether school children who want to begin their day by joining in prayer must be prohibited from doing so. Moreover, I think that the Court's task, in this as in all areas of constitutional adjudication, is not responsibly aided by the uncritical invocation of metaphors like the "wall of separation," a phrase nowhere to be found in the Constitution. What is relevant to the issue here is not the history of an established church in sixteenth-century England or in eighteenth-century America, but the history of the religious traditions of our people, reflected in countless practices of the institutions and officials of our government.

At the opening of each day's session of this Court we stand, while one of our officials invokes the protection of God. Since the days of John Marshall our Crier has said, "God save the United States and this Honorable Court." Both the Senate and the House of Representatives open their daily sessions with prayer. Each of our Presidents, from George Washington to John F. Kennedy, has upon assuming his office asked the protection and help of God.

The Court today says that the state and federal governments are without constitutional power to prescribe any particular form of words to be recited by any group of the American people on any subject touching religion. The third stanza of "The Star-Spangled Banner," made our national anthem by Act of Congress in 1931, contains these verses:

> Blest with victory and peace, may the heav'n rescued land
> Praise the Pow'r that hath made and preserved us a nation!
> Then conquer we must, when our cause it is just,
> And this be our motto, "In God is our Trust."

In 1954 Congress added a phrase to the Pledge of Allegiance to the Flag so that it now contains the words "one Nation *under* God indivisible, with liberty and justice for all." In 1952 Congress enacted legislation calling upon the President each year to proclaim a National Day of Prayer. Since 1865 the words "IN GOD WE TRUST" have been impressed on our coins.

Countless similar examples could be listed, but there is no need to belabor the obvious. It was all summed up by this Court just ten years ago in a single sentence: "We are a religious people whose institutions presuppose a Supreme Being." *Zoarch v. Clauson*, 343 U.S. 306, 313.

I do not believe that this Court, or the Congress, or the President has by the actions and practices I have mentioned established an "official religion" in violation of the Constitution. And I do not believe the state of New York has done so in this case. What each has done has been to recognize and to follow the deeply entrenched and highly cherished spiritual traditions of our nation—traditions which come down to us from those who almost two hundred years ago avowed their "firm reliance on the Protection of Divine Providence" when they proclaimed the freedom and independence of this brave new world.

I dissent.

Engel v. Vitale was neither the beginning nor the end of controversy over the First Amendment's Establishment and Free Exercise Clauses. Supreme Court justices have not been able to agree among themselves on the meaning of these clauses. Close decisions characterize freedom of religion cases before the Supreme Court.

Supreme Court cases concerning freedom of religion arise out of congressional and state laws that affect religion, as in *Engel v. Vitale* where the New York State legislature required a nondenominational prayer at the beginning of each public school day. Other types of laws affecting religion provide for governmental aid for textbooks used in private schools, the use of public school buses to transport students to parochial schools, and the use of public school teachers to teach remedial and other special classes in nonpublic schools. Since parochial and virtually all other private schools have a religious affiliation, the use of public funds in any way to support such schools presumptively violates the separation of church and state the establishment clause of the First Amendment requires.

Generally, the Supreme Court has been very cautious in permitting government aid to parochial or private schools. School voucher programs are the most controversial government aid to these schools. Government-paid vouchers defer student expenses in attending private schools, and as such constitute direct government aid to religiously affiliated schools.

THE RIGHT TO PRIVACY

The Supreme Court "found" a right to privacy in the Constitution in *Griswold v. Connecticut* (1965) and in the far more controversial case, *Roe v. Wade* (1973). The Roe decision upheld a woman's unqualified right to abortion during the first trimester of a pregnancy, and thereafter continued to limit governmental regulation of abortion under most circumstances.

The Roe decision politicized the right to privacy and spawned freedom of choice and the right to life groups that clashed at all levels of politics. Senators on both sides of the issue grilled Supreme Court nominees to take a stand and give their views on privacy. A Democratic controlled Senate Judiciary Committee defeated President Reagan's nominee to the high Court, Robert Bork, when during his 1987 hearings he proclaimed that there is no constitutional right to privacy. Thereafter nominees tried to dodge the issue with vague pronouncements about the importance of precedent but the inappropriateness of taking a stand on issues not before them in a case and controversy.

Origin and Nature of the Right to Privacy

Conservative and liberal Jurists do not disagree that the common law and constitutional precedents establish and protect an individual's right to privacy. Privacy includes, for example, protection against libel and slander in the common law dating back centuries. The Supreme Court has held that constitutional liberty and an implied right of privacy prohibits states from banning instruction in foreign languages in private schools,* and from requiring school children to go to public schools between designated ages.†

Two great legal minds, Samuel D. Warren and Louis D. Brandeis, discuss the right to privacy in the following seminal article, which they published in the Harvard Law Review in 1890. Students should particularly note the authors' emphasis that "Political, social, and economic changes entail the recognition of new rights." The major point of this reading for introductory students is, first, to be aware of the stress that the authors place upon the importance of the right to privacy. Even more important is their stress upon privacy as an evolving right that protects individuals as political, economic, and social conditions change.

26

THE RIGHT TO PRIVACY

Samuel D. Warren and Louis D. Brandeis

"It could be done only on principles of private justice, moral fitness, and public convenience, which, when applied to a new subject, make common law without a precedent; much more when received and approved by usage." — Willes, J., in *Millar v. Taylor*, 4 Burr. 2303, 2312

That the individual shall have full protection in person and in property is a principle as old as the common law; but it has been found necessary from time to time to define anew the exact nature and extent of such protection. Political, social, and economic changes entail the recognition of new rights, and the

**Meyer v. Nebraska*, 262 U.S. 390 (1923).

†Pierce v. Society of Sisters, 268 U.S. 510 (1925).

common law, in its eternal youth, grows to meet the new demands of society. Thus, in very early times, the law gave a remedy only for physical interference with life and property, for trespasses vi et armis. Then the "right to life" served only to protect the subject from battery in its various forms; liberty meant freedom from actual restraint; and the right to property secured to the individual his lands and his cattle. Later, there came recognition of man's spiritual nature, of his feelings and his intellect. Gradually the scope of these legal rights broadened; and now the right to life has come to mean the right to enjoy life, —the right to be let alone; the right to liberty secures the exercise of extensive civil privileges; and the term "property" has grown to comprise every form of possession—intangible, as well as tangible.

Thus, with the recognition of the legal value of sensations, the protection against actual bodily injury was extended to prohibit mere attempts to do such injury; that is, the putting another in fear of such injury. From the action of battery grew that of assault. Much later there came a qualified protection of the individual against offensive noises and odors, against dust and smoke, and excessive vibration. The law of nuisance was developed. So regard for human emotions soon extended the scope of personal immunity beyond the body of the individual. His reputation, the standing among his fellow-men, was considered, and the law of slander and libel arose. Man's family relations became a part of the legal conception of his life, and the alienation of a wife's affections was held remediable. Occasionally the law halted, as in its refusal to recognize the intrusion by seduction upon the honor of the family. But even here the demands of society were met. A mean fiction, the action per quod servitium amisit, was resorted to, and by allowing damages for injury to the parents' feelings, an adequate remedy was ordinarily afforded. Similar to the expansion of the right to life was the growth of the legal conception of property. From corporeal property arose the incorporeal rights issuing out of it; and then there opened the wide realm of intangible property, in the products and processes of the mind, as works of literature and art, goodwill, trade secrets, and trademarks.

This development of the law was inevitable. The intense intellectual and emotional life, and the heightening of sensations which came with the advance of civilization, made it clear to men that only a part of the pain, pleasure, and profit of life lay in physical things. Thoughts, emotions, and sensations demanded legal recognition, and the beautiful capacity for growth which characterizes the common law enabled the judges to afford the requisite protection, without the interposition of the legislature.

Recent inventions and business methods call attention to the next step which must be taken for the protection of the person, and for securing to the individual what Judge Cooley calls the right "to be let alone." Instantaneous photographs and newspaper enterprise have invaded the sacred precincts of private and domestic life; and numerous mechanical devices threaten to make good the prediction that "what is whispered in the closet shall be proclaimed from the house-tops." For years there has been a feeling that the law must afford some remedy for the unauthorized circulation of portraits of private persons; and the evil of invasion of privacy by the newspapers, long keenly felt, has been but recently discussed by an able writer. The alleged facts of a somewhat notorious case brought before an inferior tribunal in New York a few months ago, directly involved the consideration of the right of circulating portraits; and the question whether our law will recognize and protect the right to privacy in this and in other respects must soon come before our courts for consideration.

Of the desirability—indeed of the necessity—of some such protection, there can, it is believed, be no doubt. The press is overstepping in every direction the obvious bounds of propriety and of decency. . . .

The common law secures to each individual the right of determining, ordinarily, to what extent his thoughts, sentiments, and emotions shall be communicated to others. Under our system of government, he can never be compelled to express them (except when upon the witness stand); and even if he has chosen to give them expression, he generally retains the power to fix the limits of the publicity which shall be given them. The existence of this right does not depend upon the particular method of expression adopted. It is immaterial whether it be by word or by signs, in painting, by sculpture, or in music. . . .

[T]he protection afforded to thoughts, sentiments, and emotions, expressed through the medium of writing or of the arts, so far as it consists in preventing publication, is merely an instance of the enforcement of the more general right of the individual to be let alone. It is like the right not be assaulted or beaten, the right not be imprisoned, the right not to be maliciously prosecuted, the right not to be defamed. In each of these rights, as indeed in all other rights recognized by the law, there inheres the quality of being owned or possessed—and (as that is the distinguishing attribute of property) there may some propriety in speaking of those rights as property. But, obviously, they bear little resemblance to what is ordinarily comprehended under that term. The principle which protects personal writings and all other personal productions, not against theft and physical appropriation, but against publication in any form, is in reality not the principle of private property, but that of an inviolate personality. . . .

We must therefore conclude that the rights, so protected, whatever their exact nature, are not rights arising from contract or from special trust, but are rights as against the world; and, as above stated, the principle which has been applied to protect these rights is in reality not the principle of private property, unless that word be used in an extended and unusual sense. The principle which protects personal writings and any other productions of the intellect of or the emotions, is the right to privacy, and the law has no new principle to formulate when it extends this protection to the personal appearance, sayings, acts, and to personal relation, domestic or otherwise. . . .

Note the core right to privacy that Warren and Brandeis discuss in the preceding reading. Essentially, it is the right to protection from an intrusive press and other media forms, the right to one's private papers and emotions, the protection of "personal appearance, sayings, acts, and to personal relation, domestic or otherwise."

The instruments of invasion of privacy that concern the authors are not the key to understanding the right to privacy in a broad historical context. That key is the [illegible] changing nature of privacy, of "the right to be let alone," and the right to "an inviolate personality."

Legal usages, the authors argue, evolve to redefine and protect individual rights. The Supreme Court has expanded the right to privacy to protect individuals against governmental intrusions that violate changing definitions of privacy.

This is exactly what the Court's decision did in the following landmark privacy case.

27

GRISWOLD V. CONNECTICUT

381 U.S. 479 (1965)

Mr. Justice Douglas delivered the opinion of the Court.

Appellant Griswold is Executive Director of the Planned Parenthood League of Connecticut. Appellant Buxton is a licensed physician and a professor at the Yale Medical School who served as Medical Director for the League at its Center in New Haven—a center open and operating from November 1 to November 10, 1961, when appellants were arrested.

They gave information, instruction, and medical advice to married persons as to the means of preventing conception. They examined the wife and prescribed the best contraceptive device or material for her use. Fees were usually charged, although some couples were serviced free.

The statutes whose constitutionality is involved in this appeal are 53–32 and 54–196 of the General Statutes of Connecticut (1958 rev.). The former provides:

> "Any person who uses any drug, medicinal article or instrument for the purpose of preventing conception shall be fined not less than fifty dollars or imprisoned not less than sixty days nor more than one year or be both fined and imprisoned."

Section 54–196 provides:

> "Any person who assists, abets, counsels, causes, hires or commands another to commit any offense may be prosecuted and punished as if he were the principal offender."

The appellants were found guilty as accessories and fined $100 each, against the claim that the accessory statute as so applied violated the [individual liberty protected by the] Fourteenth Amendment [due process clause]. The Appellate

Division of the Circuit Court affirmed. The Supreme Court of Errors affirmed that judgment We noted probable jurisdiction. . . .

Coming to the merits, we are met with a wide range of questions that implicate the Due Process Clause of the Fourteenth Amendment. . . . We do not sit as a super-legislature to determine the wisdom, need, and propriety of laws that touch economic problems, business affairs, or social conditions. This law, however, operates directly on an intimate relation of husband and wife and their physician's role in one aspect of that relation.

The association of people is not mentioned in the Constitution nor in the Bill of Rights. The right to educate a child in a school of the parents' choice—whether public or private or parochial—is also not mentioned. Nor is the right to study any particular subject or any foreign language. Yet the First Amendment has been construed to include certain of those rights.

By *Pierce v. Society of Sisters*, [1925] the right to educate one's children as one chooses is made applicable to the States by the force of the First and Fourteenth Amendments. By *Meyer v. Nebraska*, [1923] the same dignity is given the right to study the German language in a private school. In other words, the State may not, consistently with the spirit of the First Amendment, contract the spectrum of available knowledge. . . .

The foregoing cases suggest that specific guarantees in the Bill of Rights have penumbras, formed by emanations from those guarantees that help give them life and substance. . . . Various guarantees create zones of privacy. The right of association contained in the penumbra of the First Amendment is one, as we have seen. The Third Amendment in its prohibition against the quartering of soldiers "in any house" in time of peace without the consent of the owner is another facet of that privacy. The Fourth Amendment explicitly affirms the "right of the people to be secure in their persons, houses, papers, and effects, against unreasonable searches and seizures." The Fifth Amendment in its Self-Incrimination Clause enables the citizen to create a zone of privacy which government may not force him to surrender to his detriment. The Ninth Amendment provides: "The enumeration in the Constitution, of certain rights, shall not be construed to deny or disparage others retained by the people."

The Fourth and Fifth Amendments . . . [protect] against all governmental invasions "of the sanctity of a man's home and the privacies of life. . . . [The]Fourth Amendment [creates a] "right to privacy, no less important than any other right carefully and particularly reserved to the people." . . .

The present case . . . concerns a relationship lying within the zone of privacy created by several fundamental constitutional guarantees. And it concerns a law which, in forbidding the use of contraceptives rather than regulating their manufacture or sale, seeks to achieve its goals by means having a maximum destructive impact upon that relationship. Such a law cannot stand in light of the familiar principle, so often applied by this Court, that a "governmental purpose to control or prevent activities constitutionally subject to state regulation may not be achieved by means which sweep unnecessarily broadly and thereby invade the area of protected freedoms." . . .

We deal with a right of privacy older than the Bill of Rights—older than our political parties, older than our school system. Marriage is a coming together for better or for worse, hopefully enduring, and intimate to the degree of being sacred.

It is an association that promotes a way of life, not causes; a harmony in living, not political faiths; a bilateral loyalty, not commercial or social projects. Yet it is an association for as noble a purpose as any involved in our prior decisions.

Warren and Brandeis emphasize in their Harvard Law Review article that the courts should adapt common and constitutional law to protect individuals against new threats to privacy. Justice Douglas in *Griswold v. Connecticut* (1965) draws upon the Bill of Rights to support a right to privacy, and as well finds privacy rights in Western customs and usage: "We deal with a right of privacy older than the Bill of Rights—older than our political parties, older than our school system."

Conservatives and liberal jurists alike agree on the existence of a right to privacy in our laws, customs, and usages.

Chief Justice Rehnquist represented conservative jurisprudence in his dissent in *Planned Parenthood v. Casey* (1992). He recognized the right to privacy, derivative from common law and constitutional liberty, but argued that it does not include a right to abortion:

> "The Roe Court reached too far when it analogized the right to abort a fetus to the rights involved in *Pierce v. Society of Sisters*, 268 U.S. 510 ; *Meyer v. Nebraska*, 262 U.S. 390 ; *Loving v. Virginia*, 388 U.S. 1 ; and *Griswold v. Connecticut*, 381 U.S. 479 , and thereby deemed the right to abortion to be "fundamental." None of these decisions endorsed an all-encompassing "right of privacy," as Roe claimed. Because abortion involves the purposeful termination of potential life, the abortion decision must be recognized as sui generis, different in kind from the rights protected in the earlier cases under the rubric of personal or family privacy and autonomy. And the historical traditions of the American people—as evidenced by the English common law and by the American abortion statutes in existence both at the time of the Fourteenth Amendment's adoption and Roe's issuance—do not support the view that the right to terminate one's pregnancy is "fundamental." Thus, enactments abridging that right need not be subjected to strict scrutiny."

Ironically, while the "liberal" Warren Court stirred political controversy with its school prayer and many other decisions extending civil liberties and rights to the states, it was the "conservative" Supreme Court under Chief Justice Warren Burger, appointed by Republican President Richard M. Nixon in 1969, that raised an even greater political storm by holding in *Roe v. Wade* that the Fourteenth Amendment incorporates a right to privacy that grants women the absolute right to abortion during the first trimester of pregnancy.

When the decision was handed down in 1973, a majority of states strictly regulated abortions, which could be performed if at all only to protect the life of the mother. The moral codes of many religions, particularly the Catholic church, forbid abortions under any circumstances.

Supporters of the abortion decision argued that while the issue was indeed a moral one for most people, women had a constitutionally protected right to decide whether or not they would have an abortion. Opponents not only emphatically opposed abortion on moral grounds, but also attacked the Court for acting as a super-legislature by imposing its own values upon democratically elected state legislative bodies that were regulating abortion in response to the demands of popular majorities.

The Supreme Court's abortion decision did seem to resurrect "substantive due process," a doctrine under which the Court had in the past judged the fairness of state legislation in terms not of explicitly stated constitutional standards but on the basis of its own views of the reasonableness of the laws under review The Bill of Rights does not contain a general right of privacy, although it may be fairly implied, as Justice Douglas wrote for a majority of the Court in *Griswold v. Connecticut*, 381 U.S. 479 (1965), from First Amendment freedoms of association, Fourth Amendment protections against unreasonable searches and seizures, and the Fifth Amendment shield against self-incrimination.

Whether emanating indirectly from the Bill of Rights or considered to be part of the liberty protected by the Fourteenth Amendment, the right of privacy that the Supreme Court applied in its abortion decision is highly subjective and gives the justices great leeway to impose their own concepts of privacy rights upon legislative bodies. But judicial decisions, especially those of the Supreme Court, always express the values of those making them. The justices did go beyond a strict construction of the Bill of Rights in upholding a woman's right to abortion. However, they had previously interpreted the Fourteenth Amendment Due Process Clause subjectively in each case in the step-by-step process of nationalization of most of the provisions of the Bill of Rights.

Chief Justice John Marshall in *Marbury v. Madison* (1803) held that the Supreme Court is the final judge of what the law is, which inevitably means its decisions will cause or involve the Court in major political controversies. *Roe v. Wade* is one of those controversial decisions.

28

ROE V. WADE

410 U.S. 113 (1973)

Mr. Justice Blackmun delivered the opinion of the Court:

V

The principal thrust of appellant's attack on the Texas statutes is that they improperly invade a right, said to be possessed by the pregnant woman, to choose to terminate her pregnancy. Appellant would discover this right in the concept of personal "liberty" embodied in the Fourteenth Amendment's Due Process Clause; or in personal, marital, familial, and sexual privacy said to be protected by the Bill of Rights or its penumbras, see *Griswold v. Connecticut* [1965] . . . *Eisenstadt v. Baird* [1972] . . . (White, J., concurring in result), or among those rights reserved to the people by the Ninth Amendment, *Griswold v. Connecticut*, . . . (Goldberg, J., concurring). Before addressing this claim, we feel it desirable briefly to survey, in several aspects, the history of abortion, for such insight as that history may afford us, and then to examine the state purposes and interests behind the criminal abortion laws.

VI

It perhaps is not generally appreciated that the restrictive criminal abortion laws in effect in a majority of States today are of relatively recent vintage. Those laws, generally proscribing abortion or its attempt at any time during pregnancy except when necessary to preserve the pregnant woman's life, are not of ancient or even of common-law origin. Instead, they derive from statutory changes effected, for the most part, in the latter half of the nineteenth century. . . .

VII

Three reasons have been advanced to explain historically the enactment of criminal abortion laws in the nineteenth century and to justify their continued existence.

It has been argued occasionally that these laws were the product of a Victorian social concern to discourage illicit sexual conduct. Texas, however, does not advance this justification in the present case, and it appears that no court or commentator has taken the argument seriously. The appellants and amici contend, moreover, that this is not a proper state purpose at all and suggest that, if it were, the Texas statutes are overbroad in protecting it since the law fails to distinguish between married and unwed mothers.

A second reason is concerned with abortion as a medical procedure. When most criminal abortion laws were first enacted, the procedure was a hazardous one for the woman. This was particularly true prior to the development of antisepsis. Antiseptic techniques, of course, were based on discoveries by Lister, Pasteur, and others first announced in 1867, but were not generally accepted and employed until about the turn of the century. Abortion mortality was high. Even after 1900, and perhaps until as late as the development of antibiotics in the 1940s, standard modern techniques such as dilation and curettage were not nearly so safe as they are today. Thus, it has been argued that a State's real concern in enacting a criminal abortion law was to protect the pregnant woman, that is, to restrain her from submitting to a procedure that placed her life in serious jeopardy.

Modern medical techniques have altered this situation. Appellants and various amici refer to medical data indicating that abortion in early pregnancy, this is, prior to the end of the first trimester, although not without its risk, is now relatively safe. Mortality rates for women undergoing early abortions, where the procedure is legal, appear to be as low as or lower than the rates for normal childbirth. Consequently, any interest of the State in protecting the woman from an inherently hazardous procedure, except when it would be equally dangerous for her to forgo it, has largely disappeared. Of course, important state interests in the area of health and medical standards do remain.

The State has a legitimate interest in seeing to it that abortion, like any other medical procedure, is performed under circumstances that insure maximum safety for the patient. This interest obviously extends at least to the performing physician and his staff, to the facilities involved, to the availability of aftercare, and to adequate provision for any complication or emergency that might arise. The prevalence of high mortality rates at illegal "abortion mills" strengthens, rather than weakens, the State's interest in regulating the conditions under which abortions are performed. Moreover, the risk to the woman increases as her pregnancy continues. Thus, the State retains a definite interest in protecting the woman's own health and safety when an abortion is proposed at a late stage of pregnancy.

The third reason is the State's interest—some phrase it in terms of duty—in protecting prenatal life. Some of the argument for this justification rests on the theory that a new human life is present from the moment of conception. The State's interest and general obligation to protect life then extends, it is argued, to prenatal life. Only when the life of the pregnant mother herself is at stake, balanced against the life she carries within her, should the interest of the embryo or fetus not prevail. Logically, of course, a legitimate state interest in this area need not stand or fall on acceptance of the belief that life begins at conception or at some other point prior to live birth. In assessing the State's interest, recognition may be given to the less rigid claim that as long as at least potential life is involved, the State may assert interests beyond the protection of the pregnant woman alone.

Parties challenging state abortion laws have sharply disputed in some courts the contention that a purpose of these laws, when enacted, was to protect prenatal life. . . .

It is with these interests, and the weight to be attached to them, that this case is concerned.

VIII

The Constitution does not explicitly mention any right of privacy. In a line of decisions, however, going back perhaps as far as *Union Pacific R. Co. v. Botsford* [1891] . . . , the Court has recognized that a right of personal privacy, or a guarantee of certain areas or zones of privacy, does exist under the Constitution. In varying contexts, the Court or individual Justices have, indeed, found at least the roots of that right in the First Amendment, *Stanley v. Georgia* [1969] . . . ; in the Fourth and Fifth Amendments, *Terry v. Ohio* [1968] . . . , *Katz v. United States* [1967] . . . ; in the penumbras of the Bill of Rights, *Griswold v. Connecticut* [1965] . . . ; in the Ninth Amendments, id., at 486, . . .

(Goldberg, J., concurring); or in the concept of liberty guaranteed by the first section of the Fourteenth Amendment, see *Meyer v. Nebraska* [1923].. . . These decisions make it clear that only personal rights that can be deemed "fundamental" or "implicit in the concept of ordered liberty," *Palko v. Connecticut* [1937] . . . , are included in this guarantee of personal privacy. They also make it clear that the right has some extension to activities relating to marriage, *Loving v. Virginia* [1967] . . . ; procreation, *Skinner v. Oklahoma* [1942] . . . ; contraception, *Eisenstadt v. Baird* [1972].. . .

This right of privacy, whether it be founded in the Fourteenth Amendment's concept of personal liberty and restrictions upon state action, as we feel it is, or, as the District Court determined, in the Ninth Amendment's reservation of rights to the people, is broad enough to encompass a woman's decision whether or not to terminate her pregnancy. The detriment that the State would impose upon the pregnant woman by denying this choice altogether is apparent. Specific and direct harm medically diagnosable even in early pregnancy may be involved. Maternity, or additional offspring, may force upon the woman a distressful life and future. Psychological harm may be imminent. Mental and physical health may be taxed by child care. There is also the distress, for all concerned, associated with the unwanted child, and there is the problem of bringing a child into a family already unable, psychologically and otherwise, to care for it. In other cases, as in this one, the additional difficulties and continuing stigma of unwed motherhood may be involved. All these are factors the woman and her responsible physician necessarily will consider in consultation.

On the basis of elements such as these, appellant and some amici argue that the woman's right is absolute and that she is entitled to terminate her pregnancy at whatever time, in whatever way, and for whatever reason she alone chooses. With this we do not agree. Appellant's arguments that Texas either has no valid interest at all in regulating the abortion decision, or no interest strong enough to support any limitation upon the woman's sole determination, is unpersuasive. The Court's decisions recognizing a right of privacy also acknowledge that some state regulation in areas protected by that right is appropriate. As noted above, a State may properly assert important interests in safeguarding health, in maintaining medical standards, and in protecting potential life. At some point in pregnancy, these respective interests become sufficiently compelling to sustain regulation of the factors that govern the abortion decision. The privacy right involved, therefore, cannot be said to be absolute. In fact, it is not clear to us that the claim asserted by some amici that one has an unlimited right to do with one's body as one pleases bears a close relationship to the right of privacy previously articulated in the Court's decisions. The Court has refused to recognize an unlimited right of this kind in the past. *Jacobson v. Massachusetts* [1905] . . . (vaccination); *Buck v. Bell* [1927] . . . (sterilization).

We, therefore, conclude that the right of personal privacy includes the abortion decision, but that this right is not unqualified and must be considered against important state interests in regulation.

Where certain "fundamental rights" are involved, the Court has held that regulation limiting these rights may be justified only by a "compelling state interest," . . . and that legislative enactments must be narrowly drawn to express only the legitimate state interests at stake. . . .

IX

The District Court held that the appellee failed to meet his burden of demonstrating that the Texas statute's infringement upon Roe's rights was necessary to support a compelling state interest. . . . .Appellee argues that the State's determination to recognize and protect prenatal life from and after conception constitutes a compelling state interest. As noted above, we do not agree fully with either formulation.

A. The appellee and certain amici argue that the fetus is a "person" within the language and meaning of the Fourteenth Amendment. In support of this, they outline at length and in detail the well-known facts of fetal development. If this suggestion of personhood is established, the appellant's case, of course, collapses, for the fetus' right to life is then guaranteed specifically by the Amendment. The appellant conceded as much on reargument. On the other hand, the appellee conceded on reargument that no case could be cited that holds that a fetus is a person within the meaning of the Fourteenth Amendment.

The Constitution does not define "person" in so many words. Section 1 of the Fourteenth Amendment contains three references to "person." The first, in defining "citizens," speaks of "persons born or naturalized in the United States." The word also appears both in the Due Process Clause and in the Equal Protection Clause. "Person" is used in other places in the Constitution. . . . But in nearly all these instances, the use of the word is such that it has application only postnatally. None indicates, with any assurance, that it has any possible prenatal application.

All this, together with our observation, supra, that throughout the major portion of the nineteenth century prevailing legal abortion practices were far freer than they are today, persuades us that the word "person," as used in the Fourteenth Amendment, does not include the unborn. . . .

B. The pregnant woman cannot be isolated in her privacy. She carries an embryo and, later, a fetus, if one accepts the medical definitions of the developing young in the human uterus. . . . The situation therefore is inherently different from marital intimacy, or bedroom possession of obscene material, or marriage, or procreation, or education, with which *Eisenstadt*, *Griswold*, *Stanley*, *Loving*, *Skinner*, *Pierce*, and *Meyer* were respectively concerned. As we have intimated above, it is reasonable and appropriate for a State to decide that at some point in time another interest, that of health of the mother or that of potential human life, becomes significantly involved. The woman's privacy is no longer sole and any right of privacy she possesses must be measured accordingly.

Texas urges that, apart from the Fourteenth Amendment, life begins at conception and is present throughout pregnancy, and that, therefore, the State has a compelling interest in protecting that life from and after conception. We need not resolve the difficult question of when life begins. When those trained in the respective disciplines of medicine, philosophy, and theology are unable to arrive at any consensus, the judiciary, at this point in the development of man's knowledge, is not in a position to speculate as to the answer.

It should be sufficient to note briefly the wide divergence of thinking on this most sensitive and difficult question. . . .

X

In view of all this, we do not agree that, by adopting one theory of life, Texas may override the rights of the pregnant woman that are at stake. We repeat, however, that the State does have an important and legitimate interest in preserving and protecting the health of the pregnant woman, whether she be a resident of the State or a nonresident who seeks medical consultation and treatment there, and that it has still another important and legitimate interest in protecting the potentiality of human life. These interests are separate and distinct. Each grows in substantiality as the woman approaches term and, at a point during pregnancy, each becomes "compelling."

With respect to the State's important and legitimate interest in the health of the mother, the "compelling" point, in the light of present medical knowledge, is at approximately the end of the first trimester. This is so because of the now-established medical fact, referred to above . . . that until the end of the first trimester mortality in abortion may be less than mortality in normal childbirth. It follows that, from and after this point, a State may regulate the abortion procedure to the extent that the regulation reasonably relates to the preservation and protection of maternal health. Examples of permissible state regulation in this area are requirements as to the qualifications of the person who is to perform the abortion; as to the licensure of that person; as to the facility in which the procedure is to be performed, that is, whether it must be a hospital or may be a clinic or some other place of less-than-hospital status; as to the licensing of the facility; and the like.

This means, on the other hand, that, for the period of pregnancy prior to this "compelling" point, the attending physician, in consultation with his patient, is free to determine, without regulation by the State, that, in his medical judgment, the patient's pregnancy should be terminated. If that decision is reached, the judgment may be effectuated by an abortion free of interference by the State.

With respect to the State's important and legitimate interest in potential life, the "compelling" point is at viability. This is so because the fetus then presumably has the capability of meaningful life outside the mother's womb. State regulation protective of fetal life after viability thus has both logical and biological justifications. If the State is interested in protecting fetal life after viability, it may go so far as to proscribe abortion during that period, except when it is necessary to preserve the life or health of the mother.

Measured against these standards, Art. 1196 of the Texas Penal Code, in restricting legal abortions to those "procured or attempted by medical advice for the purpose of saving the life of the mother," sweeps too broadly. The statute makes no distinction between abortions performed early in pregnancy and those performed later, and it limits to a single reason, "saving" the mother's life, the legal justification for the procedure. The statute, therefore, cannot survive the constitutional attack made upon it here. . . .

XI

To summarize and to repeat:

1. A state criminal abortion statute of the current Texas type, that excepts from criminality only a lifesaving procedure on behalf of the mother, without regard to pregnancy stage and without recognition of the other interests involved, is violative of the Due Process Clause of the Fourteenth Amendment.

(a) For the stage prior to approximately the end of the first trimester, the abortion decision and its effectuation must be left to the medical judgment of the pregnant woman's attending physician.

(b) For the stage subsequent to approximately the end of the first trimester, the State, in promoting its interest in the health of the mother, may, if it chooses, regulate the abortion procedure in ways that are reasonably related to maternal health.

(c) For the stage subsequent to viability, the State in promoting its interest in the potentiality of human life may, if it chooses, regulate, and even proscribe, abortion except where it is necessary, in appropriate medical judgment, for the preservation of the life or health of the mother.

2. The State may define the term "physician," as it has been employed in the preceding numbered paragraphs of this Part XI of this opinion, to mean only a physician currently licensed by the State, and may proscribe any abortion by a person who is not a physician as so defined.

In *Doe v. Bolton* [1973] . . . procedural requirements contained in one of the modern abortion statutes are considered. That opinion and this one, of course, are to be read together. . . .

Mr. Chief Justice Burger concurred.

Mr. Justice Douglas concurred.

Mr. Justice Stewart, concurring:

In 1963, this Court, in *Ferguson v. Skrupa*, . . . purported to sound the death knell for the doctrine of substantive due process, a doctrine under which many state laws had in the past been held to violate the Fourteenth Amendment. As Mr. Justice Black's opinion for the Court in *Skrupa* put it: "We have returned to the original constitutional proposition that courts do not substitute their social and economic beliefs for the judgment of legislative bodies, who are elected to pass laws." . . .

Barely two years later, in *Griswold v. Connecticut*, . . . the Court held a Connecticut birth control law unconstitutional. In view of what had been so recently said in *Skrupa*, the Court's opinion in *Griswold* understandably did its best to avoid reliance on the Due Process Clause of the Fourteenth Amendment as the ground for decision. Yet, the Connecticut law did not violate any provision of the Bill of Rights, nor any other specific provision of the Constitution. So it was clear to me then, and it is equally clear to me now, that the *Griswold* decision can be rationally understood only as a holding that the Connecticut statute substantively invaded the "liberty" that is protected by the Due Process Clause of the Fourteenth Amendment. As so understood, *Griswold* stands as one in a long line of pre-*Skrupa* cases decided under the doctrine of substantive due process, and I now accept it as such.

"In a Constitution for a free people, there can be no doubt that the meaning of 'liberty' must be broad indeed." . . . The Constitution nowhere mentions a specific right of personal choice in matters of marriage and family life, but the "liberty" protected by the Due Process Clause of the Fourteenth Amendment covers more than those freedoms explicitly named in the Bill of Rights. . . .

Several decisions of this Court make clear that freedom of personal choice in matters of marriage and family life is one of the liberties protected by the Due Process Clause of the Fourteenth Amendment. *Loving v. Virginia*, . . . *Griswold v. Connecticut*. . . . In *Eisenstadt v. Baird*, . . . we recognized "the right of the individual, married or single, to be free from unwarranted governmental intrusion into matters so fundamentally affecting a person as the decision whether to bear or beget a child." That right necessarily includes the right of a woman to decide whether or not to terminate her pregnancy. "Certainly the interests of a woman in giving of her physical and emotional self during pregnancy and the interest that will be affected throughout her life by the birth and raising of a child are of a far greater degree of significance and personal intimacy than the right to send a child to private school protected in *Pierce v. Society of Sisters* [1925] . . . , or the right to teach a foreign language protected in *Meyer v. Nebraska*. . . . "

Mr. Justice Rehnquist, dissenting:

. . . I have difficulty in concluding, as the Court does, that the right of "privacy" is involved in this case. Texas, by the statute here challenged, bars the performance of a medical abortion by a licensed physician on a plaintiff such as Roe. A transaction resulting in an operation such as this is not "private" in the ordinary usage of that word. . . .

If the Court means by the term "privacy" no more than that the claim of a person to be free from unwanted state regulation of consensual transactions may be a form of "liberty" protected by the Fourteenth Amendment, there is no doubt that similar claims have been upheld in our earlier decisions on the basis of the liberty. I agree with the statement of Mr. Justice Stewart in his concurring opinion that the "liberty," against deprivation of which without due process the Fourteenth Amendment protects, embraces more than the rights found in the Bill of Rights. But that liberty is not guaranteed absolutely against deprivation, only against deprivation without due process of law. The test traditionally applied in the area of social and economic legislation is whether or not a law such as that challenged has a rational relation to a valid state objective. . . . But the Court's sweeping invalidation of any restrictions on abortion during the first trimester is impossible to justify under that standard, and the conscious weighing of competing factors that the Court's opinion apparently substitutes for the established test is far more appropriate to a legislative judgment than to a judicial one.

The Court eschews the history of the Fourteenth Amendment in its reliance on the "compelling state interest" test. . . . But the Court adds a new wrinkle to this test by transposing it from the legal considerations associated with the Equal Protection Clause of the Fourteenth Amendment to this case arising under the Due Process Clause of the Fourteenth Amendment. Unless I misapprehend the consequences of this transplanting of the "compelling state interest test," the Court's opinion will accomplish the seemingly impossible feat of leaving this area of the law more confused than it found it.

While the Court's opinion quotes from the dissent of Mr. Justice Holmes in *Lochner v. New York*, the result it reaches is more closely attuned to the majority opinion of Mr. Justice Peckham in that case. As in *Lochner* and similar cases applying substantive due process standards to economic and social welfare legislation, the adoption of the compelling state interest standard will inevitably require this Court to examine the legislative policies and pass on the wisdom of these policies in the very process of deciding whether a particular state interest put forward may or may not be "compelling." The decision here to break pregnancy into three distinct terms and to outline the permissible restrictions the State may impose in each one, for example, partakes more of judicial legislation than it does of a determination of the intent of the drafters of the Fourteenth Amendment.

The fact that a majority of the States reflecting, after all the majority sentiment in those States, have had restrictions on abortions for at least a century is a strong indication, it seems to me, that the asserted right to an abortion is not "so rooted in the traditions and conscience of our people as to be ranked as fundamental," *Snyder v. Massachusetts* [1934].. . . Even today, when society's views on abortion are changing, the very existence of the debate is evidence that the "right" to an abortion is not so universally accepted as the appellant would have us believe.

To reach its result, the Court necessarily has had to find within the scope of the Fourteenth Amendment a right that was apparently completely unknown to the drafters of the Amendment. As early as 1821, the first state law dealing directly with abortion was enacted by the Connecticut Legislature. . . . By the time of the adoption of the Fourteenth Amendment in 1868, there were at least 36 laws enacted by state or territorial legislatures limiting abortion. While many States have amended or updated their laws, 21 of the laws on the books in 1868 remain in effect today. . . .

. . . The only conclusion possible from this history is that the drafters did not intend to have the Fourteenth Amendment withdraw from the States the power to legislate with respect to this matter. . . .

Mr. Justice White, joined by Mr. Justice Rehnquist, dissented.

The Court's decision in *Roe v. Wade* (1973) almost immediately mobilized pro-life forces that pressured Congress for a constitutional amendment to overturn the *Roe* decision. Elected officials were caught in a political vise on the issue, which they considered a no-win situation. Pro-lifers constituted a powerful political movement but not a majority of the American people who, after the *Roe* decision, favored the pro-choice position, although not necessarily the practice of abortion.

For their part, politicians more often than not ducked the abortion issue by making vague statements such as, "I am personally against abortion but I must uphold and respect the Supreme Court's decision on the matter." Before the *Roe* decision, many states were well on their way toward liberalizing their abortion statutes in an environment that was relatively free of political rancor. Ironically, the *Roe* decision galvanized political opposition to abortion and forced politicians, however reluctantly, to deal with the issue. As state statutes regulating abortion were struck down one after the other, the pro-life movement gathered more steam than converts.

While pressing for a constitutional amendment, the pro-lifers knew that their best hope was to convince the Supreme Court to overturn *Roe v. Wade.* Litigation had produced the decision, and litigation could overturn it if the Court's composition changed to a more conservative, pro-life viewpoint. Senate confirmation hearings for Supreme

Court nominees became a political battleground between liberals and conservatives on the abortion issue.

Ronald Reagan's election to the presidency in 1980 gave the pro-lifers renewed hopes for change. Reagan took a strong pro-life position, putting the issue at the top of his social agenda. During his eight years as president he was able to make three conservative appointments to the Supreme Court—Sandra Day O'Connor, Antonin Scalia, and Anthony M. Kennedy. Reagan and the pro-lifers had reason to hope that these new justices might tip the Court's scale in favor of overruling *Roe v. Wade.*

The suspense on both sides of the abortion issue was almost unbearable as the Court in 1989 reviewed a circuit court decision that had struck down a Missouri abortion law on the ground that it violated the principles of *Roe v. Wade.* The law prohibited the use of public facilities or employees to perform abortions, and prohibited the use of public funds for abortion counseling. The decision, *Webster v. Reproductive Health Services,* while not overruling *Roe v. Wade,* marked the beginning of a change in the Court's attitude on the abortion issue. A plurality of justices, led by Chief Justice William H. Rehnquist, began a process of modifying *Roe,* but did not take the final step, urged by Justice Scalia, of overturning it. Justice Blackmun, who had written the *Roe* opinion, dissented along with Justices Brennan and Marshall. Blackmun wrote, "The simple truth is that *Roe* would not survive the plurality's analysis, and that the plurality provides no substitute for *Roe*'s protective umbrella. I fear for the future. I fear for the liberty and equality of the millions of women who have lived and come of age in the sixteen years since *Roe* was decided. I fear for the integrity of, and public esteem for, this Court." He concluded, "For today, at least, the law of abortion stands undisturbed. For today, the women of this nation still retain the liberty to control their destinies. But the signs are evident and very ominous and a chill wind blows."

In 1992 again a sharply divided Court upheld *Roe v. Wade* by a thin majority in *Planned Parenthood v. Casey.* Sandra Day O'Connor wrote the Court's plurality opinion, which stressed the importance of following precedent unless compelling reasons supported a change.

President George Bush's appointments of Chief Justice John Roberts and Justice Samuel Alito again raised the as-yet unfulfilled hopes of conservatives that *Roe v. Wade* would be overturned.

While it seems unlikely that the Supreme Court will overrule *Roe v. Wade* in its entirety, the Rehnquist Court has allowed states to regulate abortion to a greater degree than *Roe v. Wade* would have permitted. Chief Justice Rehnquist, Justice Antonin Scalia, and other justices have rejected much of Justice Blackmun's reasoning in *Roe v. Wade*'s majority opinion. Conservatives have broadly attacked *Roe*'s affirmation of the constitutional right to privacy, first "discovered" in *Griswold v. Connecticut* (1965), to support the right to abortion.

AFFIRMATIVE ACTION

Presidents John F. Kennedy in 1961 and Lyndon B. Johnson in 1965 issued executive orders requiring affirmative action to *prevent* discrimination in government employment and contracting. These programs differed sharply from later affirmative action that established quotas for hiring, contracting, and university admissions. Originally, "affirmative action" was intended to prevent discrimination on the basis of race, not to establish "reverse discrimination" to remedy the effects of past discrimination.

Inevitably, as affirmative action spread and took on the new meaning of giving minorities special preferences in employment, government contracting, and university and college admissions, the practice became highly controversial. Critics claimed the programs were discriminatory on the basis of race in violation of the equal protection clause of the Fourteenth Amendment where state action was involved, or the equal protection component of the Fifth Amendment due process clause for federal programs. Arguably, state and federal "reverse racial discrimination" was still unconstitutional discrimination.

The seminal precedent setting affirmative action decision came in the Bakke case in 1976. The University of California medical school at Davis had an affirmative action admissions program that set aside 16 out of 100 places for a "minority group" (blacks, Chicanos, Asians, American Indians). Bakke, a white applicant whose test scores were better than those required of minority applicants, sued when the school denied him admission.

29

UNIVERSITY OF CALIFORNIA REGENTS V. BAKKE

438 U.S. 265 (1978)

Mr. Justice Powell announced the judgment of the Court.

. . . The special admissions program is undeniably a classification based on race and ethnic background. To the extent that there existed a pool of at least minimally qualified minority applicants to fill the 16 special admissions seats, white applicants could compete only for 84 seats in the entering class, rather than the 100 open to minority applicants. Whether this limitation is described as a quota or a goal, it is a line drawn on the basis of race and ethnic status.

The guarantees of the Fourteenth Amendment extend to all persons. Its language is explicit: "No State shall . . . deny to any person within its jurisdiction the equal protection of the laws." . . . The guarantee of equal protection cannot mean one thing when applied to one individual and something else when applied to a person of another color. If both are not accorded the same protection, then it is not equal.

Nevertheless, petitioner [University of California] argues that the court below [California Supreme Court, which overturned the program] erred in applying strict scrutiny to the special admissions program because white males, such as respondent, are not a "discrete and insular minority" requiring extraordinary protection from the majoritarian political process.

This rationale, however, has never been invoked in our decisions as a prerequisite to subjecting racial or ethnic distinctions to strict scrutiny. Nor has this Court held that discreteness and insularity constitute necessary preconditions to a holding that a particular [racial] classification is invidious. . . .

. . . Racial and ethnic distinctions of any sort are inherently suspect and thus call for the most exacting judicial examination. . . .

If it is the individual who is entitled to judicial protection against classifications based upon his racial or ethnic background because such distinctions impinge upon personal rights, rather than the individual only because of his membership in a particular group, then constitutional standards may be applied consistently. . . .

We have never approved a classification that aids persons perceived as members of relatively victimized groups at the expense of other innocent individuals in the absence of judicial, legislative, or administrative findings of constitutional or statutory violations. . . . After such findings have been made, the governmental interest in preferring members of the injured groups at the expense of others is substantial, since the legal rights of the victims must be vindicated. In such a case, the extent of the injury and the consequent remedy will have been judicially, legislatively, or administrative defined. Also, the remedial action usually remains subject to continuing oversight to assure that it will work the least harm possible to other innocent persons competing for the benefit. Without such findings of constitutional or statutory violations, it cannot be said that the government has any greater interest in helping one individual than in refraining from harming another. Thus, the government has no compelling justification for inflicting such harm.

Petitioner does not purport to have made, and is in no position to make, such findings. Its broad mission is education, not the formulation of any legislative policy or the adjudication of particular claims of illegality. . . .

In summary, it is evident that the Davis special admissions program involves the use of an explicit racial classification never before countenanced by this Court. It tells applicants who are not Negro, Asian, or Chicano that they are totally excluded from a specific percentage of the seats in an entering class. No matter how strong their qualifications, quantitative and extracurricular, including their own potential for contribution to educational diversity, they are never afforded the chance to compete with applicants from the preferred groups for the special admissions seats. At the same time, the preferred applicants have the opportunity to compete for every seat in the class.

The fatal flaw in petitioner's preferential program is its disregard of individual rights as guaranteed by the Fourteenth Amendment. Such rights are not absolute. But when a State's distribution of benefits or imposition of burdens hinges on ancestry or the color of a person's skin, that individual is entitled to a demonstration that the challenged classification is necessary to promote a substantial state interest. Petitioner has failed to carry this burden. For this reason, that portion of the California court's judgment holding petitioner's special admissions program invalid under the Fourteenth Amendment must be affirmed.

C

In enjoining petitioner from ever considering the race of any applicant, however, the courts below failed to recognize that the State has a substantial interest that legitimately may be served by a properly devised admissions program involving the competitive consideration of race and ethnic origin. For this reason, so much of the California court's judgment as enjoins petitioner from any consideration of the race of any applicant must be reversed.

During the 1980s the Supreme Court appeared to apply different constitutional standards to national and state and local affirmative action programs. Essentially, a close majority and sometimes plurality of the Court held that Congress has broad remedial power under the Fourteenth Amendment's Section 5 to remedy the effects of past societal discrimination by passing affirmative action programs, such as minority set-aside programs for small businesses receiving federal funds. At the same time, Supreme Court conservatives were able to marshal a majority or plurality that applied stricter constitutional standards to state and local programs. In the latter area the Court sometimes overturned state and local affirmative action programs as unjustified racial discrimination in violation of the Equal Protection Clause of the Fourteenth Amendment. Only if the states or localities could prove that their affirmative action programs were designed to remedy the effects of past discrimination would the Supreme Court uphold them. The result of these Supreme Court opinions was that Congress had far more leeway to pass affirmative action legislation than did the states or local governments.*

The Supreme Court, in a 5–4 decision, held in *Adarand Constructors v. Pena*, 515 U.S. 200 (1995), that strict judicial scrutiny would be applied to both federal and state action, requiring Congress for the first time to make findings supporting a compelling government interest in affirmative action programs.

**Compiler's note:* Major cases concerning congressional authority in affirmative action include *Fullilove v. Klutznick*, 448 U.S. 448 (1980); *Metro Broadcasting, Inc. v. Federal Communications Commission*, 497 U.S. 547 (1990). For state and local affirmative action authority see, for example, *Wygant v. Jackson Board of Education*, 476 U.S. 267 (1986); *United States v. Paradise*, 480 U.S. 149 (1987); *City of Richmond v. J. A. Croson Co.*, 488 U.S. 469 (1989).

PART TWO

POLITICAL PARTIES, ELECTORAL BEHAVIOR, AND INTEREST GROUPS

CHAPTER 4

POLITICAL PARTIES AND THE ELECTORATE

CONSTITUTIONAL BACKGROUND

Political parties and interest groups have developed outside of the original constitutional framework to channel political power in the community, and for this reason they deserve special consideration from students of American government. The Constitution was designed to structure power relationships in such a way that the arbitrary exercise of political power by any one group or individual would be prevented. One important concept held by the framers of the Constitution was that faction, that is, parties and interest groups, is inherently dangerous to political freedom and stable government. This is evident from *Federalist 10*.

30

FEDERALIST 10

James Madison

Among the numerous advantages promised by a well constructed Union, none deserves to be more accurately developed than its tendency to break and control the violence of faction. The friend of popular governments never finds himself so much alarmed for their character and fate as when he contemplates their propensity to this dangerous vice. He will not fail, therefore, to set a due value on any plan which, without violating the principles to which he is attached, provides a proper cure for it. The instability, injustice, and confusion, introduced into the public councils, have, in truth been the mortal diseases under which popular governments have everywhere perished; as they continue to be the favorite and fruitful topics from which the adversaries to liberty derive their most specious declamations. The valuable improvements made by the American constitutions on the popular models, both ancient and modern, cannot certainly be too much admired; but it would be an unwarrantable partiality, to contend that they have as effectually obviated the danger on this side, as was wished and expected. Complaints are everywhere heard from our most considerate and virtuous citizens, equally the friends of public and private faith, and of public and personal liberty, that our governments are too unstable; that the public good is disregarded in the conflicts of rival parties; and that measures are too often decided, not according to the rules of justice, and the rights of the minor party, but by the superior force of an interested and overbearing majority. However anxiously we may wish that these complaints had no foundation, the evidence of known facts will not permit us to deny that they are in some degree true. It will be found, indeed, on a candid review of our situation, that some of the distresses under which we labor, have been erroneously charged on the operation of our governments; but it will be found, at the same time, that other causes will not alone account for many of our heaviest misfortunes; and, particularly, for the prevailing and increasing distrust of public engagements, and alarm for private rights, which are echoed from one end of the continent to the other. These must be chiefly, if not wholly, effects of the unsteadiness and injustice, with which a factious spirit has tainted our public administrations.

By a faction, I understand a number of citizens, whether amounting to a majority or minority of the whole, who are united and actuated by some common impulse of passion, or of interest, adverse to the rights of other citizens, or to the permanent and aggregate interest of the community.

There are two methods of curing the mischiefs of faction: the one, by removing its causes; the other, by controlling its effects.

There are again two methods of removing the causes of faction: the one, by destroying the liberty which is essential to its existence; the other, by giving to every citizen the same opinions, the same passions, and the same interests.

It could never be more truly said, than of the first remedy, that it was worse than the disease. Liberty is to faction what air is to fire, an ailment, without which it instantly expires. But it could not be a less folly to abolish liberty, which is essential to political life because it nourishes faction, than it would be to wish the annihilation of air, which is essential to animal life, because it imparts to fire its destructive agency.

The second expedient is as impracticable, as the first would be unwise. As long as the reason of man continues fallible, and he is at liberty to exercise it, different opinions will be formed. As long as the connection subsists between his reason and his self-love, his opinions and his passions will have a reciprocal influence on each other; and the former will be objects to which the latter will attach themselves. The diversity in the faculties of men, from which the rights of property originate, is not less an insuperable obstacle to a uniformity of interests. The protection of those faculties is the first object of government. From the protection of different and unequal faculties of acquiring property, the possession of different degrees and kinds of property immediately results; and from the influence of these on the sentiments and views of the respective proprietors, ensues a division of the society into different interests and parties.

The latent causes of faction are thus sown in the nature of man; and we see them everywhere brought into different degrees of activity, according to the different circumstances of civil society. A zeal for different opinions concerning religion, concerning government, and many other points, as well of speculation as of practice; an attachment to different leaders, ambitiously contending for preeminence and power; or to persons of other descriptions, whose fortunes have been interesting to the human passions, have, in turn, divided mankind into parties, inflamed them with mutual animosity, and rendered them much more disposed to vex and oppress each other, than to cooperate for their common good. So strong is this propensity of mankind, to fall into mutual animosities, that where no substantial occasion presents itself, the most frivolous and fanciful distinctions have been sufficient to kindle their unfriendly passions, and excite their most violent conflicts. But the most common and durable source of factions has been the various and unequal distribution of property. Those who hold, and those who are without property, have ever formed distinct interests in society. Those who are creditors, and those who are debtors, fall under a like discrimination. A landed interest, a manufacturing interest, a mercantile interest, a moneyed interest, with many lesser interests, grow up of necessity in civilized nations, and divide them into different classes, actuated by different sentiments and views. The regulation of these various and interfering interests forms the principal task of modern legislation, and involves the spirit of party and faction in the necessary and ordinary operations of government.

No man is allowed to be a judge in his own cause; because his interest will certainly bias his judgment, and, not improbably, corrupt his integrity. With equal, nay, with greater reason, a body of men are unfit to be both judges and parties at the same time; yet what are many of the most important acts of legislation, but so many judicial determinations, not indeed concerning the rights of single persons, but concerning the rights of large bodies of citizens? And what are the different classes of legislators, but advocates and parties to the cause which they determine? Is a law proposed concerning private debts? It is a question to which the creditors are parties on one side, and the debtors on the other. Justice ought to hold the balance between them. Yet the parties are, and must be, themselves the judges; and the most numerous party, or, in other words, the most powerful faction, must be expected to prevail. Shall domestic manufactures be encouraged, and in what degree, by restrictions on foreign manufactures are questions which would be differently decided by the landed and the manufacturing classes; and probably by neither with a sole regard to justice and the public good. . . .

It is vain to say, that enlightened statesmen will be able to adjust these clashing interests, and render them all subservient to the public good. Enlightened statesmen will not always be at the helm; nor, in many cases, can such an adjustment be made at all, without taking into view indirect and remote considerations, which will rarely prevail over the immediate interest which one party may find in disregarding the rights of another, or the good of the whole.

The inference to which we are brought is, that the *causes* of faction cannot be removed; and that relief is only to be sought in the means of controlling its effects.

If a faction consists of less than a majority, relief is supplied by the republican principle, which enables the majority to defeat its sinister views, by regular vote. It may clog the administration, it may convulse the society; but it will be unable to execute and mask its violence under the forms of the constitution. When a majority is included in a faction, the form of popular government, on the other hand, enables it to sacrifice to its ruling passion or interest, both the public good and the rights of other citizens. To secure the public good, and private rights, against the danger of such a faction, and at the same time to preserve the spirit and the form of popular government, is then the great object to which our inquiries are directed. Let me add, that it is the great desideratum, by which alone this form of government can be rescued from the opprobrium under which it has so long labored, and be recommended to the esteem and adoption of mankind.

By what means is this object attainable? Evidently by one of two only. Either the existence of the same passion or interest in a majority, at the same time must be prevented; or the majority, having such coexistent passion or interest, must be rendered, by their number and local situation, unable to concert and carry into effect schemes of oppression. If the impulse and the opportunity be suffered to coincide, we well know, that neither moral nor religious motives can be relied on as an adequate control. They are not found to be such on the injustice and violence of individuals, and lose their efficacy in proportion to the number combined together; that is, in proportion as their efficacy becomes needful.

From this view of the subject, it may be concluded, that a pure democracy, by which I mean a society consisting of a small number of citizens, who assemble and administer the government in person, can admit of no cure from the mischiefs of faction. A common passion or interest will, in almost every case, be felt by a majority of the whole; a communication and concert, results from the form of government itself; and there is nothing to check the inducements to sacrifice the weaker party, or an obnoxious individual. Hence it is, that such democracies have ever been spectacles of turbulence and contention, have ever been found incompatible with personal security, or the rights of property; and have, in general, been as short in their lives, as they have been violent in their deaths. Theoretic politicians, who have patronized this species of government, have erroneously supposed that by reducing mankind to a perfect equality in their political rights, they would, at the same time, be perfectly equalized and assimilated in their possessions, their opinions, and their passions.

A republic, by which I mean a government in which the scheme of representation takes place, opens a different prospect, and promises the cure for which we are seeking. Let us examine the points in which it varies from pure democracy, and we shall comprehend both the nature of the cure and the efficacy which it must derive from the union.

The two great points of difference, between a democracy and a republic, are, first, the delegation of the government, in the latter, to a small number of citizens elected by the rest; secondly, the greater number of citizens, and greater sphere of country, over which the latter may be extended.

The effect of the first difference is on the one hand, to refine and enlarge the public views, by passing them through the medium of a chosen body of citizens, whose wisdom may best discern the true interest in their country, and whose patriotism and love of justice, will be least likely to sacrifice it to temporary or partial considerations. Under such a regulation, it may well happen, that the public voice, pronounced by the representatives of the people, will be more consonant to the public good, than if pronounced by the people themselves, convened for the purpose. On the other hand, the effect may be inverted. Men of factious tempers, of local prejudices, or of sinister designs, may by intrigue, by corruption, or by other means, first obtain the suffrages, and then betray the interest of the people. The question resulting is, whether small or extensive republics are most favorable to the election of proper guardians of the public weal; and it is clearly decided in favor of the latter by two obvious considerations.

In the first place, it is to be remarked, that however small the republic may be, the representatives must be raised to a certain number, in order to guard against the cabals of a few; and that however large it may be, they must be limited to a certain number, in order to guard against the confusion of a multitude. Hence, the number of representatives in the two cases not being in proportion to that of the constituents, and being proportionally greatest in the small republic, it follows that if the proportion of fit characters be not less in the large than in the small republic, the former will present a greater option, and consequently a greater probability of a fit choice.

In the next place, as each representative will be chosen by a greater number of citizens in the large than in the small republic, it will be more difficult for unworthy candidates to practice with success the vicious arts, by which elections are too often carried; and the suffrages of the people being more free, will be more likely to center in men who possess the most attractive merit, and the most diffusive and established characters. . . .

The other point of difference is, the greater number of citizens, and extent of territory, which may be brought within the compass of republican, than of democratic government; and it is this circumstance principally which renders factious combinations less to be dreaded in the former, than in the latter. The smaller the society, the fewer probably will be the distinct parties and interests composing it; the fewer the distinct parties and interests, the more frequently will a majority be found of the same party; and the smaller the number of individuals composing a majority, and the smaller the compass within which they are placed, the more easily they will concert and execute their plans of oppression. Extend the sphere, and you take in a greater variety of parties and interests; you make it less probable that a majority of the whole will have a common motive to invade the rights of other citizens; or if such a common motive exists, it will be more difficult for all who feel it to discover their own strength, and to act in unison with each other. . . .

Hence, it clearly appears, that the same advantage, which a republic has over a democracy, in controlling the effects of faction, is enjoyed by a large over a small republic—is enjoyed by the union over the states composing it. Does this advantage consist in the substitution of representatives, whose enlightened views and virtuous sentiments render them superior to local prejudices, and to schemes of injustice? It will not be denied, that the representation of the union will be most likely to possess these requisite endowments. Does it consist in the greater security afforded by a greater variety of parties, against the event of any one party being able to outnumber and oppress the rest? In an equal degree does the increased variety of parties, comprised within the union, increase this security? Does it, in fine, consist in the greater obstacles opposed to the concert and accomplishment of the secret wishes of an unjust and interested majority? Here, again, the extent of the union gives it the most palpable advantage.

The influence of factious leaders may kindle a flame within their particular states, but will be unable to spread a general conflagration through the other states; a religious sect may degenerate into a political faction in a part of the confederacy; but the variety of sects dispersed over the entire face of it, must secure the national councils against any danger from the source; a rage for paper money, for an abolition of debts, for an equal division of property, or for any other improper or wicked project, will be less apt to pervade the whole body of the union, than a particular member of it; in the same proportion as such a malady is more likely to taint a particular county or district, than an entire state.

In the extent and proper structure of the union, therefore, we behold a republican remedy for the diseases most incident to republican government. And according to the degree of pleasure and pride we feel in being republicans, ought to be our zeal in cherishing the spirit, and supporting the character of Federalists.

The following selection is taken from E. E. Schattschneider's classic treatise, *Party Government.* In this material he examines both the implications of *Federalist 10* and counterarguments to the propositions stated by Madison with regard to political parties and interest groups.

31

PARTY GOVERNMENT

E. E. Schattschneider

The Convention at Philadelphia provided a constitution with a dual attitude: it was proparty in one sense and antiparty in another. The authors of the Constitution refused to suppress the parties by destroying the fundamental liberties in which parties originate. They or their immediate successors accepted amendments that guaranteed civil rights and thus established a system of party tolerance, i.e., the right to agitate and to organize. This is the proparty aspect of the system. On the other hand, the authors of the Constitution set up an elaborate division and balance of powers within an intricate governmental structure designed to make parties ineffective. It was hoped that the parties would lose and exhaust themselves in futile attempts to fight their way through the labyrinthine framework of the government, much as an attacking army is expected to spend itself against the defensive works of a fortress. This is the antiparty part of the Constitution scheme. To quote Madison, the "great object" of the Constitution was "to preserve the public good and private right against the danger of such a faction [party] and at the same time to preserve the spirit and form of popular government."

In Madison's mind the difference between an autocracy and a free republic seems to have been largely a matter of the precise point at which parties are stopped by the government. In an autocracy parties are controlled (suppressed) at the source; in a republic parties are tolerated but are invited to strangle themselves in the machinery of government. The result in either case is much the same, sooner or later the government checks the parties but *never do the parties control the government*. Madison was perfectly definite and unmistakable in his disapproval of party government as distinguished from party tolerance. In the opinion of Madison, parties were intrinsically bad, and the sole issue for discussion was the means by which bad parties might be prevented from becoming dangerous. What never seems to have occurred to the authors of the Constitution, however, is that parties might be *used* as beneficent instruments of popular government. It is at this point that the distinction between the modern and the antique attitude is made.

The offspring of this combination of ideas was a constitutional system having conflicting tendencies. The Constitution made the rise of parties inevitable yet was incompatible with party government. This scheme, in spite of its subtlety, involved a miscalculation. Political parties refused to be content with the role assigned to them. The vigor and enterprise of the parties have therefore made American political history the story of the unhappy marriage of the parties and the Constitution, a remarkable variation of the case of the irresistible force and the immovable object, which in this instance have been compelled to live together in a permanent partnership. . . .

The Raw Materials of Politics

People who write about interests sometimes seem to assume that all interests are special and exclusive, setting up as a result of this assumption a dichotomy in which the interests on the one side are perpetually opposed to the public welfare on the other side. But there are common interests as well as special interests, and common interests resemble special interests in that they are apt to influence political behavior. The raw materials of politics are not all antisocial. Alongside of Madison's statement that differences in wealth are the most durable causes of faction there should be placed a corollary that the common possessions of the people are the most durable cause of unity. To assume that people have merely conflicting interests and nothing else is to invent a political nightmare that has only a superficial relation to reality. The body of agreement underlying the conflicts of a modern society ought to be sufficient to sustain the social order provided only that the common interests supporting this unity are mobilized. Moreover, not all differences of interest are durable causes of conflict. Nothing is apt to be more perishable than a political issue. In the democratic process, the nation moves from controversy to agreement to forgetfulness; politics is not a futile exercise like football, forever played back and forth over the same ground. The government creates and destroys interests at every turn.

There are, in addition, powerful factors inhibiting the unlimited pursuit of special aims by an organized minority. To assume that minorities will stop at nothing to get what they want is to postulate a degree of unanimity and concentration within these groups that does not often exist in real life. If every individual were capable of having only one interest to the exclusion of all others, it might be possible to form dangerous unions of monomaniacs who would go to great extremes to attain their objectives. In fact, however, people have many interests leading to a dispersion of drives certain to destroy some of the unanimity and concentration of any group. How many interests can an individual have? Enough to make it extremely unlikely that any two individuals will have the same combination of interests. Anyone who has ever tried to promote an association of people having some special interest in common will realize, first, that there are marked differences of enthusiasm within the group and, second, that interests compete with interests for the attention and enthusiasm of every individual. Every organized special interest consists of a group of busy, distracted individuals held together by the efforts of a handful of specialists and enthusiasts who sacrifice other matters in order to concentrate on one. The notion of resolute and unanimous minorities on the point of violence is largely the invention of paid lobbyists and press agents.

The result of the fact that every individual is torn by the diversity of his own interests, the fact that he is a member of many groups, is *the law of the imperfect political mobilization of interests*. That is, it has never been possible to mobilize any interest 100 percent. . . .

It is only another way of saying the same thing to state that conflicts of interests are not cumulative. If it were true that the dividing line in every conflict (or in all major conflicts) split the community identically in each case so that individuals who are opposed on one issue would be opposed to each other on all other issues also, while individuals who joined hands on one occasion would find themselves on the same side on all issues, always opposed to the same combination of antagonists, the cleavage created by the cumulative effect of these divisions would be fatal. But actually conflicts are not cumulative in this way. In real life the divisions are not so clearly marked, and the alignment of people according to interests requires an enormous shuffling back and forth from one side to the other, tending to dissipate the tensions created.

In view of the fact, therefore, (1) that there are many interests, including a great body of common interests, (2) that the government pursues a multiplicity of policies and creates and destroys interests in the process, (3) that each individual is capable of having many interests, (4) that interests cannot be mobilized perfectly, and (5) that conflicts among interests are not cumulative, it seems reasonable to suppose that the government is not the captive of blind forces from which there is no escape. There is nothing wrong about the raw materials of politics.

THE PARTY MODEL OF GOVERNMENT

The framers of the constitution believed in *mixed* government and at every point stressed the importance of limiting majority rule, which they essentially relegated to the House of Representatives. The "evil" factions of *Federalist 10* included, in modern terms, parties as well as interest groups. The framers' goal was deliberative, not democratic, government. Ultimately, the consent of the people, in Lockean terms, checked government, but popular consent was different than participation. A balanced and deliberative government would be more capable of acting in the national interest, thereby more likely to achieve the consent of all of the people, than would a process controlled by a popular majority or dominated by special interests.

Mixed government is the eighteenth-century model, while the idea of democratic government became ascendant in the nineteenth century. Madison and Hamilton in *The Federalist* admired and cited the mixed government of Rome as their paradigm. By the middle of the nineteenth century Athenian democracy supported the emerging nineteenth-century democratic and party model of government. Gary Wills has pointed out in his brilliant treatise, *Lincoln at Gettysburg*, that "America as a second Athens was an idea whose moment had come in the nineteenth century. This nation's founders first looked to Rome, not to Greece, for their model. Like most men of the eighteenth century, they thought of Athens as ruled by mobs. . . . The 'mixed government' of Rome—not Athens' direct democracy—was the model invoked in debates over the proper constitution for the United States."*

The party model of government transforms the consent of the people into the rule of the majority. Majority rule can only be accomplished through *aggregative* parties. Party as well as balanced government is a deliberative process, but, in eighteenth-century terms, party deliberations are aimed at achieving not the national interest but the selfish or factional interests of the party organization and its members. Electoral victory by whatever means becomes the primary goal of parties.

Proponents of party government push aside eighteenth-century skepticism of faction and democracy. The only politically viable way to define the national interest, party proponents argue, is through aggregative parties that give the electorate a choice between programs that will determine what the government will do.

In contrast to the eighteenth century, democratic and party government is based upon a belief in the rationality of man, and therefore the viability of a "government by discussion" through the mechanisms of political parties.† The framers were skeptical of raw politics and political incentives, which they viewed as more likely to be selfish than altruistic.

Woodrow Wilson expressed the ideas of the nineteenth century in his classic work, *Congressional Government,* written when he was a graduate student at Johns Hopkins University and published in 1885. He observed, "Whatever intention may have controlled the compromises of constitution-making in 1787, their result was to give us, not government by discussion, which is the only tolerable sort of government for a people which tries to do its own governing, but only legislation by discussion, which is no more than a small part of government by discussion."‡ Wilson admired the party government of Great Britain and he bemoaned the lack of leadership and discipline in American political parties. Lack of leadership, he wrote, "gives to our national parties their curious, conglomerate character. It would seem to be scarcely an exaggeration to say that they are homogeneous only in name. Neither of the two principal parties is of one mind with itself. Each tolerates all sorts of difference of creed and variety of aim within its own ranks. Each pretends to the same purposes and permits among its partisans the same contradictions to those purposes."§

Proponents of party government echoed Woodrow Wilson's views on many occasions long after he wrote. During much of the twentieth century political scientists and pundits called for stronger political parties, arguing that our weak party system is a major deficiency and barrier to effective democratic leadership. The American Political Science Association formed a committee on political parties that wrote a widely circulated report in 1950 that supported stronger political parties. The report, excerpted in the following selection, has become a lasting rallying point to the present day for those favoring party government.

**Compiler's note:* Gary Wills, *Lincoln at Gettysburg* (Touchstone: 1992), p. 42.

†*Compiler's note:* See Sir Ernst Barker, *Reflections on Government* (London: Oxford University Press, 1942).

‡*Compiler's note:* Woodrow Wilson, *Congressional Government* (New York: Meridian Books, Inc., 1956, from the original edition published in 1885), pp. 197–198.

§*Compiler's note:* Ibid, p. 210.

32

TOWARD A MORE RESPONSIBLE TWO-PARTY SYSTEM

Report of the Committee on Political Parties, American Political Science Association

Part I. The Need for Greater Party Responsibility

1. The Role of the Political Parties

1. *The Parties and Public Policy*. Throughout this report political parties are treated as indispensable instruments of government. That is to say, we proceed on the proposition *that popular government in a nation of more than 150 million people requires political parties which provide the electorate with a proper range of choice between alternatives of action*. The party system thus serves as the main device for bringing into continuing relationship those ideas about liberty, majority rule and leadership which Americans are largely taking for granted.

For the great majority of Americans, the most valuable opportunity to influence the course of public affairs is the choice they are able to make between the parties in the principal elections. While in an election the party alternative necessarily takes the form of a choice between candidates, putting a particular candidate into office is not an end in itself. The concern of the parties with candidates, elections and appointments is misunderstood if it is assumed that parties can afford to bring forth aspirants for office without regard to the views of those so selected. Actually, the party struggle is concerned with the direction of public affairs. Party nominations are no more than a means to this end. In short, party politics inevitably involves public policy in one way or another. *In order to keep the parties apart, one must consider the relations between each and public policy*.

This is not to ignore that in the past the American two-party system has shown little propensity for evolving original or creative ideas about public policy; that it has even been rather sluggish in responding to such ideas in the public interest; that it reflects in an enlarged way those differences throughout the country which are expressed in the operation of the federal structure of government; and that in all political organizations a considerable measure of irrationality manifests itself.

Giving due weight to each of these factors, we are nevertheless led to conclude that the choices provided by the two-party system are valuable to the American people in proportion to their definition in terms of public policy. *The reasons for the growing emphasis on public policy in party politics are to be found, above all, in the very operations of modern government.* With the extraordinary growth of the responsibilities of government, the discussion of public affairs for the most part makes sense only in terms of public policy.

2. *The New Importance of Program.* One of the most pressing requirements of contemporary politics is for the party in power to furnish a general kind of direction over the government as a whole. *The crux of public affairs lies in the necessity for more effective formulation of general policies and programs and for better integration of all of the far-flung activities of modern government.*

Only large-scale and representative political organizations possess the qualifications needed for these tasks. The ascendancy of national issues in an industrial society, the impact of the widening concern of government with problems of the general welfare, the entrance into the realm of politics of millions of new voters—all of these factors have tended to broaden the base of the parties as the largest political organizations in the country. *It is in terms of party programs that political leaders can attempt to consolidate public attitudes toward the work plans of government.*

Modern public policy, therefore, accentuates the importance of the parties, not as mere brokers between different groups and interests, but as agencies of the electorate. Because it affects unprecedented numbers of people and because it depends for its execution on extensive and widespread public support, modern public policy requires a broad political base. That base can be provided only by the parties, which reach people touched by no other political organization. . . .

In brief, our view is this: *The party system that is needed must be democratic, responsible and effective*—a system that is accountable to the public, respects and expresses differences of opinion, and is able to cope with the great problems of modern government. . . .

1. *An effective party system requires, first, that the parties are able to bring forth programs to which they commit themselves and, second, that the parties possess sufficient internal cohesion to carry out these programs. . . .*

Clearly *such a degree of unity within the parties cannot be brought about without party procedures that give a large body of people an opportunity to share in the development of the party program. . . .*

2. *The Need for an Effective Opposition Party.* The argument for a stronger party system cannot be divorced from measures designed to make the parties more fully accountable to the public. *The fundamental requirement of such accountability is a two-party system in which the opposition party acts as the critic of the party in power, developing, defining and presenting the policy alternatives which are necessary for a true choice in reaching public decisions. . . .*

Anything as close to the vital process of representative government as the party system is bound to affect the nation's political life in more than one way. Whatever impairs the essential operation of the party system also produces serious difficulties in other spheres of national existence. Inaction in the face of needed change in this central area therefore increases the dangers which may be present.

Four of these dangers warrant special emphasis. The first danger is that the inadequacy of the party system in sustaining well-considered programs and providing broad public support for them may lead to grave consequences in an explosive era. The second danger is that the American people may go too far for the safety of constitutional government in compensating for this inadequacy by shifting excessive responsibility to the President. The third danger is that with growing public cynicism and continuing proof of the ineffectiveness of the party system the nation may eventually witness the disintegration of the two major parties. The fourth danger is that the incapacity of the two parties for consistent action based on meaningful programs may rally support for extremist parties poles apart, each fanatically bent on imposing on the country its particular panacea. . . .

3. *The Danger of Overextending the Presidency.* The presidency is the greatest political office in this country. There is no other republic, in fact, that entrusts to its President as much constitutional responsibility as Americans have entrusted to the President of the United States.

He is the Chief Executive, and as such in command not only of the civilian departments of the Federal Government but also of the whole military establishment. His executive authority puts at his disposal all the administrative resources—in management, fact-finding, analysis and planning—that are available in the departmental system. By making authoritative legislative proposals and exercising his veto power, the President under the Constitution has a significant share in the work of Congress. In addition, he is the central figure in the leadership of his party, in and out of Congress.

It is still more important, perhaps, that the President is the only politically responsible organ of government that has the whole nation as constituency. Elected by the people at large, the President must look upon himself as its spokesman. In him alone all Americans find a single voice in national affairs.

It is therefore a natural tendency that time and again governmental responsibility for formulation of coherent programs and unity of action has been placed upon the President. He has been charged with the preparation of the annual budget—the work plan of the Federal Government that goes to Congress for review and final determination. He has also been charged with the presentation of the government's economic program, submitted to Congress in the periodic economic reports of the President. He cannot relinquish the burden of establishing the general lines of American foreign policy. He has been charged with the development of coordinated policies to safeguard the country's national security.

In each of these large areas, the President is called upon to prepare the ground, to initiate the process of program formulation, to come forth with proposed programs for which he is prepared to assume political responsibility. As a result, Congress has the benefit of prior effort and concrete recommendations. This division of functions reflects a sound formula, evolved in practical experience. But to apply it effectively, somewhere *dependable political support has to be built up for the governmental program* as finally adopted. *When there is no other place to get that done, when the political parties fail to do it, it is tempting once more to turn to the President.*

But the President has no magic wand. If he acts in pursuit of a broad program that has been democratically formulated in his party, nearly all of his party is likely to put itself behind the measures called for by the program. Then the question of political support presents no difficulties, which is the solution suggested in this report. Lacking his party's support for a broad program, the President is left with only one course. He can attempt to fill the void caused by the absence of an effective party program by working up a broad political program of his own.

If he does, however, he has to go out and build the necessary support for that program through his personal effort without benefit of party. There are people who say that this is a realistic way of getting somewhere with good political ideas, especially ideas bound to leave cool both Congress and the larger part of the President's party. Some others say that the scheme is not the happiest thing but the only one practically available under presidential-congressional government.

Yet can there be much doubt about the ultimate implications? When the President's program actually is the sole program in this sense, either his party becomes a flock of sheep or the party falls apart. In effect this concept of the presidency disposes of the party system by making the President reach directly for the support of a majority of the voters. It favors a President who exploits skillfully the arts of demagoguery, who uses the whole country as his political backyard, and who does not mind turning into the embodiment of personal government. . . .

4. *The Danger of Disintegration of the Two Parties*. It is a thing both familiar and deeply disturbing that many Americans have only caustic words or disdainful shrugs of the shoulder for the party system as it operates today. . . .

A chance that the electorate will turn its back upon the two parties is by no means academic. As a matter of fact, this development has already occurred in considerable part, and it is still going on. Present conditions are a great incentive for the voters to dispose of the parties as intermediaries between themselves and the government. In a way, a sizable body of the electorate has shifted from hopeful interest in the parties to the opposite attitude. This mass of voters sees itself as the President's or his opponent's direct electoral support.

Continued alienation between increasing numbers of voters and both major parties is an ominous tendency. It has a splintering effect and may lead to a system of several smaller parties. *American political institutions are too firmly grounded upon the two-party system to make its collapse a small matter.*

Orientation of the American two-party system along the lines of meaningful national programs . . . is a way of keeping differences within bounds. It is a way of reinforcing the constitutional framework within which the voter may without peril exercise his freedom of political choice.

Political parties and elections play a central role in democratic theory. Parties aggregate political and economic interests, and party competition, particularly in a two-party system, gives the electorate a choice in determining the course of government. But the American political system is not based solely on democratic theory or party government. On the contrary, the Constitution discourages political parties through the separation of powers, and dampens direct democracy through a number of devices, including the separation of powers, bicameralism, and provisions requiring extraordinary majorities to make treaties, amend the Constitution, and impeach the president. Political parties have nevertheless been present in the political process since the adoption of the Constitution. How parties may be more important to political choices in the twenty-first century is the subject of the following selection.

33

TOWARD A RESPONSIBLE PARTY SYSTEM?

Arthur Paulson

Political scientists have generally agreed about the importance of political parties to democracy. E. E. Schattschneider expressed the consensus with his oft-cited remark that "democracy is unthinkable save in terms of parties." There has been disagreement, however, about both the possibility and desirability of a responsible party system in the United States.

As long ago as 1950, the American Political Science Association Committee on Political Parties, speaking as much or more as citizens than political scientists, advocated reforms to develop a responsible party system in the United States. Their work followed upon that of Schattschneider and laid the groundwork for subsequent political scientists who would advocate reform in the direction of the responsible party model.

Advocates of a responsible two-party system have done excellent comparative analysis of party systems and presented a strong normative argument for responsible parties. But they have not demonstrated the possibility of a responsible party system in the United States. Meanwhile, critics of the responsible party model have made the same error as theorists who see only party decay and the end of realignment: Their analysis is ahistorical, superimposing the nineteenth century political party on the twenty-first century. Critics seem to assume, incorrectly, that if the nineteenth-century umbrella party is in decline, it cannot be replaced in the United States by any other form of party.

The emergence of a conservative party and a liberal party in American politics leads to speculation that the historic umbrella parties will be replaced by a responsible party system, not unlike those found in parliamentary democracies. It is a question of continuing analytic interest to political scientists, as well as a normative issue for those concerned about the outlook for American democracy in the twenty-first century.

A responsible party system exhibits the following three requisite characteristics:

1. **A responsible party system requires a functional, if not constitutional, fusion of powers between the executive and legislative branches.** In short, a responsible party system produces party government. The constitutional separation

of powers makes this characteristic of responsible parties very problematic for the United States. In the American experience, policy-making has taken on a responsible party appearance periodically, usually during periods of critical realignment.

The possibility of a responsible party system and party government is reduced further by the bicameralism of the American Congress. Whereas the American system is a Presidential democracy, with powers separated between the executive and legislative branches, the United Kingdom is the purest example of parliamentary democracy with a responsible party system, marked by a fusion of powers, in which the executive leadership of the government, the prime minister and cabinet, is the political leadership of the majority in the House of Commons. The prime minister and cabinet are themselves members of the House of Commons, and govern with its confidence. They serve terms of five years or less, so long as they maintain the support of the parliamentary majority. Finally, the British system is functionally unicameral: The House of Lords has become a symbolic appendage of the Parliament. In such a system, responsible parties can govern, or offer a loyal opposition to the government, and the executive has the votes in the legislature to deliver on its policy programs.

Periods of gridlock in policy-making in recent years have been commonly associated with divided government in the separation-of-powers system. Historically, however, there is no such necessary association. Certainly, unified government has been associated with policy-making efficiency during realigning periods such as with the Democratic majorities of the New Deal. And, just as certainly, divided government has sometimes led to policy stasis. But divided government has also often been productive. The reforms of the aptly named Progressive Era were often the product of bipartisan progressive majorities in Congress under both Republican and Democratic Presidents. The bipartisan foreign policy for two decades after World War II by definition did not require united government. The Federal Highway Act during the Eisenhower administration was a public works project of record dimensions that did nothing less than redesign the American community after passing with nearly unanimous support from both parties in Congress. The civil rights legislation of 1957–1965 was the product of a bipartisan liberal majority. Finally, Reaganomics passed a Democratic Congress with conservative majorities in both houses. All but Reaganomics were examples drawn from periods when the ideological spectrum of both major political parties spanned from liberal to conservative. Even Reaganomics required the support of conservative Democrats to pass. In all these cases, bipartisan ideological or centrist majorities were assembled.

The party system has changed, in government as in the electorate. . . . As "realignment at the top" has spread to the "bottom," that is, as the realignment in Presidential elections has spread over a thirty-year period to Congressional elections, the political parties in Congress have become ideologically polarized. Divided government now, unlike cases of divided government in much of American history, is government divided between ideologically polarized parties, and thus, is associated more definitively with gridlock. The result is that unified government will probably be more important to legislative productivity in the future than it has been in the past. The Clinton economic package of 1993, for example, passed only with a strict enforcement of party loyalty among the Democrats in Congress. Since then, with the exception of welfare reform, divided government, now with a Democratic

President and a Republican Congress, has left behind a decrease in legislative productivity. The government shutdown in 1995 is a dramatic example of the association between partisan ideological polarization and policy paralysis. Even the budget deals since then disguise the fact that controversies involving the budget in the longer term, Social Security and Medicare, and any prospective tax cut, were not addressed, resulting in a "pork," bill to the perceived advantage of incumbents of both parties. The important policy decisions were left to another day when, the leaders of each party hope, they will control both the Presidency and Congress. . . . [T]he new similarity between Presidential election and Congressional election coalitions makes it likely that elections will result in unified government more frequently than has been the case over the past thirty years. Quietly, even in the face of the separation of powers, the ideological polarization of the major parties may yet be producing at least an approximation of responsible parties and party government in the twenty-first century.

2. Responsible parties present clear ideological or programmatic alternatives, can govern when in the majority, and can offer organized loyal opposition when in the minority. American political parties have not fit the responsible party model, with the possible infrequent exception of electoral moments known as critical realignments. Instead, American parties are historically umbrella parties, nonideological coalitions of factions with diverse interests.

Critics of the responsible party model have pointed out that spatially distinct programmatic and ideological political parties are contrary to the American experience and are in any case not a prerequisite to a "responsible electorate." Indeed, according to critics, ideological polarization has been an important ingredient of party decay, not the sort of party development that would seem to be necessary for a responsible party system to emerge.

. . . . [W]hat has declined [however] is not the American political party, per se, but the locally-based, nonideological umbrella party born in the nineteenth century. What is emerging is a party system featuring two ideologically homogenized political parties offering the electorate much more polarized choices than has generally been the American experience. Historically, the function of umbrella parties has been interest aggregation, more than interest articulation, which has been the function of interest groups rather than parties. But with liberal Democrats and conservative Republicans each the dominant factions in their parties, and with liberal interest groups operating almost entirely within the Democratic Party and conservative interest groups operating almost entirely within the Republican Party, parties at the turn of the twenty-first century are increasingly engaged in interest articulation.

The ideological polarization between the major parties, however, is much more advanced on issues couched in social and cultural terms, such as race or abortion, than on economic issues. The low level of class consciousness in American political culture leaves the system still without a labor party. Both parties are ideologically classic liberal and capitalist political parties, a fact that is not likely to change in the foreseeable future. Within that context, the Democrats remain the party more likely to support government intervention in the economy, and more likely to support it at the national level. The Republicans remain the party less likely to support government intervention, and when they do, more likely to support it at the state level. It remains easier to compromise economic issues, as Walter Dean Burnham observed. But two trends may change that. First, economic issues are themselves discussed more in cultural terms. The debates about welfare reform, for example, were laden with references to moral responsibility and racial stereotypes. Second, as advanced capitalist societies develop structurally low-growth economies with rapid technological change increasing structural unemployment, economic issues will become more of the sorts of either-or issues that social and cultural issues are; in a lower-growth economy, economic issues become more zero-sum and harder to compromise. Even if both parties are capitalist parties, then, economic choices will become inherently more extreme, and lend themselves to ideological polarization.

The nationalization of American political parties facilitates the development of responsible parties. . . . The decentralized umbrella parties prior to 1964 tended to nominate candidates who did not represent clear ideological alternatives. In northeastern states, both the Democrats and Republicans nominated relatively liberal candidates; in the south, both parties (where the Republicans functioned) tended to nominate conservatives. In the more nationalized and ideologically polarized parties of the post-New Deal period, ideologically motivated issue activists have come to control nominations in candidate-centered caucuses and primaries. As a result, Republican nominees at every level of office tend to be the more conservative in every region of the country, and Democratic nominees tend to be the more liberal. The result is a national articulation of more distinct interests and issue alternatives in campaigns both for the Presidency and for Congress.

3. In a responsible party system, the executive and legislative branches have fundamentally the same electoral base. The American separation-of-powers system not only separates executive from legislative policy-making processes, it separates electoral processes and staggers elections, making possible the incidence of divided government. . . . With Presidential elections set every four years, elections for the House of Representatives every two years, and elections of one-third of the U.S. Senate every two years, the constitutional system of staggered elections separates electoral results temporally, as well as geographically. Since 1789, American voters have never voted in what the British electorate has at least every five years: a national general election.

Responsible party systems in parliamentary governments create an electoral and governing marriage between the executive and legislative "branches" whether they are constitutionally fused or not. That is, the prime minister and the parliament rely upon each other to stay in office, requiring a governing coalition that links the two to each other and to the electorate.

The debate during the [Clinton] impeachment process illustrates how unusual the American political system is among advanced democracies. The defenders of President Clinton argued that his conduct did not rise to the "constitutional" level of impeachment. Such an argument would be irrelevant in a parliamentary motion of no confidence, which is by definition political. But in a parliamentary democracy, the removal of the executive generally means either the selection of a new one by the majority, or the closing of the parliament, followed by a national election.

Although staggered elections separate the electoral foundations of the executive and legislative branches in American government, unified government has usually been the rule, anyway. Indeed, American political parties have briefly, if temporarily, resembled responsible parties, during periodic critical realignments. [Previously, I] presented the case for two propositions that, if true, would lead American parties to resemble responsible parties more frequently in the twenty-first century. First, the resolution of factional struggles in both major parties and an associated critical realignment in Presidential elections between 1964 and 1972 left in their wake an ideologically polarized party system at the national level. Second, secular realignment since that time has created party coalitions in Congressional elections very similar to the ones that emerged in Presidential elections in the 1964–1972 period. Borrowing from and editing the language of James Q. Wilson, [I have] referred to this process as "critical realignment at the top, secular realignment at the bottom."

For three decades after 1964, ideological polarization between the Democrats and Republicans in Presidential elections was not matched in Congressional elections. The south, for most of that time, violated its historic voting habits by supporting Republicans in Presidential elections, but continued to vote Democratic for the House and Senate. Electoral change in the south in Congressional elections was slow in coming, but it did evolve. Finally, in 1994, the Republicans won majorities in both houses of Congress for the first time in fifty years. More important, the Republicans ran for the House of Representatives on a national platform, the "Contract with America." Self-consciously conservative, the contract was promoted by virtually all Republican candidates for the House and particularly by Newt Gingrich. When the Republicans won the House, and he was installed as Speaker, Gingrich set himself up almost as if he were Prime Minister of the United States. His political fall since that time does reduce this trend toward nationalized and ideologically polarized parties. Indeed, the impeachment of President Clinton was continuing evidence of developing partisanship in the American Congress, which is almost parliamentary in its dimensions.

The analysis here and in the previous chapters indicates that, at the least, a responsible party system can no longer be discounted as impossible in the United States. The constitutional constraints against it have not been eliminated, nor are they likely to be. We have a new party system that increasingly resembles the responsible party model, but we do not have party government. That is, we have a party system that is increasingly appropriate to a parliamentary democracy, but we do not live in a parliamentary democracy.

The constitutional constraints, however, important as they are, do not change the fact that the ideological polarization in the American party system is something brand new, and it will have a telling impact on the political life of American democracy.

POLITICAL PARTIES IN DIVIDED GOVERNMENT

A recurring and important theme of commentators on the American political system is that the separation of powers between the president and Congress produces a deadlock of democracy. Major constitutional change to unify the president and Congress by creating a parliamentary system is unrealistic and completely out of the question. Critics of divided government have proposed more disciplined political parties to unify the president and Congress, thereby helping to overcome the effects of the separation of powers. Putting aside the fact that the separation of powers itself makes party government difficult if not impossible, in theory would disciplined political parties that unified the executive and legislative branches make an important difference? In the following selection, political scientist David Mayhew presents the provocative and important thesis that the divided government, which the separation of powers produces, works as well as the unified government that party discipline would create.

34

DIVIDED WE GOVERN

David R. Mayhew

Introduction

Since World War II, divided party control of the American national government has come to seem normal. Between the 1946 and 1990 elections, one of the two parties held the presidency, the Senate, and the House simultaneously for eighteen of those years. But control was divided for twenty-six years, it is divided right now, and we may see more such splits. Some opinion studies suggest that today's voters prefer divided control on principle: Parties jointly in power are seen to perform a service by checking each other.

Of course, divided control is not a new phenomenon. During a twenty-two-year stretch between 1874 and 1896, to take the extreme case, the two parties shared control of the government for sixteen years. But after that, the country settled into a half-century habit of unified control broken only by two-year transitions from one party's monopoly to the other's that closed out the Taft, Wilson, and Hoover administrations. It is against this immediate background that the post–World War II experience stands out.

Should we care whether party control is unified or divided? That depends on whether having one state of affairs rather than the other makes any important difference. Does it? Much received thinking says yes. The political party, according to one of political science's best-known axioms about the American system, is "the indispensable instrument that [brings] cohesion and unity, and hence effectiveness, to the government as a whole by linking the executive and legislative branches in a bond of common interest." In the words of Woodrow Wilson, "You cannot compound a successful government out of antagonisms."

At a concrete level, this means at least that significant lawmaking can be expected to fall off when party control is divided. "Deadlock" or "stalemate" will set in. Variants of this familiar claim could be cited endlessly. Randall B. Ripley argued in a 1969 study, for example: "To have a productive majority in the American system of government the President and a majority of both houses must be from the same party. Such a condition does not guarantee legislative success but is necessary for it." V. O. Key, Jr., wrote: "Common partisan control of executive and legislature does not assure energetic government, but division of party control precludes it." . . . These authors do not argue that unified party control always generates large collections of notable legislation. But they can be read to predict that it should generate, over a long period of time when contrasted with divided control, considerably more such legislation.

Another familiar claim has to do with congressional oversight. It is that Congress acting as an investigative body will give more trouble to the executive branch when a president of the opposite party holds power. That propensity can be viewed as bad or good. Woodrow Wilson might say that accelerated probing of the executive provides just another kind of unfortunate "antagonism." From another perspective, it can be expected to keep presidents and bureaucrats in line better. Either way, what causes the effect is a predicted difference between unified and divided control. Morris S. Ogul has written, "A congressman of the president's party is less likely to be concerned with oversight than a member of the opposition party." . . .

I . . . argue . . . that the above claims are wrong, or at least mostly or probably wrong. . . . But are there not . . . ways in which unified as opposed to divided party control might make a significant difference?

There are. In closing, five such ways will be introduced here by posing questions and speculating briefly about what their answers might be. In all instances the speculation ends in skepticism: Unified versus divided control has probably not made a notable difference during the postwar era. . . .

The first question is: Even if important laws win enactment just as often under conditions of divided party control, might they not be *worse* laws? Isn't "seriously defective legislation" a likelier result? That is sometimes alleged, and if true it would obviously count heavily. The subject is murky, even if kept free of ideological tests of "worseness," but the case seems to have a two-pronged logic. First, enacting coalitions under divided control, being composed of elements not "naturally" united on policy goals, might be less apt to write either clear ends or efficient means into their statutes. Second, such coalitions, absolved from unambiguous "party government" checks by the electorate down the line, might worry less about the actual effects of laws.

These are reasonable enough logics and instances, but the overall case is dubious. . . .

The second question is: Even if important individual statutes can win enactment regardless of conditions of party control, how about programmatic "coherence" across statutes? Isn't that a likelier outcome under unified party control? The argument is sometimes made. Confronted by this claim, one's first response is to note that "coherence" exists in the eyes of beholders, that beholders differ in what they see, and in any event, why is "coherence" necessary or desirable? Democracy, according to some leading models, can function well enough as an assortment of decentralized, unconnected incursions into public affairs. . . .

Still, widespread agreement does exist about the features and importance of at least two patterns of coherence across statutes, and those should be considered. One is *ideological coherence*, for which an argument might go as follows. To permit broad-ranging change of the sort recommended by ideologies that arise now and then, and to provide a graspable politics to sectors of the public who might be interested in such change, a system needs to allow ideological packaging. That is, it needs to allow, at least sometimes, the enactment of rather large collections of laws thrusting in the same ideological direction. But such packaging has already been discussed. The postwar American system has accommodated it under circumstances of both unified and divided party control—notably in the successfully enacted presidential programs of Johnson (UNI) and Reagan (DIV), and in the liberal legislative surge of 1963 through 1975–76 (UNI then DIV). Presidential programs, given their properties as drama, can probably reach the general public more effectively, but ideological surges arising from "moods" can unquestionably engage appreciable sectors of the public.

Then there is *budgetary coherence*—that is, a match between revenue and expenditure across all government programs. Whether such a match occurs is of course ultimately a matter of statutes, including appropriations bills. It goes without saying that the federal government's immense deficits have daunted and preoccupied the country's political elite as much as anything during the last decade. For some observers, the deficits have also posed a clear test of divided party control, which it has flunked. A single ruling party would have done better, the argument goes, for reasons either of ideological uniformity or electoral accountability. Lloyd N. Cutler made the latter argument in 1988: "If one party was responsible for all three power centers [House, Senate, and presidency] and produced deficits of the magnitude in which they have been produced in recent years, there would be no question of the accountability and the responsibility of that party and its elected public officials for what had happened."

Is this a valid case, finally, against divided party control? That has to remain an open question, since not much scholarship has yet appeared about the history of budgeting as it may have been affected by conditions of party control; also, highly relevant events will no doubt continue to take place. But the case is considerably less compelling than it may first look. For one thing, there is evidently no statistical relation between divided party control and deficit financing over the two centuries of American national history, or more specifically since World War II. That recent period includes the 1950s, it is useful to remember, when Eisenhower, who faced Democratic Congresses for six years, fought major political battles and drew much criticism from liberal intellectuals because he would not accept unbalanced budgets. Taking into account size of deficit or surplus, what the postwar pattern does show is a "sudden break" under Reagan. Deficits "blossomed suddenly in 1981." A time series of federal debt as a percentage of gross national product falls almost monotonically from 1946 through 1974, holds more or less steady until 1981, and then surges. The 1980s are the problem.

An explanation that seems to fit this pre-1980 versus post-1980 experience involves not conditions of party control but rather individual presidents' policies. At least since World War II, according to Paul E. Peterson, Congress "has generally followed the presidential lead on broad fiscal policies." Overall congressional appropriations—that is, for each year the total across all programs—have ordinarily come quite close to overall presidential spending requests. Changes in total revenue generated by congressional tax enactments have ordinarily approximated those proposed by presidents. . . .

The third question is: Doesn't government administration suffer as a result of divided party control? Doesn't exaggerated pulling and hauling between president and Congress undermine the implementation of laws and, in general, the functioning of agencies and the administration of programs? High-publicity Capitol Hill investigations, which have been discussed, are relevant to an answer, but the subject is broader than that. It is also vaguer and quite difficult to address. The strategy here will be to present a plausible case *for* an instance of such undermining of administration and then draw a historical comparison. This will scarcely exhaust the topic, but the instances to be compared are important in their own right as well as suggestive about conditions of party control in general.

The plausible instance is Congress's thrust toward "micro-managing" the executive branch in recent decades. That is, Congress has greatly increased its staff who monitor the administration, multiplied its days of oversight hearings, greatly expanded its use of the legislative veto (until a federal court ruled that device unconstitutional in 1983), taken to writing exceptionally detailed statutes that limit bureaucratic discretion (notably in environmental law), and tried to trim presidential power through such measures as the War Powers Act of 1973 and the Budget and Impoundment Act of 1974. Whether these moves have helped or harmed the system can be argued either way, but let us stipulate for the moment that they have undermined administration.

Has "micro-management" resulted, at least partly, from divided party control of the government? That too can be argued either way. An abundant list of alternative causes includes public and congressional reaction to the Vietnam war (as conducted by both Johnson and Nixon) and the public's rising distrust of bureaucracy. But let us hypothesize that divided party control is at least partly the cause. Here is the argument. Rather than appearing gradually, "micro-management" came into its own rather quickly under Nixon and Ford in the 1970s—especially during the Nixon-Ford term of 1973–76. To cite some quantitative evidence, days spent per year on congressional oversight hearings, and average number of pages per enacted law (an indicator of statutory detail), achieved *most* of the considerable increase they showed from 1961 through 1984 during just the four years of 1973–76.

That was during a period of divided party control. Obviously, micro-management has not flashed on whenever party control became divided (as under Eisenhower) or flashed off whenever it became unified (as under Carter). Much of it, at least, came in under Nixon-Ford and stayed. One might say that those years saw the initiation of a "regime" of micro-management—that is, a durable set of views and institutionally located practices could survive the transition to Carter and then to Reagan. Their origin is what counts. To implicate divided party control plausibly, one has to argue that two conditions were necessary for this "micro-management regime" to come into existence. First, party control had to be divided: Congress would not have inaugurated such a regime otherwise. Second, there had to occur some unusual shock to the system such as Watergate, Nixon's conduct of the war, or simply Nixon's aggressive presidency: Divided control would not have engendered such a regime otherwise. Divided control, that is, was a necessary *part* of the causal structure that triggered the regime.

That is a plausible, particular argument. Can it be generalized? The broader case would be that members of a relevant class of congressional regimes that includes the micro-management one—that is, regimes that can reasonably be alleged to undermine administration—can be expected to arise under the same circumstances. That is, they require some similar shock to the system plus a background of divided party control.

Has any other such regime ever existed? As it happens, what looks like a particularly good instance of one originated in 1938 and led a vibrant life through 1954. It was that era's "loyalty regime"—the brilliant innovation of Democratic Congressman Martin Dies of Texas, founder of the House Un-American Activities Committee. Dies pioneered a formula that carried through the Hiss, McCarran, Army-McCarthy and other investigations after the war. It was a low-cost, high-publicity, committee-centered way of waging a congressional opposition against the New Deal, the Truman administration, and then Eisenhower. Its chief technique was the hearing where someone could accuse members of the executive branch of being disloyal to the United States. No one should be surprised that that evidently had a pronounced effect on administration. Beyond its effects on the targeted personnel, it could demoralize agencies, preoccupy the White House, put a chill on unorthodox policy options, and even exile whole schools of thought from the government (as with China specialists after 1949).

It seems a good bet that this loyalty regime made as much of a mark on administration—to be sure, its own kind of mark—as has Congress's more recent micro-management regime. . . .

The fourth question is: Does the conduct of foreign policy suffer under divided party control? That might be a special concern, since "coordination" is often held to be central to effective foreign policymaking. Perhaps an excess of "deadlock" or "non-coordination" occurs under conditions of divided control. But of course such disorderliness, looked at from the other side as by opponents of Truman's China policy or Reagan's Central America policy, figures as a healthy exercise of checks and balances. Foreign policy is often a fighting matter at home. There does not seem to be any way around this. "Coordination," however much sense it may seem to make, does not and cannot dominate every other value.

Yet once past that realization, it is not clear what standards to apply. None will be proposed here. But let the reader try the following thought experiment. Choose any plausible set of standards and, using them, scan through the history of American foreign policymaking since World War II. Here is a prediction of what most readers will conclude: In general, the record was no worse when the two parties shared power. Any appraisal has to accommodate or steer around, for example, the Marshall Plan, which owed to bipartisan cooperation during a time of divided control; the Kennedy-Johnson intervention in Indochina, which, whatever else may be said about it, scarcely took its shape because of a lack of coordination; Nixon's openings to China and the Soviet Union, which were maneuvered with little Capitol Hill dissent during a time of divided control; and Bush's liberation of Kuwait in 1990–91. Given just these items, many readers may agree, considerable ingenuity would be needed to concoct a verdict spanning the four and a half decades that favors unified party control. . . .

The fifth question: Are the country's lower-income strata served less well under divided party control? One can assemble a theory that they might be, assuming for a moment that "serve" refers to direct government action rather than, say, encouragement of long-term economic growth. Separation of powers biases the American regime toward the rich, Progressive theorists used to argue at the outset of the twentieth century. The rich profit when the government does nothing, whereas the non-rich require concerted public action that can all too easily be blocked somewhere in the system's ample array of veto-points. An obvious remedy would be a constitution allowing strict majority rule. But lacking that, according to a conventional argument of political science, much depends on political parties. Their distinctive role is to impose on the country's collection of government institutions a kind of order that serves majority interests. In principle, that might be done by one party embodying the views and experiences of the non-rich (a socialist sort of argument) or by two parties bidding for the votes of the non-rich (a Downsian sort of argument). Either way, unified control is needed to deliver the goods. It allows action, rules out buck-passing, fixes responsibility, permits accountability.

That is a plausible line of argument, and the Great Society as well as the New Deal might be said to bear it out. But altogether too much of the record since World War II does not. What were the origins of the "social safety net" that the Reagan administration—during a time of divided control, for what that is worth—succeeded in widening the holes of? In fact, that net owed much of its weaving to the Nixon and Ford years—also a time of divided control. That period was the source of EEA and CETA jobs, expanded unemployment insurance, low-income energy assistance, post-1974 housing allowances, Pell grants for lower-income college students, greatly multiplied food-stamps assistance, a notable progressivizing of tax incidence, Supplementary Security Income for the aged, blind, and disabled, and Social Security increases that cut the proportion of aged below the poverty line from 25 percent in 1970 to 16 percent in 1974. The laws just kept getting passed. The Reaganite assault against both the Great Society and the 1970s pitted era against era and mood against mood. But it did not pit divided party control against unified party control or even all that clearly Republicans against Democrats.

These five questions are not the only additional ones that might be asked about unified as opposed to divided party control. This work skirts, moreover, the separate and obviously important question of whether the American system of government, with its separation-of-powers features, has been functioning adequately in recent times. Some analysts, for example John E. Chubb and Paul E. Peterson, say no: "When governments of quite different political combinations [that is, unified as well as divided control] all fail to perform effectively, it is worth considering whether the problem is the government itself and not the people or parties that run it." Energy and budgetary policies have been creaking. Each of the last two decades has ended with a riveting spectacle of government inefficacy or disorder—Carter's "malaise" crisis in 1979 and Bush's budget wrangle in 1990. Otherwise, the country is faced with declining voter turnout as well as a rise in election technologies and incumbent-serving practices that seem to be delegitimizing elected officials.

There is no end of taking steps to reform American political institutions, or of good reasons for it. But short of jettisoning the separation-of-powers core of the Constitution—an unlikely event—it would probably be a mistake to channel such concern into "party government" schemes. This work has tried to show that, surprisingly, it does not seem to make all that much difference whether party control of the American government happens to be unified or divided. One reason we assume it does is that "party government" plays a role in political science somewhere between a Platonic form and a grail. When we reach for it as a standard, we draw on abstract models, presumed European practice, and well-airbrushed American experience, but we seldom take a cold look at real American experience. We forget about Franklin Roosevelt's troubles with HUAC and the Rules Committee, Truman's and Kennedy's domestic policy defeats, McCarthy's square-off against Eisenhower, Johnson versus Fulbright on Vietnam, and Carter's energy program and "malaise."

Political parties can be powerful instruments, but in the United States they seem to play more of a role as "policy factions" than as, in the British case, governing instruments. A party as policy faction can often get its way even in circumstances of divided control: Witness the Taftite Republicans in 1947, congressional Democrats under Nixon, or the Reaganites in 1981. How, one might ask, were these temporary policy ascendancies greatly different from that of the Great Society Democrats in 1964–66?

To demand more of American parties—to ask that they become governing instruments—is to run them up against components of the American regime as fundamental as the party system itself. There is a strong pluralist component, for example, as evidenced in the way politicians respond to cross-cutting issue cleavages. There is a public-opinion component that political science's modern technologies do not seem to reach very well. The government floats in public opinion; it goes up and down on great long waves of it that often have little to do with parties. There is the obvious structural component—separation of powers—that brings on deadlock and chronic conflict, but also nudges officials toward deliberation, compromise, and super-majority outcomes. And there is a component of deep-seated individualism among American politicians, who build and tend their own electoral bases and maintain their own relations of responsibility with electorates. This seems to be a matter of political culture—perhaps a survival of republicanism—that goes way back. Unlike most politicians elsewhere, American ones at both legislative and executive levels have managed to navigate the last two centuries of history without becoming minions of party leaders. In this complicated, multi-component setting, British-style governing by party majorities does not have much of a chance.

FUNCTIONS AND TYPES OF ELECTIONS

Most people transmit their political desires to government through elections. Elections are a critical part of the democratic process, and the existence of *free* elections is a major difference between democracies and totalitarian or authoritarian forms of government. Because elections reflect popular attitudes toward governmental parties, policies, and personalities, it is useful to attempt to classify different types of elections on the basis of changes and trends that take place within the electorate. Every election is not the same. For example, the election of 1932, with the resulting Democratic landslide, was profoundly different from the election of 1960, in which Kennedy won by less than 1 percent of the popular vote.

Members of the Center for Political Studies at the University of Michigan, as well as V. O. Key, Jr., have developed a typology of elections that is useful in analyzing the electoral system. The most prevalent type of election can be classified as a "maintaining election," "one in which the pattern of partisan attachments prevailing in the preceding period persists and is the primary influence on the forces governing the vote."* Most elections fall into the maintaining category, a fact significant for the political system because such elections result in political continuity and reflect a lack of serious upheavals within the electorate and government. Maintaining elections result in the continuation of the majority political party.

At certain times in American history, what V. O. Key, Jr., has called "critical elections" take place. He discusses this type of election, which results in permanent realignment of the electorate and reflects basic changes in political attitudes.

Apart from maintaining and critical elections, a third type, in which only temporary shifts take place within the electorate, occurs, which can be called "deviating elections." For example, the Eisenhower victories of 1952 and 1956 were deviating elections for several reasons, including the personality of Eisenhower and the fact that voters could register their choice for president without changing their basic partisan loyalties at congressional and state levels. Deviating elections, with reference to the office of president, are probable when popular figures are running for the office.

In "reinstating elections," a final category that can be added to a typology of elections, there is a return to normal voting patterns. Reinstating elections take place after deviating elections as a result of the demise of the temporary forces that caused the transitory shift

---

**Compiler's note:* Angus Campbell, Philip E. Converse, Warren E. Miller, and Donald E. Stokes, *The American Voter* (New York: John Wiley & Sons, 1960), Chapter 19.

in partisan choice. The election of 1960, in which most of the Democratic majority in the electorate returned to the fold and voted for John F. Kennedy,* has been classified as a reinstating election.

35

A THEORY OF CRITICAL ELECTIONS

V. O. Key, Jr.

Perhaps the basic differentiating characteristic of democratic order consists in the expression of effective choice by the mass of the people in elections. The electorate occupies, at least in the mystique of such orders, the position of the principal organ of governance; it acts through elections. An election itself is a formal act of collective decision that occurs in a stream of connected antecedent and subsequent behavior. Among democratic orders elections, so broadly defined, differ enormously in their nature, their meaning, and their consequences. Even within a single nation the reality of election differs greatly from time to time. A systematic comparative approach, with a focus on variations in the nature of elections would doubtless be fruitful in advancing the understanding of the democratic governing process. In behavior antecedent to voting, elections differ in the proportions of the electorate psychologically involved, in the intensity of attitudes associated with campaign cleavages, in the nature of expectations about the consequences of the voting, in the impact of objective events relevant to individual political choice, in individual sense of effective connection with community decision, and in other ways. These and other antecedent variations affect the act of voting itself as well as subsequent behavior. An understanding of elections and, in turn, of the democratic process as a whole must rest partially on broad differentiations of the complexes of behavior that we call elections.

**Compiler's note:* See Philip E. Converse, Angus Campbell, Warren E. Miller, and Donald E. Stokes, "Stability and Change in 1960: A Reinstating Election," *The American Political Science Review* 55 (June 1961): 269–280.

While this is not the occasion to develop a comprehensive typology of elections, the foregoing remarks provide an orientation for an attempt to formulate a concept of one type of election—based on American experience—which might be built into a more general theory of elections. Even the most fleeting inspection of American elections suggests the existence of a category of elections in which voters are, at least from impressionistic evidence, unusually deeply concerned, in which the extent of electoral involvement is relatively quite high, and in which the decisive results of the voting reveal a sharp alteration of the preexisting cleavage within the electorate. Moreover, and perhaps this is the truly differentiating characteristic of this sort of election, the realignment made manifest in the voting in such elections seems to persist for several succeeding elections. All these characteristics cumulate to the conception of an election type in which the depth and intensity of electoral involvement are high, in which more or less profound readjustments occur in the relations of power within the community, and in which new and durable electoral groupings are formed. These comments suppose, of course, the existence of other types of complexes of behavior centering about formal elections, the systematic isolation and identification of which, fortunately, are not essential for the present discussion.

I

The presidential election of 1928 in the New England states provides a specific case of the type of critical election that has been described in general terms. In that year Alfred E. Smith, the Democratic presidential candidate, made gains in all the New England states. The rise in Democratic strength was especially notable in Massachusetts and Rhode Island. When one probes below the surface of the gross election figures it becomes apparent that a sharp and durable realignment also

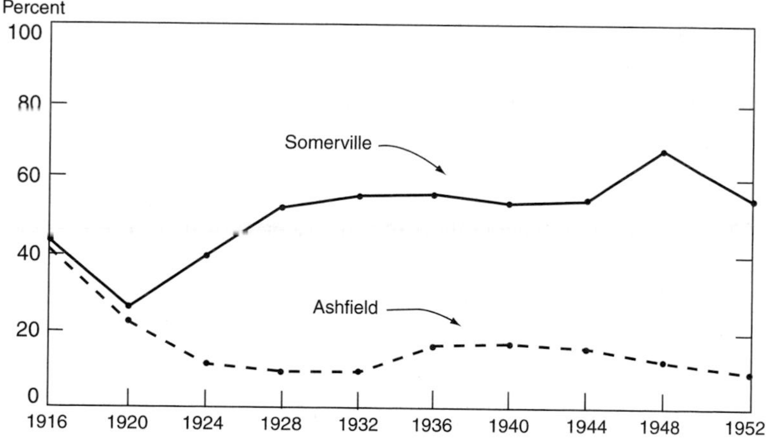

Figure A *Democratic Percentages of Major-Party Presidential Vote, Somerville and Ashfield, Massachusetts, 1916–1952*

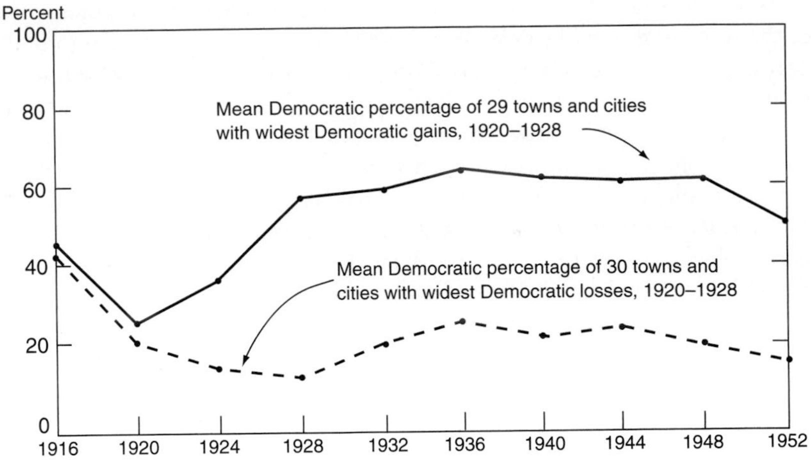

Figure B *Persistence of Electoral Cleavage of 1928 in Massachusetts*

occurred within the electorate, a fact reflective of the activation by the Democratic candidate of low-income, Catholic, urban voters of recent immigrant stock. In New England, at least, the Roosevelt revolution of 1932 was in large measure an Al Smith revolution of 1928, a characterization less applicable to the remainder of the country. . . .

Central to our concept of critical elections is realignment within the electorate both sharp and durable. With respect to these basic criteria the election of 1896 falls within the same category as that of 1928, although it differed in other respects. The persistence of the new division of 1896 was perhaps not so notable as that of 1928; yet the Democratic defeat was so demoralizing and so thorough that the party could make little headway in regrouping its forces until 1916. Perhaps the significant

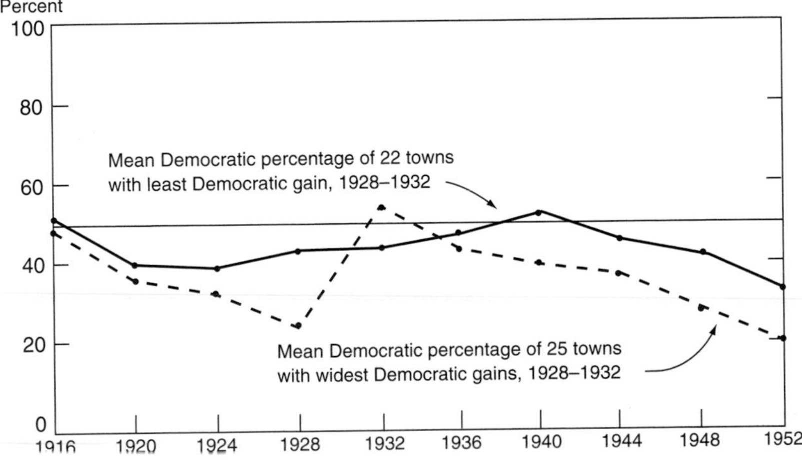

Figure C *Impact of Election of 1932 in New Hampshire*

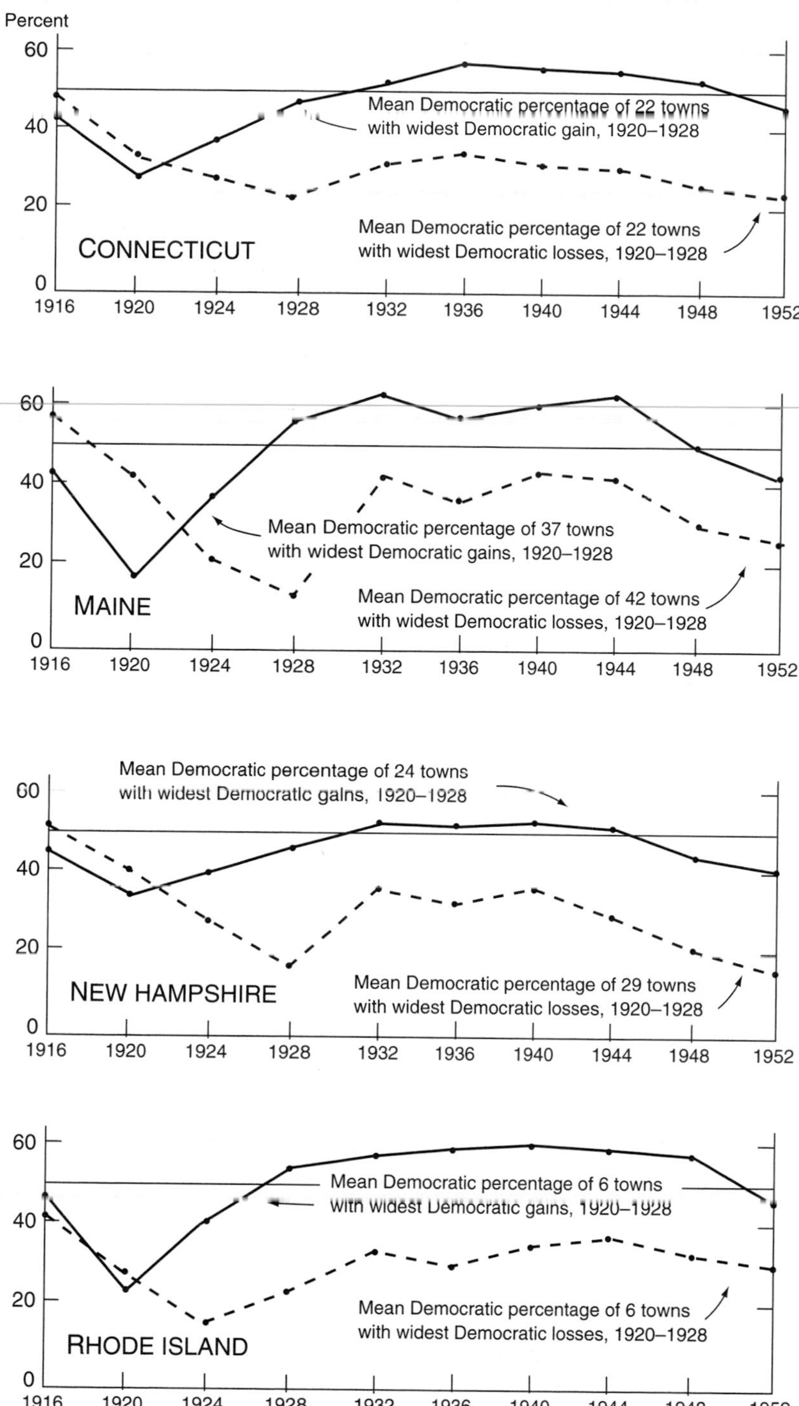

Figure D *Realignment of 1928 Connecticut, Maine, New Hampshire, and Rhode Island*

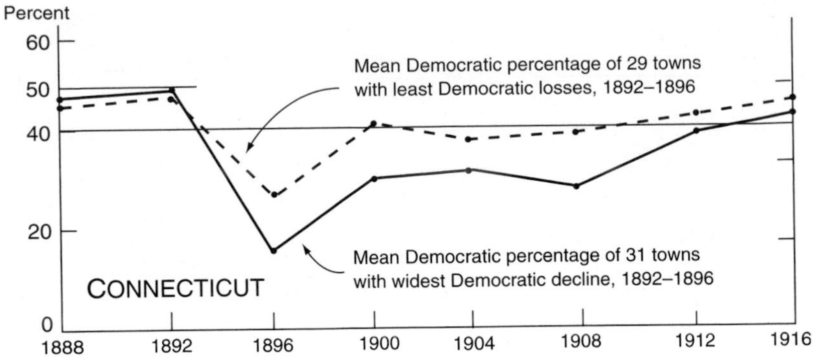

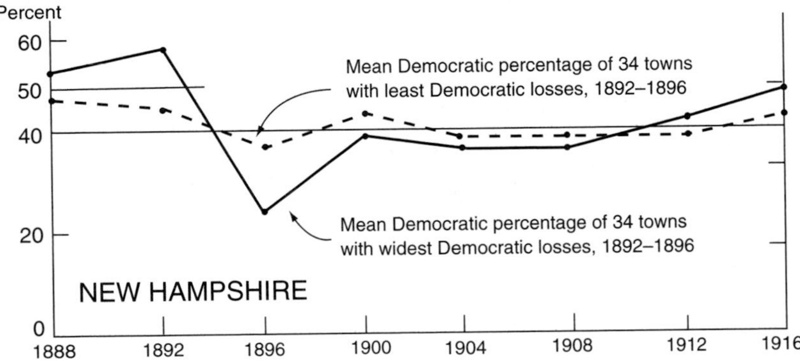

Figure E *Realignment of 1896 in Connecticut and New Hampshire*

feature of the 1896 contest was that, at least in New England, it did not form a new division in which partisan lines became more nearly congruent with lines separating classes, religions, or other such social groups. Instead, the Republicans succeeded in drawing new support, in about the same degree, from all sorts of economic and social classes. The result was an electoral coalition formidable in mass but which required both good fortune and skill in political management for its maintenance, given its latent internal contradictions. . . .

III

The discussion points toward the analytical utility of a system for the differentiation of elections. A concept of critical elections has been developed to cover a type of election in which there occurs a sharp and durable electoral realignment between parties, although the techniques employed do not yield any information of consequence about the mechanisms for the maintenance of a new alignment, once it is formed. Obviously any sort of system for the gross characterization of elections presents difficulties in application. The actual election rarely presents in pure form a case fitting completely any particular concept. Especially in a large and diverse electorate a single polling may encompass radically varying types of behavior among different categories of voters; yet a dominant characteristic often makes itself apparent. Despite such difficulties, the attempt to move toward a better understanding of elections in the terms here employed could provide a means for better integrating the study of electoral behavior with the analysis of political systems. In truth, a considerable proportion of the study of electoral behavior has only a tenuous relation to politics.

The sorts of questions here raised, when applied sufficiently broadly on a comparative basis and carried far enough, could lead to a consideration of basic problems of the nature of democratic orders. A question occurs, for example, about the character of the consequences for the political system of the temporal frequency of critical elections. What are the consequences for public administration, for the legislative process, for the operation of the economy of frequent serious upheavals within the electorate? What are the correlates of that pattern of behavior? And, for those disposed to raise such questions, what underlying changes might alter the situation? Or, when viewed from the contrary position, what consequences flow from an electorate which is disposed, in effect, to remain largely quiescent over considerable periods? Does a state of moving equilibrium reflect a pervasive satisfaction with the course of public policy? An indifference about matters political? In any case, what are the consequences for the public order? Further, what are the consequences when an electorate builds up habits and attachments, or faces situations, that make it impossible for it to render a decisive and clear-cut popular verdict that promises not to be upset by caprice at the next round of polling? What are the consequences of a situation that creates recurring, evenly balanced conflict over long periods? On the other hand, what characteristics of an electorate or what conditions permit sharp and decisive changes in the power structure from time to time? Such directions of speculation are suggested by a single criterion for the differentiation of elections. Further development of an electoral topology would probably point to useful speculation in a variety of directions.

VOTING BEHAVIOR: RATIONAL OR IRRATIONAL?

Parties are supposed to bridge the gap between the people and their government. Theoretically they are the primary vehicles for translating the wishes of the electorate into public policy, sharing this role with interest groups and other governmental instrumentalities in varying degrees. If parties are to perform this aspect of their job properly, the party system must be conducive to securing meaningful debate and action. Party organization and procedure profoundly affect the ability of parties to act in a democratically responsible manner. It should also be pointed out, however, that the electorate has a responsibility in the political process—the responsibility to act rationally, debate the issues of importance, and record a vote for one party or the other at election time. These, at least, are electoral norms traditionally discussed. But does the electorate act in this manner? Is it desirable to have 100 percent electoral participation, considering the characteristics of voting behavior? What are the determinants of electoral behavior? These questions are discussed in the following selection.

36

DEMOCRATIC PRACTICE AND DEMOCRATIC THEORY

Bernard R. Berelson, Paul F. Lazarsfeld, and William N. McPhee

Requirements for the Individual

Perhaps the main impact of realistic research on contemporary politics has been to temper some of the requirements set by our traditional normative theory for the typical citizen. "Out of all this literature of political observation and analysis, which is relatively new," says Max Beloff, "there has come to exist a picture in our minds of the political scene which differs very considerably from that familiar to us from the classical texts of democratic politics."

Experienced observers have long known, of course, that the individual voter was not all that the theory of democracy requires of him. As [British Lord James] Bryce put it [in his 1888 treatise, *The American Commonwealth*]:

> How little solidity and substance there is in the political or social beliefs of nineteen persons out of every twenty. These beliefs, when examined, mostly resolve themselves into two or three prejudices and aversions, two or three prepossessions for a particular party or section of a party, two or three phrases or catch-words suggesting or embodying arguments which the man who repeats them has not analyzed.

While our data do not support such an extreme statement, they do reveal that certain requirements commonly assumed for the successful operation of democracy are not met by the behavior of the "average" citizen. The requirements, and our conclusions concerning them, are quickly reviewed.

Interest, Discussion, Motivation

The democratic citizen is expected to be interested and to participate in political affairs. His interest and participation can take such various forms as reading and listening to campaign materials, working for the candidate or the party, arguing politics, donating money, and voting. . . . Many vote without real involvement in the election, and even the party workers are not typically motivated by ideological concerns or plain civic duty.

If there is one characteristic for a democratic system (besides the ballot itself) that is theoretically required, it is the capacity for and the practice of discussion. "It is as true of the large as of the small society," says [A.D.] Lindsay, "that its health depends on the mutual understanding which discussion makes possible; and that discussion is the only possible instrument of its democratic government." How much participation in political discussion there is in the community, what it is, and among whom—these questions have been given answers . . . earlier. . . . In this instance there was little true discussion between the candidates, little in the newspaper commentary, little between the voters and the official party representatives, some within the electorate. On the grass roots level there was more talk than debate, and, at least inferentially, the talk had important effects upon voting, in reinforcing or activating the partisans if not in converting the opposition.

An assumption underlying the theory of democracy is that the citizenry has a strong motivation for participation in political life. But it is a curious quality of voting behavior that for large numbers of people motivation is weak if not almost absent. It is assumed that this motivation would gain its strength from the citizen's perception of the difference that alternative decisions made to him. Now when a person buys something or makes other decisions of daily life, there are direct and immediate consequences for him. But for the bulk of the American people the voting decision is not followed by any direct, immediate, visible personal consequences. Most voters, organized or unorganized, are not in a position to foresee the distant and indirect consequences for themselves, let alone the society. The ballot is cast, and for most people that is the end of it. If their side is defeated, "it doesn't really matter."

Knowledge

The democratic citizen is expected to be well informed about political affairs. He is supposed to know what the issues are, what their history is, what the relevant facts are, what alternatives are proposed, what the party stands for, what the likely consequences are. By such standards the voter falls short. Even when he has the motivation, he finds it difficult to make decisions on the basis of full information when the subject is relatively simple and proximate; how can he do so when it is complex and remote? The citizen is not highly informed on details of the campaign, nor does he avoid a certain misperception of the political situation when it is to his psychological advantage to do so. The electorate's perception of what goes on in the campaign is colored by emotional feeling toward one or the other issue, candidate, party, or social group.

Principle

The democratic citizen is supposed to cast his vote on the basis of principle—not fortuitously or frivolously or impulsively or habitually, but with reference to standards not only of his own interest but of the common good as well. Here, again, if this requirement is pushed at all strongly, it becomes an impossible demand on the democratic electorate.

Many voters vote not for principle in the usual sense but "for" a group to which they are attached—their group. The Catholic vote or the hereditary vote is explainable less as principle than as a traditional social allegiance. The ordinary voter, bewildered by the complexity of modern political problems, unable to determine clearly what the consequences are of alternative lines of action, remote from the arena, and incapable of bringing information to bear on principle, votes the way trusted people around him are voting. . . .

On the issues of the campaign there is a considerable amount of "don't know"—sometimes reflecting genuine indecision, more often meaning "don't care." Among those with opinions the partisans agree on most issues, criteria, expectations, and rules of the game. The supporters of the different sides disagree on only a few issues. Not, for that matter, do the candidates themselves always join the issue sharply and clearly. The partisans do not agree overwhelmingly with their own party's position, or, rather, only the small minority of highly partisan do; the rest take a rather moderate position on the political consideration involved in an election.

Rationality

The democratic citizen is expected to exercise rational judgment in coming to his voting decision. He is expected to have arrived at his principles by reason and to have considered rationally the implications and alleged consequences of the alternative proposals of the contending parties. Political theorists and commentators have always exclaimed over the seeming contrast here between requirement and fulfillment. . . . The upshot of this is that the usual analogy between the voting "decision" and the more or less carefully calculated decisions of consumers or businessmen or courts, incidentally, may be quite incorrect. For many voters political preferences may better be considered analogous to cultural tastes—in music, literature, recreational activities, dress, ethics, speech, social behavior. Consider the parallels between political preferences and general cultural tastes. Both have their origin in ethnic, sectional, class, and family traditions. Both exhibit stability and resistance to change for individuals but flexibility and adjustment over generations for the society as a whole. Both seem to be matters of sentiment and disposition rather than "reasoned preferences." While both are responsive to changed conditions and unusual stimuli, they are relatively invulnerable to direct argumentation and vulnerable to indirect social influences. Both are characterized more by faith than by conviction and by wishful expectation rather than careful prediction or consequences. The preference for one party rather than another must be highly similar to the preference for one kind of literature or music rather than another, and the choice of the same political party every four years may be parallel to the choice of the same old standards of conduct in new social situations. In short, it appears that a sense of fitness is a more striking feature of political preference than reason and calculation.

Requirements for the System

If the democratic system depended solely on the qualifications of the individual voter, then it seems remarkable that democracies have survived through the centuries. After examining the detailed data on how individuals misperceive political reality or respond to irrelevant social influences, one wonders how a democracy ever solves its political problems. But when one considers the data in a broader perspective—how huge segments of the society adapt to political conditions affecting them or how the political system adjusts itself to changing conditions over long periods of time—he cannot fail to be impressed with the total result. Where the rational citizen seems to abdicate, nevertheless angels seem to tread. . . .

That is the paradox. *Individual voters* today seem unable to satisfy the requirements for a democratic system of government outlined by political theorists. But *the system of democracy* does meet certain requirements for a going political organization. The individual members may not meet all the standards, but the whole nevertheless survives and grows. This suggests that where the classic theory is defective is in its concentration on the *individual citizen*. What are undervalued are certain collective properties that reside in the electorate as a whole and in the political and social system in which it functions.

The political philosophy we have inherited, then, has given more consideration to the virtues of the typical citizen of the democracy than to the working of the system as a whole. Moreover, when it dealt with the system, it mainly considered the single constitutive institutions of the system, not those general features necessary if the institutions are to work as required. For example, the rule of law, representative government, periodic elections, the party system, and the several freedoms of discussion, press, association, and assembly have all been examined by political philosophers seeking to clarify and to justify the idea of political democracy. But liberal democracy is more than a political system in which individual voters and political institutions operate. For political democracy to survive, other features are required: the intensity of conflict must be limited, the rate of change must be restrained, stability in the social and economic structure must be maintained, a pluralistic social organization must exist, and a basic consensus must bind together the contending parties.

Such features of the system of political democracy belong neither to the constitutive institutions nor to the individual voter. It might be said that they form the atmosphere or the environment in which both operate. In any case, such features have not been carefully considered by political philosophers, and it is on these broader properties of the democratic political system that more reflection and study by political theory is called for. In the most tentative fashion let us explore the values of the political system, as they involve the electorate, in the light of the foregoing considerations.

Underlying the paradox is an assumption that the population is homogeneous socially and should be homogeneous politically: that everybody is about the same in relevant social characteristics; that, if something is a political virtue (like interest in the election), then everyone should have it; that there is such a thing as "the" typical citizen on whom uniform requirements can be imposed. The tendency of classic democratic literature to work with an image of "the" voter was never justified. For, as we will attempt to illustrate here, some of the most important requirements that democratic values impose on a system require a voting population that is not homogeneous but heterogeneous in its political qualities.

The need for heterogeneity arises from the contradictory functions we expect our voting system to serve. We expect the political system to adjust itself and our affairs to changing conditions; yet we demand too that it display a high degree of stability. We expect the contending interests and parties to pursue their ends vigorously and the voters to care; yet, after the election is over, we expect reconciliation. We expect the voting outcome to serve what is best for the community; yet we do not want disinterested voting unattached to the purposes and interests of different segments of that community. We want voters to express their own free and self-determined choices; yet, for the good of the community, we would like voters to avail themselves of the best information and guidance available from the groups and leaders around them. We expect a high degree of rationality to prevail in the decision; but were all irrationality and mythology absent, and all ends pursued by the most coldly rational selection of political means, it is doubtful if the system would hold together.

In short, our electoral system calls for apparently incompatible properties—which, although they cannot all reside in each individual voter, can (and do) reside in a heterogeneous electorate. What seems to be required of the electorate as a whole is a *distribution* of qualities along important dimensions. We need some people who are active in a certain respect, others in the middle, and still others passive. The contradictory things we want from the total require that the parts be different. This can be illustrated by taking up a number of important dimensions by which an electorate might be characterized.

Involvement and Indifference

How could a mass democracy work if all the people were deeply involved in politics? Lack of interest by some people is not without its benefits, too. True, the highly interested voters vote more, and know more about the campaign, and read and listen more, and participate more; however, they are also less open to persuasion and less likely to change. Extreme interest goes with extreme partisanship and might culminate in rigid fanaticism that could destroy democratic processes if generalized throughout the community. Low affect toward the election—not caring much—underlies the resolution of many political problems; votes can be resolved into a two-party split instead of fragmented into many parties (the splinter parties of the left, for example, splinter because their advocates are too interested in politics). Low interest provides maneuvering room for political shifts necessary for a complex society in a period of rapid change. Compromise might be based upon sophisticated awareness of costs and returns—perhaps impossible to demand of a mass society—but it is more often induced by indifference. Some people are and should be highly interested in politics, but not everyone is or needs to be. Only the doctrinaire would deprecate the moderate indifference that facilitates compromise.

Hence, an important balance between action motivated by strong sentiments and action with little passion behind it is obtained by heterogeneity within the electorate. Balance of this sort is, in practice, met by a distribution of voters rather than by a homogeneous collection of "ideal" citizens.

Stability and Flexibility

A similar dimension along which an electorate might be characterized is stability-flexibility. The need for change and adaptation is clear, and the need for stability ought equally to be (especially from observation of current democratic practice in, say, certain Latin American countries). . . . [I]t may be that the very people who are most sensitive to changing social conditions are those most susceptible to political change. For, in either case, the people exposed to membership in overlapping strata, those whose former life-patterns are being broken up, those who are moving about socially or physically, those who are forming new families and new friendships—it is they who are open to adjustments of attitudes and tastes. They may be the least partisan and the least interested voters, but they perform a valuable function for the entire system. Here again is an instance in which an individual "inadequacy" provides a positive service for society: The campaign can be a reaffirming force for the settled majority and a creative force for the unsettled minority. There is stability on both sides and flexibility in the middle.

Progress and Conservation

Closely related to the question of stability is the question of past versus future orientation of the system. In America a progressive outlook is highly valued, but, at the same time, so is a conservative one. Here a balance between the two is easily found in the party system and in the distribution of voters themselves from extreme conservatives to extreme liberals. But a balance between the two is also achieved by a distribution of political dispositions through time. There are periods of great political agitation (i.e., campaigns) alternating with periods of political dormancy. Paradoxically, the former—the campaign period—is likely to be an instrument of conservatism, often even of historical regression. . . .

Again, then, a balance (between preservation of the past and receptivity to the future) seems to be required of a democratic electorate. The heterogeneous electorate in itself provides a balance between liberalism and conservatism; and so does the sequence of political events from periods of drifting change to abrupt rallies back to the loyalties of earlier years.

Consensus and Cleavage . . .

[T]here are required *social* consensus and cleavage—in effect pluralism—in politics. Such pluralism makes for enough consensus to hold the system together and enough cleavage to make it move. Too much consensus would be deadening and restrictive of liberty; too much cleavage would be destructive of the society as a whole. . . . Thus again a requirement we might place on an electoral system—balance between total political war between segments of the society and total political indifference to group interests of that society—translates into varied requirements for different individuals. With respect to group or bloc voting, as with other aspects of political behavior, it is perhaps not unfortunate that "some do and some do not."

Individualism and Collectivism

Lord Bryce pointed out the difficulties in a theory of democracy that assumes that each citizen must himself be capable of voting intelligently:

> Orthodox democratic theory assumes that every citizen has, or ought to have, thought out for himself certain opinions, i.e., ought to have a definite view, defensible by argument, of what the country needs, of what principles ought to be applied in governing it, of the man to whose hands the government ought to be entrusted. There are persons who talk, though certainly very few who act, as if they believed this theory, which may be compared to the theory of some ultra-Protestants that every good Christian has or ought to have . . . worked out for himself from the Bible a system of theology.

In the first place, however, the information available to the individual voter is not limited to that directly possessed by him. True, the individual casts his own personal ballot. But, as we have tried to indicate . . . that is perhaps the most individualized action he takes in an election. His vote is formed in the midst of his fellows in a sort of group decision—if, indeed, it may be called a decision at all—and the total information and knowledge possessed in the group's present and past generations can be made available for the group's choice. Here is where opinion-leading relationships, for example, play an active role.

Second, and probably more important, the individual voter may not have a great deal of detailed information, but he usually has picked up the crucial general information as part of his social learning itself. He may not know the parties' position on the tariff, or who is for reciprocal trade treaties, or what are the differences on Asiatic policy, or how the parties split on civil rights, or how many security risks were exposed by whom. But he cannot live in an American community without knowing broadly where the parties stand. He has learned that the Republicans are more conservative and the Democrats more liberal—and he can locate his own sentiments and case his vote accordingly. After all, he must vote for one or the other party, and, if he knows the big thing about the parties, he does not need to know all the little things. The basic role a party plays as an institution in American life is more important to his voting than a particular stand on a particular issue.

It would be unthinkable to try to maintain our present economic style of life without a complex system of delegating to others what we are not competent to do ourselves, without accepting and giving training to each other about what each is expected to do, without accepting our dependence on others in many spheres and taking responsibility for their dependence on us in some spheres. And, like it or not, to maintain our present political style of life, we may have to accept much the same interdependence with others in collective behavior. We have learned slowly in economic life that it is useful not to have everyone a butcher or a baker, any more than it is useful to have no one skilled in such activities. The same kind of division of labor—as repugnant as it may be in some respects to our individualistic tradition—is serving us well today in mass politics. There is an implicit division of political labor within the electorate.

POLITICAL CAMPAIGNS AND THE ELECTORATE

The voice of the people is always heard in the electoral process, but it is not always clear exactly what the people have chosen. The candidates and their political consultants concentrate upon the projection of images rather than on the serious discussion of public issues. The media, interested in gaining as wide an audience as possible, encourage candidates to be brief in the presentation of their programs and to act with an eye to what is newsworthy in the view of television producers and newspaper editors. A maze confronts the electorate, which must be able to peer through the smoke screen of electoral politics in order to be able to vote intelligently. The following selection, from Key's oft-quoted book *The Responsible Electorate* argues that voters are not the fools that many politicians and their advisers often take them to be. The electorate, concludes the author, "behaves about as rationally and responsibly as we should expect, given the clarity of the alternatives presented to it and the character of the information available to it."

37

THE RESPONSIBLE ELECTORATE

V. O. Key, Jr.

In his reflective moments even the most experienced politician senses a nagging curiosity about why people vote as they do. His power and his position depend upon the outcome of the mysterious rites we perform as opposing candidates harangue the multitudes who finally march to the polls to prolong the rule of their champion, to thrust him, ungratefully, back into the void of private life, or to raise to eminence a new tribune of the people. What kinds of appeals enable a candidate to win the favor of the great god, The People? What circumstances move voters to shift their preferences in this direction or that? What clever propaganda tactic or slogan led to this result? What mannerism of oratory or style of rhetoric produced another outcome? What band of electors rallied to this candidate to save the day for him? What policy of state attracted the devotion of another bloc of voters? What action repelled a third sector of the electorate?

The victorious candidate may claim with assurance that he has the answers to all such questions. He may regard his success as vindication of his beliefs about why voters vote as they do. And he may regard the swing of the vote to him as indubitably a response to the campaign positions he took, as an indication of the acuteness of his intuitive estimates of the mood of the people, and as a ringing manifestation of the esteem in which he is held by a discriminating public. This narcissism assumes its most repulsive form among election winners who have championed intolerance, who have stirred the passions and hatreds of people, or who have advocated causes known by decent men to be outrageous or dangerous in their long-run consequences. No functionary is more repugnant or more arrogant than the unjust man who asserts, with a color of truth, that he speaks from a pedestal of popular approbation.

It thus can be a mischievous error to assume, because a candidate wins, that a majority of the electorate shares his views on public questions, approves his past actions, or has specific expectations about his future conduct. Nor does victory establish that the candidate's campaign strategy, his image, his television style, or his fearless stand against cancer and polio turned the trick. The election returns establish only that a winner attracted a majority of votes—assuming the existence of a modicum of rectitude in election administration. They tell us precious little about why the plurality was his.

For a glaringly obvious reason, electoral victory cannot be regarded as necessarily a popular ratification of a candidate's outlook. The voice of the people is but an echo. The output of an echo chamber bears an inevitable and invariable relation to the input. As candidates and parties clamor for attention and vie for popular support, the people's verdict can be no more than a selective reflection from among the alternatives and outlooks presented to them. Even the most discriminating popular judgment can reflect only ambiguity, uncertainty, or even foolishness if those are the qualities of the input into the echo chamber. A candidate may win despite his tactics and appeals rather than because of them. If the people can choose only from among rascals, they are certain to choose a rascal.

Scholars, though they have less at stake than do politicians, also have an abiding curiosity about why voters act as they do. In the past quarter of a century they have vastly enlarged their capacity to check the hunches born of their curiosities. The invention of the sample survey—the most widely known example of which is the Gallup poll—enabled them to make fairly trustworthy estimates of the characteristics and behaviors of large human populations. This method of mass observation revolutionized the study of politics—as well as the management of political campaigns. The new technique permitted large-scale tests to check the validity of old psychological and sociological theories of human behavior. These tests led to new hunches and new theories about voting behavior, which could in turn be checked and which thereby contributed to the extraordinary ferment in the social sciences during recent decades.

The studies of electoral behavior by survey methods cumulate into an imposing body of knowledge which conveys a vivid impression of the variety and subtlety of factors that enter into individual voting decisions. In their first stages in the 1930s the new electoral studies chiefly lent precision and verification to the working maxims of practicing politicians and to some of the crude theories of political speculators. Thus, sample surveys established that people did, indeed, appear to vote their pocketbooks. Yet the demonstration created its embarrassments because it also established that exceptions to the rule were numerous. Not all factory workers, for example, voted alike. How was the behavior of the deviants from "group interest" to be explained? Refinement after refinement of theory and analysis added complexity to the original simple explanation. By introducing a bit of psychological theory it could be demonstrated that factory workers with optimistic expectations tended less to be governed by pocketbook considerations than did those whose outlook was gloomy. When a little social psychology was stirred into the analysis, it could be established that identifications formed early in life, such as attachments to political parties, also reinforced or resisted the pull of the interest of the moment. A sociologist, bringing to play the conceptual tools of his trade, then could show that those factory workers who associate intimately with like-minded persons on the average vote with greater solidarity than do social isolates. Inquiries conducted with great ingenuity along many such lines have enormously broadened our knowledge of the factors associated with the responses of people to the stimuli presented to them by political campaigns.

Yet, by and large, the picture of the voter that emerges from a combination of the folklore of practical politics and the findings of the new electoral studies is not a pretty one. It is not a portrait of citizens moving to considered decision as they play their solemn role of making and unmaking governments. The older tradition from practical politics may regard the voter as an erratic and irrational fellow susceptible to manipulation by skilled humbugs. One need not live through many campaigns to observe politicians, even successful politicians, who act as though they regarded the people as manageable fools. Nor does a heroic conception of the voter emerge from the new analyses of electoral behavior. They can be added up to a conception of voting not as a civic decision but as an almost purely deterministic act. Given knowledge of certain characteristics of a voter—his occupation, his residence, his religion, his national origin, and perhaps certain of his attributes—one can predict with a high probability the direction of his vote. The actions of persons are made to appear to be only predictable and automatic responses to campaign stimuli.

Most findings of the analysts of voting never travel beyond the circle of the technicians; the popularizers, though, give wide currency to the most bizarre—and most dubious—theories of electoral behavior. Public-relations experts share in the process of dissemination as they sell their services to politicians (and succeed in establishing that politicians are sometimes as gullible as businessmen). Reporters pick up the latest psychological secret from campaign managers and spread it through a larger public. Thus, at one time a goodly proportion of the literate population must have placed some store in the theory that the electorate was a pushover for a candidate who projected an appropriate "father image." At another stage, the "sincere" candidate supposedly had an overwhelming advantage. And even so kindly a gentleman as General Eisenhower was said to have an especial attractiveness to those of authoritarian personality within the electorate.

Conceptions and theories of the way voters behave do not raise solely arcane problems to be disputed among the democratic and antidemocratic theorists or questions to be settled by the elegant techniques of the analysts of electoral behavior. Rather, they touch upon profound issues at the heart of the problem of the nature and workability of systems of popular government. Obviously the perceptions of the behavior of the electorate held by political leaders, agitators, and activists condition if they do not fix, the types of appeals politicians employ as they seek popular support. These perceptions—or theories—affect the nature of the input to the echo chamber, if we may revert to our earlier figure, and thereby control its output. They may govern, too, the kinds of actions that governments take as they look forward to the next election. If politicians perceive the electorate as responsive to father images, they will give it father images. If they see voters as most certainly responsive to nonsense, they will give them nonsense. If they see voters as susceptible to delusion, they will delude them. If they see an electorate receptive to the cold, hard realities, they will give it the cold, hard realities.

In short, theories of how voters behave acquire importance not because of their effects on voters, who may proceed blithely unaware of them. They gain significance because of their effects, both potentially and in reality, on candidates and other political leaders. If leaders believe the route to victory is by projection of images and cultivation of styles rather than by advocacy of policies to cope with the problems of the country, they will project images and cultivate styles to the neglect of the substance of politics. They will abdicate their prime function in a democratic system, which amounts, in essence, to the assumption of the risk of trying to persuade us to lift ourselves by our bootstraps.

Among the literary experts on politics there are those who contend that, because of the development of tricks of the manipulation of the masses, practices of political leadership in the management of voters have moved far toward the conversion of election campaigns into obscene parodies of the models set up by democratic idealists. They point to the good old days when politicians were deep thinkers, eloquent orators, and farsighted statesmen. Such estimates of the course of change in social institutions must be regarded with reserve. They may be only manifestations of the inverted optimism of aged and melancholy men who, estopped from hope for the future, see in the past a satisfaction of their yearning for greatness in our political life.

Whatever the trends may have been, the perceptions that leadership elements of democracies hold of the modes of response of the electorate must always be a matter of fundamental significance. Those perceptions determine the nature of the voice of the people, for they determine the character of the input into the echo chamber. While the output may be governed by the nature of the input, over the longer run the properties of the echo chamber may themselves be altered. Fed a steady diet of buncombe, the people may come to expect and to respond with highest predictability to buncombe. And those leaders most skilled in the propagation of buncombe may gain lasting advantage in the recurring struggles for popular favor.

[My] perverse and unorthodox argument . . . is that voters are not fools. To be sure, many individual voters act in odd ways indeed; yet in the large the electorate behaves about as rationally and responsibly as we should expect, given the clarity of the alternatives presented to it and the character of the information available to it. In American presidential campaigns of recent decades the portrait of the American electorate that develops from the data is not one of an electorate straitjacketed by social determinants or moved by subconscious urges triggered by devilishly skillful propagandists. It is rather one of an electorate moved by concern about central and relevant questions of public policy, of governmental performance, and of executive personality. Propositions so uncompromisingly stated inevitably represent overstatements. Yet to the extent that they can be shown to resemble the reality, they are propositions of basic importance for both the theory and the practice of democracy. . . .

CHAPTER 5

INTEREST GROUPS

Interest groups are vital cogs in the wheels of the democratic process. Although *Federalist 10* suggests that one major purpose of the separation-of-powers system is to break and control the "evil effects" of faction, modern political theorists take a much more sanguine view of the role that political interest groups as well as parties play in government. No longer are interest groups defined as being opposed to the "public interest." They are vital channels through which particular publics participate in the governmental process. But the Madisonian theme of *Federalist 10* that attacks "factions" continues in our political rhetoric and influences our politics. In sharp contrast to Madison and the traditional view of interest groups, group theory, as we will see in this chapter, defines democratic politics in terms of specialized interests. Interest groups are not a necessary evil but instead the core of democratic politics.

CONSTITUTIONAL BACKGROUND

Interest groups challenge Madison's carefully laid plans for limited and deliberative government in the national interest. Interest groups, or as Madison called them, factions, elevate special interests over the national interest. Madison designed the Constitution to filter factions through a process of balanced powers and representative government, which he explained in *The Federalist Papers 10, 47, 48,* and *51,* all of which are given in previous selections. The following selection discusses interest group politics in our Madisonian system.

38

MADISON'S DILEMMA

Jeffrey M. Berry

A troubling dilemma lies at the core of the American political system. In an open and free society in which people have the right to express their political views, petition their government, and organize on behalf of causes, some segments of the population are likely to pursue their own selfish interests. Dairy farmers will push Congress to adopt price subsidies even though it means families will have to pay more at the grocery store. Manufacturers and labor unions will press for tariffs and other trade barriers to protect profits and jobs. Consumers, however, will be saddled with higher prices as a result. Environmentalists will fight for increasing the number of parks and wilderness preserves, though development of those lands might provide jobs for some who are out of work. In short, people will pursue their self-interest even though the policies they advocate may hurt others and may not be in the best interest of the nation.

The dilemma is this: If the government does not allow people to pursue their self-interest, it takes away their political freedom. When we look at the nations of the world in which people are forbidden to organize and to freely express their political views, we find that there the dilemma has been solved by authoritarianism. Although the alternative permitting people to advocate whatever they want is far more preferable, it carries dangers. In a system such as ours, interest groups constantly push government to enact policies that benefit small constituencies at the expense of the general public. This dilemma is as old as the country itself, yet never more relevant than today. As lobbying has grown in recent years, anxiety has mounted over the consequences of interest group politics. Political action committees (PACs) threaten the integrity of congressional elections. Liberal citizen groups are blamed for slowing economic development with the regulatory policies they have fought for. Labor unions are held responsible because America fails to compete effectively in many world markets, while tax cuts granted to businesses seem to increase their profits at the expense of huge federal budget deficits. Beyond the sins allegedly committed by sectors of the interest group community is a broader worry. Are the sheer number of interest groups and their collective power undermining American democracy?

Many agree that interest groups are an increasingly troublesome part of American politics, yet there is little consensus on what, if anything, ought to be done about it. The dilemma remains: Interest groups are no less a threat than they are an expression of freedom.

Curing the Mischiefs of Faction

Is there no middle ground between these two alternatives? Must a government accept one or the other? Contemporary discussions of this question inevitably turn to *The Federalist*, for James Madison's analysis in essay No. 10 remains the foundation of American political theory on interest groups.

With great foresight, Madison recognized the problem that the fragile new nation would face. Although at the time he was writing the country had no political parties or lobbies as we know them, Madison correctly perceived that people would organize in some way to further their common interests. Furthermore, these groupings, or "factions" as he called them, were a potential threat to popular government. Factions were not anomalies, nor would they be occasional problems. Rather, as Madison saw it, the propensity to pursue self-interest was innate. The "causes of faction," he concluded, are "sown in the nature of man."

As any society develops, it is inevitable that different social classes will emerge, that competing interests based on differing occupations will arise, and that clashing political philosophies will take hold among the populace. This tendency was strong in Madison's eyes: He warned that free men are more likely to try to oppress each other than they are to "co-operate for their common good."

Madison worried that a powerful faction could eventually come to tyrannize others in society. What, then, was the solution for "curing the mischiefs of faction"? He rejected out of hand any restrictions on the freedoms that permitted people to pursue their own selfish interests, remarking that the remedy would be "worse than the disease." Instead, he reasoned that the effects of faction must be controlled rather than eliminating factions themselves. This control could be accomplished by setting into place the structure of government proposed in the Constitution.

In Madison's mind, a republican form of government, as designed by the framers, would provide the necessary checks on the worst impulses of factions. A republican form of government gives responsibility for decisions to a small number of representatives who are elected by the larger citizenry. Furthermore, for a government whose authority extends over a large and dispersed population, the effects of faction would be diluted by the clash of many competing interests across the country. Thus, Madison believed that in a land as large as the United States, so many interests would arise that a representative government with its own checks and balances would not become dominated by any faction. Instead, government could deal with the views of all, producing policies that would be in the common good.

Madison's cure for the mischiefs of faction was something of a leap of faith.

The structure of American government has not, by itself, prevented some interests from gaining great advantage at the expense of others. Those with large resources have always been better represented by interest groups, and the least wealthy in society have suffered because of their failure to organize. Still, even though the republican form of government envisioned by Madison has not always been strong enough to prevent abuse by factions, the beliefs underlying *Federalist No. 10* have endured.

This view that the natural diversity of interests would prevent particular groups from dominating politics found a later incarnation in American social science of the 1950s and 1960s. Pluralist scholars argued that the many (that is, plural) interests in society found representation in the policymaking process through lobbying by organizations.

The bargaining that went on between such groups and government led to policies produced by compromise and consensus. Interest groups were seen as more beneficial to the system than Madison's factions, with emphasis placed on the positive contributions made by groups in speaking for their constituents before government. Although the pluralist school was later discredited for a number of reasons (these will be outlined shortly), it furthered the Madisonian ideal: groups freely participating in the policymaking process, none becoming too powerful because of the natural conflict of interests, and government acting as a synthesizer of competing interests. This ideal remains contemporary America's hope for making interest group politics compatible with democratic values.

Interest Groups and Their Functions

One purpose in this [reading] is to reexamine the fundamental questions raised by *Federalist No. 10*. Can an acceptable balance be struck between the right of people to pursue their own interests and the need to protect society from being dominated by one or more interests? Can we achieve true pluralism, or is a severe imbalance of interest group power a chronic condition in a free and open society?

Our means of answering this question will be to look broadly at behavior among contemporary interest groups. We will often follow research questions that political scientists have asked about the internal and external operations of lobbying organizations. Data for this study come not only from the literature on interest groups, but also from interviews with Washington lobbyists. Although the topics addressed are varied, one argument runs throughout: Important changes have taken place in interest group politics in recent years, because of which renewed thought must be given to controlling the effects of faction. . . .

Understanding Interest Groups

. . . [I]nterest groups remain misunderstood and maligned organizations. Americans distrust interest groups in general but value the organizations that represent them. People join an interest group not simply because they agree with its views but because they equate those views with the "public interest." Groups that stand on opposite sides of the same issues are regarded with disdain. Intellectually we accept the legitimacy of all interest groups; emotionally we separate them into those we support and those we must view with suspicion.

The basis of any reasoned judgment about interest groups is a factual understanding of how they operate. This is not easy, for though interest groups all have the same goal to influence government, organizationally and politically they seem endlessly diverse. Yet patterns are recognizable, and . . . such factors as size, type of membership, and resources are used to distinguish basic forms of interest group behavior.

To place this analysis in perspective, we must step back to see how perceptions and attitudes of political scientists toward interest groups have changed in the latter part of the twentieth century. This is more than an interesting piece of intellectual history: A critical change in the thinking of political scientists helped broaden acceptance of the role of interest groups in public policymaking. That change, in turn, helped spur the growth of interest groups.

The Rise and Fall of Pluralism

The early forerunner of pluralism in political science was known as "group theory," most widely associated with David Truman's *The Governmental Process,* published in 1951. Truman makes a simple assertion: Politics can be understood only by looking at the interaction of groups. He casts his lot with Madison, agreeing that "tendencies toward such groupings are 'sown in the nature of man.' " He also draws on cultural anthropology and social psychology to prove his case that political man is a product of group influences. "In all societies of any degree of complexity the individual is less affected directly by the society as a whole than differentially through various of its subdivisions, or groups."

The pluralist influence in political science reached its zenith a decade later when Robert Dahl published *Who Governs?,* a study of local politics in New Haven, Connecticut. Dahl examined three areas of local politics to see just who influenced policy outcomes. His crucial finding was that in the three areas—political party nominations, urban redevelopment, and public education—different groups of people were active and influential. New Haven did not have a small, closed circle of important people who together decided all the important issues in town politics.

Dahl found policymaking in New Haven to be a process by which loose coalitions of groups and politicians would become active on issues they cared about. Although most citizens might be apathetic about most issues, many do get interested in the issues that directly affect them. Businessmen were very active in urban redevelopment; teachers, school administrators, and the Parent Teacher Association (PTA) were involved in school politics. Politicians, always on the lookout for supporters, would court groups, hoping to build their own resources. Consequently, groups representing different interests were not only active, but their support was sought and their views carried weight.

Dahl argued that a realistic definition of democracy was not 50 percent plus one getting their way on each and every issue. Rather, as he wrote in an earlier work, the " 'normal' American political process [is] one in which there is a high probability that an active and legitimate group in the population can make itself heard effectively at some crucial stage in the process of decision."

Through bargaining and compromise between affected groups and political elites, democratic decisions are reached, with no one group consistently dominating. The influence of pluralist thought, and Dahl's writings in particular, was enormous. He had gone a step further than Truman by putting his findings in such an approving light. That is, he not only seemed to be saying this is the way things are, but this is the way things should be.

Policymaking through group interaction is a positive virtue, not a threat to democracy. Placing interest groups at the center of policymaking revived democratic theory by offering an explicit defense of the American political process.

Elegantly and systematically, pluralism made sense of the bargaining between interest groups and government officials. There was a reason to it beyond the selfishness of individual groups. To most social scientists who stood in the ideological mainstream of their disciplines, pluralism was an attractive counterpoint to radical critiques of American society. Books like C. Wright Mills's *The Power Elite* (1956) had gained a good deal of attention with the claim that America was ruled by a small stratum of wealthy and powerful individuals. Members of this power elite were said to be the true decision makers in society, "democracy" being an effective illusion perpetrated on the masses. But if the power elite thesis was false, as most social scientists believed it was, what was the counter theory?

Pluralism thus became the refutation of this damning interpretation of American politics. *Who Governs?* acknowledged that political elites had disproportionate amounts of resources but said that the use of these resources in ways inimical to the system was reasonably well countered by the natural working of interest group politics. Elected officials responded to different groups on different issues, seeking out groups to enhance their own power. Group politics forced elites to be responsive to a broad range of constituencies rather than to a small group of powerful individuals. . . .

Conclusion

The events of the 1960s led many Americans to question the way their democratic system was operating. For their part, American political scientists were more and more disillusioned with the dominant theory in their discipline that purported to explain how that democracy worked. Both alienation from American government and scholarly rejection of pluralism contributed to a powerful new idea: Increased participation was needed to balance a system of interest groups that skewed policymaking toward organizations unrepresentative of the American people.

Although no new theory as such came along to replace pluralism, the idea of expanded interest group participation by the chronically underrepresented was at least a first step toward finding a new solution to the dilemma of *Federalist No. 10*. Real world events and the philosophical musings of scholars that contributed to the movement toward increased participation by interest groups could not be selective in their influence. The new interest group politics went far beyond citizen participation programs and public interest groups for those traditionally unrepresented in the governmental process. Rather, extraordinary growth in all types of lobbying organizations raised anew questions about curing the mischiefs of faction.

First Amendment Barriers to the Regulation of Interest Groups and Political Parties

James Madison pointed out in *Federalist 10* that in a free society faction, "evil" cannot be eliminated without destroying liberty at the same time. He wrote, "Liberty is to faction what air is to fire, an ailment, without which it instantly expires. But it could not be a less folly to abolish liberty, which is essential to political life because it nourishes faction, than it would be to wish the annihilation of air, which is essential to animal life, because it imparts to fire its destructive agency."

The liberty Madison referred to in *Federalist 10* was an eighteenth-century natural right, which became explicit in the First Amendment's list of freedoms of expression. The First Amendment's freedoms of speech, press, and assembly and its right to petition government for a redress of grievances protect political parties and interest groups from governmental intrusion. Neither these nor other freedoms and rights listed in the Bill of Rights are, however, absolute.

Congress as well as state legislatures have perennially attempted to regulate interest groups and, especially in the 1970s, political parties in various ways. Proponents of interest group regulation accept one prong of Madison's *Federalist 10* argument but ignore his caveat. They view interest groups as "evil" factions, but then propose a cure that invariably treads upon the liberty of groups under the First Amendment.

The following seminal case involves a constitutional challenge on First Amendment grounds to a major congressional attempt to regulate interest groups and parties in the campaign finance legislation of the 1970s. The Federal Election Campaign Act of 1971, amended in 1974, limited individual and political action committee (PAC) contributions to political candidates and parties, and also imposed limits upon spending in behalf of and by political candidates. The law created the Federal Election Commission (FEC), a regulatory body to oversee the complex provisions of the laws. Political candidates and PACs had to register with the Commission and file a detailed report on their contributions and spending.

The Supreme Court held that political spending is protected speech under the First Amendment that Congress cannot burden. However, there is sufficient public interest in establishing a level political playing field to justify limits upon political contributions and their disclosure.

Buckley v. Valeo set a precedent that has limited the authority of Congress to regulate campaign expenditures, but that limit is not inflexible. In *McConnell v. Federal Election Commission* (2002) the Supreme Court upheld broad federal regulation of campaign finance activities over some strong dissents. Justice Scalia dissenting in the McConnell case wrote: "This is a sad day for the freedom of speech. . . . [The Court today smiles] with favor upon a law that cuts to the heart of what the First Amendment is meant to protect: the right to criticize the government. For that is what the most offensive provisions of this legislation are all about. We are governed by Congress, and this legislation prohibits the criticism of Members of Congress by those entities most capable of giving such criticism loud voice: national political parties and corporations, both of the commercial and the not-for-profit sort. It forbids pre-election criticism of incumbents by corporations, even not-for-profit corporations, by use of their general funds; and forbids national-party use of 'soft' money to fund 'issue ads' that incumbents find so offensive."

39

BUCKLEY v. VALEO

424 U.S. 1 (1976)

Per Curiam

I. Contribution and Expenditure Limitations

The intricate statutory scheme adopted by Congress to regulate federal election campaigns includes restrictions on political contributions and expenditures that apply broadly to all phases of and all participants in the election process. The major contribution and expenditure limitations in the Act prohibit individuals from contributing more than $25,000 in a single year or more than $1,000 to any single candidate for an election campaign and from spending more than $1,000 a year "relative to a clearly identified candidate." Other provisions restrict a candidate's use of personal and family resources in his campaign and limit the overall amount that can be spent by a candidate in campaigning for federal office. . . .

A. General Principles

The Act's contribution and expenditure limitations operate in an area of the most fundamental First Amendment activities. Discussion of public issues and debate on the qualifications of candidates are integral to the operation of the system of government established by our Constitution. . . .

The First Amendment protects political association as well as political expression. . . .

It is with these principles in mind that we consider the primary contentions of the parties with respect to the Act's limitations upon the giving and spending of money in political campaigns. Those conflicting contentions could not more sharply define the basic issues before us. Appellees contend that what the Act regulates is conduct, and that its effect on speech and association is incidental at most. Appellants respond that contributions and expenditures are at the very core of political speech, and that the Act's limitations thus constitute restraints on First Amendment liberty that are both gross and direct. . . .

A restriction on the amount of money a person or group can spend on political communication during a campaign necessarily reduces the quantity of expression by restricting the number of issues discussed, the depth of their exploration, and the size of the audience reached. This is because virtually every means of communicating ideas in today's mass society requires the expenditure of money. . . .

The expenditure limitations contained in the Act represent substantial rather than merely theoretical restraints on the quantity and diversity of political speech. The $1,000 ceiling on spending "relative to a clearly identified candidate," 18 U.S.C. §608(e)(1) . . . would appear to exclude all citizens and groups except candidates, political parties and the institutional press from any significant use of the most effective modes of communication. Although the Act's limitations on expenditures by campaign organizations and political parties provide substantially greater room for discussion and debate, they would have required restrictions in the scope of a number of past congressional and Presidential campaigns and would operate to constrain campaigning by candidates who raise sums in excess of the spending ceiling.

By contrast with a limitation upon expenditures for political expression, a limitation upon the amount that any one person or group may contribute to a candidate or political committee entails only a marginal restriction upon the contributor's ability to engage in free communication. A contribution serves as a general expression of support for the candidate and his views, but does not communicate the underlying basis for the support. . . . While contributions may result in political expression if spent by a candidate or an association to present views to the voters, the transformation of contributions into political debate involves speech by someone other than the contributor.

Given the important role of contributions in financing political campaigns, contribution restrictions could have a severe impact on political dialogue if the limitations prevented candidates and political committees from amassing the resources necessary for effective advocacy. There is no indication, however, that the contribution limitations imposed by the Act would have any dramatic adverse effect on the funding of campaigns and political associations. The overall effect of the Act's contribution ceilings is merely to require candidates and political committees to raise funds from a greater number of persons and to compel people who would otherwise contribute amounts greater than the statutory limits to expend such funds on direct political expression, rather than to reduce the total amount of money potentially available to promote political expression.

The Act's contribution and expenditure limitations also impinge on protected associational freedoms. Making a contribution, like joining a political party, serves to affiliate a person with a candidate. In addition, it enables like-minded persons to pool their resources in furtherance of common political goals. The Act's contribution ceilings thus limit one important means of associating with a candidate or committee, but leave the contributor free to become a member of any political association and to assist personally in the association's efforts on behalf of candidates. And the Act's contribution limitations permit associations and candidates to aggregate large sums of money to promote effective advocacy. By contrast, the Act's $1,000 limitation on independent expenditures "relative to a clearly identified candidate" precludes most associations from effectively amplifying the voice of their adherents, the original basis for the recognition of First Amendment protection of the freedom of association. . . .

In sum, although the Act's contribution and expenditure limitations both implicate fundamental First Amendment interests, its expenditure ceilings impose significantly more severe restrictions on protected freedoms of political expression and association than do its limitations on financial contributions.

B. Contribution Limitations

. . . We find that, under the rigorous standard of review established by our prior decisions, the weighty interests served by restricting the size of financial contributions to political candidates are sufficient to justify the limited effect upon First Amendment freedoms caused by the $1,000 contribution ceiling. . . .

C. Expenditure Limitations

The Act's expenditure ceilings impose direct and substantial restraints on the quantity of political speech. . . . It is clear that a primary effect of these expenditure limitations is to restrict the quantity of campaign speech by individuals, groups, and candidates. The restrictions, while neutral as to the ideas expressed, limit political expression "at the core of our electoral process and of the First Amendment freedoms." . . .

1. The $1,000 Limitation on Expenditures "Relative to a Clearly Identified Candidate" . . .

. . . [T]he constitutionality of §608(e)(1) turns on whether the governmental interests advanced in its support satisfy the exacting scrutiny applicable to limitations on core First Amendment rights of political expression.

We find that the governmental interest in preventing corruption and the appearance of corruption is inadequate to justify §608(e)(1)'s ceiling on independent expenditures. . . .

It is argued, however, that the ancillary governmental interest in equalizing the relative ability of individuals and groups to influence the outcome of elections serves to justify the limitation on express advocacy of the election or defeat of candidates imposed by §608(e)(1)'s expenditure ceiling. But the concept that government may restrict the speech of some elements of our society in order to enhance the relative voice of others is wholly foreign to the First Amendment . . . The First Amendment's protection against governmental abridgment of free expression cannot properly be made to depend on a person's financial ability to engage in public discussion. . . .

For the reasons stated, we conclude that §608(e)(1)'s independent expenditure limitation is unconstitutional under the First Amendment.

2. Limitation on Expenditures by Candidates from Personal or Family Resources . . .

The ceiling on personal expenditures by candidates on their own behalf, like the limitations on independent expenditures contained in §608(e)(1), imposes a substantial restraint on the ability of persons to engage in protected First Amendment expression. . . .

The ancillary interest in equalizing the relative financial resources of candidates competing for elective office, therefore, provides the sole relevant rationale for §608(a)'s expenditure ceiling. That interest is clearly not sufficient to justify the provision's infringement of fundamental First Amendment rights. . . .

3. Limitations on Campaign Expenditures

Section 608(c) places limitations on overall campaign expenditures by candidates seeking nomination for election and election to federal office. . . .

No governmental interest that has been suggested is sufficient to justify the restriction on the quantity of political expression imposed by §608(c)'s campaign expenditure limitations. The major evil associated with rapidly increasing campaign expenditures is the danger of candidate dependence on large contributions. The interest in alleviating the corrupting influence of large contributions is served by the Act's contribution limitations and disclosure provisions rather than by §608(c)'s campaign expenditure ceilings. . . .

The interest in equalizing the financial resources of candidates competing for federal office is no more convincing a justification for restricting the scope of federal election campaigns. . . .

The campaign expenditure ceilings appear to be designed primarily to serve the governmental interests in reducing the allegedly skyrocketing costs of political campaigns. . . . The First Amendment denies government the power to determine that spending to promote one's political views is wasteful, excessive, or unwise. In the free society ordained by our Constitution it is not the government but the people—individually as citizens and candidates and collectively as associations and political committees—who must retain control over the quantity and range of debate on public issues in a political campaign.

For these reasons we hold that §608(c) is constitutionally invalid. . . .

II. Reporting and Disclosure Requirements

. . . Each political committee is required to register with the Commission, §433, and to keep detailed records of both contributions and expenditures, §§432(c), (d). . . . Each committee and each candidate also is required to file quarterly reports. . . . The reports are to contain detailed financial information. . . .

Every individual or group, other than a political committee or candidate, who makes "contributions" or "expenditures" of over $100 in a calendar year "other than by contribution to a political committee or a candidate" is required to file a statement with the Commission. . . .

A. General Principles

Unlike the overall limitations on contributions and expenditures, the disclosure requirements impose no ceiling on campaign-related activities. But we have repeatedly found that compelled disclosure, in itself, can seriously infringe on privacy of association and belief guaranteed by the First Amendment. . . .

We long have recognized that significant encroachments on First Amendment rights of the sort that compelled disclosure imposes cannot be justified by a mere showing of some legitimate governmental interest. Since *NAACP v. Alabama* [1958] we have required that the subordinating interests of the State must survive exacting scrutiny. . . .

The strict test established by *NAACP v. Alabama* is necessary because compelled disclosure has the potential for substantially infringing the exercise of First Amendment rights. But we have acknowledged that there are governmental interests sufficiently important to outweigh the possibility of infringement, particularly when the "free functioning of our national institutions" is involved. . . .

The governmental interests sought to be vindicated by the disclosure requirements are of this magnitude. They fall into three categories. First, disclosure provides the electorate with information "as to where political campaign money comes from and how it is spent by the candidate" in order to aid the voters in evaluating those who seek federal office. It allows voters to place each candidate in the political spectrum more precisely than is often possible solely on the basis of party labels and campaign speeches. The sources of a candidate's financial support also alert the voter to the interests to which a candidate is most likely to be responsive and thus facilitate predictions of future performance in office.

Second, disclosure requirements deter actual corruption and avoid the appearance of corruption by exposing large contributions and expenditures to the light of publicity. . . .

Third, and not least significant, record keeping, reporting, and disclosure requirements are an essential means of gathering the data necessary to detect violations of the contribution limitations described above.

The disclosure requirements, as a general matter, directly serve substantial governmental interests. In determining whether these interests are sufficient to justify the requirements we must look to the extent of the burden that they place on individual rights.

THE NATURE AND FUNCTIONS OF INTEREST GROUPS

Group theory is an important component of democratic political theory. The essence of group theory is that in the democratic process interest groups interact naturally and properly to produce public policy. In American political thought, the origins of this theory can be found in the theory of concurrent majority in John C. Calhoun's *Disquisition on Government.*

It is very useful to discuss the operation of interest groups within the framework of what can best be described as a *concurrent majority system.* In contemporary usage the phrase *concurrent majority* means a system in which major government policy decisions must be approved by the dominant interest groups directly affected. The word *concurrent* suggests that each group involved must give its consent before policy can be enacted. Thus a concurrent majority is a majority of each group considered separately. If we take as an example an area such as agricultural policy, in which three or four major private interest groups can be identified, we can say that the concurrent majority is reached when each group affected gives its approval before agricultural policy is passed. The extent to which such a system of concurrent majority is actually functioning is a matter that has not been fully clarified by empirical research. Nevertheless, it does seem tenable to conclude that in many major areas of public policy, it is necessary at least to achieve a concurrent majority of the *major* or *dominant* interests affected.

The *theory* of concurrent majority originated with John C. Calhoun. Calhoun, born in 1781, had a distinguished career in public service at both the national and state levels. The idea of concurrent majority evolved from the concept of state nullification of federal law. Under this states' rights doctrine, states would be able to veto any national action. The purpose of this procedure, theoretically, was to protect states in a minority from encroachment by a national majority that could act through Congress, the president, and even the Supreme Court. Those who favored this procedure had little faith in the separation-of-powers doctrine as an effective device to prevent the arbitrary exercise of national power. At the end of his career, Calhoun decided to incorporate his earlier views on state nullification into a more substantial theoretical treatise in political science; thus he wrote his famous *Disquisition on Government* (New York: D. Appleton & Co., 1853) in the decade between 1840 and 1850. He attempted to develop a general theory of constitutional (limited) government, the primary mechanism of which would be the ability of the major interest groups (states, in Calhoun's time) to veto legislation adverse to their interests. Students should overlook some of the theoretical inconsistencies in Calhoun and concentrate upon the basic justification he advances for substituting his system of concurrent majority for the separation-of-powers device. Under the latter, group interests are not necessarily taken into account, for national laws can be passed on the basis of a numerical majority. And even though this majority may reflect the interests of some groups, it will not necessarily reflect the interests of all groups affected. Calhoun argued that a system in which the major interest groups can dominate the policy process is really more in accord with constitutional democracy than the system established in our Constitution and supported in *Federalist 10.*

The group theory of John C. Calhoun has been updated and carried over into modern political science by several writers, one of the most important being David B. Truman. David Truman's selection, taken from *The Governmental Process* (1951), contains (1) a definition of the term interest group and (2) a brief outline of the frame of reference within which the operations of interest groups should be considered. A fairly articulate interest group theory of the governmental process is sketched by Truman. It will become evident to the student of American government that interest groups, like political parties, form an integral part of our political system. Further, interest group theory suggests an entirely new way of looking at government.

40

THE GOVERNMENTAL PROCESS

David B. Truman

Interest Groups

Interest group refers to any group that, on the basis of one or more shared attitudes, makes certain claims upon other groups in the society for the establishment, maintenance, or enhancement of forms of behavior that are implied by the shared attitudes. . . . [F]rom interaction in groups arise certain common habits of response, which may be called norms, or shared attitudes. These afford the participants frames of reference for interpreting and evaluating events and behaviors. In this respect all groups are interest groups because they are shared-attitude groups. In some groups at various points in time, however, a second kind of common response emerges, in addition to the frame of reference. These are shared attitudes toward what is needed or wanted in a given situation, as demands or claims upon other groups in the society. The term "interest group" will be reserved here for those groups that exhibit both aspects of the shared attitudes. . . .

Definition of the interest group in this fashion . . . permits the identification of various potential as well as existing interest groups. That is, it invites examination of an interest whether or not it is found at the moment as one of the characteristics of a particular organized group. Although no group that makes claims upon other groups in society will be found without an interest or interests, it is possible to examine interests that are not at a particular point in time the basis of interactions among individuals, but that may become such. . . .

Groups and Government: Difficulties in a Group Interpretation of Politics

Since we are engaged in an effort to develop a conception of the political process in the United States that will account adequately for the role of groups, particularly interest groups, it will be appropriate to take account of some of the factors that have been regarded as obstacles to such a conception and that have caused such groups to be neglected in many explanations of the dynamics of government. Perhaps the most important practical reason for this neglect is that the significance of groups has only fairly recently been forced to the attention of political scientists by the tremendous growth in the number of formally organized groups in the United States within the last few decades. It is difficult and unnecessary to attempt to date the beginning of such attention, but Herring in 1929, in his groundbreaking book, *Group Representation Before Congress*, testified to the novelty of the observations he reported when he stated: "There has developed in this government an extra-legal machinery of as integral and of as influential a nature as the system of party government that has long been an essential part of the government. . . . " Some implications of this development are not wholly compatible with some of the proverbial notions about representative government held by specialists as well as laymen. . . . This apparent incompatibility has obstructed the inclusion of group behaviors in an objective description of the governmental process.

More specifically, it is usually argued that any attempt at the interpretation of politics in terms of group patterns inevitably "leaves something out" or "destroys something essential" about the processes of "our" government. On closer examination, we find this argument suggesting that two "things" are certain to be ignored: the individual, and a sort of totally inclusive unity designated by such terms as "society" and "the state."

The argument that the individual is ignored in any interpretation of politics as based upon groups seems to assume a differentiation or conflict between "the individual" and some such collectivity as the group. . . .

Such assumptions need not present any difficulties in the development of a group interpretation of politics, because they are essentially unwarranted. They simply do not square with . . . evidence concerning group affiliations and individual behavior. . . . We do not, in fact, find individuals otherwise than in groups; complete isolation in space and time is so rare as to be an almost hypothetical situation. It is equally demonstrable that the characteristics of any interest group, including the activities by which we identify it, are governed by the attitudes and the circumstances that gave rise to the interactions of which it consists. There are variable factors, and, although the role played by a particular individual may be quite different in a lynch mob from that of the same individual in a meeting of the church deacons, the attitudes and behaviors involved in both are as much a part of his personality as is his treatment of his family. "The individual" and "the group" are at most merely convenient ways of classifying behavior, two ways of approaching the same phenomena, not different things.

The persistence among nonspecialists of the notion of an inherent conflict between "the individual" and "the group" or "society" is understandable in view of the doctrines of individualism that have underlain various political and economic conflicts over the past three centuries. The notion persists also because it harmonizes with a view of the isolated and independent individual as the "cause" of complicated human events. The personification of events, quite apart from any ethical considerations, is a kind of shorthand convenient in everyday speech and, like supernatural explanations of natural phenomena, has a comforting simplicity. Explanations that take into account multiple causes, including group affiliations, are difficult. The "explanation" of a national complex like the Soviet Union wholly in terms of a Stalin or the "description" of the intricacies of the American government entirely in terms of a Roosevelt is quick and easy. . . .

The second major difficulty allegedly inherent in any attempt at a group interpretation of the political process is that such an explanation inevitably must ignore some greater unity designated as society or the state. . . .

Many of those who place particular emphasis upon this difficulty assume explicitly or implicitly that there is an interest of the nation as a whole, universally and invariably held and standing apart from and superior to those of the various groups included within it. This assumption is close to the popular dogmas of democratic government based on the familiar notion that if only people are free and have access to "the facts," they will all want the same thing in any political situation. It is no derogation of democratic preferences to state that such an assertion flies in the face of all that we know of the behavior of men in a complex society. Were it in fact true, not only the interest group but even the political party should properly be viewed as an abnormality. The differing experiences and perceptions of men not only encourage individuality but also . . . inevitably result in differing attitudes and conflicting group affiliations. "There are," says Bentley in his discussion of this error of the social whole, "always some parts of the nation to be found arrayed against other parts." [From *The Process of Government* (1908).] Even in war, when a totally inclusive interest should be apparent if it is ever going to be, we always find pacifists, conscientious objectors, spies, and subversives, who reflect interests opposed to those of "the nation as a whole."

There is a political significance in assertions of a totally inclusive interest within a nation. Particularly in times of crisis, such as an international war, such claims are a tremendously useful promotional device by means of which a particularly extensive group or league of groups tries to reduce or eliminate opposing interests. Such is the pain attendant upon not "belonging" to one's "own" group that if a normal person can be convinced that he is the lone dissenter to an otherwise universally accepted agreement, he usually will conform. This pressure accounts at least in part for the number of prewar pacifists who, when the United States entered World War II, accepted the draft or volunteered. Assertion of an inclusive "national" or "public interest" is an effective device in many less critical situations as well. In themselves, these claims are part of the data of politics. However, they do not describe any actual or possible political situation within a complex modern nation. In developing a group interpretation of politics, therefore, we do not need to account for a totally inclusive interest, because one does not exist.

Denying the existence of an interest of the nation as a whole does not completely dispose of the difficulty raised by those who insist that a group interpretation must omit "the state." We cannot deny the obvious fact that we are examining a going political system that is supported or at least accepted by a large proportion of the society. We cannot account for such a system by adding up in some fashion the National Association of Manufacturers, the Congress of Industrial Organizations, the American Farm Bureau Federation, the American Legion, and other groups that come to mind when "lobbies" and "pressure groups" are mentioned. Even if the political parties are added to the list, the result could properly be designated as "a view which seems hardly compatible with the relative stability of the political system. . . ." Were such the exclusive ingredients of the political process in the United States, the entire system would have torn itself apart long since.

If these various organized interest groups more or less consistently reconcile their differences, adjust, and accept compromises, we must acknowledge that we are dealing with a system that is not accounted for by the "sum" of the organized interest groups in the society. We must go further to explain the operation of such ideals or traditions as constitutionalism, civil liberties, representative responsibility, and the like. These are not, however, a sort of disembodied metaphysical influence, like Mr. Justice Holmes's "brooding omnipresence." We know of the existence of such factors only from the behavior and the habitual interactions of men. If they exist in this fashion, they are interests. We can account for their operation and for the system by recognizing such interests as representing what . . . we called potential interest groups in the "becoming" stage of activity. "It is certainly true," as Bentley has made clear, "that we must accept a . . . group of this kind as an interest group itself." It makes no difference that we cannot find the home office and the executive secretary of such a group. Organization in this formal sense, as we have seen, represents merely a stage or degree of interaction that may or may not be significant at any particular point in time. Its absence does not mean that these interests do not exist, that the familiar "pressure groups" do not operate as if such potential groups were organized and active, or that these interests may not move from the potential to the organized stage of activity.

It thus appears that the two major difficulties supposedly obstacles to a group interpretation of the political process are not insuperable. We can employ the fact of individuality and we can account for the existence of the state without doing violence to the evidence available from the observed behaviors of men and groups. . . .

Interest Groups and the Nature of the State

Men, wherever they are observed, are creatures participating in those established patterns of interaction that we call groups. Excepting perhaps the most casual and transitory, these continuing interactions, like all such interpersonal relationships, involve power. This power is exhibited in two closely interdependent ways. In the first place, the group exerts power over its members; an individual's group affiliations largely determine his attitudes, values, and the frames of reference in terms of which he interprets his experiences. For a measure of conformity to the norms of the group is the price of acceptance within it. . . . In the second place, the group, if it is or becomes an interest group, which any group in society may be, exerts power over other groups in the society when it successfully imposes claims upon them.

Many interest groups, probably an increasing proportion in the United States, are politicized. That is, either from the outset or from time to time in the course of their development they make their claims through or upon the institutions of government. Both the forms and functions of government in turn are a reflection of the activities and claims of such groups. . . .

The institutions of government are centers of interest-based power; their connections with interest groups may be latent or overt and their activities range in political character from the routinized and widely accepted to the unstable and highly controversial. In order to make claims, political interest groups will seek access to the key points of decision within these institutions. Such points are scattered throughout the structure, including not only the formally established branches of government but also the political parties in their various forms and the relationships between governmental units and other interest groups. The extent to which a group achieves effective access to the institutions of government is the resultant of a complex of interdependent factors. For the sake of simplicity these may be classified in three somewhat overlapping categories: (1) factors relating to a group's strategic position in the society; (2) factors associated with the internal characteristics of the group; and (3) factors peculiar to the governmental institutions themselves. In the first category are: the group's status or prestige in the society, affecting the ease with which it commands deference from those outside its bounds; the standing it and its activities have when measured against the widely held but largely unorganized interests or "rules of the game"; the extent to which government officials are formally or informally "members" of the group; and the usefulness of the group as a source of technical and political knowledge. The second category includes: the degree of appropriateness of the group's organization; the degree of cohesion it can achieve in a given situation, especially in the light of competing group demands upon its membership; the skills of the leadership; and the group's resources in numbers and money. In the third category are: the operating structure of the government institutions, since such established features involve relatively fixed advantages and handicaps; and the effects of the group life of particular units or branches of the government. . . .

A characteristic feature of the governmental system in the United States is that it contains a multiplicity of points of access. The federal system establishes decentralized and more or less independent centers of power, vantage points from which to secure privileged access to the national government. Both a sign and a cause of the strength of the constituent units in the federal scheme is the peculiar character of our party system, which has strengthened parochial relationships, especially those of national legislators. National parties, and to a lesser degree those in the states, tend to be poorly cohesive leagues of locally based organizations rather than unified and inclusive structures. Staggered terms for executive officials and various types of legislators accentuate differences in the effective electorates that participate in choosing these officers. Each of these different, often opposite, localized patterns (constituencies) is a channel of independent access to the larger party aggregation and to the formal government. Thus, especially at the national level, the party is an electing-device and only in limited measure an integrated means of policy determination. Within the Congress, furthermore, controls are diffused among committee chairmen and other leaders in both chambers. The variety of these points of access is further supported by relationships stemming from the constitutional doctrine of separation of powers, from related checks and balances, and at the state and local level from the common practice of choosing an array of executive officials by popular election. At the federal level the formal simplicity of the executive branch has been complicated by a Supreme Court decision that has placed a number of administrative agencies beyond the removal power of the President. The position of these units, however, differs only in degree from that of many that are constitutionally within the Executive Branch. In consequence of alternative lines of access available through the legislature and the Executive and of divided channels for the control of administrative policy, many nominally executive agencies are at various times virtually independent of the Chief Executive.

. . . Within limits, therefore, organized interest groups, gravitating toward responsive points of decision, may play one segment of the structure against another as circumstances and strategic considerations permit. The total pattern of government over a period of time thus presents a protean complex of crisscrossing relationships that change in strength and direction with alterations in the power and standing of interests, organized and unorganized.

From Truman's definition, any group, organized or unorganized, that has a shared attitude toward goals and methods for achieving them should be classified as an interest group. Truman is essentially saying that, since people generally function as members of groups, it is more useful and accurate for the political observer to view the governmental process as the interaction of political interest groups. If one accepts the sociologist's assumption that people act and interact only as members of groups, then it is imperative that the governmental process be viewed as one of interest group interaction.

Within the framework of Truman's definition it is possible to identify both *public* and *private* interest groups. In the political process, governmental groups sometimes act as interest groups in the same sense as private organizations. In many public policies, governmental groups may have more at stake than private organizations. Thus administrative agencies, for example, may lobby as vigorously as their private counterparts to advance their own interests.

Truman contends that pluralism contains automatic checks and balances as interest groups check each other as they strive for power and dominance. The following selection introduces a classic *economic* theory of countervailing power that translates to politics as well. The famous economist John Kenneth Galbraith introduced the theory in his important work, *American Capitalism: The Concept of Countervailing Power* (1952), published shortly after the appearance of David Truman's *The Governmental Process* in 1950.

41

THE THEORY OF COUNTERVAILING POWER

John Kenneth Galbraith

. . . In fact, new restraints on private power did appear to replace [the traditional theory of capitalist] competition [which resulted in a system of economic checks and balances]. [The new restraints] were nurtured by the same process of concentration which impaired or destroyed competition. But they appeared not on the same side of the market but on the opposite side, not with competitors but with customers or suppliers. It will be convenient to have a name for this counterpart of competition and I shall call it *countervailing power*.

To begin with a broad and somewhat too dogmatically stated proposition, private economic power is held in check by the countervailing power of those who are subject to it. The first begets the second. The long trend toward concentration of industrial enterprise in the hands of a relatively few firms has brought into existence not only strong sellers, as economists have supposed, but also strong buyers as they have failed to see. The two develop together, not in precise step but in such manner that there can be no doubt that the one is in response to the other. . . .

The contention I am here making is a formidable one. It comes to this: Competition which, at least since the time of Adam Smith, has been viewed as the autonomous regulator of economic activity and as the only available regulatory mechanism apart from the state, has, in fact, been superseded. Not entirely, to be sure. There are still important markets where the power of the firm as (say) a seller is checked or circumscribed by those who provide a similar or a substitute product or service. This, in the broadest sense that can be meaningful, is the meaning of competition. The role of the buyer on the other side of such markets is essentially a passive one. It consists in looking for, perhaps asking for, and responding to the best bargain. The active restraint is provided by the competitor who offers, or threatens to offer, a better bargain. By contrast, in the typical modern market of few sellers, the active restraint is provided not by competitors but from the other side of the market by strong buyers. Given the convention against price competition, it is the role of the competitor that becomes passive.

It was always one of the basic presuppositions of competition that market power exercised in its absence would invite the competitors who would eliminate such exercise of power. In other words competition was regarded as a *self-generating* regulatory force. The doubt whether this was in fact so after a market had been preempted by a few large sellers, after entry of new firms had become difficult and after existing firms had accepted a convention against price competition, was what destroyed the faith in competition as a regulatory mechanism. Countervailing power is also a self-generating force and this is a matter of great importance. Something, although not very much, could be claimed for the regulatory role of the strong buyer in relation to the market power of sellers, did it happen that, as an accident of economic development, such strong buyers were frequently juxtaposed to strong sellers. However it is far more important that, as with the ancient presupposition concerning competition, the regulatory role of the strong buyer, in relation to the market power of the strong seller, is also self-generating. As noted, power on one side of a market creates both the need for, and the prospect of reward to, the exercise of countervailing power from the other side. In the market of small numbers, the self-generating power of competition is a chimera. That of countervailing power, by contrast, is readily assimilated to the common sense of the situation and its existence, once we have learned to look for it, is readily subject to empirical verification.

Market power can be exercised by strong buyers against weak sellers as well as by strong sellers against weak buyers. In the competitive model, competition acted as a restraint on both kinds of exercise of power. This is also the case with countervailing power. In turning to its practical manifestations, it will be convenient, in fact, to begin with a case where it is exercised by weak sellers against strong buyers. . . .

The operation of countervailing power is to be seen with the greatest clarity in the labor market where it is also most fully developed. Because of his comparative immobility, the worker has long been highly vulnerable to private economic power. The customer of any particular steel mill, at the turn of the century, could always take himself elsewhere if he felt he was being overcharged. Or he could exercise his sovereign privilege of not buying steel at all. The worker had no comparable freedom if he felt he was being underpaid. Normally he could not move and he had to have work. Not often has the power of one man over another been used more callously than in the American labor market after the rise of the large corporation. As late as the early twenties, the steel industry worked a twelve-hour day and seventy-two-hour week with an incredible twenty-four-hour stint every fortnight when the shift changed.

No such power is exercised today and for the reason that its earlier exercise stimulated the counteraction that brought it to an end. In the ultimate sense it was the power of the steel industry, not the organizing abilities of John L. Lewis and Philip Murray, that brought the United Steel Workers into being. The economic power that the worker faced in the sale of his labor—the competition of many sellers dealing with few buyers—made it necessary that he organize for his own protection. There were rewards to the power of the steel companies in which, when he had successfully developed countervailing power, he could share.

As a general though not invariable rule there are strong unions in the United States only where markets are served by strong corporations. And it is not an accident that the large automobile, steel, electrical, rubber, farm-machinery and non-ferrous metal-mining and smelting companies all bargain with powerful CIO unions. Not only has the strength of the corporations in these industries made it necessary for workers to develop the protection of countervailing power, it has provided unions with the opportunity for getting something more as well. If successful they could share in the fruits of the corporation's market power. By contrast there is not a single union of any consequence in American agriculture, the country's closest approach to the competitive model. The reason lies not in the difficulties in organization; these are considerable, but greater difficulties in organization have been overcome. The reason is that the farmer has not possessed any power over his labor force, and at least until recent times has not had any rewards from market power, which it was worth the while of a union to seek. As an interesting verification of the point, in the Great Valley of California, the large farmers of that area have had considerable power vis-à-vis their labor force. Almost uniquely in the United States, that region has been marked by persistent attempts at organization by farm workers.

The other industries which are not marked by any high degree of concentration, and accordingly are not especially powerful in their labor market, do not normally have strong unions. The textile industry, boot and shoe manufacture, lumbering and other forest industries in most parts of the country, and smaller wholesale and retail enterprises, are all cases in point. I do not advance the theory of countervailing power as a monolithic explanation of trade-union organization; in the case of bituminous-coal mining and the clothing industry, for example, the unions have emerged as a supplement to the weak market position of the operators and manufacturers. They have assumed price- and market-regulating functions that are the normal functions of management. Nevertheless, as an explanation of the incidence of trade union strength in the American economy, the theory of countervailing power clearly fits the broad contours of experience.

Since the phenomenon of countervailing power is of great practical importance, even though it has gone unrecognized in economic or political theory, we should expect, in line with our highly pragmatic approach to government, that it would have been the object of a good deal of legislation and the subject of a good deal of government policy. As the last chapter has made clear, there are strong incentives in the modern economy for developing countervailing power.

Moreover, the group that seeks countervailing power is, initially, a numerous and disadvantaged group which seeks organization because it faces, in its market, a much smaller and much more advantaged group. This situation is well calculated to excite public sympathy and, because there are numerous votes involved, to recruit political support.

In fact, the support of countervailing power has become in the last two decades perhaps the major peacetime function of the federal government. Labor has sought and received it in the protection and assistance which the Wagner Act provided to union organization. Farmers sought and received it in the form of federal price supports to their markets—a direct subsidy of market power. Unorganized workers have sought and received it in the form of minimum wage legislation. The bituminous-coal mines sought and received it in the Bituminous Coal Conservation Act of 1935 and the National Bituminous Coal Act of 1937. In a considerably more tenuous sense, investors have received it, via the Securities and Exchange Commission, in support of their position vis-à-vis the management or control of the large corporation. These measures, all designed to give a group a market power it did not have before, were among the most important legislative acts of the New Deal.

There should be no problem as to why this legislation, and the administration that sponsored it, were keenly controversial. The groups that sought the assistance of government in building countervailing power sought that power in order to use it against market authority to which they had previously been subordinate. Those whose power was thereby inhibited could hardly be expected to welcome this development or the intervention of the government to abet it.

Because the nature of countervailing power has not been firmly grasped, the government's role in relation to it has not only been imperfectly understood but also imperfectly played. One is permitted to hope that a better understanding of countervailing power will contribute to better administration in the future. . . .

The role of countervailing power in the economy marks out two broad problems in policy for the government. In all but conditions of inflationary demand, countervailing power performs a valuable—indeed an indispensable—regulatory function in the modern economy. Accordingly it is incumbent upon government to give it freedom to develop and to determine how it may best do so. The government also faces the question of where and how it will affirmatively support the development of countervailing power. It will be convenient to look first at the negative role of the government in allowing the development of countervailing power and then to consider its affirmative role in promoting it.

HOW AMERICAN GOVERNMENT AND POLITICS ENHANCE INTEREST GROUP POWER

The unique characteristics of our Madisonian government and our political process contribute to interest group power, as the following selection describes.

42

INTEREST GROUPS AND THE AMERICAN POLITICAL SYSTEM

Mark J. Rozell and Clyde Wilcox

Interest groups' high level of involvement in American elections stems, in part, from distinctive characteristics of American government, political parties, and elections. First, governmental decision making offers multiple incentives and opportunities for influencing policy. Second, the major U.S. parties are permeable to outside interests, enabling interest group activists to obtain powerful positions within local, state, and national party organizations. Third, American elections are unique: they are much more frequent than those of most other Western democracies, and far smaller percentages of citizens vote. Moreover, American elections are candidate centered: candidates must decide to run, raise their own funds, assemble their own coalitions, and reach voters with carefully targeted messages—all of which occurs outside the formal party structure.

Characteristics of American Government

At the same time that our federal system creates incentives for interest group involvement, it also places demands on interest groups, which must work within the system in order to successfully influence policy. First, because policy can be made at the national, state, and local levels, interest groups are generally called upon to be active at all three levels.

Second, interest groups are well aware that local councils and state legislatures constitute a "pipeline" of potential candidates for the House of Representatives.

Thus, they often participate in state and local races with the intention of cultivating and training potential candidates for national office.

Third, the division of powers between the executive and legislative branches means that interest groups must try to cultivate access to both the president and Congress. Given that the executive and legislative branches have different constituencies, timetables, and interests, this is a difficult enough task, but it has been made even more complex during the past forty years because the two branches have often been under the control of different parties. . . .

Fourth, because members of Congress are not bound to vote for the policies of party leaders but are independent actors, even those of the minority party are in a position to help or hurt an interest group's policy agenda. Any member of the House or Senate can introduce a bill drafted in consultation with an interest group and offer amendments in committee or on the floor to make the bill more palatable to interest groups. When a bill is up for a vote, members of Congress may vote however they choose. In the Senate, any member can put a "hold" on a bill, delaying a vote perhaps indefinitely.

[I]nterest groups often bolster their lobbying efforts by engaging in electoral activities. By helping members of Congress win elections, interest groups hope to establish relationships with senators and representatives and to get some return on their investment in the form of public policy actions. On occasion, relationships cultivated through electoral activity enable interest groups to build coalitions in support of their policy positions, even over the objections of party leaders.

Finally, the U.S. government is perhaps more willing than that of many other countries to distribute particularistic economic benefits to interest groups. Appropriations, tax, and even substantive bills such as highway bills are generally filled with specific language benefiting one or more companies or interest groups. Corporations get government contracts, special tax provisions, and exemptions from regulations (or, more commonly, delays in implementing regulations), all of which can affect their profits. In addition, members of Congress and occasionally even presidents intercede with the bureaucracy in an attempt to win favorable treatment for particular groups. The opportunity to obtain specific economic benefits is yet another incentive for interest groups to develop close relationships with policy makers—and one important way to do so is through electoral politics.

Characteristics of American Parties

Like the American government, American political parties differ from their counterparts in other democracies. In many countries, parties are closely linked with one or a few interests that they can be said to represent. In Europe, labor unions are represented by labor or social democratic parties, the Catholic Church speaks through Christian democratic parties, environmentalists have formed "green" parties, and very conservative citizens are represented by "new radical right" parties. In Israel, orthodox religious groups have their own political parties. In some countries, interest groups are represented by distinct sectors of a party. In Mexico, for example, the Partido Revolucionario Institucionalizado (PRI) has separate sectors representing agriculture, workers, and students.

In the United States, however, the parties have established relationships with a variety of interest groups that make up their core constituencies, but they also interact with groups that are nonpartisan or that are willing to back candidates of either party. . . .

Because interest groups have resources—mailing lists, newsletters, conventions, and volunteers—that can help political parties reach out to group members and other voters, parties often rely on interest groups to help them communicate with voters, often working closely with particular groups to develop and distribute distinctive messages targeting group members. When GOP leaders want to get the word out to white evangelical voters that theirs is the party of moral conservatism, they ask the Christian Coalition to carry the message in its publications, to distribute voters' guides in conservative churches, and to allow party leaders to speak at the organization's annual convention. Similarly, Democratic officials rely on unions to reach workers, on feminist organizations to reach working women, and on environmental groups to reach voters who are concerned about pollution.

Perhaps the most distinctive feature of American parties and elections is that party leaders play only a small role in selecting candidates. Through party primaries, caucuses, and conventions, interest groups can help to determine which candidates win nomination and can even work to nominate activists and members from their own groups. Although party officials are usually neutral in intraparty contests, interest groups both individually and in coalition with others are extremely active in aiding one candidate over another. . . .

Finally, unlike many European parties, which receive most or all of their campaign money from the government, American parties must raise their own money from individual and group contributions. Interest groups provide much of the money for parties through a variety of legal mechanisms. Money from interest groups helps fund party electoral activities, as well as buildings, computers, and party workers' salaries. Interest groups also contribute to party foundations and think tanks that develop policy proposals for party leaders.

Characteristics of American Elections

Elections are a necessary component of democracy, but democracies implement elections in very different ways. In most countries, elections are held at regular intervals and generally occur at the same time, both for national executive and legislative offices and for regional and local government posts. Moreover, campaigns in most countries are relatively short: in Britain, for example, the 1996 campaign lasted six weeks and included all the seats in the national legislature and most local races.

In the United States, in contrast, elections are held almost continuously. . . .

Because members of the House of Representatives stand for election every two years, representatives are constantly running for reelection—raising money, addressing voters, refining their images and their messages. And their challengers sometimes begin campaigning more than a year before the election. Senators, who are elected for six-year terms, generally campaign for at least two years, and some focus on fund raising throughout their terms. Even before a new president is sworn into office, prospective candidates from the other major party may drop in on the early presidential caucus and primary states of Iowa and New Hampshire to "test the political waters."

Another distinctive characteristic of American elections is that they are candidate centered. . . .

The difficulties of running a candidate-centered campaign render interest groups obvious allies. Interest groups can recruit candidates and encourage them to run, help finance their campaigns, and assist them in selecting campaign themes. By providing access to special communication channels such as newsletters and group gatherings, interest groups can also help candidates reach interest group members effectively and inexpensively. . . .

A third unique characteristic of American elections is the low rate of voter turnout. . . .

Low levels of voter turnout create opportunities for organized groups to greatly influence election outcomes. . . .

Finally, American elections are nearly always winner-take-all contests in single-member districts. To see why this creates an incentive for interest groups to participate in elections, consider the consequences of a 2 percent shift under two different systems: if German labor unions succeeded in increasing by 2 percent the vote share of the German Social Democratic Party, that party would gain approximately 2 percent of the seats in the Bundestag, the German parliament, because a party's share of seats in the legislature is proportional to its percentage of the popular vote. In the United States, where representation is not proportional but is based on single-member districts, a 2 percent increase in the Democratic Party's share of the vote for the U.S. House would likely enable Democrats to regain control of that body, because the increase would allow a number of Democratic candidates in close races to win the seats. Thus, a modest aggregate swing in votes may allow one party to capture most of the close contests in the United States, resulting in a much larger swing in seats. In 1994, the Republicans won control of the House by a net swing of less than 2 percent of the popular vote. . . .

Taken together, the distinctive features of American government, parties, and elections give interest groups many opportunities and incentives to participate in election campaigns. . . .

MONEY, PACs, AND ELECTIONS

Political campaigning has become increasingly expensive at all levels of government. Only presidential campaigns are publicly funded, although candidates in presidential primaries have to garner a certain amount of private contributions to qualify for federal matching funds. The rise of political action committees, which the campaign finance laws of the 1970s recognized as legitimate, has enhanced the influence of private money and interest group

power in the political process. Money and politics go together in the contemporary political environment, and political action committees are a major source of campaign funds. While PACs are perfectly legitimate organizations, authorized and even encouraged by the campaign finance laws of the 1970s, they are often portrayed as the bad guys of American politics. They are the modern-day "factions" of the James Madison attack in *Federalist 10.* The author of the following selection suggests that PAC-bashing is overdone.

43

THE MISPLACED OBSESSION WITH PACs

Larry J. Sabato

The disturbing statistics and the horror stories about political action committees seem to flow like a swollen river, week after week, year in and year out. Outrage extends across the ideological spectrum: the liberal interest group Common Cause has called the system "scandalous," while conservative former senator Barry Goldwater (R–Ariz.) has bluntly declared, "PAC money is destroying the election process. . . ."

In more and more recent campaigns, political action committees have been portrayed as the central corrupting evil in American politics. In Massachusetts in 1984, for example, all the major contenders for the U.S. Senate in both parties refused to take PAC money, and one candidate even got his Democratic opponent to sign a statement pledging to resign his seat in Congress should he "ever knowingly accept and keep a campaign contribution from a political action committee."

Candidates from Maine to California have scored points by for-swearing the acceptance of PAC gifts earlier and more fervently than their opponents. The Democratic party included in its 1984 national platform a call for banning PAC funds from all federal elections, despite its aggressiveness in attracting PAC money to itself and its candidates.

PAC-bashing is undeniably a popular campaign sport, but the "big PAC attack" is an opiate that obscures the more vital concerns and problems in campaign finance. PAC excesses are merely a symptom of other serious maladies in the area of political money, but the near-obsessive focus by public interest groups and the news media on the PAC evils has diverted attention from more fundamental matters. The PAC controversy, including the charges most frequently made against them, can help explain why PACs are best described as agents of pseudo corruption.

The PAC Era

While a good number of PACs of all political persuasions existed prior to the 1970s, it was during that decade of campaign reform that the modern PAC era began. Spawned by the Watergate-inspired revisions of the campaign finance laws, PACs grew in number from 113 in 1972 to 4,196 by 1988, and their contributions to congressional candidates multiplied more than fifteenfold, from $8.5 million in 1971–72 to $130.3 million in 1985–86.

The rapid rise of PACs has engendered much criticism, yet many of the charges made against political action committees are exaggerated and dubious. While the widespread use of the PAC structure is new, special interest money of all types has always found its way into politics. Before the 1970s it simply did so in less traceable and far more disturbing and unsavory ways. And while, in absolute terms, PACs contribute a massive sum to candidates, it is not clear that there is proportionately more interest-group money in the system than before. As political scientist Michael Malbin has argued, we will never know the truth because the earlier record is so incomplete.

The proportion of House and Senate campaign funds provided by PACs has certainly increased since the early 1970s, but individuals, most of whom are unaffiliated with PACs, together with the political parties, still supply about three-fifths of all the money spent by or on behalf of House candidates and three-quarters of the campaign expenditures for Senate contenders. So while the importance of PAC spending has grown, PACs clearly remain secondary as a source of election funding. PACs, then, seem rather less awesome when considered within the entire spectrum of campaign finance.

Apart from the argument over the relative weight of PAC funds, PAC critics claim that political action committees are making it more expensive to run for office. There is some validity to this assertion. Money provided to one candidate funds the purchase of campaign tools that the other candidate must match in order to stay competitive.

In the aggregate, American campaign expenditures seem huge. In 1988, the total amount spent by all U.S. House of Representatives candidates taken together was about $256 million, and the campaign cost of the winning House nominee averaged over $392,000. Will Rogers's 1931 remark has never been more true: "Politics has got so expensive that it takes lots of money to even get beat with."

Yet $256 million is far less than the annual advertising budgets of many individual commercial enterprises. These days it is expensive to communicate, whether the message is political or commercial. Television time, polling costs, consultants' fees, direct-mail investment, and other standard campaign expenditures have been soaring in price, over and above inflation. PACs have been fueling the use of new campaign techniques, but a reasonable case can be made that such expenses are necessary, and that more and better communication is required between candidates and an electorate that often appears woefully uninformed about politics. PACs therefore may be making a positive contribution by providing the means to increase the flow of information during elections.

PACs are also accused of being biased toward the incumbent, and except for the ideological committees, they do display a clear and overwhelming preference for those already in office. But the same bias is apparent in contributions from individuals, who ask the same reasonable, perhaps decisive, economic question: Why waste money on contenders if incumbents almost always win? On the other hand, the best challengers—those perceived as having fair-to-good chances to win—are usually generously funded by PACs. Well-targeted PAC challenger money clearly helped the GOP win a majority in the U.S. Senate in 1980, for instance, and in turn aided the Democrats in their 1986 Senate takeover.

The charge that PACs limit the number of strong challengers is true, because by giving so much money so early in the race to incumbents, they deter potential opponents from declaring their candidacies. On the other hand, the money that PACs channel to competitive challengers late in the election season may actually help increase the turnover of officeholders on election day. PAC money also tends to invigorate competitiveness in open-seat congressional races where there is no incumbent.

One line of attack on PACs that seems fairly justified is the feeling that these important components of our democratic political system are themselves undemocratic in some respects. For example, in some cases their candidate selection process completely severs the connecting link between contributor and candidate. As political scientist David Adamany has noted, this condition is most apparent in many of the politically ideological nonconnected PACs, whose lack of a parent body and whose freestyle organization make them accountable to no one and responsive mainly to their own whims. Leaders of ideological PACs, however, insist that their committees are still democratic, since contributors will simply stop giving if dissatisfied with the PACs' candidate choices.

But ideological PACs raise most of their money by direct mail, which means that the average donor's only source of information about the PAC's activities is their own communication, which, not surprisingly, tends to be upbeat and selective in reporting the committee's work. Moreover, as political scientist Frank Sorauf has stressed, since direct mail can succeed with only a 2 to 5 percent response rate, and since prospecting for new donors is continuous, decisions by even a large number of givers to drop out will have little impact on PAC fundraising.

Ideological PACs are not alone in following undemocratic practices. When the AFL-CIO overwhelmingly endorsed Democrat Walter Mondale for president in 1983, thereby making available to him the invaluable resources of most labor PACs, a CBS News/*New York Times* poll showed that less than a quarter of the union members interviewed had their presidential preferences solicited in any fashion. If a representative sampling had taken place, the AFL-CIO might not have been so pro-Mondale, since the CBS/*Times* poll indicated that Mondale was not favored by a majority of the respondents and was in fact in a statistical dead heat with Senator John Glenn (D–Ohio) for a plurality edge.

Nor can many corporate PACs be considered showcases of democracy. In a few PACs the chief executive officers completely rule the roost, and in many the CEOs have inordinate influence on PAC decisions.

PAC Money and Congressional "Corruption"

The most serious charge leveled at PACs is that they succeed in buying the votes of legislators on issues important to their individual constituencies. It seems hardly worth arguing that many PACs are shopping for congressional votes and that PAC money buys access, or opens doors, to congressmen. But the "vote-buying" allegation is generally not supported by a careful examination of the facts. PAC contributions do make a difference, at least on some occasions, in securing access and influencing the course of events, but those occasions are not nearly as frequent as anti-PAC spokesmen, even congressmen themselves, often suggest.

PACs affect legislative proceedings to a decisive degree only when certain conditions prevail. First, the less visible the issue, the more likely that PAC funds can change or influence congressional votes. A corollary is that PAC money has more effect in the early stages of the legislative process, such as agenda setting and votes in subcommittee meetings, than in later and more public floor deliberations. Press, public, and even "watchdog" groups are not nearly as attentive to initial legislative proceedings.

PAC contributions are also more likely to influence the legislature when the issue is specialized and narrow, or unopposed by other organized interests. PAC gifts are less likely to be decisive on broad national issues such as American policy in Nicaragua or the adoption of a Star Wars missile defense system. But the more technical measures seem tailor-made for the special interests. Additionally, PAC influence in Congress is greater when large PACs or groups of PACs (such as business and labor PACs) are allied. In recent years, despite their natural enmity, business and labor have lobbied together on a number of issues, including defense spending, trade policy, environmental regulation, maritime legislation, trucking legislation, and nuclear power. The combination is a weighty one, checked in many instances only by a tendency for business and labor in one industry (say, the railroads) to combine and oppose their cooperating counterparts in another industry (perhaps the truckers and teamsters).

It is worth stressing, however, that most congressmen are not unduly influenced by PAC money on most votes. The special conditions simply do not apply to most legislative issues, and the overriding factors in determining a legislator's votes include party affiliation, ideology, and constituents' needs and desires. Much has been made of the passage of large tax cuts for oil and business interests in the 1981 omnibus tax package. The journalist Elizabeth Drew said there was a "bidding war" to trade campaign contributions for tax breaks benefiting independent oil producers. Ralph Nader's Public Citizen group charged that the

$280,000 in corporate PAC money accepted by members of the House Ways and Means Committee helped to produce a bill that "contained everything business ever dared to ask for, and more." Yet as Robert Samuelson has convincingly argued, the "bidding war" between Democrats and Republicans was waged not for PAC money but for control of a House of Representatives sharply divided between Reaganite Republicans and liberal Democrats, with conservative "boll weevil" Democrats from the southern oil states as the crucial swing votes. The Ways and Means Committee actions cited by Nader were also more correctly explained in partisan terms. After all, if these special interests were so influential in writing the 1981 omnibus tax package, how could they fail so completely to derail the much more important (and, for them, threatening) tax reform legislation of 1986?

If party loyalty can have a stronger pull than PAC contributions, then surely the views of a congressman's constituents can also take precedence over those of political action committees. If an incumbent is faced with choice of either voting for a PAC-backed bill that is very unpopular in his district or forgoing the PAC's money, the odds are that any politician who depends on a majority of votes to remain in office is going to side with his constituency and vote against the PAC's interest. PAC gifts are merely a means to an end: reelection. If accepting money will cause a candidate embarrassment, then even a maximum donation will likely be rejected. The flip side of this proposition makes sense as well: if a PAC's parent organization has many members or a major financial stake in the congressman's home district, he is much more likely to vote the PAC's way—not so much because he receives PAC money but because the group accounts for an important part of his electorate. Does a U.S. senator from a dairy state vote for dairy price supports because he received a significant percentage of his PAC contributions from agriculture, or because the farm population of his state is relatively large and politically active? When congressmen vote the National Rifle Association's preferences is it because of the money the NRA's PAC distributes, or because the NRA, unlike gun-control advocates, has repeatedly demonstrated the ability to produce a sizable number of votes in many legislative districts?

If PACs have appeared more influential than they actually are, it is partly because many people believe legislators are looking for opportunities to exclaim (as one did during the Abscam scandal) "I've got larceny in my blood!" It is certainly disturbing that the National Republican Congressional Committee believed it necessary to warn its PAC-soliciting candidates: "Don't ever suggest to the PAC that it is 'buying' your vote, should you get elected." Yet knowledgeable Capitol Hill observers agree that there are few truly corrupt congressmen. Simple correlations notwithstanding, when most legislators vote for a PAC-supported bill, it is because of the merits of the case, or the entreaties of their party leaders, peers, or constituents, and not because of PAC money.

When the PAC phenomenon is viewed in the broad perspective of issues, party allegiance, and constituent interests, it is clear that merit matters most in the votes most congressmen cast. It is naive to contend that PAC money never influences decisions, but it is unjustifiably cynical to believe that PACs always, or even usually, push the voting buttons in Congress.

PACs in Perspective

As the largely unsubstantiated "vote-buying" controversy suggests, PACs are often misrepresented and unfairly maligned as the embodiment of corrupt special interests. Political action committees are a contemporary manifestation of what James Madison called "factions." In his *Federalist No. 10*, Madison wrote that through the flourishing of these competing interest groups, or factions, liberty would be preserved.

In any democracy, and particularly in one as pluralistic as the United States, it is essential that groups be relatively unrestricted in advocating their interests and positions. Not only is that the mark of a free society, it also provides a safety valve for the competitive pressures that build on all fronts in a capitalistic democracy. And it provides another means to keep representatives responsive to legitimate needs.

This is not to say that all groups pursue legitimate interests, or that vigorously competing interests ensure that the public good prevails. The press, the public, and valuable watchdog groups such as Common Cause must always be alert to instances in which narrow private interests prevail over the commonwealth—occurrences that generally happen when no one is looking.

Besides the press and various public interest organizations, there are two major institutional checks on the potential abuses wrought by factions, associations, and now PACs. The most fundamental of these is regular free elections with general suffrage. As Tocqueville commented:

> Perhaps the most powerful of the causes which tend to mitigate the excesses of political association in the United States is Universal Suffrage. In countries in which universal suffrage exists, the majority is never doubtful, because neither party can pretend to represent that portion of the community which has not voted.
>
> The associations which are formed are aware, as well as the nation at large, that they do not represent the majority: this is, indeed, a condition inseparable from their existence; for if they did represent the prepondering power, they would change the law instead of soliciting its reform.

Senator Robert Dole (R–Kan.) has said, "There aren't any poor PACs or Food Stamp PACs or Nutrition PACs or Medicare PACs," and PAC critics frequently make the point that certain segments of the electorate are underrepresented in the PAC community. Yet without much support from PACs, there are food stamps, poverty and nutrition programs, and Medicare. Why? Because the recipients of governmental assistance constitute a hefty slice of the electorate, and votes matter more than dollars to politicians. Furthermore, many citizens outside the affected groups have also made known their support of aid to the poor and elderly—making yet a stronger electoral case for these PAC-less programs.

The other major institution that checks PAC influence is the two-party system. While PACs represent particular interests, the political parties build coalitions of groups and attempt to represent a national interest. They arbitrate among competing claims, and they seek to reach a consensus on matters of overriding importance to the nation. The parties are one of the few unifying forces in an exceptionally diverse country.

If interest groups and their PACs are useful to a functioning democracy, then political parties are essential. Yet just as PACs began gathering strength in the 1970s, the parties began a steady decline in power. In the past decade the rehabilitation of the party system has begun, but there is a long way to go. A central goal of the campaign financing reform agenda should be to strengthen the political parties, and to grant them a kind of "most favored nation" preferential status in the machinery of elections and campaign finance. Reforms to bolster the parties will also serve to temper the excesses of PACs by reducing their proportional impact on the election of public officials.

However limited and checkmated by political realities PACs may be, they are still regarded by a skeptical public as thoroughly unsavory. PACs have become the embodiment of greedy special interest politics, rising campaign costs, and corruption. It does not seem to matter that most experts in the field of campaign finance take considerable exception to the prevailing characterization of political action committees. PACs have become, in the public's mind, a powerful symbol of much that is wrong with America's campaign process, and candidates for public office naturally manipulate this symbol as well as others for their own ends. It is a circumstance as old as the Republic.

PACs, however, have done little to change their image for the better. Other than the business-oriented Public Affairs Council, few groups or committees have moved to correct one-sided press coverage or educate the public on campaign financing's fundamentals. In fact, many PACs fuel the fires of discontent by refusing to defend themselves while not seeming to care about appearances. Giving to both candidates in the same race, for example—an all-too-common practice—may be justifiable in theory, but it strikes most people as unprincipled, rank influence purchasing. Even worse, perhaps, are PACs that "correct their mistakes" soon after an election by sending a donation to the winning, but not originally PAC-supported, candidate. In the seven 1986 U.S. Senate races where a Democratic challenger defeated a Republican incumbent, there were 150 instances in which a PAC gave to the GOP candidate before the election and to the victorious Democrat once the votes were counted. These practices PACs themselves should stop. Every PAC should internally ban double giving, and there should be a moratorium on gifts to previously opposed candidates until at least the halfway point of the officeholder's term.

Whether PACs undertake some necessary rehabilitative steps or not, any fair appraisal of their role in American elections must be balanced. PACs are neither political innocents nor selfless civic boosters. But, neither are they cesspools of corruption and greed, nor modern-day versions of Tammany Hall.

PACs will never be popular with idealistic reformers because they represent the rough, cutting edge of a democracy teeming with different peoples and conflicting interests. Indeed, PACs may never be hailed even by natural allies; it was the business-oriented *Wall Street Journal*, after all, that editorially referred to Washington, D.C., as "a place where politicians, PACs, lawyers, and lobbyists for unions, business or you name it shake each other down full time for political money and political support."

Viewed in perspective, the root of the problem in campaign finance is not PACs; it is money. Americans have an enduring mistrust of the mix of money (particularly business money) and politics, as Finley Peter Dunne's Mr. Dooley revealed:

> I niver knew a pollytician to go wrong ontil he'd been contaminated be contact with a business man. . . . It seems to me that th' only thing to do is to keep pollyticians an' business men apart. They seem to have a bad inflooence on each other. Whiniver I see an alderman an' a banker walkin' down th' street together I know th' Recordin' Angel will have to ordher another bottle iv ink.

As a result of the new campaign finance rules of the 1970s, political action committees superceded the "fat cats" of old as the public focus and symbol of the role of money in politics, and PACs inherited the suspicions that go with the territory. Those suspicions are valuable because they keep the spotlight on PACs and guard against undue influence. It may be regrettable that such supervision is required, but human nature—not PACs—demands it.

PART THREE

NATIONAL GOVERNMENT INSTITUTIONS

44

FEDERALIST 70

Alexander Hamilton

There is an idea, which is not without its advocates, that a vigorous executive is inconsistent with the genius of republican government. The enlightened well-wishers to this species of government must at least hope that the supposition is destitute of foundation; since they can never admit its truth, without, at the same time, admitting the condemnation of their own principles. Energy in the executive is a leading character in the definition of good government. It is essential to the protection of the community against foreign attacks; it is not less essential to the steady administration of the laws, to the protection of property against those irregular and high-handed combinations, which sometimes interrupt the ordinary course of justice, to the security of liberty against the enterprises and assaults of ambition, of faction, and of anarchy. Every man, the least conversant in Roman story, knows how often that republic was obliged to take refuge in the absolute power of a single man, under the formidable title of dictator, as well as against the intrigues of ambitious individuals, who aspired to the tyranny, and the seditions of whole classes of the community, whose conduct threatened the existence of all government, as against the invasions of external enemies, who menaced the conquest and destruction of Rome.

There can be no need, however, to multiply arguments or examples on this head. A feeble executive implies a feeble execution of the government. A feeble execution is but another phrase for a bad execution; and government ill executed, whatever it may be in theory, must be, in practice, a bad government.

Taking it for granted, therefore, that all men of sense will agree in the necessity of an energetic executive, it will only remain to inquire, what are the ingredients which constitute this energy? How far can they be combined with those other ingredients, which constitute safety in the republican sense? And how far does this combination characterize the plan which has been reported by the convention?

The ingredients which constitute energy in the executive are: unity; duration; and adequate provision for its support; competent powers.

The ingredients which constitute safety in the republican sense are: a due dependence on the people; a due responsibility.

Those politicians and statesmen, who have been the most celebrated for the soundness of their principles, and for the justness of their views, have declared in favor of a single executive, and a numerous legislature. They have, with great propriety, considered energy as the most necessary qualification of the former, and have regarded this as most applicable to power in a single hand; while they have, with equal propriety, considered the latter as the best adapted to deliberation and wisdom, and best calculated to conciliate the confidence of the people, and to secure their privileges and interests.

That unity is conducive to energy will not be disputed. Decision, activity, secrecy, and dispatch, will generally characterize the proceedings of one man, in a much more eminent degree than the proceedings of any greater number; and in proportion as the number is increased, these qualities will be diminished.

This unity may be destroyed in two ways; either by vesting the power in two or more magistrates, of equal dignity and authority; or by vesting it ostensibly in one man, subject, in whole or in part, to the control and cooperation of others, in the capacity of counsellors to him. . . .

The experience of other nations will afford little instruction on this head. As far, however, as it teaches anything, it teaches us not to be enamored of plurality in the executive. . . .

Wherever two or more persons are engaged in any common enterprise or pursuit, there is always danger of difference of opinion. If it be a public trust of office, in which they are clothed with equal dignity and authority, there is peculiar danger of personal emulation and even animosity. From either, and especially from all these causes, the most bitter dissensions are apt to spring. Whenever these happen, they lessen the respectability, weaken the authority, and distract the plans and operations of those whom they divide. If they should unfortunately assail the supreme executive magistracy of a country, consisting of a plurality of persons, they might impede or frustrate the most important measures of the government, in the most critical emergencies of state. And what is still worse, they might split the community into violent and irreconcilable factions, adhering differently to the different individuals who composed the magistracy. . . .

Upon the principles of a free government, inconveniences from the source just mentioned, must necessarily be submitted to in the formation of the legislature; but it is unnecessary, and therefore unwise, to introduce them into the constitution of the executive. It is here, too, that they may be most pernicious. In the legislature, promptitude of decision is oftener an evil than a benefit. The differences of opinion, and the jarrings of parties in that department of the government, though they may sometimes obstruct salutary plans, yet often promote deliberation and circumspection; and serve to check excesses in the majority. When a resolution, too, is once taken, the opposition must be at an end. That resolution is a law, and resistance to it punishable. But no favorable circumstances palliate, or atone for the disadvantages of dissention in the executive department. Here they are pure and unmixed. There is no point at which they cease to operate. They serve to embarrass and weaken the execution of the plan or measure to which they relate, from the first step to the final conclusion of it. They constantly counteract those qualities in the executive, which are the most necessary ingredients in its composition—vigor and expedition; and this without any counterbalancing good. In the conduct of war, in which the energy of the executive is the bulwark of the national security, everything would be to be apprehended from its plurality.

It must be confessed, that these observations apply with principal weight to the first case supposed, that is, to a plurality of magistrates of equal dignity and authority, a scheme, the advocates for which are not likely to form a numerous sect; but they apply, though not with equal, yet with considerable weight, to the project of a council, whose concurrence is made constitutionally necessary to the operations of the ostensible executive. An artful cabal in that council would be able to distract and to enervate the whole system of administration. If no such cabal should exist, the mere diversity of views and opinions would alone be sufficient to tincture the exercise of the executive authority with the spirit of habitual feebleness and dilatoriness.

But one of the weightiest objections to a plurality in the executive, and which lies as much against the last as the first plan, is, that it tends to conceal faults, and destroy responsibility. . . . It often becomes impossible, amidst mutual accusations, to determine on whom the blame or the punishment of a pernicious measure . . . ought really to fall. It is shifted from one to another with so much dexterity, and under such plausible appearances, that the public opinion is left in suspense about the real author. . . .

A little consideration will satisfy us, that the species of security sought for in the multiplication of the executive, is unattainable. Numbers must be so great as to render combination difficult; or they are rather a source of danger than security. The united credit and influence of several individuals must be more formidable to liberty than the credit and influence of either of them separately. When power, therefore, is placed in the hands of so small a number of men, as to admit of their interests and views being easily combined in a common enterprise, by an artful leader, it becomes more liable to abuse, and more dangerous when abused, than if it be lodged in the hands of one man; who, from the very circumstances of his being alone, will be more narrowly watched and more readily suspected, and who cannot unite so great a mass of influence as when he is associated with others. . . .

I will only add, that prior to the appearance of the constitution, I rarely met with an intelligent man from any of the states, who did not admit as the result of experience, that the unity of the executive of this state was one of the best of the distinguishing features of our constitution.

THE NATURE OF THE PRESIDENCY: POWER, PERSUASION, AND PARADOXES

What is the position of the presidential office today? There is little doubt that it has expanded far beyond the expectations of the framers of the Constitution. The presidency is the only governmental branch with the necessary unity and energy to meet many of the most crucial problems of twentieth-century government in the United States; people have turned to the president in times of crisis to supply the central direction necessary for survival. In the next selection, Clinton Rossiter, one of the leading American scholars of the presidency, gives his view of the role of the office.

45

THE PRESIDENCY—FOCUS OF LEADERSHIP

Clinton Rossiter

No American can contemplate the presidency . . . without a feeling of solemnity and humility—solemnity in the face of a historically unique concentration of power and prestige, humility in the thought that he has had a part in the choice of a man to wield the power and enjoy the prestige.

Perhaps the most rewarding way to grasp the significance of this great office is to consider it as a focus of democratic leadership. Free men, too, have need of leaders. Indeed, it may be argued that one of the decisive forces in the shaping of American democracy has been the extraordinary capacity of the presidency for strong, able, popular leadership. If this has been true of our past, it will certainly be true of our future, and we should therefore do our best to grasp the quality of this leadership. Let us do this by answering the essential question: For what men and groups does the president provide leadership?

First, the president is *leader of the Executive Branch*. To the extent that our federal civil servants have need of common guidance, he alone is in a position to provide it. We cannot savor the fullness of the president's duties unless we recall that he is held primarily accountable for the ethics, loyalty, efficiency, frugality, and responsiveness to the public's wishes of the two and one-third million Americans in the national administration.

Both the Constitution and Congress have recognized his power to guide the day-to-day activities of the Executive Branch, strained and restrained though his leadership may often be in practice. From the Constitution, explicitly or implicitly, he receives the twin powers of appointment and removal, as well as the primary duty, which no law or plan or circumstances can ever take away from him, to "take care that the laws be faithfully executed."

From Congress, through such legislative mandates as the Budget and Accounting Act of 1921 and the succession of Reorganization Acts, the president has received further acknowledgment of his administrative leadership. Although independent agencies such as the Interstate Commerce Commission and the National Labor Relations Board operate by design outside his immediate area of responsibility, most of the government's administrative tasks are still carried on within the fuzzy-edged pyramid that has the president at its lonely peak; the laws that are executed daily in his name and under his general supervision are numbered in the hundreds.

Many observers, to be sure, have argued strenuously that we should not ask too much of the president as administrative leader, lest we burden him with impossible detail, or give too much to him, lest we inject political considerations too forcefully into the steady business of the civil service. Still, he cannot ignore the blunt mandate of the Constitution, and we should not forget the wisdom that lies behind it. The president has no more important tasks than to set a high personal example of integrity and industry for all who serve the nation, and to transmit a clear lead downward through his chief lieutenants to all who help shape the policies by which we live.

Next, the president is *leader of the forces of peace and war*. Although authority in the field of foreign relations is shared constitutionally among three organs—president, Congress, and for two special purposes, the Senate—his position is paramount, if not indeed dominant. Constitution, laws, customs, the practice of other nations, and the logic of history have combined to place the president in a dominant position. Secrecy, dispatch, unity, continuity, and access to information—the ingredients of successful diplomacy—are properties of his office, and Congress, needless to add, possesses none of them. Leadership in foreign affairs flows today from the president—or it does not flow at all.

The Constitution designates him specifically as "Commander in Chief of the Army and Navy of the United States." In peace and war he is the supreme commander of the armed forces, the living guarantee of the American belief in "the supremacy of the civil over military authority."

In time of peace he raises, trains, supervises, and deploys the forces that Congress is willing to maintain. With the aid of the Secretary of Defense, the Joint Chiefs of Staff, and the National Security Council—all of whom are his personal choices—he looks constantly to the state of the nation's defenses. He is never for one day allowed to forget that he will be held accountable by the people, Congress, and history for the nation's readiness to meet an enemy assault.

In time of war his power to command the forces swells out of all proportion to his other powers. All major decisions of strategy, and many of tactics as well, are his alone to make or to approve. Lincoln and Franklin Roosevelt, each in his own way and time, showed how far the power of military command can be driven by a president anxious to have his generals and admirals get on with the war.

But this, the power of command, is only a fraction of the vast responsibility the modern president draws from the Commander in Chief clause. We need only think back to three of Franklin D. Roosevelt's actions in World War II—the creation and staffing of a whole array of emergency boards and offices, the seizure and operation of more than sixty strike-bound or strike-threatened plants and industries, and the forced evacuation of 70,000 American citizens of Japanese descent from the West Coast—to understand how deeply the president's authority can cut into the lives and liberties of the American people in time of war. We may well tremble in contemplation of the kind of leadership he would be forced to exert in a total war with the absolute weapon.

The president's duties are not all purely executive in nature. He is also intimately associated, by Constitution and custom, with the legislative process, and we may therefore consider him as *leader of Congress*. Congress has its full share of strong men, but the complexity of the problems it is asked to solve by a people who still assume that all problems are solvable has made external leadership a requisite of effective operation.

The president alone is in a political, constitutional, and practical position to provide such leadership, and he is therefore expected, within the limits of propriety, to guide Congress in much of its lawmaking activity. Indeed, since Congress is no longer minded or organized to guide itself, the refusal or inability of the president to serve as a kind of prime minister results in weak and disorganized government. His tasks as leader of Congress are difficult and delicate, yet he must bend to them steadily or be judged a failure. The president who will not give his best thoughts to leading Congress, more so the president who is temperamentally or politically unfitted to "get along with Congress," is now rightly considered a national liability.

The lives of Jackson, Lincoln, Wilson, and the two Roosevelts should be enough to remind us that the president draws much of his real power from his position as *leader of his party*. By playing the grand politician with unashamed zest, the first of these men gave his epic administration a unique sense of cohesion, the second rallied doubting Republican leaders and their followings to the cause of the Union, and the other three achieved genuine triumphs as catalysts of Congressional action. That gifted amateur, Dwight D. Eisenhower, has also played the role for every drop of drama and power in it. He has demonstrated repeatedly what close observers of the presidency know well: that its incumbent must devote an hour or two of every working day to the profession of Chief Democrat or Chief Republican.

It troubles many good people, not entirely without reason, to watch the president dabbling in politics, distributing loaves and fishes, smiling on party hacks, and endorsing candidates he knows to be unfit for anything but immediate delivery to the county jail. Yet if he is to persuade Congress, if he is to achieve a loyal and cohesive administration, if he is to be elected in the first place (and reelected in the second), he must put his hand firmly to the plow of politics. The president is inevitably the nation's No. 1 political boss.

Yet he is, at the same time, if not in the same breath, *leader of public opinion*. While he acts as political chieftain of some, he serves as moral spokesman for all. It took the line of presidents some time to sense the nation's need for a clear voice, but since the day when Andrew Jackson thundered against the Nullifiers of South Carolina, no effective president has doubted his prerogative to speak the people's mind on the great issues of his time, to serve, in Wilson's words, as "the spokesman for the real sentiment and purpose of the country."

Sometimes, of course, it is no easy thing, even for the most sensitive and large-minded presidents, to know the real sentiment of the people or to be bold enough to state it in defiance of loudly voiced contrary opinion. Yet the president who senses the popular mood and spots new tides even before they start to run, who practices shrewd economy in his appearances as spokesman for the nation, who is conscious of his unique power to compel discussion on his own terms and who talks the language of Christian morality and the American tradition, can shout down any other voice or chorus of voices in the land. The president is the American people's one authentic trumpet, and he has no higher duty than to give a clear and certain sound.

The president is easily the most influential leader of opinion in this country principally because he is, among all his other jobs, our Chief of State. He is, that is to say, the ceremonial head of the government of the United States, the *leader of the rituals of American democracy*. The long catalogue of public duties that the Queen discharges in England and the Governor General in Canada is the President's responsibility in this country, and the catalogue is even longer because he is not a king, or even the agent of one, and is therefore expected to go through some rather undignified paces by a people who think of him as a combination of scoutmaster, Delphic oracle, hero of the silver screen, and father of the multitudes.

The role of Chief of State may often seem trivial, yet it cannot be neglected by a president who proposes to stay in favor and, more to the point, in touch with the people, the ultimate support of all his claims to leadership. And whether or not he enjoys this role, no president can fail to realize that his many powers are invigorated, indeed are given a new dimension of authority, because he is the symbol of our sovereignty, continuity, and grandeur as a people.

When he asks a senator to lunch in order to enlist his support for a pet project, when he thumps his desk and reminds the antagonists in a labor dispute of the larger interests of the American people, when he orders a general to cease caviling or else be removed from his command, the senator and the disputants and the general are well aware—especially if the scene is laid in the White House—that they are dealing with no ordinary head of government. The framers of the Constitution took a momentous step when they fused the dignity of a king and the power of a prime minister in one elective office—when they made the president a national leader in the mystical as well as the practical sense.

Finally, the president has been endowed—whether we or our friends abroad like it or not—with a global role as a leader of the free nations. His leadership in this area is not that of a dominant executive. The power he exercises is in a way comparable to that which he holds as a leader of Congress. Senators and congressmen can, if they choose, ignore the president's leadership with relative impunity. So, too, can our friends abroad; the action of Britain and France in the Middle East is a case in point. But so long as the United States remains the richest and most powerful member of any coalition it may enter, then its president's words and deeds will have a direct bearing on the freedom and stability of a great many other countries.

Having engaged in this piecemeal analysis of the categories of presidential leadership, we must now fit the pieces back together into a seamless unity. For that, after all, is what the presidency is, and I hope this exercise in political taxonomy has not obscured the paramount fact that this focus of democratic leadership is a single office filled by a single man.

The president is not one kind of leader one part of the day, another kind in another part—leader of the bureaucracy in the morning, of the armed forces at lunch, of Congress in the afternoon, of the people in the evening. He exerts every kind of leadership every moment of the day, and every kind feeds upon and into all the others. He is a more exalted leader of ritual because he can guide opinion, a more forceful leader in diplomacy because he commands the armed forces personally, a more effective leader of Congress because he sits at the top of his party. The conflicting demands of these categories of leadership give him trouble at times, but in the end all unite to make him a leader without any equal in the history of democracy.

I think it important to note the qualification: "the history of democracy." For what I have been talking about here is not the Fuehrerprinzip of Hitler or the "cult of personality," but the leadership of free men. The presidency, like every other instrument of power we have created for our use, operates within a grand and durable pattern of private liberty and public morality, which means that the president can lead successfully only when he honors the pattern—by working towards ends to which a "persistent and undoubted majority of people has given support, and by selecting means that are fair, dignified, and familiar."

The president, that is to say, can lead us only in the direction we are accustomed to travel. He cannot lead the gentlemen of Congress to abdicate their functions; he cannot order our civil servants to be corrupt and slothful; he cannot even command our generals to bring off a coup d'état. And surely he cannot lead public opinion in a direction for which public opinion is not prepared—a truth to which our strongest presidents would make the most convincing witnesses. The leadership of free men must honor their freedom. The power of the presidency can move as a mighty host only with the grain of liberty and morality.

The president, then, must provide a steady focus of leadership—of administrators, ambassadors, generals, congressmen, party chieftains, people, and men of good will everywhere. In a constitutional system compounded of diversity and antagonism, the presidency looms up as the countervailing force of unity and harmony. In a society ridden by centrifugal forces, it is the only point of reference we all have in common. The relentless progress of this continental republic has made the presidency our truly national political institution.

There are those, to be sure, who would reserve this role to Congress, but, as the least aggressive of our presidents, Calvin Coolidge, once testified, "It is because in their hours of timidity the Congress becomes subservient to the importunities of organized minorities that the president comes more and more to stand as the champion of the rights of the whole country." The more Congress becomes, in Burke's phrase, "a confused and scuffling bustle of local agency," the more the presidency must become a clear beacon of national purpose.

It has been such a beacon at most great moments in our history. In this great moment, too, we may be confident it will burn brightly.

The constitutional and statutory *authority* of the president is indeed extraordinary. However, it is more important to point out that the actual power of the president depends upon his political abilities. The president must act within the framework of a complex and diversified political constituency. He can use the authority of his office to buttress his strength, but this alone is not sufficient. Somehow he must be able to persuade those with whom he deals to follow him; otherwise, he will be weak and ineffective.

46

PRESIDENTIAL POWER

Richard E. Neustadt

In the United States we like to "rate" a president. We measure him as "weak" or "strong" and call what we are measuring his "leadership." We do not wait until a man is dead; we rate him from the moment he takes office. We are quite right to do so. His office has become the focal point of politics and policy in our political system. Our commentators and our politicians make a specialty of taking the man's measurements. The rest of us join in when we feel "government" impinging on our private lives. In the third quarter of the twentieth century millions of us have that feeling often.

. . . Although we all make judgments about presidential leadership, we often base our judgments upon images of office that are far removed from the reality. We also use those images when we tell one another whom to choose as president. But it is risky to appraise a man in office or to choose a man for office on false premises about the nature of his job. When the job is the presidency of the United States, the risk becomes excessive. . . .

We deal here with the president himself and with his influence on governmental action. In institutional terms the presidency now includes 2,000 men and women. The president is only one of them. But *his* performance scarcely can be measured without focusing on *him*. In terms of party, or of country, or the West, so-called, his leadership involves far more than governmental action. But the sharpening of spirit and of values and of purposes is not done in a vacuum.

Although governmental action may not be the whole of leadership, all else is nurtured by it and gains meaning from it. Yet if we treat the presidency as the president, we cannot measure him as though he were the government. Not action or an outcome but his impact on the outcome is the measure of the man. His strength or weakness, then, turns on his personal capacity to influence the conduct of the men who make up government. His influence becomes the mark of leadership. To rate a president according to these rules, one looks into the man's own capabilities as seeker and as wielder of effective influence upon the other men involved in governing the country. . . .

"Presidential" . . . means nothing but the president. "Power" means *his* influence. It helps to have these meanings settled at the start.

There are two ways to study "presidential power." One way is to focus on the tactics, so to speak, of influencing certain men in given situations: how to get a bill through Congress, how to settle strikes, how to quiet Cabinet feuds, or how to stop a Suez. The other way is to step back from tactics on those "givens" and to deal with influence in more strategic terms: what is its nature and what are its sources? What can *this* man accomplish to improve the prospect that he will have influence when he wants it? Strategically, the question is not how he masters Congress in a peculiar instance, but what he does to boost his chance for mastery in any instance, looking toward tomorrow from today. The second of these two ways has been chosen for this [selection]. . . .

In form all presidents are leaders, nowadays. In fact this guarantees no more than that they will be clerks. Everybody now expects the man inside the White House to do something about everything. Laws and customs now reflect acceptance of him as the Great Initiator, an acceptance quite as widespread at the Capitol as at his end of Pennsylvania Avenue. But such acceptance does not signify that all the rest of government is at his feet. It merely signifies that other men have found it practically impossible to do *their* jobs without assurance of initiatives from him. Service for themselves, not power for the president, has brought them to accept his leadership in form. They find his actions useful in their business. The transformation of his routine obligations testifies to their dependence on an active White House. A president, these days, is an invaluable clerk. His services are in demand all over Washington. His influence, however, is a very different matter. Laws and customs tell us little about leadership in fact.

Why have our presidents been honored with this clerkship? The answer is that no one else's services suffice. Our Constitution, our traditions, and our politics provide no better source for the initiatives a president can take. Executive officials need decisions, and political protection, and a referee for fights. Where are these to come from but the White House? Congressmen need an agenda from outside, something with high status to respond to or react against. What provides it better than the program of the president? Party politicians need a record to defend in the next national campaign. How can it be made except by "their" Administration? Private persons with a public ax to grind may need a helping hand or they may need a grinding stone. In either case who gives more satisfaction than a president? And outside the United States, in every country where our policies and postures influence home politics, there will be people needing just the "right" thing said and done or just the "wrong" thing stopped in *Washington*. What symbolizes Washington more nearly than the White House?

A modern president is bound to face demands for aid and service from five more or less distinguishable sources: the Executive officialdom, from Congress, from his partisans, from citizens at large, and from abroad. The presidency's clerkship is expressive of these pressures. In effect they are constituency pressures and each president has five sets of constituents. The five are not distinguished by their membership; membership is obviously an overlapping matter. And taken one by one they do not match the man's electorate; one of them, indeed, is outside his electorate. They are distinguished, rather, by their different claims upon him. Initiatives are what they want, for five distinctive reasons. Since government and politics have offered no alternative, our laws and customs turn those wants into his obligations.

Why, then, is the president not guaranteed an influence commensurate with services performed? Constituent relations are relations of dependence. Everyone with any share in governing this country will belong to one (or two, or three) of his "constituencies." Since everyone depends on him why is he not assured of everyone's support? The answer is that no one else sits where he sits, or sees quite as he sees; no one else feels the full weight of his obligations. Those obligations are a tribute to his unique place in our political system. But just because it is unique they fall on him alone. *The same conditions that promote his leadership in form preclude a guarantee of leadership in fact.* No man or group at either end of Pennsylvania Avenue shares his peculiar status in our government and politics. That is why his services are in demand. By the same token, though, the obligations of all other men are different from his own. His Cabinet officers have departmental duties and constituents. His legislative leaders head *Congressional* parties, one in either House. His national party organization stands apart from his official family. His political allies in the states need not face Washington, or one another. The private groups that seek him out are not compelled to govern. And friends abroad are not compelled to run in our elections. Lacking his position and prerogatives, these men cannot regard his obligations as his own. They have their jobs to do; none is the same as his. As they perceive their duty they may find it right to follow him, in fact, or they may not. Whether they will feel obliged *on their responsibility* to do what he wants done remains an open question. . . .

There is reason to suppose that in the years immediately ahead the power problems of a president will remain what they have been in the decades just behind us. If so there will be equal need for presidential expertise of the peculiar sort . . . that has [been] stressed [i.e., political skill]. Indeed, the need is likely to be greater. The president himself and with him the whole government are likely to be more than ever at the mercy of his personal approach.

What may the sixties do to politics and policy and to the place of presidents in our political system? The sixties may destroy them as we know them; that goes without saying. But barring deep depression or unlimited war, a total transformation is the least of likelihoods. Without catastrophes of those dimensions nothing in our past experience suggests that we shall see either consensus of the sort available to F.D.R. in 1933 and 1942, or popular demand for institutional adjustments likely to assist a president. Lacking popular demand, the natural conservatism of established institutions will keep Congress and the party organizations quite resistant to reforms that could give him a clear advantage over them. Four-year terms for congressmen and senators might do it, if the new terms ran with his. What will occasion a demand for that? As for crisis consensus it is probably beyond the reach of the next president. We may have priced ourselves out of the market for "productive" crises on the pattern Roosevelt knew—productive in the sense of strengthening his chances for sustained support *within* the system. Judging from the fifties, neither limited war nor limited depression is productive in those terms. Anything unlimited will probably break the system.

In the absence of productive crises, and assuming that we manage to avoid destructive ones, nothing now foreseeable suggests that our next president will have assured support from any quarter. There is no use expecting it from the bureaucracy unless it is displayed on Capitol Hill. Assured support will not be found in Congress unless contemplation of their own electorates keeps a majority of members constantly aligned with him. In the sixties it is to be doubted . . . that pressure from electors will move the same majority of men in either House toward consistent backing for the president. Instead the chances are that he will gain majorities, when and if he does so, by ad hoc coalition-building, issue after issue. In that respect the sixties will be reminiscent of the fifties; indeed, a closer parallel may well be in the late forties. As for "party discipline" in English terms—the favorite cure-all of political scientists since Woodrow Wilson was a youth—the first preliminary is a party link between the White House and the leadership on both sides of the Capitol. But even this preliminary has been lacking in eight of the fifteen years since the Second World War. If ballot-splitting should continue through the sixties it will soon be "un-American" for president and Congress to belong to the same party.

Even if the trend were now reversed, there is no short-run prospect that behind each party label we would find assembled a sufficiently like-minded bloc of voters, similarly aligned in states and districts all across the country, to negate the massive barriers our institutions and traditions have erected against "discipline" on anything like the British scale. This does not mean that a reversal of the ballot-splitting trend would be without significance. If the White House and the legislative leadership were linked by party ties again, a real advantage would accrue to both. Their opportunities for mutually productive bargaining would be enhanced. The policy results might surprise critics of our system. Bargaining "within the family" has a rather different quality than bargaining with members of the rival clan. But we would still be a long way from "party government." Bargaining, not "discipline," would still remain the key to Congressional action on a president's behalf. The crucial distinctions between presidential party and Congressional party are not likely to be lost in the term of the next president.

PRESIDENTIAL POLITICS

Whether the Founding Fathers intended that the president would be a king or a clerk, they clearly did not foresee the deep involvement of the presidency in *partisan* politics. All presidents after George Washington were party chiefs, a role that grew more important as national parties expanded their electoral bases and began to act in a more disciplined fashion to facilitate their control of government. American parties have never been disciplined in the European sense, but they have managed to achieve sufficient organizational unity at national, and more importantly state and local, levels to affect and sometimes determine the course of government.

Presidential parties help to identify and translate the political demands of popular majorities into government action. Theoretically at least, presidents should be able to use their role as party chief to bridge the constitutional gap between the presidency and Congress that the separation of powers created. Before becoming party chief, politicians must capture their party's presidential nomination. Whether or not parties should choose their nominees through "brokered" conventions, in which party power brokers and "bosses" dominate, or through a grassroots process controlled by rank-and-file party members, continues to be hotly debated. Proponents of brokered conventions argue that party leaders tend to choose "better" candidates, those more representative of broad party interests and more likely to appeal to a national electorate, than candidates nominated by a grassroots process that reflects the views of a relatively narrow party electorate.

PRESIDENTIAL CHARACTER AND STYLE

The preceding selections in this chapter have focused upon the institutional aspects of the presidency and the constitutional and political responsibilities of the office. Richard Neustadt does focus upon certain personal dimensions of the power equation, the ability to persuade, but he does not deal with presidential character outside the power context. The following selection is taken from one of the most important and innovative of the recent books dealing with the presidency, in which the author, James David Barber, presents the thesis that it is the *total character* of the person who occupies the White House that is the determinant of presidential performance. As he states, "The presidency is much more than an institution." It is not only the focus of the emotional involvement of most people in politics, but also occupied by an emotional person. How that person is able to come to grips with his feelings and emotions often shapes his orientation toward issues and the way in which he makes decisions. From the very beginning the office was thought of in highly personal terms, for the framers of the Constitution, in part at least, built the office around the character of George Washington, who virtually everyone at the time thought would be the first occupant of the office. And evolution of the office since 1787 has added to its personal quotient. James David Barber provides a framework for the analysis of presidential character and its effect upon performance in the White House.

47

THE PRESIDENTIAL CHARACTER

James David Barber

When a citizen votes for a presidential candidate he makes, in effect, a prediction. He chooses from among the contenders the one he thinks (or feels, or guesses) would be the best president. He operates in a situation of immense uncertainty. If he has a long voting history, he can recall time and time again when he guessed wrong. He listens to the commentators, the politicians, and his friends, then adds it all up in some rough way to produce his prediction and his vote. Earlier in the game, his anticipations have been taken into account, either directly in the polls and primaries or indirectly in the minds of politicians who want to nominate someone he will like. But he must choose in the midst of a cloud of confusion, a rain of phony advertising, a storm of sermons, a hail of complex issues, a fog of charisma and boredom, and a thunder of accusation and defense. In the face of this chaos, a great many citizens fall back on the past, vote their old allegiances, and let it go at that. Nevertheless, the citizen's vote says that on balance he expects Mr. X would outshine Mr. Y in the presidency.

This [book] is meant to help citizens and those who advise them cut through the confusion and get at some clear criteria for choosing presidents. To understand what actual presidents do and what potential presidents might do, the first need is to see the man whole—not as some abstract embodiment of civic virtue, some scorecard of issue stands, or some reflection of a faction, but as a human being like the rest of us, a person trying to cope with a difficult environment. To that task he brings his own character, his own view of the world, his own political style. None of that is new for him. If we can see the pattern he has set for his political life we can, I contend, estimate much better his pattern as he confronts the stresses and chances of the presidency.

The presidency is a peculiar office. The founding fathers left it extraordinarily loose in definition, partly because they trusted George Washington to invest a tradition as he went along. It is an institution made a piece at a time by successive men in the White House. Jefferson reached out to Congress to put together the beginnings of political parties; Jackson's dramatic force extended electoral partisanship to its mass base; Lincoln vastly expanded the administrative reach of the office; Wilson and the

Roosevelts showed its rhetorical possibilities—in fact, every President's mind and demeanor has left its mark on a heritage still in lively development.

But the presidency is much more than an institution. It is a focus of feelings. In general, popular feelings about politics are low-key, shallow, casual. For example, the vast majority of Americans knows virtually nothing of what Congress is doing and cares less. The presidency is different. The presidency is the focus for the most intense and persistent emotions in the American polity. The president is a symbolic leader, the one figure who draws together the people's hopes and fears for the political future. On top of all his routine duties, he has to carry that off—or fail.

Our emotional attachment to presidents shows up when one dies in office. People were not just disappointed or worried when President Kennedy was killed; people wept at the loss of a man most had never even met. Kennedy was young and charismatic—but history shows that whenever a president dies in office, heroic Lincoln or debased Harding, McKinley or Garfield, the same wave of deep emotion sweeps across the country. On the other hand, the death of an ex-president brings forth no such intense emotional reaction.

The president is the first political figure children are aware of (later they add Congress, the Court, and others, as "helpers" of the president). With some exceptions among children in deprived circumstances, the president is seen as a "benevolent leader," one who nurtures, sustains, and inspires the citizenry. Presidents regularly show up among "most admired" contemporaries and forebears, and the president is the "best known" (in the sense of sheer name recognition) person in the country. At inauguration time, even presidents elected by close margins are supported by much larger majorities than the election returns show, for people rally round as he actually assumes office. There is a similar reaction when the people see their president threatened by crisis: if he takes action, there is a favorable spurt in the Gallup poll whether he succeeds or fails.

Obviously the president gets more attention in schoolbooks, press, and television than any other politician. He is one of very few who can make news by doing good things. His emotional state is a matter of continual public commentary, as is the manner in which his personal and official families conduct themselves. The media bring across the president not as some neutral administrator or corporate executive to be assessed by his production, but as a special being with mysterious dimensions.

We have no king. The sentiments English children—and adults—direct to the Queen have no place to go in our system but to the president. Whatever his talents—Coolidge-type or Roosevelt-type—the president is the only available object for such national-religious-monarchical sentiments as Americans possess.

The president helps people make sense of politics. Congress is a tangle of committees, the bureaucracy is a maze of agencies. The president is one man trying to do a job—a picture much more understandable to the mass of people who find themselves in the same boat. Furthermore, he is the top man. He ought to know what is going on and set it right. So when the economy goes sour, or war drags on, or domestic violence erupts, the president is available to take the blame. Then when things go right, it seems the president must have had a hand in it. Indeed, the flow of political life is marked off by presidents: the "Eisenhower Era," the "Kennedy Years."

What all this means is that the president's main responsibilities reach far beyond administering the Executive Branch or commanding the armed forces. The White House is first and foremost a place of public leadership. That inevitably brings to bear on the president intense moral, sentimental, and quasi-religious pressures which can, if he lets them, distort his own thinking and feeling. If there is such a thing as extraordinary sanity, it is needed nowhere so much as in the White House.

Who the president is at a given time can make a profound difference in the whole thrust and direction of national politics. Since we have only one president at a time, we can never prove this by comparison, but even the most superficial speculation confirms the commonsense view that the man himself weighs heavily among other historical factors. A Wilson reelected in 1920, a Hoover in 1932, a John F. Kennedy in 1964 would, it seems very likely, have guided the body politic along rather different paths from those their actual successors chose. Or try to imagine a Theodore Roosevelt ensconced behind today's "bully pulpit" of a presidency, or Lyndon Johnson as president in the age of McKinley. Only someone mesmerized by the lures of historical inevitability can suppose that it would have made little or no difference to government policy had Alf Landon replaced FDR in 1936, had Dewey beaten Truman in 1948, or Adlai Stevenson reigned through the 1950s. Not only would these alternative presidents have advocated different policies—they would have approached the office from very different psychological angles. It stretches credibility to think that Eugene McCarthy would have run the institution the way Lyndon Johnson did.

The burden of this [argument] is that the crucial differences can be anticipated by an understanding of a potential president's character, his world view, and his style. This kind of prediction is not easy; well-informed observers often have guessed wrong as they watched a man step toward the White House. One thinks of Woodrow Wilson, the scholar who would bring reason to politics; of Herbert Hoover, the Great Engineer who would organize chaos into progress; of Franklin D. Roosevelt, that champion of the balanced budget; of Harry Truman, whom the office would surely overwhelm; of Dwight D. Eisenhower, militant crusader; of John F. Kennedy, who would lead beyond moralisms to achievements; of Lyndon B. Johnson, the Southern conservative; and of Richard M. Nixon, conciliator. Spotting the errors is easy. Predicting with even approximate accuracy is going to require some sharp tools and close attention in their use. But the experiment is worth it because the question is critical and because it lends itself to correction by evidence.

My argument comes in layers.

First, a president's personality is an important shaper of his presidential behavior on nontrivial matters.

Second, presidential personality is patterned. His character, world view, and style fit together in a dynamic package understandable in psychological terms.

Third, a president's personality interacts with the power situation he faces and the national "climate of expectations" dominant at the time he serves. The tuning, the resonance—or lack of it—between these external factors and his personality sets in motion the dynamics of his presidency.

Fourth, the best way to predict a president's character, world view, and style is to see how they were put together in the first place. That happened in his early life, culminating in his first independent political success.

But the core of the argument . . . is that presidential character—the basic stance a man takes toward his presidential experience—comes in four varieties. The most important thing to know about a president or candidate is where he fits among these types, defined according to (a) how active he is and (b) whether or not he gives the impression he enjoys his political life.

Let me spell out these concepts briefly before getting down to cases.

Personality Shapes Performance

I am not about to argue that once you know a president's personality you know everything. But as the cases will demonstrate, the degree and quality of a president's emotional involvement in an issue are powerful influences on how he defines the issue itself, how much attention he pays to it, which facts and persons he sees as relevant to its resolution, and finally, what principles and purposes he associates with the issue. Every story of presidential decision-making is really two stories: an outer one in which a rational man calculates and an inner one in which an emotional man feels. The two are forever connected. Any real president is one whole man and his deeds reflect his wholeness.

As for personality, it is a matter of tendencies. It is not that one president "has" some basic characteristic that another president does not "have." That old way of treating a trait as a possession, like a rock in a basket, ignores the universality of aggressiveness, compliancy, detachment, and other human drives. We all have all of them, but in different amounts and in different combinations.

The Pattern of Character, World View, and Style

The most visible part of the pattern is style. *Style is the president's habitual way of performing his three political roles: rhetoric, personal relations, and homework.* Not to be confused with "stylishness," charisma, or appearance, style is how the president goes about doing what the office requires him to do—to speak, directly or through media, to large audiences; to deal face to face with other politicians, individually and in small, relatively private groups; and to read, write, and calculate by himself in order to manage the endless flow of details that stream onto his desk. No president can escape doing at least some of each. But there are marked differences in stylistic emphasis from president to president. The *balance* among the three style elements varies; one president may put most of himself into rhetoric, another may stress close, informal dealing, while still another may devote his energies mainly to study and cogitation. Beyond the balance, we want to see each president's peculiar habits of style, his mode of coping with and adapting to these presidential demands. For example, I think both Calvin Coolidge and John F. Kennedy were primarily rhetoricians, but they went about it in contrasting ways.

A president's *world view consists of his primary, politically relevant beliefs, particularly his conceptions of social causality, human nature, and the central moral conflicts of the time.*

This is how he sees the world and his lasting opinions about what he sees. Style is his way of acting; world view is his way of seeing. Like the rest of us, a president develops over a lifetime certain conceptions of reality—how things work in politics, what people are like, what the main purposes are. These assumptions or conceptions help him make sense of his world, give some semblance of order to the chaos of existence. Perhaps most important: a man's world view affects what he pays attention to, and a great deal of politics is about paying attention. The name of the game for many politicians is not so much "Do this, do that" as it is "Look here!"

"Character" comes from the Greek word for engraving; in one sense it is what life has marked into a man's being. As used here, *character is the way the president orients himself toward life*—not for the moment, but enduringly. Character is the person's stance as he confronts experience. And at the core of character, a man confronts himself. The president's fundamental self-esteem is his prime personal resource; to defend and advance that, he will sacrifice much else he values. Down there in the privacy of his heart, does he find himself superb, or ordinary, or debased, or in some intermediate range? No president has been utterly paralyzed by self-doubt and none has been utterly free of midnight self-mockery. In between, the real presidents move out on life from positions of relative strength or weakness. Equally important are the criteria by which they judge themselves. A president who rates himself by the standard of achievement, for instance, may be little affected by losses of affection.

Character, world view, and style are abstractions from the reality of the whole individual. In every case they form an integrated pattern: the man develops a combination which makes psychological sense for him, a dynamic arrangement of motives, beliefs, and habits in the service of his need for self-esteem.

The Power Situation and "Climate of Expectations"

Presidential character resonates with the political situation the president faces. It adapts him as he tries to adapt it. The support he has from the public and interest groups, the party balance in Congress, the thrust of Supreme Court opinion together set the basic power situation he must deal with. An activist president may run smack into a brick wall of resistance, then pull back and wait for a better moment. On the other hand, a president who sees himself as a quiet caretaker may not try to exploit even the most favorable power situation. So it is the relationship between president and the political configuration that makes the system tick.

Even before public opinion polls, the president's real or supposed popularity was a large factor in his performance. Besides the power mix in Washington, the president has to deal with a national climate of expectations, the predominant needs thrust up to him by the people. There are at least three recurrent themes around which these needs are focused.

People look to the president for *reassurance*, a feeling that things will be all right, that the president will take care of his people. The psychological request is for a surcease of anxiety. Obviously, modern life in America involves considerable doses of fear, tension, anxiety, worry; from time to time, the public mood calls for a rest, a time of peace, a breathing space, a "return to normalcy."

Another theme is the demand for a sense of *progress and action*. The president ought to do something to direct the nation's course—or at least be in there pitching for the people. The president is looked to as a take-charge man, a doer, a turner of the wheels, a producer of progress—even if that means some sacrifice of serenity.

A third type of climate of expectations is the public need for a sense of *legitimacy* from, and in, the presidency. The president should be a master politician who is above politics. He should have a right to his place and a rightful way of acting in it. The respectability—even religiosity—of the office has to be protected by a man who presents himself as defender of the faith. There is more to this than dignity, more than propriety. The president is expected to personify our betterness in an inspiring way, to express in what he does and is (not just in what he says) a moral idealism which, in much of the public mind, is the very opposite of "politics."

Over time the climate of expectations shifts and changes. Wars, depressions, and other national events contribute to that change, but there also is a rough cycle, from an emphasis on action (which begins to look too "political") to an emphasis on legitimacy (the moral uplift of which creates its own strains) to an emphasis on reassurance and rest (which comes to seem like drift) and back to action again. One need not be astrological about it. The point is that the climate of expectations at any given time is the political air the president has to breathe. Relating to this climate is a large part of his task.

Predicting Presidents

The best way to predict a president's character, world view, and style is to see how he constructed them in the first place. Especially in the early stages, life is experimental; consciously or not, a person tries out various ways of defining and maintaining and raising self-esteem. He looks to his environment for clues as to who he is and how well he is doing. These lessons of life slowly sink in: certain self-images and evaluations, certain ways of looking at the world, certain styles of action get confirmed by his experience and he gradually adopts them as his own. If we can see that process of development, we can understand the product. The features to note are those bearing on presidential performance.

Experimental development continues all the way to death; we will not blind ourselves to midlife changes, particularly in the full-scale prediction case, that of Richard Nixon. But it is often much easier to see the basic patterns in early life histories. Later on a whole host of distractions—especially the image-making all politicians learn to practice—clouds the picture.

In general, character has its main development in childhood, world view in adolescence, style in early adulthood. The stance toward life I call character grows out of the child's experiments in relating to parents, brothers and sisters, and peers at play and in school, as well as to his own body and the objects around it. Slowly the child defines an orientation toward experience; once established, that tends to last despite much subsequent contradiction. By adolescence, the child has been hearing and seeing how people make their worlds meaningful, and now he is moved to relate himself—his own meanings—to those around him. His focus of attention shifts toward the future; he senses that decisions about his fate are coming and he looks into the premises for those decisions. Thoughts about the way the world works and how one might work in it, about what people are like and how one might be like them or not, and about the values people share and how one might share in them too—these are typical concerns for the post-child, pre-adult mind of the adolescent.

These themes come together strongly in early adulthood, when the person moves from contemplation to responsible action and adopts a style. In most biographical accounts this period stands out in stark clarity—the time of emergence, the time the young man found himself. I call it his first independent political success. It was then he moved beyond the detailed guidance of his family; then his self-esteem was dramatically boosted; then he came forth as a person to be reckoned with by other people. The way he did that is profoundly important to him. Typically he grasps that style and hangs onto it. Much later, coming into the presidency, something in him remembers this earlier victory and reemphasizes the style that made it happen.

Character provides the main thrust and broad direction—but it does not *determine*, in any fixed sense, world view and style. The story of development does not end with the end of childhood. Thereafter, the culture one grows in and the ways that culture is translated by parents and peers shape the meanings one makes of his character. The going world view gets learned and that learning helps channel character forces. Thus it will not necessarily be true that compulsive characters have reactionary beliefs, or that compliant characters believe in compromise. Similarly for style: historical accidents play a large part in furnishing special opportunities for action—and in blocking off alternatives. For example, however much anger a young man may feel, that anger will not be expressed in rhetoric unless and until his life situation provides a platform and an audience. Style thus has a stature and independence of its own. Those who would reduce all explanation to character neglect these highly significant later channelings. For beyond the root is the branch, above the foundation the superstructure, and starts do not prescribe finishes.

Four Types of Presidential Character

The five concepts—character, world view, style, power situation, and climate of expectations—run through the accounts of presidents in [later chapters of Barber's book], which cluster the presidents since Theodore Roosevelt into four types. This is the fundamental scheme of the study. It offers a way to move past the complexities to the main contrasts and comparisons.

The first baseline in defining presidential types is *activity-passivity*. How much energy does the man invest in his presidency? Lyndon Johnson went at his day like a human cyclone, coming to rest long after the sun went down. Calvin Coolidge often slept eleven hours a night and still needed a nap in the middle of the day. In between the presidents array themselves on the high or low side of the activity line.

The second baseline is *positive-negative affect* toward one's activity—this is, how he feels about what he does. Relatively speaking, does he seem to experience his political life as happy or sad, enjoyable or discouraging, positive or negative in its main effect? The feeling I am after here is not grim satisfaction in a job well done, not some philosophical conclusion. The idea is this: is he someone who, on the surfaces we can see, gives forth the feeling that he has *fun* in political life? Franklin Roosevelt's Secretary of War, Henry L. Stimson, wrote that the Roosevelts "not only understood the *use* of power, they knew the *enjoyment* of power, too. . . . Whether a man is burdened by power or enjoys power; whether he is trapped by responsibility or made free by it; whether he is moved by other people and outer forces or moves them—that is the essence of leadership."

The positive-negative baseline, then, is a general symptom of the fit between the man and his experience, a kind of register of *felt* satisfaction.

Why might we expect these two simple dimensions to outline the main character types? Because they stand for two central features of anyone's orientation toward life. In nearly every study of personality, some form of the active-passive contrast is critical; the general tendency to act or be acted upon is evident in such concepts as dominance-submission, extraversion-introversion, aggression-timidity, attack-defense, fight-flight, engagement-withdrawal, approach-avoidance. In everyday life we sense quickly the general energy output of the people we deal with. Similarly we catch on fairly quickly to the affect dimension—whether the person seems to be optimistic or pessimistic, hopeful or skeptical, happy or sad. The two baselines are clear and they are also independent of one another: all of us know people who are very active but seem discouraged, others who are quite passive but seem happy, and so forth. The activity baseline refers to what one does, the affect baseline to how one feels about what he does.

Both are crude clues to character. They are leads into four basic character patterns long familiar in psychological research. In summary form, these are the main configurations:

Active-Positive. There is a congruence, a consistency, between much activity and the enjoyment of it, indicating relatively high self-esteem and relative success in relating to the environment. The man shows an orientation toward productiveness as a value and an ability to use his styles flexibly, adaptively, suiting the dance to the music. He sees himself as developing over time toward relatively well defined personal goals—growing toward his image of himself as he might yet be. There is an emphasis on rational mastery, on using the brain to move the feet. This may get him into trouble; he may fail to take account of the irrational in politics. Not everyone he deals with sees things his way and he may find it hard to understand why.

Active-Negative. The contradiction here is between relatively intense effort and relatively low emotional reward for that effort. The activity has a compulsive quality, as if the man were trying to make up for something or to escape from anxiety into hard work. He seems ambitious, striving upward, power-seeking. His stance toward the environment is aggressive and he has a persistent problem in managing his aggressive feelings. His self-image is vague and discontinuous. Life is a hard struggle to achieve and hold power, hampered by the condemnations of a perfectionistic conscience. Active-negative types pour energy into the political system, but it is an energy distorted from within.

Passive-Positive. This is the receptive, compliant, other-directed character whose life is a search for affection as a reward for being agreeable and cooperative rather than personally assertive. The contradiction is between low self-esteem (on grounds of being unlovable, unattractive) and a superficial optimism. A hopeful attitude helps dispel doubt and elicits encouragement from others. Passive-positive types help soften the harsh edges of politics. But their dependence and the fragility of their hopes and enjoyments make disappointment in politics likely.

Passive-Negative. The factors are consistent—but how are we to account for the man's *political* role-taking? Why is someone who does little in politics and enjoys it less there at all? The answer lies in the passive-negative's character-rooted orientation toward doing dutiful service; this compensates for low self-esteem based on a sense of uselessness. Passive-negative types are in politics because they think they ought to be. They may be well adapted to certain nonpolitical roles, but they lack the experience and flexibility to perform effectively as political leaders. Their tendency is to withdraw, to escape from the conflict and uncertainty of politics by emphasizing vague principles (especially prohibitions) and procedural arrangements. They become guardians of the right and proper way, above the sordid politicking of lesser men. Active-positive presidents want most to achieve results. Active-negatives aim to get and keep power. Passive-positives are after love. Passive-negatives emphasize their civic virtue. The relation of activity to enjoyment in a president thus tends to outline a cluster of characteristics, to set apart the adapted from the compulsive, compliant, and withdrawn types.

The first four presidents of the United States, conveniently, ran through this gamut of character types. (Remember, we are talking about tendencies, broad directions; no individual man exactly fits a category.) George Washington—clearly the most important president in the pantheon—established the fundamental legitimacy of an American government at a time when this was a matter in considerable question. Washington's dignity, judiciousness, his aloof air of reserve and dedication to duty fit the passive-negative or withdrawing type best. Washington did not seek innovation, he sought stability. He longed to retire to Mount Vernon, but fortunately was persuaded to stay on through a second term, in which, by rising above the political conflict between Hamilton and Jefferson and inspiring confidence in his own integrity, he gave the nation time to develop the organized means for peaceful change.

John Adams followed, a dour New England Puritan, much given to work and worry, an impatient and irascible man—an active-negative president, a compulsive type. Adams was far more partisan than Washington; the survival of the system through his presidency demonstrated that the nation could tolerate, for a time, domination by one of its nascent political parties. As president, an angry Adams brought the United States to the brink of war with France, and presided over the new nation's first experiment in political representation: the Alien and Sedition Acts, forbidding, among other things, unlawful combinations "with intent to oppose any measure or measures of the government of the United States," or "any false, scandalous, and malicious writing or writings against the United States, or the president of the United States, with intent to defame . . . or to bring them or either of them, into contempt or disrepute."

Then came Jefferson. He too had his troubles and failures—in the design of national defense, for example. As for his presidential character (only one element in success or failure), Jefferson was clearly active-positive. A child of the Enlightenment, he applied his reason to organizing connections with Congress aimed at strengthening the more popular forces. A man of catholic interests and delightful humor, Jefferson combined a clear and open vision of what the country could be with a profound political sense, expressed in his famous phrase, "Every difference of opinion is not a difference of principle."

The fourth president was James Madison, "Little Jemmy," the constitutional philosopher thrown into the White House at a time of great international turmoil. Madison comes closest to the passive-positive, or compliant, type; he suffered from irresolution, tried to compromise his way out, and gave in too readily to the "warhawks" urging combat with Britain. The nation drifted into war, and Madison wound up ineptly commanding his collection of amateur generals in the streets of Washington. General Jackson's victory at New Orleans saved the Madison administration's historical reputation; but he left the presidency with the United States close to bankruptcy and secession.

These four presidents—like all presidents—were persons trying to cope with the roles they had won by using the equipment they had built over a lifetime. The president is not some shapeless organism in a flood of novelties, but a man with a memory in a system with a history. Like all of us, he draws on his past to shape his future. The pathetic hope that the White House will turn a Caligula into a Marcus Aurelius is as naive as the fear that ultimate power inevitably corrupts. The problem is to understand—and to state understandably—what in the personal past foreshadows the presidential future. . . .

Each President defines a unique leadership posture that is a strategic choice to enhance political authority and credibility. A President's leadership posture can be an asset or liability, depending upon a President's correct assessment of the politics of his Presidency. President Bush's central premise was that he would not allow others to define his leadership. The following selection by a leading presidential scholar analyzes how George W. Bush defined his presidential leadership style

48

LEADERSHIP BY DEFINITION: REFLECTIONS ON GEORGE W. BUSH'S POLITICAL STANCE

Stephen Skowronek

There are good reasons for caution in evaluating a sitting president. Major initiatives are pending; crucial choices are yet to be made; access is limited; events still hold sway. Arguably, however, certain qualities of leadership are best captured in the moment. One of these is the president's leadership posture, the terms of political engagement he projects to those he intends to move along his chosen course.

The principal impression, often the only impression, Americans get of their president is conveyed through this stance. George W. Bush is a president known to evoke intense reactions from friends and foes alike. Perhaps it is because his leadership posture has been so striking and the reactions to it so visceral that little thought has been given to its claims and how they figure in a more general assessment of American national politics. This is the stuff that tends to get lost with time, the sort of thing that grandparents try to convey to grandchildren when conjuring their impressions of a president long gone. More often than not, they give up in frustration, saying "you just had to be there."

One reason for the difficulty is that a president's leadership posture is closely related to other qualities—personal character, governing style, "the times"—that, though ineffable in their own way, serve today as the parlance of leadership studies. No doubt, each has a part to play in determining the political stance a president adopts, and yet a discussion of any one of these factors, or all of them together, will quickly trail off in other directions. The problem is not that we don't have good specifications of these factors or that they don't generate insights into the operations of the American presidency, but that a leadership posture does not readily reduce to them. Thus, when it comes to articulating what we experience most directly in our president, it seems advisable to work the other way around, to consider first what a leadership posture is—its own core attributes—and then circle back to see how related factors contribute to the one currently on display. . . .

All told, then, there does seem to be good reason to think about a president's leadership posture as something distinct. It is less about what is given in the situation—a man and a set of circumstances—than about what is created in the attempt to seize the moment. Calling attention to this points in turn to what seems to be at the crux of the matter: a leadership posture is, first and foremost, an assertion of political authority. It projects a timely warrant for the exercise of power and bids for deference. . . .

Leadership by Definition

I take my cues in describing this president's leadership posture from his 2000 campaign autobiography, *A Charge to Keep*. In the first lines of the book's foreword, George W. Bush states his precept for political leadership: he vows never to allow himself to be defined by others. The cocky defiance of that opening salvo has long since become familiar. By the same token, one cannot read these lines now without being struck by how well they encapsulate the political stance of this presidency: George W. Bush leads by definition.

I do not mean to ignore the irony that Bush's vow introduced a book that was, in fact, put together by others. Principle responsibility for defining Bush, including the elevated value in this self-presentation of definition per se, lay with ghost writer and campaign aide Karen Hughes. It is precisely because this genre of writing fuses the personal and the strategic in a collective political project, precisely because a campaign biography self-consciously fashions a candidate's life story to maximize his appeal to others, that it can serve as a useful access point to the leadership posture assumed. In this instance, it is also a rare point of access. Bush does not say a lot about himself, at least not on the record, nor is he known as an especially profound thinker. In reading further, however, it turns out that there was a lot more thinking behind Bush's stance than his tart one liner.

A Charge to Keep is a treatise on the value of definition in leadership. It not only organizes Bush's life story around a series of "defining moments" but also provides instruction on the high costs of losing definition. Chapter by chapter, the reader discovers that definition has been the central preoccupation of this man's political education. In the early pages, for example, Bush recalls watching uneasily "as Bill Clinton's catchphrase—'It's the economy, stupid'—became the defining message of the [1992] campaign, even though economists said, and the economy showed, that recovery was underway." Toward the end of the book, that story is repeated: "During the 1988 campaign, my dad was able to define himself. In 1992, Bill Clinton and Ross Perot defined him, and he lost in a long and miserable year." Just a few pages before, the greatness of Ronald Reagan—the man who defeated his father for the Republican presidential nomination in 1980—is traced to his clear and simple assertion of purpose: "His presidency was a defining one." Chapters earlier, we learn that "failure to define the mission" led to the ruin of Lyndon Johnson, and, more important for Bush and his generation, to years of self-doubt and drift in the nation at large.

What is displayed on these pages is an acute sensitivity to the problem of political definition, a view of politics as a struggle for definition, an understanding of leadership as the assertion and control of definitions. This is a man who has pondered the fate of recent leaders and concluded that their success turned on their ability to define themselves and the others around them. This is a man who has come to believe that definitions effectively asserted can create their own reality.

The reader of *A Charge to Keep* knows exactly what kind of leader this aspirant intends to be: the kind who lays out terms and upholds them against all comers. Bush's political persona as a man who acts with unflinching resolve on stated purposes follows directly: it was a stance adopted to make him, by definition, a leader. To be sure, all leaders seek to define themselves one way or another.

To set Bush apart as one who has led by definition is to observe something a bit different about him, something that is, to say the very least, an exaggeration of what most others offer. With Bush, definition was not just another attribute of leadership; it was the litmus test of leadership, the signal mark of the genuine article. There was more to it than the sense of a man who was clear about his terms; there was the sense of a man who was wholly self-determined. The charge was not just to identify with a party or a set of national priorities; leadership by definition implied a willingness to stand fully committed up front, fully revealed in one's commitments, and ready to act. Some leaders protect options with subtlety, others acknowledge complexity and prescribe sober intelligence. There was no hedge in Bush's stance: "I don't do nuance." Definition conveys certainty and self-confidence. The posture is that of a man of set mind, one who knows what to do and leads by doing it. Strength is projected through conviction and validated through persistence. Decision making is inner-directed, predictably contained by preformed standards; the "hard work" lies just beyond that, in "getting the job done." As Bush has shown, one who leads by definition need not be indifferent to the rough and tumble of the political process or stand above the gritty arts of political maneuver, but enlisting necessary compromises in service to the definition is part of the maneuvering. . . .

Leadership by definition works to absorb deviation and create in its place a sense of relentless movement forward toward fulfillment of the goal. Each tactical shift is a necessary regrouping in preparation for the next push down the prescribed path; the posture remains intact so long as others sense that the leader's inner compass is still strong and guiding the course. Leadership by definition becomes in this way a driving, multi-front offensive to affirm terms and call forth the corresponding reality.

It is tempting to interpret this as the leadership posture of a hard-line ideologue. There is certainly something of the ideologue in Bush, but the label misses as much as it clarifies, and in so doing, it fails to capture either the challenge or the full potential of his political stance. Consider, for example, the ideological obfuscation of "compassionate conservatism" where a government-friendly social sensitivity, even entitlement, is endorsed alongside a clear reaffirmation of the orthodoxy of the Republican party of our day. The leadership challenge of definition is not to achieve ideological precision; it is to deploy a political persona strong enough to bring order to seemingly incongruous norms, to stabilize the political balance implicit in the program on the strength of the leader's personal convictions. Definition did not make Bush a purist; it made him a stalwart. What it projected was unwavering commitment to stated purposes, a leader completely identified with his cause and thoroughly devoted to its success.

PRESIDENTIAL LEADERSHIP AND POLITICAL PARTIES

Our eighteenth-century constitutional system of divided government weakens political parties. The Founding Fathers did not intend for either the president or Congress to govern through parties. As the following selection reveals, modern presidents have taken a leaf from the founders' notebook by relying more on administrative than party government.

49

THE PRESIDENCY AND POLITICAL PARTIES

Sidney M. Milkis

The relationship between the presidency and the American party system has always been difficult. The architects of the Constitution established a nonpartisan president who, with the support of the judiciary *and Senate*, was intended to play the leading institutional role in checking and controlling the "violence of faction" that the framers feared would rend the fabric of representative democracy. Even after the presidency became a more partisan office during the early part of the nineteenth century, its authority continued to depend on an ability to transcend party politics. The president is nominated by a party but, unlike the British prime minister, is not elected by it.

The inherent tension between the presidency and the party system reached a critical point during the 1930s. The institutionalization of the modern presidency, arguably the most significant constitutional legacy of Franklin D. Roosevelt's New Deal, ruptured severely the limited, albeit significant, bond that linked presidents to their parties. In fact, the modern presidency was crafted with the intention of reducing the influence of the party system on American politics. In this sense Roosevelt's extraordinary party leadership contributed to the decline of the American party system. This decline continued—even accelerated—under the administrations of subsequent presidents, notably Lyndon B. Johnson and Richard M. Nixon. Under Ronald Reagan, however, the party system showed at least some signs of transformation and renewal. Reagan and his successor, George H. W. Bush, supported efforts by Republicans in the national committee and congressional campaign organizations to restore some of the importance of political parties by refashioning them into highly untraditional but politically potent national organizations. George W. Bush further advanced and benefited from the more national and programmatic party that arose with the resurgence and transformation of conservatism during the Reagan presidency. It remains to be seen, however, whether national programmatic parties can perform the parties' historic function of moderating presidential ambition and mobilizing public support for political principles and programs.

New Deal Party Politics, Presidential Reform, and the Decline of the American Party System

The New Deal seriously questioned the adequacy of the traditional natural rights liberalism of John Locke and the framers, which emphasized the need to limit constitutionally the scope of government's responsibilities. The modern liberalism that became the public philosophy of the New Deal entailed a fundamental reappraisal of the concept of rights. As Roosevelt first indicated in his 1932 campaign speech at the Commonwealth Club in San Francisco, effective political reform would require, at a minimum, the development of "an economic declaration of rights, an economic constitutional order," grounded in a commitment to guarantee a decent level of economic well-being for the American people. Although equality of opportunity had traditionally been promoted by limited government interference in society, recent economic and social changes, such as the closing of the frontiers and the growth of industrial combinations, demanded that America now recognize "the new terms of the old social contract."

The establishment of a new constitutional order would require a reordering of the political process. The traditional patterns of American politics, characterized by constitutional mechanisms that impeded collective action, would have to give way to a more centralized and administrative government. As Roosevelt put it, "The day of enlightened administration has come."

The concerns Roosevelt expressed in the Commonwealth Club speech are an important guide to understanding the New Deal and its effects on the party system. The pursuit of an economic constitutional order presupposed a fundamental change in the relationship between the presidency and the party system. In Roosevelt's view, the party system, which was essentially based on state and local organizations and interests and was thus suited to congressional primacy, would have to be transformed into a national, executive-oriented system organized on the basis of public issues.

In this understanding, Roosevelt was no doubt influenced by the thought of Woodrow Wilson. The reform of parties, Wilson believed, depended on extending the influence of the presidency. The limits on partisanship inherent in American constitutional government notwithstanding, the president represented his party's "vital link of connection" with the nation: "He can dominate his party by being spokesman for the real sentiment and purpose of the country, by giving the country at once the information and statements of policy which will enable it to form its judgments alike of parties and men." . . .

In the final analysis, the "benign dictatorship" that Roosevelt sought to impose on the Democratic party was more conducive to corroding the American party system than to reforming it. His prescription for party reform—extraordinary presidential leadership—posed a serious, if not intractable, dilemma: on the one hand, the decentralized character of politics in the United States [could] be modified only by strong presidential leadership; on the other, a president determined to alter fundamentally the connection between the executive and the party eventually [would] shatter party unity. . . .

The most significant institutional reforms of the New Deal did not promote party government but fostered instead a program that would help the president to govern in the absence of party government. This program, as embodied in the 1937 executive reorganization bill, would have greatly extended presidential authority over the executive branch, including the independent regulatory commissions. The president and the executive agencies would also be delegated extensive authority to govern, making unnecessary the constant cooperation of party members in Congress. As the Report of the President's Committee on Administrative Management put it, with administrative reform the "brief exultant commitment" to progressive government that was expressed in the elections of 1932 and, especially, 1936 would now be more firmly established in "persistent, determined, competent, day by day administration of what the Nation has decided to do." . . .

Interestingly, the administrative reform bill, which was directed to making politics less necessary, became, at Roosevelt's urging, a party government-style "vote of confidence" for the administration in Congress. Roosevelt initially lost this vote in 1938, when the reorganization bill was defeated in the House of Representatives, but he did manage, through the purge campaign and other partisan actions, to keep administrative reform sufficiently prominent in party councils that a compromise version passed in 1939. Although considerably weaker than Roosevelt's original proposal, the 1939 Executive Reorganization Act was a significant measure. It not only provided authority for the creation of the Executive Office of the President, which included the newly formed White House Office and a strengthened and refurbished Bureau of the Budget, but also enhanced the president's control of the expanding activities of the executive branch. As such, this legislation represents the genesis of the institutional presidency, which was equipped to govern independently of the constraints imposed by the regular political process.

The civil service reform carried out by the Roosevelt administration was another important part of the effort to replace partisan politics with executive administration. The original reorganization proposals of 1937 had contained provisions to make the administration of the civil service more effective and to expand the merit system. The reorganization bill passed in 1939 was shorn of this controversial feature; but Roosevelt found it possible to accomplish extensive civil service reform through executive action. He did so by extending merit protection to personnel appointed by the administration during its first term, four-fifths of whom had been brought into government outside of merit channels. Patronage appointments had traditionally been used to nourish the party system; the New Deal celebrated an administrative politics that fed instead an executive department oriented to expanding liberal programs. As the administrative historian Paul Van Riper has noted, the new practices created a new kind of patronage, "a sort of intellectual and ideological patronage rather than the more traditional partisan type."

Roosevelt's leadership transformed the Democratic party into a way station on the road to administrative government. As the presidency developed into an elaborate and ubiquitous institution, it preempted party leaders in many of their limited, but significant, duties: providing a link from government to interest groups, staffing the executive department, contributing to policy development, and organizing election campaigns, [and communicating with the public]. Moreover, New Deal administrative reform was directed not just to creating presidential government but to embedding progressive principles (considered tantamount to political rights) in a bureaucratic structure that would insulate reform and reformers from electoral change.

Lyndon Johnson's Great Society and the Transcendence of Partisan Politics

Presidential leadership during the New Deal prepared the executive branch to be a government unto itself and established the presidency rather than the party as the locus of political responsibility. This shift was greatly augmented by World War II and the cold war. With the Great Depression giving way to war, another expansion of presidential authority took place, as part of the national security state, further weakening the executive's ties with the party system. As the New Deal prepared for war, Roosevelt spoke not only of the government's obligation to guarantee "freedom from want" but also its responsibility to provide "freedom from fear"—to protect the American people, and the world, against foreign aggression. This obligation to uphold "human rights" became a new guarantee of security, which presupposed a further expansion of national administrative power.

But the modern presidency was created to chart the course for, and direct the voyage to, a more liberal America. Roosevelt's pronouncement of a "second bill of rights" proclaimed and began this task, but it fell to Johnson, as one journalist noted, to "codify the New Deal vision of a good society."

Johnson's attempt to create the Great Society marked a significant extension of programmatic liberalism and accelerated the effort to transcend partisan politics. Roosevelt's ill-fated efforts to guide the affairs of his party were well remembered by Johnson, who came to Congress in 1937 in a special House election as an enthusiastic supporter of the New Deal. He took Roosevelt's experience to be the best example of the generally ephemeral nature of party government in the United States, and he fully expected the cohesive Democratic support he received from Congress after the 1964 election to be temporary. Thus Johnson, like Roosevelt, looked beyond the party system toward the politics of "enlightened administration." . . .

Richard Nixon, Nonpartisanship, and the Demise of the Modern Presidency

Considering that the New Deal and Great Society were established by replacing traditional party politics with administration, it is not surprising that when a conservative challenge to liberal reform emerged, it entailed the creation of a conservative "administrative presidency." This development further contributed to the decline of partisan politics.

Until the 1960s, opponents of the welfare state were generally opposed to the modern presidency, which had served as the fulcrum of liberal reform. Nevertheless, by the end of the Johnson administration, it became clear that a strong conservative movement would require an activist program of retrenchment in order to counteract the enduring effects of the New Deal and Great Society. Opponents of liberal public policy, primarily housed in the Republican party, decided that, ideologically, the modern presidency could be a two-edged sword.

The administrative actions of the Nixon presidency were a logical extension of the practices of Roosevelt and Johnson. The centralization of authority in the White House and the reduction of the regular Republican organization to perfunctory status during the Nixon years was hardly new. The complete autonomy of the Committee for the Re-Election of the President (CREEP) from the regular Republican organization in the 1972 campaign was but the final stage of a long process of White House preemption of the national committee's political responsibilities. And the administrative reform program that was pursued after Nixon's reelection, in which executive authority was concentrated in the hands of White House operatives and four cabinet "supersecretaries," was the culmination of a long-standing tendency in the modern presidency to reconstitute the executive branch as a formidable and independent instrument of government.

Thus, just as Roosevelt's presidency anticipated the Great Society, Johnson's presidency anticipated the administrative presidency of Richard Nixon. Indeed, the strategy of pursuing policy goals through administrative capacities that had been created for the most part by Democratic presidents was considered especially suitable by a minority Republican president who faced a hostile Congress and bureaucracy intent on preserving those presidents' programs. Nixon actually surpassed previous modern presidents in viewing the party system as an obstacle to effective governance.

Yet, mainly because of the Watergate scandal, Nixon's presidency had the effect of strengthening opposition to the unilateral use of presidential power, even as it further attenuated the bonds that linked presidents to the party system. The evolution of the modern presidency now left the office in complete institutional isolation. This isolation continued during the Ford and Carter years, so much so that by the end of the 1970s scholars were lamenting the demise of the presidency as well as of the party system.

The Reagan Presidency and the Revitalization of Party Politics

The development of the modern presidency fostered a serious decline in the traditional local and patronage-based parties. Yet some developments during the Reagan presidency suggested that a phoenix had emerged from the ashes. The erosion of old-style partisan politics had allowed a more national and issue-oriented party system to develop, forging new links between presidents and their parties.

The Republican party in particular developed a formidable organizational apparatus, which displayed unprecedented strength at the national level. . . .

The revival of the Republican party as a force against government by administration seemed to complete the development of a new American party system. The nomination and election of Ronald Reagan, a far more ideological conservative than Nixon, galvanized the Republican commitment to programs, such as "regulatory relief" and "new federalism," that severely challenged the institutional legacy of the New Deal. Had such a trend continued, the circumvention of the regular political process by administrative action may well have been displaced by the sort of full-scale debate about political questions usually associated with critical realignments.

Reagan broke with the tradition of the modern presidency and identified closely with his party. The president worked hard to strengthen the Republicans' organizational and popular base, surprising his own political director with his "total readiness" to shoulder such partisan responsibilities as making numerous fund-raising appearances for the party and its candidates. Apparently, after having spent the first fifty years of his life as a Democrat, Reagan brought the enthusiasm of a convert to Republican activities.

The experience of the Reagan administration suggests how the relationship between the president and the party can be mutually beneficial. Republican party strength provided Reagan with the support of a formidable institution, solidifying his personal popularity and facilitating the support of his program in Congress. As a result, the Reagan presidency was able to suspend the paralysis that seemed to afflict [the executive office] in the 1970s, even though the Republicans still lacked control of the House of Representatives. In turn, Reagan's popularity served the party by strengthening its fund-raising efforts and promoting a shift in voters' party loyalties, placing the Republicans by 1985 in a position of virtual parity with the Democrats for the first time since the 1940s. It may be, then, that the 1980s marked the watershed both for a new political era and for a renewed link between presidents and the party system.

Nevertheless, the emergence of strong national party organizations in the 1980s could not fundamentally alter the limited possibilities for party government under the American Constitution, a fact that would continue to encourage modern presidents, particularly those intent on ambitious policy reform, to emphasize popular appeal and administrative action rather than "collective responsibility." It is not surprising, therefore, that the Reagan presidency frequently pursued its program with acts of administrative discretion that short-circuited the legislative process and weakened efforts to carry out broad-based party policies. The Iran-contra scandal, for example, was not simply a matter of the president's being asleep on his watch;

rather, it also revealed the Reagan administration's determination to assume a more forceful anti-communist posture in Central America in the face of a recalcitrant Congress and bureaucracy. . . .

As such, Reagan did not transform Washington completely. Rather, he strengthened the Republican beachhead in the nation's capital, solidifying his party's recent dominance of the presidency and providing better opportunities for conservatives in the Washington community. Reagan's landslide reelection in 1984 did not prevent the Democrats from maintaining control of the House of Representatives; nor did his plea to the voters during the 1986 congressional campaign to elect Republican majorities prevent the Democrats from recapturing control of the Senate.

Reagan's two terms witnessed a revitalization of the struggle between the executive and legislative branches; indeed, his conservative program became the foundation for more fundamental philosophical and policy differences between them than in the past. The Iran-contra affair and the battles to control regulatory policy were marked not just by differences between the president and Congress about policy, but also by each branch's efforts to weaken the other. The efforts of Republicans to compensate for their inability to control Congress by seeking to circumvent legislative restrictions on presidential conduct were matched by Democratic initiatives to burden the executive with smothering legislative oversight. The opposition to liberal reform, then, did not end in a challenge to national administrative power but in a raw and disruptive battle to control its services.

Reagan's Legacy and the Accession of George Bush

. . . The 1988 election also revealed the limits of the Reagan revolution, reflecting in its outcome the underlying pattern that had characterized American politics since 1968: Republican dominance in the White House, Democratic ascendancy almost everywhere else. In fact, the 1988 election represented an extreme manifestation of this pattern. Never before had a president been elected while the other party gained ground in the House, Senate, the state legislatures, and the state governorships. Never before had voters given a newly elected president fewer fellow partisans in Congress than they gave George H. W. Bush. . . .

In sum, the closer ties that Reagan and Bush tried to forge between the modern presidency and the Republican party did not alter the unprecedented partisan and electoral divisions that characterized the era of divided government. Indeed, the persistence of divided government itself retarded the restoration of partisanship to the presidency. During the early days of his presidency, Bush attempted to reach out to Democrats in Congress in order to restore the badly frayed consensus in American politics. But he gave no reasonable defense of his pragmatism. [Once] he abandoned his antitax pledge and lost his top political strategist to illness, Bush's presidency floated adrift. His search for agreement with Congress in the absence of any clear principles threatened the modern presidency with the same sort of isolation and weakness that had characterized the Ford and Carter years. . . .

Bill Clinton and the Politics of Divided Democracy

. . . The 1992 election contained both optimistic and pessimistic portents for the modern presidency. The Democrats ran an effective campaign; the party not only captured the presidency but also preserved its majorities in the House and Senate, ending twelve years of divided rule in American politics. Indeed, Bill Clinton's victory over Bush seemed to represent more than a rejection of the incumbent president; in part, it expressed the voters' hope that the institutional conflict they had witnessed during the era of divided government would now come to an end. This hope was encouraged by Clinton's promise to govern as a "new Democrat," as an "agent of change" who would restore consensus to American politics. Nevertheless, the strong support for the independent candidate H. Ross Perot, who garnered 19 percent of the popular vote (the most serious challenge to the two-party system, since Theodore Roosevelt's 1912 Progressive party campaign), reflected the continuing erosion of partisan loyalties in the electorate. Indeed, Perot, a successful businessman, who had never held political office of any kind, and his campaign, dominated by thirty-minute "infomercials" and hour-long appearances on talk shows, set a new standard for direct plebiscitary appeals that threatened to sound the death knell of the party campaign. "Perot hints broadly at an even bolder new order," historian Alan Brinkley wrote in 1992, "in which the president, checked only by direct expressions of popular desire, will roll up his sleeves and solve the nation's problems." . . .

In the end, the American people invested their hope for constructive change more cautiously, in the possibility that Clinton embodied a new form of Democratic politics that could correct and renew the progressive tradition as shaped by the New Deal. As Clinton declared frequently during the campaign, he championed ideas that represented a new philosophy of government, a "new covenant," that in the name of responsibility and community would seek to constrain the demands for economic rights that had been unleashed by the New Deal.

Clinton pledged to dedicate his party to the new concept of justice he espoused. But his commitment to control government spending and recast the welfare state was obscured during the early days of his presidency by many traditional liberal actions. No sooner had he been inaugurated than Clinton announced his intention to issue executive orders to reverse the policy of Reagan and Bush of forbidding abortion counseling at federally funded clinics (the so-called "gag rule")—and to lift the long-standing ban on homosexuals in the military. These policies could be carried out "with a stroke of the pen," Clinton believed, leaving him free, as he promised during his quest for the presidency, to focus "like a laser" on the economy.

There was no prospect, however, that such divisive social issues could be resolved through executive orders. To be sure, the development of the administrative presidency gave presidents more power to exercise domestic policy autonomously. Yet with the expansion of national administration to issues that shaped the direction and character of American public life, this power proved to be illusory. . . .

The apologetic stance that Clinton displayed in the face of traditional liberal causes was, to a point, understandable; it was a logical response to the modern institutional separation between the presidency and the party. The moderate wing of the Democratic party that he represented—including the Democratic Leadership Council—was a minority wing. The majority of liberal interest group activists and Democratic members of Congress still preferred "entitlements" to "obligations" and "regulations" to "responsibilities." The media-driven caucuses and primaries . . . had given him the opportunity to seize the Democratic label as an outsider candidate but offered no means to effect a transformation of his party when he took office. To bring about the new mission of progressivism that he advocated during the election, Clinton would have to risk a brutal confrontation with the major powers in the Democratic party.

No president had risked such a confrontation with his party since Roosevelt's failed purge campaign in 1938. It is not surprising, therefore, that Clinton's allies in the Democratic Leadership Council urged him to renew his "credentials as an outsider" by going over the heads of the party leadership in Congress and taking his message directly to the people. The new president could "break gridlock," they argued, only by appealing to the large number of independents in the electorate who had voted for Perot—that is, by "forging new and sometimes bipartisan coalitions around an agenda that moves beyond the polarized left-right debate."

In the fall of 1993, Clinton took a page from his former political associates in his successful campaign to secure congressional approval of the North American Free Trade Agreement (NAFTA) with Canada and Mexico. The fight for NAFTA caused Clinton to defend free enterprise ardently and to oppose the protectionism of labor unions, which still represented one of the most important constituencies in the national Democratic party. . . .

But health care, not trade policy, became the defining issue of Clinton's early presidency. The administration's health care program promised to "guarantee all Americans a comprehensive package of benefits over the course of an entire lifetime." . . . Although the administration made conciliatory overtures to the plan's opponents, hoping to forge a bipartisan cooperation on Capitol Hill and a broad consensus among the general public, the possibilities for comprehensive reform hinged on settling differences about the appropriate role of government that had divided the parties and the country for the past two decades. In the end, this proved impractical. The health care bill died in the 103rd Congress. . . .

By proposing such an ambitious health care reform bill, Clinton angered conservatives. By failing to deliver on his promise to provide a major overhaul of the health care system, he dismayed the ardent liberals of his party. Most significant, the defeat of the president's health care program created the overwhelming impression that he had not lived up to his campaign promise to transcend the bitter philosophical and partisan battles of the Reagan and Bush years.

The president and his party paid dearly for this failure in the 1994 election. . . .

The dramatic Republican triumph in the 1994 midterm election brought back divided government and with it the institutional confrontation that Clinton had promised to resolve. Indeed, the first session of the 104th Congress quickly degenerated into the same sort of administrative politics that had corroded the legitimacy of political institutions in the United States since Nixon's presidency. This time, however, the struggle between the branches assumed a novel form: institutional confrontation between a Democratic White House and a Republican Congress. . . .

Throughout his 1996 reelection campaign, Clinton held firmly to the centrist ground he had staked out after the 1994 election, campaigning on the same "New" Democratic themes of "opportunity, responsibility, and community" that had served him well during his first run for the White House. He won 49 percent of the popular vote to Dole's 41 percent and Perot's 8 percent, along with 379 electoral votes to Dole's 159.

Clinton was the first Democratic president to be elected to a second term since FDR, but his candidate-centered campaign, abetted by a strong economy, did little to help his party. The Democrats lost two seats in the Senate, and gained but a modest nine seats in the House, thus failing to gain control of either legislative body. In truth, Clinton's campaign testified to the fragility of the nationalized party system that arose during the 1980s. The president's remarkable political comeback in 1995 was supported by so-called "soft" money that was designated for party building activities and thus not covered by campaign finance laws. These funds were used mostly to mount television advertising campaigns that championed the president's independence from partisan squabbles. Indeed, Clinton scarcely endorsed the election of a Democratic Congress in 1996; moreover, he raised funds for the party's congressional candidates only late in the campaign. Adding insult to injury, the administration's controversial fund-raising methods led to revelations during the final days of the election that might have reduced Clinton's margin of victory and undermined the Democrats' effort to retake the House.

Clinton's wayward effort to forge a "third way" is suggestive of the modern presidency's dominant but uneasy place in contemporary American politics. The disjuncture between the bitter partisanship within the Capitol and the weakening of partisan affiliation outside of it won Clinton—along with his skill in combining doctrines—a certain following in the country. His gift for forging compromise was displayed in May 1997, when the White House and the Republican leadership agreed on a tentative plan to balance the budget by 2002. In part, this uneasy compromise was made possible by a revenue windfall caused by the robust economy, which enabled the negotiators to avoid the sort of hard choices over program cuts and taxes that had animated the bitter struggles of the 104th Congress. Even so, this rapprochement, which brought about the first balanced budget in three decades, testified to the potential of modern presidents to advance principles and policies that defy the sharp cleavages characteristic of the nationalized party system.

Yet as the Monica Lewinsky scandal, resulting in the House impeachment and Senate trial of Clinton, dramatically revealed, what Woodrow Wilson termed the "extraordinary isolation" of the modern presidency has its limits. Hoping to become a great president in the tradition of Franklin Roosevelt, Clinton became the first elected president to be impeached by the House of Representatives. (Andrew Johnson, the only other president to suffer such an indignity, inherited the executive office after Lincoln was assassinated.). . . .

After a five week trial, the president's accusers failed to gain a simple majority, much less the constitutionally mandated two-thirds, for the charges against Clinton. But whatever authority the president had at the beginning of the administration to establish a new covenant of rights and responsibilities between citizens and their government was shattered by the public disrespect for his morality. Indeed, the virulent partisanship that characterized the impeachment process forced Clinton to seek fellowship among his fellow Democrats in Congress and to abandon his plans to pursue entitlement reform as the capstone of his presidency. In the wake of the impeachment debacle, Clinton positioned himself as the champion of Social Security and Medicare, urging Congress to invest a significant share of the mounting budget surplus in these traditional liberal programs. Clinton's extraordinary resilience, it seemed, was achieved at the cost of failure to fulfill his promise to correct and renew the progressive tradition.

The 2000 Election, September 11, and Beyond: George W. Bush, the War on Terrorism, and Ratification of the Modern Presidency

The 2000 election testified to the modern presidency's fragile governing authority. Neither the Democratic nominee, Vice President Gore, nor the Republican, Governor Bush of Texas, took positions that suggested a way out of the fractious state of American politics. Instead, both candidates took centrist pragmatic positions during the general election campaign that were designed to shore up the principal programs of the welfare state. The activists of the Democratic and Republican parties differed starkly on issues such as abortion and the environment, reflecting their fundamental disagreements about the role of government and the relationship between church and state. But the two candidates sought to distance themselves from their parties, seeking a strategic center between Democratic liberalism and Republican conservatism. The election ended in a virtual tie, a deadlock resolved in Bush's favor by the Supreme Court. Even the conclusion to the election failed to arouse popular passions. The controversy bitterly divided party activists, but not the American people, many of whom, following the recent pattern of low turnout elections and public indifference toward politics, had stayed away from the polls.

Like his predecessor, Bill Clinton, candidate Bush sought to forge a "third way," signifying the modern presidency's dominant but uneasy place in American politics. Bush campaigned as a "compassionate conservative," who would pursue centrist, pragmatic solutions to problems such as education and poverty; indeed, Bush's speeches, which proclaimed the values of "responsibility," "community," and "education," faintly echoed Clinton's campaign rhetoric in the 1992 and 1996 elections.

Important differences marked Bush's and Clinton's stances toward partisanship, however. Clinton never made clear how his third-way politics would serve the principles of the Democratic Party; in fact, he and the DLC were highly ambivalent, if not avowedly hostile, toward partisanship. But in compassionate conservatism, Bush embraced a doctrine that he and his close advisors hoped would strengthen the appeal of the Republican Party. Bush's rhetoric and policy proposals, his top political strategist, Karl Rove, claimed, were a deliberate attempt to play to conservative values "without being reflexively antigovernment." In fact, as Michael Gerson, Bush's principal speech writer, argued, the president's rhetoric did not try to "split the difference between liberalism and conservatism," but rather conveyed how "activist government could be used for conservative ends.

Like Reagan, Bush has sought to rally conservatives to a National Republican party that proclaims to be against national administration, a claim expressed most loudly in conservative activists' militant opposition to new taxes. But Bush could not simply follow in Reagan's footsteps. The ambition to redefine Republican conservatism and achieve an enduring Republican political order evident in Bush's rhetoric entailed a difficult balancing act between partisanship geared to satisfy core constituencies and the bipartisan cooperation necessary to reach out to new groups.

At the beginning of his administration, Bush chose to identify with his party's strong ideological leaders in Congress, hoping to solidify his base of support before reaching out to independent voters. In the meantime, however, the president's emphasis on traditional conservative issues such as tax cuts, regulatory relief, energy production, and missile defense risked alienating moderate Republicans, a small but pivotal group in the closely divided House and Senate.

Bush reaped both the rewards and costs of his early strategy of partisan conservatism. The president persuaded Congress to enact the leading conservative plank in his 2000 platform, a ten-year, $1.5 trillion tax cut. But the Republicans lost control of the Senate in May 2001 when Senator James Jeffords of Vermont announced that he was transferring his allegiance from the Republican to the Democratic caucus. Within days, every Senate committee and subcommittee was transformed into Democratic hands.

Stung by Jeffords' defection and the loss of the Senate to the Democrats, Bush sought to reach out to moderate voters with initiatives that impinged on issues traditionally "owned" by Democrats. Bush strayed from Reaganites' visceral dislike of government not only in his commitment to faith-based initiatives (which were heavily favored by Christian conservative groups) and education reform (which received the overwhelming approval of strategically important state governors), but also in his support for adding a prescription drug program to Medicare (which attracted the support of the interest group behemoth American Association of Retired Persons). The Bush White House's pragmatism was joined to partisan calculation. It's position on Medicare, for example, was allied to the partisan gamble that political capital could be gained with conservatives by combining a commitment to expanded benefits with provisions that would set the program on the road to privatization. As House Majority Leader, Tom Delay (R–Texas), put it, the prescription drug legislation, enacted in November, 2003, contained initiatives like health savings accounts, a tax benefit that would discourage individuals to shelter income for a variety of health-related expenses, that presented Republicans with "a historic opportunity to put a conservative imprint on a major entitlement program."

Indeed, the Bush administration has been more attentive to party building than any White House since the consolidation of the modern presidency during the 1930s. Bush's active recruitment of Republican candidates and diligent fundraising have considerably strengthened the party organization; and his public displays of religiosity and ostentatious use of moral language have served to consolidate a Republican identity of moral and religious conservatism that has energized Republican partisans. These efforts have yielded handsome political benefits. The president's dramatic intervention in the 2002 midterm elections helped Republicans achieve historic victories in the House and Senate. Not only did the 2002 election mark the first time in more than a century that the president's party had regained control of the Senate at midterm, it also represented the first time since FDR that a president saw his party gain seats in both houses of Congress in a first term midterm election.

Bush could not take all the credit for Republican gains. Since the late 1970s the party had been developing into a formidable national organization, in which the Republican National Committee rather than state and local organizations, was the principal agent of party-building activities. This top down approach to party building appeared to many critics to be too centralized and too dependent on television advertising to perform the party's traditional role of mobilizing voters and popular support for government programs. But the Bush White House and the leading strategists of the Republican National Committee, believing that they had been out organized "on the ground" by Democrats in the 2000 election, began to put together a massive grassroots mobilizing strategy in 2002. Democrats since the New Deal had relied on auxiliary organizations such as labor unions to get out the vote. But campaign strategists in the Bush administration worked in collaboration with the RNC to create a national organization to mobilize voters under the direction of the Republican Party.

Building on the successes in the 2002 elections, Bush and his advisors designed and implemented the most ambitious grassroots campaign in the party's history for the 2004 elections. Indeed, one could argue that they built the first "national party machine" in American history, an elaborate network of almost a million and a half campaign volunteers concentrated in the sixteen most competitive states, which was credited as a key to Bush's narrow but decisive victory over his opponent, Senator John Kerry of Massachusetts, in the presidential election, and with helping to increase Republicans' command of the Senate and House. Bush thus surpassed Reagan, whose party leadership never led to Republican majorities in both the House of Representatives and Senate.

The Bush White House has been especially successful in significantly increasing the Republican Party's "base"—that is, loyal Republicans who participate actively in politics, and tend to stay with you through think and thin. Significantly, the GOP grass roots campaigns in 2002 and 2004 targeted not "swing voters" but "lazy Republicans"—those who White House and RNC strategists identified as likely to support the GOP at all levels, but who were unreliable in their voting habits. Although Bush's poll numbers have dropped considerably during his troubled second term, the travails of Katrina and nation building in Iraq would have led to a much more serious political debacle, where it not for the expanded, fiercely loyal Republican base that he and his political strategists have so assiduously cultivated. Even as Bush's job approval rating declined to 40% in May 2006, a full 74% of Republicans continued to support the president. The durability of Republican support for Bush testifies to the strength of the coalition he has helped build.

In fact, the 2004 campaign may have marked a culmination of sorts in the development of a "new" party system—the national Republican and Democratic parties appeared to instigate a serious partisan dispute that captured the attention of the American people and mobilized a large turnout. Prior to 2004, the "new" national party system had strengthened partisan discipline in Washington, D.C., most notably in Congress, and had been a valuable source of campaign services—especially campaign funds—for candidates. But it had failed to stir the passions and allegiance of the American people, attested to by declining partisan identification and anemic voting rates. In contrast, the 2004 campaign seemed passionate, polarized, and participatory. Thus the Republican "Grass roots mobilization" —and earnest Democratic efforts to compete with it—represent the best evidence that a "new" party system has come of age. Significantly, both the Republican grass roots organization and the Get-Out-the-Vote campaign of Americans Coming Together (ACT), the auxiliary ("shadow party") group that assumed principal responsibility for the Kerry campaign's voter mobilization effort, were organized outside of the regular state and local party organizations. Both camps sought to recruit new insurgent leadership in the states and localities, as the new foot soldiers of a nationalized party system. Beyond its immediate electoral effectiveness, then, Republican mobilization efforts in 2004 may provide a plausible blueprint for a revitalized party politics that draws more people into the political process and renews linkages between citizens and elected officials.

Although Bush's partisan leadership marks the most systematic effort by a modern president to create a strong national party, the prospects for "a new party system" that can hold the modern presidency to account are still very uncertain. In fact, there is a real sense in which the "new" party system may be a creature of, and dependent on, the modern presidency. As Rove put it, the national parties that have emerged since the 1980s are "of great importance in the tactical and mechanical aspects of electing a president." But they are "less important in developing a political and policy strategy for the White House." In effect, he said, parties served as a critical "means to the president's end." The emergence of the modern executive office presupposed that "the White House had to determine the administration's objectives" and by implication the party's.

Bush, in fact, with the steadfast support of Republican leaders in Congress, has exploited party beliefs and organization to advance a conservative executive centered administrative state. This started with Reagan, but Bush has trumped Reagan in his commitment to big government conservatism. Already executive-centered in its approach to politics and policy, the Bush White House became even more insulated from Congress and the Republican Party after September 11, 2001, as it planned and fought the war against terrorism. The most dramatic example of this executive aggrandizement has been the Bush administration's foreign policy, especially its "preemption doctrine," pursued with such controversy in Iraq. But the Bush White House has also shown ambition to use national administrative power in domestic affairs, far beyond the exigencies of homeland security. Rather than eliminate the Department of Education, as the Reagan administration proposed to do, the Bush administration pushed the No Child Left Behind law through Congress in 2001, which holds the national schools accountable to standards set by the federal government. Equally important, rather than curtail New Deal and Great Society entitlements, such and Medicare and Social Security, Bush and his political allies have sought to recast them in a conservative image. Hoping to build on the enactment of the prescription drug program, Bush proposed not to cut social security benefits, as Reagan had once attempted and paid dearly for, but, rather, to "privatize" them, allowing workers under age 55 to divert some of their Social Security payroll taxes into personal retirement accounts. This reform, the White House claimed, would yield a better rate of return on funds dedicated to Social Security benefits;

more fundamentally, the personal retirement accounts would recast the core New Deal entitlement as a vehicle by which individuals would assume greater responsibility to plan for their own retirement. Nonetheless, the national government would still force people to save, control the investment choices they made, and regulate the rate of withdrawals. Although Bush's social security plan foundered on the rocks of his administration's declining political fortunes during his second term, the president's aggressive pursuit of entitlement reform revealed his commitment to remake national administrative power to serve conservative political objectives.

The efforts to consolidate a conservative administrative state on Bush's watch may represent, to use E.E. Schattschneider's phrase, a "displacement of conflict," in which the struggle between champions and opponents of the administrative state has given way to a battle between liberals and conservatives for its services. But, as Stephen Skowronek has suggested, the extricable connection between the new party system and executive power provides some support for a possibility that the nationalized party might "in effect become whatever the president needs it to be, and whatever capacity it had to hold its leaders to account would accordingly be lost." The traditional decentralized parties, nourished by the patronage system, acted as a gravitational pull on presidential ambition; the new national parties, sustained not only by the national party committees, but also by advocacy groups, think tanks, and the mass media, encourage presidents to advance bold programs and policies.

The Bush-Cheney 2004 campaign highlighted Republicans' dedication to executive aggrandizement. It was "framed" not so much as a choice between Republican and Democratic principles as a choice between George Bush and John Kerry, as a critical but practical decision about which individual, in the aftermath of 9/11, was most likely to manage the imposing tasks of economic and homeland security. This is not to deny that the Bush campaign's emphasis on wartime leadership was skillfully tied to national security and traditional values that appealed to Republican partisans; but the centrality of presidential leadership tended to emphasize loyalty to Bush, rather than to a collective party organization with a past and a future. As Matthew Dowd, the top strategist for the 2004 Bush-Cheney campaign, suggested, "Leadership is a window into the soul—people want someone they can count on in tough times, and [after 9-11] Bush filled this paternalistic role." Given the president's campaign message, the impressive grassroots operation may have been less a means for mobilizing support for shared values and partisan goals than for mobilizing public approval for the president's personal leadership in the War on Terrorism.

The Democratic campaign, too, emphasized personal administrative competence. As a prominent figure in the Kerry campaign admitted, in explaining the National Democratic Convention's emphasis on Kerry's military service—defined by the candidate's acceptance of the nomination with the emphatic pronouncement that he was, "Reporting for Duty!—the Democratic campaign did not emphasize party principles, but focused instead on presenting the Democratic senator as a "plausible alternative" to the incumbent president, one who displayed the "strength required of a leader in post–9-11 America." Kerry's "flip-flopping" appeared to defy this campaign theme; but the Democratic candidate's inability to effectively engage Bush in a debate over the War on Terrorism was less a matter of indecisiveness than it was his and the Democrats' embrace of modern presidential prerogative. Like many Democrats in the Congress,

Kerry justified his vote for the Iraqi resolution in 2002 by claiming that it did not declare war, but, instead, delegated to the president authority to go to war and determine its scope and duration. Kerry raised substantial arguments against going to war with Iraq, but he voted for the Iraqi resolution because he accepted presidential superiority over Congress, and presidential independence from party politics, in foreign affairs. As he argued at the time of his vote, "We are affirming a president's right and responsibility to keep the American people safe, and the president must take that grant of responsibility seriously." This acceptance of executive aggrandizement badly hamstrung Kerry's effort to challenge Bush on the central issue of the 2004 presidential election.

Consequently, although both the Republicans and Democrats engaged in innovative and effective practices in raising campaign funds, getting their message out, and mobilizing voters during the 2004 elections, it remains unclear that these proto-national machines (or popular allegiance to them) will endure beyond the election. Ultimately, as Dowd acknowledged, "both parties' organizing force has focused on President Bush—the Republicans in defense of his leadership; the Democrats in opposition—hostility—to it. After the election, both parties will be challenged to sustain a collective commitment independently of their devotion to, or hatred of Bush." As is already evident, both the Democrats and Republicans will be hard pressed to meet this challenge in the 2006 and 2008 elections.

Nonetheless, the national programmatic parties, especially the GOP, are strong institutions, more than twenty years in the making. The new party system is more amenable to presidential governance to be sure, but not completely subordinate to it. The failed Harriet Miers Supreme Court nomination, congressional Republicans' strongly negative response to the Dubai Ports deal, and their resistance to Bush's efforts to "compromise" on the issue of policy regarding undocumented immigrant workers all suggest that the party still retains considerable capacity to resist presidential domination. The major question for the next several years is whether the profound revival of the modern presidency's governing authority in the wake of 9/11 has brought a national party system to fruition or continued the long-term development of a modern presidency that renders collective partisanship impractical.

THE CONSTITUTIONAL PRESIDENCY AND EMERGENCY POWERS

Presidential Emergency Powers Pre and Post 9-11-2001

In the aftermath of the terrorist acts of September 11, 2001, that brought down New York's World Trade Towers, destroyed part of the Pentagon, and threatened the White House and the U.S. Capitol, President Bush sought wide prerogative and new statutory powers to deal with the war on terrorism. The terrorist acts were unprecedented but the presidential quest for the power to cope with a national emergency was not new.

Constitutional Precedents

The presidential quest for emergency powers is always greatest in time of war, and the war that presented the greatest threat to the country was the Civil War. President Lincoln exercised both prerogative, or unilateral, power as well as statutory power, derived from congressional laws, to act to preserve and protect the Union. As President Bush and the executive branch, and Congress, respond to terrorist threats, the Constitution and constitutional precedents speak to how far they can go in suspending civil liberties and civil rights in order to detain and arrest suspected terrorists.

The first precedent is *Ex Parte Merryman*, a federal Circuit Court case in which Supreme Court Chief Justice Taney presided when "riding circuit," a practice that existed until the end of the nineteenth century where Supreme Court justices not only supervised circuit courts but, as required by law, actively participated in their cases. The case arose in Maryland during the Civil War. President Lincoln in 1861 secretly authorized the suspension of the writ of habeas corpus in the vicinity of the military line in Maryland. Union forces arrested Lieutenant John Merryman of the Maryland Calvary, and also arrested and detained without trial numerous delegates to the Maryland legislature. Union General Winfield Scott and his officers suspected the detainees of anti-Union sentiments and, in the case of Merryman, actions in helping to expel Pennsylvania forces from Maryland.

Section 9, Clause 2 of the U.S. Constitution provides:

> "The privilege of the Writ of Habeas Corpus shall not be suspended, unless when in Cases of Rebellion or Invasion the public Safety may require it."

Merryman's appeal for a writ of habeas corpus came before Chief Justice Taney who, in chambers acting for the Maryland Circuit Court to which the habeas corpus appeal had been made, granted it.

Taney wrote in part:

> "The Constitution provides, as I have before said, that 'no person shall be deprived of life, liberty, or property, without due process of law.' It declares that 'the right of the people to be secure in their persons, houses, papers, and effects against unreasonable searches and seizures shall not be violated, and no warrant shall issue but upon probable cause, supported by oath or affirmation, and particularly describing the place to be searched and the persons or things to be seized.' It provides that the party accused shall be entitled to a speedy trial in a court of justice.
>
> And these great and fundamental laws, which Congress itself could not suspend, have been disregarded and suspended, like the writ of *habeas corpus*, by a military order, supported by force of arms. Such is the case now before me; and I can only say that if the authority which the Constitution has confided to the judiciary department and judicial officers may thus upon any pretext or under any circumstances be usurped by the military power at its discretion, the people of the United States are no longer living under a Government of laws, but every citizen holds life, liberty, and property at the will and pleasure of the army officer in whose military district he may happen to be found."

The following Supreme Court decision complements *Ex Parte Merryman* and is a historic precedent governing presidential emergency powers during times of national crisis. President Lincoln ordered trials by military tribunals in the District of Indiana in cases of suspected rebels and rebel sympathizers. He suspended the writ of habeas corpus to appeal the decisions of the tribunals to civil courts.

50

EX PARTE MILLIGAN

71 U.S. 2 (1866)

Mr. Justice Davis delivered the opinion of the court.

On the 10th day of May, 1865, Lambdin P. Milligan presented a petition to the Circuit Court of the United States for the District of Indiana, to be discharged from an alleged unlawful imprisonment. The case made by the petition is this: Milligan is a citizen of the United States; has lived for twenty years in Indiana; and, at the time of the grievances complained of, was not, and never had been in the military or naval service of the United States. On the 5th day of October, 1864, while at home, he was arrested by order of General Alvin P. Hovey, commanding the military district of Indiana; and has ever since been kept in close confinement.

On the 21st day of October, 1864, he was brought before a military commission, convened at Indianapolis, by order of General Hovey, tried on certain charges and specifications; found guilty, and sentenced to be hanged; and the sentence ordered to be executed on Friday, the 19th day of May, 1865. . . .

Milligan insists that said military commission had no jurisdiction to try him upon the charges preferred, or upon any charges whatever; because he was a citizen of the United States and the State of Indiana, and had not been, since the commencement of the late Rebellion, a resident of any of the States whose citizens were arrayed against the government, and that the right of trial by jury was guaranteed to him by the Constitution of the United States.

The prayer of the petition was, that under the act of Congress, approved March 3d, 1863, entitled, "An act relating to habeas corpus and regulating judicial proceedings in certain cases," he may be brought before the court, and either turned over to the proper civil tribunal to be proceeded against according to the law of the land or discharged from custody altogether. . . .

The importance of the main question presented by this record cannot be overstated; for it involves the very framework of the government and the fundamental principles of American liberty. . . .

It was admitted at the bar that the Circuit Court had jurisdiction to entertain the application for the writ of habeas corpus and to hear and determine it; and it could not be denied; for the power is expressly given in the 14th section of the Judiciary Act of 1789, as well as in the later act of 1863. . . .

It is true, that it is usual for a court, on application for a writ of habeas corpus, to issue the writ, and, on the return, to dispose of the case; but the court can elect to waive the issuing of the writ and consider whether, upon the facts presented in the petition, the prisoner, if brought before it, could be discharged. . . .

. . . Milligan claimed his discharge from custody by virtue of the act of Congress "relating to habeas corpus, and regulating judicial proceedings in certain cases," approved March 3d, 1863. Did that act confer jurisdiction on the Circuit Court of Indiana to hear this case? . . .

Milligan, in his application to be released from imprisonment, averred the existence of every fact necessary under the terms of this law to give the Circuit Court of Indiana jurisdiction. If he was detained in custody by the order of the President, otherwise than as a prisoner of war; if he was a citizen of Indiana and had never been in the military or naval service, and the grand jury of the district had met, after he had been arrested, for a period of twenty days, and adjourned without taking any proceedings against him, then the court had the right to entertain his petition and determine the lawfulness of his imprisonment. . . .

The controlling question in the case is this: Upon the facts stated in Milligan's petition, and the exhibits filed, had the military commission mentioned in it jurisdiction, legally, to try and sentence him? . . .

No graver question was ever considered by this court, nor one which more nearly concerns the rights of the whole people; for it is the birthright of every American citizen when charged with crime, to be tried and punished according to law. . . .

Have any of the rights guaranteed by the Constitution been violated in the case of Milligan? and if so, what are they?

Every trial involves the exercise of judicial power; and from what source did the military commission that tried him derive their authority? Certainly no part of judicial power of the country was conferred on them; because the Constitution expressly vests it "in one supreme court and such inferior courts as the Congress may from time to time ordain and establish," and it is not pretended that the commission was a court ordained and established by Congress. They cannot justify on the mandate of the President; because he is controlled by law, and has his appropriate sphere of duty, which is to execute, not to make, the laws; and there is "no unwritten criminal code to which resort can be had as a source of jurisdiction."

But it is said that the jurisdiction is complete under the "laws and usages of war."

It can serve no useful purpose to inquire what those laws and usages are, whence they originated, where found, and on whom they operate; they can never be applied to citizens in states which have upheld the authority of the government, and where the courts are open and their process unobstructed. This court has judicial knowledge that in Indiana the Federal authority was always unopposed, and its courts always open to hear criminal accusations and redress grievances; and no usage of war could sanction a military trial there for any offence whatever of a citizen in civil life, in nowise [71 U.S. 2, 122] connected with the military service. Congress could grant no such power; and to the honor of our national legislature be it said, it has never been provoked by the state of the country even to attempt its exercise. One of the plainest constitutional provisions was, therefore, infringed when Milligan was tried by a court not ordained and established by Congress, and not composed of judges appointed during good behavior. . . .

Another guarantee of freedom was broken when Milligan was denied a trial by jury. . . . The sixth amendment affirms that "in all criminal prosecutions the accused shall enjoy the right to a speedy and public trial by an impartial jury," language broad enough to embrace all persons and cases; but the fifth, recognizing the necessity of an indictment, or presentment, before any one can be held to answer for high crimes, "except in cases arising in the land or naval forces, or in the militia, when in actual service, in time of war or public danger"; and the framers of the Constitution, doubtless, meant to limit the right of trial by jury, in the sixth amendment, to those persons who were subject to indictment or presentment in the fifth. . . .

It is claimed that martial law covers with its broad mantle the proceedings of this military commission. . . .

It is difficult to see how the safety for the country required martial law in Indiana. If any of her citizens were plotting treason, the power of arrest could secure them, until the government was prepared for their trial, when the courts were open and ready to try them. It was as easy to protect witnesses before a civil as a military tribunal; and as there could be no wish to convict, except on sufficient legal evidence, surely an ordained and establish court was better able to judge of this than a military tribunal composed of gentlemen not trained to the profession of the law. . . .

It is proper to say, although Milligan's trial and conviction by a military commission was illegal, yet, if guilty of the crimes imputed to him, and his guilt had been ascertained by an established court and impartial jury, he deserved severe punishment. Open resistance to the measures deemed necessary to subdue a great rebellion, by those who enjoy the protection of government, and have not the excuse even of prejudice of section to plead in their favor, is wicked; but that resistance becomes an enormous crime when it assumes the form of a secret political organization, armed to oppose the laws, and seeks by stealthy means to introduce the enemies of the country into peaceful communities, there to light the torch of civil war, and thus overthrow the power of the United States. Conspiracies like these, at such a juncture, are extremely perilous; and those concerned in them are dangerous enemies to their country, and should receive the heaviest penalties of the law, as an example to deter others from similar criminal conduct. It is said the severity of the laws caused them; but Congress was obliged to enact severe laws to meet the crisis; and as our highest civil duty is to serve our country when in danger, the late war has proved that rigorous laws, when necessary, will be cheerfully obeyed by a patriotic people, struggling to preserve the rich blessings of a free government. . . .

The Chief Justice [Salmon P. Chase] delivered the following opinion.

Four members of the court, concurring with their brethren in the order heretofore made in this cause, but unable to concur in some important particulars with the opinion which has just been read, think it their duty to make a separate statement of their views of the whole case.

We do not doubt that the Circuit Court for the District of Indiana had jurisdiction of the petition of Milligan for the writ of habeas corpus. . . .

The opinion which has just been read . . . asserts not only that the military commission held in Indiana was not authorized by Congress, but that it was not in the power of Congress to authorize it; from which it may be thought to follow, that Congress has no power to indemnify the officers who composed the commission against liability in civil courts for acting as members of it.

We cannot agree to this.

We agree in the proposition that no department of the government of the United States—neither President, nor Congress, nor the Courts—possesses any power not given by the Constitution.

We assent, fully, to all that is said, in the opinion, of the inestimable value of the trial by jury, and of the other constitutional safeguards of civil liberty. And we concur, also, in what is said of the writ of habeas corpus, and of its suspension, with two reservations: (1.) That, in our judgment, when the writ is suspended, the Executive is authorized to arrest as well as to detain; and (2.) that there are cases in which, the privilege of the writ being suspended, trial and punishment by military commission, in states where civil courts are open, may be authorized by Congress, as well as arrest and detention. . . .

In Indiana, for example, at the time of the arrest of Milligan and his co-conspirators, it is established by the papers in the record, that the state was a military district, was the theatre of military operations, had been actually invaded, and was constantly threatened with invasion. It appears, also, that a powerful secret association, composed of citizens and others, existed within the state, under military organization, conspiring against the draft, and plotting insurrection, the liberation of the prisoners of war at various depots, the seizure of the state and national arsenals, armed cooperation with the enemy, and war against the national government.

We cannot doubt that, in such a time of public danger, Congress had power, under the Constitution, to provide for the organization of a military commission, and for trial by that commission of persons engaged in this conspiracy. . . .

We think that the power of Congress, in such times and in such localities, to authorize trials for crimes against the security and safety of the national forces, may be derived from its constitutional authority to raise and support armies and to declare war, if not from its constitutional authority to provide for governing the national forces.

We have no apprehension that this power, under our American system of government, in which all official authority is derived from the people, and exercised under direct responsibility to the people, is more likely to be abused than the power to regulate commerce, or the power to borrow money. And we are unwilling to give our assent by silence to expressions of opinion which seem to us calculated, though not intended, to cripple the constitutional powers of the government, and to augment the public dangers in times of invasion and rebellion.

51

PRESIDENTIAL POWERS IN TIMES OF EMERGENCY: COULD TERRORISM RESULT IN A CONSTITUTIONAL DICTATOR?

John W. Dean

At present, the President has opted to exercise only a few of his emergency powers. Under the National Emergencies Act, at this time, he is only utilizing provisions relating to the military.

Will the President choose to use additional powers? It depends on the future. Because we don't know what shape this undeclared war on terrorism will take, we can't know what powers this president—or any successor—might need to cope with the problems of terrorism.

An American President, should he need them, possesses awesome powers. Those powers potentially include what political scientists have described as the powers of a "constitutional dictatorship." No President has ever had to go that far—although they have come close.

Now, however, it is not difficult to conceive of scenarios where terrorist groups, hell-bent on our destruction and refusing to abide by any known rules of war, could employ weapons of mass destruction or bio-terrorism in a manner that could threaten our existence as a nation. What happens then?

Democracy In Crisis: Will It Transform Into Another Form of Government?

Democracy works best in times of peace, when there is debate, compromise, and deliberation in forming governing rules, regulations, and policies. When confronted with a major crisis—particularly one that is, like terrorism, of an unfamiliar nature—the nation will turn to the President for initiative and resolute leadership. If our very existence and way of life are threatened, Americans will want their President to do whatever is necessary.

The history of democratic governments, from the ancient republics of Greece and Rome to the modern states that have replaced earlier totalitarian governments, show that governing by committees, or legislative bodies, never works in times of crisis. Fortunately, our Founders were aware of this when they designed our system.

Alexander Hamilton explained in Federalist No. 70 that the essential nature of the chief executive is his "energy," which "is a leading [element] in the definition of good government. It is essential to the protection of the community against foreign attacks; it is no less essential to the steady administration of the laws; to the protection of property against those irregular and high-handed combinations, which sometimes interrupt the ordinary course of justice; to the security of liberty against the enterprises and assaults of ambition, of faction, and of anarchy."

While our constitution contains no express provision for "emergency" or "crisis" situations, such a provision is not necessary. The U.S. Supreme Court made clear in *Ex Parte Milligan*, following the Civil War, that "the government, within the Constitution, has all the powers granted to it which are necessary to preserve its existence." Or as one commentator has added, "self-preservation is the first law of any nation."

Past presidents—principally Abraham Lincoln, Woodrow Wilson, and Franklin Roosevelt—by exercising their powers in time of emergency, have expanded their authority as necessary to meet emergencies they faced. They have, in essence, made the law in times of crisis, not always in the manner envisioned.

Lincoln launched the Civil War unilaterally, without Congressional action, following the secession of seven Southern states. Only later did he obtain Congressional approval. His critics called him a dictator. But he got the job done that had to be done.

Wilson asked for and received near dictatorial powers from Congress when attacks by Germany against American ships and submarines plunged the nation into World War I. He had to raise and equip a large army to fight on foreign soil. To do so, he demanded and received unprecedented new power and authority.

When Franklin Roosevelt was inaugurated in 1933, the world-wide Great Depression had reached its depths. The new President promised action, and during his first 100 days, Congress gave him what he needed to enable him to use federal powers to rout the Depression and rescue every sector of the economy, as well as state and local government, from economic ruin.

Later, following the 1941 attack on Pearl Harbor, which forced the United States into World War II, FDR's exertion of his presidential powers would far exceed anything Wilson or Lincoln had done. Through the strength of his personality, Roosevelt lead the nation from that day of "infamy" through battles in Europe, Africa, Asia and the Pacific to total victory.

While FDR continued to ask Congress for what he needed, he gave them no choice as to whether they would accede. For example, in demanding that Congress repeal provisions in the Price Control Act (prohibiting ceilings on certain food products), he told the Congress: "In the event the Congress should fail to act, and act adequately, I shall accept the responsibility, and I will act." And he reminded the Congress: "The President has the power . . . to take measures necessary to avert a disaster which would interfere with winning of the war."

We've been blessed with strong presidents in times of national crisis. They were men who demonstrated a capacity for leadership, and men who acted undemocratically, but only to preserve our democracy.

We've been fortunate, for the distinction between a "constitutional dictator" and a strong president is remarkably thin, if not non-existent. As Writ columnist Michael Dorf has noted, there are few checks on our Commander in Chief.

Constitutional Dictatorships: What Happens to Democracies in Emergencies

Rossiter looked at the phenomenon of constitutional dictatorships in the aftermath of World War II, for he was concerned that "more rather than fewer periods of crisis" lay ahead. In *Constitutional Dictatorship*, he examines the experiences of crisis governments ranging from the ancient constitutional state of Rome to four modern states (Germany, France, Great Britain, and the United States), focusing on four major crises in the United States: the Civil War, the two World Wars, and the Great Depression.

Professor Albert Sturm, a student of Rossiter's work, has also written of constitutional dictatorships. In a 1949 essay "Emergencies and the Presidency" in the *Journal of Politics*, for example, Sturm found that these "temporary concentrations of power in an executive" for meeting emergencies, which have been "employed by vigorous democracies since ancient times," are necessary for "the preservation of the established system in the face of temporary crisis." Typically, such authority lasts only as long as the crisis, Sturm notes, and it is sanctioned by the "existing constitutional system."

Constitutional Dictatorship: Could It Happen Here?

Of course, the very concept of a "dictatorship" is offensive and inimical to our political thinking as citizens of a democracy. And Rossiter acknowledges that no American government has ever been a true constitutional dictatorship, as that concept is understood by students of government. Rather, he uses the term, in the American context, as "convenient hyperbole"—an exaggeration meant to underscore how many, and how extensive, have been the powers American presidents have necessarily arrogated to themselves in wartime.

Nevertheless, Rossiter, and other students of constitutional dictatorships, do not rule out the idea that one could ever exist in America. Indeed, they raised questions in the aftermath of World War II that are still relevant today as we find ourselves in an undeclared war, and the first stages of emergency government.

Recall that FDR took the nation from a "limited" national emergency on September 8, 1939, to an "unlimited" emergency by May 27, 1941, and then to total war by December 7, 1941. Anyone who does not believe the war on terrorism will escalate, as well, is in denial.

Rossiter does not address the question of whether Americans could tolerate the undemocratic ways of a constitutional dictatorship. Instead, he is interested in the question of whether we could survive the alternative. He asks, that is, if we could "afford not to resort to undemocratic methods when such methods are essential to the preservation of the state?" To raise the question suggests the answer.

Terrorism Could Indeed Result In A Constitutional Dictatorship

"Constitutional dictatorship is a dangerous thing," Rossiter advises. Such governments are the result of necessity, of the sheer imperative of survival. The greatest danger with such a form of government, and its related institutions and laws, is that they can remain after the crisis has abated.

These are not decisions that should be made by the President and Congress each time the crisis escalates; rather, we should think about them carefully in advance in order to make prudent decisions later.

One need only look at the haste and thoughtlessness with which we have adopted the potentially dangerous USA Patriot Act, most of which Republicans and Democrats alike had earlier rejected, to understand why legislating in the aftershock of terrorism should be avoided if possible.

Our present emergency laws and regulations are a hodgepodge, a patchwork quilt. They respond to precedents from past great crises, and that is wise, but unfortunately these precedents do not contemplate a protracted war on terrorism, or an enemy unlike any we have ever confronted.

Congress has the power to determine whether it wants the American equivalent of a constitutional dictator in the White House. The only way to be certain that we don't make that decision during a crisis, is to revise and codify our emergency laws now—before fear and anger in the aftermath of a possible attack might cause us to make bad decisions, and too easily trade liberty for security in numerous areas.

As I write this column, President Bush has announced that he will address the nation about his plans for restructuring the government for fighting the war on terrorism. None of Professor Rossiter's observations about our history is more chilling than his finding that each national crisis has left the nation a little less democratic than before. With the President's announcement, it is not too soon to consider whether, in fighting terrorism, we really want a constitutional dictator to lead us. I certainly don't, nor do I know anyone who does, but if a future attack comes, and is devastating, the pressure to resort to constitutional dictatorship may be irresistible.

CHAPTER 7

THE BUREAUCRACY

American bureaucracy today is an important fourth branch of the government. Too frequently this administrative branch is lumped under the heading of "the Executive" and considered to be subordinate to the president. But the following selections will reveal that the bureaucracy is often autonomous, acting outside of the control of Congress, the president, and even the judiciary. This fact raises an important problem for our constitutional democracy: How can the bureaucracy be kept responsible if it does not fit into the constitutional framework that was designed to guarantee limited and responsible government?

CONSTITUTIONAL BACKGROUND

While the Constitution carefully outlined the responsibilities and powers of the president, Congress, and to a lesser extent the Supreme Court, it did not mention the bureaucracy. The position of the bureaucracy in the separation-of-powers scheme developed by custom and statutory law rather than by explicit constitutional provisions. The following selection makes it clear that, although the Constitution did not provide for an administrative branch, it did have a bearing upon the development of the bureaucracy. Perhaps the most important result of constitutional democracy is that the administrative agencies have become pawns in the constant power struggle between the president and Congress.

52

CONSTITUTIONAL DEMOCRACY AND BUREAUCRATIC POWER

Peter Woll

The administrative branch today stands at the very center of our governmental process; it is the keystone of the structure. And administrative agencies exercise legislative and judicial as well as executive functions—a fact that is often overlooked. . . .

How should we view American bureaucracy? Ultimately, the power of government comes to rest in the administrative branch. Agencies are given the responsibility of making concrete decisions carrying out vague policy initiated in Congress or by the president. The agencies can offer expert advice, closely attuned to the most interested pressure groups, and they often not only determine the policies that the legislature and executive recommend in the first place, but also decisively affect the policy-making process. Usually it is felt that the bureaucracy is politically "neutral," completely under the domination of the president, Congress, or the courts. We will see that this is not entirely the case, and that the president and Congress have only sporadic control over the administrative process.

The bureaucracy is a semi-autonomous branch of the government, often dominating Congress, exercising strong influence on the president, and only infrequently subject to review by the courts. If our constitutional democracy is to be fully analyzed, we must focus attention upon the administrative branch. What is the nature of public administration? How are administration and politics intertwined? How are administrative constituencies determined? What is the relationship between agencies and their constituencies? What role should the president assume in relation to the administrative branch? How far should Congress go in controlling agencies which in fact tend to dominate the legislative process? Should judicial review be expanded? What are the conditions of judicial review? How do administrative agencies perform judicial functions, and how do these activities affect the ability of courts to oversee their actions? These questions confront us with what is called the problem of administrative responsibility: that is, how can we control the activities of the administrative branch? In order to approach an understanding of this difficult problem, it is necessary to appreciate the nature of the administrative process and how it interacts with other branches of the government and with the general public. It is also important to understand the nature of our constitutional system, and the political context within which agencies function.

We operate within the framework of a constitutional democracy. This means, first, that the government is to be limited by the separation of powers and Bill of Rights. Another component of the system, federalism, is designed in theory to provide states with a certain amount of authority when it is not implied at the national level. Our separation of powers, the system of checks and balances, and the federal system help to explain some of the differences between administrative organization here and in other countries. But the Constitution does not explicitly provide for the administrative branch, which has become a new fourth branch of government. This raises the question of how to control the bureaucracy when there are no clear constitutional limits upon it. The second aspect of our system, democracy, is of course implied in the Constitution itself, but has expanded greatly since it was adopted. We are confronted, very broadly speaking, first with the problem of constitutional limitation, and secondly with the problem of democratic participation in the activities of the bureaucracy. The bureaucracy must be accommodated within the framework of our system of constitutional democracy. This is the crux of the problem of administrative responsibility.

Even though the Constitution does not explicitly provide for the bureaucracy, it has had a profound impact upon the structure, functions, and general place that the bureaucracy occupies in government. The administrative process was incorporated into the constitutional system under the heading of "The Executive Branch." But the concept of "administration" at the time of the adoption of the Constitution was a very simple one, involving the "mere execution" of "executive details," to use the phrases of Hamilton in *The Federalist*. The idea, at that time, was simply that the president as Chief Executive would be able to control the Executive Branch in carrying out the mandates of Congress. In *Federalist 72*, after defining administration in this very narrow way, Hamilton stated:

> . . . The persons, therefore, to whose immediate management the different administrative matters are committed ought to be considered as Assistants or Deputies of the Chief Magistrate, and on this account, they ought to derive their offices from his appointment, at least from his nomination, and ought to be subject to his superintendence.

It was clear that Hamilton felt the president would be responsible for administrative action as long as he was in office. This fact later turned up in what can be called the "presidential supremacy" school of thought, which held and still holds that the president is *constitutionally* responsible for the administrative branch, and that Congress should delegate to him all necessary authority for this purpose. Nevertheless, whatever the framers of the Constitution might have planned if they could have foreseen the nature of bureaucratic development, the fact is that the system they constructed in many ways supported bureaucratic organization and functions independent of the president. The role they assigned to Congress in relation to administration assured this result, as did the general position of Congress in the governmental system as a check or balance to the power of the president. Congress has a great deal of authority over the administrative process.

If we compare the power of Congress and the president over the bureaucracy it becomes clear that they both have important constitutional responsibility. Congress retains primary control over the organization of the bureaucracy. It alone creates and destroys agencies, and determines whether they are to be located within the executive branch or outside it. This has enabled Congress to create a large number of *independent* agencies beyond presidential control. Congress has the authority to control appropriations and may thus exercise a great deal of power over the administrative arm, although increasingly the Bureau of the Budget and the president have the initial, and more often than not the final, say over the budget. Congress also has the authority to define the jurisdiction of agencies. Finally, the Constitution gives to the legislature the power to interfere in high-level presidential appointments, which must be "by and with the advice and consent of the Senate."

Congress may extend the sharing of the appointive power when it sets up new agencies. It may delegate to the president pervasive authority to control the bureaucracy. But one of the most important elements of the separation of power is the electoral system, which gives to Congress a constituency which is different from and even conflicting with that of the president. This means that Congress often decides to set up agencies beyond presidential purview. Only rarely will it grant the president any kind of final authority to structure the bureaucracy. During World War II, on the basis of the War Powers Act, the president had the authority to reorganize the administrative branch. Today he has the same authority, provided that Congress does not veto presidential proposals within a certain time limit. In refusing to give the president permanent reorganization authority, Congress is jealously guarding one of its important prerogatives.

Turning to the constitutional authority of the president over the bureaucracy, it is somewhat puzzling to see that it gives him a relatively small role. He appoints certain officials by and with the advice and consent of the Senate. He has directive power over agencies that are placed within his jurisdiction by Congress. His control over patronage, once so important, has diminished sharply under the merit system. The president is Commander-in-Chief of all military forces, which puts him in a controlling position over the Defense Department and agencies involved in military matters. In the area of international relations, the president is by constitutional authority the "Chief Diplomat," to use [presidential scholar Clinton] Rossiter's phrase. This means that he appoints Ambassadors (by and with the advice and consent of the Senate), and generally directs national activities in the international arena—a crucially important executive function. But regardless of the apparent intentions of some of the framers of the Constitution as expressed by Hamilton in *The Federalist,* and in spite of the predominance of the presidency in military and foreign affairs, the fact remains that we seek in vain for explicit constitutional authorization for the president to be "Chief Administrator."

This is not to say that the president does not have an important responsibility to act as chief of the bureaucracy, merely that there is no constitutional mandate for this. As our system evolved, the president was given more and more responsibility until he became, in practice, Chief Administrator. At the same time the constitutional system has often impeded progress in this direction. The president's Committee on

Administrative Management in 1937, and later the Hoover Commissions of 1949 and 1955, called upon Congress to initiate a series of reforms increasing presidential authority over the administrative branch. It was felt that this was necessary to make democracy work. The president is the only official elected nationally, and if the administration is to be held democratically accountable, he alone can stand as its representative. But meaningful control from the White House requires that the president have a comprehensive program which encompasses the activities of the bureaucracy. He must be informed as to what they are doing, and be able to control them. He must understand the complex responsibilities of the bureaucracy. Moreover, he must be able to call on sufficient political support to balance the support which the agencies draw from private clientele groups and congressional committees. This has frequently proven a difficult and often impossible task for the president. He may have the *authority* to control the bureaucracy in many areas, but not enough power.

On the basis of the Constitution, Congress feels it quite proper that when it delegates legislative authority to administrative agencies it can relatively often place these groups outside the control of the president. For example, in the case of the Interstate Commerce Commission . . . Congress has delegated final authority to that agency to control railroad mergers and other aspects of transportation activity, without giving the president the right to veto. The president may feel that a particular merger is undesirable because it is in violation of the antitrust laws, but the Interstate Commerce Commission is likely to feel differently. In such a situation, the president can do nothing because he does not have the *legal authority* to take any action. If he could muster enough political support to exercise influence over the ICC, he would be able to control it, but the absence of legal authority is an important factor in such cases and diminishes presidential power. Moreover, the ICC draws strong support from the railroad industry, which has been able to counterbalance the political support possessed by the president and other groups that have wished to control it. Analogous situations exist with respect to other regulatory agencies.

Besides the problem of congressional and presidential control over the bureaucracy, there is the question of judicial review of administrative decisions. The rule of law is a central element in our Constitution. The rule of law means that decisions judicial in nature should be handled by common law courts, because of their expertise in rendering due process of law. When administrative agencies engage in adjudication their decisions should be subject to judicial review—at least, they should if one supports the idea of the supremacy of law. Judicial decisions are supposed to be rendered on an independent and impartial basis, through the use of tested procedures, in order to arrive at the accurate determination of the truth. Administrative adjudication should not be subject to presidential or congressional control, which would mean political determination of decisions that should be rendered in an objective manner. The idea of the rule of law, derived from the common law and adopted within the framework of our constitutional system, in theory limits legislative and executive control over the bureaucracy.

The nature of our constitutional system poses very serious difficulties to the development of a system of administrative responsibility. The Constitution postulates that the functions of government must be separated into different branches with differing constituencies and separate authority. The idea is that the departments should oppose each other, thereby preventing the arbitrary exercise of political power. Any combination of functions was considered to lead inevitably to arbitrary government. This is a debatable point, but the result of the Constitution is quite clear. The administrative process, on the other hand, often combines various functions of government in the same hands. Attempts are made, of course, to separate those who exercise the judicial functions from those in the prosecuting arms of the agencies. But the fact remains that there is a far greater combination of functions in the administrative process than can be accommodated by strict adherence to the Constitution.

It has often been proposed, as a means of alleviating what may be considered the bad effects of combined powers in administrative agencies, to draw a line of control from the original branches of the government to those parts of the bureaucracy exercising similar functions. Congress would control the legislative activities of the agencies, the president the executive aspects, and the courts the judicial functions. This would maintain the symmetry of the constitutional system. But this solution is not feasible, because other parts of the Constitution, giving different authority to these three branches, make symmetrical control of this kind almost impossible. The three branches of the government are not willing to give up whatever powers they may have over administrative agencies. For example, Congress is not willing to give the president complete control over all executive functions, nor to give the courts the authority to review all the decisions of the agencies. At present, judicial review takes place only if Congress authorizes it, except in those rare instances where constitutional issues are involved.

Another aspect of the problem of control is reflected in the apparent paradox that the three branches do not always use to the fullest extent their authority to regulate the bureaucracy, even though they wish to retain their power to do so. The courts, for example, have exercised considerable self-restraint in their review of administrative decisions. They are not willing to use all their power over the bureaucracy. Similarly, both Congress and the president will often limit their dealings with the administrative branch for political and practical reasons.

In the final analysis, we are left with a bureaucratic system that has been fragmented by the Constitution, and in which administrative discretion is inevitable. The bureaucracy reflects the general fragmentation of our political system. It is often the battleground for the three branches of government, and for outside pressure groups which seek to control it for their own purposes.

THE POLITICAL ROOTS AND CONSEQUENCES OF BUREAUCRACY

With the exception of those bureaucratic executive departments that all governments need, such as State, Treasury, and Defense departments, American bureaucracy has been created largely by *private*-sector political demands. In response to those demands,

Congress has over the years created more and more executive departments and agencies to solve economic, political, and social problems. It is important to realize that the bureaucracy is not, as many of its critics have suggested, a conspiracy by government officials to increase their power. The following selection traces the rise of the administrative state and particularly notes how political pluralism has affected the character of the bureaucracy by dividing it into clientele sectors.

53

THE RISE OF THE BUREAUCRATIC STATE

James Q. Wilson

During its first 150 years, the American republic was not thought to have "bureaucracy," and thus it would have been meaningless to refer to the "problems" of a "bureaucratic state." There were, of course, appointed civilian officials: Though only about 3,000 at the end of the Federalist period, there were about 95,000 by the time Grover Cleveland assumed office in 1881, and nearly half a million by 1925. Some aspects of these numerous officials were regarded as problems—notably, the standard by which they were appointed and the political loyalties to which they were held—but these were thought to be matters of proper character and good management. The great political and constitutional struggles were not over the power of the administrative apparatus, but over the power of the President, of Congress, and of the states.

The Founding Fathers had little to say about the nature or function of the executive branch of the new government. The Constitution is virtually silent on the subject and the debates in the Constitutional Convention are almost devoid of reference to an administrative apparatus. This reflected no lack of concern about the matter, however. Indeed, it was in part because of the Founders' depressing experience with chaotic and inefficient management under the Continental Congress and the Articles of Confederation that they had assembled in Philadelphia. Management by committees composed of part time amateurs had cost the colonies dearly in the War of Independence and few, if any, of the Founders wished to return to that system. The argument was only over how the heads of the necessary departments of government were to be selected, and whether these heads should be wholly subordinate to the President or whether instead they should form some sort of council that would advise the President and perhaps share in his authority. In the end, the Founders left it up to Congress to decide the matter.

There was no dispute in Congress that there should be executive departments, headed by single appointed officials, and, of course, the Constitution specified that these would be appointed by the President with the advice and consent of the Senate. The only issue was how such officials might be removed. After prolonged debate and by the narrowest of majorities, Congress agreed that the President should have the sole right of removal, thus confirming that the infant administrative system would be wholly subordinate—in law at least—to the President. Had not Vice-President John Adams, presiding over a Senate equally divided on the issue, cast the deciding vote in favor of presidential removal, the administrative departments might conceivably have become legal dependencies of the legislature, with incalculable consequences for the development of the embryonic government.

The "Bureaucracy Problem"

The original departments were small and had limited duties. The State Department, the first to be created, had but nine employees in addition to the Secretary. The War Department did not reach 80 civilian employees until 1801; it commanded only a few thousand soldiers. Only the Treasury Department had substantial powers—it collected taxes, managed the public debt, ran the national bank, conducted land surveys, and purchased military supplies. Because of this, Congress gave the closest scrutiny to its structure and its activities.

The number of administrative agencies and employees grew slowly but steadily during the 19th and early 20th centuries and then increased explosively on the occasion of World War I, the Depression, and World War II. It is difficult to say at what point in this process the administrative system became a distinct locus of power or an independent source of political initiatives and problems. What is clear is that the emphasis on the sheer size of the administrative establishment—conventional in many treatments of the subject—is misleading.

The government can spend vast sums of money—wisely or unwisely—without creating that set of conditions we ordinarily associate with the bureaucratic state. For example, there could be massive transfer payments made under government auspices from person to person or from state to state, all managed by a comparatively small staff of officials and a few large computers. In 1971, the federal government paid out $54 billion under various social insurance programs, yet the Social Security Administration employs only 73,000 persons, many of whom perform purely routine jobs.

And though it may be harder to believe, the government could in principle employ an army of civilian personnel without giving rise to those organizational patterns that we call bureaucratic. Suppose, for instance, that we as a nation should decide to have in the public schools at least one teacher for every two students. This would require a vast increase in the number of teachers and schoolrooms, but almost all of the persons added would be performing more or less identical tasks, and they could be organized into very small units (e.g., neighborhood schools). Though there would be significant overhead costs, most citizens would not be aware of any increase in the "bureaucratic" aspects of education—indeed, owing to the much greater time each teacher would have to devote to each pupil and his or her parents, the citizenry might well conclude that there actually had been a substantial reduction in the amount of "bureaucracy."

To the reader predisposed to believe that we have a "bureaucracy problem," these hypothetical cases may seem farfetched. Max Weber, after all, warned us that in capitalist and socialist societies alike, bureaucracy was likely to acquire an "overtowering" power position. Conservatives have always feared bureaucracy, save perhaps the police. Humane socialists have frequently been embarrassed by their inability to reconcile a desire for public control of the economy with the suspicion that a public bureaucracy may be as immune to democratic control as a private one. Liberals have equivocated, either dismissing any concern for bureaucracy as reactionary quibbling about social progress or embracing that concern when obviously nonreactionary persons (welfare recipients, for example) express a view toward the Department of Health and Human Services indistinguishable from the view businessmen take of the Internal Revenue Service.

Political Authority

There are at least three ways in which political power may be gathered undesirably into bureaucratic hands: by the growth of an administrative apparatus so large as to be immune from popular control, by placing power over a governmental bureaucracy of any size in private rather than public hands, or by vesting discretionary authority in the hands of a public agency so that the exercise of that power is not responsive to the public good. These are not the only problems that arise because of bureaucratic organization. From the point of view of their members, bureaucracies are sometimes uncaring, ponderous, or unfair; from the point of view of their political superiors, they are sometimes unimaginative or inefficient; from the point of view of their clients, they are sometimes slow or unjust. No single account can possibly treat all that is problematic in bureaucracy; even the part I discuss here—the extent to which political authority has been transferred undesirably to an unaccountable administrative realm—is itself too large for a single essay. But it is, if not the most important problem, then surely the one that would most have troubled our Revolutionary leaders, especially those that went on to produce the Constitution. It was, after all, the question of power that chiefly concerned them, both in redefining our relationship with England and in finding a new basis for political authority in the Colonies.

To some, following in the tradition of [Max] Weber, bureaucracy is the inevitable consequence and perhaps necessary concomitant of modernity. A money economy, the division of labor, and the evolution of legal-rational norms to justify organizational authority require the efficient adaptation of means to ends and a high degree of predictability in the behavior of rulers. To this, Georg Simmel added the view that organizations tend to acquire the characteristics of those institutions with which they are in conflict, so that as government becomes more bureaucratic, private organizations—political parties, trade unions, voluntary associations—will have an additional reason to become bureaucratic as well.

By viewing bureaucracy as an inevitable (or, as some would put it, "functional") aspect of society, we find ourselves attracted to theories that explain the growth of bureaucracy in terms of some inner dynamic to which all agencies respond and which makes all barely governable and scarcely tolerable. Bureaucracies grow, we are told, because of Parkinson's Law: Work and personnel expand to consume the available resources. Bureaucracies behave, we believe, in accord with various other maxims, such as the Peter Principle: In hierarchical organizations, personnel are promoted up to that point at which their incompetence becomes manifest—hence, all important positions are held by incompetents. More elegant, if not essentially different, theories have been propounded by scholars. The tendency of all bureaus to expand is explained by William A. Niskanen by the assumption, derived from the theory of the firm, that "bureaucrats maximize the total budget of their bureau during their tenure"—hence, "all bureaus are too large." What keeps them from being not merely too large but all-consuming is that fact that a bureau must deliver to some degree on its promised output, and if it consistently underdelivers, its budget will be cut by unhappy legislators. But since measuring the output of a bureau is often difficult—indeed, even *conceptualizing* the output of the State Department is mind-boggling—the bureau has a great deal of freedom within which to seek the largest possible budget.

Such theories, both the popular and the scholarly, assign little importance to the nature of the tasks an agency performs, the constitutional framework in which it is embedded, or the preferences and attitudes of citizens and legislators. Our approach will be quite different: Different agencies will be examined in historical perspective to discover the kinds of problems—if any, to which their operations give rise, and how those problems were affected—perhaps determined—by the tasks which they were assigned, the political system in which they operated, and the preferences they were required to consult. What follows will be far from a systematic treatment of such matters, and even farther from a rigorous testing of any theory of bureaucratization. Our knowledge of agency history and behavior is too sketchy to permit that.

Bureaucracy and Size

During the first half of the 19th century, the growth in the size of the federal bureaucracy can be explained, not by the assumption of new tasks by the government or by the imperialistic designs of the managers of existing tasks, but by the addition to existing bureaus of personnel performing essentially routine, repetitive tasks for which the public demand was great and unavoidable. The principal problem facing a bureaucracy thus enlarged was how best to coordinate its activities toward given and noncontroversial ends.

The increase in the size of the executive branch of the federal government at this time was almost entirely the result of the increase in the size of the Post Office. From 1816 to 1861, federal civilian employment in the executive branch increased nearly eightfold (from 4,837 to 36,672), but 86 percent of this growth was the result of additions to the postal service. The Post Office Department was expanding as population and commerce expanded. By 1869 there were 27,000 post offices scattered around the nation; by 1901, nearly 77,000. In New York alone, by 1894 there were nearly 3,000 postal employees, the same number required to run the entire federal government at the beginning of that century. . . .

The Military Establishment

Not all large bureaucracies grow in response to demands for service. The Department of Defense, since 1941 the largest employer of federal civilian officials, has become, as the governmental keystone of the "military-industrial complex," the very archetype of an administrative entity that is thought to be so vast and so well-entrenched that it can virtually ignore the political branches of government, growing and even acting on the basis of its own inner imperatives. . . .

A "Military-Industrial Complex"?

The argument for the existence of an autonomous, bureaucratically led military-industrial complex is supported primarily by events since 1950. Not only has the United States assumed during this period worldwide commitments that necessitate a larger military establishment, but the advent of new, high-technology weapons has created a vast industrial machine with an interest in sustaining a high level of military expenditures, especially on weapons research, development, and acquisition. This machine, so the argument goes, is allied with the Pentagon in ways that dominate the political officials nominally in charge of the armed forces. There is some truth in all this. We have become a world military force, though that decision was made by elected officials in 1949–1950 and not dictated by a (then nonexistent) military-industrial complex. High-cost, high-technology weapons have become important and a number of industrial concerns will prosper or perish depending on how contracts for those weapons are let. The development and purchase of weapons is sometimes made in a wasteful, even irrational, manner. And the allocation of funds among the several armed services is often dictated as much by inter-service rivalry as by strategic or political decisions. . . .

Bureaucracy and Clientelism

After 1861, the growth in the federal administrative system could no longer be explained primarily by an expansion of the postal service and other traditional bureaus. Though these continued to expand, new departments were added that reflected a new (or at least greater) emphasis on the enlargement of the scope of government. Between 1861 and 1901, over 200,000 civilian employees were added to the federal service, only 52 percent of whom were postal workers. Some of these, of course, staffed a larger military and naval establishment stimulated by the Civil War and the Spanish-American War. By 1901 there were over 44,000 civilian defense employees, mostly workers in government-owned arsenals and shipyards. But even those could account for less than one fourth of the increase in employment during the preceding 40 years.

What was striking about the period after 1861 was that the government began to give formal, bureaucratic recognition to the emergence of distinctive interest in a diversifying economy. As Richard L. Schott has written, "whereas earlier federal departments had been formed around specialized governmental functions (foreign affairs, war, finance, and the like), the new departments of this period—Agriculture, Labor, and Commerce—were devoted to the interests and aspirations of particular economic groups."

The original purpose behind these clientele-oriented departments was neither to subsidize nor to regulate, but to promote, chiefly by gathering and publishing statistics and (especially in the case of agriculture) by research. . . .

Public Power and Private Interests

. . . The New Deal was perhaps the high water mark of at least the theory of bureaucratic clientelism. Not only did various sectors of society, notably agriculture, begin receiving massive subsidies, but the government proposed, through the National Industry Recovery Act (NIRA) to cloak with public power a vast number of industrial groupings and trade associations so that they might control production and prices in ways that would end the depression. The NIRA's Blue Eagle fell before the Supreme Court—the wholesale delegation of public power to private interests was declared unconstitutional. But the piecemeal delegation was not, as the continued growth of specialized promotional agencies attests. The Civil Aeronautics Board, for example, erroneously thought to be exclusively a regulatory agency, was formed in 1938 "to promote" as well as regulate civil aviation and it has done so by restricting entry and maintaining above-market rate fares.

Agriculture, of course, provides the leading case of clientelism. Theodore J. Lowi finds "at least 10 separate, autonomous, local self-governing systems" located in or closely associated with the Department of Agriculture that control to some significant degree the flow of billions of dollars in expenditures and loans. Local committees of farmers, private farm organizations, agency heads, and committee chairmen in Congress dominate policymaking in this area—not, perhaps, to the exclusion of the concerns of other publics, but certainly in ways not powerfully constrained by them.

"Cooperative Federalism"

The growing edge of client-oriented bureaucracy can be found, however, not in government relations with private groups, but in the relations among governmental units. In dollar volume, the chief clients of federal domestic expenditures are state and local government agencies. . . .

The degree to which such grants, and the federal agencies that administer them, constrain or even direct state and local bureaucracies is a matter of dispute. No general answer can be given—federal support of welfare programs has left considerable discretion in the hands of the states over the size of benefits and some discretion over eligibility rules, whereas federal support of highway construction carries with it specific requirements as to design, safety, and (since 1968) environmental and social impact.

A few generalizations are possible, however. The first is that the states and not the cities have been from the first, and remain today, the principal client group for grants-in-aid. It was not until the Housing Act of 1937 that money was given in any substantial amount directly to local governments and though many additional programs of this kind were later added, as late as 1970 less than 12 percent of all federal aid went directly to cities and towns. The second general observation is that the 1960s mark a major watershed in the way in which the purposes of federal aid are determined. Before that time, most grants were for purposes initially defined by states—to build highways and airports, to fund unemployment insurance programs, and the like. Beginning in the 1960s, the federal government, at the initiative of the President and his advisors, increasingly came to define the purposes of these grants—not necessarily over the objection of the states, but often without any initiative from them. Federal money was to be spent on poverty, ecology, planning, and other "national" goals for which, until the laws were passed, there were few, if any, well-organized and influential constituencies. Whereas federal money was once spent in response to the claims of distinct and organized clients, public or private, in the contemporary period federal money has increasingly been spent in ways that have created such clients.

And once rewarded or created, they are rarely penalized or abolished. . . .

Self-Perpetuating Agencies

If the Founding Fathers were to return to examine bureaucratic clientelism, they would, I suspect, be deeply discouraged. James Madison clearly foresaw that American society would be "broken into many parts, interests and classes of citizens" and that this "multiplicity of interest" would help ensure against "the tyranny of the majority," especially in a federal regime with separate branches of government. Positive action would require a "coalition of a majority"; in the process of forming this coalition, the rights of all would be protected, not merely by self-interested bargains, but because in a free society such a coalition "could seldom take place on any other principles than those of justice and the general good." To those who wrongly believed that Madison thought of men as acting only out of base motives, the phrase is instructive: Persuading men who disagree to compromise their differences can rarely be achieved solely by the parceling out of relative advantage; the belief is also required that what is being agreed to is right, proper, and defensible before public opinion.

Most of the major new social programs of the United States, whether for the good of the few or the many, were initially adopted by broad coalitions appealing to general standards of justice or to conceptions of the public weal. This is certainly the case with most of the New Deal legislation—notably such programs as Social Security—and with most Great Society legislation—notably Medicare and aid to education; it was also conspicuously the case with respect to post–Great Society legislation pertaining to consumer and environmental concerns. State occupational licensing laws were supported by majorities instead in, among other things, the contribution of these statutes to public safety and health.

But when a program supplies particular benefits to an existing or newly created interest, public or private, it creates a set of political relationships that make exceptionally difficult further alteration of that program by coalitions of the majority. What was created in the name of the common good is sustained in the name of the particular interest. Bureaucratic clientelism becomes self-perpetuating, in the absence of some crisis or scandal, because a single interest group to which the program matters greatly is highly motivated and well-situated to ward off the criticisms of other groups that have a broad but weak interest in the policy.

In short, a regime of separated powers makes it difficult to overcome objections and contrary interests sufficiently to permit the enactment of a new program or the creation of a new agency. Unless the legislation can be made to pass either with little notice or at a time of crisis or extraordinary majorities—and sometimes even then—the initiation of new programs requires public interest arguments. But the same regime works to protect agencies, once created, from unwelcome change because a major change is, in effect, new legislation that must overcome the same hurdles as the original law, but this time with one of the hurdles—the wishes of the agency and its client—raised much higher. As a result, the Madisonian system makes it relatively easy for the delegation of public power to private groups to go unchallenged and, therefore, for factional interests that have acquired a supportive public bureaucracy to rule without submitting their interests to the effective scrutiny and modification of other interests. . . .

CHAPTER 8

CONGRESS

The United States Congress, exercising supreme legislative power, was at the beginning of the nineteenth century the most powerful political institution in the national government. It was feared by the framers of the Constitution, who felt that unless it was closely guarded and limited it would easily dominate both the presidency and the Supreme Court. Its powers were carefully enumerated, and it was made a bicameral body. This latter provision not only secured representation of different interests but also limited the power of the legislature which, when hobbled by two houses often working against each other, could not act as swiftly and forcefully as a single body could. Although still important, the power and prestige of Congress have declined while the powers of the president and the Supreme Court, not to mention those of the vast governmental bureaucracy, have increased. Congressional power, its basis, and the factors influencing the current position of Congress vis-à-vis coordinate governmental departments are discussed in this chapter.

CONSTITUTIONAL BACKGROUND: REPRESENTATION OF POPULAR, GROUP, AND NATIONAL INTERESTS

Article I, Section 1 of the Constitution states that "all legislative powers herein granted shall be vested in a Congress of the United States, which shall consist of a Senate and House of Representatives." Section 8 specifically enumerates congressional powers, and provides that Congress shall have power "to make all laws which shall be necessary and proper for carrying into execution the foregoing powers, and all other powers vested by this Constitution in the government of the United States, or in any department or officer thereof."

Apart from delineating the powers of Congress, Article I provides that the House shall represent the people, and the Senate the states through appointment of members by the state legislatures. The representative function of Congress is written into the Constitution, and at the time of the framing of the Constitution much discussion centered on the nature of representation and what constituted adequate representation in a national legislative body. Further, relating in part to the question of representation, the framers of the Constitution had to determine what the appropriate tasks for each branch of the legislature were and to what extent certain legislative activities should be within the exclusive or initial jurisdiction of the House or the Senate. All these questions depended to some extent upon the conceptualization the framers had of the House as representative of popular interests on a short-term basis and the Senate as a reflection of conservative interests on a long-term basis. These selections from *The Federalist* indicate the thinking of the framers about the House of Representatives and the Senate.

54

FEDERALIST 53, 56, 57, 58, 62, 63

James Madison

Federalist 53

. . . No man can be a competent legislator who does not add to an upright intention and a sound judgment a certain degree of knowledge of the subjects on which he is to legislate. A part of this knowledge may be acquired by means of information, which lie within the compass of men in private, as well as public stations. Another part can only be attained, or at least thoroughly attained, by actual experience in the station which requires the use of it. The period of service ought, therefore, in all such cases, to bear some proportion to the extent of practical knowledge requisite to the due performance of the service. . . .

In a single state the requisite knowledge relates to the existing laws, which are uniform throughout the state, and with which all the citizens are more or less conversant. . . . The great theater of the United States presents a very different scene. The laws are so far from being uniform that they vary in every state; whilst the public affairs of the union are spread throughout a very extensive region, and are extremely diversified by the local affairs connected with them, and can with difficulty be correctly learnt in any other place than in the central councils, to which a knowledge of them will be brought by representatives of every part of the empire. Yet some knowledge of the affairs, and even of the laws of all the states, ought to be possessed by the members from each of the states. . . .

A branch of knowledge which belongs to the acquirements of a federal representative, and which has not been mentioned, is that of foreign affairs. In regulating our own commerce he ought to be not only acquainted with the treaties between the United States and other nations, but also with the commercial policy and laws of other nations. He ought not to be altogether ignorant of the law of nations; for that, as far as it is a proper object of municipal legislation, is submitted to the federal government. And although the House of Representatives is not immediately to participate in foreign negotiations and arrangements, yet from the necessary connection between the several branches of public affairs, those particular subjects will frequently deserve attention in the ordinary course of legislation, and will sometimes demand particular legislative sanction and cooperation. Some portion of this knowledge may, no doubt, be acquired in a man's closet; but some of it also can only be acquired to best effect, by a practical attention to the subject, during the period of actual service in the legislature. . . .

Federalist 56

The . . . charge against the House of Representatives is, that it will be too small to possess a due knowledge of the interests of its constituents.

As this objection evidently proceeds from a comparison of the proposed number of representatives, with the great extent of the United States, the number of their inhabitants, and the diversity of their interests, without taking into view, at the same time, the circumstances which will distinguish the Congress from other legislative bodies, the best answer that can be given to it, will be a brief explanation of these peculiarities.

It is a sound and important principle that the representative ought to be acquainted with the interests and circumstances of his constituents. But this principle can extend no farther than to those circumstances and interests to which the authority and care of the representative relate. An ignorance of a variety of minute and particular objects, which do not lie within the compass of legislation, is consistent with every attribute necessary to a due performance of the legislative trust. In determining the extent of information required in the exercise of a particular authority, recourse then must be had to the objects within the purview of that authority.

What are to be the objects of federal legislation? Those which are of most importance, and which seem most to require knowledge, are commerce, taxation, and the militia.

A proper regulation of commerce requires much information, as has been elsewhere remarked; but as far as this information relates to the laws, and local situation of each individual state, a very few representatives would be sufficient vehicles of it to the federal councils.

Taxation will consist, in great measure, of duties which will be involved in the regulation of commerce. So far the preceding remark is applicable to this object. As far as it may consist of internal collections, a more diffusive knowledge of the circumstances of the state may be necessary. But will not this also be possessed in sufficient degree by a very few intelligent men, diffusively elected within the state? . . .

With regard to the regulation of the militia there are scarcely any circumstances in reference to which local knowledge can be said to be necessary. . . . The art of war teaches general principles of organization, movement, and discipline, which apply universally.

The attentive reader will discern that the reasoning here used, to prove the sufficiency of a moderate number of representatives, does not, in any respect, contradict what was urged on another occasion, with regard to the extensive information which the representatives ought to possess, and the time that might be necessary for acquiring it. . . .

Federalist 57

. . . The House of Representatives is so constituted as to support in the members an habitual recollection of their dependence on the people. Before the sentiments impressed on their minds by the mode of their elevation, can be effaced by the exercise of power, they will be compelled to anticipate the moment when their power is to cease, when their exercise of it is to be reviewed, and when they must descend to the level from which they were raised; there for ever to remain unless a faithful discharge of their trust shall have established their title to a renewal of it.

I will add, as a . . . circumstance in the situation of the House of Representatives, restraining them from oppressive measures, that they can make no law which will not have its full operation on themselves and their friends, as well as on the great mass of the society. This has always been deemed one of the strongest bonds by which human policy can connect the rulers and the people together. It creates between them that communion of interest, and sympathy of sentiments, of which few governments have furnished examples; but without which every government degenerates into tyranny. If it be asked, what is to restrain the House of Representatives from making legal discriminations in favor of themselves, and a particular class of the society? I answer, the genius of the whole system; the nature of just and constitutional laws; and, above all, the vigilant and manly spirit which actuates the people of America; a spirit which nourishes freedom, and in return is nourished by it.

If this spirit shall ever be so far debased as to tolerate a law not obligatory on the legislature, as well as on the people, the people will be prepared to tolerate anything but liberty.

Such will be the relation between the House of Representatives and their constituents. Duty, gratitude, interest, ambition itself, are the cords by which they will be bound to fidelity and sympathy with the great mass of the people. It is possible that these may all be insufficient to control the caprice and wickedness of men. But are they not all that government will admit, and that human prudence can devise? Are they not the genuine, and the characteristic means, by which republican government provides for the liberty and happiness of the people? . . .

Federalist 58

. . . In this review of the constitution of the House of Representatives . . . one observation . . . I must be permitted to add . . . as claiming, in my judgment, a very serious attention. It is, that in all legislative assemblies, the greater the number composing them may be, the fewer will be the men who will in fact direct their proceedings. In the first place, the more numerous any assembly may be, of whatever characters composed, the greater is known to be the ascendancy of passion over reason. In the next place, the larger the number, the greater will be the proportion of members of limited information and of weak capacities. Now it is precisely on characters of this description that the eloquence and address of the few are known to act with all their force. In the ancient republics, where the whole body of the people assembled in person, a single orator, or an artful statesman, was generally seen to rule with as complete a sway as if a sceptre had been placed in his single hands. On the same principle, the more multitudinous a representative assembly may be rendered, the more it will partake of the infirmities incident to collective meetings of the people. Ignorance will be the dupe of cunning; and passion the slave of sophistry and declamation. The people can never err more than in supposing, that by multiplying their representatives beyond a certain list, they strengthen the barrier against the government of a few. Experience will for ever admonish them, that, on the contrary, after securing a sufficient number for the purposes of safety, of local information, and of diffusive sympathy with the whole society, they will counteract their own views by every addition to their representatives. The countenance of the government may become more democratic; but the soul that animates it will be more oligarchic. The machine will be enlarged, but the fewer, and often the more secret, will be the springs by which its motions are directed. . . .

Federalist 62

Having examined the constitution of the House of Representatives . . . I enter next on the examination of the Senate.

The heads under which this member of the government may be considered are—I. The qualifications of senators; II. The appointment of them by the state legislatures; III. The equality of representation in the Senate; IV. The number of senators, and the term for which they are to be elected; V. The powers vested in the Senate.

I

The qualifications proposed for senators, as distinguished from those of representatives, consist in a more advanced age and a longer period of citizenship. A senator must be thirty years of age at least; as a representative must be twenty-five. And the former must have been a citizen nine years; as seven years are required for the latter. The propriety of these distinctions is explained by the nature of the senatorial trust; which, requiring greater extent of information and stability of character, requires at the same time, that the senator should have reached a period of life most likely to supply these advantages. . . .

II

It is equally unnecessary to dilate on the appointment of senators by the state legislators. Among the various modes which might have been devised for constituting this branch of the government, that which has been proposed by the convention is probably the most congenial with the public opinion. It is recommended by the double advantage of favoring a select appointment, and of giving to the state governments such an agency in the formation of the federal government, as must secure the authority of the former, and may form a convenient link between the two systems.

III

The equality of representation in the Senate is another point, which, being evidently the result of compromise between the opposite pretensions of the large and the small states, does not call for much discussion. If indeed it be right, that among a people thoroughly incorporated into one nation, every district ought to have a proportional share in the government: and that among independent and sovereign states bound together by a simple league, the parties, however unequal in size, ought to have an equal share in the common councils, it does not appear to be without some reason, that in a compound republic, partaking both of the national and federal character, the government ought to be founded on a mixture of the principles of proportional [as found in the House of Representatives] and equal representation [in the Senate]. . . .

. . . The equal vote allowed to each state, is at once a constitutional recognition of the portion of sovereignty remaining in the individual states, and an instrument for preserving that residuary sovereignty. So far the equality ought to be no less acceptable to the large than to the small states; since they are not less solicitous to guard by every possible expedient against an improper consolidation of the states into one simple republic.

Another advantage accruing from this ingredient in the constitution of the senate is, the additional impediment it must prove against improper acts of legislation. No law or resolution can now be passed without the concurrence, first, of a majority of the people, and then, of a majority of the states. It must be acknowledged that this complicated check on legislation may, in some instances, be injurious as well as beneficial; and that the peculiar defense which it involves in favor of the smaller states, would be more rational, if any interests common to them, and distinct from those of the other states, would otherwise be exposed to peculiar danger. But as the larger states will always be able, by their power over the supplies, to defeat unreasonable exertions of this prerogative of the lesser states; and as the facility and excess of law-making seem to be the diseases to which our governments are most liable, it is not impossible, that this part of the constitution may be more convenient in practice than it appears to many in contemplation.

IV

The number of senators, and the duration of their appointment, come next to be considered. In order to form an accurate judgment on both these points, it will be proper to inquire into the purposes which are to be answered by the Senate; and, in order to ascertain these, it will be necessary to review the inconveniences which a republic must suffer from the want of such an institution.

First

It is a misfortune incident to republican government, though in a lesser degree than to other governments, that those who administer it may forget their obligations to their constituents, and prove unfaithful to their important trust. In this point of view, a senate, as a second branch of the legislative assembly, distinct from, and dividing the power with, a first, must be in all cases a salutary check on the government. It doubles the security to the people by requiring the concurrence of two distinct bodies in schemes of usurpation or perfidy, where the ambition or corruption of one would otherwise be sufficient. . . . [A]s the improbability of sinister combinations will be in proportion to the dissimilarity in the genius of the two bodies, it must be politic to distinguish them from each other by every circumstance which will consist with a due harmony in all proper measures, and with the genuine principles of republican government.

Second

The necessity of a senate is not less indicated by the propensity of all single and numerous assemblies, to yield to the impulse of sudden and violent passions, and to be seduced by factious leaders into intemperate and pernicious resolutions. Examples on this subject might be cited without number; and from proceedings within the United States, as well as from the history of other nations. But a position that will not be contradicted need not be proved. All that need be remarked is that a body which is to correct this infirmity ought itself to be free from it, and consequently ought to be less numerous. It ought, moreover, to possess great firmness, and consequently ought to hold its authority by a tenure of considerable duration.

Third

Another defect to be supplied by a senate lies in a want of due acquaintance with objects and principles of legislation. It is not possible that an assembly of men, called, for the most part, from pursuits of a private nature, continued in appointments for a short time, and led by no permanent motive to devote the intervals of public occupation to a study of the laws, the affairs, and the comprehensive interests of their country, should, if left wholly to themselves, escape a variety of important errors in the exercise of their legislative trust. . . .

Fourth

The mutability in the public councils, arising from a rapid succession of new members, however qualified they may be, points out, in the strongest manner, the necessity of some stable institution in the government. Every new election in the states is found to change one-half of the representatives. From this change of men must proceed a change of opinions; and from a change of opinions, a change of measures. But a continued change even of good measures is inconsistent with every rule of prudence, and every prospect of success. . . .

Federalist 63

A fifth desideratum, illustrating the utility of a senate, is the want of a due sense of national character. Without a select and stable member of the government, the esteem of foreign powers will not only be forfeited by an unenlightened and variable policy . . . ; but the national councils will not possess that sensibility to the opinion of the world, which is perhaps not less necessary in order to merit, than it is to obtain, its respect and confidence. . . .

I add, as a sixth defect, the want in some important cases of a due responsibility in the government to the people, arising from that frequency of elections, which in other cases produces this responsibility. . . .

Responsibility, in order to be reasonable, must be limited to objects within the power of the responsible party, and in order to be effectual, must relate to operations of that power, of which a ready and proper judgment can be formed by the constituents. The objects of government may be divided into two general classes; the one depending on measures, which have singly an immediate and sensible operation; the other depending on a succession of well chosen and well connected measures, which have a gradual and perhaps unobserved operation. The importance of the latter description to the collective and permanent welfare of every country, needs no explanation. And yet it is evident that an assembly elected for so short a term as to be unable to provide more than one or two links in a chain of measures, on which the general welfare may essentially depend, ought not to be answerable for the final result, any more than a steward or tenant, engaged for one year, could be justly made to answer for plans or improvements, which could not be accomplished in less than half a dozen years. Nor is it possible for the people to estimate the share of influence, which their annual assemblies may respectively have on events resulting from the mixed transactions of several years. It is sufficiently difficult, at any rate, to preserve a personal responsibility in the members of a numerous body, for such acts of the body as have an immediate, detached, and palpable operation on its constituents.

The proper remedy for this defect must be an additional body in the legislative department, which, having sufficient permanency to provide for such objects as require a continued attention, and a train of measures, may be justly and effectually answerable for the attainment of those objects.

Thus far I have considered the circumstances, which point out the necessity of a well constructed senate, only as they relate to the representatives of the people. To a people as little blinded by prejudice, or corrupted by flattery, as those whom I address,

I shall not scruple to add, that such an institution may be sometimes necessary, as a defense to the people against their own temporary errors and delusions. As the cool and deliberate sense of the community ought, in all governments, and actually will, in all free governments, ultimately prevail over the views of its rulers; so there are particular moments in public affairs, when the people, stimulated by some irregular passion, or some illicit advantage, or misled by the artful misrepresentations of interested men, may call for measures which they themselves will afterwards be the most ready to lament and condemn. In these critical moments, how salutary will be the interference of some temperate and respectable body of citizens, in order to check the misguided career, and to suspend the blow meditated by the people against themselves, until reason, justice and truth can regain their authority over the public mind? What bitter anguish would not the people of Athens have often avoided, if their government had contained so provident a safeguard against the tyranny of their own passions? Popular liberty might then have escaped the indelible reproach of decreeing to the same citizens the hemlock on one day, and statues on the next.

It may be suggested that a people spread over an extensive region cannot, like the crowded inhabitants of a small district, be subject to the infection of violent passions; or to the danger of combining in the pursuit of unjust measures. I am far from denying that this is a distinction of peculiar importance. I have, on the contrary, endeavored in a former paper to show that it is one of the principal recommendations of a confederated republic. At the same time this advantage ought not to be considered as superseding the use of auxiliary precautions. It may even be remarked that the same extended situation, which will exempt the people of America from some of the dangers incident to lesser republics, will expose them to the inconveniency of remaining for a longer time under the influence of those misrepresentations which the combined industry of interested men may succeed in distributing among them. . . .

CONGRESS AND THE WASHINGTON POLITICAL ESTABLISHMENT

CONGRESS EMERGES AS A PROFESSIONAL BODY SHAPED BY REELECTION AND INTERNAL POWER INCENTIVES

Woodrow Wilson's classic *Congressional Government* (1885), derived from his doctoral dissertation at Johns Hopkins University, where he received a Ph.D. in 1886, described a Congress that was unknown at the time except to Capitol Hill insiders. Wilson's groundbreaking book is a seminal work on Congress that all students should know.

During the 1880s Congress was beginning to emerge from an institution "citizen legislators" dominated to a venue in which professional politicians advanced their political careers. Member reelection and internal power incentives began to shape Congress and led directly to the rise of multiple committees to serve these incentives. Committees were the "little legislatures" that collectively defined Congress.

The British Empire dominated the nineteenth century and its parliamentary government became a model for democracy throughout the world. Party government was the keystone of British democracy, but the Madisonian model considered parties to be "evil" factions that opposed the national interest. According to this model, the deliberative process that the separation of powers and checks and balances encouraged should define the national interest, not party partisanship. Somewhat ironically for a future American president, Wilson was an anglophile who greatly admired the parliamentary and party model of government.

The more the young Wilson studied Congress the more dismayed he became. Committee denomination of Congress reflected a decentralization and fragmentation of the legislative process that advanced special interests and defeated the collective will of popular majorities that parties should represent. The conclusion of Congressional Government calls for more party control of Congress to connect it to public opinion. But, as Wilson describes Congress in the following selection, committees define its politics, not disciplined parties. Capitol Hill politics reflect an ebb and flow and committee and party control, but the cycles of committee power are longer than those of party dominance.

55

CONGRESSIONAL GOVERNMENT

*Woodrow Wilson**

The House of Representatives

"No more vital truth was ever uttered than that freedom and free institutions cannot long be maintained by any people who do not understand the nature of their own government."

Like a vast picture thronged with figures of equal prominence and crowded with elaborate and obtrusive details, Congress is hard to see satisfactorily and

**Compiler's note:* Woodrow Wilson, *Congressional Government: A Study in American Politics* (Houghton Mifflin, 1901), pp. 58 ff., as edited.

appreciatively at a single view and from a single stand-point. Its complicated forms and diversified structure confuse the vision, and conceal the system which underlies its composition. It is too complex to be understood without an effort, without a careful and systematic process of analysis. Consequently, very few people do understand it, and its doors are practically shut against the comprehension of the public at large. If Congress had a few authoritative leaders whose figures were very distinct and very conspicuous to the eye of the world, and who could represent and stand for the national legislature in the thoughts of that very numerous, and withal very respectable, class of persons who must think specifically and in concrete forms when they think at all, those persons who can make something out of men but very little out of intangible generalizations, it would be quite within the region of possibilities for the majority of the nation to follow the course of legislation without any very serious confusion of thought. I suppose that almost everybody who just now gives any heed to the policy of Great Britain, with regard even to the reform of the franchise and other like strictly legislative questions, thinks of Mr. Gladstone and his colleagues rather than of the House of Commons, whose servants they are. The question is not, What will Parliament do? but, What will Mr. Gladstone do? And there is even less doubt that it is easier and more natural to look upon the legislative designs of Germany as locked up behind Bismarck's heavy brows than to think of them as dependent upon the determinations of the Reichstag, although as a matter of fact its consent is indispensable even to the plans of the imperious and domineering Chancellor.

But there is no great minister or ministry to represent the will and being of Congress in the common thought. The Speaker of the House of Representatives stands as near to leadership as any one; but his will does not run as a formative and imperative power in legislation much beyond the appointment of the committees who are to lead the House and do its work for it, and it is, therefore, not entirely satisfactory to the public mind to trace all legislation to him. He may have a controlling hand in starting it; but he sits too still in his chair, and is too evidently not on the floor of the body over which he presides, to make it seem probable to the ordinary judgment that he has much immediate concern in legislation after it is once set afoot. Everybody knows that he is a staunch and avowed partisan, and that he likes to make smooth, whenever he can, the legislative paths of his party; but it does not seem likely that all important measures originate with him, or that he is the author of every distinct policy. And in fact he is not. He is a great party chief, but the hedging circumstances of his official position as presiding officer prevent his performing the part of active leadership. He appoints the leaders of the House, but he is not himself its leader.

The leaders of the House are the chairmen of the principal Standing Committees. Indeed, to be exactly accurate, the House has as many leaders as there are subjects of legislation; for there are as many Standing Committees as there are leading classes of legislation, and in the consideration of every topic of business the House is guided by a special leader in the person of the chairman of the Standing Committee, charged with the superintendence of measures of the particular class to which that topic belongs. It is this multiplicity of leaders, this many-headed leadership, which makes the organization of the House too complex to afford uninformed people and unskilled observers any easy clue to its methods of rule. For the chairmen of the Standing Committees do not constitute a coöperative body like a ministry. They do not consult and concur in the adoption of homogeneous and mutually helpful measures; there is no thought of acting in concert. Each Committee goes its own way at its own pace. It is impossible to discover any unity or method in the disconnected and therefore unsystematic, confused, and desultory action of the House, or any common purpose in the measures which its Committees from time to time recommend. . . .

Often the new member goes to Washington as the representative of a particular line of policy, having been elected, it may be, as an advocate of free trade, or as a champion of protection; and it is naturally his first care upon entering on his duties to seek immediate opportunity for the expression of his views and immediate means of giving them definite shape and thrusting them upon the attention of Congress. His disappointment is, therefore, very keen when he finds both opportunity and means denied him. He can introduce his bill; but that is all he can do, and he must do that at a particular time and in a particular manner. . . . For if he supposes, as he naturally will, that after his bill has been sent up to be read by the clerk he may say a few words in its behalf, and in that belief sets out upon his long-considered remarks, he will be knocked down by the rules as surely as he was on the first occasion when he gained the floor for a brief moment. The rap of Mr. Speaker's gavel is sharp, immediate, and peremptory. He is curtly informed that no debate is in order; the bill can only be referred to the appropriate Committee.

This is, indeed, disheartening; it is his first lesson in committee government, and the master's rod smarts; but the sooner he learns the prerogatives and powers of the Standing Committees the sooner will he penetrate the mysteries of the rules and avoid the pain of further contact with their thorny side. The privileges of the Standing Committees are the beginning and the end of the rules. Both the House of Representatives and the Senate conduct their business by what may figuratively, but not inaccurately, be called an odd device of *disintegration*. The House virtually both deliberates and legislates in small sections. Time would fail it to discuss all the bills brought in, for they every session number thousands; and it is to be doubted whether, even if time allowed, the ordinary processes of debate and amendment would suffice to sift the chaff from the wheat in the bushels of bills every week piled upon the clerk's desk. Accordingly, no futile attempt is made to do anything of the kind. The work is parceled out, most of it to the forty-seven Standing Committees which constitute the regular organization of the House, some of it to select committees appointed for special and temporary purposes. Each of the almost numberless bills that come pouring in on Mondays is "read a first and second time,"—simply perfunctorily read, that is, by its title, by the clerk, and passed by silent assent through its first formal courses, for the purpose of bringing it to the proper stage for commitment, and referred without debate to the appropriate Standing

Committee. Practically, no bill escapes commitment—save, of course, bills introduced by committees, and a few which may now and then be crowded through under a suspension of the rules, granted by a two-thirds vote—though the exact disposition to be made of a bill is not always determined easily and as a matter of course. Besides the great Committee of Ways and Means and the equally great Committee on Appropriations, there are Standing Committees on Banking and Currency, on Claims, on Commerce, on the Public Lands, on Post-Offices and Post-Roads, on the Judiciary, on Public Expenditures, on Manufactures, on Agriculture, on Military Affairs, on Naval Affairs, on Mines and Mining, on Education and Labor, on Patents, and on a score of other branches of legislative concern; but careful and differential as is the topical division of the subjects of legislation which is represented in the titles of these Committees, it is not always evident to which Committee each particular bill should go. Many bills affect subjects which may be regarded as lying as properly within the jurisdiction of one as of another of the Committees; for no hard and fast lines separate the various classes of business which the Committees are commissioned to take in charge. Their jurisdictions overlap at many points, and it must frequently happen that bills are read which cover just this common ground. Over the commitment of such bills sharp and interesting skirmishes often take place. There is active competition for them, the ordinary, quiet routine of matter-of-course reference being interrupted by rival motions seeking to give very different directions to the disposition to be made of them. To which Committee should a bill "to fix and establish the maximum rates of fares of the Union Pacific and Central Pacific Railroads" be sent,—to the Committee on Commerce or to the Committee on the Pacific Railroads? Should a bill which prohibits the mailing of certain classes of letters and circulars go to the Committee on Post-Offices and Post-Roads, because it relates to the mails, or to the Committee on the Judiciary, because it proposes to make any transgression of its prohibition a crime? What is the proper disposition of any bill which thus seems to lie within two distinct committee jurisdictions?

The fate of bills committed is generally not uncertain. As a rule, a bill committed is a bill doomed. When it goes from the clerk's desk to a committee-room it crosses a parliamentary bridge of sighs to dim dungeons of silence whence it will never return. The means and time of its death are unknown, but its friends never see it again. Of course no Standing Committee is privileged to take upon itself the full powers of the House it represents, and formally and decisively reject a bill referred to it; its disapproval, if it disapproves, must be reported to the House in the form of a recommendation that the bill "do not pass." But it is easy, and therefore common, to let the session pass without making any report at all upon bills deemed objectionable or unimportant, and to substitute for reports upon them a few bills of the Committee's own drafting; so that thousands of bills expire with the expiration of each Congress, not having been rejected, but having been simply neglected. There was not time to report upon them.

Of course it goes without saying that the practical effect of this Committee organization of the House is to consign to each of the Standing Committees the entire direction of legislation upon those subjects which properly come to its consideration. As to those subjects it is entitled to the initiative, and all legislative action with regard to them is under its overruling guidance. It gives shape and course to the determinations of the House. . . .

These are some of the plainer points of the rules. They are full of complexity, and of confusion to the uninitiated, and the confusions of practice are greater than the confusions of the rules. For the regular order of business is constantly being interrupted by the introduction of resolutions offered "by unanimous consent," and of bills let in under a "suspension of the rules." Still, it is evident that there is one principle which runs through every stage of procedure, and which is never disallowed or abrogated,—the principle that the Committees shall rule without let or hindrance. And this is a principle of extraordinary formative power. It is the mould of all legislation. . . .

The prerogatives of the Committees represent something more than a mere convenient division of labor. There is only one part of its business to which Congress, as a whole, attends,—that part, namely, which is embraced under the privileged subjects of revenue and supply. The House never accepts the proposals of the Committee of Ways and Means, or of the Committee on Appropriations, without due deliberation; but it allows almost all of its other Standing Committees virtually to legislate for it. In form, the Committees only digest the various matter introduced by individual members, and prepare it, with care, and after thorough investigation, for the final consideration and action of the House; but, in reality, they dictate the course to be taken, prescribing the decisions of the House not only, but measuring out, according to their own wills, its opportunities for debate and deliberation as well. The House sits, not for serious discussion, but to sanction the conclusions of its Committees as rapidly as possible. It legislates in its committee-rooms; not by the determinations of majorities, but by the resolutions of specially-commissioned minorities; so that it is not far from the truth to say that Congress in session is Congress on public exhibition, whilst Congress in its committee-rooms is Congress at work. . . .

The author of the following selection agrees with David Mayhew (see selection 61) that the principal goal of members of Congress is reelection. That incentive, the author suggests, has led Congress to create a vast federal bureaucracy to implement programs that ostensibly benefit constituents. Congress has delegated substantial authority to administrative departments and agencies to carry out programs, inevitably resulting in administrative decisions that frequently step on constituents' toes. Congress, which has gained credit for establishing the programs in the first place, steps in once again to receive credit for handling constituent complaints against the bureaucracy. The author's provocative thesis is that both the establishment and maintenance of a vast federal bureaucracy is explained by the congressional reelection incentive.

56

THE RISE OF THE WASHINGTON ESTABLISHMENT

Morris P. Fiorina

Dramatis Personae

In this [selection] I will set out a theory of the Washington establishment(s). The theory is quite plausible from a common-sense standpoint, and it is consistent with the specialized literature of academic political science. Nevertheless, it is still a theory, not proven fact. Before plunging in let me bring out in the open the basic axiom on which the theory rests: the self-interest axiom.

I assume that most people most of the time act in their own self-interest. This is not to say that human beings seek only to amass tangible wealth but rather to say that human beings seek to achieve their own ends—tangible and intangible—rather than the ends of their fellow men. I do not condemn such behavior nor do I condone it (although I rather sympathize with Thoreau's comment that "if I knew for a certainty that a man was coming to my house with the conscious design of doing me good, I should run for my life."). I only claim that political and economic theories which presume self-interested behavior will prove to be more widely applicable than those which build on more altruistic assumptions.

What does the axiom imply when used in the specific context of this [selection], a context peopled by congressmen, bureaucrats, and voters? I assume that the primary goal of the typical congressman is reelection. Over and above the [six-figure] salary plus "perks" and outside money, the office of congressman carries with it prestige, excitement, and power. It is a seat in the cockpit of government. But in order to retain the status, excitement, and power (not to mention more tangible things) of office, the congressman must win reelection every two years. Even those congressmen genuinely concerned with good public policy must achieve reelection in order to continue their work. Whether narrowly self-serving or more publicly oriented, the individual congressman finds reelection to be at least a necessary condition for the achievement of his goals.

Moreover, there is a kind of natural selection process at work in the electoral arena. On average, those congressmen who are not primarily interested in reelection will not achieve reelection as often as those who are interested. We, the people, help to weed out congressmen whose primary motivation is not reelection. We admire politicians who courageously adopt the aloof role of the disinterested statesman, but we vote for those politicians who follow our wishes and do us favors.

What about the bureaucrats? A specification of their goals is somewhat more controversial—those who speak of appointed officials as public servants obviously take a more benign view than those who speak of them as bureaucrats. The literature provides ample justification for asserting that most bureaucrats wish to protect and nurture their agencies. The typical bureaucrat can be expected to seek to expand his agency in terms of personnel, budget, and mission. One's status in Washington (again, not to mention more tangible things) is roughly proportional to the importance of the operation one oversees. And the sheer size of the operation is taken to be a measure of importance. As with congressmen, the specified goals apply even to those bureaucrats who genuinely believe in their agency's mission. If they believe in the efficacy of their programs, they naturally wish to expand them and add new ones. All of this requires more money and more people. The genuinely committed bureaucrat is just as likely to seek to expand his agency as the proverbial empire-builder.

And what of the third element in the equation, us? What do we, the voters who support the Washington system, strive for? Each of us wishes to receive a maximum of benefits from government for the minimum cost. This goal suggests maximum government efficiency, on the one hand, but it also suggests mutual exploitation on the other. Each of us favors an arrangement in which our fellow citizens pay for our benefits.

With these brief descriptions of the cast of characters in hand, let us proceed.

Tammany Hall Goes to Washington

What should we expect from a legislative body composed of individuals whose first priority is their continued tenure in office? We should expect, first, that the normal activities of its members are those calculated to enhance their chances of reelection. And we should expect, second, that the members would devise and maintain institutional arrangements which facilitate their electoral activities. . . .

For most of the twentieth century, congressmen have engaged in a mix of three kinds of activities: lawmaking, pork barreling, and casework. Congress is first and foremost a lawmaking body, at least according to constitutional theory. In every postwar session Congress "considers" thousands of bills and resolutions, many hundreds of which are brought to a record vote. . . . Naturally the critical consideration in taking a position for the record is the maximization of approval in the home district. If the district is unaffected by and unconcerned with the matter at hand, the congressman may then take into account the general welfare of the country. (This sounds cynical, but remember that "profiles in courage" are sufficiently rare that their occurrence inspires books and articles.) Abetted by political scientists of the pluralist school, politicians have propounded an ideology which maintains that the good of the country on any given issue is simply what is best for a majority of congressional districts. This ideology provides a philosophical justification for what congressmen do while acting in their own self-interest.

A second activity favored by congressmen consists of efforts to bring home the bacon to their districts. Many popular articles have been written about the pork barrel, a term originally applied to rivers and harbors legislation but now generalized to cover all manner of federal largesse. Congressmen consider new dams, federal buildings, sewage treatment plants, urban renewal projects, etc. as sweet plums to be plucked. Federal projects are highly visible, their economic impact is easily detected by constituents, and sometimes they even produce something of value to the district. The average constituent may have some trouble translating his congressman's vote on some civil rights issue into a change in his personal welfare. But the workers hired and supplies purchased in connection with a big federal project provide benefits that are widely appreciated. The historical importance congressmen attach to the pork barrel is reflected in the rules of the House. That body accords certain classes of legislation "privileged" status: they may come directly to the floor without passing through the Rules Committee, a traditional graveyard for legislation. What kinds of legislation are privileged? Taxing and spending bills, for one: the government's power to raise and spend money must be kept relatively unfettered. But in addition, the omnibus rivers and harbors bills of the Public Works Committee and public lands bills from the Interior Committee share privileged status. The House will allow a civil rights or defense procurement or environmental bill to languish in the Rules Committee, but it takes special precautions to insure that nothing slows down the approval of dams and irrigation projects.

A third major activity takes up perhaps as much time as the other two combined. Traditionally, constituents appeal to their congressman for myriad favors and services. Sometimes only information is needed, but often constituents request that their congressman intervene in the internal workings of federal agencies to affect a decision in a favorable way, to reverse an adverse decision, or simply to speed up the glacial bureaucratic process. On the basis of extensive personal interviews with congressmen, Charles Clapp writes:

> Denied a favorable ruling by the bureaucracy on a matter of direct concern to him, puzzled or irked by delays in obtaining a decision, confused by the administrative maze through which he is directed to proceed, or ignorant of whom to write, a constituent may turn to his congressman for help. These letters offer great potential for political benefit to the congressman since they affect the constituent personally. If the legislator can be of assistance, he may gain a firm ally; if he is indifferent, he may even lose votes.

Actually congressmen are in an almost unique position in our system, a position shared only with high-level members of the executive branch. Congressmen possess the power to expedite and influence bureaucratic decisions. This capability flows directly from congressional control over what bureaucrats value most: higher budgets and new program authorizations. In a very real sense each congressman is a monopoly supplier of bureaucratic unsticking services for his district.

Every year the federal budget passes through the appropriations committees of Congress. Generally these committees make perfunctory cuts. But on occasion they vent displeasure on an agency and leave it bleeding all over the Capitol. The most extreme case of which I am aware came when the House committee took away the entire budget of the Division of Labor Standards in 1947 (some of the budget was restored elsewhere in the appropriations process). Deep and serious cuts are made occasionally, and the threat of such cuts keeps most agencies attentive to congressional wishes. Professors Richard Fenno and Aaron Wildavsky have provided extensive documentary and interview evidence of the great respect (and even terror) federal bureaucrats show for the House Appropriations Committee. Moreover, the bureaucracy must keep coming back to Congress to have its old programs reauthorized and new ones added. Again, most such decisions are perfunctory, but exceptions are sufficiently frequent that bureaucrats do not forget the basis of their agencies' existence. . . . The bureaucracy needs congressional approval in order to survive, let alone expand. Thus, when a congressman calls about some minor bureaucratic decision or regulation, the bureaucracy considers his accommodation a small price to pay for the goodwill its cooperation will produce, particularly if he has any connection to the substantive committee or the appropriations subcommittee to which it reports.

From the standpoint of capturing voters, the congressman's lawmaking activities differ in two important respects from his pork-barrel and casework activities. First, programmatic actions are inherently controversial. Unless his district is homogeneous, a congressman will find his district divided on many major issues. Thus when he casts a vote, introduces a piece of nontrivial legislation, or makes a speech with policy content he will displease some elements of his district. Some constituents may applaud the congressman's civil rights record, but others believe integration is going too fast. Some support foreign aid, while others believe it's money poured down a rat hole. Some advocate economic equality, others stew over welfare cheaters. On such policy matters the congressman can expect to make friends as well as enemies. Presumably he will behave so as to maximize the excess of the former over the latter, but nevertheless a policy stand will generally make some enemies.

In contrast, the pork barrel and casework are relatively less controversial. New federal projects bring jobs, shiny new facilities, and general economic prosperity, or so people believe. Snipping ribbons at the dedication of a new post office or dam is a much more pleasant pursuit than disposing of a constitutional amendment on abortion. Republicans and Democrats, conservatives and liberals, all generally prefer a richer district to a poorer one. Of course, in recent years the river damming and stream-bed straightening activities of the Army Corps of Engineers have aroused some opposition among environmentalists. Congressmen happily reacted by absorbing the opposition and adding environmentalism to the pork barrel: water treatment plants are currently a hot congressional item.

Casework is even less controversial. Some poor, aggrieved constituent becomes enmeshed in the tentacles of an evil bureaucracy and calls upon Congressman St. George to do battle with the dragon. Again Clapp writes:

> A person who has a reasonable complaint or query is regarded as providing an opportunity rather than as adding an extra burden to an already busy office. The

> party affiliation of the individual even when known to be different from that of the congressman does not normally act as a deterrent to action. Some legislators have built their reputations and their majorities on a program of service to all constituents irrespective of party. Regularly, voters affiliated with the opposition in other contests lend strong support to the lawmaker whose intervention has helped them in their struggle with the bureaucracy.

Even following the revelation of sexual improprieties, Wayne Hays won his Ohio Democratic primary by a two-to-one margin. According to a *Los Angeles Times* feature story, Hay's constituency base was built on a foundation of personal service to constituents:

> They receive help in speeding up bureaucratic action on various kinds of federal assistance—black lung benefits to disabled miners and their families, Social Security payments, veterans' benefits and passports.
>
> Some constituents still tell with pleasure of how Hays stormed clear to the seventh floor of the State Department and into Secretary of State Dean Rusk's office to demand, successfully, the quick issuance of a passport to an Ohioan.

Practicing politicians will tell you that word of mouth is still the most effective mode of communication. News of favors to constituents gets around and no doubt is embellished in the process.

In sum, when considering the benefits of his programmatic activities, the congressman must tote up gains and losses to arrive at a net profit. Pork barreling and casework, however, are basically pure profit.

A second way in which programmatic activities differ from casework and the pork barrel is the difficulty of assigning responsibility to the former as compared with the latter. No congressman can seriously claim that he is responsible for the 1964 Civil Rights Act, the ABM, or the 1972 Revenue Sharing Act. Most constituents do have some vague notion that their congressman is only one of hundreds and their senator one of an even hundred. Even committee chairmen may have a difficult time claiming credit for a piece of major legislation, let alone a rank-and-file congressman. Ah, but casework, and the pork barrel. In dealing with the bureaucracy, the congressman is not merely one vote of 435. Rather, he is a nonpartisan power, someone whose phone calls snap an office to attention. He is not kept on hold. The constituent who receives aid believes that his congressman and his congressman alone got results. Similarly, congressmen find it easy to claim credit for federal projects awarded their districts. The congressman may have instigated the proposal for the project in the first place, issued regular progress reports, and ultimately announced the award through his office. Maybe he can't claim credit for the 1965 Voting Rights Act, but he can take credit for Littletown's spanking new sewage treatment plant.

Overall then, programmatic activities are dangerous (controversial), on the one hand, and programmatic accomplishments are difficult to claim credit for, on the other. While less exciting, casework and pork barreling are both safe and profitable. For a reelection-oriented congressman the choice is obvious.

The key to the rise of the Washington establishment (and the vanishing marginals) is the following observation: the growth of an activist federal government has stimulated a change in the mix of congressional activities. Specifically, a lesser proportion of congressional effort is now going into programmatic activities and a greater proportion into pork-barrel and casework activities. As a result, today's congressmen make relatively fewer enemies and relatively more friends among the people of their districts.

To elaborate, a basic fact of life in twentieth-century America is the growth of the federal role and its attendant bureaucracy. Bureaucracy is the characteristic mode of delivering public goods and services. *Ceteris paribus*, the more government attempts to do for people, the more extensive a bureaucracy it creates. As the scope of government expands, more and more citizens find themselves in direct contact with the federal government. Consider the rise in such contacts upon passage of the Social Security Act, work relief projects and other New Deal programs. Consider the millions of additional citizens touched by the veterans' programs of the postwar period. Consider the untold numbers whom the Great Society and its aftermath brought face to face with the federal government. In 1930 the federal bureaucracy was small and rather distant from the everyday concerns of Americans. By 1975 it was neither small nor distant.

As the years have passed, more and more citizens and groups have found themselves dealing with the federal bureaucracy. They may be seeking positive actions—eligibility for various benefits and awards of government grants. Or they may be seeking relief from the costs imposed by bureaucratic regulations—on working conditions, racial and sexual quotas, market restrictions, and numerous other subjects. While not malevolent, bureaucracies make mistakes, both of commission and omission, and normal attempts at redress often meet with unresponsiveness and inflexibility and sometimes seeming incorrigibility. Whatever the problem, the citizen's congressman is a source of succor. The greater the scope of government activity, the greater the demand for his services.

Private monopolists can regulate the demand for their product by raising or lowering the price. Congressmen have no such (legal) option. When the demand for their services rises, they have no real choice except to meet that demand—to supply more bureaucratic unsticking services—so long as they would rather be elected than unelected. This vulnerability to escalating constituency demands is largely academic, though. I seriously doubt that congressmen resist their gradual transformation from national legislators to errand boy-ombudsmen. As we have noted, casework is all profit. Congressmen have buried proposals to relieve the casework burden by establishing a national ombudsman or Congressman Reuss's proposed Administrative Counsel of the Congress. One of the congressmen interviewed by Clapp stated:

> Before I came to Washington I used to think that it might be nice if the individual states had administrative arms here that would take care of necessary liaison between citizens and the national government. But a congressman running for reelection is interested in building fences by providing personal services. The system is set to reelect incumbents regardless of party, and incumbents wouldn't dream of giving any of this service function away to any subagency. As an elected member I feel the same way.

In fact, it is probable that at least some congressmen deliberately stimulate the demand for their bureaucratic fixit services. Recall that the new Republican in district A travels about his district saying:

> I'm your man in Washington. What are your problems? How can I help you?

And in district B, did the demand for the congressman's services rise so much between 1962 and 1964 that a "regiment" of constituency staff became necessary? Or, having access to the regiment, did the new Democrat stimulate the demand to which he would apply his regiment?

In addition to greatly increased casework, let us not forget that the growth of the federal role has also greatly expanded the federal pork barrel. The creative pork barreler need not limit himself to dams and post offices—rather old-fashioned interests. Today, creative congressmen can cadge LEAA money for the local police, urban renewal and housing money for local politicians, educational program grants for the local education bureaucracy. And there are sewage treatment plants, worker training and retraining programs, health services, and programs for the elderly. The pork barrel is full to overflowing. The conscientious congressman can stimulate applications for federal assistance (the sheer number of programs makes it difficult for local officials to stay current with the possibilities), put in a good word during consideration, and announce favorable decisions amid great fanfare.

In sum, everyday decisions by a large and growing federal bureaucracy bestow significant tangible benefits and impose significant tangible costs. Congressmen can affect these decisions. Ergo, the more decisions the bureaucracy has the opportunity to make, the more opportunities there are for the congressman to build up credits.

The nature of the Washington system is . . . quite clear. Congressmen (typically the majority Democrats) earn electoral credits by establishing various federal programs (the minority Republicans typically earn credits by fighting the good fight). The legislation is drafted in very general terms, so some agency, existing or newly established, must translate a vague policy mandate into a functioning program, a process that necessitates the promulgation of numerous rules and regulations and, incidentally, the trampling of numerous toes. At the next stage, aggrieved and/or hopeful constituents petition their congressman to intervene in the complex (or at least obscure) decision processes of the bureaucracy. The cycle closes when the congressman lends a sympathetic ear, piously denounces the evils of bureaucracy, intervenes in the latter's decisions, and rides a grateful electorate to ever more impressive electoral showings. Congressmen take credit coming and going. They are the alpha and the omega.

The popular frustration with the permanent government in Washington is partly justified, but to a considerable degree it is misplaced resentment. Congress is the linchpin of the Washington establishment. The bureaucracy serves as a convenient lightning rod for public frustration and a convenient whipping boy for congressmen. But so long as the bureaucracy accommodates congressmen, the latter will oblige with ever larger budgets and grants of authority. Congress does not just react to big government—it creates it. All of Washington prospers. More and more bureaucrats promulgate more and more regulations and dispense more and more money. Fewer and fewer congressmen suffer electoral defeat. Elements of the electorate benefit from government programs, and all of the electorate is eligible for ombudsman services. But the general, long-term welfare of the United States is no more than an incidental by-product of the system.

COMMITTEE CHAIRMEN AS POLITICAL ENTREPRENEURS

Congressional scholars have pointed out how the personal power incentive on Capitol Hill supports and expands committee government. Congressional committees became a dominant force in the legislative process toward the end of the nineteenth century. In 1885 Woodrow Wilson was able to state categorically in his famous work, *Congressional Government:*

> The leaders of the House are the chairmen of the principal Standing Committees. Indeed, to be exactly accurate, the House has as many leaders as there are subjects of legislation; for there are as many Standing Committees as there are leading classes of legislation, and in the consideration of every topic of business the House is guided by a special leader in the person of the chairman of the Standing Committee, charged with the superintendence of measures of the particular class to which that topic belongs. It is this multiplicity of leaders, this many-headed leadership, which makes the organization of the House too complex to afford uninformed people and unskilled observers any easy clue to its methods of rule. For the chairmen of the Standing Committees do not constitute a cooperative body like a ministry. They do not consult and concur in the adoption of homogeneous and mutually helpful measures; there is no thought of acting in concert. Each Committee goes its own way at its own pace. It is impossible to discover any unity or method in the disconnected and therefore unsystematic, confused, and desultory action of the House, or any common purpose in the measures which its Committees from time to time recommend.

With regard to the Senate he noted:

> It has those same radical defects of organization which weaken the House. Its functions also, like those of the House, are segregated in the prerogatives of numerous Standing Committees. In this regard Congress is all of a piece. There is in the Senate no more opportunity than exists in the House for gaining such recognized party leadership as would be likely to enlarge a man by giving him a sense of power, and to steady and sober him by filling him with a grave sense of responsibility. So far as its organization controls it, the Senate . . . proceedings bear most of the characteristic features of committee rule.

The Legislative Reorganization Act of 1946 was designed to streamline congressional committee structure and provide committees and individual members of Congress with increased expert staff; however, although the number of standing committees was reduced, subcommittees have increased so that the net numerical reduction is not as great as was originally intended. Further, because Congress still conducts its business through committees, (1) the senior members of the party with the majority in Congress dominate the formulation of public policy through the seniority rule; (2) policy formulation is fragmented, with each committee maintaining relative dominance over policy areas within its jurisdiction; and (3) stemming from this fragmentation, party control is weakened, especially when the president attempts to assume legislative dominance.

Although Congress is often pictured as powerless in confrontation with the executive branch, the fact is that the chairmen of powerful congressional committees often dominate administrative agencies over which they have jurisdiction. They are an important part of the broad Washington establishment. This is particularly true of the chairmen of appropriations committees and subcommittees; because of their control of the purse strings, they are able to wield far more influence over the bureaucracy than are the chairmen of other committees. The appropriations committees have a direct weapon—money—that they can wield against administrative adversaries. And the chairmen of all committees have seniority that often exceeds that of the bureaucrats with whom they are dealing. The secretaries and assistant secretaries of executive departments are political appointees who rarely stay in government more than two years, whereas powerful members of Congress have been around for one or more decades. This gives the latter expertise that those working within the political levels of the bureaucracy often lack. Political appointees in the bureaucracy must rely upon their professional staff in order to match the expertise of senior members of Congress. The power of the chairmen of the appropriations committees often leads them to interfere directly in administrative operations. They become, in effect, part of the bureaucracy, often dominating it and determining what programs it will implement. The constant interaction between committee chairs and agencies results in "government without passing laws," to use the phrase of Michael W. Kirst.*

While committees remain an important part of the Washington power establishment, their chairmen often becoming informal "prime ministers" dominating the policy arenas their committees control, though the chairmen are no longer the feudal barons Woodrow Wilson portrayed. But congressional committees, more than political parties, continue to define the legislative process. The dispersion of committee power adds new dimensions to divided government. As the president confronts Congress he must deal with multiple power centers, making presidential leadership even more complex and difficult.

57

CONGRESS AND THE QUEST FOR POWER

Lawrence C. Dodd[1]

The postwar years have taught students of Congress a very fundamental lesson: Congress is a dynamic institution. The recent congressional changes picture an institution that is much like a kaleidoscope. At first glance the visual images and

---

[1]*Author's Note:* For critical assistance at various stages in the writing of this essay, I would like to thank Arnold Fleischmann, Michael N. Green, Bruce I. Oppenheimer, Diana Phillips, Russ Renka, Terry Sullivan, and numerous graduate and undergraduate students who shared with me their questions and insights.

**Compiler's note*: See Michael W. Kirst, *Government Without Passing Laws* (Chapel Hill: University of North Carolina Press, 1969).

structural patterns appear frozen in a simple and comprehensive mosaic. Upon closer and longer inspection the realization dawns that the picture is subject to constant transformations. These transformations seem to flow naturally from the prior observations, yet the resulting mosaic is quite different and is not ordered by the same static principles used to interpret and understand the earlier one. The appreciation and understanding of the moving image requires not only comprehending the role of each colorful geometric object in a specific picture, not developing a satisfactory interpretation of the principles underlying a specific picture or change in specific aspects of the picture, but grasping the dynamics underlying the structural transformations themselves. So it is with Congress. To understand and appreciate it as an institution we must focus not only on particular aspects of internal congressional structure and process, nor on changes in particular patterns. We must seek to understand the more fundamental dynamics that produce the transformations in the congressional mosaic. This essay represents an attempt to explain the dynamics of congressional structure. . . .

I

As with politicians generally, members of Congress enter politics in a quest for personal power. This quest may derive from any number of deeper motives: a desire for ego gratification or for prestige, a search for personal salvation through good works, a hope to construct a better world or to dominate the present one, or a preoccupation with status and self-love. Whatever the source, most members of Congress seek to attain the power to control policy decisions that impose the authority of the state on the citizenry at large.

The most basic lesson that any member of Congress learns on entering the institution is that the quest for power by service within Congress requires reelection. First, reelection is necessary in order to remain in the struggle within Congress for "power positions." Staying in the struggle is important not only in that it provides the formal status as an elected representative without which an individual's influence on national legislative policy lacks legal authority; the quest for power through election and reelection also signals one's acceptance of the myth of democratic rule and thus one's acceptability as a power seeker who honors the society's traditional values. Second, reelection, particularly by large margins, helps create an aura of personal legitimacy. It indicates that one has a special mandate from the people, that one's position is fairly secure, that one will have to be "reckoned with." Third, long-term electoral success bestows on a member of Congress the opportunity to gain the experience and expertise, and to demonstrate the legislative skill and political prescience, that can serve to justify the exercise of power.

Because reelection is so important, and because it may be so difficult to ensure, its pursuit can become all-consuming. The constitutional system, electoral laws, and social system together have created political parties that are weak coalitions. A candidate for Congress normally must create a personal organization rather than rely on her or his political party. The "electoral connection" that intervenes between the desire for power and the realization of power may lead members to emphasize form over substance, position taking, advertising, and credit claiming rather than problem solving. In an effort to sustain electoral success, members of Congress may fail to take controversial and clear positions, fail to make hard choices, fail to exercise power itself. Yet members of Congress generally are not solely preoccupied with reelection. Most members have relatively secure electoral margins. This security stems partially from the fact that members of Congress are independent of political parties and are independent from responsibility for selecting the executive, and thus can be judged more on personal qualities than on partisan or executive affiliations. Electoral security is further reinforced because members of Congress personally control financial and casework resources that can help them build a loyalty from their constituents independent of policy or ideological considerations. The existence of secure electoral margins thus allows members to devote considerable effort toward capturing a "power position" within Congress and generating a mystique of special authority that is necessary to legitimize a select decision-making role for them in the eyes of their nominal peers.

The concern of members of Congress with gaining congressional power, rather than just securing reelection, has had a considerable influence on the structure and life of Congress. Were members solely preoccupied with reelection, we would expect them to spend little time in Washington and devote their personal efforts to constituent speeches and district casework. One would expect Congress to be run by a centralized, efficient staff who, in league with policy-oriented interest groups, would draft legislation, investigate the issues, frame palatable solutions, and present the members with the least controversial bills possible. Members of Congress would give little attention to committee work, and then only to committees that clearly served reelection interests. The primary activity of congresspeople in Congress, rather, would be extended, televised floor debates and symbolic roll call votes, all for show. Such a system would allow the appearance of work while providing ample opportunity for the mending of home fences. Alternatively, were only a few members of Congress concerned about power, with others concerned with reelection, personal finances, or private lives, one might expect a centralized system with a few leaders exercising power and all others spending their time on personal or electoral matters.

Virtually all members of the U.S. Congress are preoccupied with power considerations. They are unwilling—unless forced by external events—to leave the major decisions in either a centralized, autonomous staff system or a central leadership. Each member wants to exercise power—to make the key policy decisions. This motive places every member in a personal conflict with every other member: to the extent that one member realizes her or his goal personally to control all key decisions, all others must lose. Given this widespread power motive, an obvious way to resolve the conflict is to disperse power—or at least power positions—as widely as possible. One logical solution, in other words, is to place basic policy-making responsibility in a series of discrete and relatively autonomous committees and subcommittees, each having control over the decisions in a specified jurisdictional area. Each member can belong to a small number of committees and, within them, have a significant and perhaps dominant influence on policy. Although such a system denies every member the opportunity to control all policy decisions, it ensures that most members, particularly if they stay in Congress long enough to obtain a subcommittee or committee chair, and if they generate the mystique of special authority necessary to allow them to activate the power potential of their select position, can satisfy a portion of their power drive.

Within Congress, as one would expect in light of the power motive, the fundamental structure of organization is a committee system. Most members spend most of their time not in their district but in Washington, and most of their Washington time not on the floor in symbolic televised debate but rather in the committee or subcommittee rooms, in caucus meetings, or in office work devoted to legislation. While the staff, particularly the personal staff, may be relegated to casework for constituents, the members of Congress sit through hearing after hearing, debate after debate, vote after vote seeking to shape in subcommittee, committee, and floor votes the contours of legislation. This is not to suggest, of course, that members of Congress do not engage in symbolic action or personal casework and do not spend much time in the home district; they do, in their effort at reelection. Likewise, staff do draft legislation, play a strong role in committee investigations, and influence the direction of public policy; they do this, however, largely because members of Congress just do not have enough time in the day to fulfill their numerous obligations. Seen in this perspective, Congress is not solely, simply, or primarily a stage on which individuals intentionally and exclusively engage in meaningless charades. Whatever the end product of their effort may be, members of Congress have actively sought to design a congressional structure and process that would maximize their ability to exercise personal power within Congress and, through Congress, within the nation at large.

The congressional committee structure reflects rather naturally the various dimensions that characterize the making of public policy. There are authorization committees that create policies and programs, specify their duties and powers, and establish absolute funding levels. There are appropriations committees that specify the actual funding level for a particular fiscal year. There are revenue committees that raise the funds to pay for the appropriations necessary to sustain the authorized programs. In addition, since Congress itself is an elaborate institution that must be serviced, there are housekeeping committees—those that provide for the day-to-day operation of Congress. In the House of Representatives there is also an internal regulation committee, the House Rules Committee, that schedules debate and specifies the rules for deliberation on specific bills.

These committees vary greatly in the nature and comprehensiveness of their impact on national policy making. The housekeeping committees tend to be service committees and carry little national weight except through indirect influence obtained from manipulating office and staff resources that other members may want so desperately as to modify their policy stances on other committees. A second set of committees, authorization committees such as Interior or Post Office, have jurisdictions that limit them to the concerns of fairly narrow constituencies; these are "reelection committees" that allow members to serve their constituencies' parochial interests but offer only limited potential to effect broad-scale public policy. A third group of committees are policy committees, such as Education and Labor or

International Relations, that consider fairly broad policy questions, though questions that have fairly clear and circumscribed jurisdictional limits. A fourth set of committees are the "power" committees, which make decisions on issues such as the scheduling of rules (the House Rules Committee), appropriations (House and Senate Appropriations committees), or revenues (House Ways and Means or Senate Finance) that allow them to affect most or all policy areas. Within a pure system of committee government, power committees are limited in the comprehensiveness of their control over the general policy-making process. No overarching control committee exists to coordinate the authorization, appropriations, or revenue process.

Because an essential type of legislative authority is associated with each congressional committee, members find that service on any committee can offer some satisfaction of their power drive. There are, nevertheless, inherent differences in the power potential associated with committees, differences that are tied to the variation in legislative function and in the comprehensiveness of a committee's decisional jurisdiction. This variation between committees is sufficient to make some committees more attractive as a place to gain power. Because members are in a quest for power, not simply reelection, they generally will seek to serve on committees whose function and policy focus allow the broadest personal impact on policy.

Maneuvering for membership on the more attractive committees is constrained by two fundamental factors. First, there are a limited number of attractive committee slots, and much competition will exist for these vacancies. Most members cannot realize their goal to serve on and gain control of these committees. For this reason, much pressure exists to establish norms by which members "prove" themselves deserving of membership on an attractive committee. Such norms include courtesy to fellow members, specialization in limited areas of public policy, a willingness to work hard on legislation, a commitment to the institution, adherence to the general policy parameters seen as desirable by senior members of Congress who will dominate the committee nominations process, and a willingness to reciprocate favors and abide by the division of policy domains into the set of relatively independent policy-making entities. Members who observe these norms faithfully will advance to the more desirable committees because they will have shown themselves worthy of special privilege, particularly if they also possess sufficient congressional seniority.

Seniority is particularly important because of the second constraint on the process—the fact that service on the more powerful committees may limit one's ability to mend electoral fences. On the more comprehensive committees, issues often can be more complex and difficult to understand, necessitating much time and concentration on committee work; members may not be able to get home as often or as easily. Issues will be more controversial and will face members with difficult and often unpopular policy choices; members will be less able to engage in the politics of form over substance. The national visibility of the members will be greater, transforming them into public figures whose personal lives may receive considerable attention. Indiscretions that normally might go unreported will become open game for the press and can destroy careers. Thus, although it is undoubtedly true that service on the more comprehensive committees may bring with it certain attributes that can help reelection (campaign contributions from interest groups, name identification and status, a reputation for power that may convince constituents that "our member can deliver"), service on the more attractive committees does thrust members into a more unpredictable world. Although members generally will want to serve on the most powerful committees, it will normally be best for them to put off such service until they have a secure electoral base and to approach their quest for power in sequential steps.

Because of the constraints operating within a system of committee government, congressional careers reflect a set of stages. The first stage entails an emphasis on shoring up the electoral base through casework, service on constituent-oriented reelection committees, and gaining favor within Congress by serving on the housekeeping committees. Of course, the first stage is never fully "completed": there is never a time at which a member of Congress is "guaranteed" long-term reelection or total acceptance within Congress, so both constituent and congressional service are a recurring necessity. But a point is normally reached—a point defined by the circumstances of the member's constituency, the opportunities present in Congress, and the personality and competence of the member—when he or she will feel secure enough, or perhaps unhappy enough, to attempt a move to a second stage. In the second stage members broaden their horizons and seek service on key policy committees that draft important legislation regulating such national policy dimensions as interstate commerce, education, or labor. In this stage, representatives begin to be "legislators," to preoccupy themselves with national policy matters. Because of the limited number of positions on power committees, many members will spend most, perhaps the rest, of their career in this stage, moving up by committee seniority to subcommittee and committee chairs on the policy committees. As they gain expertise in the specific policy area, and create a myth of special personal authority, they will gain power in some important but circumscribed area of national policy. For members who persist, however, and/or possess the right attributes of electoral security and personal attributes, a third stage exists: service on a power committee—Rules, Ways and Means, or Finance, Appropriations, and, in the Senate, Foreign Relations. Service on these committees is superseded, if at all, only by involvement in a fourth stage: service in the party leadership as a floor leader or Speaker. Few individuals ever have the opportunity to realize this fourth and climactic step; in a system of committee government, in fact, this step will be less sought and the battles less bitter than one might expect, considering the status associated with them, because power will rest primarily in committees rather than in the party. Although party leadership positions in a system of committee government do carry with them a degree of responsibility, particularly the obligation to mediate conflicts between committees and to influence the success of marginal legislation on the house floor, members will generally be content to stay on a power committee and advance to subcommittee and committee chair positions rather than engage in an all-out effort to attain party leadership positions.

This career path, presented here in an idealized and simplified fashion, is a general "power ladder" that members attempt to climb in their quest for power within Congress. Some members leave the path voluntarily to run for the Senate (if in the House), to run for governor, to serve as a judge, or to serve as president. Some for special reasons bypass one or another stage, choose to stay at a lower rung, are defeated, or retire. Despite exceptions, the set of stages is a very real guide to the long-term career path that members seek to follow. Implicit within this pattern is the very real dilemma discussed earlier: progress up the career ladder brings with it a greater opportunity for significant personal power, but also greater responsibility. As members move up the power ladder, they move away from a secure world in which reelection interest can be their dominant concern and into a world in which concerns with power and public policy predominate. They take their chance and leave the security of the reelection stage because of their personal quest for power, without which reelection is a largely meaningless victory.

The attempt to prove oneself and move up the career ladder requires enormous effort. Even after one succeeds and gains a power position, this attainment is not in itself sufficient to guarantee the personal exercise of power. To utilize fully the power prerogatives that are implicit in specific power positions, a member must maintain the respect, awe, trust, and confidence of committee and house colleagues; he or she must sustain the aura of personal authority that is necessary to legitimize the exercise of power. Although the norm of seniority under a system of pure committee government will protect a member's possession of a power position, seniority is not sufficient to guard personal authority. In order to pass legislation and dominate policy decisions in a committee's jurisdictional area, a committee chair must radiate an appearance of special authority. The member must abide by the norms of the house and the committee, demonstrate legislative competence, and generate policy decisions that appear to stay within the general policy parameters recognized as acceptable by the member's colleagues. Among reelection efforts, efforts to advance in Congress to power positions, efforts to sustain and nurture personal authority, and efforts to exercise power, the members of Congress confront an incredible array of crosscutting pressures and internal dilemmas—decisions about how to balance external reelection interests with the internal institutional career, how to maximize the possibility of power within Congress by service on particular committees, how to gain and nurture authority within committees by specific legislative actions. The world of the congressman or congresswoman is complicated further, however, by a very special irony.

II

As a form of institutional organization, committee government possesses certain attributes that recommend it. By dividing policy concerns among a variety of committees it allows members to specialize in particular policy areas; this division provides a congressional structure through which the members can be their own expert advisers and maintain a degree of independence from lobbyists or outside specialists. Specialization also provides a procedure whereby members can become acquainted with particular programs and agencies and follow their behavior over a period of years, thus allowing informed oversight of the implementation of public policy. The dispersion of power implicit in committee government is important, furthermore, because it brings a greater number of individuals into the policy-making process and thus allows a greater range of policy innovation. In addition, as stressed above, committee government also serves the immediate power motive of congresspeople by creating so many power positions that all members can seek to gain power in particular policy domains.

Despite its assets, committee government does have severe liabilities, flaws that undermine the ability of Congress to fulfill its constitutional responsibilities to make legislative policy and oversee the implementation of that policy. First, committee government by its very nature lacks strong, centralized leadership, thereby undermining its internal decision-making capacity and external authority. Internally, Congress needs central leadership because most major questions of public policy (such as economic or energy policy) cut across individual committee jurisdictions. Since each committee and subcommittee may differ in its policy orientation from all others, and since the support of all relevant committees will be essential to an overall program, it is difficult, if not impossible, to enact a coherent general approach to broad policy questions. A central party leader or central congressional steering committee with extensive control over the standing committees could provide the leadership necessary to assist the development and passage of a coherent policy across the various committees, but committee government rejects the existence of strong centralized power. The resulting dispersion of power within Congress, and the refusal to allow strong centralized leadership, ensures that congressional decisions on major policy matters (unless aided and pushed by an outside leader) will be incremental at best, immobilized and incoherent as a norm. And to the extent that a Congress governed by committees can generate public policy, it faces the external problem of leadership, the inability of outside political actors, the press, or the public to identify a legitimate spokesperson for Congress on any general policy question. The wide dispersion of power positions allows numerous members to gain a degree of dominance over specific dimensions of a policy domain; all of these members can speak with some authority on a policy question, presenting conflicting and confusing approaches and interpretations. In cases where Congress does attempt to act, Congress lacks a viable mechanism through which to publicize and justify its position in an authoritative manner. Should Congress be in a conflict with the president, who can more easily present a straightforward and publicized position, Congress almost certainly will lose out in the eyes of public opinion. Lacking a clearly identifiable legislative leader in its midst, Congress is unable to provide the nation with unified, comprehensible, or persuasive policy leadership.

Closely related to the lack of leadership is a lack of fiscal coordination. Nowhere within a system of committee government is there a mechanism to ensure that the decisions of authorization, appropriations, and revenue committees have some reasonable relationship to one another. The authorization committees make their decisions about the programs to authorize largely independent of appropriations committee decisions about how much money the government will spend. The appropriations committees decide on spending levels largely independent of revenue committee decisions on taxation. Since it is always easier to promise (or authorize) than to deliver (or spend), program goals invariably exceed the actual financial outlays and thus the actual delivery of service. And since it is easier to spend money than to make or tax money, particularly for politicians, expenditures will exceed the revenues to pay the bills. Moves to coordinate the authorization, appropriations, and revenue processes are inconsistent with committee government, since such an effort would necessarily create a central mechanism with considerable say over all public policy and thus centralize power in a relatively small number of individuals. Committee government thus by its very nature is consigned to frustration: the policies that it does produce will invariably produce higher expectations than they can deliver; its budgets, particularly in periods of liberal, activist Congresses, will produce sizable and unplanned deficits in which expenditures far exceed revenues. The inability of committee government to provide realistic program goals and fiscal discipline will invite the executive to intervene in the budget process in order to provide fiscal responsibility and coordination. The result, of course, will be a concomitant loss of the congressional control over the nation's purse strings.

A third detriment associated with committee government, and one that is exacerbated by the absence of leadership and committee coordination, is the lack of accountability and responsibility. A fundamental justification of congressional government is that it allows political decision making to be responsive to the will of a national majority. Committee government distributes this decision-making authority among a largely autonomous set of committees. Since seniority protects each committee's membership from removal and determines who will chair each committee, a committee's members can feel free to follow their personal policy predilections and stop any legislation they wish that falls within their committee's jurisdiction, or propose any that they wish. Within a system of committee government, resting as it does on the norm of seniority, no serious way exists to hold a specific committee or committee chair accountable to the majority views of Congress or the American people, should those views differ from the views held within a particular committee. Because of the process whereby members are selected to serve on major committees—a process that emphasizes not their compatibility with the majority's policy sentiment but rather their adherence to congressional norms, general agreement with the policy views of senior congresspeople, and possession of seniority—the top committees (especially at the senior ranks) are quite likely to be out of step with a congressional or national majority. This lack of representativeness is particularly likely if patterns of electoral security nationwide provide safe seats (and thus seniority) to regions or localities that are unrepresentative of the dominant policy perspectives of the country. Responsiveness is further undermined because the absence of strong central leaders, and a widespread desire among members for procedural protection of their personal prerogatives, require reliance on rigid rules and regulations to govern the flow of legislation and debate, rules such as the Senate's cloture rule that allows the existence of filibusters. Under a system of party government, where limiting rules may exist on the books, strong party leaders can mitigate their effects. In a system of committee government, rules become serious hurdles that can block the easy flow of legislation, particularly major, controversial legislation, thereby decreasing the ability of Congress to respond rapidly to national problems.

Committee government thus undermines the justification of Congress as an institution that provides responsive, representative government. Since institutions derive their power not solely from constitutional legalisms but from their own mystique of special authority that comes from their legitimizing myths, committee government undercuts not only Congress's ability to exercise power but also the popular support that is necessary to maintain its power potential.

The lack of accountability and the damage to Congress's popular support are augmented by a fourth characteristic of committee government—a tendency toward insulation of congressional decision making. This insulation derives from three factors. First, members of committees naturally try to close committee sessions from public purview, limiting thereby the intrusion of external actors such as interest groups or executive agencies and thus protecting committee members' independent exercise of power within committees. Second, the creation of a multiplicity of committees makes it difficult for the public or the press to follow policy deliberations even if they are open. Third, it is difficult if not impossible to create clear jurisdictional boundaries between committees. The consequent ambiguity that exists between jurisdictional boundaries will often involve committees themselves in extensive disputes over the control of particular policy domains, further confusing observers who are concerned with policy deliberations. By closing its committee doors, creating a multiplicity of committees, and allowing jurisdictional ambiguities, a system of committee government isolates Congress from the nation at large. Out of sight and out of mind, Congress loses the attention, respect, and understanding of the nation and becomes an object of scorn and derision, thus further undermining the authority or legitimacy of its pronouncements and itself as an institution.

Finally, committee government undermines the ability of Congress to perform that one function for which committee government would seem most suited—aggressive oversight of administration. According to the classic argument, the saving grace of committee government is that the dispersion of power and the creation of numerous policy experts ensure congressional surveillance of the bureaucracy. Unfortunately, this argument ignores the fact that the individuals on the committees that pass legislation will be the very people least likely to investigate policy implementation. They will be committed to the program, as its authors or most visible supporters, and will not want to take actions that might lead to a destruction of the program. The impact of publicity and a disclosure of agency or program shortcomings, after all, is very unpredictable and difficult to control and may create a public furor against the program. The better part of discretion is to leave the agency largely to its own devices and rely on informal contacts and special personal arrangements, lest the glare of publicity and the discovery of shortcomings force Congress to deauthorize a pet program, casting aspersions on those who originally drafted the legislation. Members of Congress are unwilling to resolve this problem by creating permanent and powerful oversight committees because such committees, by their ability to focus attention on problems of specific agencies and programs, would threaten the authority of legislative committees to control and direct policy in their allotted policy area. Committee government thus allows a failure of executive oversight.

In the light of these five problems, the irony of committee government is that it attempts to satisfy members' individual desires for personal power by dispersing internal congressional authority so widely that the resulting institutional impotence cripples the ability of Congress to perform its constitutional roles, thereby dissipating the value of internal congressional power. Members of Congress thus are not only faced with the daily dilemma of balancing reelection interests with their efforts at upward power mobility within Congress; their lives are also complicated by a cruel paradox, the ultimate incompatibility of widely dispersed power within Congress, on the one hand, and a strong role for Congress in national decision making, on the other. This inherent tension generates an explosive dynamic within Congress as an organization and between Congress and the executive.

In the short run, as members of Congress follow the immediate dictates of the personal power motive, they are unaware of, or at least unconcerned with, the long-term consequences of decentralized power; they support the creation of committee government. The longer committee government operates, the more unhappy political analysts and the people generally become with the inability of Congress to make national policy or ensure policy implementation. With Congress deadlocked by immobilism, political activists within Congress and the nation at large turn to the president (as the one alternative political figure who is popularly elected and thus should be responsive to popular sentiments) and encourage him (or her, if we ever break the sex barrier) to provide policy leadership and fiscal coordination, to open up congressional decision making to national political forces and ensure congressional responsiveness, and to oversee the bureaucracy. Presidents, particularly those committed to activist legislation, welcome the calls for intervention and will see their forthright role as an absolute necessity to the well-being of the Republic. Slowly at first, presidents take over the roles of chief legislator, chief budgetary officer, overseer of the bureaucracy, chief tribune, and protector of the people. Eventually the president's role in these regards becomes so central that he feels free to ignore the wishes of members of Congress, even those who chair very important committees, and impose presidential policy on Congress and the nation at large.

The coming of a strong, domineering, imperial president who ignores Congress mobilizes its members into action. They see that their individual positions of power within Congress are meaningless unless the institution can impose its legislative will on the nation. They search for ways to regain legislative preeminence and constrain the executive. Not being fools, members identify part of the problem as an internal institutional one and seek to reform Congress. Such reform efforts come during or immediately following crises in which presidents clearly and visibly threaten fundamental power prerogatives of Congress. The reforms will include attempts to provide for more centralized congressional leadership, fiscal coordination, congressional openness, better oversight mechanisms, clarification of committee jurisdictions, procedures for policy coordination, and procedures to encourage committee accountability. Because the quest for personal power continues as the underlying motivation of individual members, the reforms are basically attempts to strengthen the value of internal congressional power by increasing the power of Congress *vis-à-vis* the executive. The reform efforts, however, are constrained by consideration of personal power prerogatives of members of Congress. The attempt to protect personal prerogatives while centralizing power builds structural flaws into the centralization mechanisms, flaws that would not be present were the significance of congressional structure for the national power of Congress itself the only motive. The existence of these flaws provides the openings through which centralization procedures are destroyed when institutional crises pass and members again feel free to emphasize personal power and personal careers. In addition, because policy inaction within Congress often will be identified as the immediate cause of presidential power aggrandizement, and because policy immobilism may become identified with key individuals or committees that have obstructed particular legislation, reform efforts also may be directed toward breaking up the authority of these individuals or committees and dispersing it among individuals and committees who seem more amenable to activist policies. This short-term dispersal of power, designed to break a legislative logjam (and, simultaneously, to give power to additional individuals), will serve to exacerbate immobilism in the long run when the new mechanisms of centralization are destroyed.

Viewed in a broad historical perspective, organizational dynamics within Congress, and external relations of Congress to the president, have a "cyclical" pattern. At the outset, when politicians in a quest for national power first enter Congress, they decentralize power and create committee government. Decentralization is followed by severe problems of congressional decision making, presidential assumption of legislative prerogatives, and an eventual presidential assault on Congress itself. Congress reacts by reforming its internal structure: some reform efforts will involve legislation that attempts to circumscribe presidential action; other reforms will attempt to break specific points of deadlock by further decentralization and dispersal of congressional authority; eventually, however, problems of internal congressional leadership and coordination will become so severe that Congress will be forced to undertake centralizing reforms. As Congress moves to resolve internal structural problems and circumscribe presidential power, presidents begin to cooperate so as to defuse the congressional counterattack; to do otherwise would open a president to serious personal attack as anti-congressional and thus anti-democratic, destroying the presidency's legitimizing myth as a democratic institution and identifying presidential motivations as power aggrandizement rather than protection of the Republic. As the immediate threat to congressional prerogatives recedes, members of Congress (many of whom will not have served in Congress during the era of institutional crisis) become preoccupied with their immediate careers and press once again for greater power dispersal within Congress and removal of centralizing mechanisms that inhibit committee and subcommittee autonomy. Decentralization reasserts itself and Congress becomes increasingly leaderless, uncoordinated, insulated, unresponsive, unable to control executive agencies. Tempted by congressional weakness and hounded by cries to "get the country moving," the executive again reasserts itself and a new institutional crisis eventually arises. A review of American history demonstrates the existence of this cycle rather clearly, particularly during the twentieth century. . . .

CONGRESS AND THE ELECTORAL CONNECTION

Edmund Burke was a quintessential eighteenth-century statesman and political philosopher. He served in the House of Commons during the 1760s, representing a county that was essentially "owned" by a wealthy peer. After the King dissolved Parliament in 1774 Burke was invited to stand for election in the thriving commercial city of Bristol, known as the "capital of Western England." Wealthy merchants controlled the city politically, and sought in their representative in Parliament a person who would open the trade with America that had been lost as a result of the American Revolution.

Following his electoral victory in October of 1774 Burke delivered to his constituents the following speech, which became a political classic. His speech perfectly reflects the underlying philosophy of the framers of the Constitution that government should be *deliberative* and carried out in the *national interest.*

58

SPEECH TO THE ELECTORS OF BRISTOL

Edmund Burke

. . . I owe myself, in all things, to all the freemen of this city. My particular friends have a demand on me that I should not deceive their expectations. Never was cause or man supported with more constancy, more activity, more spirit. I have been supported with a zeal, indeed, and heartiness in my friends, which (if their object had been at all proportioned to their endeavors) could never be sufficiently commended. They supported me upon the most liberal principles. They wished that the members for Bristol should be chosen for the city, and for their country at large, and not for themselves.

So far they are not disappointed. If I possess nothing else, I am sure I possess the temper that is fit for your service. . . .

I shall ever retain, what I now feel, the most perfect and grateful attachment to my friends—and I have no enmities, no resentments. I never can consider fidelity to engagements and constancy in friendships but with the highest approbation, even when those noble qualities are employed against my own pretensions. The gentleman who is not so fortunate as I have been in this contest enjoys, in this respect, a consolation full of honor both to himself and to his friends. They have certainly left nothing undone for his service. . . .

I am sorry I cannot conclude without saying a word on a topic touched upon by my worthy colleague.[1] I wish that topic had been passed by at a time when I have so little leisure to discuss it. But since he has thought proper to throw it out, I owe you a clear explanation of my poor sentiments on that subject.

He tells you that "the topic of instructions has occasioned much altercation and uneasiness in this city"; and he expresses himself (if I understand him rightly) in favor of the coercive authority of such instructions.

Certainly, Gentlemen, it ought to be the happiness and glory of a representative to live in the strictest union, the closest correspondence, and the most unreserved communication with his constituents. Their wishes ought to have great weight with him; their opinions high respect; their business unremitted attention. It is his duty to sacrifice his repose, his pleasure, his satisfactions, to theirs—and above all, ever, and in all cases, to prefer their interest to his own.

But his unbiased opinion, his mature judgment, his enlightened conscience, he ought not to sacrifice to you, to any man, or to any set of men living. These he does not derive from your pleasure—no, nor from the law and the constitution. They are a trust from Providence, for the abuse of which he is deeply answerable. Your representative owes you, not his industry only, but his judgment; and he betrays, instead of serving you, if he sacrifices it to your opinion.

My worthy colleague says his will ought to be subservient to yours. If that be all, the thing is innocent. If government were a matter of will upon any side, yours, without question, ought to be superior. But government and legislation are matters of reason and judgment, and not of inclination; and what sort of reason is that in which the determination precedes the discussion, in which one set of men deliberate and another decide, and where those who form the conclusion are perhaps three hundred miles distant from those who hear the arguments?

To deliver an opinion is the right of all men; that of constituents is a weighty and respectable opinion, which a representative ought always to rejoice to hear, and which he ought always most seriously to consider. But *authoritative* instructions, *mandates* issued, which a member is bound blindly and implicitly to obey, to vote, and to argue for, though contrary to the clearest conviction of his judgment and conscience; these are things utterly unknown to the laws of this land, and which arise from a fundamental mistake of the whole order and tenor of our constitution.

Parliament is not a congress of ambassadors from different and hostile interests, which interests each must maintain, as an agent and advocate, against other agents and advocates; but Parliament is a *deliberative* assembly of one nation, with one interest, that of the whole—where not local purposes, not local prejudices,

---

[1]Henry Cruger, also elected for Bristol.

ought to guide, but the general good, resulting from the general reason of the whole. You choose a member, indeed; but when you have chosen him he is not a member of Bristol, but he is a member of *Parliament*. If the local constituent should have an interest or should form a hasty opinion evidently opposite to the real good of the rest of the community, the member for that place ought to be as far as any other from any endeavor to give it effect. . . . Your faithful friend, your devoted servant, I shall be to the end of my life: a flatterer you do not wish for. . . .

From the first hour I was encouraged to court your favor, to this happy day of obtaining it, I have never promised you anything but humble and persevering endeavors to do my duty. The weight of that duty, I confess, makes me tremble; and whoever well considers what it is, of all things in the world, will fly from what has the least likeness to a positive and precipitate engagement. To be a good member of Parliament is, let me tell you, no easy task—especially at this time, when there is so strong a disposition to run into the perilous extremes of servile compliance or wild popularity. To unite circumspection with vigor is absolutely necessary, but it is extremely difficult. We are now members for a rich commercial city; this city, however, is but a part of a rich commercial nation, the interests of which are various, multiform, and intricate. We are members for that great nation, which, however, is itself but part of a great *empire*, extended by our virtue and our fortune to the farthest limits of the East and of the West. All these wide-spread interests must be considered—must be compared—must be reconciled, if possible. We are members for a *free* country; and surely we all know that the machine of a free constitution is no simple thing, but as intricate and as delicate as it is valuable. We are members in a great and ancient *monarchy*; and we must preserve religiously the true, legal rights of the sovereign, which form the keystone that binds together the noble and well-constructed arch of our empire and our constitution. A constitution made up of balanced powers must ever be a critical thing. As such I mean to touch that part of it which comes within my reach. . . .

Throughout the 1970s public opinion polls consistently revealed that Congress was held in low esteem by the American people. Very little has changed over the years in the way voters view Congress. Only 25 percent of voters polled by the *New York Times* and CBS before the Fall 2006 congressional elections expressed approval of Congress, and 77 percent said members of congress did not deserve reelection.

The origins of voter disillusionment with Congress began in the 1970s. The book *Who Runs Congress?*, published by the Ralph Nader Congress Project, reflected and at the same time helped to crystallize public disenchantment with Capitol Hill.* The book emphasized the need for citizens to take on Congress to prevent a further flagging of the institution. In his introduction, Ralph Nader summarized the contents of the book by stating that "the people have indeed abdicated their power, their money, and their democratic birthright to

Compiler's note: Mark J. Green et al., Eds., *Who Runs Congress?* (New York: Bantam/Grossman, 1972).

Congress. As a result, without the participation of the people, Congress has surrendered its enormous authority and resources to special interest groups, waste, insensitivity, ignorance, and bureaucracy."* The theme of the 1972 Nader project, that Congress was in crisis, continues to be accepted by the vast majority of people.

While Ralph Nader and his colleagues feel that the major cause of the demise of Congress is its detachment from the people, Richard Fenno, in the following selection, adopts a different viewpoint. He feels that people fault the *institution* of Congress, not their individual representatives on Capitol Hill. In fact, he points out that there is a close connection between legislators and constituents, and often, a feeling of affection by voters for their representatives. Fenno feels that we apply different standards in judging individual members of Congress than we do in assessing the institution, being far more lenient in the former than the latter case. The individual is judged for his or her personality, style, and representativeness, while the institution is judged by its ability to recognize and solve the nation's problems. But the institution cannot be thought of apart from the members that compose it. It is they who have given it its unique character. It is the individual member who, more often than not, has supported a decentralized and fragmented legislature because of the members' incentive to achieve personal power and status on Capitol Hill.

59

IF, AS RALPH NADER SAYS, CONGRESS IS "THE BROKEN BRANCH," HOW COME WE LOVE OUR CONGRESSMEN SO MUCH?

Richard F. Fenno, Jr.

Off and on during the past two years, I accompanied ten members of the House of Representatives as they traveled around in their home districts. In every one of those districts I heard a common theme, one that I had not expected. Invariably, the representative I was with—young or old, liberal or conservative, Northerner,

**Compiler's note*: Ibid., p.1.

Southerner, Easterner, or Westerner, Democrat or Republican—was described as "the best congressman in the United States." Having heard it so often, I now accept the description as fact. I am even prepared to believe the same thing (though I cannot claim to have heard it with my own ears) of the members of the Senate. Each of our 435 representatives and 100 senators is, indeed, "the best congressman in the United States." Which is to say that each enjoys a great deal of support and approbation among his or her constituents. Judging by the election returns, this isn't much of an exaggeration. In [recent elections], 96 percent of all House incumbents who ran were reelected; and 85 percent of all Senate incumbents who ran were reelected. These convincing figures are close to the average reelection rates of incumbents for the past ten elections. We do, it appears, love our congressmen.

On the other hand, it seems equally clear that we do not love our Congress. Louis Harris reported in 1970 that only one-quarter of the electorate gave Congress a positive rating on its job performance—while nearly two-thirds expressed themselves negatively on the subject. . . . There [is] considerable concern—dramatized recently by the critical Nader project—for the performance of Congress as an institution. On the evidence, we seem to approve of our legislators a good deal more than we do our legislature. And therein hangs something of a puzzle. If our congressmen are so good, how can our Congress be so bad? If it is the individuals that make up the institution, why should there be such a disparity in our judgments? What follows are a few reflections on this puzzle.

A first answer is that we apply different standards of judgment, those that we apply to the individual being less demanding than those we apply to the institution. For the individual, our standard is one of representativeness—of personal style and policy views. Stylistically, we ask that our legislator display a sense of identity with us so that we, in turn, can identify with him or her—via personal visits to the district, concern for local projects and individual "cases," and media contact of all sorts, for example. On the policy side, we ask only that his general policy stance does not get too frequently out of line with ours. And, if he should become a national leader in some policy area of interest to us, so much the better. These standards are admittedly vague. But because they are locally defined and locally applied, they are consistent and manageable enough so that legislators can devise rules of thumb to meet them. What is more, by their performance they help shape the standards, thereby making them easier to meet. Thus they win constituent recognition as "the best in the United States." And thus they establish the core relationship for a representative democracy.

For the institution, however, our standards emphasize efforts to solve national problems—a far less tractable task than the one we (and he) set for the individual. Given the inevitable existence of unsolved problems, we are destined to be unhappy with congressional performance. The individual legislator knows when he has met our standards of representativeness; he is reelected. But no such definitive measure of legislative success exists. And, precisely because Congress is the most familiar and most human of our national institutions, lacking the distant majesty of the Presidency and the Court, it is the easy and natural target of our criticism. We have met our problem solvers, and they are us.

Furthermore, such standards as we do use for judging the institutional performance of Congress are applied inconsistently. In 1963, when public dissatisfaction was as great as in 1970, Congress was criticized for being obstructionist, dilatory and insufficiently cooperative with regard to the Kennedy programs. Two years later, Congress got its highest performance rating of the decade when it cooperated completely with the executive in rushing the Great Society program into law. But by the late 1960s and early 1970s the standard of judgment had changed radically—from cooperation to counterbalance in Congressional relations with the Executive. Whereas, in 1963, Harris had found "little in the way of public response to the time-honored claim that the Legislative Branch is . . . the guardian against excessive Executive power," by 1968 he found that three-quarters of the electorate wanted Congress to act as the watchdog of the Executive and not to cooperate so readily with it. The easy passage of the Tonkin Resolution reflects the cooperative standards set in the earlier period; its repeal reflects the counterbalancing standards of the recent period. Today we are concerned about Ralph Nader's "broken branch" which, we hear, has lost—and must reclaim from the Executive—its prerogatives in areas such as war-making and spending control. To some degree, then, our judgments on Congress are negative because we change our minds frequently concerning the kind of Congress we want. A Congress whose main job is to cooperate with the Executive would look quite different from one whose main job is to counterbalance the Executive.

Beneath the differences in our standards of judgment, however, lies a deeper dynamic of the political system. Senators and representatives, for their own reasons, spend a good deal more of their time and energy polishing and worrying about their individual performance than they do working at the institution's performance. Though it is, of course, true that their individual activity is related to institutional activity, their first-order concerns are individual, not institutional. Foremost is their desire for reelection. Most members of Congress like their job, want to keep it, and know that there are people back home who want to take it away from them. So they work long and hard at winning reelection. Even those who are safest want election margins large enough to discourage opposition back home and/or to help them float further political ambitions. No matter what other personal goals representatives and senators wish to accomplish—increased influence in Washington and helping to make good public policy are the most common—reelection is a necessary means to those ends.

We cannot criticize these priorities—not in a representative system. If we believe the representative should mirror constituency opinion, we must acknowledge that it requires considerable effort for him to find out what should be mirrored. If we believe a representative should be free to vote his judgment, he will have to cultivate his constituents assiduously before they will trust him with such freedom. Either way we will look favorably on his efforts. We come to love our legislators, in the *second* place, because they so ardently sue for our affections.

As a courtship technique, moreover, they re-enforce our unfavorable judgments about the institution. Every representative with whom I traveled criticized the Congress and portrayed himself, by contrast, as a fighter against its manifest evils. Members run *for* Congress by running *against* Congress. They refurbish their individual reputations as "the best congressman in the United States" by attacking the collective reputation of the Congress of the United States. Small wonder the voters feel so much more warmly disposed and so much less fickle toward the individuals than toward the institution. One case in point: the House decision to grant President Nixon a spending ceiling plus authority to cut previously appropriated funds to maintain that ceiling. One-half the representatives I was with blasted the House for being so spineless that it gave away its power of the purse to the President. The other half blasted the House for being so spineless in exercising its power of the purse that the President had been forced to act. Both groups spoke to supportive audiences; and each man enhanced his individual reputation by attacking the institution. Only by raising both questions, however, could one see the whole picture. Once the President forced the issue, how come the House didn't stand up to him and protect its crucial institutional power over the purse strings? On the other hand, if economic experts agreed that a spending ceiling was called for, how come the House didn't enact it and make the necessary budget cuts in the first place? The answer to the first question lies in the proximity of their reelection battles, which re-enforced the tendency of all representatives to think in individualistic rather than institutional terms. The answer to the second question lies in the total absence of institutional machinery whereby the House (or, indeed, Congress) can make overall spending decisions.

Mention of the institutional mechanisms of Congress leads us to a *third* explanation for our prevailing pattern of judgments. When members of Congress think institutionally—as, of course they must—they think in terms of a structure that will be most congenial to the pursuit of their individual concerns—for reelection, for influence, or for policy. Since each individual has been independently designated "the best in the United States," each has an equal status and an equal claim to influence within the structure. For these reasons, the members naturally think in terms of a very fragmented, decentralized institution, providing a maximum of opportunity for individual performance, individual influence, and individual credit.

The 100-member Senate more completely fits this description than the 435 member House. The smaller body permits a more freewheeling and creative individualism. But both chambers tend strongly in this direction, and representatives as well as senators chafe against centralizing mechanisms. Neither body is organized in hierarchical—or even in well-coordinated—patterns of decision-making. Agreements are reached by some fairly subtle forms of mutual adjustment—by negotiation, bargaining, and compromise. And interpersonal relations—of respect, confidence, trust—are crucial building blocks. The members of Congress, in pursuit of their individual desires, have thus created an institution that is internally quite complex. Its structure and processes are, therefore, very difficult to grasp from the outside.

In order to play out some aspects of the original puzzle, however, we must make the effort. And the committee system, the epitome of fragmentation and decentralization, is a good place to start. The performance of Congress as an institution is very largely the performance of its committees. The Nader project's "broken branch" description is mostly a committee-centered description because that is where the countervailing combination of congressional expertise and political skill resides. To strengthen Congress means to strengthen its committees. To love Congress means to love its committees. Certainly when we have not loved our Congress, we have heaped our displeasure upon its committees. The major legislative reorganizations, of 1946 and 1970, were committee-centered reforms—centering on committee jurisdictions, committee democracy, and committee staff support. Other continuing criticisms—of the seniority rule for selecting committee chairmen, for example—have centered on the committees.

Like Congress as a whole, committees must be understood first in terms of what they do for the individual member. To begin with, committees are relatively more important to the individual House member than to the individual senator. The representative's career inside Congress is very closely tied to his committee. For the only way such a large body can function is to divide into highly specialized and independent committees. Policy-making activity funnels through these committees; so does the legislative activity and influence of the individual legislator. While the Senate has a set of committees paralleling those of the House, a committee assignment is nowhere near as constraining for the career of the individual senator. The Senate is more loosely organized, senators sit on many more committees and subcommittees than representatives, and they have easy access to the work of committees of which they are not members. Senators, too, can command and utilize national publicity to gain influence beyond the confines of their committee. Whereas House committees act as funnels for individual activity, Senate committees act as facilitators of individual activity. The difference in functions is considerable—which is why committee chairmen are a good deal more important in the House than in the Senate and why the first modifications of the seniority rule should have come in the House rather than the Senate. My examples will come from the House.

Given the great importance of his committee to the career of the House member, it follows that we will want to know how each committee can affect such careers. . . .

Where a committee's members are especially interested in pyramiding their individual influence, they will act so as to maintain the influence of their committee (and, hence, their personal influence) within the House. They will adopt procedures that enhance the operating independence of the committee. They will work hard to remain relatively independent of the Executive Branch. And they will try to underpin that independence with such resources as specialized expertise, internal cohesion, and the respect of their House colleagues. Ways and Means and Appropriations are committees of this sort. By contrast, where a committee's members are especially interested in getting in on nationally controversial policy action, they will not be much concerned about the independent influence of their committee. They will want to ally themselves closely with any and all groups outside the committee who share their policy views. They want to help enact what they individually regard as good public policy; and if that means ratifying policies shaped elsewhere—in the Executive Branch particularly—so be it. And, since their institutional independence is not a value for them, they make no special effort to acquire such underpinnings as expertise, cohesion, or chamber respect. Education and Labor and Foreign Affairs are committees of this sort.

These two types of committees display quite different strengths in their performance. Those of the first type are especially influential. Ways and Means probably makes a greater independent contribution to policy making than any other House committee. Appropriations probably exerts a more influential overview of executive branch activities than any other House committee. The price they pay, however, is a certain decrease in their responsiveness to noncommittee forces—as complaints about the closed rule on tax bills and executive hearings on appropriations bills will attest. Committees of the second type are especially responsive to noncommittee forces and provide easy conduits for outside influence in policy making. Education and Labor was probably more receptive to President Johnson's Great Society policies than any other House committee; it successfully passed the largest part of the program. Foreign Affairs has probably remained as thoroughly responsive to Executive Branch policies, in foreign aid for instance, as any House committee. The price they pay, however, is a certain decrease in their influence—as complaints about the rubber-stamp Education and Labor Committee and about the impotent Foreign Affairs Committee will attest. In terms of the earlier discussions of institutional performance standards, our hopes for a cooperative Congress lie more with the latter type of committee; our hopes for a counterbalancing Congress lie more with the former.

So, committees differ. And they differ to an important degree according to the desires of their members. This ought to make us wary of blanket descriptions. Within the House, Foreign Affairs may look like a broken branch, but Ways and Means does not. And, across chambers, Senate Foreign Relations (where member incentives are stronger) is a good deal more potent than House Foreign Affairs. With the two Appropriations committees, the reverse is the case. It is not just that "the broken branch" is an undiscriminating, hence inaccurate, description. It is also that blanket descriptions lead to blanket prescriptions. And it just might be that the wisest course of congressional reform would be to identify existing nodes of committee strength and nourish them rather than to prescribe, as we usually do, reforms in equal dosages for all committees.

One lesson of the analysis should be that member incentives must exist to support any kind of committee activity. Where incentives vary, it may be silly to prescribe the same functions and resources for all committees. The Reorganization Act of 1946 mandated all committees to exercise "continuous watchfulness" over the executive branch—in the absence of any supporting incentive system. We have gotten overview activity only where random individuals have found an incentive for doing so—not by most committees and certainly not continuously. Similarly, I suspect that our current interest in exhorting all committees to acquire more information with which to combat the executive may be misplaced. Information is relatively easy to come by—and some committees have a lot of it. What is hard to come by is the incentive to use it, not to mention the time and the trust necessary to make it useful. I am not suggesting a set of reforms but rather a somewhat different strategy of committee reforms—less wholesale, more retail.

Since the best-known target of wholesale committee reform is the seniority rule, it deserves special comment. If our attacks on the rule have any substance to them, if they are anything other than symbolic, the complaint must be that some or all committee chairmen are not doing a good job. But we can only find out whether this is so by conducting a committee-by-committee examination. Paradoxically, our discussions of the seniority rule tend to steer us away from such a retail examination by mounting very broad, across-the-board kinds of arguments against chairmen as a class—arguments about their old age, their conservatism, their national unrepresentativeness. Such arguments produce great cartoon copy, easy editorial broadsides, and sitting-duck targets for our congressmen on the stump. But we ought not to let the arguments themselves, nor the Pavlovian public reactions induced by our cartoonists, editorial writers, and representatives, pass for good institutional analysis. Rather, they have diverted us from that task.

More crucial to a committee's performance than the selection of its chairman is his working relationship with the other committee members. Does he agree with his members on the functions of the committee? Does he act to facilitate the achievement of their individual concerns? Do they approve of his performance as chairman? Where there is real disagreement between chairman and members, close analysis may lead us to fault the members and not the chairman. If so, we should be focusing our criticisms on the members. If the fault lies with the chairman, a majority of the members have the power to bring him to heel. They need not kill the king; they can constitutionalize the monarchy. While outsiders have been crying "off with his head," the members of several committees have been quietly and effectively constitutionalizing the monarchy. Education and Labor, Post Office, and Interior are recent examples where dissatisfied committee majorities have subjected their chairmen to majority control. Where this has not been done, it is probably due to member satisfaction, member timidity, member disinterest, or member incompetence. And the time we spend railing against the seniority rule might be better spent finding out, for each congressional committee, just which of these is the case. If, as a final possibility, a chairman and his members are united in opposition to the majority party or to the rest of us, the seniority rule is not the problem. More to the point, as I suspect is usually the case, the reasons and the ways individual members get sorted onto the various committees is the critical factor. In sum, I am not saying that the seniority rule is a good thing, I am saying that, for committee performance, it is not a very important thing.

What has all this got to do with the original puzzle—that we love our congressmen so much more than our Congress? We began with a few explanatory guesses. Our standards of judgment for individual performance are more easily met: the individual member works harder winning approval for himself than for his institution; and Congress is a complex institution, difficult for us to understand. The more we try to understand Congress—as we did briefly with the committee system—the more we are forced to peel back the institutional layers until we reach the individual member. At that point, it becomes hard to separate, as we normally do, our judgments about congressmen and Congress. The more we come to see institutional performance as influenced by the desires of the individual member, the more the original puzzle ought to resolve itself. For as the independence of our judgments decreases, the disparity between them ought to grow smaller. But if we are to hold this perspective on Congress, we shall need to understand the close individual-institution relationship—chamber by chamber, party by party, committee by committee, legislator by legislator.

This is not a counsel of despair. It is a counsel of sharper focus and a more discriminating eye. It counsels the mass media, for example, to forego "broken branch" type generalizations about Congress in favor of examining a committee in depth, or to forego broad criticism of the seniority rule for a close look at a committee chairman. It counsels the rest of us to focus more on the individual member and to fix the terms of our dialogue with him more aggressively. It counsels us to fix terms that will force him to think more institutionally and which will hold him more accountable for the performance of the institution. "Who Runs Congress," asks the title of the Nader report, "the President, Big Business or You?" From the perspective of this paper, it is none of these. It is the members who run Congress. And we get pretty much the kind of Congress they want. We shall get a different kind of Congress when we elect different kinds of congressmen or when we start applying different standards of judgment to old congressmen. Whether or not we ought to have a different kind of Congress is still another, much larger, puzzle.

Richard F. Fenno, Jr., explains in selection 59 that the public holds Congress and its members to different standards. *Congress-bashing*, to use the author's colorful term from the following selection, is popular not only with the public but, more importantly, with those who shape public opinion, including political journalists and pundits, network news anchors and television commentators, self-proclaimed public interest representatives, and, perhaps most importantly of all, members of Congress themselves who have found that running against Congress is a successful campaign tactic.

The author of the following selection, a prominent congressional scholar, describes the popular support of Congress-bashing and concludes that criticism of Congress has gone too far.

60

CONGRESS-BASHING FOR BEGINNERS

Nelson W. Polsby

On a shelf not far from where I am writing these words sit a half a dozen or so books disparaging Congress and complaining about the congressional role in the constitutional separation of powers. These books date mostly from the late 1940s and the early 1960s, and typically their authors are liberal Democrats. In those years, Congress was unresponsive to liberal Democrats and, naturally enough, aggrieved members of that articulate tribe sought solutions in structural reform.

In fact, instead of reforms weakening Congress what they—and we—got was a considerably strengthened presidency. This was mostly a product of World War II and not the result of liberal complaints. Before World War II Congress would not enact even the modest recommendations of the Brownlow Commission to give the president a handful of assistants with "a passion for anonymity," and it killed the National Resources Planning Board outright. After World War II everything changed: Congress gave the president responsibility for smoothing the effects of the business cycle, created a Defense Department and two presidential agencies—the NSC and the CIA—that enhanced the potential for presidential dominance of national security affairs, and laid the groundwork for the growth of a presidential branch, politically responsive to both Democratic and Republican presidents.

Congress and the Goring of Oxen

Though it took time for the presidential branch to grow into its potential, the growth of this branch, separate and at arm's length from the executive branch that it runs in the president's behalf, is the big news of the postwar era—indeed, of the last half-century in American government. It is customary today to acknowledge that Harry Truman's primary agenda, in the field of foreign affairs, was quite successfully enacted even though Congress was dominated by a conservative coalition, and what Truman wanted in the way of peacetime international involvement was for the United States quite unprecedented. Dwight Eisenhower's agenda was also largely international in its impact. Looking back, it seems that almost all Eisenhower really cared about was protecting the international position of the United States from diminution by Republican isolationists. Everything else was expendable.

Congress responded sluggishly and in its customary piecemeal fashion. It was right around John Kennedy's first year in office that liberals rediscovered that old roadblock in Congress, a "deadlock of democracy," as one of them put it. It was Congress that had thwarted the second New Deal after 1937, the packing of the Supreme Court, and Harry Truman's domestic program; it was Congress that had stalled civil rights and buried Medicare; it was Congress that had sponsored the Bricker Amendment to limit the president's power to make treaties. Are memories so short that we do not recall these dear, departed days when Congress was the graveyard of the forward-looking proposals of liberal presidents? Then, Congress was a creaky eighteenth-century machine unsuited to the modern age, and Congress-bashers were liberal Democrats.

To be sure, Congress had a few defenders, mostly Republicans and Dixiecrats, who found in its musty cloakrooms and windy debates a citadel (as one of them said) of old-time legislative virtues, where the historic functions of oversight and scrutiny were performed, where the run-away proposals of the presidency could be subjected to the sober second thoughts of the people's own elected representatives, and so on.

Why rehash all this? In part, it is to try to make the perfectly obvious point that Congress-bashing then was what people did when they controlled the presidency but didn't control Congress. And that, in part, is what Congress-bashing is about now. Today, Republicans and conservatives are doing most (although not all) of the complaining. It is worth a small bet that a fair number of editorial pages claimed that the separation of powers made a lot of sense during the Kennedy-Johnson years—but no longer say the same today. On the other side, backers of FDR's scheme to pack the Court have turned into vigorous defenders of the judicial status quo since Earl Warren's time.

There is nothing wrong with letting the goring of oxen determine what side we take in a political argument. In a civilized country, however, it makes sense to keep political arguments civil, and not to let push come to shove too often. There is something uncivil, in my view, about insisting upon constitutional reforms to cure political ailments. What liberal critics of Congress needed was not constitutional reform. What they needed was the 89th Congress, which, in due course, enacted much of the agenda that the Democratic party had built up over the previous two decades. History didn't stop with the rise of the presidential branch and the enactment of the second New Deal/New Frontier/Great Society. President Johnson overreached. He concealed from Congress the costs of the Vietnam War. He created a credibility gap.

This, among other things, began to change Congress. The legislative branch no longer was altogether comfortable relying on the massaged numbers and other unreliable information coming over from the presidential branch. They began to create a legislative bureaucracy to cope with this challenge. They beefed up the General Accounting Office and the Congressional Research Service. They created an Office of Technology Assessment and a Congressional Budget Office. They doubled and redoubled their personal staffs and committee staffs.

Sentiments supporting this expansion began, oddly enough, after a landslide election in which the Democratic party swept the presidency and both houses of Congress. So mistrust between the branches in recent history has by no means been entirely a partisan matter. Nevertheless, Richard Nixon's presidency, conducted entirely in unhappy harness with a Democratic Congress, did not improve relations between the two branches of government. Johnson may have been deceitful, but Nixon, especially after his reelection in 1972, was positively confrontational.

It was Nixon's policy to disregard comity between the branches. This, and not merely his commission of impeachable offenses, fueled the impeachment effort in Congress. That effort was never wholly partisan. Republicans as well as Democrats voted articles of impeachment that included complaints specifically related to obstruction of the discharge of congressional responsibilities.

It is necessary to understand this recent history of the relations between Congress and the president in order to understand the provenance of the War Powers Act, the Boland Amendment, numerous other instances of congressional micromanagement, the unprecedented involvement of the NSC in the Iran-contra affair, and like manifestations of tension and mistrust between Congress and the president. These tensions are, to a certain degree, now embedded in law and in the routines of responsible public officials; they cannot be made to disappear with a wave of a magic wand. They are, for the most part, regrettable in the consequences they have had for congressional-presidential relations, but they reflect real responses to real problems in these relations. Congressional responses, so far as I can see, have been completely legal, constitutional, and—in the light of historical circumstances—understandable. The best way to turn the relations between the legislative and the presidential branches around would be for the presidential side to take vigorous initiatives to restore comity. As head of the branch far more capable of taking initiatives, and the branch far more responsible for the underlying problem, this effort at restoration is in the first instance up to the President.

President Bush and the Item Veto

In this respect, President Bush is doing a decent job, giving evidence of reaching out constructively. It is not my impression that the Bush administration has done a lot of Congress-bashing. After all, what Bush needs isn't a weakened Congress so much as a Republican Congress. Over the long run (though probably not in time to do Bush much good) Republicans are bound to regret despairing of the latter and therefore seeking the former. We have seen enough turns of the wheel over the last half-century to be reasonably confident that sooner or later Republicans will start to do better in congressional elections. The presidential item veto, the Administration's main Congress-bashing proposal, won't help Republicans in Congress deal with a Democratic president when the time comes, as sooner or later it will, for a Democrat to be elected president.

The item veto would effectively take congressional politics out of the legislative process, and would weaken Congress a lot. It would encourage members of Congress, majority and minority alike, to be irresponsible and to stick the president with embarrassing public choices. It would reduce the incentives for members to acquire knowledge about public policy or indeed to serve.

By allocating legislative responsibilities to Congress, the Constitution as originally (and currently) designed forces representatives of diverse interest to cooperate. Because what Congress does as a collectivity matters, legislative work elicits the committed participation of members. The item veto would greatly trivialize the work product of Congress by requiring the president's acquiescence on each detail of legislation. Members would lose their independent capacity to craft legislation. Their individual views and knowledge would dwindle in importance; only the marshalling of a herd capable of overturning a veto would matter in Congress.

The item veto is, in short, a truly radical idea. It is also almost certainly unconstitutional. To espouse it requires a readiness to give up entirely on the separation of powers and on the constitutional design of the American government. There are plenty of people, some of them well-meaning, who are ready to do that. I am not, nor should people who identify themselves as conservatives or liberals or anywhere in the political mainstream.

The separation of powers is actually a good idea. It gives a necessary weight to the great heterogeneity of our nation—by far the largest and most heterogeneous nation unequivocally to have succeeded at democratic self-government in world history. It would take a medium-sized book to make all the qualifications and all the connections that would do justice to this argument. The conclusion is worth restating anyway: the item veto is a root-and-branch attack on the separation of powers; it is a very radical and a very bad idea.

Term Limitations

Less serious in its impact, but still destructive, is the proposal to limit the terms of members of Congress. This proposal relies heavily for its appeal upon ignorance in the population at large about what members of Congress actually do. For in order to take seriously the idea of limiting congressional terms, one must believe that the job of a representative in Congress is relatively simple, and quickly and easily mastered. It is not.

The job of a member of Congress is varied and complex. It includes: (1) Managing a small group of offices that attempt on request to assist distressed constituents, state and local governments, and enterprises in the home district that may have business with the federal government. This ombudsman function gives members an opportunity to monitor the performance of the government in its dealings with citizens and can serve to identify areas of general need. (2) Serving on committees that oversee executive-branch activity on a broad spectrum of subjects (such as immigration, copyright protection, telecommunications, or health policy) and that undertake to frame issues of national scope for legislative action. This entails mastering complicated subject matter; working with staff members, expert outsiders, and colleagues to build coalitions; understanding justifications; and answering objections. (3) Participating in general legislative work. Members have to vote on everything, not merely on the work of their own committees. They have to inform themselves of the merits of bills, and stand ready to cooperate with colleagues whose support they will need to advance their own proposals. (4) Keeping track of their own political business. This means watching over and occasionally participating in the politics of their own states and localities, and mending fences with interest groups, friends and neighbors, backers, political rivals, and allies. (5) Educating all the varied people with whom they come in contact about issues that are high on the agenda and about reasonable expectations of performance. This includes the performance of the government, the Congress, and the member.

Plenty of members never try to master the job, or try and fail, and these members would be expendable. The objection might still be raised that constituents, not an excess of constitutional limitations, ought to decide who represents whom in Congress. But that aside, what about the rather substantial minority of members who learn their jobs, do their homework, strive to make an impact on public policy, and—through long experience and application to work—actually make a difference? Can we, or should we, dispense with them as well?

It is a delusion to think that good public servants are a dime a dozen in each congressional district, and that only the good ones would queue up to take their twelve-year fling at congressional office. But suppose they did. In case they acquired expertise, what would they do next? Make money, I suppose. Just about the time that their constituents and the American people at large could begin to expect a payoff because of the knowledge and experience that these able members had acquired at our expense, off they would go to some Washington law firm.

And what about their usefulness in the meantime? It would be limited, I'm afraid, by the greater expertise and better command of the territory by lobbyists, congressional staff, and downtown bureaucrats—career people one and all. So this is, once again, a proposal merely to weaken the fabric of Congress in the political system at large, and thereby to limit the effectiveness of the one set of actors most accessible to ordinary citizens.

The standard objection to this last statement is that members of Congress aren't all that accessible. Well, neither is Ralph Nader, who has long overstayed the dozen years that contemporary Congress-bashers wish to allocate to members. Neither is the author of *Wall Street Journal* editorials in praise of limitations. And it must be said that a very large number of members take their representational and ombudsman duties very seriously indeed. This includes holders of safe seats, some of whom fear primary-election opposition, some of whom are simply conscientious. A great many of them do pay attention—close attention—to their constituents. That is one of the reasons—maybe the most important reason—that so many of them are reelected. Much Congress-bashing these days actually complains about high reelection rates, as though a large population of ill-served constituents would be preferable.

Congressional Salaries

While we have Ralph Nader on our minds, it is certainly appropriate to pay our disrespects to his completely off-the-wall effort, temporarily successful, at the head of a crazed phalanx of self-righteous disk jockeys and radio talk-show hosts, to deprive members of Congress of a salary increase. The issue of congressional salaries is a straightforward one. Many members, being well-to-do, don't need one. But some do. The expenses of maintaining two places of residence—in Washington and at home—make membership in Congress nearly unique and singularly expensive among upper-middle-class American jobs. Here is the point once more: it is a job, requiring skill and dedication to be done properly. Moreover, membership in Congress brings responsibilities. National policy of the scope and scale now encompassed by acts of the federal government requires responsible, dedicated legislators. People with far less serious responsibilities in the private sector are ordinarily paid considerably better than members of Congress. Think, for example, how far down the organizational chart at General Motors or at CBS or at some other large corporation one would have to go before reaching executives making what members of Congress do, and compare their responsibilities with those of Congress and its members. Actually, most corporations won't say what their compensation packages are like. But at a major auto company, people who make around $100,000 a year are no higher than upper middle management, and certainly don't have responsibilities remotely comparable to those of members of Congress.

There is a case for decent congressional salaries to be made on at least two grounds: one is the rough equity or opportunity-cost ground that we ought not financially to penalize people who serve, and the second is the ground of need for those members who have the expense of families or college educations to think of, and who have no extraordinary private means. The long-run national disadvantage of failing to recognize the justice of these claims is of course a Congress deprived of people for whom these claims are exigent, normal middle-class people with family responsibilities and without money of their own. These are not the sorts of people a sane electorate should wish to prevent from serving.

Members of Congress, knowing very well of the irrational hostilities that the proposal of a congressional pay raise can stir up, have taken the unfortunate precaution of holding hostage the salaries of federal judges, who are now ludicrously underpaid by the admittedly opulent standards of the legal profession, and senior civil servants. An unhealthy impasse has been created owing, at bottom, to Congress-bashing of the most unattractive kind, which exploits the ignorance of ordinary citizens of the dimensions of the members' working lives, and incites citizens to a mindless social envy, in which it is assumed that paying a decent professional salary to professional officeholders is automatically some sort of rip-off.

Members of Congress now make about $98,000. The bottom salary for major-league baseball players is $100,000. Some law firms in New York start new graduates of good law schools at $90,000 or more. How can we argue that members of Congress and others at the top of the federal government should not be paid at least a modest premium above these beginners' wages? There is, evidently, no talking sense to the American people on this subject.

I believe we can dismiss out of hand the charge that large numbers of members individually, or Congress collectively, live in a world all their own, divorced from realities of everyday life. The sophomores who have written attacks of this sort in recent years in the *Atlantic*, *Newsweek*, and elsewhere simply don't know what they are talking about. They abuse their access to large audiences by neglecting to explain the real conditions that govern the lives of members, conditions that provide ample doses of everyday life.

No doubt scandals involving various members have in recent times made Congress as an institution vulnerable to criticism. But much of this criticism is irresponsible and irrelevant. Suppose we were to discover instances of cupidity, unusual sexual activity, and abuses of power among the rather sizable staff of an important daily newspaper? Or a symphony orchestra? Or, God forbid, a university? I suppose that would shake our confidence in at least part of the collective output, but one would hope for relevant discriminations. One might distrust the ticket office, perhaps, but not the symphony's performance of Mozart; the stock tips, perhaps, but not the Washington page; the basketball program, but not the classics department. I do not think that the existence of scandal excuses us from attempting to draw sensible conclusions about institutions and their performance.

This sort of balanced and discriminating analysis isn't what proposals for item vetoes, limitations on terms of service, or depressed rates of pay are all about. They are about the ancient but now slightly shopworn American custom of Congress-bashing.

A commonly held assumption about members of Congress is that their primary incentive is to engage in activities that strengthen their prospects for reelection. David

Mayhew, one proponent of this theory, argues in his book *Congress: The Electoral Connection* that both the formal and informal organizations of Congress are oriented principally toward the reelection of its members. For example, the dispersion of committees, which number close to three hundred, maximizes the opportunities of committee chairs to use their power to distribute benefits directly to their districts and states and to take positions on issues that will be appealing to their constituents. Moreover, the weak party structure of Capitol Hill allows individual members to go their own ways in dealing with their diverse constituencies. Unified congressional parties, argues Mayhew, would not allow Congress the necessary flexibility to advertise, claim credit, and take positions to gain electoral support. In the following selection Mayhew illustrates the kinds of activities Senate and House members engage in to maximize their electoral support.

61

CONGRESS: THE ELECTORAL CONNECTION

David R. Mayhew

Whether they are safe or marginal, cautious or audacious, congressmen must constantly engage in activities related to reelection. There will be differences in emphasis, but all members share the root need to do things—indeed, to do things day in and day out during their terms. The next step here is to present a typology, a short list of the *kinds* of activities congressmen find it electorally useful to engage in. The case will be that there are three basic kinds of activities. It will be important to lay them out with some care. . . .

One activity is *advertising,* defined here as any effort to disseminate one's name among constituents in such a fashion as to create a favorable image but in messages having little or no issue content. A successful congressman builds what amounts to a brand name, which may have a generalized electoral value for other politicians in the same family. The personal qualities to emphasize are experience, knowledge, responsiveness, concern, sincerity, independence, and the like. Just getting one's name across is difficult enough; only about half the electorate, if asked, can supply their House members' names. It helps a congressman to be known. "In the main, recognition carries a positive valence; to be perceived at all is to be perceived favorably." A vital advantage enjoyed by House incumbents is that they are much better known among voters than their November challengers. They are better known because they spend a great deal of time, energy, and money trying to make themselves better known. There are standard routines—frequent visits to the constituency, nonpolitical speeches to home audiences, the sending out of infant care booklets and letters of condolence and congratulations. Of 158 House members questioned . . . 121 said that they regularly sent newsletters to their constituents; 48 wrote separate news or opinion columns for newspapers; 82 regularly reported to their constituencies by radio or television; 89 regularly sent out mail questionnaires. Some routines are less standard. Congressman George E. Shipley (D., Ill.) claims to have met personally about half his constituents (i.e., some 200,000 people). For over twenty years Congressman Charles C. Diggs, Jr. (D., Mich.) has run a radio program featuring himself as a "combination disc jockey-commentator and minister." Congressman Daniel J. Flood (D., Pa.) is "famous for appearing unannounced and often uninvited at wedding anniversaries and other events." Anniversaries and other events aside, congressional advertising is done largely at public expense. Use of the franking privilege has mushroomed in recent years; in early 1973 one estimate predicted that House and Senate members would send out about 476 million pieces of mail in the year 1974, at a public cost of $38.1 million—or about 900,000 pieces per member with a subsidy of $70,000 per member. By far the heaviest mailroom traffic comes in Octobers of even-numbered years. There are some differences between House and Senate members in the ways they go about getting their names across. House members are free to blanket their constituencies with mailings for all boxholders; senators are not. But senators find it easier to appear on national television—for example, in short reaction statements on the nightly news shows. Advertising is a staple congressional activity, and there is no end to it. For each member there are always new voters to be apprised of his worthiness and old voters to be reminded of it.

A second activity may be called *credit claiming,* defined here as acting so as to generate a belief in a relevant political actor (or actors) that one is personally responsible for causing the government, or some unit thereof, to do something that the actor (or actors) considers desirable. The political logic of this, from the congressman's point of view, is that an actor who believes that a member can make pleasing things happen will no doubt wish to keep him in office so that he can make pleasing things happen in the future. The emphasis here is on individual accomplishment (rather than, say, party or governmental accomplishment) and on the congressman as doer (rather than as, say, expounder of constituency views). Credit claiming is highly important to congressmen, with the consequence that much of congressional life is a relentless search for opportunities to engage in it.

Where can credit be found? If there were only one congressman rather than 535, the answer would in principle be simple enough. Credit (or blame) would attach in Downsian fashion to the doing of the government as a whole. But there are 535. Hence it becomes necessary for each congressman to try to peel off pieces of governmental accomplishment for which he can believably generate a sense of responsibility. For the average congressman the staple way of doing this is to traffic in what may be called "particularized benefits." Particularized governmental benefits, as the term will be used here, have two properties: (1) Each benefit is given out to a specific individual, group, or geographical constituency, the recipient unit being of a scale that allows a single congressman to be recognized (by relevant political actors and other congressmen) as the claimant for the benefit (other congressmen being perceived as indifferent or hostile). (2) Each benefit is given out in apparently ad hoc fashion (unlike, say, social security checks) with a congressman apparently having a hand in the allocation. A particularized benefit can normally be regarded as a member of a class. That is, a benefit given out to an individual, group, or constituency can normally be looked upon by congressmen as one of a class of similar benefits given out to sizable numbers of individuals, groups, or constituencies. Hence the impression can arise that a congressman is getting "his share" of whatever it is the government is offering. (The classes may be vaguely defined. Some state legislatures deal in what their members call "local legislation.")

In sheer volume the bulk of particularized benefits come under the heading of "casework"—the thousands of favors congressional offices perform for supplicants in ways that normally do not require legislative action. High school students ask for essay materials, soldiers for emergency leaves, pensioners for location of missing checks, local governments for grant information, and on and on. Each office has skilled professionals who can play the bureaucracy like an organ—pushing the right pedals to produce the desired effects. But many benefits require new legislation, or at least they require important allocative decisions on matters covered by existent legislation. Here the congressman fills the traditional role of supplier of goods to the home district. It is a believable role; when a member claims credit for a benefit on the order of a dam, he may well receive it. Shiny construction projects seem especially useful. . . .

The third activity congressmen engage in may be called *position taking*, defined here as the public enunciation of a judgmental statement on anything likely to be of interest to political actors. The statement may take the form of a roll call vote. The most important classes of judgmental statements are those prescribing American governmental ends (a vote cast against the war; a statement that "the war should be ended immediately") or governmental means (a statement that "the way to end the war is to take it to the United Nations"). The judgments may be implicit rather than explicit, as in: "I will support the president on this matter." But judgments may range far beyond these classes to take in implicit or explicit statements on what almost anybody should do or how he should do it: "The great Polish scientist Copernicus has been unjustly neglected"; "The way for Israel to achieve peace is to give up the Sinai." The congressman as position taker is a speaker rather than a doer. The electoral requirement is not that he make pleasing things happen but that he make pleasing judgmental statements. The position itself is the political commodity.

Especially on matters where governmental responsibility is widely diffused it is not surprising that political actors should fall back on positions as tests of incumbent virtue. For voters ignorant of congressional processes the recourse is an easy one. The following comment [by a Congressman] is highly revealing: "Recently, I went home and began to talk about the———act. I was pleased to have sponsored that bill, but it soon dawned on me that the point wasn't getting through at all. What was getting through was that the act might be a help to people. I changed the emphasis: I didn't mention my role particularly, but stressed my support of the legislation."

The ways in which positions can be registered are numerous and often imaginative. There are floor addresses ranging from weighty orations to mass-produced "nationality day statements." There are speeches before home groups, television appearances, letters, newsletters, press releases, ghostwritten books, *Playboy* articles, even interviews with political scientists. On occasion congressmen generate what amount to petitions; whether or not to sign the 1956 Southern Manifesto defying school desegregation rulings was an important decision for southern members. Outside the roll call process the congressman is usually able to tailor his positions to suit his audiences. A solid consensus in the constituency calls for ringing declarations. . . .

Probably the best position-taking strategy for most congressmen at most times is to be conservative—to cling to their own positions of the past where possible and to reach for new ones with great caution where necessary. Yet in an earlier discussion of strategy the suggestion was made that it might be rational for members in electoral danger to resort to innovation. The form of innovation available is entrepreneurial position taking, its logic being that for a member facing defeat with his old array of positions it makes good sense to gamble on some new ones. It may be that congressional marginals fulfill an important function here as issue pioneers—experimenters who test out new issues and thereby show other politicians which ones are usable. An example of such a pioneer is Senator Warren Magnuson (D., Wash.), who responded to a surprisingly narrow victory in 1962 by reaching for a reputation in the area of consumer affairs. Another example is Senator Ernest Hollings (D., S.C.), a servant of a shaky and racially heterogeneous southern constituency who launched "hunger" as an issue in 1969—at once pointing to a problem and giving it a useful nonracial definition. One of the most successful issue entrepreneurs of recent decades was the late Senator Joseph McCarthy (R., Wis.); it was all there—the close primary in 1946, the fear of defeat in 1952, the desperate casting about for an issue, the famous 1950 dinner at the Colony Restaurant where suggestions were tendered, the decision that "Communism" might just do the trick.

The effect of position taking on electoral behavior is about as hard to measure as the effect of credit claiming. Once again there is a variance problem; congressmen do not differ very much among themselves in the methods they use or the skills they display in attuning themselves to their diverse constituencies. All of them, after all, are professional politicians. . . .

There can be no doubt that congressmen believe positions make a difference. An important consequence of this belief is their custom of watching each other's elections to try to figure out what positions are salable. Nothing is more important in Capitol Hill politics than the shared conviction that election returns have proven a point. . . .

These, then, are the three kinds of electorally oriented activities congressmen engage in—advertising, credit claiming, and position taking. . . .

David Mayhew's thesis, part of which is presented in the preceding selection, is that the Washington activities of members of Congress are, with few exceptions, geared toward reelection. In contrast, Richard Fenno argues that the Washington careers of members of Congress may or may not be related to reelection. In his early work on Congress, Fenno pointed out that the *incentives* of members of Congress fall generally into three categories: (1) reelection, (2) internal power and influence on Capitol Hill, and (3) good public policy. While the incentives of House and Senate members cannot always be placed neatly into one of these categories, Fenno's research suggested that the behavior of members in *Congress* tends to be dominated by one of these incentives.*

Committee selection, in particular, is made to advance reelection, increase power and status on Capitol Hill, or make a good public policy. For example, such committees as Interior and Insular Affairs in the House serve the reelection incentives of their members by channeling specific benefits, such as water and conservation projects, into their districts. Members seeking influence in the House prefer such committees as Ways and Means and Appropriations, both of which reflect the role of the House in the constitutional system and represent it in the outside world. Representatives on the Ways and Means and the Appropriations committees, particularly the chairs and ranking minority members, can use their positions effectively to bolster their reputations for power in the House. "Good public policy" committees are those that are used to reflect ideological viewpoints, such as the House Education and Labor Committee, rather than to give particular benefits to constituents or to augment internal influence.

While members of Congress have varying degrees of success in their pursuit of internal power and good public policy, they are overwhelmingly successful in achieving reelection. The power of incumbency is truly formidable. Over 95 percent of House incumbents are regularly reelected, usually by margins in excess of 55 percent and frequently without opposition. Senators are somewhat more vulnerable than representatives, for Senate seats are attractive targets of opportunity for political parties, interest groups, and ambitious politicians. Nevertheless, Senate incumbents, too, have great advantages over challengers, and normally well over 80 percent of them are easily reelected. Certainly, as David Mayhew points out in selection 61, members of Congress have shaped the legislative environment to enhance their reelection prospects.

Generally, as members of Congress gain seniority, their Washington careers become separated from their constituency activities. The incumbency effect, buttressed by an effective organization within their constituency, leaves them free to pursue goals on Capitol Hill that are not specifically aimed at gaining votes. In the following selection Richard Fenno discusses the linkage between the constituency and Washington activities of House and Senate members.

**Compiler's note*: Richard F. Fenno, Jr., *Congressmen in Committees* (Boston: Little, Brown and Co., 1973).

62

HOME STYLE AND WASHINGTON CAREER

Richard F. Fenno, Jr.

. . . When we speak of constituency careers, we speak primarily of the pursuit of the goal of reelection. When we speak of Washington careers, we speak primarily of the pursuit of the goals of influence in the House and the making of good public policy. Thus the intertwining of careers is, at bottom, an intertwining of member goals.

So long as they are in the expansionist stage of their constituency careers, House members will be especially attentive to their home base. They will pursue the goal of reelection with single-minded intensity and will allocate their resources disproportionately to that end. . . . [F]irst-term members go home more frequently, place a larger proportion of their staff in the district, and more often leave their families at home than do their senior colleagues. Building a reelection constituency at home and providing continuous access to as much of that constituency as possible requires time and energy. Inevitably, these are resources that might otherwise be allocated to efforts in Washington. "The trouble is," said one member near the end of his second term,

> I haven't been a congressman yet. The first two years, I spent all of my time getting myself reelected. The last two years, I spent getting myself a district so that I could get reelected. So I won't be a congressman until next year.

By being "a congressman" he means pursuing goals above and beyond that of reelection (i.e., power in the House and good public policy).

In a House member's first years, the opportunities for gaining inside power and policy influence are limited. Time and energy and staff can be allocated to home without an acute sense of conflict. At rates that vary from congressman to congressman, however, the chances to have some institutional or legislative effect improve. As members stretch to avail themselves of the opportunity, they may begin to experience some allocative strain. It requires time and energy to develop a successful career in Washington just as it does to develop a successful career in the district. Because it may not be possible to allocate these resources to House and home, each to an optimal degree, members may have to make allocative and goal choices.

A four-term congressman with a person-to-person home style described the dilemma of choice:

> I'm beginning to be a little concerned about my political future. I can feel myself getting into what I guess is a natural and inevitable condition—the gradual erosion of my local orientation. I'm not as enthused about tending my constituency relations as I used to be and I'm not paying them the attention I should be. There's a natural tension between being a good representative and taking an interest in government. I'm getting into some heady things in Washington, and I want to make an input into the government. It's making me a poorer representative than I was. I find myself avoiding the personal collisions that arise in the constituency—turning away from that one last handshake, not bothering to go to that one last meeting. I find myself forgetting people's names. And I find myself caring less about it than I used to. Right now, it's just a feeling I have. In eight years I have still to come home less than forty weekends a year. This is my thirty-sixth trip this year. What was it Arthur Rubinstein said? "If I miss one practice, I notice it. If I miss two practices, my teacher notices it. If I miss a week of practice, my audience notices it." I'm at stage one right now—or maybe stage one and stage two. But I'm beginning to feel that I could be defeated before long. And I'm not going to change. I don't want the status. I want to contribute to government.

The onset of a Washington career is altering his personal goals and his established home style. He is worried about the costs of the change; but he is willing to accept some loss of reelection support in exchange for his increased influence in Congress.

The dilemma faces every member of Congress. It is built into the twin requirements that Congress be a representative and a legislative institution. Some members believe they can achieve reelection at home together with influence or policy in Washington without sacrificing either. During Congressman O's first year as a subcommittee chairman, I asked him whether his new position would make it more difficult to tend to district matters. He replied,

> If you mean, am I getting Potomac fever, the answer is, no. If you mean, has the change in my official duties here made me a better congressman, the answer is, yes. If you mean has it taken away from my activity in the constituency, the answer is no.

Congressman O, we recall, has been going home less; but he has been increasing the number and the activity of his district staff. Although he speaks confidently of his allocative solution, he is not unaware of potential problems. "My staff operation runs by itself. They don't need me. Maybe I should worry about that. You aren't going back and say I'm ripe for the plucking are you? I don't think I am."

A three-term member responded very positively when I paraphrased the worries of the congressman friend of his who had quoted Arthur Rubinstein:

> You can do your job in Washington and in your district if you know how. My quarrel with [the people like him] of this world is that they don't learn to be good politicians before they get to Congress. They get there because some people are sitting around the table one day and ask them to do it. They're smart, but they don't learn to organize a district. Once you learn to do that, it's much easier to do your job in Washington.

This member, however, has not yet tasted the inside influence of his friend. Moreover, he does not always talk with such assurance. His district is not so well organized that he has reduced his personal attentiveness to it.

> Ralph Krug [the congressman in the adjacent district] tells me I spoil my constituents. He says, "You've been elected twice, you know your district; once a month is enough to come home." But that's not my philosophy. Maybe it will be someday. . . . My lack of confidence is still a pressure which brings me home. This is my political base. Washington is not my political base. I feel I have to come home to get nourished, to see for myself what's going on. It's my security blanket—coming home.

For now, he feels no competing pulls; but he is not unaware of his friend's dilemma.

Members pose the dilemma with varying degrees of immediacy. No matter how confident members may be of their ability to pursue their Washington and their constituency careers simultaneously, however, they all recognize the potentiality of conflict and worry about coping with it. It is our guess that the conflict between the reelection goal on the one hand and the power or policy goals on the other hand becomes most acute for members as they near the peak of influence internally. For, at this stage of their Washington career, the resource requirements of the Washington job make it nearly impossible to meet established expectations of attentiveness at home. Individuals who want nothing from their Washington careers except the status of being a member of Congress will never pursue any other goal except reelection. For these people, the dilemma of which we speak is minimal. Our concern is with those individuals who find, sooner or later, that they wish to pursue a mix of goals in which reelection must be weighed along with power or policy.

One formula for managing a mix of goals that gives heavy weight to a Washington career is to make one's influence in Washington the centerpiece of home style. The member says, in effect, "I can't come home to present myself in person as much as I once did, because I'm so busy tending to the nation's business; but my seniority, my influence, my effectiveness in Washington is of great benefit to you." He asks his supportive constituents to adopt a new set of expectations, one that would put less of a premium on access. Furthermore, he asks these constituents to remain sufficiently intense in their support to discourage challengers—especially those who will promise access. All members do some of this when they explain their Washington activity—especially in connection with "explaining power." And, where possible, they quote from favorable national commentary in their campaign literature. But [very few Congressmen] have made Washington influence the central element of [their] home style.

One difficulty of completely adopting such a home style is that the powerful Washington legislator can actually get pretty far out of touch with his supportive constituents back home. One of the more senior members of [Congress], and a leader of his committee, recounted the case when his preoccupation with an internal legislative impasse affecting Israel caused him to neglect the crucial Jewish element of his primary constituency—a group "who contribute two-thirds of my money." A member of the committee staff had devised an amendment to break the deadlock.

> Peter Tompkins looked at it and said to me, "Why don't we sponsor it?" So we put it forward, and it became known as the Crowder-Tompkins Amendment. I did it because I respected the staff man who suggested it and because I wanted to get something through that was reasonable. Well, a member of the committee called people back home and said, "Crowder is selling out." All hell broke loose. I started

> getting calls at two and three in the morning from my friends asking me what I was doing. So I went back home and discussed the issue with them. When I walked into the room, it made me feel sad and shocked to feel their hostility. They wanted me to know that they would clobber me if they thought I was selling out. Two hours later, we walked out friends again. I dropped the Crowder-Tompkins Amendment. That's the only little flare up I've ever had with the Jewish community. But it reminded me of their sensitivity to anything that smacks of discrimination.

The congressman survived. But he would not have needed so forceful a reminder of his strongest supporters' concerns were he nearer the beginning of his constituency career. But, of course, neither would he have been a committee leader, and neither would the imperatives of a House career bulked so large in his mix of goals.

Another way to manage conflicting reelection and Washington career goals might be to use one's Washington influence to alter support patterns at home. That is, instead of acting—as is the normal case—to reenforce home support, to keep what he had "last time," the congressman might act to displace that old support with compensating new support. He might even accomplish this inadvertently, should his pursuit of power or policy attract, willy-nilly, constituents who welcome his new mix of goals. The very Washington activity that left him out of touch with previously supportive constituents might put him in touch with newly supportive ones. A newly acquired position of influence in a particular policy area or a new reputation as an effective legislator might produce such a feedback effect. . . .

. . . [There is] a tendency for successful home styles to harden over time and to place stylistic constraints on the congressman's subsequent behavior. The pursuit of a Washington career helps us explain this constituency phenomenon. That is, to the degree that a congressman pursues power or policy goals in the House, he will have that much less time or energy to devote to the consideration of alternative home styles. His predisposition to "do what we did last time" at home will be further strengthened by his growing preoccupation with Washington matters. Indeed, the speed with which a congressman begins to develop a Washington career will affect the speed with which his home style solidifies. . . .

In all of this speculation about career linkages, we have assumed that most members of Congress develop, over time, a mix of personal goals. We particularly assume that most members will trade off some of their personal commitment to reelection in order to satisfy a personal desire for institutional or policy influence. It is our observation . . . that House members do, in fact, exhibit varying degrees of commitment to reelection. All want reelection in the abstract, but not all will pay any price to achieve it; nor will all pay the same price. . . .

One senior member contemplated retirement in the face of an adverse redistricting but, because he had the prospect of a committee chairmanship, he decided to run and hope for the best. He wanted reelection because he wanted continued influence; but he was unwilling to put his present influence in jeopardy by pursuing reelection with the same intensity that marked his earlier constituency career. As he put it,

> Ten years ago, I whipped another redistricting. And I did it by neglecting my congressional duties. . . . Today I don't have the time, and I'm not going to neglect my duties. . . . If I do what is necessary to get reelected and thus become chairman of

> the committee, I will lose the respect and confidence of my fellow committee members because of being absent from the hearings and, occasionally, the votes.

He did not work hard at reelection, and he won by his narrowest margin ever. But he succeeded in sustaining a mix of personal goals very different from an earlier one. . . .

The congressman's home activities are more difficult and taxing than we have previously recognized. Under the best of circumstances, the tension involved in maintaining constituency contact and achieving legislative competence is considerable. Members cannot be in two places at once, and the growth of a Washington career exacerbates the problem. But, more than that, the demands in both places have grown recently. The legislative workload and the demand for legislative expertise are steadily increasing. So is the problem of maintaining meaningful contact with their several constituencies. Years ago, House members returned home for months at a time to live among their supportive constituencies, soak up the home atmosphere, absorb local problems at first hand. Today, they race home for a day, a weekend, a week at a time. [Few] maintain a family home in their district. [Many] stay with relatives or friends or in barely furnished rooms when they are at home. The citizen demand for access, for communication, and for the establishment of trust is as great as ever. So members go home. But the quality of their contact has suffered. "It's like a one-night stand in a singles bar." It is harder to sustain a genuine two-way communication than it once was. House member worries about the home relationship—great under any circumstances, but greater now—contribute to the strain and frustration of the job. Some cope; but others retire. It may be those members who cannot stand the heat of the home relationship who are getting out of the House kitchen. If so, people prepared to be more attentive to home . . . are likely to replace them.

The interplay between home careers and Washington careers continues even as House members leave Congress. For, in retirement or in defeat, they still face a choice—to return home or to remain in Washington. The subject of post-congressional careers is too vast to be treated here. But students of home politics can find, in these choices, indications of the depth and durability of home attachments in the face of influential Washington careers. It is conventional wisdom in the nation's capital that senators and representatives "get Potomac fever" and that "they don't go back to Pocatello" when their legislative careers end. Having pursued the goals of power and policy in Washington with increasing success, they prefer, it is said, to continue their Washington career in some nonlegislative job rather than to go back home. In such a choice, perhaps, we might find the ultimate displacement of the constituency career with the Washington career.

An examination of the place of residence of 370 individuals who left the House between 1954 and 1974, and who were alive in 1974, sheds considerable doubt on this Washington wisdom. It appears that most House members do, indeed, "go back to Pocatello." Of the 370 former members studied, 253 (68 percent) resided in their home states in 1974; 91 lived in the Washington, D.C., area; and 26 resided someplace else. Of those 344 who chose either Washington or home, therefore, nearly three-quarters chose home. This simple fact underscores the very great strength of the home attachments we have described in this [selection].

No cross section of living former members will tell us for sure how many members lingered in Washington for a while before eventually returning home. Only a careful tracing of all individual cases, therefore, will give us a full and accurate description of the Washington-home choice. Even so, among the former members most likely to be attracted to Washington—those who left Congress from 1970 to 1974—only 37 percent have chosen to remain there. A cursory glance at all those who have chosen to prolong their Washington careers, however, tells us what we might expect—that they have already had longer congressional careers than those who returned home. Our data also tell us that these members are younger than those who choose to return home. Thus, we speculate, the success of a member's previous career in Congress and the prospect that he or she still has time to capitalize on that success in the Washington community are positive inducements to stay. And these inducements seem unaffected by the manner of his or her leaving Congress—whether by electoral defeat (for renomination or reelection) or retirement. Those who were defeated, however, had shorter congressional careers and were younger than those who had voluntarily retired.

CHAPTER 9

THE JUDICIARY

Much of English history leading up to the Glorious Revolution of 1688 was a struggle for parliamentary supremacy. First came Magna Carta in 1215, to be followed by the Petition of Right in 1628 and finally the English Bill of Rights in 1689.

However, over the same period the English monarchs, not parliaments, created an elaborate system of courts to protect individual rights to life, liberty, and property and to administer equitable principles of justice to resolve individual disputes where appropriate.

ENGLISH COMMON LAW PRECEDENTS

With regard to our federal judiciary we are truly all Englishmen. Our federal and most state judiciaries have deep English roots in English common law, and judicial powers in common law and equity are English in origin. Law school students in their first year learn contracts, property, and torts, all derived from common law.

We will not get into the distinction between common law and equity, but students should be aware at least that what "the law" is all about are remedies for wrongs and injustices to individuals from the acts of persons acting in a private capacity, and from government actions.

A major distinction between the English and American constitutional system is the power of our judiciary, and the particularly the Supreme Court, to exercise judicial review over congressional laws, as well as presidential and state actions. Courts cannot initiate cases, but can only act on cases and controversies properly brought before them. To challenge government actions parties must demonstrate that they have suffered a personally distinctive injury to a legally protected right. Courts apply law; hence cases and controversies must present legal issues to the courts.

What students should be aware of is that our judicial system, like the courts of Britain that have evolved over centuries, has enormous and extensive powers to remedy legal wrongs and prevent injustice. Judicial independence from the political branches of the government emerged as a central principle of government from the time the Monarch began to establish common law and equity courts as early as the twelfth century.

Before the English "Glorious Revolution" of 1688, which established the principle of parliamentary supremacy, the Lord Chief Justice of England, Sir Edward Coke, proclaimed in Dr. Bonham's Case (1610):

> And it appears in our books, that in many cases, the common law will control acts of parliament, and sometimes adjudge them to be utterly void: for when an act of parliament is against common right and reason, or repugnant, or impossible to be performed, the common law will control it, and adjudge such act to be void[.]

As parliamentary supremacy became firmly established, English courts could not overturn parliamentary laws through the exercise of judicial review. Nevertheless, as the great English jurist William Blackstone wrote in his seminal Commentaries on the Laws of England (1765–1769), the courts were essential to the preservation of constitutional government.

63

COMMENTARIES ON THE LAWS OF ENGLAND 1765*

William Blackstone

A third subordinate right of every Englishman is that of applying to the courts of justice for redress of injuries. Since the law is in England the supreme arbiter of every man's life, liberty, and property, courts of justice must at all times be open to the subject, and the law be duly administered therein.

The emphatical words of *magna carta*, spoken in the person of the king, who in judgment of law (says sir Edward Coke) is ever present and repeating them in all his courts, are these; "*nulli vendemus, nulli negabimus, aut differemus rectum vel justitiam [We neither sell nor deny, nor delay, to any person, equity or justice]*: and

Compiler's note: William Blackstone, *Commentaries on the Laws of England: A Facsimile of the First Edition of 1765–1769*. (Chicago: University of Chicago Press, 1979), *The Founders' Constitution* Volume 5, Amendment V, Document 8, http://press-pubs.uchicago.edu/founders/documents/amendV_due_process8.html.

therefore every subject," continues the same learned author, "for injury done to him *in bonis [goods or property], in terries [land], vel persona [character]*, by any other subject, be he ecclesiastical or temporal without any exception, may take his remedy by the course of the law, and have justice and right for the injury done to him, freely without sale, fully without any denial, and speedily without delay."

It were endless to enumerate all the *affirmative* acts of parliament wherein justice is directed to be done according to the law of the land: and what that law is, every subject knows; or may know if he pleases: for it depends not upon the arbitrary will of any judge; but is permanent, fixed, and unchangeable, unless by authority of parliament.

I shall however just mention a few *negative* statutes, whereby abuses, perversions, or delays of justice, especially by the prerogative, are restrained. It is ordained by *magna carta*, that no freeman shall be outlawed, that is, put out of the protection and benefit of the laws, but according to the law of the land. By [statute] it is enacted, that no commands or letters shall be sent under the great seal, or the little seal, the signet, or privy seal, in disturbance of the law; or to disturb or delay common right: and, though such commandments should come, the judges shall not cease to do right. And by [statute] it is declared, that the pretended power of suspending, or dispensing with laws, or the execution of laws, by regal authority without consent of parliament, is illegal.

Not only the substantial part, or judicial decisions, of the law, but also the formal part, or method of proceeding, cannot be altered but by parliament: for if once those outworks were demolished, there would be no inlet to all manner of innovation in the body of the law itself.

The king, it is true, may erect new courts of justice; but then they must proceed according to the old established forms of the common law. For which reason it is [by statute that] upon the dissolution of the court of Starchamber, that neither his majesty, nor his privy council, have any jurisdiction, power, or authority by English bill, petition, articles, libel (which were the course of proceeding in the Starchamber, borrowed from the civil law) or by any other arbitrary way whatsoever, to examine, or draw into question, determine or dispose of the lands or goods of any subjects of this kingdom; but that the same ought to be tried and determined in the ordinary courts of justice, and by *course of law*.

CONSTITUTIONAL BACKGROUND: JUDICIAL INDEPENDENCE AND JUDICIAL REVIEW

An independent judicial system is an important part of constitutional government. The Constitution provides for an independent Supreme Court by giving its justices life tenure and guaranteed compensation.

The Supreme Court ultimately defines and applies the Constitution. Through judicial review, both legislative and executive decisions may be overruled by the courts if they are unconstitutional. The courts also interpret statutory law to decide, for example, the permissible scope of executive or state actions under federal law.

Alexander Hamilton, in the following selection from *The Federalist,* stresses judicial independence and judicial power to exercise constitutional review of legislative acts.

64

FEDERALIST 78

Alexander Hamilton

We proceed now to an examination of the judiciary department of the proposed government.

In unfolding the defects of the existing confederation, the utility and necessity of a federal judicature have been clearly pointed out. It is the less necessary to recapitulate the considerations there urged; as the propriety of the institution in the abstract is not disputed; the only questions which have been raised being relative to the manner of constituting it, and to its extent. To these points, therefore, our observations shall be confined.

The manner of constituting it seems to embrace these several objects: 1st. The mode of appointing the judges; 2nd. The tenure by which they are to hold their places; 3rd. The partition of the judiciary authority between different courts, and their relations to each other.

First

As to the mode of appointing the judges: This is the same with that of appointing the officers of the union in general, and has been so fully discussed . . . that nothing can be said here which would not be useless repetition.

Second

As to the tenure by which the judges are to hold their places: This chiefly concerns their duration in office; the provisions for their support; the precautions for their responsibility.

According to the plan of the convention, all the judges who may be appointed by the United States are to hold their offices *during good behavior;* which is conformable to the most approved of the state constitutions. . . . The standard of good behavior for the continuance in office of the judicial magistracy is certainly one of the most valuable of the modern improvements in the practice of government. In a monarchy, it is an excellent barrier to the despotism of the prince; in a republic, it is a no less excellent barrier to the encroachments and oppressions of the representative body. And it is the best expedient which can be devised in any government, to secure a steady, upright, and impartial administration of the laws.

Whoever attentively considers the different departments of power must perceive, that, in a government in which they are separated from each other, the judiciary, from the nature of its functions, will always be the least dangerous to the political rights of the constitution; because it will be least in a capacity to annoy or injure them. The executive not only dispenses the honors, but holds the sword of the community. The legislature not only commands the purse, but prescribes the rules by which the duties and rights of every citizen are to be regulated. The judiciary, on the contrary, has no influence over either the sword or the purse; no direction either of the strength or of the wealth of the society; and can take no active resolution whatever. It may truly be said to have neither FORCE NOR WILL, but merely judgment; and must ultimately depend upon the aid of the executive arm for the efficacious exercise even of this faculty.

This simple view of the matter suggests several important consequences: It proves incontestably, that the judiciary is beyond comparison, the weakest of the three departments of power, that it can never attack with success either of the other two; and that all possible care is requisite to enable it to defend itself against their attacks. It equally proves, that, though individual oppression may now and then proceed from the courts of justice, the general liberty of the people can never be endangered from that quarter; I mean so long as the judiciary remains truly distinct from both the legislature and executive. For I agree, that "there is no liberty, if the power of judging be not separated from the legislative and executive powers." It proves, in the last place, that as liberty can have nothing to fear from the judiciary alone, but would have everything to fear from its union with either of the other departments; that, as all the effects of such a union must ensue from a dependence of the former on the latter, notwithstanding a nominal and apparent separation; that as, from the natural feebleness of the judiciary, it is in continual jeopardy of being overpowered, awed or influenced by its coordinate branches; that, as nothing can contribute so much to its firmness and independence as PERMANENCY IN OFFICE, this quality may therefore be justly regarded as an indispensable ingredient in its constitution; and, in a great measure, as the CITADEL of the public justice and the public security.

The complete independence of the courts of justice is peculiarly essential in a limited constitution. By a limited constitution, I understand one which contains certain specified exceptions to the legislative no *ex post facto* laws, and the like. Limitations of this kind can be preserved in practice no other way than through the medium of the courts of justice, whose duty it must be to declare all acts contrary to the manifest tenor of the constitution void. Without this, all the reservations of particular rights or privileges would amount to nothing.

Some perplexity respecting the right of the courts to pronounce legislative acts void, because contrary to the constitution, has arisen from an imagination that the doctrine would imply a superiority of the judiciary to the legislative power. It is urged that the authority which can declare the acts of another void, must necessarily be superior to the one whose acts may be declared void. As this doctrine is of great importance in all the American constitutions, a brief discussion of the grounds on which it rests cannot be unacceptable.

There is no position which depends on clearer principles than that every act of a delegated authority, contrary to the tenor of the commission under which it is exercised, is void. No legislative act, therefore, contrary to the constitution, can be valid. To deny this would be to affirm, that the deputy is greater than his principal; that the servant is above his master; that the representatives of the people are superior to the people themselves; that men, acting by virtue of powers, may do not only what their powers do not authorize, but what they forbid.

If it be said that the legislative body are themselves the constitutional judges of their powers, and that the construction they put upon them is conclusive upon the other departments, it may be answered, that this cannot be the natural presumption, where it is not to be collected from any particular provisions in the constitution. It is not otherwise to be supposed that the constitution could intend to enable the representatives of the people to substitute their will to that of their constituents. It is far more rational to suppose that the courts were designed to be an intermediate body between the people and the legislature, in order, among other things, to keep the latter within the limits assigned to their authority. The interpretation of the laws is the proper and peculiar province of the courts. A constitution is, in fact, and must be, regarded by the judges as a fundamental law. It must therefore belong to them to ascertain its meaning, as well as the meaning of any particular act proceeding from the legislative body. If there should happen to be an irreconcilable variance between the two, that which has the superior obligation and validity ought, of course, to be preferred; in other words, the constitution ought to be preferred to the statute, the intention of the people to the intention of their agents.

Nor does this conclusion by any means suppose a superiority of the judicial to the legislative power. It only supposes that the power of the people is superior to both; and that where the will of the legislature declared in its statutes, stands in opposition to that of the people declared in the constitution, the judges ought to be governed by the latter, rather than the former. They ought to regulate their decisions by the fundamental laws, rather than by those which are not fundamental. . . .

It can be no weight to say, that the courts, on the pretense of a repugnancy, may substitute their own pleasure to the constitutional intentions of the legislature. This might as well happen in the case of two contradictory statutes; or it might as well happen in every adjudication upon any single statute. The courts must declare the sense of the law; and if they should be disposed to exercise WILL instead of

JUDGMENT, the consequence would equally be the substitution of their pleasure to that of the legislative body. The observation, if it proved anything, would prove that there ought to be no judges distinct from the body.

If then the courts of justice are to be considered as the bulwarks of a limited constitution, against legislative encroachments, this consideration will afford a strong argument for the permanent tenure of judicial officers, since nothing will contribute so much as this to that independent spirit in the judges, which must be essential to the faithful performance of so arduous a duty.

This independence of the judges is equally requisite to guard the constitution and the rights of individuals, from the effects of those ill-humors which the arts of designing men, or the influence of particular conjunctures, sometimes disseminate among the people themselves, and which, though they speedily give place to better information, and more deliberate reflection, have a tendency, in the meantime, to occasion dangerous innovations in the government, and serious oppression of the minor party in the community. . . . Until the people have, by some solemn and authoritative act, annulled or changed the established form, it is binding upon themselves collectively, as well as individually; and no presumption, or even knowledge of their sentiments, can warrant their representatives in a departure from it, prior to such an act. But it is easy to see, that it would require an uncommon portion of fortitude in the judges to do their duty as faithful guardians of the constitution, where legislative invasions of it had been instigated by the major voice of the community.

But it is not with a view to infractions of the constitution only, that the independence of the judges may be an essential safeguard against the effects of occasional ill-humors in the society. These sometimes extend no farther than to the injury of the private rights of particular classes of citizens, by unjust and partial laws. Here also the firmness of the judicial magistracy is of vast importance in mitigating the severity, and confining the operation of such laws. It not only serves to moderate the immediate mischiefs of those which may have been passed, but it operates as a check upon the legislative body in passing them; who, perceiving that obstacles to the success of an iniquitous intention are to be expected from the scruples of the courts, are in a manner compelled by the very motives of the injustice they mediate, to quality their attempts. . . .

That inflexible and uniform adherence to the rights of the constitution, and of individuals, which we perceive to be indispensable in the courts of justice, can certainly not be expected from judges who hold their offices by a temporary commission. Periodical appointments, however regulated, or by whomsoever made, would, in some way or other, be fatal to their necessary independence. If the power of making them was committed either to the executive or legislature, there would be danger of an improper compliance to the branch which possessed it; if to both, there would be an unwillingness to hazard the displeasure of either; if to the people, or to persons chosen by them for the special purpose, there would be too great a disposition to consult popularity to justify a reliance that nothing would be consulted but the constitution and the laws.

There is yet a further and a weighty reason for the permanency of judicial offices, which is deducible from the nature of the qualifications they require. It has been frequently remarked, with great propriety, that a voluminous code of laws is one of the inconveniences necessarily connected with the advantages of a free government. To avoid an arbitrary discretion in the courts, it is indispensable that they should be bound down by strict rules and precedents, which serve to define and point out their duty in every particular case that comes before them; and it will readily be conceived, from the variety of controversies which grow out of the folly and wickedness of mankind, that the records of those precedents must unavoidably swell to a very considerable bulk, and must demand long and laborious study to acquire a competent knowledge of them. Hence it is, that there can be but few men in the society, who will have sufficient skill in the laws to qualify them for the stations of judges. And making the proper deductions for the ordinary depravity of human nature, the number must be still smaller, of those who unite the requisite integrity with the requisite knowledge. . . .

From *Federalist 78* students can observe that the intent of the framers of the Constitution, at least as expressed and represented by Hamilton, was to give to the courts the power of judicial review over legislative acts. But the Constitution did not explicitly establish the power of judicial review. Although the cause of this omission is not known, it is reasonable to assume that the framers felt that judicial power implied judicial review. Further, it is possible that the framers did not expressly mention judicial review because they had to rely on the states for adoption of the Constitution; judicial power would extend to the states as well as to the coordinate departments of the national government.

The power of the Supreme Court to invalidate an act of Congress was stated by John Marshall in *Marbury v. Madison*, 1 Cranch 137 (1803). At issue was a provision in the Judiciary Act of 1789 that extended the *original jurisdiction* of the Supreme Court by authorizing it to issue writs of mandamus in cases involving public officers of the United States and private persons, a power not conferred upon the Court in the Constitution. Marbury had been appointed a justice of the peace by President John Adams under the Judiciary Act of 1801, passed by the Federalists after Jefferson and the Republican party won the elections in the fall of 1800 so that President Adams could fill various newly created judicial posts with Federalists before he left office in March 1801.

Marbury was scheduled to receive one of these commissions, but when Jefferson took office on March 4, with Madison as his secretary of state, it had not been delivered. Marbury filed a suit with the Supreme Court requesting it to exercise its original jurisdiction and issue a writ of mandamus (a writ to compel an official to perform his or her duty) to force Madison to deliver the commission, an act which both Jefferson and Madison were opposed to doing. In his decision, Marshall, a prominent Federalist, stated that although Marbury had a legal right to his commission, and although mandamus was the proper remedy, the Supreme Court could not extend its original jurisdiction beyond the limits specified in the Constitution; therefore, that section of the Judiciary Act of 1789 permitting the court to issue such writs to public officers was unconstitutional. Incidentally, the Republicans were so outraged at Adams' last-minute appointments that there were threats that Marshall would be impeached if he issued a writ of mandamus directing Madison to deliver the commission. This is not to suggest that Marshall let such considerations influence him; however, politically his decision was thought to be a masterpiece of reconciling his position as a Federalist with the political tenor of the times.

65

MARBURY V. MADISON

1 Cranch 137 (1803)

Mr. Chief Justice Marshall delivered the opinion of the Court, saying in part:

. . . The authority, therefore, given to the Supreme Court, by the [Judiciary Act of 1789] . . . establishing the judicial courts of the United States, to issue writs of mandamus to public officers, appears not to be warranted by the Constitution [because it adds to the original jurisdiction of the Court delineated by the framers of the Constitution in Article III; had they wished this power to be conferred upon the Court it would be so stated, in the same manner that the other parts of the Court's original jurisdiction are stated];. . . it becomes necessary to inquire whether a jurisdiction so conferred can be exercised.

The question whether an act repugnant to the Constitution can become the law of the land, is a question deeply interesting to the United States; but, happily, not of an intricacy proportioned to its interests. It seems only necessary to recognize certain principles supposed to have been long and well established, to decide it.

That the people have an original right to establish, for their future government, such principles as, in their opinion, shall most conduce to their own happiness, is the basis on which the whole American fabric has been erected. The exercise of this original right is a very great exertion; nor can it nor ought it to be frequently repeated. The principles, therefore, so established, are deemed fundamental. And as the authority from which they proceed is supreme, and can seldom act, they are designed to be permanent.

This original and supreme will organizes the government, and assigns to different departments their respective powers. It may either stop here, or establish certain limits not to be transcended by those departments.

The government of the United States is of the latter description. The powers of the legislature are defined and limited; and that those limits may not be mistaken, or forgotten, the Constitution is written. To what purpose are powers limited, and to what purpose is that limitation committed to writing, if these limits may, at any time, be passed by those intended to be restrained? The distinction between a government with limited powers is abolished, if those limits do not confine the persons on whom they are imposed, and if acts prohibited and acts allowed, are of equal obligation. It is a proposition too plain to be contested, that the Constitution controls any legislative act repugnant to it; or, that the legislature may alter the Constitution by an ordinary act.

Between these alternatives there is no middle ground. The Constitution is either a superior paramount law, unchangeable by ordinary means, or it is on a level with ordinary legislative acts, and, like other acts, is alterable when the legislature shall please to alter it.

If the former part of the alternative be true, then a legislative act contrary to the Constitution, is not law; if the latter part be true, then written constitutions are absurd attempts, on the part of the people, to limit a power in its own nature illimitable.

Certainly all those who have framed written constitutions contemplate them as forming the fundamental and paramount law of the nation, and, consequently, the theory of every such government must be, that an act of the legislature, repugnant to the constitution, is void.

This theory is essentially attached to a written constitution, and is consequently to be considered, by this court, as one of the fundamental principles of our society. It is not, therefore, to be lost sight of in the further consideration of this subject.

If an act of the legislature, repugnant to the Constitution, is void, does it, notwithstanding its invalidity, bind the courts, and oblige them to give it effect? Or, in other words, though it be not law, does it constitute a rule as operative as if it was a law? This would be to overthrow in fact what was established in theory; and would seem, at first view, an absurdity too gross to be insisted on. It shall, however, receive a more attentive consideration.

It is emphatically the province and duty of the judicial department to say what the law is. Those who apply the rule to particular cases, must of necessity expound and interpret that rule. If two laws conflict with each other, the courts must decide on the operation of each.

So if the law be in opposition to the Constitution; if both the law and the Constitution apply to a particular case, so that the court must either decide that case conformably to the law, disregarding the Constitution, or conformably to the Constitution, disregarding the law, the court must determine which of these conflicting rules governs the case. This is of the very essence of judicial duty.

If, then, the courts are to regard the Constitution, and the Constitution is superior to any ordinary act of the legislature, the Constitution, and not such ordinary act, must govern the case to which they both apply.

Those, then, who controvert the principle that the Constitution is to be considered, in court, as a paramount law, are reduced to the necessity of maintaining that courts must close their eyes on the Constitution, and see only the law.

This doctrine would subvert the very foundation of all written constitutions. It would declare that an act which, according to the principles and theory of our government, is entirely void, is yet, in practice, completely obligatory. It would declare that if the legislature shall do what is expressly forbidden, such act, notwithstanding the express prohibition, is in reality effectual. It would be giving to the legislature a practical and real omnipotence, with the same breath which professes to restrict their powers within narrow limits. It is prescribing limits, and declaring that those limits may be passed at pleasure.

That it thus reduces to nothing what we have deemed the greatest improvement on political institutions, a written constitution, would of itself be sufficient, in America, where written constitutions have been viewed with so much reverence, for rejecting the construction. But the peculiar expressions of the Constitution of the United States furnish additional arguments in favor of its rejection.

The judicial power of the United States is extended to all cases arising under the Constitution.

Could it be the intention of those who gave this power, to say that in using it the Constitution should not be looked into? That a case arising under the Constitution should be decided without examining the instrument under which it arises?

This is too extravagant to be maintained.

In some cases, then, the Constitution must be looked into by the judges. And if they can open it at all, what part of it are they forbidden to read or obey?

There are many other parts of the Constitution which serve to illustrate this subject.

It is declared that "no tax or duty shall be laid on articles exported from any State." Suppose a duty on the export of cotton, of tobacco, or of flour; and a suit instituted to recover it. Ought judgment to be rendered in such a case? Ought the judges to close their eyes on the Constitution, and only see the law?

The Constitution declares "that no bill of attainder or *ex post facto* law shall be passed."

If, however, such a bill should be passed, and a person should be prosecuted under it, must the court condemn to death those victims whom the Constitution endeavors to preserve?

"No person," says the Constitution, "shall be convicted of treason unless on the testimony of two witnesses to the same overt act, or on confession in open court."

Here the language of the Constitution is addressed especially to the courts. It prescribes, directly for them, a rule of evidence not to be departed from. If the legislature should change that rule, and declare one witness, or a confession out of court, 392
sufficient for conviction, must the constitutional principle yield to the legislative act?

From these, and many other selections which might be made, it is apparent that the framers of the Constitution contemplated that instrument as a rule for the government of courts, as well as of the legislature.

Why otherwise does it direct the judges to take an oath to support it? This oath certainly applies in an especial manner to this conduct in their official character. How immoral to impose it on them, if they were to be used as the instruments, and the knowing instruments, for violating what they swear to support!

The oath of office, too, imposed by the legislature, is completely demonstrative of the legislative opinion on this subject. It is in these words: "I do solemnly swear that I will administer justice without respect to persons, and do equal right to the poor and to the rich; and that I will faithfully and impartially discharge all the duties incumbent on me as_____, according to the best of my abilities and understanding, agreeably to the Constitution and laws of the United States."

Why does a judge swear to discharge his duties agreeably to the Constitution of the United States, if that Constitution forms no rule for his government—if it is closed upon him, and cannot be inspected by him?

If such be the real state of things, this is worse than solemn mockery. To prescribe, or to take this oath, becomes equally a crime.

It is also not entirely unworthy of observation, that in declaring what shall be the supreme law of the land, the Constitution itself is first mentioned; and not the laws of the United States generally, but those only which shall be made in pursuance of the Constitution, have that rank.

Thus, the particular phraseology of the Constitution of the United States confirms and strengthens the principle, supposed to be essential to all written constitutions, that a law repugnant to the Constitution is void; and that courts, as well as other departments, are bound by that instrument.

The rule must be discharged.

Marbury v. Madison unequivocally established the Supreme Court's supremacy over Congress. But the history of the Supreme Court is not one of activism in overruling congressional laws. Judicial review has been most significant and controversial in overturning state actions.

With the exception of the major confrontation between the Supreme Court and President Franklin D. Roosevelt during the New Deal in the 1930's, the Court only occasionally tangled with the President or Congress over its first two hundred years. But Chief Justice Rehnquist's Court took on Congress in a series of important cases as the twentieth century ended and the twenty-first century began. It resurrected a dormant commerce clause to limit congressional power to enact gun control legislation (*Lopez*, 1995) and the regulation of violence against women (*Morrison*, 2000). It overturned the Religious Freedom Restoration Act of 1993 in which Congress attempted to overrule a Supreme Court decision (*City of Boerne*, 1997). The Supreme Court also limited congressional authority to enact affirmative action programs (*Adarand*, 1995).*

POWERS AND LIMITATIONS OF THE SUPREME COURT

Paul A. Freund, in his book *On Understanding the Supreme Court* (1949), notes that the Supreme Court has a definite political role. He asks:

> Is the law of the Supreme Court a reflection of the notions of "policy" held by its members? The question recalls the controversy over whether judges "make" or "find" the law.

---

*Compiler's note: Chapter 2 discusses the Lopez case and has an excerpt from *United States v. Morrison* (Reading 14).

A generation or two ago it was thought rather daring to insist that judges make law. Old Jeremiah Smith, who began the teaching of law at Harvard after a career on the New Hampshire Supreme Court, properly deflated the issue. "Do judges make law?" he repeated. "Course they do. Made some myself." Of course Supreme Court Justices decide cases on the basis of their ideas of policy.

It would be difficult to conceive how a Court having the power to interpret the Constitution could fail to make policy, that is, could fail to make rulings that have general impact upon the community as a whole. The essential distinction between policymaking and adjudication is that the former has a general effect while the latter touches only a specifically designated person or group.

The Supreme Court's decisions may have a "policy" effect, but they are always based on constitutional or statutory law. Courts interpret law, they do not make it. There are other constraints on the judiciary. The Supreme Court and lower courts are limited to the consideration of cases and controversies brought before them by outside parties. Courts cannot initiate law. Moreover, all courts, and the Supreme Court in particular, exercise judicial self-restraint in certain cases to avoid difficult and controversial issues and to avoid outside pressure to limit the powers of the judiciary. John P. Roche, in the next selection, deals with the background, the nature, and the implications of judicial doctrines of self-restraint.

66

JUDICIAL SELF-RESTRAINT

John P. Roche

Every society, sociological research suggests, has its set of myths which incorporate and symbolize its political, economic, and social aspirations. Thus, as medieval society had the Quest for the Holy Grail and the cult of numerology, we, in our enlightened epoch, have as significant manifestations of our collective hopes the dream of impartial decision-making and the cult of "behavioral science." While in my view these latter two are but different facets of the same fundamental drive, namely, the age-old effort to exorcise human variables from human action, our concern here is with the first of them, the pervasive tendency in the American political and constitutional tradition directed toward taking the politics out of politics, and substituting some set of Platonic guardians for fallible politicians.

While this dream of objectivizing political Truth is in no sense a unique American phenomenon, it is surely true to say that in no other democratic nation has the effort been carried so far and with such persistence. Everywhere one turns in the United States, he finds institutionalized attempts to narrow the political sector and to substitute allegedly "independent" and "impartial" bodies for elected decision-makers. The so-called "independent regulatory commissions" are a classic example of this tendency in the area of administration, but unquestionably the greatest hopes for injecting pure Truth-serum into the body politic have been traditionally reserved for the federal judiciary, and particularly for the Supreme Court. The rationale for this viewpoint is simple: "The people must be protected from themselves, and no institution is better fitted for the role of chaperone than the federal judiciary, dedicated as it is to the supremacy of the rule of law."

Patently central to this function of social chaperonage is the right of the judiciary to review legislative and executive actions and nullify those measures which derogate from eternal principles of truth and justice as incarnated in the Constitution. Some authorities, enraged at what the Supreme Court has found the Constitution to mean, have essayed to demonstrate that the framers did not intend the Court to exercise this function, to have, as they put it, "the last word." I find no merit in this contention; indeed, it seems to me undeniable not only that the authors of the Constitution intended to create a federal government, but also that they assumed *sub silentio* that the Supreme Court would have the power to review both national and state legislation.

However, since the intention of the framers is essentially irrelevant except to antiquarians and polemicists, it is unnecessary to examine further the matter of origins. The fact is that the United States Supreme Court, and the inferior federal courts under the oversight of the high Court, have enormous policy-making functions. Unlike their British and French counterparts, federal judges are not merely technicians who live in the shadow of a supreme legislature, but are fully equipped to intervene in the process of political decision making. In theory, they are limited by the Constitution and the jurisdiction it confers, but, in practice, it would be a clumsy judge indeed who could not, by a little skillful exegesis, adapt the Constitution to a necessary end. This statement is in no sense intended as a condemnation; on the contrary, it has been this perpetual reinvigoration by reinterpretation, in which the legislature and the executive as well as the courts play a part, that has given the Constitution its survival power. Applying a Constitution which contains at key points inspired ambiguity, the courts have been able to pour the new wine in the old bottle. Note that the point at issue is not the legitimacy or wisdom of judicial legislation; it is simply the enormous scope that this prerogative gives to judges to substitute their views for those of past generations, or, more controversially, for those of a contemporary Congress and President.

Thus it is naive to assert that the Supreme Court is limited by the Constitution, and we must turn elsewhere for the sources of judicial restraint. The great power exercised by the Court has carried with it great risks, so it is not surprising that American political history has been sprinkled with demands that the judiciary be emasculated. The really startling thing is that, with the notable exception of the McCardle incident in 1869, the Supreme Court has emerged intact from each of these encounters. Despite the plenary power that Congress, under Article III of the

Constitution, can exercise over the appellate jurisdiction of the high Court, the national legislature has never taken sustained and effective action against its House of Lords. It is beyond the purview of this analysis to examine the reasons for Congressional inaction; suffice it here to say that the most significant form of judicial limitation has remained self-limitation. This is not to suggest that such a development as statutory codification has not cut down the area of interpretive discretion, for it obviously has. It is rather to maintain that when the justices have held back from assaults on legislative or executive actions, they have done so on the basis of self-established rationalizations. . . .

The remainder of this paper is therefore concerned with two aspects of this auto-limitation: first, the techniques by which it is put into practice; and, second, the conditions under which it is exercised. . . .

Techniques of Judicial Self-Restraint

The major techniques of judicial self-restraint appear to fall under the two familiar rubrics: procedural and substantive. Under the former fall the various techniques by which the Court can avoid coming to grips with substantive issues, while under the latter would fall those methods by which the Court, in a substantive holding, finds that the matter at issue in the litigation is not properly one for judicial settlement. Let us examine these two categories in some detail.

Procedural Self-Restraint

Since the passage of the Judiciary Act of 1925, the Supreme Court has had almost complete control over its business. United States Supreme Court *Rule 38*, which governs the *certiorari* policy, states, (§ 5) that discretionary review will be granted only "where there are special and important reasons therefor." Professor Fowler Harper has suggested in a series of detailed and persuasive articles on the application of this discretion [*University of Pennsylvania Law Review*, vols. 99–101; 103] that the Court has used it in such a fashion as to duck certain significant but controversial problems. While one must be extremely careful about generalizing in this area, since the reasons for denying *certiorari* are many and complex, Harper's evidence does suggest that the Court in the period since 1949 has refused to review cases involving important civil liberties problems which on their merits appeared to warrant adjudication. As he states at one point: "It is disconcerting when the Court will review a controversy over a patent on a pin ball machine while one man is deprived of his citizenship and another of his liberty without Supreme Court review of a plausible challenge to the validity of government action.". . .

Furthermore, the Supreme Court can issue *certiorari* on its own terms. Thus in *Dennis v. United States*, appealing the Smith Act convictions of the American communist leadership, the Court accepted the evidential findings of the Second Circuit as final and limited its review to two narrow constitutional issues. This, in effect, burked the basic problem: whether the evidence was sufficient to demonstrate that the

Communist Party, U.S.A., was *in fact* clear and present danger to the security of the nation, or whether the communists were merely shouting "Fire!" in an empty theater.

Other related procedural techniques are applicable in some situations. Simple delay can be employed, perhaps in the spirit of the Croatian proverb that "delay is the handmaiden of justice.". . . However, the technique of procedural self-restraint is founded on the essentially simple gadget of refusing jurisdiction, or of procrastinating the acceptance of jurisdiction, and need not concern us further here.

Substantive Self-Restraint

Once a case has come before the Court on its merits, the justices are forced to give some explanation for whatever action they may take. Here self-restraint can take many forms, notably, the doctrine of political questions, the operation of judicial parsimony, and—particularly with respect to the actions of administrative officers of agencies—the theory of judicial inexpertise.

The doctrine of political questions is too familiar to require much elaboration here. Suffice it to say that if the Court feels that a question before it, e.g., the legitimacy of a state government, the validity of a legislative apportionment, or the correctness of executive action in the field of foreign relations, is one that is not properly amenable to judicial settlement, it will refer the plaintiff to the "political" organs of government for any possible relief. The extent to which this doctrine is applied seems to be a direct coefficient of judicial egotism, for the definition of a political question can be expanded or contracted in accordian-like fashion to meet the exigencies of the times. A juridical definition of the term is impossible, for at root the logic that supports it is circular: political questions are matters not soluble by the judicial process; matters not soluble by the judicial process are political questions. As an early dictionary explained, violins are small cellos, and cellos are large violins.

Nor do examples help much in definition. While it is certainly true that the Court cannot *mandamus* a legislature to apportion a state in equitable fashion, it seems equally true that the Court is without the authority to force state legislators to implement unsegregated public education. Yet in the former instance the Court genuflected to the "political" organs and took no action, while in the latter it struck down segregation as violative of the Constitution.

Judicial parsimony is another major technique of substantive self-restraint. In what is essentially a legal application of Occam's razor, the court has held that it will not apply any more principles to the settlement of a case than are absolutely necessary, e.g., it will not discuss the constitutionality of a law if it can settle the instant case by statutory construction. Furthermore, if an action is found to rest on erroneous statutory construction, the review terminates at that point: the Court will not go on to discuss whether the statute, properly construed, would be constitutional. A variant form of this doctrine, and a most important one, employs the "case of controversy" approach, to wit, the Court, admitting the importance of the issue, inquires as to whether the litigant actually has standing to bring the matter up. . . .

A classic use of parsimony to escape from a dangerous situation occurred in connection with the evacuation of the Nisei from the West Coast in 1942. Gordon

Hirabayashi, in an attempt to test the validity of the regulations clamped on the American-Japanese by the military, violated the *curfew* and refused to report to an evacuation center. He was convicted on both counts by the district court and sentenced to three months for each offense, the sentences to run concurrently. When the case came before the Supreme Court, the justices sustained his conviction for violating the curfew, but refused to examine the validity of the evacuation order on the ground that it would not make any difference to Hirabayashi anyway; he was in for ninety days no matter what the Court did with evacuation.

A third method of utilizing substantive self-restraint is particularly useful in connection with the activities of executive departments or regulatory agencies, both state and federal. I have entitled it the doctrine of judicial *inexpertise*, for it is founded on the unwillingness of the Court to revise the findings of experts. The earmarks of this form of restraint are great deference to the holdings of the expert agency usually coupled with such a statement as "It is not for the federal courts to supplant the [Texas Railroad] Commission's judgment even in the face of convincing proof that a different result would have been better." In this tradition, the Court has refused to question *some* exercises of discretion by the National Labor Relations Board, the Federal Trade Commission, and other federal and state agencies. But the emphasis on *some* gives the point away; in other cases, apparently on all fours with those in which it pleads its technical *inexpertise*, the Court feels free to assess evidence *de novo* and reach independent judgment on the technical issues involved. . . .

In short, with respect to expert agencies, the Court is equipped with both offensive and defensive gambits. It if chooses to intervene, one set of precedents is brought out, while if it decides to hold back, another set of equal validity is invoked. Perhaps the best summary of this point was made by Justice Harlan in 1910, when he stated bluntly that "the Courts have rarely, if ever, felt themselves so restrained by technical rules that they could not find some remedy, consistent with the law, for acts . . . that violated natural justice or were hostile to the fundamental principles devised for the protection of the essential rights of property."

This does not pretend to be an exhaustive analysis of the techniques of judicial self-restraint; on the contrary, others will probably find many which are not given adequate discussion here. The remainder of this paper, however, is devoted to the second area of concern: the conditions under which the Court refrains from acting.

The Conditions of Judicial Self-Restraint

The conditions which lead the Supreme Court to exercise auto-limitation are many and varied. In the great bulk of cases, this restraint is an outgrowth of sound and quasi-automatic legal maxims which defy teleological interpretation. It would take a master of the conspiracy theory of history to assign meaning, for example, to the great majority of *certiorari* denials; the simple fact is that these cases do not merit review. However, in a small proportion of cases, purpose does appear to enter the picture, sometimes with a vengeance. It is perhaps unjust to the Court to center our attention on this small proportion, but it should be said in extenuation that these cases often involve extremely significant political and social issues. In the broad picture, the refusal to grant *certiorari* in 1943 to the Minneapolis Trotskyites convicted under the Smith Act is far more meaningful than the similar refusal to grant five hundred petitions to prison "lawyers" who have suddenly discovered the *writ of habeas corpus*. Likewise, the holding that the legality of Congressional apportionment is a "political question" vitally affects the operation of the whole democratic process.

What we must therefore seek are the conditions under which the Court holds back in this *designated category of cases*. Furthermore, it is important to realize that there are positive consequences of negative action; as Charles Warren has implied, the post–Civil War Court's emphasis on self-restraint was a judicial concomitant of the resurgence of states' rights. Thus self-restraint may, as in wartime, be an outgrowth of judicial caution, or it may be part of a purposeful pattern of abdicating national power to the states.

Ever since the first political scientist discovered Mr. Dooley, the changes have been run on the aphorism that the Supreme Court "follows the election returns," and I see no particular point in ringing my variation on this theme through again. Therefore, referring those who would like a more detailed explanation to earlier analyses, the discussion here will be confined to the bare bones of my hypothesis.

The power of the Supreme Court to invade the decision-making arena, I submit, is a consequence of that fragmentation of political power which is normal in the United States. No cohesive majority, such as normally exists in Britain, would permit a politically irresponsible judiciary to usurp decision-making functions, but, for complex social and institutional reasons, there are few issues in the United States on which cohesive majorities exist. The guerrilla warfare which usually rages between Congress and the President, as well as the internal civil wars which are endemic in both the legislature and the administration, give the judiciary considerable room for maneuver. If, for example, the Court strikes down a controversial decision of the Federal Power Commission, it will be supported by a substantial bloc of congressmen; if it supports the FPC's decision, it will also receive considerable congressional support. But the important point is that either way it decides the case, there is no possibility that Congress will exact any vengeance on the Court for its action. A disciplined majority would be necessary to clip the judicial wings, and such a majority does not exist on this issue.

On the other hand, when monolithic majorities do exist on issues, the Court is likely to resort to judicial self-restraint. A good case here is the current tidal wave of anti-communist legislation and administrative action, the latter particularly with regard to aliens, which the Court has treated most gingerly. About the only issues on which there can be found cohesive majorities are those relating to national defense, and the Court has, as Clinton Rossiter demonstrated in an incisive analysis [*The Supreme Court and the Commander-in-Chief*, Ithaca, 1951], traditionally avoided problems arising in this area irrespective of their constitutional merits. Like the slave who accompanied a Roman consul on his triumph whispering "You too are mortal," the shade of Thad Stevens haunts the Supreme Court chamber to remind the justices what an angry Congress can do.

To state the proposition in this brief compass is to oversimplify it considerably I have, for instance, ignored the crucial question of how the Court knows when a majority *does* exist, and I recognize that certain aspects of judicial behavior cannot be jammed into my hypothesis without creating essentially spurious epicycles. However, I am not trying to establish a monistic theory of judicial action; group action, like that of individuals, is motivated by many factors, some often contradictory, and my objective is to elucidate what seems to be one tradition of judicial motivation. In short, judicial self-restraint and judicial power seem to be opposite sides of the same coin: it has been by judicious application of the former that the latter has been maintained. A tradition beginning with Marshall's *coup* in *Marbury v. Madison* and running through *Mississippi v. Johnson* and *Ex Parte Vallandigham* to *Dennis v. United States* suggests that the Court's power has been maintained by a wise refusal to employ it in unequal combat.

John Roche's theory is that the Supreme Court, in a system in which politics is often carried out through litigation, has survived through the judicious application of self-restraint. The Court has retreated when confronted by monolithic political majorities, a rare occurrence. Political pluralism undermines the ability of political majorities to form. This creates a power vacuum, which allows the Court to step in and decide the outcome of controversies that normally the political process would resolve.

THE USE OF THE STANDING DOCTRINE AS PROCEDURAL SELF-RESTRAINT

Article III limits the Supreme Court and the federal judiciary to "cases" and "controversies." In federal cases the Supreme Court has the final authority to decide what is a case and controversy. The jurisprudence of "standing" attempts to define the circumstances under which plaintiffs bringing lawsuits have "standing" to sue, or the right to take them to court. Multiple cases have addressed the standing issue and attempted to develop consistent and understandable precedents defining standing.

In a nutshell, to have standing a plaintiff must be able to demonstrate to the satisfaction of the court individual injury to a legally protected right or interest that judicial action can redress. Plaintiffs cannot sue for "third parties" unless the third party is incompetent to sue, as in the case of a minor, *and* the plaintiff has a direct and substantial relationship to the third party.

The standing doctrine protects courts from frivolous lawsuits and from suits that raise hypothetical issues that are not ripe for judicial review. Strict standing requirements limit judicial actions to cases that involve real and substantial contested party interests.

The standing doctrine is subjective, and can be used to exercise judicial self-restraint *or* activism. Supreme Court justices can and often do disagree sharply on what constitutes standing to sue. Standing cannot and does not have a dictionary definition. In controversial cases standing is highly subjective as activist justices readily find that plaintiffs meet standing requirements while justices who desire judicial self-restraint find that the plaintiffs do not have standing. Justices use standing as a way to either take or refuse a case depending upon whether or not they want to rule on it.

JUDICIAL DECISION MAKING

Judicial decision making is not quasi-scientific, always based clearly upon legal principles and precedent, with the judges set apart from the political process. The interpretation of law, whether constitutional or statutory, involves a large amount of discretion. The majority of the Court can always read its opinion into law if it so chooses.

Justice William J. Brennan, Jr., who served on the Supreme Court for 33 years (1956–1990), discusses in the following reading the general role of the Court and the procedures it follows in decision making. The particulars of these procedures change over time, but the overall framework remains.

67

HOW THE SUPREME COURT ARRIVES AT DECISIONS

William J. Brennan, Jr.

Throughout its history the Supreme Court has been called upon to face many of the dominant social, political, economic and even philosophical issues that confront the nation. But Solicitor General Cox only recently reminded us that this does not mean that the Court is charged with making social, political, economic or philosophical decisions.

Quite the contrary, the Court is not a council of Platonic guardians for deciding our most difficult and emotional questions according to the Justices' own notions of what is just or wise or politic. To the extent that this is a government function at all, it is the function of the people's elected representatives.

The Justices are charged with deciding according to law. Because the issues arise in the framework of concrete litigation they must be decided on facts embalmed in a record made by some lower court or administrative agency. And while the Justices may and do consult history and the other disciplines as aids to constitutional decisions, the text of the Constitution and relevant precedents dealing with that text are their primary tools.

It is indeed true, as Judge Learned Hand once said, that the judge's authority depends upon the assumption that he speaks with the mouth of others: the momentum of his utterances must be greater than any which his personal reputation and character can command; if it is to do the work assigned to it—if it is to stand against the passionate resentments arising out of the interests he must frustrate—he must preserve his authority by cloaking himself in the majesty of an over-shadowing past, but he must discover some composition with the dominant trends of his times.

Answers Unclear

However, we must keep in mind that, while the words of the Constitution are binding, their application to specific problems is not often easy. The Founding Fathers knew better than to pin down their descendants too closely.

Enduring principles rather than petty details were what they sought.

Thus the Constitution does not take the form of a litany of specifics. There are, therefore, very few cases where the constitutional answers are clear, all one way or all the other, and this is also true of the current cases raising conflicts between the individual and governmental power—an area increasingly requiring the Court's attention.

Ultimately, of course, the Court must resolve the conflicts of competing interests in these cases, but all Americans should keep in mind how intense and troubling these conflicts can be.

Where one man claims a right to speak and the other man claims the right to be protected from abusive or dangerously provocative remarks the conflict is inescapable.

Where the police have ample external evidence of a man's guilt, but to be sure of their case put into evidence a confession obtained through coercion, the conflict arises between his right to a fair prosecution and society's right to protection against his depravity.

Where the orthodox Jew wishes to open his shop and do business on the day which non-Jews have chosen, and the Legislature has sanctioned, as a day of rest, the Court cannot escape a difficult problem of reconciling opposed interests.

Finally, the claims of the Negro citizen, to borrow Solicitor General Cox's words, present a "conflict between the ideal of liberty and equality expressed in the Declaration of Independence, on the one hand, and, on the other hand, a way of life rooted in the customs of many of our people."

Society Is Disturbed

If all segments of our society can be made to appreciate that there are such conflicts, and that cases which involve constitutional rights often require difficult choices, if this alone is accomplished, we will have immeasurably enriched our common understanding of the meaning and significance of our freedoms. And we will have a better appreciation of the Court's function and its difficulties.

How conflicts such as these ought to be resolved constantly troubles our whole society. There should be no surprise, then, that how properly to resolve them often produces sharp division within the Court itself. When problems are so fundamental, the claims of the competing interests are often nicely balanced, and close divisions are almost inevitable.

Supreme Court cases are usually one of three kinds: the "original" action brought directly in the Court by one state against another state or states, or between a state or states and the federal government. Only a handful of such cases arise each year, but they are an important handful.

A recent example was the contest between Arizona and California over the waters of the lower basin of the Colorado River. Another was the contest between the federal government and the newest state of Hawaii over the ownership of lands in Hawaii.

The second kind of case seeks review of the decisions of a federal Court of Appeals—there are eleven such courts—or of a decision of a federal District Court—there is a federal District Court in each of the fifty states.

The third kind of case comes from a state court—the Court may review a state court judgment by the highest court of any of the fifty states, if the judgment rests on the decision of a federal question.

When I came to the Court seven years ago the aggregate of the cases in the three classes was 1,600. In the term just completed there were 2,800, an increase of 75 percent in seven years. Obviously, the volume will have doubled before I complete ten years of service.

How is it possible to manage such a huge volume of cases? The answer is that we have the authority to screen them and select for argument and decision only those which, in our judgment, guided by pertinent criteria, raise the most important and far-reaching questions. By that device we select annually around 6 percent—between 150 and 170 cases—for decision.

Petition and Response

That screening process works like this: when nine Justices sit, it takes five to decide a case on the merits. But it takes only the votes of four of the nine to put a case on the argument calendar for argument and decision. Those four voters are hard to come by—only an exceptional case raising a significant federal question commands them.

Each application for review is usually in the form of a short petition, attached to which are any opinions of the lower courts in the case. The adversary may file a response—also, in practice usually short. Both the petition and response identify the federal questions allegedly involved, argue their substantiality, and whether they were properly raised in the lower courts.

Each Justice receives copies of the petition and response and such parts of the record as the parties may submit. Each Justice then, without any consultation at this stage with the others, reaches his own tentative conclusion whether the application should be granted or denied.

The first consultation about the case comes at the Court conference at which the case is listed on the agenda for discussion. We sit in conference almost every Friday during the term. Conferences begin at ten in the morning and often continue until six, except for a half-hour recess for lunch.

Only the Justices are present. There are no law clerks, no stenographers, no secretaries, no pages—just the nine of us. The junior Justice acts as guardian of the door, receiving and delivering any messages that come in or go from the conference.

Order of Seating

The conference room is a beautifully oak-paneled chamber with one side lined with books from floor to ceiling. Over the mantel of the exquisite marble fireplace at one end hangs the only adornment in the chamber—a portrait of Chief Justice John Marshall. In the middle of the room stands a rectangular table, not too large but large enough for the nine of us comfortably to gather around it.

The Chief Justice sits at the south end and Mr. Justice Black, the senior Associate Justice, at the north end. Along the side to the left of the Chief Justice sit Justices Stewart, Goldberg, White and Harlan. On the right side sit Justice Clark, myself and Justice Douglas in that order.

We are summoned to conference by a buzzer which rings in our several chambers five minutes before the hour. Upon entering the conference room each of us shakes hands with his colleagues. The handshake tradition originated when Chief Justice Fuller presided many decades ago. It is a symbol that harmony of aims if not of views is the Court's guiding principle.

Each of us has his copy of the agenda of the day's cases before him. The agenda lists the cases applying for review. Each of us before coming to the conference has noted on his copy his tentative view whether or not review should be granted in each case.

The Chief Justice begins the discussion of each case. He then yields to the senior Associate Justice and discussion proceeds down the line in order of seniority until each Justice has spoken.

Voting goes the other way. The junior Justice votes first and voting then proceeds up the line to the Chief Justice, who votes last.

Each of us has a docket containing a sheet for each case with appropriate places for recording the votes. When any case receives four votes for review, that case is transferred to the oral argument list. Applications in which none of us sees merits may be passed over without discussion.

Now how do we process the decisions we agree to review?

There are rare occasions when the question is so clearly controlled by an earlier decision of the Court that a reversal of the lower court judgment is inevitable. In these rare instances we may summarily reverse without oral argument.

Each Side Gets Hour

The case must very clearly justify summary disposition, however, because our ordinary practice is not to reverse a decision without oral argument. Indeed, oral argument of cases taken for review, whether from the state or federal courts, is the usual practice. We rarely accept submissions of cases on briefs.

Oral argument ordinarily occurs about four months after the application for review is granted. Each party is usually allowed one hour, but in recent years we have limited oral argument to a half-hour in cases thought to involve issues not requiring longer arguments.

Counsel submit their briefs and record in sufficient time for the distribution of one set to each Justice two or three weeks before the oral argument. Most of the members of the present Court follow the practice of reading the briefs before the argument. Some of us often have a bench memorandum prepared before the argument. This memorandum digests the facts and the arguments of both sides, highlighting the matters about which we may want to question counsel at the argument.

Often I have independent research done in advance of argument and incorporate the results in the bench memorandum.

We follow a schedule of two weeks of argument from Monday through Thursday, followed by two weeks of recess for opinion writing and the study of petitions for review. The argued cases are listed on the conference agenda on the Friday following argument. Conference discussions follow the same procedure I have described for the discussions of *certiorari* petitions.

Opinion Assigned

Of course, it is much more extended. Not infrequently discussion of particular cases may be spread over two or more conferences.

Not until the discussion is completed and a vote taken is the opinion assigned. The assignment is not made at the conference but formally in writing some few days after the conference.

The Chief Justice assigns the opinions in those cases in which he has voted with the majority. The senior Associate Justice voting with the majority assigns the opinion in the other cases. The dissenters agree among themselves who shall write the dissenting opinion. Of course, each Justice is free to write his own opinion, concurring or dissenting.

The writing of an opinion always takes weeks and sometimes months. The most painstaking research and care are involved.

Research, of course, concentrates on relevant legal materials—precedents particularly. But Supreme Court cases often require some familiarity with history, economics, the social and other sciences, and authorities in these areas, too, are consulted when necessary.

When the author of an opinion feels he has an unanswerable document he sends it to a print shop, which we maintain in our building. The printed draft may be revised several times before his proposed opinion is circulated among the other Justices. Copies are sent to each member of the Court, those in the dissent as well as those in the majority.

Some Change Minds

Now the author often discovers that his work has only begun. He receives a return, ordinarily in writing, from each Justice who voted with him and sometimes also from the Justices who voted the other way. He learns who will write the dissent if one is to be written. But his particular concern is whether those who voted with him are still of his view and what they have to say about his proposed opinion.

Often some who voted with him at conference will advise that they reserve final judgment pending the circulation of the dissent. It is a common experience that dissents change votes, even enough votes to become the majority.

I have had to convert more than one of my proposed majority opinions into a dissent before the final decision was announced. I have also, however, had the more satisfying experience of rewriting a dissent as a majority opinion for the Court.

Before everyone has finally made up his mind a constant interchange by memoranda, by telephone, at the lunch table continues while we hammer out the final form of the opinion. I had one case during the past term in which I circulated ten printed drafts before one was approved as the Court opinion.

Uniform Rule

The point of this procedure is that each Justice, unless he disqualifies himself in a particular case, passes on every piece of business coming to the Court. The Court does not function by means of committees or panels. Each Justice passes on each petition, each time, no matter how drawn, in long hand, by typewriter, or on a press. Our Constitution vests the judicial power in only one Supreme Court. This does not permit Supreme Court action by committees, panels, or sections.

The method that the Justices use in meeting an enormous caseload varies. There is one uniform rule: Judging is not delegated. Each Justice studies each case in sufficient detail to resolve the question for himself. In a very real sense, each decision is an individual decision of every Justice.

The process can be a lonely, troubling experience for fallible human beings conscious that their best may not be adequate to the challenge.

"We are not unaware," the late Justice Jackson said, "that we are not final because we are infallible; we know that we are infallible only because we are final."

One does not forget how much may depend on his decision. He knows that usually more than the litigants may be affected, that the course of vital social, economic and political currents may be directed.

This then is the decisional process in the Supreme Court. It is not without its tensions, of course—indeed, quite agonizing tensions at times.

I would particularly emphasize that, unlike the case of a Congressional or White House decision, Americans demand of their Supreme Court judges that they produce a written opinion, the collective expression of the judges subscribing to it, setting forth the reason which led them to the decision.

These opinions are the exposition, not just to lawyers, legal scholars and other judges, but to our whole society, of the bases upon which a particular result rests—why a problem, looked at as disinterestedly and dispassionately as nine human beings trained in a tradition of the disinterested and dispassionate approach can look at it, is answered as it is.

It is inevitable, however, that Supreme Court decisions—and the Justices themselves—should be caught up in public debate and be the subjects of bitter controversy.

An editorial in *The Washington Post* did not miss the mark by much in saying that this was so because

> one of the primary functions of the Supreme Court is to keep the people of the country from doing what they would like to do—at times when what they would like to do runs counter to the Constitution. . . . The function of the Supreme Court is not to count constituents; it is to interpret a fundamental charter which imposes restraints on constituents. Independence and integrity, not popularity, must be its standards.

Freund's View

Certainly controversy over its work has attended the Court throughout its history. As Professor Paul A. Freund of Harvard remarked, this has been true almost since the Court's first decision:

> When the Court held, in 1793, that the state of Georgia could be sued on a contract in the federal courts, the outraged Assembly of that state passed a bill declaring that any federal marshal who should try to collect the judgment would be guilty of a felony and would suffer death, without benefit of clergy, by being hanged. When the Court decided that state criminal convictions could be reviewed in the Supreme Court, Chief Justice Roane of Virginia exploded, calling it a "most monstrous and unexampled decision. It can only be accounted for by that love of power which history informs us infects and corrupts all who possess it, and from which even the eminent and upright judges are not exempt."

But public understanding has not always been lacking in the past. Perhaps it exists today. But surely a more informed knowledge of the decisional process should aid a better understanding.

It is not agreement with the court's decisions that I urge. Our law is the richer and the wiser because academic and informed lay criticism is part of the stream of development.

Consensus Needed

It is only a greater awareness of the nature and limits of the Supreme Court's function that I seek.

The ultimate resolution of questions fundamental to the whole community must be based on a common consensus of understanding of the unique responsibility assigned to the Supreme Court in our society.

The lack of that understanding led Mr. Justice Holmes to say fifty years ago:

> We are very quiet there, but it is the quiet of a storm center, as we all know. Science has taught the world skepticism and has made it legitimate to put everything to the test of proof. Many beautiful and noble reverences are impaired, but in these days no one can complain if any institution, system, or belief is called on to justify its continuance in life. Of course we are not excepted and have not escaped.

Painful Accusation

Doubts are expressed that go to our very being. Not only are we told that when Marshall pronounced an Act of Congress unconstitutional he usurped a power that the Constitution did not give, but we are told that we are the representatives of a class—a tool of the money power.

I get letters, not always anonymous, intimating that we are corrupt. Well, gentlemen, I admit that it makes my heart ache. It is very painful, when one spends all the energies of one's soul in trying to do good work, with no thought but that of solving a problem according to the rules by which one is bound, to know that many see sinister motives and would be glad of evidence that one was consciously bad.

But we must take such things philosophically and try to see what we can learn from hatred and distrust and whether behind them there may not be a germ of inarticulate truth. The attacks upon the Court are merely an expression of the unrest that seems to wonder vaguely whether law and order pay. When the ignorant are taught to doubt they do not know what they safely may believe. And it seems to me that at this time we need education in the obvious more than investigation of the obscure.

INTERPRETING THE CONSTITUTION

Justice William J. Brennan, Jr., in his discussion of how the Supreme Court arrives at decisions in the preceding selection, points out that inevitably Supreme Court decisions and the justices are the subjects of public debate and often bitter controversy. It is not surprising that when Supreme Court justices and lower-court judges as well follow the early dictum of Chief Justice John Marshall, which he stated in *Marbury v. Madison* in 1803, that "It is emphatically the province and duty of the judicial department to say what the law is," they will become the center of political storms stirred up by those who feel the Court has overstepped its bounds.

While the Supreme Court may not enter unequal political combat, as John Roche contends in selection 66, it has made many highly controversial decisions since Roche wrote his article in 1955. One conservative law scholar has gone so far as to state, "In the years since *Brown v. Board of Education* (1954) nearly every fundamental change in domestic social policy has been brought about not by the decentralized democratic (or, more accurately, republican) process contemplated by the Constitution, but simply by the Court's decree."*

Conservatives, clearly unhappy with the trend in Supreme Court decision making not only during the Warren era (1953–1969) but also under the chief justiceship of Warren Burger (1969–1986), charged that the Court's "loose" constitutional interpretations have been contrary to the wishes of the majority of the people and have made a mockery of the Constitution itself. Responding to their conservative constituencies, Republican presidential candidates Richard M. Nixon in 1968, Ronald Reagan in 1980, and George W. Bush in 2000, promised to take action to reverse the Supreme Court's alleged liberalism by appointing conservative justices.

Ironically, one of Nixon's appointees, Harry Blackmun, authored the Court's controversial abortion decision in 1973 (see selection 28). Another Nixon appointee, Lewis Powell, joined the more liberal justices in the *Bakke* case to allow universities and the colleges to take race into account in their admissions processes, a tacit although far from direct support for the affirmative action programs conservatives so strongly opposed. Nixon found, as had Dwight D. Eisenhower, who appointed Earl Warren to be chief justice in 1953, that presidents have no control over their appointees once they are on the Court.

For his part in the conservative cause, President Ronald Reagan, while choosing Sandra Day O'Connor as the first woman Supreme Court justice, tried to make certain beforehand that she would support conservative positions on such issues as abortion. Reagan added three conservative Supreme Court justices and had an even greater impact upon the lower federal judiciary, which he "stacked" with conservative judges. President George W. Bush's appointments of Chief Justice John Roberts in 2005, and Samuel Alito in 2006, both conservatives, promise a new conservative tone on the Court.

Debate over the role of the Supreme Court intensified during Reagan's second term. His attorney general, Edwin Meese, in a speech given before the American Bar Association, attacked the Supreme Court for interpreting the Constitution according to its own values rather than the intent of the Founding Fathers. In response, Associate Justice William J. Brennan, speaking to a Georgetown University audience, called the attorney general "arrogant" and "doctrinaire," stating that it is impossible to "gauge accurately the intent of the framers on the application of principle to specific, contemporary questions." Another Supreme Court justice, John Paul Stevens, joined the attack on Meese.

The arguments in the 1980s over the proper role of the Supreme Court recalled the debate in the early days of the Republic between proponents of "strict" construction of the Constitution on the one hand and "loose" construction on the other. No less an intellectual and political giant than Thomas Jefferson favored the former approach, arguing that judges should not interpret the Constitution to reflect their own political values. He particularly opposed Chief Justice John Marshall's "loose" construction of congressional authority under Article I and the Implied Powers Clause, which supported an expansion of national power over the states. Prior to Marshall's historic decisions in *McCulloch v. Maryland* (1819)

---

*Compiler's note: Lino A. Graglia, "How the Constitution Disappeared," *Commentary*, February 1986, p. 19.

and *Gibbons v. Ogden (1824),* which flexibly interpreted the Constitution to support broad congressional powers over the states (see selections 12–13), Alexander Hamilton had provided the rationale for loose construction in *The Federalist.* He suggested that Congress should be able to carry out its enumerated powers by whatever means it considered to be necessary and proper.

An old adage states that where one stands on political issues depends upon whose ox is being gored. Liberal supporters of Franklin D. Roosevelt attacked the conservative Supreme Court during the early New Deal when it was systematically declaring the core of FDR's program to be unconstitutional. After his overwhelming 1936 electoral victory Roosevelt attempted to "pack" the Court by seeking congressional approval of legislation that would give him the authority to appoint one new justice for each justice over 70 years of age. The legislation would have given him at the time the authority to appoint a Supreme Court majority because there were seven septuagenarian justices on the Court. Conservatives attacked Roosevelt's plan, charging that it was an unconstitutional and even un-American attempt to undermine the Supreme Court's independence. They wanted the Court to continue acting as a superlegislature as long as it advocated conservative views. However, when the tables were turned, and the Court became the advocate of "liberal" views during the Warren era, conservatives were quick to attack it for acting as a superlegislature against the will of the majority, which was the same argument liberals had used against the Court in the 1930s.

THE CONTEMPORARY DEBATE OVER CONSTITUTIONAL INTERPRETATION

Debate over constitutional interpretation arises because the Constitution itself is, in the words of Chief Justice John Marshall in *McCulloch v. Maryland,* one of enumerated, not defined, powers. "A Constitution," Marshall wrote, "to contain an accurate detail of all the subdivisions of which its great powers will admit, and of all the means of which they may be carried into execution, would partake of the prolixity of a legal code, and could scarcely be embraced by the human mind. It would probably never be understood by the public. Its nature, therefore, requires, that only its great outlines should be marked. . . ."

Ultimately, the Supreme Court defines the Constitution. Ironically, the Supreme Court's authority to be the final arbiter of constitutional issues is nowhere explicitly defined in the Constitution. But, as previous selections have pointed out, eighteenth-century American jurisprudence and political philosophy supported the concept of a higher law and the authority of courts to apply it to legislative actions.

In the following selections, excerpted from the abortion case, *Planned Parenthood of Southeastern Pennsylvania v. Casey* (1992), Supreme Court justices give contrasting opinions on how the Court should interpret the Constitution and its own constitutional precedents. The justices address the question of whether or not the original abortion decision, *Roe v. Wade* (1973), should be modified or overruled. The constitutional provision being interpreted is the "liberty" of the Due Process Clause of the Fourteenth Amendment. As the different justices grapple with the question of how liberty should be defined in the Constitution, students will become aware of the highly subjective character of constitutional interpretation.

68

CONSTITUTIONAL LIBERTY AND THE RIGHT TO ABORTION

Justice Sandra Day O'Connor

I

Liberty finds no refuge in a jurisprudence of doubt. Yet 19 years after our holding that the Constitution protects a woman's right to terminate her pregnancy in its early stages, *Roe v. Wade*, that definition of liberty is still questioned. Joining the respondents as *amicus curiae*, the United States, as it has done in five other cases in the last decade, again asks us to overrule *Roe*.

At issue in these cases are five provisions of the Pennsylvania Abortion Control Act of 1982 as amended in 1988 and 1989. . . . The Act requires that a woman seeking an abortion give her informed consent prior to the abortion procedure, and specifies that she be provided with certain information at least 24 hours before the abortion is performed. For a minor to obtain an abortion, the Act requires the informed consent of one of her parents, but provides for a judicial bypass option if the minor does not wish to or cannot obtain a parent's consent. Another provision of the Act requires that, unless certain exceptions apply, a married woman seeking an abortion must sign a statement indicating that she has notified her husband of her intended abortion. The Act exempts compliance with these three requirements in the event of a "medical emergency," which is defined in § 3203 of the Act. In addition to the above provisions regulating the performance of abortions, the Act imposes certain reporting requirements on facilities that provide abortion services. . . .

After considering the fundamental constitutional questions resolved by *Roe*, principles of institutional integrity, and the rule of *stare decisis*, we are led to conclude this: the essential holding of *Roe v. Wade* should be retained and once again reaffirmed.

It must be stated at the outset and with clarity that *Roe*'s essential holding, the holding we reaffirm, has three parts. First is a recognition of the right of the woman to choose to have an abortion before viability and to obtain it without undue interference from the State. Before viability, the State's interests are not strong enough to support a prohibition of abortion or the imposition of a substantial obstacle to the woman's effective right to elect the procedure. Second is a confirmation of the

State's power to restrict abortions after fetal viability, if the law contains exceptions for pregnancies which endanger a woman's life or health. And third is the principle that the State has legitimate interests from the outset of the pregnancy in protecting the health of the woman and the life of the fetus that may become a child. These principles do not contradict one another; and we adhere to each.

II

Constitutional protection of the woman's decision to terminate her pregnancy derives from the Due Process Clause of the Fourteenth Amendment. It declares that no State shall "deprive any person of life, liberty, or property, without due process of law." The controlling word in the case before us is "liberty." Although a literal reading of the Clause might suggest that it governs only the procedures by which a State may deprive persons of liberty, for at least 105 years. . . the Clause has been understood to contain a substantive component as well, one "barring certain government actions regardless of the fairness of the procedures used to implement them.". . . "[T]he guaranties of due process, though having their roots in Magna Carta's '*per legem terrae*' and considered as procedural safeguards 'against executive usurpation and tyranny,' have in this country 'become bulwarks also against arbitrary legislation.'". . .

The most familiar of the substantive liberties protected by the Fourteenth Amendment are those recognized by the Bill of Rights. We have held that the Due Process Clause of the Fourteenth Amendment incorporates most of the Bill of Rights against the States. It is tempting, as a means of curbing the discretion of federal judges, to suppose that liberty encompasses no more than those rights already guaranteed to the individual against federal interference by the express provisions of the first eight amendments to the Constitution. But of course this Court has never accepted that view.

It is also tempting, for the same reason, to suppose that the Due Process Clause protects only those practices, defined at the most specific level, that were protected against government interference by other rules of law when the Fourteenth Amendment was ratified. . . . But such a view would be inconsistent with our law. It is a premise of the Constitution that there is a realm of personal liberty which the government may not enter. We have vindicated this principle before. Marriage is mentioned nowhere in the Bill of Rights and interracial marriage was illegal in most States in the 19th century, but the Court was no doubt correct in finding it to be an aspect of liberty protected against state interference by the substantive component of the Due Process Clause in *Loving*.. . .

Neither the Bill of Rights nor the specific practices of States at the time of the adoption of the Fourteenth Amendment marks the outer limits of the substantive sphere of liberty which the Fourteenth Amendment protects. See U.S. Const., Amend. 9. As the second Justice Harlan recognized in [*Poe v. Ullman*]:

> [T]he full scope of the liberty guaranteed by the Due Process Clause cannot be found in or limited by the precise terms of the specific guarantees elsewhere

> provided in the Constitution. This 'liberty' is not a series of isolated points pricked out in terms of the taking of property; the freedom of speech, press, and religion; the right to keep and bear arms; the freedom from unreasonable searches and seizures; and so on. It is a rational continuum which, broadly speaking, includes a freedom from all substantial arbitrary impositions and purposeless restraints,. . . and which also recognizes, what a reasonable and sensitive judgment must, that certain interests require particularly careful scrutiny of the state needs asserted to justify their abridgment. . . .

The inescapable fact is that adjudication of substantive due process claims may call upon the Court in interpreting the Constitution to exercise that same capacity which by tradition courts always have exercised: reasoned judgment. Its boundaries are not susceptible of expression as a simple rule. That does not mean we are free to invalidate state policy choices with which we disagree; yet neither does it permit us to shrink from the duties of our office. . . .

Men and women of good conscience can disagree, and we suppose some always shall disagree, about the profound moral and spiritual implications of terminating a pregnancy, even in its earliest stage. Some of us as individuals find abortion offensive to our most basic principles of morality, but that cannot control our decision. Our obligation is to define the liberty of all, not to mandate our own moral code. . . .

It was . . . personal liberty that *Roe* sought to protect. . . .

While we appreciate the weight of the arguments made on behalf of the State in the case before us, arguments which in their ultimate formulation conclude that *Roe* should be overruled, the reservations any of us may have in reaffirming the central holding of *Roe* are outweighed by the explication of individual liberty we have given combined with the force of *stare decisis*. We turn now to that doctrine.

III

The obligation to follow precedent begins with necessity, and a contrary necessity marks its outer limit. With Cardozo, we recognize that no judicial system could do society's work if it eyed each issue afresh in every case that raised it. Indeed, the very concept of the rule of law underlying our own Constitution requires such continuity over time that a respect for precedent is, by definition, indispensable. At the other extreme, a different necessity would make itself felt if a prior judicial ruling should come to be seen so clearly as error that its enforcement was for that very reason doomed. . . .

So in this case we may inquire whether *Roe*'s central rule has been found unworkable; whether the rule's limitation on state power could be removed without serious inequity to those who have relied upon it or significant damage to the stability of the society governed by the rule in question; whether the law's growth in the intervening years has left *Roe*'s central rule a doctrinal anachronism discounted by society; and whether *Roe*'s premises of fact have so far changed in the ensuing two decades as to render its central holding somehow irrelevant or unjustifiable in dealing with the issue it addressed. . . .

The sum of the precedential inquiry to this point shows *Roe*'s underpinnings unweakened in any way affecting its central holding. While it has engendered disapproval, it has not been unworkable. An entire generation has come of age free to assume *Roe*'s concept of liberty in defining the capacity of women to act in society, and to make reproductive decisions; no erosion of principle going to liberty or personal autonomy has left *Roe*'s central holding a doctrinal remnant; *Roe* portends no developments at odds with other precedent for the analysis of personal liberty; and no changes of fact have rendered viability more or less appropriate as the point at which the balance of interests tips. Within the bounds of normal *stare decisis* analysis, then, and subject to the considerations on which it customarily turns, the stronger argument is for affirming *Roe*'s central holding, with whatever degree of personal reluctance any of us may have, not for overruling it.

In a less significant case, *stare decisis* analysis could, and would, stop at the point we have reached. But the sustained and widespread debate *Roe* has provoked calls for some comparison between that case and others of comparable dimension that have responded to national controversies and taken on the impress of the controversies addressed. Only two such decisional lines from the past century present themselves for examination, and in each instance the result reached by the Court accorded with the principles we apply today.

The first example is that line of cases identified with *Lochner v. New York*, which imposed substantive limitations on legislation limiting economic autonomy in favor of health and welfare regulation, adopting, in Justice Holmes' view, the theory of *laissez-faire*. *Id.* (Holmes, J., dissenting). The *Lochner* decisions were exemplified by *Adkins v. Children's Hospital of D.C.*, 261 U.S. 525 (1923), in which this Court held it to be an infringement of constitutionally protected liberty of contract to require the employers of adult women to satisfy minimum wage standards. Fourteen years later, *West Coast Hotel Co. v. Parrish* signalled the demise of *Lochner* by overruling *Adkins*. In the meantime, the Depression had come and, with it, the lesson that seemed unmistakable to most people by 1937, that the interpretation of contractual freedom protected in *Adkins* rested on fundamentally false factual assumptions about the capacity of a relatively unregulated market to satisfy minimal levels of human welfare. As Justice Jackson wrote of the constitutional crisis of 1937 shortly before he came on the bench, "The older world of *laissez-faire* was recognized everywhere outside the Court to be dead." The facts upon which the earlier case had premised a constitutional resolution of social controversy had proved to be untrue, and history's demonstration of their untruth not only justified but required the new choice of constitutional principle that *West Coast Hotel* announced. Of course, it was true that the Court lost something by its misperception, or its lack of prescience, and the Court-packing crisis only magnified the loss; but the clear demonstration that the facts of economic life were different from those previously assumed warranted the repudiation of the old law.

The second comparison that 20th century history invites is with the cases employing the separate-but-equal rule for applying the Fourteenth Amendment's equal protection guarantee. They began with *Plessy v. Ferguson*, holding that legislatively mandated racial segregation in public transportation works no denial of equal protection, rejecting the argument that racial separation enforced by the legal machinery of American society treats the black race as inferior. . . . As one commentator observed, the question before the Court in *Brown* was "whether discrimination inheres in that segregation which is imposed by law in the twentieth century in certain specific states in the American Union. And that question has meaning and can find an answer only on the ground of history and of common knowledge about the facts of life in the times and places aforesaid."

The Court in *Brown* addressed these facts of life by observing that whatever may have been the understanding in *Plessy*'s time of the power of segregation to stigmatize those who were segregated with a "badge of inferiority," it was clear by 1954 that legally sanctioned segregation had just such an effect, to the point that racially separate public educational facilities were deemed inherently unequal. Society's understanding of the facts upon which a constitutional ruling was sought in 1954 was thus fundamentally different from the basis claimed for the decision in 1896. While we think *Plessy* was wrong the day it was decided, see *Plessy* (Harlan, J., dissenting), we must also recognize that the *Plessy* Court's explanation for its decision was so clearly at odds with the facts apparent to the Court in 1954 that the decision to reexamine *Plessy* was on this ground alone not only justified but required.

West Coast Hotel and *Brown* each rested on facts, or an understanding of facts, changed from those which furnished the claimed justifications for the earlier constitutional resolutions. Each case was comprehensible as the Court's response to facts that the country could understand, or had come to understand already, but which the Court of an earlier day, as its own declarations disclosed, had not been able to perceive. As the decisions were thus comprehensible they were also defensible, not merely as the victories of one doctrinal school over another by dint of numbers (victories though they were), but as applications of constitutional principle to facts as they had not been seen by the Court before. In constitutional adjudication as elsewhere in life, changed circumstances may impose new obligations, and the thoughtful part of the Nation could accept each decision to overrule a prior case as a response to the Court's constitutional duty. . . .

VI

Our Constitution is a covenant running from the first generation of Americans to us and then to future generations. It is a coherent succession. Each generation must learn anew that the Constitution's written terms embody ideas and aspirations that must survive more ages than one. We accept our responsibility not to retreat from interpreting the full meaning of the covenant in light of all of our precedents. We invoke it once again to define the freedom guaranteed by the Constitution's own promise, the promise of liberty.

69

LIBERTY, PRIVACY, AND THE RIGHT TO ABORTION

Chief Justice William H. Rehnquist

. . . We have held that a liberty interest protected under the Due Process Clause of the Fourteenth Amendment will be deemed fundamental if it is "implicit in the concept of ordered liberty." *Palko v. Connecticut*. . . .

In construing the phrase "liberty" incorporated in the Due Process Clause of the Fourteenth Amendment, we have recognized that its meaning extends beyond freedom from physical restraint. . . .

In *Roe v. Wade*, the Court recognized a "guarantee of personal privacy" which "is broad enough to encompass a woman's decision whether or not to terminate her pregnancy." We are now of the view that, in terming this right fundamental, the Court in *Roe* read the earlier opinions upon which it based its decision much too broadly. Unlike marriage, procreation and contraception, abortion "involves the purposeful termination of potential life." The abortion decision must therefore "be recognized as *sui generis*, different in kind from the others that the Court has protected under the rubric of personal or family privacy and autonomy." One cannot ignore the fact that a woman is not isolated in her pregnancy, and that the decision to abort necessarily involves the destruction of a fetus.

Nor do the historical traditions of the American people support the view that the right to terminate one's pregnancy is "fundamental." The common law which we inherited from England made abortion after "quickening" an offense. At the time of the adoption of the Fourteenth Amendment, statutory prohibitions or restrictions on abortion were commonplace; in 1868, at least 28 of the then-37 States and 8 Territories had statutes banning or limiting abortion. By the turn of the century virtually every State had a law prohibiting or restricting abortion on its books. By the middle of the present century, a liberalization trend had set in. But 21 of the restrictive abortion laws in effect in 1868 were still in effect in 1973 when *Roe* was decided, and an overwhelming majority of the States prohibited abortion unless necessary to preserve the life or health of the mother. On this record, it can scarcely be said that any deeply rooted tradition of relatively unrestricted abortion in our history supported the classification of the right to abortion as "fundamental" under the Due Process Clause of the Fourteenth Amendment. . . .

70

LIBERTY AND ABORTION: A STRICT CONSTRUCTIONIST'S VIEW

Justice Antonin Scalia

. . . Laws against bigamy. . . which entire societies of reasonable people disagree with—intrude upon men and women's liberty to marry and live with one another. But bigamy happens not to be a liberty specially "protected" by the Constitution.

That is, quite simply, the issue in this case: not whether the power of a woman to abort her unborn child is a "liberty" in the absolute sense; or even whether it is a liberty of great importance to many women. Of course it is both. The issue is whether it is a liberty protected by the Constitution of the United States. I am sure it is not. I reach that conclusion not because of anything so exalted as my views concerning the "concept of existence, of meaning, of the universe, and of the mystery of human life." Rather, I reach it for the same reason I reach the conclusion that bigamy is not constitutionally protected—because of two simple facts: (1) the Constitution says absolutely nothing about it, and (2) the longstanding traditions of American society have permitted it to be legally proscribed. . . .

The emptiness of the "reasoned judgment" that produced *Roe* is displayed in plain view by the fact that, after more than 19 years of effort by some of the brightest (and most determined) legal minds in the country, after more than 10 cases upholding abortion rights in this Court, and after dozens upon dozens of *amicus* briefs submitted in this and other cases, the best the Court can do to explain how it is that the word "liberty" *must* be thought to include the right to destroy human fetuses is to rattle off a collection of adjectives that simply decorate a value judgment and conceal a political choice. The right to abort, we are told, inheres in "liberty" because it is among "a person's most basic decisions," it involves a "most intimate and personal choic[e]," it is "central to personal dignity and autonomy," it "originate[s] within the zone of conscience and belief," it is "too intimate and personal" for state interference, it reflects "intimate views" of a "deep, personal character," it involves "intimate relationships," and notions of "personal autonomy and bodily integrity," and it concerns a particularly "important decisio[n]." But it is obvious to anyone applying "reasoned judgment" that the same adjectives can be applied to many forms of conduct that this Court. . . has held are *not* entitled to constitutional protection—because, like abortion, they are forms of conduct that have long been criminalized in American society. Those adjectives might be applied, for example, to homosexual sodomy, polygamy, adult incest, and suicide, all of which are equally "intimate" and "deep[ly] personal" decisions involving "personal autonomy and bodily integrity," and all of which can constitutionally be proscribed because it is our unquestionable constitutional tradition that they are proscribable. It is not reasoned judgment that supports the Court's decision; only personal predilection. . . .

[W]hether it would "subvert the Court's legitimacy" or not, the notion that we would decide a case differently from the way we otherwise would have in order to show that we can stand firm against public disapproval is frightening. It is a bad enough idea, even in the head of someone like me, who believes that the text of the Constitution, and our traditions, say what they say and there is no fiddling with them. But when it is in the mind of a Court that believes the Constitution has an evolving meaning; that the Ninth Amendment's reference to "othe[r]" rights is not a disclaimer, but a charter for action; and that the function of this Court is to "speak before all others for constitutional ideals" unrestrained by meaningful text or tradition—then the notion that the Court must adhere to a decision for as long as the decision faces "great opposition" and the Court is "under fire" acquires a character of almost czarist arrogance. We are offended by these marchers who descend upon us, every year on the anniversary of *Roe*, to protest our saying that the Constitution requires what our society has never thought the Constitution requires. These people who refuse to be "tested by following" must be taught a lesson. We have no Cossacks, but at least we can stubbornly refuse to abandon an erroneous opinion that we might otherwise change—to show how little they intimidate us. . . .

We should get out of this area, where we have no right to be, and where we do neither ourselves nor the country any good by remaining.

APPENDIX 1

THE DECLARATION OF INDEPENDENCE

In CONGRESS, July 4, 1776,

The unanimous Declaration of the thirteen united States of America

When in the Course of human events it becomes necessary for one people to dissolve the political bonds which have connected them with another, and to assume among the Powers of the earth, the separate and equal station to which the Laws of Nature and of Nature's God entitle them, a decent respect to the opinions of mankind requires that they should declare the causes which impel them to the separation.

We hold these truths to be self-evident, that all men are created equal, that they are endowed by their Creator with certain unalienable Rights, that among these are Life, Liberty and the pursuit of Happiness. That to secure these rights, Governments are instituted among Men, deriving their just powers from the consent of the governed. That whenever any Form of Government becomes destructive of these ends, it is the Right of the People to alter or to abolish it, and to institute new Government, laying its foundation on such principles and organizing its powers in such form, as to them shall seem most likely to effect their Safety and Happiness. Prudence, indeed, will dictate that Governments long established should not be changed for light and transient causes; and accordingly all experience hath shown, that mankind are more disposed to suffer, while evils are sufferable, than to right themselves by abolishing the forms to which they are accustomed. But when a long train of abuses and usurpations, pursuing invariably the same Object evinces a design to reduce them under absolute Despotism, it is their right, it is their duty, to throw off such Government, and to provide new Guards for their future security.—Such has been the patient sufferance of these Colonies; and such is now the necessity which constrains them to alter their former Systems of Government. The history of the present King of Great Britain is a history of repeated

---

Compiler's note: This text retains the spelling, capitalization, and punctuation of the original.

injuries and usurpations, all having in direct object the establishment of an absolute Tyranny over these States. To prove this, let Facts be submitted to a candid world.

He has refused his Assent to Laws, the most wholesome and necessary for the public good.

He has forbidden his Governors to pass Laws of immediate and pressing importance, unless suspended in their operation till his Assent should be obtained; and when so suspended, he has utterly neglected to attend to them.

He has refused to pass other Laws for the accommodation of large districts of people, unless those people would relinquish the right of Representation in the Legislature, a right inestimable to them and formidable to tyrants only.

He has called together legislative bodies at places unusual, uncomfortable, and distant from the depository of their Public Records, for the sole purpose of fatiguing them into compliance with his measures.

He has dissolved Representative Houses repeatedly, for opposing with manly firmness his invasions on the rights of the people.

He has refused for a long time, after such dissolutions, to cause others to be elected; whereby the Legislative powers, incapable of Annihilation, have returned to the People at large for their exercise; the State remaining in the mean time exposed to all the dangers of invasion from without, and convulsions within.

He has endeavored to prevent the population of these States; for that purpose obstructing the Laws for Naturalization of Foreigners; refusing to pass others to encourage their migration hither, and raising the conditions of new Appropriations of Lands.

He has obstructed the Administration of Justice, by refusing his Assent to Laws for establishing Judiciary powers.

He has made Judges dependent on his Will alone, for the tenure of their offices, and the amount and payment of their salaries.

He has erected a multitude of New Offices, and sent hither swarms of Officers to harass our People, and eat out their substance.

He has kept among us, in times of peace, Standing Armies without the Consent of our legislatures.

He has affected to render the Military independent of and superior to the Civil power.

He has combined with others to subject us to a jurisdiction foreign to our constitution, and unacknowledged by our laws; giving his Assent to their Acts of pretended Legislation:

For quartering large bodies of armed troops among us:

For protecting them, by a mock Trial, from Punishment for any Murders which they should commit on the Inhabitants of these States:

For cutting off our Trade with all parts of the world:

For imposing Taxes on us without our Consent:

For depriving us in many cases, of the benefits of Trial by Jury:

For transporting us beyond Seas to be tried for pretended offenses:

For abolishing the free System of English Laws in a neighbouring Province, establishing therein an Arbitrary government, and enlarging its Boundaries so as to render it at once an example and fit instrument for introducing the same absolute rule into these Colonies:

For taking away our Charters, abolishing our most valuable Laws, and altering fundamentally the Forms of our Governments:

For suspending our own Legislatures, and declaring themselves invested with Power to legislate for us in all cases whatsoever.

He has abdicated Government here, by declaring us out of his Protection and waging War against us.

He has plundered our seas, ravaged our Coasts, burnt our towns, and destroyed the Lives of our people.

He is at this time transporting large armies of foreign mercenaries to compleat the works of death, desolation and tyranny, already begun with circumstances of Cruelty & perfidy scarcely paralleled in the most barbarous ages, and totally unworthy the Head of a civilized nation.

He has constrained our fellow Citizens taken Captive on the high Seas to bear Arms against their Country, to become the executioners of their friends and Brethren, or to fall themselves by their Hands.

He has excited domestic insurrections amongst us, and has endeavored to bring on the inhabitants of our frontiers, the merciless Indian Savages, whose known rule of warfare, is an undistinguished destruction of all ages, sexes and conditions.

In every stage of these Oppressions We have Petitioned for Redress in the most humble terms: Our repeated Petitions have been answered only by repeated injury. A Prince, whose character is thus marked by every act which may define a Tyrant, is unfit to be the ruler of a free People.

Nor have We been wanting in attention to our British brethren. We have warned them from time to time of attempts by their legislature to extend an unwarrantable jurisdiction over us. We have reminded them of the circumstances of our emigration and settlement here. We have appealed to their native justice and magnanimity, and we have conjured them by the ties of our common kindred to disavow these usurpations, which, would inevitably interrupt our connections and correspondence. They too have been deaf to the voice of justice and consanguinity. We must, therefore, acquiesce in the necessity, which denounces our Separation, and hold them, as we hold the rest of mankind, Enemies in War, in Peace Friends.

We, therefore, the Representatives of the united States of America, in General Congress, Assembled, appealing to the Supreme Judge of the world for the rectitude of our intentions, do, in the Name, and by Authority of the good People of these Colonies, solemnly publish and declare, That these United Colonies are, and of Right ought to be, Free and Independent States; that they are Absolved from all Allegiance to the British-Crown, and that all political connection between them and the State of Great-Britain, is and ought to be totally dissolved; and that as Free and Independent States, they have full Power to levy War, conclude Peace, contract Alliances, establish Commerce, and to do all other Acts and Things which Independent States may of right do. And for the support of this Declaration, with a firm reliance on the Protection of Divine Providence, we mutually pledge to each other our Lives, our Fortunes, and our sacred Honor.

Signed by Order and in Behalf of the Congress,

John Hancock, President

Attest. Charles Thomson, Secretary

New-Hampshire.

Josiah Bartlett, Matthew Thornton.
W$^{m.}$.Wimple,

Massachusetts-Bay.

Sam$^{l.}$ Adams, Rob$^{t.}$Treat Paine,
John Adams, Elbridge Gerry.

Rhode-Island.

Step. Hopkins, William Ellery.

Connecticut.

Roger Sherman,
Sam'^{El} Huntington,
W^{m}. Williams,
Oliver Wolcott.

New-York.

W$^{m.}$ Floyd,
Phil. Livingston, Lewis Morris.
Fran$^{s.}$ Lewis,

New-Jersey.

Rich$^{d.}$ Stockton,
Jno. Witherspoon,
John Hart,
Abra. Clark.
Fra$^{s.}$ Hopkinson,

Pennsylvania.

Rob$^{t.}$ Morris,
Benjamin Rush,
Benja. Franklin,
John Morton,
Ja$^{s.}$ Smith,
Geo. Taylor,
James Wilson,
Geo. Ross.
Geo. Clymer,

Delaware.

Caesar Rodney,
Geo. Read
Tho. M'kean.

Maryland.

Samuel Chase,
W^{m}. Paca,
Thos. Stone,
Charles Caroll, of Carrollton.

Virginia.

George Wythe,
Richard Henry Lee,
Th. Jefferson,
Thos. Nelson, j^{r}.,
Francis Lightfoot Lee,
Carter Braxton.
Benj^{a}. Harrison,

North-Carolina.

W^{m}. Hooper,
Joseph Hewes,
John Penn.

South-Carolina.

Edward Rutledge,
Thos. Heyward, jun^{r}.,
Thomas Lynch, jun^{r}.,
Arthur Middleton.

Georgia.

Button Gwinnett,
Lyman Hall,
Geo. Walton.

APPENDIX 2

THE CONSTITUTION OF THE UNITED STATES

We, the People of the United States, in Order to form a more perfect Union, establish Justice, insure domestic Tranquility, provide for the common defense, promote the general Welfare, and secure the Blessings of Liberty to ourselves and our Posterity, do ordain and establish this Constitution for the United States of America.

Article I

Section 1.

All legislative Powers herein granted shall be vested in a Congress of the United States, which shall consist of a Senate and House of Representatives.

Section 2.

1. The House of Representatives shall be composed of Members chosen every second Year by the People of the several States, and the Electors in each State shall have the Qualifications requisite for Electors of the most numerous Branch of the State Legislature.
2. No Person shall be a Representative who shall not have attained to the Age of twenty five Years, and been seven Years a Citizen of the United States, and who shall not, when elected, be an Inhabitant of that State in which he shall be chosen.
3. [Representatives and direct Taxes* shall be apportioned among the several States which may be included within this Union, according to their respective Numbers,

Compiler's note: The Sixteenth Amendment replaced this with respect to income taxes.

which shall be determined by adding to the whole Number of free Persons, including those bound to Service for a Term of Years, and excluding Indians not taxed, three fifths of all other Persons.]* The actual Enumeration shall be made within three Years after the first Meeting of the Congress of the United States, and within every subsequent Term of ten years, in such Manner as they shall by Law direct. The Number of Representatives shall not exceed one for every thirty Thousand, but each State shall have at Least one Representative; and until such enumeration shall be made, the State of New-Hampshire shall be entitled to chuse three, Massachusetts eight, Rhode-Island and Providence Plantations one, Connecticut five, New-York six, New-Jersey four, Pennsylvania eight, Delaware one, Maryland six, Virginia ten, North-Carolina five, South-Carolina five, and Georgia three.

4. When vacancies happen in the Representation from any State, the Executive Authority thereof shall issue Writs of Election to fill such Vacancies.
5. The House of Representatives shall choose their Speaker and other Officers; and shall have the sole Power of Impeachment.

Section 3.

1. The Senate of the United States shall be composed of two Senators from each State, [chosen by the Legislature]† thereof, for six Years; and each Senator shall have one Vote.
2. Immediately after they shall be assembled in Consequence of the first Election, they shall be divided as equally as may be into three Classes. The Seats of the Senators of the first Class shall be vacated at the Expiration of the second Year, of the second Class at the Expiration of the fourth Year, and of the third Class at the Expiration of the sixth Year, so that one third may be chosen every second Year; [and if Vacancies happen by Resignation, or otherwise, during the Recess of the Legislature of any State, the Executive thereof may make temporary Appointments until the next Meeting of the Legislature, which shall then fill such Vacancies].‡
3. No person shall be a Senator who shall not have attained to the Age of thirty Years, and been nine Years a Citizen of the United States, and who shall not, when elected, be an Inhabitant of that State for which he shall be chosen.
4. The Vice President of the United States shall be President of the Senate, but shall have no Vote, unless they be equally divided.
5. The Senate shall choose their other Officers, and also a President pro tempore, in the absence of the Vice President, or when he shall exercise the Office of President of the United States.
6. The Senate shall have the sole Power to try all Impeachments. When sitting for that Purpose, they shall be on Oath or Affirmation. When the President of the United States is tried, the Chief Justice shall preside: And no Person shall be convicted without the Concurrence of two thirds of the Members present.
7. Judgment in Cases of Impeachment shall not extend further than to removal from Office, and disqualification to hold and enjoy any Office of honor, Trust or Profit under the United States: but the Party convicted shall nevertheless be liable and subject to Indictment, Trial, Judgment and Punishment, according to Law.

**Compiler's note:* Repealed by the Fourteenth Amendment.

†*Compiler's note:* Repealed by the Seventeenth Amendment, Section 1.

‡*Compiler's note:* Changed by the Seventeenth Amendment.

Section 4.

1. The Times, Places and Manner of holding Elections for Senators and Representatives, shall be prescribed in each State by the Legislature thereof; but the Congress may at any time by Law make or alter such Regulations, except as to the Places of chusing Senators.
2. The Congress shall assemble at least once in every Year, and such Meeting shall [be on the first Monday in December,]* unless they shall by Law appoint a different Day.

Section 5.

1. Each House shall be the Judge of the Elections, Returns and Qualifications of its own Members, and a Majority of each shall constitute a Quorum to do Business; but a smaller number may adjourn from day to day, and may be authorized to compel the Attendance of absent Members, in such Manner, and under such Penalties as each House may provide.
2. Each House may determine the Rules of its Proceedings, punish its Members for disorderly Behaviour, and, with the Concurrence of two thirds, expel a Member.
3. Each House shall keep a Journal of its Proceedings, and from time to time publish the same, excepting such Parts as may in their Judgment require Secrecy; and the Yeas and Nays of the Members of either House on any question shall, at the Desire of one fifth of those Present, be entered on the Journal.
4. Neither House, during the Session of Congress, shall, without the Consent of the other, adjourn for more than three days, nor to any other Place than that in which the two Houses shall be sitting.

Section 6.

1. The Senators and Representatives shall receive a Compensation for their Services, to be ascertained by Law, and paid out of the Treasury of the United States. They shall in all Cases, except Treason, Felony and Breach of the Peace, be privileged from Arrest during their Attendance at the Session of their respective Houses, and in going to and returning from the same; and for any Speech or Debate in either House, they shall not be questioned in any other Place.
2. No Senator or Representative shall, during the Time for which he was elected, be appointed to any civil Office under the Authority of the United States, which shall have been created, or the Emoluments whereof have been increased during such time; and no Person holding any Office under the United States, shall be a Member of either House during his Continuance in Office.

Section 7.

1. All Bills for raising Revenue shall originate in the House of Representatives; but the Senate may propose or concur with Amendments as on other Bills.
2. Every Bill which shall have passed the House of Representatives and the Senate, shall, before it become a Law, be presented to the President of the United States; If he

**Compiler's note:* Changed by the Twentieth Amendment, Section 2.

approve he shall sign it, but if not he shall return it, with his Objections to that House in which it shall have originated, who shall enter the Objections at large on their Journal, and proceed to reconsider it. If after such Reconsideration two thirds of that House shall agree to pass the Bill, it shall be sent, together with the Objections, to the other House, by which it shall likewise be reconsidered, and if approved by two thirds of that House, it shall become a Law. But in all such Cases the Votes of both Houses shall be determined by Yeas and Nays, and the Names of the Persons voting for and against the Bill shall be entered on the Journal of each House respectively. If any Bill shall not be returned by the President within ten Days (Sundays excepted) after it shall have been presented to him, the Same shall be a Law, in like Manner as if he had signed it, unless the Congress by their Adjournment prevent its Return, in which Case it shall not be a Law.

3. Every Order, Resolution, or Vote to which the Concurrence of the Senate and House of Representatives may be necessary (except on a question of Adjournment) shall be presented to the President of the United States; and before the Same shall take Effect, shall be approved by him, or being disapproved by him, shall be repassed by two thirds of the Senate and House of Representatives, according to the Rules and Limitations prescribed in the Case of a Bill.

Section 8.

1. The Congress shall have Power To lay and collect Taxes, Duties, Imposts and Excises, to pay the Debts and provide for the common Defence and general Welfare of the United States; but all Duties, Imposts and Excises shall be uniform throughout the United States;
2. To borrow money on the credit of the United States;
3. To regulate Commerce with foreign Nations, and among the several States, and with the Indian Tribes;
4. To establish an uniform Rule of Naturalization, and uniform Laws on the subject of Bankruptcies throughout the United States;
5. To coin Money, regulate the Value thereof, and of foreign Coin, and fix the Standard of Weights and Measures;
6. To provide for the Punishment of counterfeiting the Securities and current Coin of the United States;
7. To establish Post Offices and post Roads;
8. To promote the Progress of Science and useful Arts, by securing for limited Times to Authors and Inventors the exclusive Right to their respective Writings and Discoveries;
9. To constitute Tribunals inferior to the supreme Court;
10. To define and punish Piracies and Felonies committed on the high Seas, and Offences against the Law of Nations;
11. To declare War, grant Letters of Marque and Reprisal, and make Rules concerning Captures on Land and Water;
12. To raise and support Armies, but no Appropriation of Money to that Use shall be for a longer Term than two Years;
13. To provide and maintain a Navy;
14. To make rules for the Government and Regulation of the land and naval Forces;
15. To provide for calling forth the Militia to execute the Laws of the Union, suppress Insurrections and repel Invasions;
16. To provide for organizing, arming, and disciplining the Militia, and for governing such Part of them as may be employed in the Service of the United States, reserving to the

States respectively, the Appointment of the Officers, and the Authority of training the Militia according to the discipline prescribed by Congress;

17. To exercise exclusive Legislation in all Cases whatsoever, over such District (not exceeding ten Miles square) as may, by Cession of particular States, and the acceptance of Congress, become the Seat of the Government of the United States, and to exercise like Authority over all Places purchased by the Consent of the Legislature of the State in which the Same shall be, for the Erection of Forts, Magazines, Arsenals, dock-Yards, and other needful Buildings;—And
18. To make all Laws which shall be necessary and proper for carrying into Execution the foregoing Powers, and all other Powers vested by this Constitution in the Government of the United States, or in any Department or Officer thereof.

Section 9.

1. The Migration or Importation of such Persons as any of the States now existing shall think proper to admit, shall not be prohibited by the Congress prior to the Year one thousand eight hundred and eight, but a Tax or duty may be imposed on such Importation, not exceeding ten dollars for each Person.
2. The Privilege of the Writ of Habeas Corpus shall not be suspended, unless when in Cases of Rebellion or Invasion the public Safety may require it.
3. No Bill of Attainder or ex post facto Law shall be passed.
4. No Capitation, or other direct, Tax shall be laid, unless in Proportion to the Census or Enumeration herein before directed to be taken.*
5. No Tax or Duty shall be laid on Articles exported from any State.
6. No Preference shall be given by any Regulation of Commerce or Revenue to the Ports of one State over those of another: nor shall Vessels bound to, or from, one State, be obliged to enter, clear, or pay Duties in another.
7. No Money shall be drawn from the Treasury, but in Consequence of Appropriations made by Law; and a regular Statement and Account of the Receipts and Expenditures of all public Money shall be published from time to time.
8. No Title of Nobility shall be granted by the United States: And no Person holding any Office of Profit or Trust under them, shall, without the Consent of the Congress, accept of any present, Emolument, Office, or Title, of any kind whatever, from any King, Prince, or foreign State.

Section 10.

1. No State shall enter into any Treaty, Alliance, or Confederation; grant Letters of Marque and Reprisal; coin Money; emit Bills of Credit; make any Thing but gold and silver Coin a Tender in Payment of Debts, pass any Bill of Attainder, ex post facto Law, or Law impairing the Obligation of Contracts, or grant any Title of Nobility.
2. No State shall, without the Consent of the Congress, lay any Imposts or Duties on Imports or Exports, except what may be absolutely necessary for executing its inspection Laws: and the net Produce of all Duties and Imposts, laid by any State on Imports or Exports, shall be for the Use of the Treasury of the United States; and all such Laws shall be subject to the Revision and Controul of the Congress.

**Compiler's note:* Changed by the Sixteenth Amendment.

3. No State shall, without the Consent of Congress, lay any duty of Tonnage, keep Troops, or Ships of War in time of Peace, enter into any Agreement or Compact with another State, or with a foreign Power, or engage in War, unless actually invaded, or in such imminent Danger as will not admit of delay.

Article II

Section 1.

1. The executive Power shall be vested in a President of the United States of America. He shall hold his Office during the Term of four Years, and, together with the Vice President, chosen for the same Term, be elected, as follows:
2. Each State shall appoint, in such Manner as the Legislature thereof may direct, a Number of Electors, equal to the whole Number of Senators and Representatives to which the State may be entitled in the Congress; but no Senator or Representative, or Person holding an Office of Trust or Profit under the United States, shall be appointed an Elector.

   [The Electors shall meet in their respective States, and vote by Ballot for two persons, of whom one at least shall not be an Inhabitant of the same State with themselves. And they shall make a List of all the Persons voted for, and of the Number of Votes for each; which List they shall sign and certify, and transmit sealed to the Seat of the Government of the United States, directed to the President of the Senate. The President of the Senate shall, in the Presence of the Senate and House of Representatives, open all the Certificates, and the Votes shall then be counted. The Person having the greatest Number of Votes shall be the President, if such Number be a Majority of the whole Number of Electors appointed; and if there be more than one who have such Majority, and have an equal Number of Votes, then the House of Representatives shall immediately choose by Ballot one of them for President; and if no Person have a Majority, then from the five highest on the List the said House shall in like Manner choose the President. But in choosing the President, the Votes shall be taken by States, the Representation from each State having one Vote; A quorum for this Purpose shall consist of a Member or Members from two thirds of the States, and a Majority of all the States shall be necessary to a Choice. In every Case, after the Choice of the President, the Person having the greatest Number of Votes of the Electors shall be the Vice President. But if there should remain two or more who have equal Votes, the Senate shall choose from them by Ballot the Vice-President.]*
3. The Congress may determine the Time of choosing the electors, and the Day on which they shall give their Votes; which Day shall be the same throughout the United States.
4. No person except a natural born Citizen, or a Citizen of the United States, at the time of the Adoption of this Constitution, shall be eligible to the Office of President; neither shall any Person be eligible to that Office who shall not have attained to the Age of thirty five Years, and been fourteen Years a Resident within the United States.

---

*Compiler's note: This paragraph was superseded in 1804 by the Twelfth Amendment.

5. In Case of the Removal of the President from Office, or of his Death, Resignation, or Inability to discharge the Powers and Duties of the said Office, the Same shall devolve on the Vice President, and the Congress may by Law provide for the Case of Removal, Death, Resignation or Inability, both of the President and Vice President, declaring what Officer shall then act as President, and such Officer shall act accordingly, until the Disability be removed, or a President shall be elected.*
6. The President shall, at stated Times, receive for his Services, a Compensation, which shall neither be increased nor diminished during the Period for which he shall have been elected, and he shall not receive within that Period any other Emolument from the United States, or any of them.
7. Before he enter on the Execution of his Office, he shall take the following Oath or Affirmation:—"I do solemnly swear (or affirm) that I will faithfully execute the Office of President of the United States, and will to the best of my Ability, preserve, protect and defend the Constitution of the United States."

Section 2.

1. The President shall be Commander in Chief of the Army and Navy of the United States, and of the Militia of the several States, when called into the actual Service of the United States; he may require the Opinion in writing, of the principal Officer in each of the executive Departments, upon any Subject relating to the Duties of their respective Offices, and he shall have Power to Grant Reprieves and Pardons for Offenses against the United States, except in Cases of Impeachment.
2. He shall have Power, by and with the Advice and Consent of the Senate, to make Treaties, provided two thirds of the Senators present concur; and he shall nominate, and by and with the Advice and Consent of the Senate, shall appoint Ambassadors, other public Ministers and Consuls, Judges of the supreme Court, and all other Officers of the United States, whose Appointments are not herein otherwise provided for, and which shall be established by Law: but the Congress may by Law vest the Appointment of such inferior Officers, as they think proper, in the President alone, in the Courts of Law, or in the Heads of Departments.
3. The President shall have Power to fill up all Vacancies that may happen during the Recess of the Senate, by granting Commissions which shall expire at the End of their next Session.

Section 3.

He shall from time to time give to the Congress Information of the State of the Union, and recommend to their Consideration such Measures as he shall judge necessary and expedient; he may, on extraordinary Occasions, convene both Houses, or either of them, and in Case of Disagreement between them, with Respect to the Time of Adjournment, he may adjourn them to such Time as he shall think proper; he shall receive Ambassadors and other public Ministers; he shall take Care that the Laws be faithfully executed, and shall Commission all the Officers of the United States.

**Compiler's note:* Changed by the Twenty-fifth Amendment.

Section 4.

The President, Vice President and all civil Officers of the United States, shall be removed from Office on Impeachment for, and Conviction of, Treason, Bribery, or other high Crimes and Misdemeanors.

Article III

Section 1.

The judicial Power of the United States, shall be vested in one supreme Court, and in such inferior Courts as the Congress may from time to time ordain and establish. The Judges, both of the supreme and inferior Courts, shall hold their Offices during good Behaviour, and shall, at stated Times, receive for their Services, a Compensation, which shall not be diminished during their Continuance in Office.

Section 2.

1. The judicial Power shall extend to all Cases, in Law and Equity, arising under this Constitution, the Laws of the United States, and Treaties made, or which shall be made, under their Authority;—to all Cases affecting Ambassadors, other public Ministers and Consuls;—to all Cases of admiralty and maritime Jurisdiction;—to Controversies to which the United States shall be a Party;—to Controversies between two or more States;—[between a State and Citizens of another State];* —between Citizens of different States;—between Citizens of the same State claiming Lands under Grants of different States, and [between a State, or the Citizens thereof, and foreign States, Citizens or Subjects].†
2. In all Cases affecting Ambassadors, other public Ministers and Consuls, and those in which a State shall be Party, the supreme Court shall have original Jurisdiction. In all the other Cases before mentioned, the supreme Court shall have appellate Jurisdiction, both as to Law and Fact, with such Exceptions, and under such Regulations as the Congress shall make.
3. The Trial of all Crimes, except in Cases of Impeachment, shall be by Jury; and such Trial shall be held in the State where the said Crimes shall have been committed: but when not committed within any state, the Trial shall be at such Place or Places as the Congress may by Law have directed.

Section 3.

1. Treason against the United States, shall consist only in levying War against them, or in adhering to their Enemies, giving them Aid and Comfort. No Person shall be convicted of Treason unless on the Testimony of two Witnesses to the same overt Act, or on Confession in open Court.

**Compiler's note:* Restricted by the Eleventh Amendment.

†Compiler's note: Restricted by the Eleventh Amendment.

2. The Congress shall have power to declare the Punishment of Treason, but no Attainder of Treason shall work Corruption of Blood, or Forfeiture except during the Life of the Person attained.

Article IV

Section 1.

Full Faith and Credit shall be given in each State to the public Acts, Records, and judicial Proceedings of every other State. And the Congress may by general Laws prescribe the Manner in which such Acts, Records and Proceedings shall be proved, and the Effect thereof.

Section 2.

1. The Citizens of each State shall be entitled to all Privileges and Immunities of Citizens in the several States.
2. A Person charged in any State with Treason, Felony, or other Crime, who shall flee from Justice, and be found in another State, shall on demand of the executive Authority of the State from which he fled, be delivered up, to be removed to the State having Jurisdiction of the Crime.
3. [No Person held to Service or Labour in one State, under the Laws thereof, escaping into another, shall, in Consequence of any Law or Regulation therein, be discharged from such Service or Labour, but shall be delivered up on Claim of the Party to whom such Service or Labour may be due.]*

Section 3.

1. New States may be admitted by the Congress into this Union; but no new State shall be formed or erected within the Jurisdiction of any other State; nor any State be formed by the Junction of two or more States, or Parts of States, without the Consent of the Legislatures of the States concerned as well as of the Congress.
2. The Congress shall have Power to dispose of and make all needful Rules and Regulations respecting the Territory or other Property belonging to the United States; and nothing in this Constitution shall be so construed as to Prejudice any Claims of the United States, or of any particular State.

Section 4.

The United States shall guarantee to every State in this Union a Republican Form of Government, and shall protect each of them against Invasion; and on Application of the Legislature, or of the Executive (when the Legislature cannot be convened) against domestic Violence.

**Compiler's note:* This paragraph has been superseded by the Thirteenth Amendment.

Article V

The Congress, whenever two thirds of both Houses shall deem it necessary, shall propose Amendments to this Constitution, or, on the Application of the Legislatures of two thirds of the several States, shall call a Convention for proposing Amendments, which, in either Case, shall be valid to all Intents and Purposes, as Part of this Constitution, when ratified by the Legislature of three fourths of the several States, or by Conventions in three fourths thereof, as the one or the other Mode of Ratification may be proposed by the Congress; Provided that no Amendment which may be made prior to Year One thousand eight hundred and eight shall in any Manner affect the first and fourth Clauses in the Ninth Section of the first Article; and that no State, without its Consent, shall be deprived of its equal Suffrage in the Senate.

Article VI

1. All Debts contracted and Engagements entered into, before the Adoption of this Constitution, shall be as valid against the United States under this Constitution, as under the Confederation.
2. This Constitution, and the Laws of the United States which shall be made in Pursuance thereof; and all Treaties made, or which shall be made, under the Authority of the United States, shall be the supreme Law of the Land; and the Judges in every State shall be bound thereby, any Thing in the Constitution or Laws of any State to the Contrary notwithstanding.
3. The Senators and Representatives before mentioned, and the Members of the several State Legislatures, and all executive and judicial Officers, both of the United States and of the several States, shall be bound by Oath or Affirmation, to support this Constitution; but no religious Test shall ever be required as a Qualification to any Office or public Trust under the United States.

Article VII

The Ratification of the conventions of nine States, shall be sufficient for the Establishment of this Constitution between the States so ratifying the Same.

DONE in Convention by the Unanimous Consent of the States present the Seventeenth Day of September in the Year of our Lord one thousand seven hundred and Eighty seven and of the Independence of the United States of America the Twelfth.

In Witness whereof We have hereunto subscribed our Names,

Go. Washington—
Presid't. and deputy from Virginia
Attest William Jackson, Secretary [followed by 38 names from 12 states]

Amendments

Articles in Addition to, and Amendment of, the Constitution of the United States of America, Proposed by Congress, and Ratified by the Legislatures of the several States, Pursuant to the Fifth Article of the Original Constitution.

Article I*

Congress shall make no law respecting an establishment of religion, or prohibiting the free exercise thereof; or abridging the freedom of speech, or of the press; or the right of the people peaceably to assemble, and to petition the Government for a redress of grievances.

Article II

A well regulated Militia, being necessary to the security of a free State, the right of the people to keep and bear Arms, shall not be infringed.

Article III

No Soldier, shall, in time of peace be quartered in any house, without the consent of the Owner, nor in time of war, but in a manner to be prescribed by law.

Article IV

The right of the people to be secure in their persons, houses, papers, and effects, against unreasonable searches and seizures, shall not be violated, and no Warrants shall issue, but upon probable cause, supported by Oath or affirmation, and particularly describing the place to be searched, and the persons or things to be seized.

Article V

No person shall be held to answer for a capital, or otherwise infamous crime, unless on a presentment or indictment of a Grand Jury, except in cases arising in the land or naval forces, or in the Militia, when in actual service in time of War or public danger; nor shall any person be subject for the same offence to be twice put in jeopardy of life or limb; nor shall be compelled in any criminal case to be witness against himself, nor be deprived of life, liberty, or property, without due process of law; nor shall private property be taken for public use, without just compensation.

Article VI

In all criminal prosecutions, the accused shall enjoy the right to a speedy and public trial, by an impartial jury of the State and district wherein the crime shall have been committed, which district shall have been previously ascertained by law, and to be informed of the

---

**Compiler's note:* The first ten amendments were adopted in 1791.

nature and cause of the accusation; to be confronted with the witnesses against him; to have compulsory process for obtaining witnesses in his favor, and to have the Assistance of Counsel for his defence.

Article VII

In suits at common law, where the value in controversy shall exceed twenty dollars, the right of trial by jury shall be preserved, and no fact tried by a jury, shall be otherwise reexamined in any Court of the United States, than according to the rules of the common law.

Article VIII

Excessive bail shall not be required, nor excessive fines imposed, nor cruel and unusual punishments inflicted.

Article IX

The enumeration in the Constitution, of certain rights, shall not be construed to deny or disparage others retained by the people.

Article X

The powers not delegated to the United States by the Constitution, nor prohibited by it to the States, are reserved to the States respectively, or to the people.

Article XI*

The Judicial power of the United States shall not be construed to extend to any suit in law or equity, commenced or prosecuted against one of the United States by Citizens of another State, or by Citizens or Subjects of any Foreign State.

Article XII†

The Electors shall meet in their respective states and vote by ballot for President and Vice-President, one of whom, at least, shall not be an inhabitant of the same state with themselves; they shall name in their ballots the person voted for as President, and in distinct ballots the person voted for as Vice-President, and they shall make distinct lists of all persons voted for as

---

**Compiler's note:* Adopted in 1798.

†*Compiler's note:* Adopted in 1804.

President, and of all persons voted for as Vice-President, and of the number of votes for each, which lists they shall sign and certify, and transmit sealed to the seat of the government of the United States, directed to the President of the Senate;—The President of the Senate shall, in presence of the Senate and House of Representatives, open all the certificates and the votes shall then be counted;—The person having the greatest number of votes for President, shall be the President, if such number be a majority of the whole number of Electors appointed; and if no person have such majority, then from the persons having the highest numbers not exceeding three on the list of those voted for as President, the House of Representatives shall choose immediately, by ballot, the President. But in choosing the President, the votes shall be taken by states, the representation from each state having one vote; a quorum for this purpose shall consist of a member or members from two-thirds of the states, and a majority of all the states shall be necessary to a choice. [And if the House of Representatives shall not choose a President whenever the right of choice shall devolve upon them, before the fourth day of March next following, then the Vice-President shall act as President, as in the case of the death or other constitutional disability of the President].* —The person having the greatest number of votes as Vice-President, shall be the Vice-President, if such number be a majority of the whole number of Electors appointed, and if no person have a majority, then from the two highest numbers on the list, the Senate shall choose the Vice-President; a quorum for the purpose shall consist of two-thirds of the whole number of Senators, and a majority of the whole number shall be necessary to a choice. But no person constitutionally ineligible to the office of President shall be eligible to that of Vice-President of the United States.

Article XIII†

Section 1.

Neither slavery nor involuntary servitude, except as a punishment for crime whereof the party shall have been duly convicted, shall exist within the United States, or any place subject to their jurisdiction.

Section 2.

Congress shall have power to enforce this article by appropriate legislation.

Article XIV‡

Section 1.

All persons born or naturalized in the United States, and subject to the jurisdiction thereof, are citizens of the United States and of the State wherein they reside. No state shall make or enforce any law which shall abridge the privileges or immunities of citizens of the United

---

**Compiler's note:* Superseded by the Twentieth Amendment, Section 3.

†*Compiler's note:* Adopted in 1865.

‡*Compiler's note:* Adopted in 1868.

States; nor shall any State deprive any person of life, liberty, or property, without due process of law; nor deny to any person within its jurisdiction the equal protection of the laws.

Section 2.

Representatives shall be apportioned among the several States according to their respective numbers, counting the whole number of persons in each State, excluding Indians not taxed. But when the right to vote at any election for the choice of electors for President and Vice-President of the United States, Representatives in Congress, the Executive and Judicial officers of a State, or the members of the Legislature thereof, is denied to any of the male inhabitants of such State, being twenty-one years of age, and citizens of the United States, or in any way abridged, except for participation in rebellion, or other crime, the basis of representation therein shall be reduced in the proportion which the number of such male citizens shall bear to the whole number of male citizens twenty-one years of age in such State.

Section 3.

No person shall be a Senator or Representative in Congress, or elector of President and Vice-President, or hold any office, civil or military, under the United States, or under any State, who, having previously taken an oath, as a member of Congress, or as an officer of the United States, or as a member of any State legislature, or as an executive or judicial officer of any State, to support the Constitution of the United States, shall have engaged in insurrection or rebellion against the same, or given aid or comfort to the enemies thereof. But Congress may by a vote of two-thirds of each House, remove such disability.

Section 4.

The validity of the public debt of the United States, authorized by law, including debts incurred for payment of pensions and bounties for services in suppressing insurrection or rebellion, shall not be questioned. But neither the United States nor any State shall assume or pay any debt or obligation incurred in aid of insurrection or rebellion against the United States, or any claim for the loss or emancipation of any slave; but all such debts, obligations and claims shall be held illegal and void.

Section 5.

The Congress shall have power to enforce, by appropriate legislation, the provisions of this article.

Article XV*

Section 1.

The right of citizens of the United States to vote shall not be denied or abridged by the United States or by any State on account of race, color, or previous condition of servitude.

**Compiler's note:* Adopted in 1870.

Section 2.

The Congress shall have power to enforce this article by appropriate legislation.

Article XVI*

The Congress shall have power to lay and collect taxes on incomes, from whatever source derived, without apportionment among the several States, and without regard to any census or enumeration.

Article XVII†

The Senate of the United States shall be composed of two Senators from each State, elected by the people thereof, for six years; and each Senator shall have one vote. The electors in each State shall have the qualifications requisite for electors of the most numerous branch of the State legislatures.

When vacancies happen in the representation of any State in the Senate, the executive authority of such State shall issue writs of election to fill such vacancies: *Provided*, That the legislature of any State may empower the executive thereof to make temporary appointments until the people fill the vacancies by election as the legislature may direct.

This amendment shall not be so construed as to affect the election or term of any Senator chosen before it becomes valid as part of the Constitution.

Article XVIII‡

Section 1.

After one year from the ratification of this article the manufacture, sale, or transportation of intoxicating liquors within, the importation thereof into, or the exportation thereof from the United States and all territory subject to the jurisdiction thereof for beverage purposes is hereby prohibited.

Section 2.

The Congress and the several States shall have concurrent power to enforce this article by appropriate legislation.

**Compiler's note:* Adopted in 1913.

†Compiler's note: Adopted in 1913.

‡Compiler's note: Adopted in 1919. Repealed by Section 1 of the Twenty-first Amendment.

Section 3.

This article shall be inoperative unless it shall have been ratified as an amendment to the Constitution by the legislatures of the several States, as provided in the Constitution, within seven years from the date of the submission hereof to the States by the Congress.

Article XIX*

The right of citizens of the United States to vote shall not be denied or abridged by the United States or by any State on account of sex.

Congress shall have power to enforce this article by appropriate legislation.

Article XX†

Section 1.

The terms of the President and Vice-President shall end at noon on the 20th day of January, and the terms of Senators and Representatives at noon on the 3d day of January, of the years in which such terms would have ended if this article had not been ratified; and the terms of their successors shall then begin.

Section 2.

The Congress shall assemble at least once in every year, and such meeting shall begin at noon on the 3d day of January, unless they shall by law appoint a different day.

Section 3.

If, at the time fixed for the beginning of the term of the President, the president elect shall have died, the Vice-President elect shall become President. If a President shall not have been chosen before the time fixed for the beginning of his term, or if the President elect shall have failed to qualify, then the Vice-President elect shall act as President until a President shall have qualified; and the Congress may by law provide for the case wherein neither a President elect nor a Vice-President elect shall have qualified, declaring who shall then act as President, or the manner in which one who is to act shall be selected, and such person shall act accordingly until a President or Vice-President shall have qualified.

**Compiler's note:* Adopted in 1920.

†Compiler's note: Adopted in 1933.

Section 4.

The Congress may by law provide for the case of the death of any of the persons from whom the House of Representatives may choose a President whenever the right of choice shall have devolved upon them, and for the case of the death of any of the persons from whom the Senate may choose a Vice-President whenever the right of choice shall have devolved upon them.

Section 5.

Section 1 and 2 shall take effect on the 15th day of October following the ratification of this article.

Section 6.

This article shall be inoperative unless it shall have been ratified as an amendment to the Constitution by the legislatures of three-fourths of the several States within seven years from the date of its submission.

Article XXI*

Section 1.

The eighteenth article of amendment to the Constitution of the United States is hereby repealed.

Section 2.

The transportation or importation into any State, Territory, or possession of the United States for delivery or use therein of intoxicating liquors, in violation of the laws thereof, is hereby prohibited.

Section 3.

This article shall be inoperative unless it shall have been ratified as an amendment to the Constitution by conventions in the several States, as provided in the Constitution, within seven years from the date of the submission hereof to the States by the Congress.

Article XXII†

Section 1.

No person shall be elected to the office of the President more than twice, and no person who has held the office of President, or acted as President, for more than two years of a term to which some other person was elected President shall be elected to the office of the

---

**Compiler's note:* Adopted in 1933.

†Compiler's note: Adopted in 1951.

President more than once. But this Article shall not apply to any person holding the office of President when this Article was proposed by the Congress, and shall not prevent any person who may be holding the office of President, or acting as President, during the term within which this Article becomes operative from holding the office of President or acting as President during the remainder of such term.

Section 2.

This article shall be inoperative unless it shall have been ratified as an amendment to the Constitution by the legislatures of three-fourths of the several States within seven years from the date of its submission to the States by the Congress.

Article XXIII*

Section 1.

The District constituting the seat of Government of the United States shall appoint in such manner as the Congress may direct:

A number of electors of President and Vice-President equal to the whole number of Senators and Representatives in Congress to which the District would be entitled if it were a State, but in no event more than the least populous State; they shall be in addition to those appointed by the States, but they shall be considered, for the purposes of the election of President and Vice-President, to be electors appointed by a State; and they shall meet in the District and perform such duties as provided by the twelfth article of amendment.

Section 2.

The Congress shall have power to enforce this article by appropriate legislation.

Article XXIV†

Section 1.

The right of citizens of the United States to vote in any primary or other election for President or Vice-President, for electors for President or Vice-President, or for Senator or Representative in Congress, shall not be denied or abridged by the United States or any state by reasons of failure to pay any poll tax or other tax.

Section 2.

The Congress shall have power to enforce this article by appropriate legislation.

---

*Compiler's note: Adopted in 1961.
†Compiler's note: Adopted in 1964.

Article XXV*

Section 1.

In case of the removal of the President from office or of his death or resignation, the Vice-President shall become President.

Section 2.

Whenever there is a vacancy in the office of the Vice-President, the President shall nominate a Vice-President who shall take office upon confirmation by a majority vote of both Houses of Congress.

Section 3.

Whenever the President transmits to the President pro tempore of the Senate and the Speaker of the House of Representatives his written declaration that he is unable to discharge the powers and duties of his office, and until he transmits to them a written declaration to the contrary, such powers and duties shall be discharged by the Vice-President as Acting President.

Section 4.

Whenever the Vice-President and a majority of either the principal officers of the Executive departments or of such other body as Congress may by law provide transmit to the President pro tempore of the Senate and the Speaker of the House of Representatives their written declaration that the President is unable to discharge the powers and duties of his office, the Vice-President shall immediately assume the powers and duties of the office as Acting President.

Thereafter, when the President transmits to the President pro tempore of the Senate and the Speaker of the House of Representatives his written declaration that no inability exists, he shall resume the powers and duties of his office unless the Vice-President and a majority of either the principal officers of the Executive departments or of such other body as Congress may by law provide transmit within four days to the President pro tempore of the Senate and the Speaker of the House of Representatives their written declaration that the President is unable to discharge the powers and duties of his office. Thereupon Congress shall decide the issue, assembling within forty-eight hours for that purpose if not in session. If the Congress, within twenty-one days after receipt of the latter written declaration, or, if Congress is not in session, within twenty-one days after Congress is required to assemble, determines by two-thirds vote of both houses that the President is unable to discharge the powers and duties of his office, the Vice-President shall continue to discharge the same as Acting President; otherwise, the President shall resume the powers and duties of his office.

*_Compiler's note:_ Adopted in 1967.

Article XXVI*

Section 1.

The right of citizens of the United States, who are 18 years of age or older, to vote shall not be denied or abridged by the United States or any state on account of age.

Section 2.

The Congress shall have power to enforce this article by appropriate legislation.

Article XXVII†

Section 1.

No law varying the compensation for services of the Senators and Representatives, shall take effect, until an election of Representatives shall have intervened.

**Compiler's note:* Adopted in 1971.

†*Compiler's note:* Adopted in 1992.

CREDITS

James David Barber, from *The Presidential Character*, Second Edition and Third Edition (Prentice-Hall, Inc.). Copyright © 1972, 1977, 1985 by James David Barber. Reprinted by permission of the author.

Bernard R. Berelson, Paul F. Lazarsfeld, and William N. McPhee, *Voting: A Study of Opinion Formation in a Presidential Campaign*, pp. 305–333. Copyright © University of Chicago Press. Used with permission.

Jeffrey M. Berry, excerpts taken from pp. 1–4, 8–11, 15–16 of *The Interest Group Society*. Copyright © 1997 by Jeffrey M. Berry. Reprinted by permission of Pearson Education, Inc.

David S. Broder, excerpts from "A Republic Served" in *Democracy Derailed*. Copyright © 2000 by David Broder. Reprinted by permission of Harcourt, Inc.

Richard F. Fenno, Jr., *Home Style: House Members in Their Districts* (Boston: Little, Brown and Company, 1978). Copyright © 1978 by Little, Brown and Company, Inc. Reprinted by permission.

Richard F. Fenno, Jr., "If as Ralph Nader Says, Congress Is 'The Broken Branch,' How Come We Love Our Congressmen So Much?" Originally written as part of an editorial project entitled "The Role of Congress: A Study of the Legislative Branch." Copyright © 1972 by Time, Inc. and Richard F. Fenno, Jr. Reprinted by permission.

Morris P. Fiorina, *Congress: Keystone of the Washington Establishment*. Copyright © 1977. Reprinted by permission of Yale University Press.

Ross J. S. Hoffman and Paul Levack, from *Burke's Politics* by Ross J. S. Hoffman and Paul Levack. Copyright © 1949 by Alfred A. Knopf, a division of Random House, Inc. Used by permission.

V. O. Key, Jr., "A Theory of Critical Elections," *The Journal of Politics* 17 (February 1955): 1. Copyright © 1955. Used with permission.

V. O. Key, Jr., from *The Responsible Electorate: Rationality in Presidential Voting, 1936–1960*, pp. 1–7, Cambridge, Mass.: Harvard University Press. Copyright © 1966 by the President and Fellows of Harvard College. Used with permission.

David Mayhew, *Congress: The Electoral Connection*. Copyright © 1974. Reprinted by permission of Yale University Press.

David Mayhew, *Divided We Govern: Party Control, Lawmaking, and Investigations, 1946–1990*. Copyright © 1991. Reprinted by permission of Yale University Press.

Sidney Milkis, "The Presidency and Political Parties." Copyright © Sidney Milkis. Used with permission.

Richard E. Neustadt, excerpts from *Presidential Power* by Richard E. Neustadt. Copyright © 1986 Pearson Education. Used with permission.

Arthur Paulson, *Realignment and Party Revival*, pp. 296–301. Copyright © 2000 Greenwood Press. Reproduced with permission of Greenwood Publishing Group, Inc., Westport, CT.

Nelson W. Polsby, "Congress-Bashing for Beginners." Reprinted by permission of the author from *The Public Interest*, No. 1200 (Summer 1990), pp. 15–23. Copyright © 1990 by National Affairs, Inc.

John P. Roche, "The Founding Fathers," *APSR*, December 1961. Copyright © 1961 by the American Political Science Association. Reprinted by permission.

Clinton Rossiter, "The Presidency Focus of Leadership." *New York Times*, Copyright © New York Times Company, Inc.

Mark J. Rozell and Clyde Wilcox, *Interest Groups in American Campaigns*, pp. 12–19. Copyright © 1999 Congressional Quarterly Inc. Used with permission.

Larry J. Sabato, *Paying for Elections: The Campaign Finance Thicket*. Copyright © 1989 Century Foundation. Reprinted by permission.

Stephen Skowronek, "Leadership by Definition: First Term Reflections on George W. Bush's Political Stance," *Perspectives on Politics*, Dec. 2005, Vol. 3, No. 4. Copyright © 2005. Reprinted by permission of Cambridge University Press.

Laurence H. Tribe and Michael C. Dorf, "How Not to Read the Constitution" from *On Reading the Constitution*, pp. 7–8, 13–15, 20, Cambridge, Mass.: Harvard University Press. Copyright © 1991 by the President and Fellows of Harvard College. Used with permission.

David B. Truman, from *The Government Process* (New York: Alfred A. Knopf, 1951). Reprinted by permission of the author.

James Q. Wilson, "The Rise of the Bureaucratic State." Reprinted with permission of the author from *The Public Interest*, No. 41 (Fall 1975). Copyright © 1975 by National Affairs, Inc.